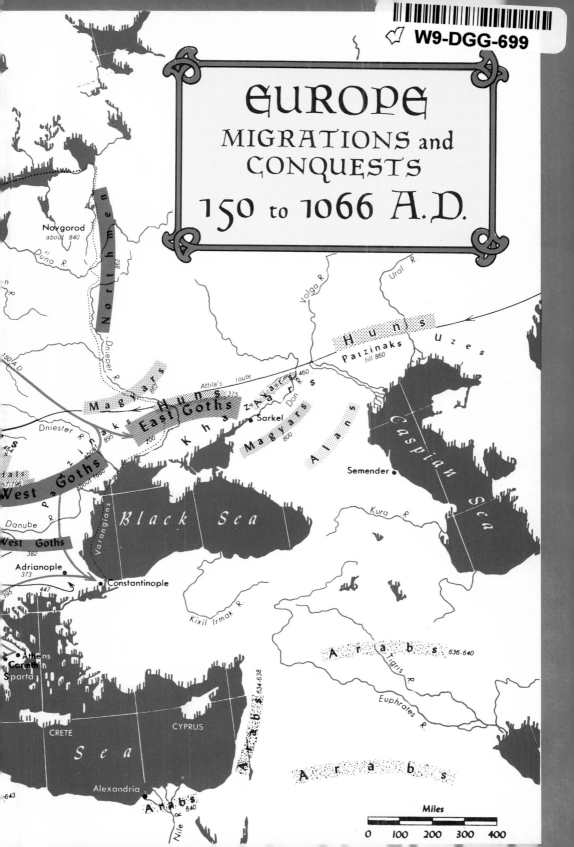

EUROPE
MIGRATIONS and CONQUESTS
150 to 1066 A.D.

Novgorod
about 840

Duna R.

n R.

Northmen
898

Dnieper R.

Volga R.

Ural R.

150 A.D.

Magyars
800

Huns

Patzinaks
895

Attila's route
375

East Goths
800

Khazars

Don R.
460

Sarkel

Huns

Patzinaks
till 860

Uzes

Magyars
800

Alans

Caspian Sea

Dniester R.

Patzinaks

454 s

ats
57-196

West Goths

West Goths
382

Danube R.

Adrianople
373

395

447

Varangians

Semender

Kura R.

Black   Sea

Constantinople

Kizil Irmak R.

Athens
Corinth
Sparta

Arabs
636-640

Tigris R.

Euphrates R.

634-638

CYPRUS

CRETE

Sea

Arabs

Arabs

-643

Alexandria

Arabs
640

Nile R.

Miles

0   100   200   300   400

SIXTH
EDITION

WESTERN CIVILIZATIONS
Their History and Their Culture

Volume 1

WESTERN

CIVILIZATIONS
Their History and Their Culture

Edward McNall Burns

SIXTH EDITION

Volume 1
*The Dawn of History through
the Reformation*

W. W. NORTON & COMPANY, INC.
New York

TO the memory of *My Mother*

Who first inspired in me the desire to know

Library of Congress Catalog Card No. 63-8026

Format Design by Nancy H. Dale
Cartography by Liam Dunne, E. D. Weldon, and Donald Pitcher

PRINTED IN THE UNITED STATES OF AMERICA
FOR THE PUBLISHERS BY THE VAIL-BALLOU PRESS, INC.
3456789

Contents

v

Part 2. *The Classical Civilizations of Greece and Rome*

Part 3. The Early Middle Ages

Part 4. The Later Middle Ages and the Transition to the Modern World

Illustrations

Illustrations in Color

ix

Illustrations in the Text

Maps and Charts

Maps in Color

Maps and Charts in the Text

Preface

SINCE THE publication of the Fifth Edition of this book much has occurred to bring into sharper focus the dramatic events of the modern world. We are now able to see more clearly the revolutionary trends of our times. To describe and assess the significance of such developments as the decline and revival of Western Europe, the ascendancy of the Soviet Union and the United States, the power struggle between East and West, the nationalist revolt against imperialism, the role of neutralism, the recurring international crises, the exploration of space, and the awesome achievements in the fields of atomic and thermonuclear energy, a new edition of *Western Civilizations* becomes necessary. But the present edition is not a mere enlargement of its predecessors. The entire book has been re-examined. Much new material has been added, but some of the old has been eliminated, and rewriting has been done throughout. Notable changes include: an increase of political history, especially of the medieval and early modern periods; the addition of new material on international relations; the insertion of interpretive summaries at the end of many chapters and sections; and a complete revision of reading lists with the inclusion of critical evaluations of important works. Books obtainable in paperbound editions have been specially identified. The entire problem of illustrative materials has been restudied: some of the older pictures have been enlarged, and new ones, obtained in many cases from European sources, have been added, including thirteen full-page and double-page spreads. The color plates, which so greatly enhanced the value of the previous edition, have been retained.

The purpose of this book is to present a compact survey of man's struggles, ideals, and achievements from ancient times to the present. Because of limitations of space, however, the record has had to be confined primarily to western Asia, northern Africa, Europe, and the Americas. In general, developments in that portion of the world east of Persia have been brought into the picture only in so far as they have been closely related to the history of the West. But within the limits thus described, the object has been to portray the drama of civilization as a whole. No major acts or scenes of that drama have been ignored or slighted. The civilizations before the Greeks have been treated not as a mere prologue but as significant stages in man's unending struggle to solve his problems. If there is any basic philosophic interpretation underlying the narrative, it is the conviction that most of human progress thus far has resulted from the growth of intelligence and respect for the rights of man, and that therein lies the chief hope for a better world in the future.

Western Civilizations was published originally in 1941. Second, third, fourth, and fifth editions were issued in 1947, 1949, 1954, and 1958, respectively. The present edition is the first to be brought out in both a one-volume and a two-volume format. Also available for use with the Sixth Edition is a new Study Guide, whose distinguishing feature is the inclusion of many extracts from original sources.

As its title indicates, this book is not exclusively or even primarily a political history. Political narrative is recognized as important, but it is not the whole substance of history. In the main, the facts of political history are subordinated to the development of institutions and ideas or are presented as the groundwork of cultural, economic, and social movements. The author believes that the effects of the Black Death were no less important than the Hundred Years' War, and that it is of greater value to understand the significance of Newton and Darwin than it is to be able to name the kings of France. In accordance with this broader conception of history, more space has been given to the teachings of Aristotle and the Stoics than to the military exploits of Alexander the Great or Julius Caesar.

In preparing this work the author has profited from the assistance and counsel of many individuals whose services no words of appreciation can adequately measure. He is indebted, first of all, to the hundreds of college teachers who have used the book and have contributed suggestions for its improvement. Of particular value have been the recommendations of Professor Sooren Frankian and his staff at Los Angeles City College. The author wishes to acknowledge an even greater debt of gratitude to Professor Philip L. Ralph of Lake Erie College, who has not only read and criticized the manuscript in its entirety but has written the sections on music. Professor Ross J. S. Hoffman of Fordham University has also criticized most of the manuscript and has made numerous invaluable suggestions for removing its imperfections. Dean Harry M. Orlinsky of the Jewish Institute of Religion has helped with the revision of the chapter on the Hebrews and has saved the author from numerous pitfalls. Professor Peter Charanis of Rutgers University has given expert assistance with the ancient and medieval sections, and Professor Henry R. Winkler, Dean Samuel C. McCulloch, Dr. F. Gunther Eyck, and the late Dr. Norman L. Stamps with the modern. The chapters on ancient history have been read and criticized by Professor J. W. Swain of the University of Illinois and those on the medieval world and the Renaissance by Professor Edgar N. Johnson of Brandeis University. The sections on modern literature have been examined critically by Professor Rudolf Kirk, Chairman of the Rutgers Department of English, and by Professor Clara Marburg

PREFACE Kirk of Douglass College. Professor David L. Cowen of Rutgers University has watched with unusual vigilance to eliminate errors and recommend improvements throughout the book. Others who have given valuable aid with one or more chapters include Dr. August Meier, formerly Assistant to the President of Fisk University; Professors Mark M. Heald, L. Ethan Ellis, Sidney Ratner, George P. Schmidt, and the late Irving S. Kull of Rutgers University; and Professors Oscar J. Falnes and Henry H. B. Noss of New York University. The author is indebted to Professor Helmut H. von Erffa of the Rutgers Department of Art for help in interpreting some of the illustrations and to the Padres of the Santa Barbara Mission for assistance in translating medieval Latin. Mrs. Beulah H. Scheer has helped with the preparation of the chronological charts. The assistance of Professor Albert W. Holzmann and Dr. F. Gunther Eyck with the German pronunciations; of Professor Remigio U. Pane with the Spanish and Italian pronunciations; and of Dr. Madeleine Charanis, Dr. Lucy Huang, and Professor Ardath W. Burks with the French, Chinese, and Japanese pronunciations, respectively, is gratefully acknowledged. The author is indebted, finally, to Mr. H. Gilbert Kelley, Reference Librarian of Rutgers University, for assistance with factual knowledge, and above all to his wife, Marie Bentz Burns, for her arduous labors of research, typing, proofreading, and preparing the index, and for her patience, devotion, and understanding.

EDWARD McNALL BURNS

Santa Barbara, California

Picture Acknowledgments

The corporations, public agencies, and individuals listed below have generously provided photographs or other materials to illustrate *Western Civilizations*. Specific contributions are indicated in the list of illustrations by the name of the donor in full or by code letters after the title of the picture furnished.

American Museum of Natural History (AMNH)
American Philosophical Society
American School of Classical Studies, Athens (Agora Excavations)
American Telephone and Telegraph Company
Wayne Andrews
Arabian-American Oil Company
Arena Chapel, Padua
Baltimore & Ohio Railroad (B&O RR)
Bayeux Public Library
John Barrington Bayley
Belgian Government Tourist Bureau (BGTB)
British Information Services (BIS)
British Museum
British Transport Commission
British Travel Association
H. Stafford Bryant, Jr.
Chase Manhattan Bank Museum of Moneys of the World (Chase)
Stephen C. Clark
Electronic Music Center of Columbia and Princeton Universities
Ford Motor Company
Henry Ford Museum, Dearborn
Foreign Operations Administration
Alison Frantz
Free Europe Press
French Embassy, Press and Information Division (FEPI)

French Government Tourist Office (FGTO)
French National Railroad (FNR)
Germanic Museum, Nuremberg
German Railroads
German Tourist Information Office (GTIO)
Greek Information Office (GIO)
Henry E. Huntington Library and Art Gallery (Huntington)
Iglesia San Tomé, Toledo, Spain
International Harvester Company
Israel Government Tourist Office (IGTO)
Israel Office of Information (IOA)
Italian State Tourist Office (ISTO)
Jewish Museum of New York, Frank J. Darmstaedter (JMNY)
P. Kidson and U. Pariser, *Sculpture at Chartres* (Alec Tiranti, Ltd.)
L. S. B. Leakey
Robert Lehman
Lever Brothers
Marshall MacDuffie
Mauritshuis, The Hague
Metropolitan Museum of Art, New York (MMA)
Minneapolis Institute of Art
Morgan Library, New York (Morgan)
Museum of Fine Arts, Boston
Museum of Modern Art, New York (Modern)
National Archives

PICTURE ACKNOWLEDGMENTS

National Gallery of Art
National Museum, Naples
Richard J. Neutra
New York Public Library, Picture Collection and Print Collection (NYPL)
Oriental Institute, University of Chicago
Phillips Memorial Gallery
Pitti Palace, Florence
Prado, Madrid
Her Majesty the Queen
Rutgers University, Department of Art (Rutgers)
Santa Maria della Grazie, Milan
Seattle World's Fair
A. A. Schechter Associates
Sistine Chapel
Spanish Tourist Office (STO)

Sperry-Rand Corporation
Standard Oil Company of New Jersey
Swiss National Tourist Office
Tennessee Valley Authority
Alec Tiranti, Ltd.
Trans World Airlines (TWA)
Uffizi Gallery, Florence (Uffizi)
United Nations
United States Army
United States Lines Company
United States Marine Corps
United States Navy
University Prints (UP)
V. W. van Gogh
Whitney Museum of American Art
Yale University Press

FROM SPECIAL COLLECTIONS AND GIFTS IN THE METROPOLITAN MUSEUM OF ART, NEW YORK

BEQUEST OF BENJAMIN ALTMAN, 1913: Arm chair upholstered in Beauvais tapestry after design by Berain.

BEQUEST OF WILLIAM K. VANDERBILT, 1920: Secretaire: ebony with black marble top; black and gold lacquer panels; ormolu mounts, with the cipher of Marie Antoinette.

BEQUEST OF MRS. H. O. HAVEMEYER, 1929. THE H. O. HAVEMEYER COLLECTION: *Portrait of a Young Man*, Bronzino; *Boy with a Greyhound*, Veronese; *Portrait of a Gentleman*, Ingres; *Pink and Green*, Degas; *Montagne Sainte Victoire with Aqueduct*, Cézanne; *Still Life*, Cézanne.

GIFT OF HENRY PAYNE BINGHAM, 1937: *Venus and Adonis*, Peter Paul Rubens.

GIFT OF ANN PAYNE BLUMENTHAL, 1941: Arm chair (*bergère*).

JULES S. BACHE COLLECTION: *Madonna and Child*, Luca della Robbia; *Portrait of a Young Man*, Bellini (1949); *Portrait of a Lady*, Domenico Veneziano (1949).

THE ALFRED STIEGLITZ COLLECTION, 1949: *Sea and Gulls*, John Marin.

BEQUEST OF SAMUEL A. LEWISOHN, 1951: *la Orana Maria*, Gauguin.

BEQUEST OF MARY WETMORE SHIVELY IN MEMORY OF HER HUSBAND, HENRY L. SHIVELY: *Portrait of Louis XV as a Child, in Royal Costume*, Hyacinthe Rigaud.

FROM SPECIAL COLLECTIONS AND GIFTS IN THE MUSEUM OF MODERN ART, NEW YORK

MRS. SIMON GUGGENHEIM FUND: *Piano Lesson*, Henri Matisse; *Three Musicians*, Pablo Picasso; *I and the Village*, Marc Chagall.

ACQUIRED THROUGH THE LILLIE P. BLISS BEQUEST: *The Starry Night*, Vincent van Gogh; *The Table*, Georges Braque.

MRS. JOHN D. ROCKEFELLER, JR., FUND: *Around the Fish*, Paul Klee.

SIXTH
EDITION

WESTERN CIVILIZATIONS
Their History and Their Culture

THE DAWN OF HISTORY

PART

1

THE DAWN OF HISTORY

No one knows the place of origin of the human species. There is evidence, however, that it may have been south central Africa or possibly central or south central Asia. Here climatic conditions were such as to favor the evolution of a variety of human types from primate ancestors. From their place or places of origin members of the human species wandered to southeastern and eastern Asia, northern Africa, Europe, and eventually to America. For hundreds of centuries they remained primitive, leading a life which was at first little better than that of the higher animals. About 5000 B.C. a few of them, enjoying special advantages of location and climate, developed superior cultures. These cultures, which attained knowledge of writing and considerable advancement in the arts and sciences and in social organization, began in that part of the world known as the Near Orient. This region extends from the western border of India to the Mediterranean Sea and to the farther bank of the Nile. Here flourished, at different periods between 5000 and 300 B.C., the mighty empires of the Egyptians, the Babylonians, the Assyrians, the Chaldeans, and the Persians, together with the smaller states of such peoples as the Cretans, the Sumerians, the Phoenicians, and the Hebrews. In other parts of the world the beginnings of civilization were retarded. There was nothing that could be called civilized life in China until about 2000 B.C. And, except on the island of Crete, there was no civilization in Europe until more than 1000 years later.

A CHRONOLOGICAL TABLE *

	Geological Period		Characteristic Forms of Life	Culture Periods
3 billion— years ago	Precambrian		One-celled organisms First invertebrates: worms, algae	
510 million— years ago	Paleozoic	Cambrian	Mollusks, sponges Insects, first vertebrates	
		Ordovician	Corals, sharks, seaweed	
		Silurian	Lungfish, crustaceans Earliest amphibians	
		Devonian	Large amphibians Ferns	
		Mississippian		
		Pennsylvanian		
		Permian		

* Adapted from time scale issued by Geological Names Committee, 1958.

	Geological Period			Characteristic Forms of Life	Culture Periods
180 million—years ago	Mesozoic	Triassic		Giant reptiles	
		Jurassic		Diversified reptiles, birds Marsupials, bony fishes	
90 million—years ago		Cretaceous		Trees	
	Cenozoic	Tertiary	Paleocene	Early mammals, first primates	
			Eocene	Primitive apes, ancestors of monkeys	
			Oligocene	Ancestors of great apes	
			Miocene	Ancestors of man, modern mammals	
			Pliocene	Early human species, other primates	
1 million—years ago		Quaternary	Pleistocene	Present day animals and races of men	Lower Paleolithic
			Recent		Upper Paleolithic
					Neolithic
7000—years ago					Civilized man

Zinjanthropus Boisei skull, discovered by Prof. L.S.B. and Mary Leakey, noted British archeologists. It is a fossil hominid skull of general Australopithicene type, found on a "living floor" in bed I at Olduvai, Tanganyika. Age: 1,750,000 years. This discovery conclusively links fossil man to the pebble-tool implements of the period, found previously in the same area.

Reconstruction of the Skulls of Four Types of Stone Age Men: Java, Peking, Neanderthal, Cro-Magnon.

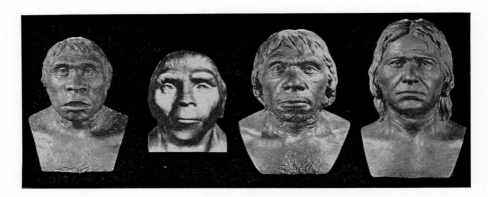

Early Paleolithic Tools. From left to right, a fist hatchet, a carving tool, and a side scraper.

Late Paleolithic Tools and Implements. From left to right, a bone harpoon point, a flint knife blade or spear point, and beads or pendants of elks' teeth.

The Stone Age or Preliterate Cultures

> Our debt to prehistoric man is an impressive one. Practically all
> the basic discoveries of techniques that mark present-day modes
> of life, and that are now commonplace—excepting only metal-
> working, power machinery and electricity—were made during the
> time man's economy was characterized by the use of stone tools.
> —Melville J. Herskovits, *Man and His Works*

The entire span of human history can be divided roughly into two
periods, the Age of Stone and the Age of Metals. The former is
sometimes called the Preliterate Age, or the period before the invention of writing. The latter coincides with the period of history
based upon written records. The Preliterate Age covered at least 95
per cent of man's existence and did not come to an end until about
5000 B.C. The Age of Metals practically coincides with the history
of civilized nations. The Age of Stone is subdivided into the Paleolithic, or Old Stone Age, and the Neolithic, or New Stone Age.
Each takes its name from the type of stone tools and weapons char-
acteristically manufactured during the period. Thus during the
greater part of the Paleolithic Age implements were commonly
made by chipping pieces off a large stone or flint and using the core
that remained as a hand ax or "fist hatchet." Toward the end of the
period the chips themselves were used as knives or spearheads, and
the core thrown away. The Neolithic Age witnessed the supplant-
ing of chipped stone tools by implements made by grinding and
polishing stone.

*Periods of
man's
history*

The names of the periods mentioned leave much to be desired.
They were invented at a time when the study of early cultures was
in its infancy. It is now recognized that sharp dividing lines cannot
always be drawn between stages of culture on the basis of their
methods of making stone tools and weapons. This is particularly
true of the later stages. Moreover, types of tools and weapons have
not in all cases been the most significant traits distinguishing one
culture from another. Nevertheless, the method of naming has been
found convenient and will doubtless continue to be used.

*Significance of
names of the
periods*

5

1. The Culture of Lower Paleolithic Men

The Paleolithic period can be dated from roughly 1,750,000 B.C. to 10,000 B.C. It is commonly divided into two stages, an earlier or Lower Paleolithic and a later or Upper Paleolithic. The Lower Paleolithic was much the longer of the two, covering about 75 per cent of the entire Old Stone Age. During this time at least four species of men inhabited the earth. The oldest was apparently a creature called by anthropologists *Zinjanthropus boisei*, whose skeletal remains were found in the Great Rift valley of Tanganyika in Central Africa. Fortunately, volcanic ash covered some of the tools he had used and also preserved a fragment of his skull and a shin bone. By means of the potassium-argon method, which makes it possible to measure the loss of radioactivity in a mineral, geologists have estimated the age of the rock in which the human relics were found as 1,750,000 years. That Zinjanthropus was a true ancestral human being is indicated by evidence that he walked erect and that he used crude tools. It must not be supposed, of course, that these tools represented any high degree of manufacturing skill or inventive talent. For the most part, they consisted of objects taken from nature: bones of large animals, limbs from trees, and chunks of stone, perhaps broken or crudely chipped.

Two other early inhabitants of the Lower Paleolithic were Java man and Peking man. Java man, whose scientific name is *Pithecanthropus erectus*, was long thought to be the oldest of manlike creatures, but it is now generally agreed that the date of his origin was about 500,000 B.C. His skeletal remains were found on the island of Java in 1891. Originally only a skull-cap, a thigh bone, three teeth and a jaw bone were discovered; in recent years, however, other fragments have been unearthed, with the result that it is now possible to reconstruct the entire skull of Pithecanthropus. It has been established that his cranial capacity was nearly double that of a male gorilla, but only two-thirds that of modern man.

The remains of Peking man or *Sinanthropus pekinensis* were found in China, about forty miles southwest of Peking (Peiping) between 1926 and 1930. Since the latter date, fragments of no fewer than 32 skeletons of the Sinanthropus type have been located, making possible a complete reconstruction of at least the head of this ancient species. Anthropologists generally agree that Sinanthropus and Pithecanthropus are of approximately the same antiquity, and that both probably descended from the same ancestral type. Until recently many scientists believed that the so-called Piltdown man, whose fragmentary "remains" were found in England in 1911, was a contemporary of the Java and Peking species. But in 1953 it was revealed that "Piltdown man" was a hoax. The fragments, which included a skull-cap and a jaw bone, had been skillfully altered. The jaw bone was actually that of an ape, chemically treated to make it appear aged, while the skull-cap was only about 50,000 years old.

Much more dependable evidence exists of another Paleolithic man, although he did not make his appearance until the period was well advanced. This specimen was Fontéchevade man, so called from the cave in which his remains were found in 1947 in Charente, in southwestern France. Although the finds included only fragments of skulls, enough of them were intact to make possible accurate measurements. Moreover, the geological layer in which they were found, and also the one immediately above, was complete and undisturbed, so that little trouble could arise in assigning them to a chronological era. In certain respects Fontéchevade man resembled modern man more closely even than some ancestors of later origin. For example, the skull-cap dimensions were about the same as those of living Europeans. More interesting, the heavy eyebrow ridges, so characteristic of most early men, were lacking, and the construction of the forehead was remarkably similar to that of our own. On the other hand, the brain case was exceptionally thick, and the cranium was low-vaulted. Fontéchevade man derived his large brain capacity from the extraordinary breadth of his cranium, not from its height.

Fonté-chevade man

During the last 25,000 years of the Lower Paleolithic period a fourth species of ancient man made his appearance. He was *Homo neanderthalensis*, famous as an early cave man. His skeletal fragments were first discovered in the valley of the Neander, near Düsseldorf, northwestern Germany, in 1856. Since then numerous other discoveries have been made, in some cases complete skeletons, in such widely separated regions as Belgium, Spain, Italy, Yugoslavia, Russia, and Palestine. So closely did Neanderthal man resemble modern man that he is classified as a member of the same genus, the genus *Homo*. The resemblance, however, was by no means perfect. Neanderthal men, on the average, were only about five feet, four inches in height. They had receding chins and heavy eyebrow ridges. Although their foreheads sloped back and their brain cases were low-vaulted, their average cranial capacity was slightly greater than that of modern Caucasians. What this may have signified with respect to their intelligence cannot be determined.

Neanderthal man

The knowledge we possess of the culture of Lower Paleolithic men is scanty indeed. The skills they achieved and the learning they acquired must have been pitiful in quantity even when compared with the accomplishments of modern primitive men. Yet Pithecanthropus and his successors were not mere apes, forgetting in a moment the chance triumphs they had made. They undoubtedly had the capacity for speech, which enabled them to communicate with their fellows and to pass on what they had learned to succeeding generations. We are justified in assuming also that they possessed reasoning ability, however crudely it may have been developed. Practically from the beginning, therefore, they were probably tool-

Lower Paleolithic culture

7

using creatures, employing their wits to fashion implements and weapons. Perhaps at first these would be nothing but limbs broken from trees to be used as clubs. Eventually it was discovered that stones could be chipped in such a way as to give them cutting edges. The butt was then held in the palm of the hand. Thus evolved the so-called hand ax or fist hatchet, which appears to have served the combined purposes of a cleaver, saw, scraper, and knife.

*Improvements
made by Nean-
derthal man*

Before the end of the Lower Paleolithic period, Neanderthal man seems largely to have abandoned the use of the fist hatchet. Improved methods of chipping stone enabled him to rely primarily upon the flakes themselves. The result was the development of spearheads, borers, and much superior knives and scrapers. Indications have been found also of a degree of advancement in nonmaterial culture. In the entrances to caves where Neanderthal man lived, or at least took refuge, evidence has been discovered of flint-working floors and stone hearths where huge fires appear to have been made. These would suggest the origins of co-operative group life and possibly the crude beginnings of social institutions. More significance may be attached to Neanderthal man's practice of bestowing care upon the bodies of his dead, interring with them in shallow graves tools and other objects of value. Perhaps this practice indicates the development of a religious sense, or at least a belief in some form of survival after death.

2. Upper Paleolithic Culture

*The Upper Pa-
leolithic period*

About 30,000 B.C. the culture of the Old Stone Age passed from the Lower Paleolithic stage to the Upper Paleolithic. The Upper Paleolithic period lasted for only about 200 centuries, or from 30,000 to 10,000 B.C. A new and superior type of human being dominated the earth in this time. Biologically these men were closely related to modern man. Their foremost predecessors, Neanderthal men, had ceased to exist as a distinct variety. What became of the Neanderthalers is not known. According to one school of opinion, they were probably exterminated by their conquerors or perished through failure of their food supply. According to another school, they lost their identity merely through interbreeding with the newcomers. One branch of them in a remote area of the world may actually have been the ancestors of the new race that now became dominant.

*Cro-Magnon
man*

The name used to designate the prevailing breed of Upper Paleolithic men is Cro-Magnon, from the Cro-Magnon cave in Dordogne, France, where some of the most typical remains were discovered. Cro-Magnon men were tall, broad-shouldered, and erect, the males averaging over six feet. They had high foreheads, well-developed chins, and a cranial capacity about equal to the modern average. The heavy eyebrow ridges so typical of earlier species were lacking. Whether Cro-Magnon men left any survivors is a debatable question. They do not seem to have been exterminated but appear to have been driven into mountainous regions and to have been absorbed ultimately into later races.

Upper Paleolithic culture was markedly superior to that which had gone before. Not only were tools and implements better made, but they existed in greater variety. They were not fashioned merely from flakes of stone and an occasional shaft of bone; other materials were used in abundance, particularly reindeer horn and ivory. Examples of the more complicated tools included the bone needle, the fishhook, the harpoon, the dart thrower, and, at the very end, the bow and arrow. That Upper Paleolithic man wore clothing is indicated by the fact that he made buttons and toggles of bone and horn and invented the needle. He did not know how to weave cloth, but animal skins sewn together proved a satisfactory substitute. Large numbers of perforated animal teeth and shells have also been found, suggesting that he made pendants and necklaces to adorn his person. It is certain that he cooked his food, for enormous hearths, evidently used for roasting flesh, have been discovered. In the vicinity of one at Solutré, in southern France, was a mass of charred bones, estimated to contain the remains of 100,000 large animals. Although Cro-Magnon man built no houses, except a few simple huts in regions where natural shelters did not abound, his life was not wholly nomadic. Evidences found in the caves that were his usual homes indicate that he must have used them, seasonally at least, for years at a time.

Upper Paleo-lithic culture: tools and weapons

With respect to nonmaterial elements there are also indications that Upper Paleolithic culture represented a marked advancement. Group life was now more regular and more highly organized than ever before. The profusion of charred bones at Solutré and elsewhere probably indicates co-operative enterprise in the hunt and sharing of the results in great community feasts. The amazing workmanship displayed in tools and weapons and highly developed techniques in the arts could scarcely have been achieved without some division of labor. It appears certain, therefore, that Upper Paleolithic communities included professional artists and skilled craftsmen. In order to acquire such talents, certain members of the communities must have gone through long periods of training and given all their time to the practice of their specialties. In consequence they would have to be supported by the rest of the group. Thus an aristocracy would arise, and possibly the highest members of it would enjoy enough prestige to become rulers with limited authority.

Evidences of social development

Substantial proof exists that Cro-Magnon man had highly developed notions of a world of unseen powers. He bestowed more care upon the bodies of his dead than did Neanderthal man, painting the corpses, folding the arms over the heart, and depositing pend-

Sympathetic magic

9

ants, necklaces, and richly carved weapons and tools in the graves. He formulated an elaborate system of sympathetic magic designed to increase his supply of food. Sympathetic magic is based upon the principle that imitating a desired result may bring about that result. Applying this principle, Cro-Magnon man made paintings on the walls of his caves depicting the capture of reindeer in the hunt, or he carved images of the cave bear with javelins piercing its side. At other times he fashioned clay models of the bison or mammoth and mutilated them with dart thrusts. The purpose of such representations was quite evidently to facilitate the very results portrayed and thereby to increase the hunter's success and make easier the struggle for existence. Possibly incantations or ceremonies accompanied the making of the pictures or images, and it is likely that the work of producing them was carried on while the actual hunt was in progress.

*Evidences
of intellectual
progress*

The Upper Paleolithic period witnessed some slight intellectual progress. Cro-Magnon man could count, and the first mathematical records in the history of mankind made their appearance. These consisted of various objects: a notched javelin or dart thrower, for example, or a stag tooth scored horizontally with a sharp tool and worn as a pendant. All of them were probably records of animals slain in the hunt. A bare possibility exists that Cro-Magnon man developed a primitive system of writing. Various interesting signs have been discovered which give the appearance of being characters of a written language. They were probably nothing more, however, than conventionalized symbols of natural objects. Plenty of other evidence can be found that the art of this period often showed a tendency toward conventionalization. The possibility that a knowledge of writing existed at this time must therefore be regarded as remote.

*Upper
Paleolithic art*

The supreme achievement of Cro-Magnon man was his art—an achievement so original and resplendent that it ought to be counted

Examples of Upper Paleolithic Engraving and Sculpture. The two objects at the top and upper right are dart throwers. At the lower right is the famous Venus of Willendorf.

among the Seven Wonders of the World. Nothing else illustrates so well the great gulf between his culture and that of his predecessors. Upper Paleolithic art included nearly every branch that the material culture of the time made possible. Sculpture, painting, carving, and engraving were all represented. The ceramic arts and architecture were lacking, for pottery had not yet been invented, and no buildings were erected except of simple design. UPPER PALEOLITHIC CULTURE

The art *par excellence* of Cro-Magnon man was painting. Here were exhibited the greatest number and variety of his talents—his discrimination in the use of color, his meticulous attention to detail, his capacity for the employment of scale in depicting a group, and above all his genius for naturalism. The art of modern primitive folk resembles the art of a child; it portrays things not as they are, but in accordance with naïve preconceptions in the mind. The art of Upper Paleolithic man was remarkably free from such tendencies and showed a firm resolution to copy the world of nature with utmost fidelity. Especially noteworthy was the painter's skill in representing movement. A large proportion of his murals depicted animals running, leaping, browsing, chewing the cud, or facing the hunter at bay. Ingenious devices were often employed to give the impression of motion. Chief among them was the drawing or painting of additional outlines to indicate the areas into which the legs or the head of the animal had moved. But the scheme was so shrewdly executed that no appearance whatever of artificiality resulted. *Painting*

Cave-man art throws a flood of light on many problems relating to primitive mentality and folkways. To a certain extent it was undoubtedly an expression of a true aesthetic sense. Cro-Magnon man did obviously take some delight in the graceful line or symmetrical pattern or brilliant color. The fact that he painted and tattooed the body and wore ornaments gives evidence of this. But his chief works of art can scarcely have been produced for the sake of creating beautiful objects. Such a possibility must be excluded for several reasons. To begin with, the best of the paintings and drawings are usually to be found on the walls and ceilings of the darkest and most inaccessible parts of the caves. The gallery of paintings at Niaux, for instance, is more than half a mile from the entrance of the cavern. No one could see the artists' creations except in the imperfect light of torches or of primitive lamps which must have smoked and sputtered badly, since the only illuminating fluid was animal fat. Furthermore, there is evidence that Cro-Magnon man was largely indifferent toward his work of art after it was finished. He did not cherish it with the passing of the years, nor did he spend much time in admiring it. On the contrary, he was likely to use the very same surface for a new production. Numerous examples have been found of paintings or drawings superimposed upon earlier ones of the same or of different types. Evidently the important thing was not the finished work itself, but the act of making it. *Significance of Upper Paleolithic art*

Cave Drawings at Lascaux, France. Characteristic examples of the realism of Cro-Magnon man's art.

Art as a serious business

For Paleolithic man, art was a serious business. The real purpose of nearly all of it was apparently not to delight the senses but to make easier the struggle for existence by increasing the supply of animals useful for food. The artist himself was not an aesthete but a magician, and his art was a form of magic designed to promote the hunter's success. In this purpose lay its chief significance and the foundation of most of its special qualities. It suggests, for example, the real reason why game animals were almost the exclusive subjects of the great murals and why plant life and inanimate objects were seldom represented. It aids us in understanding Cro-Magnon man's neglect of the finished paintings and his predominant interest in the process by which they were made. Finally, magical purposes go far toward explaining the spectacular genius of the artist himself, for the very existence of the community was believed to depend upon the competent performance of his duties, and consequently no effort would be spared in giving him a thorough training.

The end of Upper Paleolithic culture

Upper Paleolithic culture came to an untimely end about 10,000 B.C. Internal decay, exemplified by the decline of art, seems to have been one of the causes. The factors responsible cannot be determined exactly. Impatience with the old methods, a striving after "short cuts" that resulted in standardization and loss of originality, may have been one of them. A more obvious and doubtless more effective cause of the decline of the culture as a whole was partial destruction

12

of the food supply. As the last great glacier retreated farther and farther northward, the climate of southern Europe became too warm for the reindeer, and they gradually migrated to the shores of the Baltic. The mammoth, whether for the same or for different reasons, became extinct. Representatives of the magnificent Cro-Magnon race probably followed the reindeer northward, but apparently they did not continue their cultural achievements.

3. Neolithic Culture

The last stage of preliterate culture is known as the Neolithic period, or the New Stone Age. The name is applied because stone weapons and tools were now generally made by grinding and polishing instead of by chipping or fracturing as in the preceding periods. The bearers of Neolithic culture were new varieties of modern man who poured into Africa and southern Europe from western Asia. Since no evidence exists of their later extermination or wholesale migration, they must be regarded as the immediate ancestors of most of the peoples now living in Europe.

The meaning of the term Neolithic

It is impossible to fix exact dates for the Neolithic period. The culture was not well established in Europe until about 3000 B.C., though it certainly originated earlier. There is evidence that it existed in Egypt as far back as 5000 B.C., and that it probably began at an equally early date in southwestern Asia. There is also variation in the dates of its ending. It was superseded in the Nile valley by the first historic civilization soon after the year 4000.[1] Except on the island of Crete it did not come to an end anywhere in Europe before 2000, and in northern Europe much later still. In a few regions of the world it has not terminated yet. The natives of some islands of the Pacific, the Arctic regions of North America, and the jungles of Brazil are still in the Neolithic culture stage except for a few customs acquired from explorers and missionaries.

The varying dates of the Neolithic stage

In many respects the New Stone Age was the most significant in the history of the world thus far. The level of material progress rose to new heights. Neolithic man had a better mastery of his environment than any of his predecessors. He was less likely to perish from a shift in climatic conditions or from the failure of some part of his food supply. This decided advantage was the result primarily of the development of agriculture and the domestication of animals. Whereas all of the men who had lived heretofore were mere food-gatherers, Neolithic man was a *food-producer*. Tilling the soil and keeping flocks and herds provided him with much more dependable food resources and at times yielded him a surplus. These circumstances made possible a more rapid increase of population,

The Neolithic revolution

[1] All dates in Egyptian history prior to 2000 are approximations and may represent a margin of error of several centuries.

promoted a settled existence, and fostered the growth of institutions. Such were the elements of a great social and economic revolution whose importance it would be almost impossible to exaggerate.

The new culture also derives significance from the fact that it was the first to be distributed over the *entire* world. Although some earlier cultures, especially those of Neanderthal and Cro-Magnon men, were widely dispersed, they were confined chiefly to the accessible mainland areas of the Old World. Neolithic man penetrated into every habitable area of the earth's surface—from Arctic wastes to the jungles of the tropics. He apparently made his way from a number of centers of origin to every nook and cranny of both hemispheres. He traveled incredible distances by water as well as by land, and eventually occupied every major island of the oceans, no matter how remote. Even Hawaii, situated 4000 miles from the Asiatic mainland, proved not to be beyond his reach. Whether he launched his vessel or raft for some visible goal, and then drifted out of his course and by a lucky accident was washed ashore before he starved to death, or whether he got there by skill or intent, it is certain that he did arrive, for when the white men came the natives of the Hawaiian Islands had essentially the same pattern of culture as Neolithic men everywhere else.

The factors responsible for this wide distribution cannot be determined with precision. It has been established that Neolithic man invented boats and rafts, without which he could never have escaped the confines of Asia, Africa, and Europe. But why he should have forced his way into steaming jungles, mountain fastnesses, and bleak and barren areas like Labrador and Patagonia remains an impenetrable mystery. We can only conjecture that increasing population required a constant search for new hunting areas and possibly for grazing and agricultural lands. Younger and more venturesome individuals would be forever striking out into new regions in the hope of improving their economic condition.

The historian would have difficulty in overestimating the importance of the Neolithic migrations. The net result was that they distributed a similar pattern of culture over the entire world. The few elements of earlier cultures which had managed to survive were almost completely inundated. Their disappearance means that we now have no way of discovering more than a small part of what went on in Paleolithic man's mind—whether he believed that government is an evil or that private property is sacred or that the world was created out of nothing. The fact that we find particular notions in the primitive mind of today does not prove that they are inseparable from the blood and sinew of the species, for it is necessary to remember that all existing primitive races are the beneficiaries or the victims of a common heritage.

The invention of boats and rafts was not the only example of **14** Neolithic man's mechanical ingenuity. He developed the arts of knitting, of spinning, and of weaving cloth. He made the first pottery and knew how to produce fire artificially by friction. He built houses of wood and sun-dried mud. Toward the end of the period he discovered the possibilities of metals, and a few implements of copper and gold were added to his stock. Since nothing was yet known of the arts of smelting and refining, the use of metals was limited to the more malleable ones occasionally found in the pure state in the form of nuggets.

Neolithic Dwellings. Examples shown are restorations of Swiss lake dwellings. They were commonly erected on poles or stilts for purposes of defense.

But the real foundation stones of the Neolithic culture were the domestication of animals and the development of agriculture. Without these it is inconceivable that the culture would have attained the complexity it did. More than anything else they were responsible for the settled mode of existence, for the growth of villages and social institutions. They stimulated the rise of a division of labor and encouraged the practice of exchange. They compelled man constantly to seek new methods of harnessing nature and thereby led to an increase in his physical equipment and his store of knowledge.

Importance of agriculture and the domestication of animals

The first animal to be domesticated is generally thought to have been the dog, on the assumption that he would be continually hanging around the hunter's camp to pick up bones and scraps of meat. Eventually it would be discovered that he could be put to use in hunting, or possibly in guarding the camp. After achieving success in domesticating the dog, Neolithic man would logically turn his attention to other animals, especially to those he used for food. Before the period ended, at least five species—the cow, the dog, the goat, the sheep, and the pig—had been made to serve his needs. Not all of them in all parts of the world, however. The Neolithic tribes of the New World domesticated no animals at all, except the hairless dog in some parts of Mexico, the llama and the alpaca in the Andean highland, and the guinea pig and the turkey in a few other regions.

Origins of the domestication of animals

The exact spot where agriculture originated has never been positively determined. All we know is that wild grasses which were probably the ancestors of the cereal grains have been found in a number of places. Types of wheat grow wild in Asia Minor, in the Caucasus, and in Mesopotamia. Wild ancestors of barley have been

The beginning of agriculture

15

reported from North Africa, from Persia, from Asia Minor, and from Turkestan. Though it is probable that these were the first crops of Neolithic agriculture, they were by no means the only ones. Millet, vegetables, and numerous fruits were also grown. Flax was cultivated in the Old World for its textile fiber, and in some localities the growing of the poppy for opium had already begun. In the New World maize (Indian corn) was the only cereal crop, but the American Indians cultivated numerous other products, including tobacco, beans, squashes, pumpkins, and potatoes.

Historically, the most important feature of Neolithic culture was probably the development of institutions. An institution may be defined as a combination of group beliefs and activities organized in a relatively permanent fashion for the purpose of fulfilling some group need. It ordinarily includes a body of customs and traditions, a code of rules and standards, and physical extensions such as buildings, punitive devices, and facilities for communication and indoctrination. Since man is a social being, some of these elements probably existed from earliest times, but institutions in their fully developed form seem to have been an achievement of the Neolithic Age.

The nature of institutions

One of the most ancient of human institutions is the family. Sociologists do not agree upon how it should be defined. Historically, however, the family has always meant a more or less permanent unit composed of parents and their offspring, which serves the purposes of care of the young, division of labor, acquisition and transmission of property, and preservation and transmission of beliefs and customs. The family is not now, and never has been, exclusively biological in character. Like most institutions, it has evolved through a long period of changing conventions which have given it a variety of functions and forms.

Definition of the family

The family during Neolithic times appears to have existed in both polygamous and monogamous forms. The term polygamy is used by sociologists to mean any type of plural marriage—either a plurality of husbands or a plurality of wives. The scientific name for the former is *polyandry*, and for the latter *polygyny*. Polyandry seems always to have been rare. At the present time it is confined to a few Eskimo communities, to the Wahuma tribes of East Africa, and to southern India and Tibet. It appears to develop under conditions of extreme poverty where a number of men must pool their resources in order to purchase or support a wife, or where female infanticide is practiced as a means of controlling population growth. The latter custom soon results in an excess of males. Polygyny arises under a variety of conditions. In some cases it results from a preponderance of females. For example, the Arctic seal-hunter's life is so hazardous that in some villages the number of men may be less than half the number of women. In a few instances polygyny has been resorted to as a means of producing a rapid increase in the

Polygamy

population. Since one man can procreate far more offspring than one woman can bear, such peoples as the ancient Hebrews encouraged the taking of extra wives in order that the group might multiply rapidly and thereby protect itself against absorption or annihilation by hostile neighbors. Still a third factor in the origin of polygyny has been the love of display. Rulers and other rich men have maintained a plurality of wives as a form of conspicuous consumption. King Solomon kept a harem of 700 wives and 300 concubines, not necessarily because of a voracious sexual appetite, but in order to impress other monarchs with his ability to support such a large establishment. He was interested also, of course, in political alliances with as many as possible of the surrounding monarchs, and marrying their daughters was a convenient means of establishing these.

A second institution developed in more complex form by Neolithic man was religion. On account of its infinite variations, it is hard to define, but perhaps the following would be accepted as an accurate definition of the institution in at least its basic character: "Religion is everywhere an expression in one form or another of a sense of dependence on a power outside ourselves, a power which

The nature of primitive religion; rites and ceremonies

Megalithic Monuments at Stonehenge, England. The practice of erecting megaliths, or huge stone pillars and structures, was common in Neolithic cultures. Those at Stonehenge are probably the remains of a temple of sun worship.

we may speak of as a spiritual or moral power."[2] Modern anthropologists emphasize the fact that early religion was not so much a matter of belief as a matter of rites. For the most part, the rites came first; the myths, dogmas, and theologies were later rationalizations. Primitive man was universally dependent upon nature—on the regular succession of the seasons, on the rain falling when it

[2] A. R. Radcliffe-Brown, *Structure and Function in Primitive Society*, p. 157.

should, on the growth of plants and the reproduction of animals. Unless he performed sacrifices and rites these natural phenomena, according to his notion, would not occur. For this reason he developed rain-making ceremonies in which water was sprinkled on ears of corn to imitate the falling of the rain. The ceremonial dances of the American Indians often had a similar import. The members of a whole village or even a whole tribe would attire themselves in animal skins and mimic the habits and activities of some species they depended upon for food. They apparently had a vague feeling that by imitating the life pattern of the species they were helping to guarantee its continuance.

The element of fear

But there was also another element conspicuously present in primitive religion. This was the element of fear. Modern primitive men, at least, live in an almost constant state of alarm and dread. As an old Eskimo medicine man said to the explorer Knud Rasmussen: "We do not believe; we fear." [3] Everything strange and unfamiliar is fraught with danger. The savage fears not only sickness and death but also hunger, drought, storms, the spirits of the dead, and the animals he has killed. Every misfortune, loss, or failure is the harbinger of other misfortunes and failures unless the evil influence that caused them is appeased, paralyzed, or annihilated. To accomplish such ends, charms, incantations, and other devices of magic potency seem to be a vital necessity.

Ceremonies to ward off evil

It follows that a large part of primitive man's religion consists of ceremonial precautions to ward off evil. For example, no savage will risk swimming across a dangerous river without first endeavoring by prayers or incantations to win its favor. An Eskimo who has killed a polar bear must present it with tools and weapons pleasing to it; if the bear is a female, women's knives and needle cases are given. Bestowal of these gifts is considered necessary to appease the wrath of the bear's soul and keep it from wreaking damage. In West Africa, the hunter who has killed a hippopotamus disembowels it, strips himself naked, crawls inside the carcass, and bathes his entire body with the animal's blood. Throughout the procedure he prays to the spirit of the hippo that it will bear him no ill-will for having killed it, and that it will not incite other hippopotami to attack his canoe in revenge.[4]

Neolithic man's prelogical mind

Between the sort of religion just described and the theological religions of Judaism, Christianity, and Islam there seems only the vaguest connection. Most Neolithic men were and still are in a prelogical stage. Their thinking resembles more closely that of a child than it does the thinking of civilized man. They draw no sharp distinction between animate and inanimate objects or between the natural and the supernatural. They recognize no miracles, for nothing is impossible or absurd. In like manner, there are no

[3] Lucien Lévy-Bruhl, *Primitives and the Supernatural*, p. 22.
[4] Lucien Lévy-Bruhl, *How Natives Think*, p. 238.

accidents, for every happening has its mystic significance. Should a child fall into the fire, someone has bewitched him, and the parents will not rest until they have found the culprit. Most primitive men today have little conception of natural cause. Some tribes reject completely the idea of natural death. Others have no notion of natural birth. They see no definite connection between sexual intercourse and reproduction. The union of male and female is merely to prepare the way for a spirit to enter the woman's body and make her pregnant.

Probably the first intellectual revolution in the history of mankind was the transition from the prelogical basis of primitive religion to the type of religious thinking which rests upon a belief in benevolent gods and a philosophical explanation of the universe. How the transition was accomplished, no one knows. Apparently some tribes developed the idea that supernatural beings in manlike form would be more capable of hearing and answering entreaties than disembodied spirits or ghosts. Since prehistoric man almost universally assumed that the spirit of a human being survived the death of his body, and since medicine men were widely revered, it seems possible that the spirits of some of these may have been transferred to mountain tops or to homes in the sky and worshiped as gods. Perhaps in some other cases the awakening of an ethical sense led to a belief in one or more gods as the upholders of righteousness and justice. Such ideas would doubtless come to the minds of exceptional men almost from the beginning, with the result that in particular areas a belief in a single divinity of goodness might well co-exist with the most primitive fears of ghosts and witches. Whatever their origin, personal deities were venerated by the earliest civilizations, and it seems certain that beliefs concerning them did come into existence during the Neolithic culture stage.

The transition to theological religion

Still another of the great institutions to be developed by Neolithic man was the state. By way of definition, the state may be described as an organized society occupying a definite territory and possessing an authoritative government independent of external control. The essence of the state is sovereignty, or the power to make and administer laws and to preserve social order by punishing men for infractions of those laws. A state must not be confused with a nation. The latter is an ethnic concept, used to designate a people bound together by ties of language, customs, or racial origin or by common memories or a belief in a common destiny. A nation may or may not occupy a definite territory and does not possess the element of sovereignty. It may not even have an independent government, as for example the Poles during the long period when they were under Austrian, German, and Russian rule. At the present time most nations are also states, but this condition has resulted largely from the breaking up of the Russian, Austrian, German, and Turkish empires at the end of World War I.

The state defined

*Absence of the
state in many
primitive so-
cieties*

Except in time of crisis, the state does not exist in a very large proportion of primitive societies—a fact which probably indicates that its genesis was rather late in the Neolithic culture stage. Most savage communities have no permanent system of courts, no police agencies, and no governments with coercive power. Custom takes the place of law, the blood-feud is the mode of administering justice, and there is very little conception of crime against the community. To primitive man, offenses are mostly what we call "torts," or private wrongs between individuals or families, in the punishment of which no public authority takes part. The acceptance of *wergeld,* or blood-money, is a common practice, and even felonies such as murder are regarded merely as offenses against the victim's family. Since the family of the victim has been deprived of a valuable member, the proper satisfaction is a money payment. If this is not offered, the family may retaliate in kind by killing the offender or a member of the offender's family. Practically the only wrongs against society are violations of *taboos,* or religious prohibitions, but the punishment for these is religious, not political.

*A variety of
causes of the
origin of the
state*

The origin of the state was probably the consequence of a variety of factors. We are certainly justified in assuming the development of agriculture to have been one of the most important. In sections like the Nile valley, where a numerous population lived by cultivating intensively a limited area of fertile soil, a high degree of social organization was absolutely essential. Ancient customs would not suffice for the definition of rights and duties in such a society, with its high standard of living, its unequal distribution of wealth, and its wide scope for the clash of personal interests. New measures of social control would become necessary, which could scarcely be achieved in any other way than by setting up a government of sovereign authority and submitting to it; in other words, by establishing a state. The result would not be accomplished in a single day or even in a single year. The initial forms of public control would be few and tentative, but they would be gradually extended, until finally a state, not necessarily despotic, but with full authority, would come into being.

A number of ancient states evidently owed their origin to war activities. That is, they were founded for purposes of conquest, for defense against invasion, or to make possible the expulsion of an invader from the country. The Hebrew monarchy seems to have been a product of the first of these reasons. With the war for the conquest of Canaan none too successful, the Hebrew people besought their leader Samuel to give them a king, that they might be "like all the nations" with a powerful ruler to keep them in order and to lead them to victory in battle. One has only to observe the effects of modern warfare, both offensive and defensive, in strengthening and enlarging the powers of government to see how similar influences might have operated to bring the state into existence in the first place.

Some modern anthropologists attach great importance to leadership as a factor in the origin of the state. They point out that in time of crisis an individual of commanding qualities often steps out from the crowd and takes control. In a shipwreck, for example, one of the men in a lifeboat assumes authority, rationing the water and food, if any, and keeping his companions in order. Among the Bushmen of Australia and among the Eskimos, no political institutions exist at all under ordinary circumstances. But when an emergency arises, someone takes the leadership for the duration of the crisis, and what was originally an informal band of hunters takes on the character of a rudimentary state. Among peoples leading a more settled existence the leader has frequently become a sort of political boss, presiding over a "machine," and dispensing feasts and other favors. Sometimes he is revered as almost divine, as a symbol of the unity and interdependence of the group. It is assumed that the members live through him as the body of an individual lives through its head.

The factor of leadership

Although evidence can be found to support all of the above hypotheses, they should not be regarded as the exclusive explanations. Religion doubtless contributed to the origin of states in some areas. Medicine men, or shamans, frequently exercise a kind of sovereignty. Though they may command no physical force, their power to impose religious penalties and to strike terror into the hearts of their followers gives them a degree of coercive authority. In all probability some of them made themselves kings. It is conceivable that in other cases the state arose from the natural expansion of group life, with its resulting complexities and conflicts. As the population increased in limited areas, customary law and family administration of justice proved inadequate, and political organization became necessary as a substitute. In the domain of politics as in every other sphere concerned with social origins, no one explanation can be made to accommodate all the facts.

Other causes

Selected Readings

• *Items so designated are available in paperbound editions.*

Boas, Franz, *The Mind of Primitive Man*, New York, 1927. Excellent on the traits common to all men.
Ceram, C. W., *Gods, Graves and Scholars*, New York, 1952. Popular but scholarly.
• Childe, V. G., *Man Makes Himself*, London, 1936. (Mentor)
Dawson, Christopher, *The Age of the Gods*, New York, 1937.
Folsom, J. K., *The Family*, New York, 1934.
Gillin, John, *The Ways of Men*, New York, 1948.
Herskovits, M. J., *Man and His Works*, New York, 1948. One of the best

introductions to anthropology.

Hooton, E. A., *Up from the Ape*, rev., New York, 1947.

Lévy-Bruhl, Lucien, *How Natives Think*, London, 1926.

———, *Primitives and the Supernatural*, New York, 1935. A superlative study of primitive "Logic."

· Linton, Ralph, *The Tree of Culture*, New York, 1955. (Vintage)

· Lowie, R. H., *Primitive Society*, New York, 1925. (Torchbooks) Interesting but tends to generalize in terms of modern institutions.

MacCurdy, G. G., *Human Origins*, New York, 1924, 2 vols.

· Malinowski, Bronislaw, *Crime and Custom in Savage Society*, New York, 1951. (Littlefield, Adams) The most provocative and valuable study on the subject.

· Nevins, Allan, *The Gateway to History*, New York, 1938. (Rev., Anchor)

Osborn, H. F., *Men of the Old Stone Age*, New York, 1915.

Peake, Harold, and Fleure, H. J., *Hunters and Artists*, New Haven, 1927.

Radcliffe-Brown, A. R., *Structure and Function in Primitive Society*, Glencoe, Ill., 1952. Stimulating and informative.

· Radin, Paul, *Primitive Man as Philosopher*, New York, 1927. (Dover)

· ———, *Primitive Religion*, New York, 1937. (Dover)

· Ralph, P. L., *The Story of Our Civilization*, New York, 1959. (Dutton)

Renard, Georges, *Life and Work in Prehistoric Times*, New York, 1929.

· Somervell, D. C., ed., A. J. Toynbee, *A Study of History*, New York, 1947–57, 2 vols. (Galaxy, 6 vols.) An excellent condensation of a really great work.

Tyler, J. M., *The New Stone Age in Northern Europe*, New York, 1921.

The Nature and Origin of Civilizations

He who knows the story of the transition from the prehistoric hunters of the Nile jungle to the sovereigns and statesmen, the architects, engineers, and craftsmen, the sages and social prophets of a great organized society, which wrought these monumental wonders along the Nile at a time when all Europe was still living in Stone Age barbarism and there was none to teach a civilization of the past—he who knows all this knows the story of the *first rise of a civilization of profound moral vision anywhere on the globe.*

—James H. Breasted, *The Dawn of Conscience*

1. Cultures and Civilizations

The stages of man's advancement described thus far have been referred to as *cultures*. This word is commonly used to designate societies or periods which have not yet attained to a knowledge of writing and whose general level of achievement is comparatively primitive. But the term has other meanings. It is sometimes applied to intellectual and artistic accomplishments, to literature, art, music, philosophy, and science. It is employed by some historians to designate the whole complex pattern of ideas, achievements, traditions, and characteristics of a nation or empire at a particular time.

Culture defined

The term *civilization* also carries a variety of meanings. The German philosopher of history Oswald Spengler referred to civilizations as decadent phases of highly developed cultures. When a great people or empire was in its prime, he characterized its social and intellectual pattern as a culture. When it passed its prime and became ossified and stagnant, he described it as a "civilization." The noted British historian Arnold J. Toynbee also sees world history as a succession of cultural units. But he designates each of the primary ones, throughout its development, as a "civilization." He distinguishes between civilizations and "primitive societies" largely on a quantitative basis. The latter are "relatively short-lived, are restricted to relatively narrow geographical areas, and embrace relatively small numbers of human beings." [1]

The meaning of civilization

The term *civilization* has still another meaning. Since each culture has peculiar features of its own, and since some cultures are more highly developed than others, we can speak quite properly

[1] *A Study of History* (D. C. Somervell, ed.), Vol. I, p. 35.

of a civilization as a superior culture. We can say that a culture deserves to be called a civilization when it has reached a stage of advancement in which writing has come to be used to a considerable extent, some progress has been made in the arts and sciences, and political, social, and economic institutions have developed sufficiently to conquer at least some of the problems of order, security, and efficiency in a complex society. This is the sense in which the term will be used throughout the remainder of this book.

2. Factors Responsible for the Origin and Growth of Civilizations

What causes contribute to the rise of civilizations? What factors account for their growth? Why do some civilizations reach much higher levels of development than others? Inquiry into these questions is one of the chief pursuits of social scientists. Some decide that factors of geography are the most important. Others stress economic resources, food supply, contact with older civilizations, and so on. Usually a variety of causes is acknowledged, but one is commonly singled out as deserving special emphasis.

Probably the most popular of the theories accounting for the rise of superior cultures are those which come under the heading of geography. Prominent among them is the hypothesis of climate. The climatic theory, advocated in days past by such notables as Aristotle and Montesquieu, received its most eloquent exposition in the writings of an American geographer, Ellsworth Huntington. Dr. Huntington acknowledged the importance of other factors, but he insisted that no nation, either ancient or modern, rose to the highest cultural status except under the influence of a climatic stimulus. He described the ideal climate as one in which the mean temperature seldom falls below the mental optimum of 38 degrees or rises above the physical optimum of 64 degrees. But temperature is not alone important. Moisture is also essential, and the humidity should average about 75 per cent. Finally, the weather must not be uniform: cyclonic storms, or ordinary storms resulting in weather changes from day to day, must have sufficient frequency and intensity to clear the atmosphere every once in a while and produce those sudden variations in temperature which seem to be necessary to exhilarate and revitalize man.[2]

Much can be said in favor of the climatic hypothesis. Certainly some parts of the earth's surface, under existing atmospheric conditions, could never cradle a superior culture. They are either too hot, too humid, too cold, or too dry. Such is the case of regions beyond the Arctic Circle, the larger desert areas, and the jungles of India, Central America, and Brazil. Evidence is available, more-

24 [2] Ellsworth Huntington, *Civilization and Climate*, third edition, pp. 220–23.

over, to show that some of these places have not always suffered
under climate so adverse as that now prevalent. Various inhospitable
sections of Asia, Africa, and America contain unmistakable traces
of more salubrious days in the past. Here and there are the ruins
of towns and cities where now the supply of water seems totally
inadequate. Roads traverse deserts which at present are impassable.
Bridges span river beds which have had no water in them for years.
These and similar phenomena, observed by travelers in desert regions, appear to furnish proof that the climatic factor in history
cannot be ignored.

The best-known evidences of the cultural importance of climatic
change are those pertaining to the civilization of the Mayas. Mayan
civilization flourished in Guatemala, Honduras, and on the peninsula
of Yucatan in Mexico from about 400 to 1500 A.D. Numbered among
its achievements were the making of paper, the invention of the
zero, the perfection of a solar calendar, and the development of a
system of writing partly phonetic. Great cities were built; marked
progress was made in astronomy; and sculpture and architecture
were advanced to high levels. At present most of the civilization is
in ruins. No doubt many factors conspired to produce its untimely
end, including deadly wars between tribes, but climatic change was
also probably involved. The remains of most of the great cities are
now surrounded by jungles, where malaria is prevalent and agriculture difficult. That the Mayan civilization or any other could have
grown to maturity under conditions like these is hard to believe.
It seems probable, therefore, that the climate of the Mayan region
some five or six centuries ago was different from what it is now.

The Mayan civilization

But the hypothesis is open to criticism on several counts. Evidences of climatic change on a significant scale are still very far from
conclusive. There is nothing to indicate, for example, that the
climate of Greece and Rome in ancient times was more invigorating
than it is at present. Moisture conditions in ancient Greece were
undoubtedly more favorable, but there is no proof of alterations in
temperature. Nor can the decline of civilization in Egypt and
Mesopotamia be accounted for by radical changes in atmospheric
conditions. Most of the evidence seems to show that economic and
social factors, such as the exhaustion of resources and the growth of
slavery and habits of indolence, had far greater effects.

Criticism of the climatic hypothesis

Related to the climatic hypothesis is the soil-exhaustion theory.
A group of modern conservationists has hit upon this theory as
the sole explanation of the decay and collapse of the great empires
of the past and as a universal threat to the nations of the present and
future. At best it is only a partial hypothesis, since it offers no theory
of the birth or growth of civilizations. But its proponents seem to
think that almost any environment not ruined by man is capable
of nourishing a superior culture. The great deserts and barren areas
of the earth, they maintain, are not natural but artificial, created

The soil-ex-haustion theory

by man through bad grazing and farming practices. Conservationists discover innumerable evidences of waste and neglect that have wrought havoc in such areas as Mesopotamia, Palestine, Greece, Italy, China, and Mexico. The majestic civilizations that once flourished in these countries were ultimately doomed by the simple fact that their soil would no longer provide sufficient food for the population. As a consequence, the more intelligent citizens migrated elsewhere and left their inferiors to sink slowly into stagnation and apathy. But the fate that overtook the latter was not of their making alone. The whole nation had been guilty of plundering the forests, mining the soil, and pasturing flocks on the land until the grass was eaten down to the very roots. Among the tragic results were floods alternating with droughts, since there were no longer any forests to regulate the run-off of rain or snow. At the same time, much of the top soil on the close-cropped or excessively cultivated hillsides was blown away or washed into the rivers to be carried eventually down to the sea. The damage done was irreparable, since about 300 years are required to produce a single inch of top soil.

Yet another of the geographic theories is the contention that the topography of the earth's surface has been the main conditioning element in the rise of civilizations. A famous champion of this theory was Karl Ritter, a German who lived in the first half of the nineteenth century. Ritter maintained that the form and shape of continents are of great importance in providing advantages for cultural growth. Continents possessing an irregular coast line and diversified geographic conditions furnish the only favorable environments for the progress of nations. The more compact and homogeneous a continent is, the more backward will be its inhabitants. Over the whole territory their culture will be uniform, and the absence of good harbors will limit contact with the world outside. The result will be stagnation. By contrast, peoples living on a continent such as Europe, with its sharply broken coast line and its varied geographic features, enjoy notable advantages. Their land is accessible by water to its very heart. Numerous bays and harbors and islands off the coast render seafaring easy and break the isolation that would be otherwise inevitable. As a consequence, it is not strange that Europe has been able to develop "the highest of all civilizations." [3]

The topographical theory

Even more famous as an exponent of the topographical theory was the English historian Henry Thomas Buckle (1821–1862). Buckle divided the principal environments of man into two classes: (1) those that stimulate the imagination, and (2) those that sharpen the understanding. To illustrate the former he submitted the example

[3] Quoted by Franklin Thomas, "Some Representative Contributions of Anthropogeography to Modern Political Theory," Merriam, Barnes, and others, *A History of Political Theories, Recent Times*, p. 464.

of India, where the works of nature are of "startling magnitude," overawing man and impressing him with a sense of his own insignificance. The natives therefore torture themselves, invent cruel and terrifying gods, and practice a religion of hideous orgies. They are pessimists and fatalists, denying all value to life and repudiating the ability of man to understand and control his world. As an example of the second class of environments, Buckle referred to Greece, where the face of nature is more ordinary and "less threatening to man." Such an environment, he argued, promotes the elevation of man, generates an attitude of optimism, and stimulates a feeling of confidence in the powers of the human mind. He considered it no miracle, therefore, that Greece should have been able to produce one of the world's most distinguished cultures and some of the greatest critical thinkers of all time.[4]

The topographical theory seems to have comparatively little to confirm it. No geologist would agree that coastal indentations and the altitude of mountain ranges have altered much within the range *Criticism of* of historic time. Greece has no fewer harbors now than in the age *the topographi-* of Pericles, nor has Mount Olympus risen in recent years to any *cal theory* proportions of "startling magnitude." Yet the modern Greeks do not match their ancestors in intellectual accomplishment. If the influence of topography was at one time conducive to rational thinking and to the development of confidence and joy in achievement, why should that influence have ceased to operate? The theory does not explain either how a country like Switzerland could become one of the leading centers of enlightenment of the present day. On the other hand, there is no gainsaying the fact that a long and irregular coast line is an asset in the development of trade, and therefore an important advantage in the diffusion and reception of knowledge.

According to some philosophers of history, most of the great historic cultures were founded by nomads. The foremost exponent of this theory was a German, Franz Oppenheimer. He and his *The nomad* followers contended that nomads were the original conquerors of *theory* primitive cultures and the founders of the state and of complex society. Exploitation of the labor of the vanquished and confiscation of their wealth, he asserted, enabled the conquerors to live in ease and luxury. They established themselves as a nobility and bought or commandeered for their own entertainment whatever talent the country afforded. In time they came to encourage actively the progress of learning and the arts as symbols of their life of leisure and their privileged position. They alone had time to enjoy such things, and, besides, patronage of artists and men of letters served as a convenient form of luxurious display.

Oppenheimer maintained that the diet of the herdsman, consisting

[4] H. T. Buckle, *The History of Civilization in England*, second edition, pp. 93–106.

as it does of meat and milk, is highly nourishing. The nomad, consequently, has boundless energy. He infuses new life into stagnant peoples wherever he goes. Brutal and domineering though he may be, he nevertheless builds the organization, imposes the discipline, and creates the inequalities of rank and class which seem to be necessary as foundations for cultural growth. Moreover, the customs and diet of pastoral folk are conducive to rapid increases of population. The form of marriage is commonly polygamous, and a plentiful supply of the milk of animals "shortens the period of nursing for the mothers, and consequently permits a greater number of children to be born and to grow into maturity." [5] The result is that nomads periodically burst their territorial confines and invade and conquer the lands of more settled peoples.

Evidence of a sort can be discovered in abundance to corroborate this theory. Not a few of the great cultures of the past appear to have been founded by conquering nomads. Three great reservoirs of humanity seem time after time to have let loose inundations of peoples that poured into the more fertile areas of the Old World. From the grasslands north of the Arabian Desert came the Babylonians, Assyrians, and Chaldeans successively to conquer the Tigris-Euphrates valley. From the steppes of central Asia issued the Medes, Persians, and Indians, and probably most of the ancestors of the nations of Europe. The Arabian Desert itself was the starting point of the Hebrew migrations into the land of Canaan and of the conquests of the Moslems. All of these focal areas are unsuited to agriculture; to this day they are inhabited by nomads. It follows that the peoples mentioned must originally have lived under the pastoral economy, even though some of them had abandoned their flocks and herds at the time they made their principal conquests.

*Evidence
to confirm the
nomad theory*

But the nomad theory has its shortcomings as an explanation of the rise of superior cultures. Certainly it cannot be used to account for the origin of all of them. The Egyptian civilization, for example, appears to have been established by people who derived their livelihood primarily from agriculture. The Phoenicians, who came from Babylonia about 2000 B.C. to found a maritime culture in the Lebanon valley, must have been long accustomed to the peaceful arts of tilling the soil before their migration. Moreover, there is reason to believe that most of the great inventions and discoveries which provided the original basis of civilization were made by peaceful, agricultural peoples. Such folk seem to have originated irrigation, mathematics, and astronomy, and systems of writing. The American economist and philosopher Thorstein Veblen declared that nomadic peoples made no significant contributions whatever, with the exceptions of poetry and religious creeds and cults.[6] But the fact remains that conquering nomads did infuse new energy into the

The nomad theory criticized

---

[5] F. Oppenheimer, *The State*, pp. 42–43.
28   [6] Thorstein Veblen, *The Instinct of Workmanship*, p. 167.

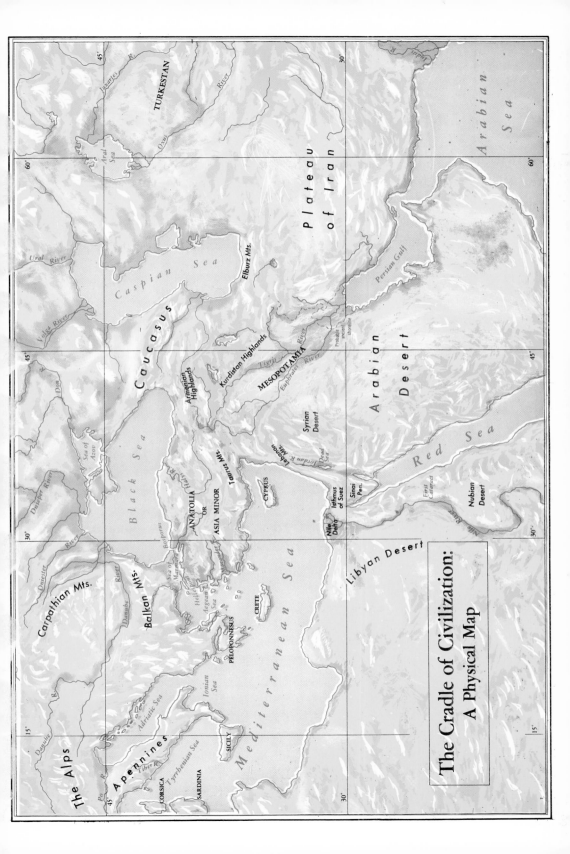

The Cradle of Civilization:
A Physical Map

Egyptian Pottery Jar, with Painted Decoration, *ca.* 3600 B.C. It was filled with food or water and placed in the tomb to provide for the needs of the body in the afterlife.

An Egyptian Official and His Son. Painted limestone, *ca.* 2500 B.C.

Painted limestone figures, *ca.* 1300 B.C.

Tomb model of an Egyptian fishing boat, *ca.* 2000 B.C.

Wall painting of an Egyptian house, *ca.* 1400 B.C.

Farm Hand Plowing. Egyptian tomb figures, *ca.* 1900 B.C.

Gold and Inlay Pendant of Princess Sit Hat-Hor Yunet. Egyptian, Twelfth Dynasty.

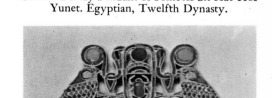

cultures of settled areas and probably goaded the inhabitants into activity which ultimately resulted in achievements. Moreover, the circumstances surrounding the original expansion of such peoples as the Babylonians, the Assyrians, the Hebrews, and the Moslems leave little doubt that the conditions of nomadic existence were partly responsible for the fact that they founded civilizations.

The most recent hypothesis of the origin of civilizations is the adversity theory of the distinguished British historian, Arnold J. Toynbee. According to this theory, conditions of hardship or adversity are the real causes which have brought into existence superior cultures. Such conditions constitute a *challenge* which not only stimulates men to try to overcome it but generates additional energy for new achievements. The challenge may take the form of a desert, a jungle area, rugged topography, or a grudging soil. The Hebrews and Arabs were challenged by the first, the Indians of the Andean Highland by the last. The challenge may also take the form of defeat in war or even enslavement. Thus the Carthaginians, as a result of defeat in the First Punic War, were stimulated to conquer a new empire in Spain; while centuries later, Oriental captives enslaved by the Romans strengthened and propagated their religious heritage until Rome herself succumbed to it. In general it is true that the greater the challenge, the greater the achievement; nevertheless, there are limits. The challenge must not be too severe, else it will deal a crushing blow to all who attempt to meet it. Such environments as Greenland, Labrador, and Tierra del Fuego have climate and soil conditions so absolutely bleak and inhospitable that they could never give birth to civilizations.

The adversity theory of Arnold J. Toynbee

The majority of historians believe that the genesis of civilizations cannot be explained except on the basis of a complex of causes. Not any one factor, but a combination of several must be taken into account. Among these factors they place uppermost the geographic and economic elements of favorable climate, fertile soil, access to good harbors, and an abundance of mineral resources. They also accord a high place to opportunities for interchange of ideas with other peoples of a comparable level of advancement. Civilizations do not develop in isolated corners of the world. The backwardness of Australia, New Zealand, and South Africa before the coming of Europeans was probably due to this cause. These sections were favorably situated so far as climate and resources were concerned, but they were too remote to be affected by the stimulus of progress elsewhere. It is common also for historians to emphasize the concentration of population in limited areas and the invention of new skills and processes, such as pictographic writing and the smelting of metals, as factors in the origin of high cultures. Historians also recognize the importance of religion as an influence in the transition from primitive to civilized life. The earliest forms of social regulation were probably for religious purposes. Religion provided

A number of factors must be taken into account in explaining the origin of civilizations

29

the oldest law codes and systems of morality and perhaps also the foundations of philosophy and science. Priests constituted the most ancient class of educated men, and there is reason to believe that it was they who invented the first systems of writing.

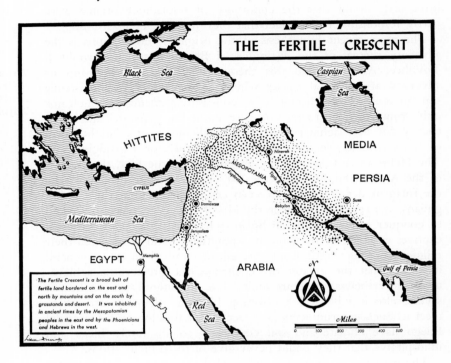

THE FERTILE CRESCENT

The Fertile Crescent is a broad belt of fertile land bordered on the east and north by mountains and on the south by grasslands and desert. It was inhabited in ancient times by the Mesopotamian peoples in the east and by the Phoenicians and Hebrews in the west.

3. Why the Earliest Civilizations Began Where They Did

The Nile and the Tigris-Euphrates valleys probably the centers of the oldest civilizations

Which of the great civilizations of antiquity was the oldest is still a sharply debated question. The judgment of many scholars inclines toward the Egyptian, though a respectable body of authority supports the claims of the Tigris-Euphrates valley. Still other experts prefer Elam, a region lying east of the Tigris-Euphrates valley and bordering on the Persian Gulf. While the opinion of no competent scholar is to be brushed lightly aside, there is nevertheless stronger warrant for believing that the Nile and Tigris-Euphrates valleys were the homes of the oldest historic cultures. These two areas were geographically the most favored sections in the general region of the so-called Fertile Crescent.[7] Here larger numbers of artifacts of undoubted antiquity have been found than

[7] The Fertile Crescent is that wide belt of productive land which extends northwestward from the Persian Gulf and then down the Mediterranean coast almost to Egypt. It forms a semicircle around the northern part of the Arabian desert.

in any other sections of the Near Orient. Furthermore, progress in the arts and sciences had reached unparalleled heights in both of these areas as early as 3000 B.C., when most of the rest of the world was steeped in ignorance. If the foundations of this progress were really laid elsewhere, it seems strange that they should have disappeared, although of course there is no telling what the spade of the archaeologist may uncover in the future. The possibility that the world's earliest civilizations may have originated in India or China must be excluded. No evidence exists of anything other than primitive culture in India before 3250 B.C., and the peak of cultural development was not reached until much later. No true civilization flourished in China before 1500 B.C.

Of the several causes responsible for the earliest rise of civilizations in the Nile and Tigris-Euphrates valleys, geographic factors would seem to have been the most important. Both regions had the notable advantage of a limited area of exceedingly fertile soil. Although it extended for a distance of 750 miles, the valley of the Nile was not more than ten miles wide in some places, and its maximum width was thirty-one miles. The total area was less than 10,000 square miles, or roughly the equivalent of the State of Maryland. Through countless centuries the river had carved a vast canyon or trench, bounded on either side by cliffs ranging in height from a few hundred to a thousand feet. The floor of the canyon was covered with a rich alluvial deposit, which in places reached a depth in excess of thirty feet. The soil was of such amazing productivity that as many as three crops per year could be raised on the same land. This broad and fertile canyon constituted the cultivable area of ancient Egypt. Here several million people were concentrated. In Roman times the population of the valley approximated seven million, and probably it was not much smaller in the days of the Pharaohs. Beyond the cliffs there was nothing but desert—the Libyan desert on the west and the Arabian on the east. In the ancient Egyptian language "highlander" was synonymous with foreigner. To "go up" was the equivalent of going abroad, while to "descend" was the popular expression for returning home from the alien world.[8]

A limited area of fertile soil in the Nile valley

In the Tigris-Euphrates valley similar conditions prevailed. As in Egypt, the rivers provided excellent facilities for inland transportation and were alive with fish and waterfowl for a plentiful supply of protein food. The distance between the Tigris and Euphrates rivers at one point was less than twenty miles, while nowhere in the lower valley did it exceed forty-five miles. Since the surrounding country was desert, the people were kept from scattering over too great an expanse of territory. The result, as in Egypt, was the welding of the inhabitants into a compact society, under conditions that facilitated a ready interchange of ideas and discoveries. As the

A similar condition in Mesopotamia

---

[8] J. H. Breasted, *History of Egypt*, p. 11.

population increased, the need for agencies of social control became ever more urgent. Numbered among such agencies were government, schools, legal and moral codes, and institutions for the production and distribution of wealth. At the same time conditions of living became more complex and artificial and necessitated the keeping of records of things accomplished and the perfection of new techniques. Among the consequences were the invention of writing, the practice of smelting metals, the performance of mathematical operations, and the development of astronomy and the rudiments of physics. With these achievements the first great ordeal of civilization was passed.

Climatic advantages in Egypt

Climatic influences also played their part in both regions. The atmosphere of Egypt is dry and invigorating. Even the hottest days produce none of the oppressive discomfort which is often experienced during the summer seasons in more northern countries. The mean temperature in winter varies from 56 degrees in the Delta to 66 degrees in the valley above. The summer mean is 83 degrees and an occasional maximum of 122 is reached, but the nights are always cool and the humidity is extremely low. Except in the Delta, rainfall occurs in negligible quantities, but the deficiency of moisture is counteracted by the annual inundations of the Nile from July to October. Also very significant from the historical standpoint is the total absence of malaria in Upper Egypt, while even in the coastal region it is practically unknown. The direction of the prevailing winds is likewise a favorable factor of more than trivial importance. For more than three-quarters of the year the wind comes from the north, blowing in opposition to the force of the Nile current. The effect of this is to simplify immensely the problem of transportation. Upstream traffic, with the propulsion of the wind to counteract the force of the river, presents no greater difficulty than downstream traffic. This factor in ancient times must have been of enormous advantage in promoting communication among a numerous people, some of whom were separated by hundreds of miles.

Climatic influences in Mesopotamia

Climatic conditions in Mesopotamia do not seem to have been quite so favorable as in Egypt. The summer heat is more relentless; the humidity is somewhat higher; and tropical diseases take their toll. Nevertheless, the torrid winds from the Indian Ocean, while enervating to human beings, blow over the valley at just the right season to bring the fruit of the date palm to a full ripeness. More than anything else the excellent yield of dates, the dietary staple of the Orient, encouraged the settlement of large numbers of people in the valley of the two rivers. Finally, the melting of the snows in the mountains of the north produced an annual flooding of the Babylonian plain similar to that in Egypt. The effect was to enrich the soil with moisture and to cover it over with a layer of mud of unusual fertility.

Most significant of all of the geographic influences, however, was the fact that the scanty rainfall in both regions provided a spur to initiative and inventive skill. In spite of the yearly floods of the rivers there was insufficient moisture left in the soil to produce abundant harvests. A few weeks after the waters had receded, the earth was baked to a stony hardness. Irrigation was accordingly necessary if full advantage was to be taken of the richness of the soil. As a result, in both Egypt and Mesopotamia elaborate systems of dams and irrigation canals were constructed as long ago as five thousand years. The mathematical skill, engineering ability, and social co-operation necessary for the development of these projects were available for other uses and so fostered the achievement of civilization.

The importance of scanty rainfall as a spur to initiative

The question remains to be answered, which of the two civilizations, the Egyptian or the Mesopotamian, was the older? This question thus far has defied a satisfactory answer. It is possible to present various facts which seem to suggest the priority of Egypt. Most important of all, the dwellers in the Nile valley enjoyed geographic advantages which were denied to the natives of Mesopotamia: a less enervating atmosphere, a climate comparatively free from disease, and the availability of metals and good building stone. Egypt, moreover, was well protected from invasion and from intermixture with more backward peoples. On the east and west were trackless deserts, on the north was a harborless coast line, and on the south the rocky barriers of a series of cataracts prevented the inroads of African savages. Only at the two northern corners could the valley be penetrated easily. By contrast, Mesopotamia was relatively unprotected. Not one of its boundaries afforded any appreciable degree of security. It stood as a constant temptation to the hungry hordes of nomads in the surrounding mountains and deserts. As a consequence, the progress of cultural evolution was subject to frequent interruptions by the invasions of pillaging tribes.

Evidence for the priority of Egypt

Until recently most historians appeared to take it for granted that the Egyptian civilization was the older. They based their assumption upon the conclusions of two of the world's most renowned Egyptologists, James H. Breasted and Alexandre Moret. Between the two world wars of the twentieth century, however, facts were unearthed which seemed to prove a substantial Mesopotamian influence in the Nile valley as early as 3500 B.C. This influence was exemplified by the use of cylinder seals, methods of building construction, art motifs, and elements of a system of writing of undoubted Mesopotamian origin. That such achievements could have radiated into Egypt from the Tigris-Euphrates valley at so early a date indicated beyond doubt that the Mesopotamian civilization was one of vast antiquity. It did not necessarily prove, though, that it was older than the Egyptian. For the achievements mentioned were not taken over and copied slavishly. Instead, the Egyptians

Uncertainty as to which civilization was older

33

modified them radically to suit their own culture pattern. On the basis of this evidence, it would seem that the only conclusion which can be safely drawn is that both civilizations were very old, and that for the most part they developed concurrently.

Selected Readings

· *Items so designated are available in paperbound editions.*

Baikie, James, *A History of Egypt*, London, 1929, Vol. I.

Boas, Franz, *The Mind of Primitive Man*, New York, 1927. Valuable as a study of the traits common to all men.

Breasted, James H., *The Dawn of Conscience*, New York, 1934. An excellent treatise on the origin of religious and ethical concepts.

———, *History of Egypt*, New York, 1912. Still one of the best histories of ancient Egypt.

Buckle, Henry T., *History of Civilization in England*, 2nd ed., New York, 1863.

Burton, H. E., *The Discovery of the Ancient World*, New Haven, 1932.

Butterfield, Herbert, *History and Human Relations*, New York, 1952.

Cambridge Ancient History, New York, 1923, Vol. I.

· Childe, V. G., *New Light on the Most Ancient East*. (Evergreen)

· Clough, Shepard B., *The Rise and Fall of Civilization: An Inquiry into the Relationship Between Economic Development and Civilization*, New York, 1951. (Columbia)

Hall, H. R., *Ancient History of the Near East*, New York, 1913.

Huntington, Ellsworth, *Civilization and Climate*, 3rd edn., New Haven, 1924. Provocative but dogmatic.

Magoffin, R. V. D., and Davis, E. C., *The Romance of Archaeology*, New York, 1929.

· Muller, H. J., *The Uses of the Past*, New York, 1952. (Galaxy) A thoughtful analysis.

Myres, J. L., *The Dawn of History*, New York, 1911.

· Nevins, Allan, *The Gateway to History*, New York, 1938. (rev., Anchor)

Smith, G. E., *The Ancient Egyptians and the Origin of Civilization*, rev., New York, 1923. Narrow and dogmatic.

Spengler, Oswald, *The Decline of the West*, 1-vol. edn., New York, 1934. The gist of his philosophy is contained in the Introduction.

· Somervell, D. C., ed., A. J. Toynbee, *A Study of History*, New York, 1947–57, 2 vols. (Galaxy, 6 vols.) An excellent abridgement of a monumental work.

Trever, A. A., *History of Ancient Civilization*, New York, 1936, Vol. I.

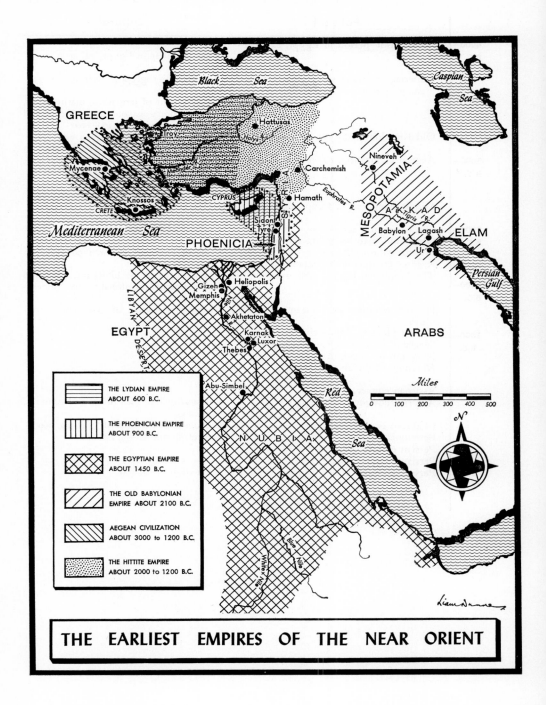

GREECE

Black Sea

Troy
Hattusas

Mycenae

Meander R.

Knossos

CRETE

CYPRUS

Mediterranean Sea

Sidon
Tyre

PHOENICIA

Caspian Sea

Nineveh

Carchemish

Hamath

Euphrates R.

MESOPOTAMIA

A K K A D

Tigris R.

Babylon
Lagash

ELAM

Ur

Persian Gulf

Heliopolis

Gizeh
Memphis

Akhetaton

Karnak
Luxor

Thebes

EGYPT

LIBYAN DESERT

Abu-Simbel

ARABS

Red Sea

N U B I A

White Nile

Blue Nile

Miles

0   100   200   300   400   500

N

THE LYDIAN EMPIRE
ABOUT 600 B.C.

THE PHOENICIAN EMPIRE
ABOUT 900 B.C.

THE EGYPTIAN EMPIRE
ABOUT 1450 B.C.

THE OLD BABYLONIAN
EMPIRE ABOUT 2100 B.C.

AEGEAN CIVILIZATION
ABOUT 3000 to 1200 B.C.

THE HITTITE EMPIRE
ABOUT 2000 to 1200 B.C.

Liam Dunne

THE EARLIEST EMPIRES OF THE NEAR ORIENT

	Political	Cultural
4000— **B.C.**	Pre-dynastic period in Egypt, *ca.* 4000–3200	Solar calendar in Egypt, *ca.* 4000
	Sumerian supremacy in Mesopotamia, *ca.* 4000–2000	Egyptian hieroglyphic writing, *ca.* 3500
		Development of irrigation, mathematics, rudimentary astronomy in Egypt and Mesopotamia, *ca.* 3500–2500
	Old Kingdom in Egypt, *ca.* 3200–2300	Cuneiform writing, *ca.* 3200 B.C.
3000— **B.C.**	Aegean civilization, *ca.* 3000–1000	Invention of principle of alphabet in Egypt, *ca.* 3000
		Construction of great pyramids in Egypt, *ca.* 2700
		Philosophy in Egypt, *ca.* 2500
	Middle Kingdom in Egypt, 2100–1788	
2000— **B.C.**	Hittite empire, 2000–1200	Code of Dungi, *ca.* 2000
	Old Babylonian kingdom, 1900–1600	
	Hyksos conquer Egypt, 1750–1580	Code of Hammurabi, *ca.* 1790
	Kassites conquer Babylonians, *ca.* 1600	
	The Empire in Egypt, 1580–1090	Egyptian temple architecture, 1580–1090
1500— **B.C.**		Development of alphabet by Phoenicians, *ca.* 1500
	Hebrew conquest of Canaan, *ca.* 1300–900	Realistic sculpture of Assyrians, 1300–600
1000— **B.C.**	United Hebrew Monarchy, 1025–935	
	Secession of Ten Tribes of Israel, 935	
	Kingdom of Israel, 935–722	
	Kingdom of Judah, 935–586	
	Assyrian empire, 722–612	
	Assyrian conquest of Egypt, 670	Division of day into hours and minutes, *ca.* 600
	Chaldean empire, 612–539	Calculation of length of year, *ca.* 600
	Babylonian captivity, 586–539	Deuteronomic Code, *ca.* 600
	Persian empire, 559–330	
	Persian conquest of Egypt, 525	
500— **B.C.**	Persian Empire under Darius, 521–486	Book of Job, *ca.* 500

NEAR ORIENT   *Dates are B.C. unless given as A.D.*

Economic	Religious
	Creation and Flood epics in Mesopotamia, *ca.* 4000
Development of serfdom in Mesopotamia and in Egypt, *ca.* 3500	Egyptian sun worship, *ca.* 3500
	Ethical religion in Egypt, *ca.* 3000
	Egyptian belief in personal immortality, *ca.* 2500
Large-scale industry in Egypt and Crete, *ca.* 2000	
	Demon worship and witchcraft in Babylonia, *ca.* 1900
Slavery in Egypt, *ca.* 1580	
Introduction of use of iron by Hittites, *ca.* 1500	
	Religious revolution of Ikhnaton, 1375
World trade of Phoenicians, *ca.* 1000–500	Hebrew worship of Yahweh, *ca.* 1000
	Ten Commandments, *ca.* 700
Slavery in Assyria, *ca.* 750	Prophetic Revolution, 700–500
	Hebrew doctrine of universal monotheism, *ca.* 600
Invention of coinage by Lydians, *ca.* 600	Astral religion of Chaldeans, 600–500
World trade of Chaldeans, 600–500	Divination and astrology, 600–500
	Zoroastrianism, *ca.* 600–300
	Babylonian Captivity of Jews, 586–539
Royal Road of Persians, *ca.* 500	
	Mithraism, *ca.* 300 B.C–275 A.D.
	Gnosticism, *ca.* 100 B.C.–100 A.D.
	Rise of Christianity, *ca.* 25 A.D.

The Egyptian Civilization

How great is that which thou has done, O lord of gods. Thy
plans and thy counsels are those which come to pass throughout.
Thou sentest me forth in valor, thy strength was with me. No
land stood before me, at the mention of thee. I overthrew those
who invaded my boundary, prostrated in their place. . . . It was
ordained because of thy victory-bringing commands, it was given
because of thy kingdom-bestowing power.
—Utterance of King Ramses III before his father, Amon-
Re, ruler of the gods, from The Great Inscription in
the Second Court relief in Medinet Habu temple

*The rise
of civilization
in Egypt*

The Neolithic culture stage came to an end in some parts of the
world soon after 5000 B.C. It seems to have disappeared first of all in
the Nile valley, but the area watered by the Tigris and Euphrates
rivers was not far behind. Progress toward a higher cultural level
appears to have been especially rapid in Egypt; not only that, but
the achievements of the Egyptians laid the foundation for a great
deal of the work of other peoples. It is therefore appropriate that we
begin our study of the historic cultures with the rise of civilization
on the banks of the Nile.

1. The Pre-Dynastic Period

*Meaning of the
pre-dynastic
period*

Since there was no enduring unified state in the valley of the
Nile until about 3200 B.C., the centuries from 5000 to 3200 are
referred to as the pre-dynastic period.[1] In the early part of this
period the country seems to have consisted of a number of "nomes,"
or city-states each of them independent, although evidently co-
operating with others for economic ends. Shortly after the beginning
of the fourth millennium a fusion of states took place to form two
large kingdoms, one in the north and one in the south. How the
consolidations were effected no one knows, but possibly they were
accomplished through voluntary agreement or peaceful acquiescence
in the rule of some capable prince. There is little evidence of military
conquest. These kingdoms endured until the end of the pre-dynastic
period, although they seem to have been united for a brief interval
soon after their establishment.

The racial complexion of pre-dynastic Egypt was essentially the

[1] Some authorities give the year 3400 as the approximate date for the beginning of the First Dynasty. Although recent research seems to favor about 3200,
it should be remembered that all dates prior to 2000 are largely a matter of
conjecture.

same as in later epochs. The inhabitants belonged to the Mediterranean branch of the Caucasian race; but they were not a pure strain, and there is nothing to indicate that racial factors as such were of importance in the development of their culture. They were a short, dark, long-headed people, with straight, black hair, deep-set eyes, and slightly aquiline noses. Some of them showed traces of Negroid and Libyan intermixture and possibly of the blood of Semites and other western Asiatic peoples. Their language contained evidences of Semitic elements, which would likewise indicate close relations with some of the natives of Asia.

The racial character of the Egyptians

The pre-dynastic period was by no means insignificant in the cultural history of Egypt. Outstanding progress was made in the arts and crafts and even in some of the sciences. Tools, weapons, and ornaments were expertly fashioned from flint, copper, and gold. New processes of finishing, glazing, and decorating pottery were discovered, with the result that the Egyptians of this period were able to make vessels of as high utility and artistic excellence as any produced by their later descendants. Other important achievements included the development of an efficient system of irrigation, the reclamation of swamp lands, and the weaving of a very superior quality of linen cloth.

Material progress in pre-dynastic Egypt

But these were not all of their accomplishments. There is evidence that the pre-dynastic Egyptians evolved a system of laws based upon custom, which were held in such high repute that they were later considered binding even upon the Pharaoh himself. A system of writing appears also to have come into use. Although no actual specimen of such writing has ever been found, the examples that have survived from the First Dynasty partake of so complex a nature that they must have originated much earlier. Finally, the Egyptians of this period invented the first solar calendar in the history of man. It seems to have been based upon the annual reappearance of Sirius, the "Dog Star," and it provided for twelve months of thirty days each, with five feast days added at the end of the year. According to the computations of modern Egyptologists, this calendar was put into effect about the year 4200 B.C. The existence of a reasonably accurate calendar at this time argues that a considerable development of mathematics, and possibly the other sciences, had already been attained.

Intellectual progress

2. Political History under the Pharaohs

About 3200 B.C. the kingdoms of Northern and Southern Egypt were combined into a single political unit, apparently for the second time, although the earlier union was of very brief duration. The traditional founder of the new state was Menes, who therefore became known as the founder of the First Dynasty. Five other dynasties followed in regular order until 2300 B.C. During the first two

Founding of the Old Kingdom

39

dynasties the capital was maintained at Thinis in Upper Egypt. The
Third Dynasty transferred the seat of government to Memphis on
the southern edge of the Delta, in order to secure the advantage of
a more central location of administrative functions. Here it remained
for approximately five centuries. The period from about 2800 to
2300 B.C. is accordingly called the Memphite period, while the entire age of the first six dynasties is known as the period of the Old
Kingdom.

*The govern-
ment of the Old
Kingdom*

The government of the Old Kingdom did not actually approach
the degree of personal absolutism that is commonly believed to have
existed. It was nearer a theocracy than an autocracy. The absolutism of the king was exercised not in his own behalf but as the
vicar of the god. It was the god as the personification of justice and
social order who actually ruled, according to the prevailing conception; the monarch was his agent. It is true, of course, that the king
was himself considered divine, the son of the sun god Re. He was
held in such high respect that he could not be mentioned by name,
but had to be referred to as "Pharaoh," from the Egyptian "per-o"
meaning "great house" or "royal house." He was forbidden to marry
anyone outside of his immediate family, lest the divine blood be
contaminated by an inferior strain. It is to be noted, however, that
in all his official actions his authority was limited by the ancient law,
which was believed to embody the divine will. He was not above the
law, but subject to it. To compare him, therefore, with the divine-
right monarchs of more modern times is to misunderstand his function.

*Union
of church and
state*

No separation of church and state existed in the Old Kingdom.
The Pharaoh's chief subordinates were the priests, and he was himself the chief priest. But he had other agents also: a vizier or prime
minister, a royal treasurer, a chief architect, a superintendent of public works, a chief justice, and forty-two nomarchs. The last were the
governors of the nomes or local districts into which the country was
divided. Originally they were appointed by the Pharaoh and were
supposed to execute his will, but gradually they made their positions
hereditary and usurped for themselves more and more prerogatives
of sovereignty. Since the nomes were survivals of the old city-states,
sectional feeling lingered and encouraged the local governors to
defy the central authority.

*Responsibilities
of the Pharaoh*

The position of Pharaoh was hereditary, but the privilege of succession to the office involved responsibilities. Usually the crown
prince served an apprenticeship under his father as superintendent of
public works or vizier. He thus came to the throne as an enlightened
and educated statesman, familiar with the needs of the country and
schooled in the great public enterprises of mining, construction of
public works, and irrigation. It was well that he was thus prepared,
for as king he was obliged by custom to devote a great deal of his
time to inspection and management of the various projects designed

to promote the national interest. The divinity that doth hedge a king did not exempt the Pharaoh from arduous service for the public welfare.

What has been said already about the importance of Egyptian law suggests that judicial procedure of fairly high quality must have been followed. Such was the case. Although the Old Kingdom had no well-defined class of professional judges, the administrative officials who served at times in a judicial capacity were learned in the law and boasted of their even-handed justice in deciding cases. Altogether six courts, to which different administrative officials were assigned from time to time as judges, composed the judicial branch of the government. Over them all was the chief justice, who sometimes held the position of vizier as well. Appeals could also be taken to the Pharaoh himself under certain circumstances. Apparently no class of cases was excluded from the regular jurisdiction of the courts. Records show that even cases of treason in the king's household were tried with the same scrupulous regard for legal procedure that was exhibited in the trials of petty offenders. The Pharaohs of the Old Kingdom had not yet learned the infamous distinction between political "crimes" and ordinary crimes which has been drawn by the rulers of some modern states.

The courts and judicial procedure

The government of the Old Kingdom was founded upon a policy of peace and non-aggression. In this respect it was almost unique among ancient states. The Pharaoh had no standing army, nor was there anything that could be called a national militia. Each nome had its local militia, but it was commanded by the civil officials, and when called into active service it generally devoted its energies to labor on the public works. In case of a threat of invasion the various local units were assembled at the call of the Pharaoh and placed under the command of one of his civil subordinates. At no other time did the head of the government have a military force at his disposal. The Egyptians of the Old Kingdom were content for the most part to work out their own destinies and to let other nations alone. The reasons for this attitude are to be found in the protected position of their country, in their possession of land of inexhaustible fertility, and in the fact that their state was a product of co-operative need instead of being grounded in exploitation.

The non-militaristic character of the Old Kingdom

After a solid millennium of peace and relative prosperity the Old Kingdom came to an end about 2300 B.C. Several causes appear to have been responsible: the usurpation of power by the nomarchs; the persistence of particularism, or "states' rights" sentiment; the growth of individualism; and the financial burdens imposed upon the people by Pharaohs with grandiose schemes for national development. The period which followed is called the Feudal Age. Save for intervals of order and progress it was marked by anarchy, aggrandizement of the power of the nobles, social revolution of the masses, and invasion by Negroid and Asiatic tribes. It did not end

End of the Old Kingdom

*The Middle
Kingdom
(2100-1788
B.C.)*

until the rise of the Eleventh Dynasty about 2100—an event which ushered in the next great stage in Egyptian history, which is known as the Middle Kingdom.

The government of the Middle Kingdom was notably weaker than that of the Old Kingdom. Dynasties of Pharaohs continued a nominal rule, but extensive authority gravitated into the hands of the nomarchs and nobles of lesser rank. The glory of these men was to govern as benevolent despots, performing in their local bailiwicks the functions rightfully belonging to the head of the state. In time they too were assailed by the masses, with the result that after 2000 B.C. the Pharaohs of the Twelfth Dynasty were able to regain a measure of their former power. The people themselves were rewarded by appointments to government positions and by grants of land and vested rights in particular occupations. The whole population, regardless of birth or rank, appears to have been accorded privileges hitherto reserved for the few. For this reason the government of the Twelfth Dynasty is sometimes referred to as the first democratic kingdom in history. The period of its rule was a golden age of social justice and intellectual achievement, although the forms of theocracy still survived.

*The invasion of
the Hyksos*

With the end of the Twelfth Dynasty, Egypt entered another era of internal chaos and foreign invasion which lasted for more than two centuries, or from 1788 to 1580 B.C. The contemporary records are scanty, but they seem to show that the internal disorder was the result of a counter-revolt of the nobles. The Pharaohs were again reduced to impotence, and much of the social progress of the preceding age was destroyed. About 1750 the land was invaded by the Hyksos, or the "Shepherd Kings," a mixed horde originating in western Asia. They extended a nominal rule over the whole country, although their effective sovereignty was probably confined to the Delta. Their military prowess is commonly ascribed to the fact that they possessed horses and war chariots, but their victory was certainly made easier by the dissension among the Egyptians themselves. Their rule had profound effects upon Egyptian history. Not only did they familiarize the Egyptians with new methods of warfare; but by providing them with a common grievance in the face of foreign tyranny they also enabled them to forget their differences and unite in a common cause. Thus the path was cleared for the restoration of strong government over the whole country.

*Expulsion of
the Hyksos and
founding of the
Empire*

Near the end of the seventeenth century the rulers of Upper Egypt launched a revolt against the Hyksos, a movement which was eventually joined by most of the natives of the valley. By 1580 all of the conquerors who had not been killed or enslaved had been driven from the country. The hero of this victory, Ahmose I, founder of the Eighteenth Dynasty, now made himself despot of Egypt. The regime he established was much more highly consolidated than any that had hitherto existed. In the great resurgence of nationalism which had accompanied the struggle against the Hyksos, local patriotism was annihilated and with it the power of the nobles. Most of the nomarchs had opposed the rise of Ahmose; his final triumph made their position untenable and left them with no alternative but to surrender their claims to sovereignty.

The period which followed the accession of Ahmose is called the period of the Empire. It lasted from 1580 to 1090 B.C., during which *The growth of* time the country was ruled by three dynasties of Pharaohs in *imperialism* succession, the Eighteenth, Nineteenth, and Twentieth. No longer was the prevailing state policy pacific and isolationist; a spirit of aggressive imperialism rapidly pervaded the nation. The causes of this change are not far to seek. The military ardor generated by the successful war against the Hyksos whetted an appetite for further victories. A vast military machine had been created to expel the invader, which proved to be too valuable an adjunct to the Pharaoh's power to be discarded immediately. Besides, there were fears, either real or imaginary, of new invasions from western Asia.

The first steps in the direction of the new policy were taken by the immediate successors of Ahmose in making extensive raids into Palestine and claiming sovereignty over Syria. The lust for empire reached its zenith some years later during the reign of Thutmose III, *Egyptian con-* who came to the throne in 1479 B.C. With one of the most formidable *quests* armies of ancient times he speedily annihilated all opposition in Syria and eventually made himself master of a vast domain extending from the Euphrates to the farther cataracts of the Nile. Phoenicians, Canaanites, Hittites, and Assyrians acknowledged his suzerainty or paid him tribute. But he never succeeded in welding the conquered peoples into loyal subjects, and his death was the signal for widespread revolt in Syria. His successors suppressed the uprising and managed to hold the empire together for some time, but ultimate disaster could not be averted. More territory had been annexed than could be managed successfully; the influx of wealth into Egypt weakened the national fiber by fostering corruption and luxury; while the constant revolts of the vanquished eventually sapped the strength of the state beyond all hope of recovery. By the twelfth century most of the conquered provinces had been permanently lost.

The government of the Empire resembled that of the Old Kingdom, except for the fact that it was more absolute. Military power rather than national unity was now the basis of the Pharaoh's rule. *The govern-* A professional army was always available with which to overawe his *ment of the* subjects. His eldest son, who in the Old Kingdom had served an *Empire* apprenticeship as vizier, was now the highest ranking officer in the standing army. Scarcely any vestige of local authority remained. The nation was divided into more than fifty administrative units, many of them purely arbitrary, and over each was appointed a "count" or governor as the direct representative of the monarch's rule. Most of the former nobles now became courtiers or members of the royal bureaucracy under the complete domination of the king. The Pharaoh was not yet a divine-right monarch, but the actual extent of his power had begun to approach that of more modern despots.

The last of the great Pharaohs was Ramses III, who ruled from 1198 to 1167 B.C. He was succeeded by a long line of nonentities who inherited his name but not his ability. By the middle of the twelfth century Egypt had fallen a prey to numerous ills of barbarian invasion and social decadence. Libyans and Nubians were swarming over the country and gradually debasing cultural standards. About the same time the Egyptians themselves appear to have lost their creative talent; their intellects seem to have been led astray by the seductions of magic and superstition; and the inevitable result was domination of the national life by a crude religious formalism. To win immortality by magic devices was now the commanding interest of men of every class. The process of decline was hastened also by the growing power of the priests, who finally usurped the royal prerogatives and dictated the Pharaoh's decrees.

The last of the Pharaohs

From the middle of the tenth century to nearly the end of the eighth a dynasty of Libyan barbarians occupied the throne of the Pharaohs. The Libyans were followed by a line of Ethiopians or Nubians, who came in from the desert regions west of the Upper Nile. In 670 Egypt was conquered by the Assyrians, who succeeded in maintaining their supremacy for only eight years. After the collapse of Assyrian rule in 662 the Egyptians regained their independence, and a brilliant renaissance of culture ensued. It was doomed to an untimely end, however, for in 525 B.C. the country was conquered by the Persians. The ancient civilization was never again revived.

The downfall of Egypt

3. Egyptian Religion

Religion played a dominant role in the life of the ancient Egyptians. The Greek description of the Egyptians as "the most religious of men" is something of an exaggeration, and yet there is no denying that belief in the supernatural was as important to the culture of the Nile valley as to any other civilization, past or present. Religion left its impress upon almost every department of Egyptian life. The art was an expression of religious symbolism. The literature and philosophy were suffused with religious teachings. The government of the Old Kingdom was to a large extent a theocracy, and even the military Pharaohs of the Empire professed to rule in the name of the god. Economic energy and material resources in considerable amounts were squandered in providing elaborate tombs and in maintaining a costly ecclesiastical system.

The importance of religion in Egypt

The religion of the ancient Egyptians evolved through various stages from simple polytheism to philosophic monotheism. In the beginning each city or district appears to have had its local deities, who were guardian gods of the locality or personifications of nature powers. The unification of the country under the Old Kingdom resulted not only in a consolidation of territory but in a fusion of divinities as well. All of the guardian deities were merged into the great sun god Re or Ra. In later times, with the establishment of a Theban dynasty in control of the government, this deity was commonly called Amon or Ammon-Re from the name of the chief god of Thebes. The gods who personified the vegetative powers of nature were fused into a deity called Osiris, who was also the god of the Nile. Throughout Egyptian history these two great powers who ruled the universe, Re and Osiris, vied with each other for supremacy. Other deities, as we shall see, were recognized also, but they occupied a distinctly subordinate place.

During the period of the Old Kingdom the solar faith, embodied in the worship of Re, was the dominant system of belief. It served as an official religion whose chief function was to give immortality to the state and to the people collectively. The Pharaoh was the living representative of this faith on earth; through his rule the rule of the god was maintained. The belief prevailed also that mummifying the Pharaoh's body and keeping it in an everlasting tomb would contribute to the eternal existence of the nation. But Re was not only a guardian deity. He was in addition the god of righteousness, justice, and truth and the upholder of the moral order of the universe. He offered no spiritual blessings or even material rewards to men as individuals, nor did he concern himself in any other ways with ordinary human welfare. The solar faith was not a religion for the masses as such, except in so far as their welfare coincided with that of the state.

The cult of Osiris, as we have already observed, began its existence as a nature religion. The god personified the growth of vegetation and the life-giving powers of the Nile. The career of Osiris was wrapped about with an elaborate legend. In the remote past, according to belief, he had been a benevolent ruler, who taught his people agriculture and other practical arts and gave them laws. After a time he was treacherously slain by his wicked brother Set, and his body cut into pieces. His wife Isis, who was also his sister, went in search of the pieces, put them together, and miraculously restored his body to life. The risen god regained his kingdom and continued his beneficent rule for a time, but eventually descended to the nether world to serve as judge of the dead. Horus, his posthumous son, finally grew to manhood and avenged his father's death by killing Set.

Originally this legend seems to have been little more than a nature myth. The death and resurrection of Osiris symbolized the recession

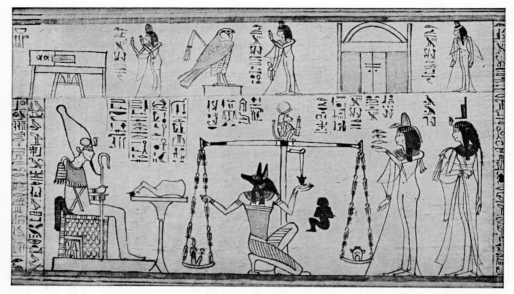

Funerary Papyrus. The scene shows the heart of a princess of the XXIst Dynasty being weighed in a balance before the god Osiris. On the other side of the balance are the symbols for life and truth.

Significance of the Osiris legend of the Nile in the autumn and the coming of the flood in the spring. But in time the Osiris legend began to take on a deeper significance. The human qualities of the deities concerned—the paternal solicitude of Osiris for his subjects, the faithful devotion of his wife and son— appealed to the emotions of the average Egyptian, who was now able to see his own tribulations and triumphs mirrored in the lives of the gods. More important still, the death and resurrection of Osiris came to be regarded as conveying a promise of personal immortality for man. As the god had triumphed over death and the grave, so might the individual also who followed him faithfully inherit everlasting life. Finally, the victory of Horus over Set appeared to foreshadow the ultimate ascendancy of good over evil.

With the growing perception of these implications, the cult of Osiris gradually became the more popular branch of the Egyptian *The popularity of the cult of Osiris* religion. The worship of the sun god Re required such lofty powers of abstraction that it made little appeal to the average man. Especially during the period of the Middle Kingdom, when individualism rose to its greatest heights, the popular cult received more than its share of attention. The result was not altogether fortunate. Osiris was essentially a god of the dead; he bestowed no rewards upon men in this life. As a consequence of his worship the minds of the Egyptian masses were oriented more and more toward the after-life. Too much emphasis came to be placed upon winning salvation in the world to come, and not enough upon co-operation

46

with Re to promote the reign of righteousness in this world. The solar faith did not die out during the time of the Middle Kingdom, but it was clearly reduced to second place.

Egyptian ideas of the hereafter attained their full development in the later history of the Middle Kingdom. Soon after the beginning of this period the religion had come to include the conception of a *ba*, or "soul," in addition to the idea of a *ka*, or "double." Both were regarded as surviving the death of the individual. The *ba* took flight in the form of a bird. The *ka* wandered off in much the same way that the "other self" might travel to distant places in a dream while the body was locked in sleep. Both the *ba* and the *ka* would eventually return and revivify the body if it were still in existence. For this reason elaborate preparations had to be made to prevent the extinction of one's earthly remains. Not only were bodies mummified but wealthy men left munificent endowments to provide their mummies with food and other essentials. As the religion advanced toward maturity, however, a less naïve conception of the after-life was adopted. The dead were now believed to appear before Osiris to be judged according to their deeds on earth. The process of judgment occupied three stages. In the first, the deceased was required to declare his innocence of forty-two sins, including murder, theft, untruthfulness, greed, adultery, blasphemy, loss of temper, pride, and dishonesty in business transactions. Having thus acquitted himself of this catalogue of vices, the deceased was then obliged to assert his virtues. He must avow that he had satisfied the needs of the gods, that he had given "bread to the hungry, water to the thirsty, clothing to the naked, and a ferry to him who was without a boat." [2] In the third and final stage the heart of the defendant was weighed in the balance against a feather, the symbol of truth, in order to determine the accuracy of his testimony. According to the Egyptian notion, the heart represented the conscience, which would betray the person who testified falsely.

Egyptian ideas of the hereafter

See color plates at pages 29, 60, 61

All of the departed who met the tests included in this system of judgment entered a celestial realm of physical delights and simple pleasures. Here in marshes of lilies and lotus-flowers they would hunt wild geese and quail with never-ending success. Or they might build houses in the midst of orchards with luscious fruits of unfailing yield. They would find lily-lakes on which to sail, pools of sparkling water in which to bathe, and shady groves inhabited by singing birds and every manner of gentle creatures. The unfortunate victims whose hearts revealed their vicious lives were condemned to perpetual hunger and thirst in a place of darkness, forever cut off from the glorious light of Re.

Rewards and punishments

The Egyptian religion attained its highest perfection about the end of the Middle Kingdom and the beginning of the Empire. By this time the solar faith and the cult of Osiris had been merged in such a way as to preserve the best features of both. The province of

The perfection of the Egyptian religion

[2] J. H. Breasted, *The Dawn of Conscience*, p. 259.

Re as the god of the living, as the champion of good in this world, was accorded almost equal importance with the functions of Osiris as the giver of personal immortality and the judge of the dead. The religion was now quite clearly an ethical one. Men repeatedly avowed their desire to do justice because such conduct was pleasing to the great sun god.

Priestcraft and superstition

Very soon after the establishment of the Empire the religion which has just been described underwent a serious debasement. Its ethical significance was largely destroyed, and superstition and magic gained the ascendancy. The chief cause seems to have been that the long and bitter war for the expulsion of the Hyksos fostered the growth of irrational attitudes and correspondingly depreciated the intellect. The result was a marked increase in the power of the priests, who preyed upon the fears of the masses to promote their own advantage. Greedy for gain, they inaugurated the practice of selling magical charms, which were supposed to have the effect of preventing the heart of the deceased from betraying his real character. They also sold formulas which, inscribed on rolls of papyrus and placed in the tomb, were alleged to be effective in facilitating the passage of the dead to the celestial realm. The aggregate of these formulas constituted what is referred to as the Book of the Dead. Contrary to the general impression, it was not an Egyptian Bible, but merely a collection of mortuary inscriptions. Some of them proclaimed the moral purity of the deceased; others threatened the gods with disaster unless the persons whose names they bore were granted eternal reward. All of them were purchased in the belief that they guaranteed an entrance into the kingdom of Re. Good deeds and a clear conscience were now considered outmoded.

See color plates at page 61

The religious revolution of Ikhnaton

This degradation of the religion at the hands of the priests into a system of magical practices finally resulted in a great reformation or religious revolution. The leader of this movement was the Pharaoh Amenhotep IV, who began his reign about 1375 B.C. After some fruitless attempts to correct the most flagrant abuses, he resolved to crush the system entirely. He drove the priests from the temples, hacked the names of the traditional deities from the public monuments, and commanded his people to worship a new god whom he called "Aton," an ancient designation for the physical sun. He changed his own name from Amenhotep ("Amen rests") to Ikhnaton, which meant "Aton is satisfied." Ikhnaton is the name by which he is commonly known in history.

Ikhnaton's doctrines

More important than these physical changes was the new set of doctrines enunciated by the reforming Pharaoh. According to eminent authorities, he taught first of all a religion of universal monotheism; Aton, he declared, was the only god in existence, the god not merely of Egypt but of the whole universe.[3] He restored

[3] J. H. Breasted, *A History of Egypt*, p. 376; see also Alexandre Moret, *From Tribe to Empire*, pp. 298-300.

the ethical quality of the national religion at its best by insisting that Aton was the author of the moral order of the world and the re-warder of men for integrity and purity of heart. He envisaged the new god as an eternal creator and sustainer of all that is of benefit to man, and as a heavenly father who watches with benevolent care over all his creatures. Conceptions like these of the unity, righteous-ness, and benevolence of God were not attained again until the time of the Hebrew prophets some 600 years later.

The revolution of Ikhnaton was not an enduring success. The Pharaohs who followed him as rulers of the Empire were not in-spired by the same devoted idealism. Such was particularly the *The results of* case of the famous Tutenkhamen, who allowed the corrupt and *Ikhnaton's* mercenary priests to regain their power. The result was a revival *revolution* and a gradual extension of the same old superstitions which had prevailed before Ikhnaton's reign. For the great masses of the nation the ethical significance of the religion was permanently lost, and they were thrown back once more to ignorance and priestly greed. Among the educated classes, however, the influence of Ikhnaton's teachings lingered for some time. Although the god Aton was no longer recognized, the qualities he represented continued to be held in high esteem. What happened was that the attributes of Aton were now transferred by the educated minority to Ammon-Re. The traditional solar deity was acclaimed as the only god and the em-bodiment of righteousness, justice, and truth. He was worshiped, moreover, as a merciful and loving being "who heareth prayers, who giveth the hand to the poor, who saveth the weary." [4] It should be noted also that to this religion of ethical monotheism was added an element of personal salvation through repentance. The religious philosophers of the time developed the new idea that the god would refrain from punishing the penitent sinner who humbly implored forgiveness.

Adherence by the intelligent few to these noble ideas was not enough to save the religion from complete degeneracy and ruin. The spread of superstition, the popularity of magic, and the para- *Decay sets* lyzing grip of a degenerate priesthood were far too deadly in their *in once more* effects to be overcome by exalted doctrines. In the end the whole system of belief and worship was engulfed by formalism and ig-norance and by fetishism (worship of magical objects), animal wor-ship, necromancy (black magic: foretelling the future by com-muning with the dead), and other magical crudities. The commer-cialism of the priests was more rampant than ever, and the chief function of the organized religion had come to be the sale of formulas and charms which would stifle the conscience and trick the gods into granting eternal salvation. The tragedy was com-pounded by the fact that as the religion decayed it exerted a baneful effect upon the rest of the culture. Philosophy, art, and government

[4] J. H. Breasted, *The Dawn of Conscience*, p. 316.

were so closely linked with religion that all of them went down together.

4. Egyptian Intellectual Achievements

*The general
character of
Egyptian
philosophy*

I. PHILOSOPHY The philosophy of ancient Egypt was chiefly ethical and political, although traces of broader philosophic conceptions are occasionally to be found. The idea that the universe is controlled by mind or intelligence, for example, is a notion that appeared from time to time in the writings of priests and sages. It was first expressed in an inscription known as the *Memphite Drama*, dating from the end of the fourth millennium, and it was revived by Ikhnaton two thousand years later. This idea is so far removed from ordinary anthropomorphic beliefs of ancient peoples that it may seem surprising to find it developed by one of the earliest civilizations; but such was the case. Other philosophic ideas of the ancient Egyptians included the conception of an eternal universe, the notion of constantly recurring cycles of events, and the doctrine of natural cause and effect.

*The earliest
ethical philoso-
phy*

The earliest examples of ethical philosophy are contained in the *Maxims* of Ptahhotep, who served as vizier under one of the Pharaohs of the Fifth Dynasty about 2500 B.C. The work consists of some forty paragraphs of sage advice left by the vizier for the instruction of his son. About half of them are aphorisms of practical wisdom intended for the guidance of the young man in the pursuit of worldly success. Others, however, inculcate morality of a very high order. The son is enjoined to be gracious, tolerant, kindly, and cheerful, but above all to be righteous and just, even to the sacrifice of his own advantage, for "the power of righteousness is that it endures." The author also counsels the avoidance of greed, sensuality, and pride and urges moderation and restraint.[5] Elementary though these maxims are, they are nevertheless highly significant, for they are the first expressions of moral idealism in all the world's literature.

*The appearance
of disillusion-
ment and skepti-
cism*

During the Middle Kingdom ethical philosophy displayed a more sophisticated trend. Indeed, its most prominent characteristics were attitudes of pessimism and disillusionment. One reason was that the ancient faith in the religion of Re had broken down. Men no longer believed that preserving the material remains of the Pharaoh would insure the immortality of the nation. Another was that the collapse of the united kingdom and the prevalence of social disorder and foreign invasion produced a feeling of insecurity and hopelessness. Above all, the growth of intellectual maturity made the older conceptions of life and the world appear naïve and groundless. The consequence was a tendency toward the opposite extreme of believing in nothing.

[5] *Ibid.*, pp. 129–39.

A characteristic example of the new philosophic trend was the *Song of the Harp-Player,* which one of the Pharaohs of the Eleventh Dynasty had engraved on the wall of his tomb-chapel about 2100 B.C. It expresses a philosophy of complete skepticism regarding an existence in the after-world: "None cometh from thence that he may tell us how they fare." The gods are not recognized, except that Re is conceived as a blind, impersonal force. No importance is attached to the traditional rewards of virtue and effort; fame, riches, and power are empty delusions. Death is the common fate of Pharaoh and servant alike, and no one knows the day or the hour of its coming. The logical course for man to pursue is therefore to follow desire, to seek his pleasure while he may. But self-indulgence is not enough. One should also strive to gain a good name, by giving "bread to him who hath no field," and by other benevolent works.[6]

INTELLECTUAL ACHIEVEMENTS —PHILOSOPHY

The Song of the Harp-Player

The first of a series of Egyptian philosophers whose interests were predominantly political was a priest of Heliopolis who lived during the years that followed the collapse of the Old Kingdom. His name (Khekheperre-soneb) is of such formidable length that he is generally referred to simply as the Priest of Heliopolis. He was the author of the earliest arraignment of society and the first indictment of the upper classes for their injustice to the poor. "The poor man," he declared, "has no strength to save himself from him that is stronger than he." Misery reigns throughout the land. Those who are born to lead are degenerate and cowardly. Society itself is corrupt and complacent. The author recommended no specific reforms, but, as Breasted suggests, many of his reflections would be appropriate in the writings of social critics of our own day.

Political philosophy

With the accession of the Eleventh Dynasty about 2100 B.C., Egypt returned to a semblance of order and prosperity. It was natural that the political philosophy of the time should reflect the welcome change. The most famous specimen of this philosophy is a work which has been given the title of the *Plea of the Eloquent Peasant.* Its authorship is unknown, but it was probably written at the behest of an intelligent Pharaoh who wanted to inculcate high standards of official morality in his subordinates and impress the people with the justice of his rule. It is composed in narrative form and relates the story of a peasant who has been robbed by an unscrupulous official. The victim appeals to the official's superiors, who, at the instance of the Pharaoh, encourage him to unburden himself of all his grievances and to expound his conception of administrative justice. In the course of his pleas the peasant contends that officers of state have the following duties: to act as the father of the orphan, the husband of the widow, and the brother of the forsaken; to ward off the robber and protect the wretched; to execute punishment upon whom it is due; to judge impartially and to speak no falsehood; and to promote such an order of harmony

The Plea of the Eloquent Peasant

[6] *Ibid.,* pp. 163–67.

and prosperity that no one may suffer from hunger or cold or thirst. Few nobler conceptions of the functions of rulers have ever been set forth by political philosophers. We are not to suppose that the sentiments expressed were actually those of the peasant. The story is fictitious. The philosophy it contains reflects the ideals of an enlightened Pharaoh.

II. SCIENCE The branches of science which first absorbed the attention of the Egyptians were astronomy and mathematics. Both were developed for practical ends—to compute the time of the Nile inundations, to lay out the plans for pyramids and temples, and to solve the intricate problems of irrigation and public control of economic functions. The Egyptians were not pure scientists; they had little interest in the nature of the physical universe as such— a fact which probably accounts for their failure to advance very far in the science of astronomy. They perfected a solar calendar, as we have already learned, mapped the heavens, identified the prin- cipal fixed stars, and achieved some success in determining accurately the positions of stellar bodies. Nearly all of these accomplishments were made in the pre-dynastic period and in the Old Kingdom. In later times the interest in astronomy waned.

The character of Egyptian sci- ence; astronomy

The science of mathematics was more highly developed. The Egyptians laid the foundations for at least two of the common mathematical subjects—arithmetic and geometry. They devised the arithmetical operations of addition, subtraction, and division, al- though they never discovered how to multiply except through a series of additions. They invented the decimal system, but they had no symbol for zero. Fractions caused them some difficulty: all those with a numerator greater than one had to be broken down into a series, each with *one* as the numerator, before they could be used in mathematical calculations. The only exception was the fraction two-thirds, which the scribes had learned to use as it stood. The Egyptians also achieved a surprising degree of skill in mensuration, computing with accuracy the areas of triangles, rectangles, and hexagons. The ratio of the circumference of a circle to its diameter they calculated to be 3.16. They learned how to compute the volume of the pyramid and the cylinder, and even the volume of the hemisphere.

Achievements in mathematics

See color plates at page 61

The third branch of science in which the Egyptians did some remarkable work was medicine, although progress was slow until the age of the Middle Kingdom. Early medical practice was con- servative and profusely corrupted by superstition, but a document dating from about 1700 B.C. reveals a fairly adequate conception of scientific diagnosis and treatment. Egyptian physicians were frequently specialists: some were oculists; others were dentists, surgeons, specialists in diseases of the stomach, and so on. In the course of their work they made many discoveries of lasting value.

Medicine

52

They recognized the importance of the heart and had some appreciation of the significance of the pulse. They acquired a degree of skill in the treatment of fractures and performed simple operations. Unlike some peoples of later date they ascribed disease to natural causes. They discovered the value of cathartics, noted the curative properties of numerous drugs, and compiled the first *materia medica*, or catalogue of medicines. Many of their remedies, both scientific and magical, were carried into Europe by the Greeks and are still employed by the peasantry of isolated regions.

In other scientific fields the Egyptians contributed little. Although they achieved feats which rival modern engineering, they possessed but the scantiest knowledge of physics. They knew the principle of the inclined plane, but they were ignorant of the pulley. To their credit also must be assigned considerable progress in metallurgy, the invention of the sundial, and the making of paper and glass. With all their deficiencies as pure scientists, they really equaled the Romans in actual accomplishment and went far ahead of anything done by the Hebrews and Persians.

III. WRITING AND LITERATURE The Egyptians developed their first form of writing during the pre-dynastic period. This system, known as the *hieroglyphic*, from the Greek words meaning sacred carving, was originally composed of pictographic signs denoting concrete objects. Gradually certain of these signs were conventionalized and used to represent abstract concepts. Other characters were introduced to designate separate syllables which could be combined to form words. Finally, twenty-four symbols, each representing a single consonant sound of the human voice, were added early in the Old Kingdom. Thus the hieroglyphic system of writing had come to include at an early date three separate types of characters, the pictographic, syllabic, and alphabetic.

The ultimate step in this evolution of writing would have been the complete separation of the alphabetic from the non-alphabetic characters and the exclusive use of the former in written communication. The Egyptians were reluctant to take this step. Their traditions of conservatism impelled them to follow old habits. Although they made frequent use of the consonant signs, they did not commonly employ them as an independent system of writing. It was left for the Phoenicians to do this some 1500 years later. Nevertheless, the Egyptians must be credited with the invention of the principle of the alphabet. It was they who first perceived the value of single symbols for the individual sounds of the human voice. The Phoenicians merely copied this principle, based their own system of writing upon it, and diffused the idea among neighboring nations. In the ultimate sense it is therefore true that the Egyptian alphabet was the parent of every other that has ever been used in the Western world. The Egyptians also devised two other systems of

Other scientific accomplishments

The hieroglyphic system

The principle of the alphabet

writing in addition to the hieroglyphic: the *hieratic*, which was a cursive or running hand employed for business purposes; and the *demotic*, which was a simpler and more popular form of hieratic.

Egyptian literature was largely philosophical and religious. The former type has already been discussed. By far the best specimens *Egyptian reli-* of the latter were the *Memphite Drama*, the *Royal Sun Hymn* of *gious literature* Ikhnaton, and the hymns of personal piety which have survived from the period of the Empire. The *Memphite Drama*, written about 3000 B.C., was a theological dialogue in which various gods discoursed on the doctrines of the solar religion. The object of the work was apparently to promote the national worship of the sun god Re. Its pervading theme was the idea that Re was the arbiter of human destiny, the author of good, and the giver of life to the "peaceful" and of death to the "guilty." The *Royal Hymn* of Ikhnaton, composed by the great reforming Pharaoh of the fourteenth century B.C., was a stately ode in praise of the majesty, providence, and justice of Aton, "the sole God, beside whom there is no other." It was the supreme embodiment of the Egyptian conception of universal monotheism.

Literature of a deeper emotional quality was exemplified by the hymns of personal piety, written during the two or three hundred *The hymns of* years that followed the death of Ikhnaton. They likewise avow a *personal piety* belief in one God, but they call him by the more ancient name of Amon, and celebrate his loving kindness rather than his splendor and majesty. He is acclaimed as the "Lord of sweetness who giveth breath to every one he loveth" and bestows his tender care upon his humblest creatures. He is merciful, wise, and just, and forgives those who call upon his name. "Punish me not for my many sins" is a common supplication addressed to him. The following is a typical excerpt from one of these hymns:

> Thou, O Amon, art the lord of the silent
> Who cometh at the cry of the poor.
> When I cry to thee in my affliction,
> Then thou comest and savest me.
> That thou mayest give breath to him who is bowed down,
> And mayest save me lying in bondage.[7]

In addition to the philosophical and religious works, there were many writings of a lighter sort. Folk songs of the common people *Popular litera-* at their labors, stories of travel and adventure, odes of victory in *ture* battle, and charming love lyrics that suggest the style and imagery of the Biblical Song of Solomon are among the several types which have come down to us. Most famous of the individual compositions was the *Tale of the Two Brothers*, considered by some authorities as the source of the Old Testament narrative of Joseph and Poti-

54   [7] *Ibid.,* p. 315.

phar's wife. The popular literature of Egypt is especially significant for its influence, since much of its content was copied by later Oriental peoples, and for the light which it throws upon the society of the common man. It portrays the average Egyptian in his prevailing moods of cheerful resignation and joy in the simpler pleasures. It reveals a society comparatively free from the grosser forms of tyranny and ignorance. We are given the impression of a standard of living that was not indescribably poor and mean, in which the middle classes, at least, could acquire the rudiments of an education and thereby escape from a life of drudgery and pain.

5. The Meaning of Egyptian Art

No single interpretation will suffice to explain the meaning of Egyptian art. Its purposes were varied, and the ideals it was supposed to represent changed with the shifting tendencies of political and social history. In general, it expressed the aspirations of a collectivized national life. It was not art for art's sake, nor did it serve to convey the individual's reactions to the problems of his personal world. Yet there were times when the conventions of a communal society were broken down, and the supremacy was accorded to a spontaneous individual art that sensed the beauty of the flower or caught the radiant idealism of a youthful face. Seldom was the Egyptian genius for faithful reproduction of nature entirely suppressed. Even the rigid formalism of the official architecture was commonly relieved by touches of naturalism—columns in imitation of palm trunks, lotus blossom capitals, and occasional statues of Pharaohs which were not conventionalized types but true individual portraits.

The character of Egyptian art

See color plates at page 61

In most civilizations where the interests of society are exalted above those of its members, architecture is at once the most typical and the most highly developed of the arts. Egypt was no exception. Whether in the Old Kingdom, Middle Kingdom, or Empire it was the problems of building construction which absorbed the talent of the artist. Although painting and sculpture were by no means primitive, they nevertheless had as their primary function the embellishment of temples. Only at times did they rise to the status of independent arts.

Architecture

The characteristic examples of Old Kingdom architecture were the pyramids, the first of which were built at least as early as 2700 B.C. An amazing amount of labor and skill were expended in their construction. The Greek historian Herodotus estimated that 100,000 men must have been employed for twenty years to complete the single pyramid of Khufu at Gizeh. Its total height exceeds 480 feet, and the more than two million limestone blocks it contains are fitted together with a precision which few modern masons could duplicate. Each of the blocks weighs about two and a half tons. They

The pyramids

Gateway of the Great Temple at Luxor. The purpose of the temple was to portray the divine origin of the Pharaoh as the son of Ammon-Re.

were evidently hewn out of rock cliffs with drills and wedges and then dragged up earthen ramps by gangs of men and pried into place.

Significance of the pyramids

The significance of the pyramids is not easy to comprehend. They may have been intended for the economic purpose of providing employment opportunities. Such a theory would assume that the population had increased to overcrowding, and that the resources of agriculture, mining, industry, and commerce were no longer adequate to provide a livelihood for all the people. But whatever the validity of this theory, it is hardly a complete explanation. The pyramids also had a political and religious significance. Their construction was an act of faith, the expression of an ambition to endow the state with permanence and stability. As indestructible tombs of the rulers they were believed to guarantee immortality to the people, for the Pharaoh was the embodiment of the national life. It is possible also that they were intended to serve as symbols of sun worship. As the tallest structures in Egypt they would catch the first light of the rising sun and reflect it to the valley below.

During the Middle Kingdom and the Empire the temple displaced the pyramid as the leading architectural form. No longer was preservation of the material remains of the Pharaoh considered so important, nor was there quite the same credulous faith in the identification of the ruler with the nation. On the other hand, there was the same interest in structures of massive proportions which would express the national strength and the belief in the eternity of the culture. But these structures were not tombs. The most famous examples of them were the great temples at Karnak and Luxor, built during the period of the Empire. Many of their gigantic, richly carved columns still stand as silent witnesses of a splendid architectural talent.

The temples

Egyptian temples were characterized first of all by massive size.
The temple at Karnak, with a length of about 1300 feet, covered the
largest area of any religious edifice ever built. Its central hall alone
could contain almost any of the Gothic cathedrals of Europe. But

Characteristics of temple architecture

even its enormous bulk was not enough to satisfy the passion for
grandeur. Artificial devices were employed to make the building
seem larger than it really was. As an example, the height of the
ceiling was progressively diminished from the entrance toward the
rear to create the illusion of a long perspective and therefore of a
vast expanse of floor. The columns used in the temples had stupen-
dous proportions. The largest of them were seventy feet high, with
diameters in excess of twenty feet. It has been estimated that the
capitals which surmounted them could furnish standing room for
a hundred men.

The Egyptians deliberately chose to give their temples hugeness
of size and solidity of construction. They did not completely sacrifice grace and proportion—much of the decoration was instinct with
life, and the design frequently bespoke a high regard for symmetry.
But impressions of grandeur and massiveness were quite evidently

The passion for hugeness

Hypostyle Hall in the Temple at Karnak. Hugeness, to express the national strength and belief in eternity, was a dominant feature of Egyptian temple architecture. Note also the deeply incised carvings on the columns.

the vital considerations, especially in the temples of the Empire. Such
a conclusion is rendered obvious by the fact that the materials used
in temple construction were by no means of a flimsy or insubstantial
character. Walls several feet thick and columns of enormous diameter were not made necessary by a choice of materials that were
likely to crumble; on the contrary, the Egyptians used nothing but
the hardest of stone. We are therefore led to the belief that the real
purpose of their building style was to symbolize conceptions of national pride, imperial glory, and the strength and permanence of the
state. Many other imperialistic peoples, the Assyrians and the
Romans for example, have sought to express the majesty of their **57**

accomplishments in buildings of imposing magnitude. Perhaps the tendency in much modern architecture to identify beauty with hugeness is a reflection of a similar pride in conquest.

As already mentioned, Egyptian sculpture and painting served primarily as adjuncts to architecture. The former was heavily laden *Egyptian sculp-* with conventions which restricted its style and meaning. Statues *ture* of Pharaohs were commonly of colossal size. Those produced during the Empire ranged in height from seventy-five to ninety feet. Some of them were colored to resemble life, and the eyes were frequently inlaid with rock crystal. The figures were nearly always rigid, with the arms folded across the chest or fixed to the sides of the body and with the eyes staring straight to the front. Countenances were generally represented as impassive, utterly devoid of emotional expression. Anatomical distortion was frequently practiced: the natural length of the thighs might be increased, the squareness of the shoulders accentuated, or all of the fingers of the hand made equal in length. A familiar example of non-naturalistic sculpture was the Sphinx. This represented the head of a Pharaoh on the body of a lion. The purpose was probably to symbolize the notion that the Pharaoh possessed the lion's qualities of strength and courage. The figures of sculpture in relief were even less in conformity with nature. The

Colossus of Ramses II (XIXth Dynasty). Though almost modern in its sharp, cubist lines, this statue is typically Egyptian in the imperturbable expression of the face and the conventionalized treatment of shoulders, arms, and legs.

Relief Portrait of Seti I (XIXth Dynasty). The face is almost the only individualized part of this portrait. Observe the frontality of the shoulders, the conventionalized position of the feet, and the equal length of the fingers.

head was presented in profile, with the eye fullface; the torso was shown in the frontal position, while the legs were rendered in profile. Such were the general tendencies, but it should be noted that they were not universal. Occasionally the artist succeeded in a partial defiance of conventions, as is evidenced by the production of some highly individual likenesses of the later Pharaohs. The most notable example was a beautiful limestone head of Ikhnaton, found some years ago at Amarna, which clearly portrayed the quality of dreamy mysticism inherent in the soul of the great reformer.

The meaning of Egyptian sculpture is not hard to perceive. The colossal size of the statues of Pharaohs was doubtless intended to symbolize their power and the power of the state they represented. It is significant that the size of these statues increased as the empire expanded and the government became more absolute. The conventions of rigidity and impassiveness, which dominated not only the statues of rulers but even the sculptures of less formal description such as the figure of *The Seated Scribe*, were meant to express the timelessness and stability of the national life. Here was a nation which, according to the ideal, was not to be torn loose from its moorings by the uncertain mutations of fortune but was to remain fixed and imperturbable. The portraits of its chief men consequently must betray no anxiety, fear, or triumph, but an unvarying calmness throughout the ages. In similar fashion, the anatomical distortion can probably be interpreted as a deliberate attempt to express some national ideal. There is certainly no reason to believe that it was practiced through ignorance of the laws of proportion or inability to copy the natural form. Very likely it was intended as a denial of mortality. The eternal existence of the people might very easily be thought to depend upon investing their leaders with attributes which would serve to protest their death as ordinary human beings. The most eloquent device for this purpose was representation of the body of a Pharaoh with the head of a god, but the other examples of non-naturalistic portrayal probably had a similar object.

The meaning of Egyptian sculpture

See color plates at pages 29, 60, 61

Though most of Egyptian painting has perished, that which survives is largely free from political and religious conventions. Certainly it was not dominated by them to the extent that architecture and sculpture were. The reason is perhaps to be found in the fact that painting developed late and did not have time to become weighted down with a mass of traditions. Religion did exert its influence, but in a positive manner. The best paintings were those created during the reign of Ikhnaton and immediately after. The gospel of the reforming king, with its reverence for nature as the handiwork of God, fostered a revival of realism in art which was particularly evident in painting. As a result, the murals of this period exhibit a decided talent for representation of the striking phenomena of the world of experience. They have particular merit as examples of the portrayal of movement. They caught the instant

Painting

59

Fishing and Fowling: Wall Painting Thebes, XVIIIth Dynasty. Most of the women appear to belong to the prosperous classes, while the simple garb and insignificant size of the men indicates that they are probably slaves.

action of the wild bull leaping in the swamp, the headlong flight of the frightened stag, and the effortless swimming of ducks in the pond. Even the paintings in the great temple of Luxor made a similar appeal to the senses; the blue ceiling studded with stars and the flowers and trees emblazoned on the columns and walls bore witness to the artist's appreciation of the beauty of his natural environment.

6. Social and Economic Life

The absence of a caste system

The social organization of Egypt was distinguished by a surprising degree of fluidity. No inflexible caste system ever developed. All men were equal in the sight of the law. Although degrees of economic inequality naturally existed, no man's status was unalterably fixed, unless he was a member of the royal family. Even serfs appear to have been capable of rising above their humble condition. Freemen quite regularly made the transition from one social order to another. Such a structure of society differed in marked degree from the stratified social regimes in other parts of the Orient—in India and Mesopotamia, for example.

The principal classes

During the greater part of the history of Egypt the population was divided into five classes: the royal family; the priests; the nobles; the middle class of scribes, merchants, artisans, and farmers; and the serfs. During the Empire a sixth class, the professional soldiers, was added, ranking immediately below the nobles. Thousands of slaves were captured in this period also, and these formed for a time a seventh class. Despised by freemen and serfs alike, they

Jeweled Headdress of Gold, Carnelian, and Glass. Egyptian, 1475 B.C.

Thutmose III as Amon, 1450 B.C. The Pharaoh wears the crown and the beard of the god, and carries a scimitar and the symbol of "life."

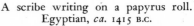

A scribe writing on a papyrus roll. Egyptian, ca. 1415 B.C.

Silversmiths Working on a Stand and a Jar. Egyptian, ca. 1450 B.C.

Girl Musicians Playing a Harp, Lute, Pair of Oboes, and Lyre. Egyptian, ca. 1410 B.C.

Scarab or Beetle-Shaped Charm of a Pharaoh, ca. 1395 B.C. The beetle was sacred in ancient Egypt.

Shawabty ("to answer") Figures, ca. 1400 B.C. These were put in the tomb to do any degrading work the rich man might be called upon to do in the next world. Rich men were buried with hundreds of such figures.

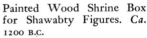

Painted Wood Shrine Box for Shawabty Figures. Ca. 1200 B.C.

Head of Ramses II, 1324–1258 B.C.

Part of the Egyptian "Book of the Dead." A collection of magic formulas to enable the deceased to gain admission to the realm of Osiris and to enjoy its eternal benefits.

Stele or Grave Marker. It shows the deceased being presented to the Sun god on his throne. She is holding her heart in her hand.

A hieroglyphic character for the idea "Millions of Years," 500–330 B.C.

Bronze Bull, Symbol of Strength. Arabian, VI cent. B.C.

A carved sandstone capital, *ca.* 370 B.C., representing a bundle of papyrus reeds.

All pictures courtesy MMA.

were forced to labor in the government quarries and on the temple estates. Gradually, however, they were enrolled in the army and even in the personal service of the Pharaoh. With these developments they ceased to constitute a separate class. The position of the various ranks of society shifted from time to time. In the Old Kingdom the nobles and priests among all of the Pharaoh's subjects held the supremacy. During the Middle Kingdom the classes of commoners came into their own. Scribes, merchants, artisans, and serfs rebelled against the nobles and wrested concessions from the government. Particularly impressive is the dominant role played by the merchants and industrialists in this period. The establishment of the Empire, accompanied as it was by the extension of government functions, resulted in the ascendancy of a new nobility, made up primarily of bureaucrats. The priests also waxed in power with the growth of magic and superstition.

The gulf which separated the standards of living of the upper and lower classes of Egypt was just about as wide as it is today in Europe and America. The wealthy nobles lived in splendid *The gulf be-* villas that opened into fragrant gardens and shady groves. Their *tween rich and* food had all the richness and variety of sundry kinds of meat, *poor*

 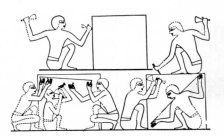

Making Sun-dried Bricks. Nile mud (generally mixed with chaff or straw) is being worked with a hoe, carried away in buckets and dumped in a pile. Lying on the ground in a row are three bricks, from the last of which a wooden mold, used in shaping them, is being lifted. An overseer with a stick is seated close by. The finished bricks are carried off by means of a yoke across the shoulders. From

a wall-painting at Thebes about 1500 B.C.

Stonecutters Dressing Blocks. Men with mallets and chisels are dressing down blocks to true surfaces. Below, two of them test the accuracy of the dressed surface. After two edges of the block are determined, a cord is stretched between two pegs to help gauge how much remains to be chiseled away.

poultry, cakes, fruit, wine, beer, and sweets. They ate from vessels of alabaster, gold, and silver and adorned their persons with expensive fabrics and costly jewels. By contrast, the life of the poor was wretched indeed. The laborers in the towns inhabited congested slums composed of mud-brick hovels with roofs of thatch. Their only furnishings were stools and boxes and a few crude pottery

The Egyptian family

The educational system

Agriculture, trade, and industry

jars. The peasants on the great estates enjoyed a less crowded but no more abundant life.

The basic social unit among the Egyptians was the monogamous family. No man, not even the Pharaoh, could have more than one lawful wife. Concubinage, however, was a socially reputable institution. Women occupied an unusually enviable status; in fact, the Egyptian family was almost matriarchal. Descent was traced through the female line, and the authority of the maternal grandfather over the children was greater than that of their own father. Almost alone among Oriental peoples the Egyptians permitted women to succeed to the throne. Another extraordinary social practice was close inbreeding. The ruler as son of the great sun god was required to marry his sister or some other female of his immediate family lest the divine blood be contaminated. The rest of the population commonly followed the identical custom. As yet, historians have been unable to discover any positive traces of racial degeneration produced by this practice, probably for the reason that the Egyptian stock was genetically sound to begin with.

The educational system of this ancient people was about what one would expect in a highly integrated society. Attached to the treasury were a number of public schools equipped for the training of the thousands of scribes whose services were necessary in the keeping of records and accounts and in the administration of government functions. Many of them were also employed in a private capacity by the owners of the landed estates and by the leaders of the business world. Admission to these schools was open to any promising youth regardless of class. Apparently the instruction was provided free of charge by the government because of the vital need for trained men. None but thoroughly utilitarian subjects had any place in the curriculum; the purpose was not education in the broader sense, but practical training. In spite of their limitations, these schools did provide for the poor but talented youth an avenue of escape from a life of hopeless drudgery.

The Egyptian economic system rested primarily upon an agrarian basis. Agriculture was diversified and highly developed, and the soil yielded excellent crops of wheat, barley, millet, vegetables, fruits, flax, and cotton. Theoretically the land was the property of the king, but in the earlier periods he granted most of it to his subjects, so that in actual practice it was largely in the possession of individuals. Commerce did not amount to much before 2000 B.C., but after that date it grew rapidly to a position of first-rate importance. A flourishing trade was carried on with the island of Crete, with Phoenicia, Palestine, and Syria. The chief articles of export consisted of wheat, linen fabrics, and fine pottery. Imports were confined largely to gold, silver, ivory, and lumber. Of no less significance than commerce was manufacturing as a branch of the economic life. As early as 3000 B.C. large numbers of people were already engaged

Sowing Seed and Working It into the Soil. From a bag which he wears over his left shoulder, the sower casts seed under the feet of cattle yoked to a plow. The plow is here used to harrow the soil. While one laborer guides the cows with a stick, another guides the plow straight and keeps the plowshare in the ground by bearing down on the handles. Sheep are then driven across the field to trample in the seed. From wall paintings at Sheikh Saïd, about 2700 B.C.

in industrial pursuits, mostly in separate crafts. In later times factories were established, employing twenty or more persons under one roof, and with some degree of division of labor. The leading industries were quarrying, shipbuilding, and the manufacture of pottery, glass, and textiles.

From an early date the Egyptians made progress in the perfection of instruments of business. They knew the elements of accounting and bookkeeping. Their merchants issued orders and receipts for goods. They invented deeds for property, written contracts, and wills. While they had no system of coinage, they had nevertheless attained a money economy. Rings of copper or gold of definite weight circulated as media of exchange. This Egyptian ring-money is apparently the oldest currency in the history of civilizations. Probably it was not used except for the larger transactions. The simple dealings of the peasants and poorer townsfolk doubtless continued on a basis of barter. *The development of instruments of business*

The Egyptian economic system was always collectivistic. From the very beginning the energies of the people had been drawn into socialized channels. The interests of the individual and the interests of society were conceived as identical. The productive activities of the entire nation revolved around the huge state enterprises, and the government remained by far the largest employer of labor. It should be noted, though, that during the Old and Middle Kingdoms this collectivism was not all-inclusive; a considerable sphere was left for private initiative. Merchants conducted their own businesses; many of the craftsmen had their own shops; and as time went on, larger and larger numbers of peasants gained the status of independent farmers. The government continued to operate the quarries and mines, to build pyramids and temples, and to farm the royal estates. *Economic collectivism*

The extreme development of state control came with the founding of the Empire. The growth of a military absolutism and the increasing frequency of wars of conquest augmented the need for revenue and for unlimited production of goods. To fulfill this need

63

the government extended its control over every department of economic life. The entire agricultural land again became the property of the Pharaoh, in fact as well as in theory. Although large sections of it were granted to favorites of the king, most of it was worked by royal serfs and slaves. The free middle class of earlier days now largely disappeared. The services of craftsmen were conscripted for the erection of magnificent temples and for the manufacture of implements of war, while foreign trade became a state monopoly. As the Empire staggered toward its downfall, the government absorbed more and more of the economic activities of the people.

Except during the reign of Ikhnaton, a corrupt alliance existed between the Pharaohs of the Empire and the priests. Greedy for power and plunder, the members of the ecclesiastical hierarchy supported the kings in their ambitions for despotic rule. As a reward they were granted exemption from taxation and a generous share of the national wealth. War captives were turned over to them in such numbers that they actually held two per cent of the population of the country as temple slaves. In addition, they received from their generous patrons one-seventh of the arable land, hundreds of thousands of cattle, and nearly a hundred ships. They employed a great host of artisans in the manufacture of amulets and funerary equipment, which they sold at tremendous profit to the misguided worshipers. Without question these priestly enterprises meant a serious drain on the national resources and thereby contributed to economic and social decay. Too large a proportion of the wealth of Egypt was being squandered on sterile projects of the church and the state, on otherworldly preparations, and on the conquest of an empire.

7. The Egyptian Achievement and Its Importance to Us

Few civilizations of ancient times surpassed the Egyptian in importance to the modern world. Even the influence of the Hebrews was not much greater. From the land of the Pharaohs came the germ and the stimulus for numerous intellectual achievements of later centuries. Important elements of philosophy, mathematics, science, and literature had their beginnings there. The Egyptians also developed one of the oldest systems of jurisprudence and political theory. They perfected the achievements of irrigation, engineering, and the making of pottery, glass, and paper. They were one of the first peoples to have any clear conception of art for other than utilitarian purposes, and they originated architectural principles that were destined for extensive use in subsequent history. Notable among these were the column, the colonnade, the lintel, the obelisk, and the clerestory, or low wall with windows looking out upon the roof of the main part of the building.

More significant still were the Egyptian contributions in the fields of religion and individual and social ethics. Aside from the Persians, the dwellers on the banks of the Nile were the only people of the ancient world to build a national religion around the doctrine of personal immortality. Egyptian priests and sages likewise were the first to preach universal monotheism, the providence of God, forgiveness of sins, and rewards and punishments after death. Finally, Egyptian ethical theory was the source from which various nations derived standards of personal and social morality; for it embraced not only the ordinary prohibitions of lying, theft, and murder, but included also the exalted ideals of justice, benevolence, and the equal rights of all men.

Selected Readings

· Items so designated are available in paperbound editions.

Alfred, Cyril, The Egyptians, New York, 1961.
Baikie, James, A History of Egypt, London, 1929.
Breasted, James H., The Dawn of Conscience, New York, 1934. An excellent account of the development of religious and ethical concepts.
———, History of Egypt, New York, 1912. Still one of the best histories of ancient Egypt.
Cottrell, Leonard, Life Under the Pharaohs, New York, 1960.
Engberg, R. M., The Dawn of Civilization, Chicago, 1937.
Erman, Adolf, Life in Ancient Egypt, New York, 1894.
Frankfort, Henri, The Intellectual Adventure of Ancient Man, Chicago, 1946. One of the best accounts of early intellectual development.
Hall, H. R., Ancient History of the Near East, New York, 1913.
Mason, W. A., History of the Art of Writing, New York, 1920.
Maspero, G. C. C., Art in Ancient Egypt, New York, 1912.
Moret, Alexandre, The Nile and Egyptian Civilization, New York, 1928. Interesting in its contrasts with Breasted.
Peet, T. E., Comparative Study of the Literatures of Egypt, Palestine, and Mesopotamia, New York, 1931.
Petrie, W. M. F., Social Life in Ancient Egypt, Boston, 1923.
———, Religious Life in Ancient Egypt, Boston, 1924.
Robinson, Victor, The Story of Medicine, New York, 1932.
Shorter, A. W., Everyday Life in Ancient Egypt, London, 1932. One of the few works of its kind, therefore valuable.
———, Introduction to Egyptian Religion, New York, 1932.
Smith, G. E., The Ancient Egyptians and the Origin of Civilization, New York, 1923.
Steindorf, G., and K. C. Steele, When Egypt Ruled the East, Chicago, 1942. A useful supplement to Breasted.
Ullman, B. L., Ancient Writing, New York, 1932.
Wilson, J. A., The Burden of Egypt, Chicago, 1951. An excellent interpretation.

Source Materials

Breasted, J. H., Ancient Records of Egypt, 5 vols.
· ———, Development of Religion and Thought in Ancient Egypt. (Torchbooks)
Budge, E. A. W., Osiris and the Egyptian Resurrection, 2 vols.
Pritchard, J. B., ed., Ancient Near Eastern Texts, Princeton, 1950.

CHAPTER 4

The Mesopotamian Civilization

If a son strike his father, they shall cut off his fingers.
If a man destroy the eye of another man, they shall destroy his eye.
If one break a man's bone, they shall break his bone.
If one destroy the eye of a freeman or break the bone of a free-
man, he shall pay one mina of silver.
If one destroy the eye of a man's slave or break a bone of a man's
slave he shall pay one-half his price.
—*The Code of Hammurabi*, lines 195–199.

*Origin
and comparison
with Egypt*

The other of the most ancient civilizations was that which began
in the Tigris-Euphrates valley at least as early as 4000 B.C. For convenience historians refer to this civilization as the Mesopotamian,
although the name Mesopotamia is sometimes applied only to the
northern portion of the land between the two rivers. The Mesopotamian civilization was distinctly unlike the Egyptian. Its political history was marked by sharper interruptions. Its racial composition was less homogeneous, and its social and economic structure
gave wider scope to individual initiative.

*Religious and
social
differences*

The differences in ideals and in religious and social attitudes were
perhaps more fundamental. The Egyptian culture was predominantly
ethical, the Mesopotamian legalistic. The Egyptian outlook upon
life, except during the Middle Kingdom, was generally one of cheerful resignation, comparatively free from the cruder superstitions.
By contrast, the Mesopotamian view was gloomy, pessimistic, and
enthralled by morbid fears. Where the native of Egypt believed in
immortality and dedicated a large part of his energy to preparation
for the life to come, his Mesopotamian contemporary lived in the
present and regarded his fate beyond the grave with indifference.
Finally, the civilization of the Nile valley embodied concepts of
monotheism, a religion of love, and social equalitarianism; that of
the Tigris-Euphrates was more selfish and cynical. Its religion seldom evolved beyond the stage of primitive polytheism, and its ideal
of justice was largely confined to literal observance of the terms of
a contract.

1. Political History

The pioneers in the development of the Mesopotamian civilization were a people known as the Sumerians, who settled in the lower

Tigris-Euphrates valley between 5000 and 4000 B.C. Their precise origin is unknown, but they seem to have come from the plateau of central Asia. They spoke a language unrelated to any now known, although their culture bore a certain resemblance to the earliest civilization of India. With little or no difficulty they subjugated the natives already in the lower valley, a mysterious people who were just emerging from the Neolithic stage.

About 2400 B.C. the Sumerians were conquered by Sargon I, the ruler of a nation of Semites who had established themselves in a section of the valley known as Akkad. This was the prelude to the founding of the first great Semitic empire in western Asia, for soon afterward Sargon conquered the Elamites and all of northern Syria to the Mediterranean Sea. But like so many states that have had their roots in conquest, this empire was short-lived. Sargon's death was the signal for the first of a series of Sumerian revolts. Although these revolts were suppressed, they weakened the state and paved the way for its overthrow by the Guti, a fierce barbarian people from the north. Finally, about 2100 B.C., the Sumerians, under the leadership of the city of Ur, rebelled successfully against the rule of the Guti and established their power over all of Sumer and Akkad. The most noted king of the new state was Dungi, who assumed the grandiloquent title of "king of the four regions of the earth" and attempted to duplicate the military accomplishments of Sargon I.

The new Sumerian empire did not survive the death of Dungi. It was annexed by the Elamites in the twenty-first century and about 1800 B.C. was conquered by a Semitic people known as the Amorites, who had come in from the fringes of the Arabian desert. Since they made the village of Babylon the capital of their empire they are commonly called the Babylonians, or the Old Babylonians to distinguish them from the Neo-Babylonians or Chaldeans who occupied the valley much later. The rise of the Old Babylonians inaugurated the second important stage of the Tigris-Euphrates civilization. Although most of the Sumerian culture survived, Sumerian dominance was now at an end. The Babylonians established an autocratic state and during the reign of their most famous king, Hammurabi, extended their dominion north to Assyria. But after his time their empire gradually declined until it was finally overthrown by the Kassites about 1750 B.C.

*The rise and
fall of the Old
Babylonians*

With the downfall of Old Babylonia a period of retrogression set in which lasted for six hundred years. The Kassites were barbarians with no interest in the cultural achievements of their predecessors. Their lone contribution was the introduction of the horse into the Tigris-Euphrates valley. The old culture would have died out entirely if it had not been for its partial adoption by another Semitic people who as early as 3000 B.C. had founded a tiny kingdom on the plateau of Assur some 500 miles up the Tigris River. These people came to be called the Assyrians, and their ultimate rise to power marked the beginning of the third stage in the development of the Mesopotamian civilization. About 1300 B.C. they began to expand and soon afterward made themselves masters of the whole northern valley. In the tenth century they overturned what was left of Kassite power in Babylonia. Their empire reached its height in the eighth and seventh centuries under Sargon II (722–705 B.C.), Sennacherib (705–681), and Assurbanipal (668–626). It had now come to include nearly all of the civilized world of that time. One after another, Syria, Phoenicia, the Kingdom of Israel, and Egypt had fallen victims of Assyrian military prowess. Only the little Kingdom of Judah was able to withstand the hosts of Nineveh, probably because of an outbreak of pestilence in the ranks of Sennacherib's army.[1]

*The downfall
of the Assyrians
and the rise of
the Chaldeans*

Brilliant though the successes of the Assyrians were, they did not endure. So rapidly were new territories annexed that the empire soon reached an unmanageable size. The Assyrians' genius for government was far inferior to their appetite for conquest. Subjugated nations chafed under the cruel despotism that had been forced upon them and, as the empire gave signs of cracking from within, determined to regain their freedom. The death blow was delivered by the Kaldi or Chaldeans, a nation of Semites who had settled southeast of the valley of the two rivers. Under the leadership of Nabopolassar, who had served the Assyrian emperors in the capacity of a provincial governor, they organized a revolt and finally captured Nineveh in 612 B.C.

*The Chaldean
empire*

Nabopolassar was succeeded by his son Nebuchadnezzar, who ruled until 562 B.C. During the reign of the latter the Chaldeans rose to the mastery of a new cosmopolitan empire in the Near Orient. The last vestiges of Assyrian authority were annihilated in all of the more valuable sections of the Fertile Crescent. Even the Kingdom of Judah, which had successfully defied the Assyrian "wolves," fell an easy victim to the relentless energy of Nebuchadnezzar. The temple at Jerusalem was looted and burned, King Zedekiah was blinded, and he and several thousand of his countrymen were carried off into captivity in Babylon.

*The downfall of
the Chaldeans*

But the empire of the Chaldeans did not long survive the death of its greatest ruler. During the reigns of his successors the nation turned to the indulgence of antiquarian interests—to the worship of the achievements of the Old Babylonians, whom they ignorantly revered as their ancestors. Jealous contention arose between the kings and the priests; and the Medes, a tributary nation on the eastern border, began to give trouble. But the major reason for the downfall of the Chaldean empire was the insatiable greed of its founder. It was this lust for power and glory that led him to repeat the blunders of the Assyrian monarchs before him in conquering

---

[1] Hebrew prophets declared that an angel of the Lord visited the camp of the Assyrians by night and slew 185,000 of them. II Kings 19:35.

an unwieldy empire and in humiliating proud peoples. The hand-writing on the wall which Belshazzar is supposed to have seen at his famous feast should have been intended for Nebuchadnezzar.[2]

In 539 B.C. the empire of the Chaldeans fell, after an existence of less than a century. It was overthrown by Cyrus the Persian, as he himself declared, "without a battle and without fighting." The easy victory appears to have been made possible by assistance from the Jews and by a conspiracy of the priests of Babylon to deliver the city to Cyrus as an act of vengeance against the Chaldean king, whose policies they did not like. Members of other influential classes appear also to have looked upon the Persians as deliverers.

The Persian conquest

Although the Persian state incorporated all of the territories that had once been embraced by the Mesopotamian empires, it included many other provinces besides. It was the vehicle, moreover, of a new and different culture. The downfall of Chaldea must therefore be taken as marking the end of Mesopotamian political history.

2. Sumerian Origins of the Civilization

More than to any other people, the Mesopotamian civilization owed its character to the Sumerians. Much of what used to be ascribed to the Babylonians and Assyrians is now known to have been developed by the nation that preceded them. The system of writing was of Sumerian origin; likewise the religion, the laws, and a great deal of the science and commercial practice. Only in the evolution of government and military tactics and in the develop-ment of the arts was the originating talent of the later conquerors particularly manifest.

The Sumerians the chief originators of Mesopotamian civilization

Through the greater part of their history the Sumerians lived in a loose confederation of city-states, united only for military pur-poses. At the head of each was a *patesi*, who combined the functions of chief priest, commander of the army, and superintendent of the irrigation system. Occasionally one of the more ambitious of these rulers would extend his power over a number of cities and assume the title of king. Not until the time of Dungi, about 2000 B.C., how-ever, were all of the Sumerian people united under a single authority of the same nationality as themselves.

The Sumerian political system

The Sumerian economic pattern was relatively simple and per-mitted a wider scope for individual enterprise than was generally allowed in Egypt. The land was never the exclusive property of the king either in theory or in practice. Neither was trade or industry a monopoly of the government. On the other hand, the masses of the people had little they could call their own. Many of them were serfs, but even those who were technically free were little better off, forced as they were to pay high rents and to labor on the public works. Slavery in the strict sense of the word was not an important

The Sumerian economic pat-tern

[2] Compare the Old Testament account in Daniel 5:24-31.

Diorama of a Part of Ur about 2000 B.C. A modern archaeologist's conception. Walls are omitted to show interiors at left.

institution. Most of those referred to as slaves were really serfs, who had mortgaged their persons for debt. They do not appear to have been an especially degraded class. They could own property, work for wages when their master did not need them, and even marry free women. Doubtless the great majority of them were of Sumerian nationality, a fact which helps to explain their rather liberal treatment.

Agriculture

Agriculture was the chief economic pursuit of most of the citizens, and the Sumerians were excellent farmers. By virtue of their knowledge of irrigation they produced amazing crops of cereal grains and subtropical fruits. Since most of the land was divided into large estates held by the rulers, the priests, and the army officers, the average rural citizen was either a tenant farmer or a serf. Commerce was the second most important source of the nation's wealth. A flourishing trade was established with all of the surrounding countries, revolving around the exchange of metals and timber from the north and west for the agricultural products and manufactured goods from the lower valley. Nearly all of the familiar adjuncts of business were highly developed; bills, receipts, notes, and letters of credit were regularly used. Custom required that deals should be confirmed by written agreements, signed by witnesses. Merchants employed salesmen who traveled to distant regions and sold goods on commission. In all major transactions bars or ingots of gold and silver served as money, the standard unit of exchange being the silver shekel, approximately equal in weight to a modern 50-cent piece but with a purchasing power much greater.

Sumerian law

The most distinctive achievement of the Sumerians was their system of law. It was the product of a gradual evolution out of local usage, but it was finally incorporated into a comprehensive code by Dungi after the middle of the third millennium. Only a few fragments of this law have survived in their original form, but the famous code of Hammurabi, the Babylonian king, is now recognized to have been nothing more than a revision of the code of Dungi. Ultimately this code became the basis of the laws of nearly all of the Semites—Babylonians, Assyrians, Chaldeans, and Hebrews.

The following may be regarded as the essential features of the Sumerian law:

(1) The *lex talionis*, or law of retaliation in kind—"an eye for an eye, a tooth for a tooth, a limb for a limb," etc.

(2) Semi-private administration of justice. It was incumbent upon the victim himself or his family to bring the offender to justice. The court served principally as an umpire in the dispute between the plaintiff and defendant, not as an agency of the state to maintain public security, although constables attached to the court might assist in the execution of the sentence.

(3) Inequality before the law. The code divided the population into three classes: patricians or aristocrats; burghers or commoners; serfs and slaves. Penalties were graded according to the rank of the victim, but also in some cases according to the rank of the offender. The killing or maiming of a patrician was a much more serious offense than a similar crime committed against a burgher or a slave. On the other hand, when a patrician was the offender he was punished *more severely* than a man of inferior status would be for the same crime. The origin of this curious rule was probably to be found in considerations of military discipline. Since the patricians were army officers and therefore the chief defenders of the state, they could not be permitted to give vent to their passions or to indulge in riotous conduct.

(4) Inadequate distinction between accidental and intentional homicide. A person responsible for killing another accidentally did not escape penalty, as he would under modern law, but had to pay a fine to the family of the victim, apparently on the theory that children were the property of their fathers and wives the property of their husbands.

Quite as much as their law the religion of the Sumerians illuminates their social attitudes and the character of their culture. They did not succeed in developing a very exalted religion; yet it occupied an important place in their lives. To begin with, it was polytheistic and anthropomorphic. They believed in a number of gods and goddesses, each a distinct personality with human attributes. Shamash, the sun god; Enlil, the lord of the rain and wind; and Ishtar, the goddess of the female principle in nature, were only a few of them. Although the Sumerians had a special deity of the plague in tne person of the god Nergal, their religion was really monistic, in the sense that they regarded all of their deities as capable of both good and evil. Shamash, for example, as the god of the sun gave warmth and light for the benefit of man; but he might also send his burning rays to bake the soil and to wither the tender plants before they had time to yield their fruits. Religious dualism, in-

The character of Sumerian religion

71

*A religion for
this world, not
for the next*

*A religion
neither ethical
nor spiritual*

*The Creation
and Flood epics*

volving a belief in entirely separate divinities of good and evil, did not appear in the Mesopotamian civilization until much later.

The Sumerian religion was a religion for this world exclusively; it offered no hope for a life to come. The after-life was a mere temporary existence in a dreary, shadowy place which later came to be called Sheol. Here the ghosts of the dead lingered for a time, perhaps a generation or so, and then disappeared. No one could look forward to resurrection in another world and a joyous eternal existence as a recompense for the evils of this life; the victory of the grave was complete. In accordance with these beliefs the Sumerians bestowed no particular care upon the bodies of their dead. No mummification was practiced, and no elaborate tombs were built. Corpses were commonly interred beneath the floor of the house without a coffin and with very few articles for the use of the ghost.

Neither spiritual nor ethical content had any place of conspicuous importance in this religion. As we have seen, the gods were not spiritual beings but creatures cast in the human mold, with most of the weaknesses and passions of mortal men. Nor were the purposes of the religion any more spiritual. It provided no blessings in the form of solace, uplift of the soul, or oneness with God. If it benefited man at all, it did so only in the form of material gain—abundant harvests and prosperity in business. Similarly, the doctrines and forms of worship were almost devoid of ethical significance. The religion did not prescribe or enforce standards of morality. The obligations imposed upon the individual were mainly ritualistic. Though the gods were often angry with men and vented their wrath upon them, that wrath was due not to breaches of the divine commandments, but to the failure of men to show proper respect to the deities and to provide for their needs.

The true nature of the Sumerian religion is revealed in the famous Creation and Flood epics, which provided the framework for the much later Hebrew stories in the Old Testament. The Creation epic related the magic triumph of the god Marduk over the jealous and cowardly gods who had created him, the formation of the world out of the body of one of his slain rivals, and finally, in order that the gods might be fed, the making of man out of clay and dragon's blood. The whole account was crude and revolting, with nothing in it to appeal to a spiritual or moral sense. Almost as barbarous was the Sumerian version of the Flood. Grown jealous of man, the gods decided to destroy the whole race of mortals by drowning. One of their number, however, betrayed the secret to a favorite inhabitant of the earth, instructing him to build an ark for the salvation of himself and his kind. The flood raged for seven days, until the whole earth was covered with water. Even the gods "crouched like a dog on the wall." Finally the tumult was stilled and the waters subsided. The favored man and his brothers came forth from the ark and offered grateful sacrifice. Hungry from their long deprivation

Male Votive Figure, Sumer. This statue of white gypsum, colored with bitumen, shows the conventionalized treatment of hair and beard and the huge, staring eyes common to Mesopotamian art. Observe also the immense thumbs and the fingers of equal length.

of food, the gods "scented the sweet savour, and gathered like flies above the sacrifice," and decided never again to be so foolish as to risk the destruction of man.

In the field of intellectual endeavor the Sumerians achieved no great distinction. They did, however, produce a system of writing which was destined to be used for a thousand years after the downfall of their nation. This was the celebrated *cuneiform* writing, consisting of wedge-shaped characters imprinted on clay tablets with a square-tipped reed. Although at first a pictographic system, it was gradually transformed into an aggregate of syllabic and phonetic signs, some three hundred and fifty in number. No alphabet was ever developed out of it. The Sumerians wrote nothing that could be called philosophy, but they did make some feeble beginnings in science. They discovered the processes of multiplication and division and even the extraction of square and cube root. Their systems of numeration and of weights and measures were duodecimal, with the number sixty as the most common unit. They invented the water clock and the lunar calendar, the latter an inaccurate division of the year into months based upon cycles of the moon. In order to bring it into harmony with the solar year, an extra month had to be added from time to time. Astronomy was little more than astrology, and medicine was a curious compound of herbalism and magic. The repertory of the physician consisted primarily of charms to exorcise the evil spirits which were believed to be the cause of disease.

Intellectual achievements

As artists the Sumerians excelled in metal work, gem carving, and sculpture. They produced some remarkable specimens of naturalistic

73

Fragments of Jewelry Found at Ur in Two Graves of Ladies-in-Waiting to the Queen. The materials used are gold, carnelian, and lapis lazuli. Dating from 3500–2800 B.C., it is the oldest jewelry in the world.

Sumerian art

art in their weapons, vessels, jewelry, and human and animal representations, which revealed alike a technical skill and a gift of imagination. Evidently religious conventions had not yet imposed any paralyzing influence, and consequently the artist was still free to follow his own impulses. Architecture, on the other hand, was distinctly inferior, probably because of the limitations enforced by the scarcity of good building materials. Since there was no stone in the valley, the architect had to depend upon sun-dried brick. The characteristic Sumerian edifice, extensively copied by their Semitic successors, was the *ziggurat*, a terraced tower set on a platform and surmounted by a shrine. Its construction was massive, its lines were monotonous, and little architectural ingenuity was exhibited in it. The royal tombs and private houses showed more originality. It was in them that the Sumerian inventions of the arch, the vault, and the dome were regularly employed, and the column was used occasionally.

3. Old Babylonian "Contributions"

The shortcomings of the Old Babylonians

Although the Old Babylonians were an alien nation, they had lived long enough in close contact with the Sumerians to be influenced profoundly by them. They had no culture of their own worthy of the name when they came into the valley, and in general they simply appropriated what the Sumerians had already developed. With so excellent a foundation to build upon, they should have made remarkable progress; but such was not the case. When they ended their history, the state of civilization in the Tigris-Euphrates valley was no more advanced than when they began.

Changes in the system of law

First among the significant changes which the Old Babylonians made in their cultural inheritance may be mentioned the political and legal. As military conquerors holding in subjection numerous vanquished nations, they found it necessary to establish a consolidated state. Vestiges of the old system of local autonomy were swept away, and the power of the king of Babylon was made supreme. A system of royal taxation was adopted as well as compulsory military service. The system of law was also changed to conform to the new conditions. The list of crimes against the state was enlarged, and the king's officers assumed a more active role in apprehending and punishing offenders, although it was still impossible for any criminal to be pardoned without the consent of the victim or the victim's family. The severity of penalties was decidedly increased, particularly for crimes involving any suggestion of treason or sedition. Such apparently trivial offenses as "gadding about" and "disorderly conduct of a tavern" were made punishable by death, probably on the assumption that they would be likely to foster disloyal activities. Whereas under the Sumerian law the harboring of fugitive slaves was punishable merely by a fine, the Babylonian law made it a capital crime. According to the Sumerian code, the slave who disputed his master's rights over him was to be sold; the Code of Hammurabi prescribed that he should have his ear cut off. Adultery was also made a capital offense, whereas under the Sumerian law it did not even necessarily result in divorce. In a few particulars the new system of law revealed some improvement. Wives and children sold for debt could not be held in bondage for longer than four years, while a female slave who had borne her master a child could not be sold at all.

The Old Babylonian laws also reflect a somewhat more extensive development of business than that which existed in the preceding culture. That those who traded for profit enjoyed a privileged position in society is evidenced by the fact that the commercial provisions of Hammurabi's code were based upon the principle of "Let the buyer beware." The Babylonian rulers did not believe in a regime of free competition, however. Trade, banking, and industry were subject to elaborate regulation by the state. There were laws regarding partnership, storage, and agency; laws respecting deeds, wills, and the taking of interest on money; and a great host of others. For a deal to be negotiated without a written contract or without witnesses was punishable by death. Agriculture, which was still the occupation of a majority of the citizens, did not escape regulation either. The code provided penalties for failure to cultivate a field and for neglect of dikes and canals. Both government ownership and private tenure of land were permitted; but, regardless of the status of the owner, the tenant farmer was required to pay two-thirds of all he produced as rent.

Economic development

Religion at the hands of the Old Babylonians underwent numerous changes both superficial and profound. Deities that had been venerated by the Sumerians were now neglected, and new ones exalted in their stead. Marduk, originally the local god of the town of Babylon, was elevated to the highest position in the pantheon. Ishtar remained the chief goddess. Tammuz, her brother and lover, who had been of no special significance in the Sumerian religion, now became the third most important divinity. His death in the autumn and resurrection in the spring symbolized the death and rebirth of vegetation. But the death and resurrection of the god had more than a symbolic meaning; vaguely at least they were con-

Changes in the religion

ceived as the real causes of the nature processes themselves, and the god's rites were a form of magic. They carried no spiritual significance, however, conveying no promise of the resurrection of man from the dead or of personal immortality. The Old Babylonians were no more otherworldly in their outlook than the Sumerians.

The increase in superstition

Equally noteworthy was an increase in superstition. Astrology, divination, and other forms of magic took on added significance. A morbid consciousness of sin gradually displaced the essentially amoral attitude of the Sumerians. In addition, an increased emphasis was placed upon the worship of demons. Nergal, the god of the plague, came to be envisaged as a hideous monster seeking every chance to strike down his victims. Hordes of other demons and malevolent spirits lurked in the darkness and rode through the air bringing terror and destruction to all in their path. Against them there was no defense except sacrifices and magic charms. If the Old Babylonians did not invent witchcraft, they were at least the first "civilized" people to magnify it to serious proportions. Their laws invoked the death penalty against it, and there is evidence that the power of witches was widely feared. Whether the growth of demonology and witchcraft was due to the increasing unhealthfulness of the climate of the Tigris-Euphrates valley, or to the gloomy mentality of the people themselves, is a question which cannot be answered; but it is probable that the former is the chief explanation.

The decline of intellect and the arts

There seems to be little doubt that intellectually and artistically the Mesopotamian civilization suffered a partial decline during the period of Babylonian rule. This was not the first instance of cultural retrogression in history, but it was one of the most pronounced. Nothing of any importance was added to the scientific discoveries of the Sumerians, and some of them appear to have been neglected or forgotten. Literature showed some improvement over the earlier writings, especially in the famous Gilgamesh epic, a story of the mighty deeds of a supernatural adventurer. Although most of the legends themselves were of Sumerian origin, it was Babylonian poets who wove them into powerful descriptive style. A kind of prototype of the Book of Job, the so-called *Babylonian Job*, was also written in this period. It relates the story of a pious sufferer who is afflicted he knows not why, and it contains some mature reflections on the helplessness of man and the impenetrable mysteries of the universe.

Panel of Glazed Brick, Babylon, Sixth Century B.C. An ornamental relief on a background of earth brown. The lion is in blue, white, and yellow glazes.

As an example of Oriental philosophy it is not without merit. The graphic arts, on the other hand, definitely deteriorated. The Babylonians lacked the creative interest and talent to duplicate the fresh and ingenious carving and engraving of the Sumerians. Moreover, sculpture fell under the domination of religious and political conventions, with the result that originality was stifled.

4. The Metamorphosis under Assyria

Of all the peoples of the Mesopotamian area after the time of the Sumerians, the Assyrians went through the most completely independent evolution. For several centuries they had lived a comparatively isolated existence on top of their small plateau in the upper valley of the Tigris. Eventually they came under the influence of the Babylonians, but not until after the course of their own history had been partially fixed. As a consequence, the period of Assyrian supremacy (from about 1300 B.C. to 612 B.C.) had more nearly a peculiar character than any other era of Mesopotamian history.

The evolution of Assyrian supremacy

The Assyrians were pre-eminently a nation of warriors; not because they were racially different from any of the other Semites, but because of the special conditions of their own environment. Their situation was strikingly similar to that of the modern Japanese, except that they lived on a plateau instead of on a group of islands. The limited resources of their original home and the constant danger of attack from hostile nations around them forced the development of warlike habits and imperial ambitions. It is therefore not strange that their greed for territory should have known no limits. The more they conquered, the more they felt they had to conquer, in order to protect what they had already gained. Every success excited ambition and riveted the chains of militarism more firmly than ever. Disaster was inevitable.

A nation of warriors

The exigencies of war determined the whole character of the Assyrian system. The state was a great military machine. The army commanders were at once the richest and the most powerful class in the country. Not only did they share in the plunder of war, but they were frequently granted huge estates as rewards for victory. At least one of them, Sargon II, dared to usurp the throne. The military establishment itself represented the last word in preparedness. The standing army greatly exceeded in size that of any other nation of the Near Orient. New and improved armaments and techniques of fighting gave to the Assyrian soldiers unparalleled advantages. Iron swords, heavy bows, long lances, battering rams, fortresses on wheels, and metal breastplates, shields, and helmets were only a few examples of their superior equipment.

Features of the Assyrian militarism

But swords and spears and engines of war were not their only instruments of combat. As much as anything else the Assyrians depended upon frightfulness as a means of overcoming their enemies.

Terrorism

77

Upon soldiers captured in battle, and sometimes upon non-combatants as well, they inflicted unspeakable cruelties—skinning them alive, impaling them on stakes, cutting off ears, noses, and sex organs, and then exhibiting the mutilated victims in cages for the benefit of cities that had not yet surrendered. Accounts of these cruelties are not taken from atrocity stories circulated by their enemies; they come from the records of the Assyrians themselves. Their chroniclers boasted of them as evidences of valor, and the people believed in them as guaranties of security and power. It is clear why the Assyrians were the most hated of all the nations of antiquity.

The tragedy of Assyrian militarism

There is much grist for the mill of the pacifist in the military history of Assyria. There has never been a better illustration of the unwisdom of conquest and the folly of brute force. Seldom has the decline of an empire been so swift and so complete; for in spite of her magnificent armaments and her wholesale destruction of her foes, Assyria's period of imperial splendor lasted little more than a century. Nation after nation conspired against her and finally accomplished her downfall. Her enemies took frightful vengeance. The whole land was so thoroughly sacked and the people so completely enslaved or exterminated that it has been difficult to trace any subsequent Assyrian influence upon history. The power and security which military strength was supposed to provide proved a mockery in the end. If Assyria had been utterly defenseless, her fate could hardly have been worse.

Neglect of the arts of peace

With so complete an absorption in military pursuits, it was inevitable that the Assyrians should have neglected in some measure the arts of peace. Such progress as they did make was largely conditioned by the factors of war. There was no further development of industry and commerce, for the Assyrians scorned such pursuits as beneath the dignity of a soldierly people. As compared with the thousands of business tablets left by the Old Babylonians, only a few hundred have ever been found at Nineveh. The minimum of manufacturing and trade which had to be carried on was left to the Arameans, a people closely related to the Phoenicians and the Hebrews. The Assyrians themselves preferred to derive their living from agriculture. The land system included both public and private holdings. The temples held the largest share of the landed wealth. Although the estates of the crown were likewise extensive, they were constantly being diminished by grants to the army officers. Numerous private citizens were also the owners of freehold estates.

Defects in the economic system

Neither the economic nor the social order was sound. The frequent military campaigns depleted the energies and resources of the nation. In the course of time the army officers became a pampered aristocracy, delegating their duties to their subordinates and devoting themselves to luxurious pleasures. The stabilizing influence of a prosperous and intelligent middle class was precluded by the rule that only foreigners could engage in commercial activities. Yet more serious was the treatment accorded to the lower classes, the serfs and the slaves. The former comprised the bulk of the rural population. Some of them cultivated definite portions of their master's estates and retained a part of what they produced for themselves. Others were "empty" men, without even a plot to cultivate and dependent on the need for seasonal labor to provide for their means of subsistence. All were extremely poor and were subject to the additional hardships of labor on the public works and compulsory military service. The slaves, who were chiefly an urban working class, were really of two different types: the domestic slaves, who performed household duties and sometimes engaged in business for their masters; and the war captives. The former were not numerous and were allowed a great deal of freedom, even to the extent of owning property. The latter suffered much greater miseries. Bound by heavy shackles, they were compelled to labor to the point of exhaustion in building roads, canals, and palaces.

Whether the Assyrians adopted the law of the Old Babylonians has never been settled. Undoubtedly they were influenced by it, but several of the features of Hammurabi's code are entirely absent. *Assyrian law* Notable among these are the *lex talionis* and the system of gradation of penalties according to the rank of the victim and the offender. Whereas the Babylonians prescribed the most drastic punishments for crimes suggestive of treason or sedition, the Assyrians reserved theirs for such offenses as abortion and unnatural vice, probably for the military reason of preventing a decline in the birth rate. Another contrast is the more complete subjection of Assyrian women. Wives were treated as chattels of their husbands, the right of divorce was placed entirely in the hands of the male, a plurality of wives was permitted, and all married women were forbidden to appear in public with their faces unveiled. Here, according to Professor Olmstead, was the beginning of the Oriental seclusion of women.[3]

That a military nation like the Assyrians should not have taken first rank in intellectual achievement is easily understandable. The atmosphere of a military campaign is not favorable to reflection or *Scientific* disinterested research. Yet the demands of successful campaigning *achievements* may lead to a certain accumulation of knowledge, for practical problems have to be solved. Under such circumstances the Assyrians accomplished some measure of scientific progress. They appear to have divided the circle into 360 degrees and to have estimated locations on the surface of the earth in something resembling latitude and longitude. They recognized and named five planets and achieved some success in predicting eclipses. Since the health of armies is important, medicine received considerable attention. More than five hundred drugs, both vegetable and mineral, were catalogued and their uses indicated. Symptoms of various diseases were described and were generally interpreted as due to natural causes, although

[3] A. T. E. Olmstead, *History of Assyria*, p. 553.

The Lion Hunt. A typical specimen of Assyrian sculpture in relief.
The Assyrians were masters in depicting scenes of violence and animal ferocity.

incantations and the prescription of disgusting compounds to drive
out demons were still commonly employed as methods of treatment.

In the domain of art the Assyrians surpassed the Old Babylonians
and at least equaled the work of the Sumerians, although in different form. Sculpture was the art most highly developed, particularly
in the low reliefs. These portrayed dramatic incidents of war and
the hunt with the utmost fidelity to nature and a vivid description
of movement. The Assyrians delighted in depicting the cool bravery
of the hunter in the face of terrific danger, the ferocity of lions at
bay, and the death agonies of wounded beasts. Unfortunately this
art was limited almost entirely to the two themes of war and sport.
Its purpose was to glorify the exploits of the ruling class. Architecture ranked second to sculpture from the standpoint of artistic
excellence. Assyrian palaces and temples were built of stone, obtained
from the mountainous areas of the north, instead of the mud brick
of former times. Their principal features were the arch and the
dome. The column was also used but never very successfully. The
chief demerit of this architecture was its hugeness, which the Assyrians appeared to regard as synonymous with beauty.

Assyrian culture reached its height in the seventh century during
the reign of Assurbanipal. A man of considerable refinement, he
was almost the only ruler of the nation to devote any attention
to the patronage of learning and the arts. He ordered his scribes
to collect all the copies of Babylonian writings that could be found
on every conceivable subject and bring them to the royal library
at Nineveh. Where necessary he authorized revisions to be made
in order to bring the ancient learning into harmony with more recent

*The excellence
of Assyrian art*

*Assurbanipal,
patron of cul-
ture*

80

Assyrian Winged Bull, now in Oriental Institute, University of Chicago. Its precise significance is unknown, but it may have been intended to symbolize the Assyrian militarists' worship of strength and speed.

knowledge. Under Assurbanipal's patronage the royal library came to contain more than 22,000 tablets. Many of them were magic formulas, but included in the lot were thousands of letters, business documents, and military chronicles. The king himself was the author of an autobiography and of numerous letters that displayed some literary talent. But the most important of the original compositions of the Assyrians were their narratives of military campaigns, which, in their highly embellished and deliberately exaggerated form, represent one of the earliest attempts at patriotic historical writing.

5. The Chaldean Renascence

The Mesopotamian civilization entered its final stage with the overthrow of Assyria and the establishment of Chaldean supremacy. This stage is often called the Neo-Babylonian, because Nebuchadnezzar and his followers restored the capital at Babylon and attempted to revive the culture of Hammurabi's time. As might have been expected, their attempt was not wholly successful. The Assyrian metamorphosis had altered that culture in various profound and ineffaceable ways. Besides, the Chaldeans themselves had a history of their own which they could not entirely escape. Nevertheless, they did manage to revive certain of the old institutions and ideals. They restored the ancient law and literature, the essentials of the Old Babylonian form of government, and the economic system of their supposed ancestors with its dominance of industry and trade. Farther than this they were unable to go.

The Chaldean or final stage in Mesopotamian civilization

It was in religion that the failure of the Chaldean renascence was most conspicuous. Although Marduk was restored to his traditional place at the head of the pantheon, the system of belief was little more than superficially Babylonian. What the Chaldeans really did was to develop an astral religion. The gods were divested of their limited human qualities and exalted into transcendent, omnipotent beings. They were actually identified with the planets themselves. Marduk became Jupiter, Ishtar became Venus, and so on. Though

The astral religion of the Chaldeans

81

still not entirely aloof from man, they certainly lost their character as beings who could be cajoled and threatened and coerced by magic. They ruled the universe almost mechanically. While their immediate intentions were sometimes discernible, their ultimate purposes were inscrutable.

Two significant results flowed from these amazing conceptions. The first was an attitude of fatalism. Since the ways of the gods were past finding out, all that man could do was to resign himself to his fate. It behooved him therefore to submit absolutely to the gods, to trust in them implicitly, in the vague hope that the results in the end would be good. Thus arose for the first time in history the conception of piety as submission—a conception which was adopted in several other religions, as we shall see in succeeding chapters. For the Chaldeans it implied no otherworldly significance; one did not resign himself to calamities in this life in order to be justified in the next. The Chaldeans had no interest in a life to come. Submission might bring certain earthly rewards, but in the main, as they conceived it, it was not a means to an end at all. It was rather the expression of an attitude of despair, of humility in the face of mysteries that could not be fathomed.

The growth of fatalism

The second great result which came from the growth of an astral religion was the development of a stronger spiritual consciousness. This is revealed in the penitential hymns of unknown authors and in the prayers which were ascribed to Nebuchadnezzar and other kings as the spokesmen for the nation. In most of them the gods are addressed as exalted beings who are concerned with justice and righteous conduct on the part of men, although the distinction between ceremonial and genuine morality is not always sharply drawn. It has been asserted by one author that these hymns could have been used by the Hebrews with little modification except for the substitution of the name of Yahweh for that of the Chaldean god.[4]

The development of a spiritual consciousness

With the gods promoted to so lofty a plane, it was perhaps inevitable that man should have been abased. Creatures possessed of mortal bodies could not be compared with the transcendent, passionless beings who dwelt in the stars and guided the destinies of the earth. Man was a lowly creature, sunk in iniquity and vileness, and hardly even worthy of approaching the gods. The consciousness of sin already present in the Babylonian and Assyrian religions now reached a stage of almost pathological intensity. In the hymns the sons of men are compared to prisoners, bound hand and foot, languishing in darkness. Their transgressions are "seven times seven." Their misery is increased by the fact that their evil nature has prompted them to sin unwittingly.[5] Never before had men been

The abasement of man

[4] Morris Jastrow, *The Civilization of Babylonia and Assyria*, p. 217.
[5] *Ibid.*, pp. 471–74.

regarded as so hopelessly depraved, nor had religion been fraught with so gloomy a view of life.

Curiously enough, the pessimism of the Chaldeans does not appear to have affected their morality very much. So far as the evidence goes, they indulged in no rigors of asceticism. They did not mortify the flesh, nor did they even practice self-denial. Apparently they took it for granted that man could not avoid sinning, no matter how hard he tried. They seem to have been just as deeply engrossed in the material interests of life and in the pursuit of the pleasures of sense as any of the earlier nations. Indeed, it seems that they were even more greedy and sensual. Occasional references were made in their prayers and hymns to reverence, kindness, and purity of heart as virtues, and to oppression, slander, and anger as vices, but these were intermingled with ritualistic conceptions of cleanness and uncleanness and with expressions of desire for physical satisfactions. When the Chaldeans prayed, it was not always that their gods would make them good, but more often that they would grant long years, abundant offspring, and luxurious living.

Chaldean morality

Aside from religion, the Chaldean culture differed from that of the Sumerians, Babylonians, and Assyrians chiefly in regard to scientific achievements. Without doubt the Chaldeans were the most capable scientists in all of Mesopotamian history, although their accomplishments were limited primarily to astronomy. They worked out the most elaborate system for recording the passage of time which had yet been devised, with their invention of the seven-day week and their division of the day into twelve double-hours of 120 minutes each. They kept accurate records of their observation of eclipses and other celestial occurrences for more than 350 years—until long after the downfall of their empire. Two of their most spectacular achievements were made by individual astronomers whose names have come down to us. In the sixth century Nabu-Rimannu calculated the correct length of the year within about twenty-six minutes, and about a hundred years later Kidinnu discovered and proved the periodic change in the inclination of the earth's axis.

Chaldean science

The motivating force behind Chaldean astronomy was religion. The chief purpose of mapping the heavens and collecting astronomical data was to discover the future which the gods had prepared for the race of men. Since the planets were gods themselves, that future could best be divined in the movements of the heavenly bodies. Astronomy was therefore primarily astrology. Sciences other than astronomy continued in a backward state, probably because they were not definitely related to religion. Medicine in particular showed little advance beyond the stage it had reached under the Assyrians. The same was true of the remaining aspects of Chaldean culture. Art differed only in its greater magnificence. Literature, dominated

The religious basis of Chaldean science

by the antiquarian spirit, revealed a monotonous lack of originality. The writings of the Old Babylonians were extensively copied and re-edited, but they were supplemented by little that was new.

6. The Mesopotamian Legacy

*Mesopotamian
influence:
(1) upon the
modern
world*

Notwithstanding the relatively inferior quality of the Mesopotamian civilization, its influence has been scarcely less than that of Egypt. From one or another of the four Mesopotamian nations we get a considerable number of our most common culture elements: the seven-day week; the fact that the dials on our watches and clocks contain numerals up to twelve, corresponding to the Chaldean division of the day into twelve double-hours; the belief in horoscopes; the superstition of planting crops according to the phases of the moon; the twelve signs of the zodiac; the circle of 360 degrees; and the arithmetical process of multiplication.

*(2) upon the
Persians, Phoe-
nicians, Canaan-
ites, and He-
brews*

The influence exerted upon various nations of antiquity was even more significant. The Persians were profoundly affected by Chaldean culture. The Hittites, who aided the Kassites in overthrowing the Babylonians about 1750 B.C., adopted the clay tablets, the cuneiform writing, the Gilgamesh epic, and much of the religion of the nation they conquered. The Babylonian religion also had its effect upon the Phoenicians, as is evidenced by their worship of Astarte (Ishtar) and Tammuz. From the Sumerians or Old Babylonians the Canaanites derived a large part of their law as well as a good many of their religious beliefs. But the principal heirs of Mesopotamian culture were the Hebrews. Possibly as far back as 1800 B.C. some of their ancestors had lived for a time in the northwestern portion of the valley between the two rivers. Numerous Mesopotamian traits were also acquired indirectly through contact with the Canaanites and Phoenicians. It was probably in this manner that the Hebrews came into possession of the Creation and Flood legends and a system of law which had its ultimate origin in the Mesopotamian civilization. An even greater influence was exerted during the period of the Captivity, from 586 to 539 B.C. During these years the Jews were brought into direct association for the first time with a rich and powerful nation. In spite of their hatred of their captors they unconsciously adopted many of their ways. There is evidence, for example, that they acquired some of the Chaldean penchant for trade. In addition, much of the symbolism, pessimism, fatalism, and demonology of the Chaldeans passed into the religion of Judah, transforming it markedly from the character it had had in the time of the Prophets.[6]

Mesopotamian institutions and beliefs also exerted their influence upon the Greeks and the Romans, although for the most part in-

[6] The Hebrew calendar to this day contains a month named in honor of the god Tammuz.

directly. The Stoic philosophy with its doctrines of determinism and pessimism may have reflected that influence in some measure, since its originator, Zeno, was a Semite, probably a Phoenician. A better case could possibly be made for the Mesopotamian origin of such Roman practices as divination, worship of the planets as gods, and the use of the arch and the vault. Several of these elements were introduced to the Romans by the Etruscans, a people of western Asiatic origin. Others were brought in by the Romans themselves as a result of their military campaigns in Asia Minor. That there were natives of the Mesopotamian region resident in Rome, in the later centuries of her history at least, is evidenced by the fact that the Romans used the name "Chaldeans" as synonymous with "astrologers" and sought the aid of such persons on numerous occasions in divining the future.

READINGS

(3) upon the Greeks and the Romans

See color plates at page 189

Selected Readings

· *Items so designated are available in paperbound editions.*

Cambridge Ancient History, Vols. I and III.
Contenau, G., *Everyday Life in Babylonia and Assyria*, New York, 1954. Based on recent archaeological evidence and well illustrated.
Delaporte, L. J., *Mesopotamia: The Babylonian and Assyrian Civilization*, New York, 1925.
· Frankfort, Henri, *The Birth of Civilization in the Near East*, Bloomington, 1951. (Anchor) Brief but useful.
———, *The Intellectual Adventure of Ancient Man*, Chicago, 1946. Contains evidence of the pessimism of the Mesopotamian peoples.
Goodspeed, G. S., *A History of the Babylonians and Assyrians*, New York, 1921. A good introductory work.
Hall, H. R., and Woolley, C. L., *Ur Excavations*, Philadelphia, 1927–39, 5 vols.
Hogarth, D. G., *The Ancient East*, New York, 1915.
Hrozny, Bedrich, *Ancient History of Western Asia, India and Crete*, Prague, 1953.
Jastrow, Morris, *The Civilization of Babylonia and Assyria*, Philadelphia, 1915.
Johns, C. H. W., *Relations between the Laws of Babylonia and the Laws of the Hebrew Peoples*, New York, 1915.
Olmstead, A. T. E., *History of Assyria*, New York, 1923. The standard work. Perhaps a little too favorable.
Woolley, C. L., *The Sumerians*, New York, 1928. A pioneer work, brief and interestingly written.

Source Materials

Barton, G. A., *The Royal Inscriptions of Sumer and Akkad.*
Harper, R. F. ed. and tr., *Assyrian and Babylonian Literature.*
———, ed., *The Code of Hammurabi.*
Johns, C. H. W., *Assyrian Deeds and Documents*, 4 vols.
Luckenbill, D. D., ed., *Ancient Records of Assyria and Babylonia*, 2 vols.
Rogers, R. W., ed. and tr., *Cuneiform Parallels to the Old Testament*, 2 vols.

CHAPTER 5

The Civilization of Ancient Persia

That would we choose, Ahura-Mazdah and Righteousness the
beautiful, so that we may think and speak and do whatever is the
best of deeds for both worlds. For the reward for the best deed
we strive, that security and fodder be preserved for the Kine,
whatever we be instructed or uninstructed, whether rulers of subjects. Truly to the best of rulers is the Kingdom, for we ascribe
the Kingdom to Ahura-Mazdah and to Best Righteousness. As a
man or a woman knows what is right, with fervor let him execute
what is right, for himself and for whomsoever he can bring to
understanding.

—A. T. Olmstead, *Seven-fold Yasna*

Persia
produces a new
civilization

The Chaldeans, as we have seen, were the last of the nations with
a culture essentially Mesopotamian. In 539 B.C. the Persians conquered the valley of the two rivers and soon afterward the whole
empire of the Chaldean kings. But the Persians established what
was really a new civilization. While they adopted much from the
Chaldeans, they made no effort to preserve the old culture intact,
and they introduced a great many new elements from other sources.
Their religion was entirely different, while their art was com-
pounded of elements taken from nearly every people they conquered. Neither did they continue the Chaldean interest in science
nor the development of business and industry. Finally, it should
be remembered that the empire of the Persians included a great
many territories which had never been subject to the Chaldean
kings.

1. The Empire and Its History

The Persian
background

Comparatively little is known of the Persians before the sixth
century B.C. Up to that time they appear to have led an obscure
and peaceful existence on the eastern shore of the Persian Gulf. Their
homeland afforded only modest advantages. On the east it was
hemmed in by high mountains, and its coast line was destitute of
harbors. The fertile valleys of the interior, however, were capable
of providing a generous subsistence for a limited population. Save
for the development of an elaborate religion, the people had made
little progress. They had no system of writing, but they did have
a spoken language closely related to Sanskrit and to the languages
of ancient and modern Europe. It is for this reason alone and not

because of race that they are accurately referred to as an Indo-European people. At the dawn of their history they were not an independent nation but were vassals of the Medes, a kindred people who ruled over a great empire north and east of the Tigris River.

In 559 B.C. a prince by the name of Cyrus became king of a southern Persian tribe. About five years later he made himself ruler of all the Persians and then developed an ambition for dominion over neighboring peoples. As Cyrus the Great he has gone down in history as one of the most sensational conquerors of all time. Within the short space of twenty years he founded a vast empire, larger than any that had previously existed. It is impossible to believe that his successes were due entirely to the force of his own personality. To begin with, he was accepted by the Medes as their king soon after he became ruler of the Persians. The reasons for this are not entirely known. According to various traditions he was the grandson or the son-in-law of the Median king. Perhaps a vague feeling of national kinship impelled Medes and Persians to unite under a common leader. At any rate, Cyrus' "conquest" of the Medes was achieved with such slight opposition that it meant little more than a change of dynasties. Cyrus profited also from the dissension within the Chaldean state, as we noted in the preceding chapter, and from the decrepit condition of other Near Eastern empires. Moreover, the geographic conditions of the Persian homeland were particularly conducive to expansion. The limited area of fertile land, the lack of other resources, and the rich bordering countries inviting conquest were factors which made it virtually inevitable that the nation would break through the confines of its original territory just as soon as the pinch of poverty began to be felt.

The rise of Cyrus

The first of the real conquests of Cyrus was the kingdom of Lydia, which occupied the western half of Asia Minor and was separated from the lands of the Medes only by the Halys River, in what is now northern Turkey. Perceiving the ambitions of the Persians, Croesus, the famous Lydian king, determined to wage a preventive war to preserve his own nation from conquest. He formed alliances with Egypt and Sparta and then consulted the Greek oracle at Delphi as to the advisability of an immediate attack. According to Herodotus, the oracle replied that if he would cross the Halys and assume the offensive he would destroy a great army. He did, but that army was his own. His forces were completely overwhelmed, and his prosperous little kingdom was annexed as a province of the Persian state. Seven years later, in 539 B.C., Cyrus took advantage of discontent and conspiracies in the Chaldean empire to capture the city of Babylon. His victory was an easy one, for he had the assistance of the Jews within the city and of the Chaldean priests, who were dissatisfied with the policies of their king. The conquest of the Chaldean capital made possible the rapid extension of control

The conquests of Cyrus

over the whole empire and thereby added the Fertile Crescent to the domains of Cyrus.

*The successors
of Cyrus*

The great conqueror died in 529 B.C., apparently as the result of wounds received in a war with barbarian tribes. Soon afterward a succession of troubles overtook the state he had founded. Like so many other empire builders both before and since, he had devoted too much energy to conquest and not enough to internal development. He was succeeded by his son Cambyses, who conquered Egypt in 525 B.C. During the new king's absence revolt spread throughout his Asiatic possessions. Chaldeans, Elamites, and even the Medes strove to regain their independence. The chief minister of the realm, abetted by the priests, organized a movement to gain possession of the throne for a pretender who was one of their puppets. Upon learning of conditions at home, Cambyses set out from Egypt with his most dependable troops, but he was murdered on the way. The most serious of the revolts was finally crushed by Darius, a powerful noble, who killed the pretender and seized the throne for himself.

*Darius the
Great*

Darius I, or the Great, as he is somewhat inaccurately called, ruled over the empire from 521 to 486 B.C. The early years of his reign were occupied in suppressing the revolts of subject peoples and in improving the administrative organization of the state. In both of these tasks he achieved considerable success, but his ambitions for power carried him a little too far. Under the pretext of checking the incursions of the Scythians, he crossed the Hellespont, conquered a large part of the Thracian coast, and thereby aroused the hostility of the Athenians. In addition, he increased the oppression of the Ionian Greeks on the shore of Asia Minor, who had fallen under Persian domination with the conquest of Lydia. He interfered with their trade, collected heavier tribute from them, and forced them to serve in his armies. The immediate result was a revolt of the Ionian cities with the assistance of Athens. And when Darius attempted to punish the Athenians for their part in the rebellion, he found himself involved in a war with nearly all the states of Greece.

*The fall of the
Persian empire*

The decisive defeat of the Persians in this war proved to be the turning point in their history. The offensive power of the empire was now definitely shattered, and since the interests of the people had been centered upon military glory, the one unifying influence was broken. The nation sank slowly into stagnation and decay. The last century and a half of its existence was marked by frequent assassinations, revolts of provincial governors, and barbarian invasions, until finally in 330 B.C. its independence was annihilated by the armies of Alexander the Great.

Much has been written about the liberality and efficiency of the Persian government, but it seems doubtful that it was greatly **88** superior to the governments of some earlier empires. While it is true

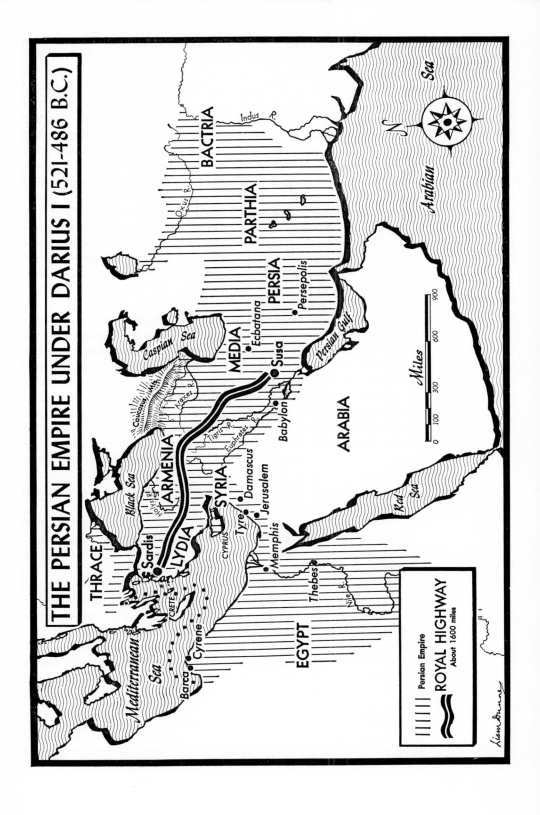

THE PERSIAN EMPIRE UNDER DARIUS I (521-486 B.C.)

Sea

Arabian Sea

BACTRIA

Indus R.

Oxus R.

PARTHIA

Caspian Sea

PERSIA

Persepolis

Ecbatana

MEDIA

Susa

Arabian Sea

Caucasus Mts.

Araxes R.

Halys R.

Tigris R.

Euphrates R.

Babylon

Persian Gulf

ARABIA

Miles

900

600

300

100

0

Black Sea

ARMENIA

SYRIA

Damascus

Jerusalem

Tyre

CYPRUS

Memphis

Red Sea

THRACE

Sardis

LYDIA

CRETE

Thebes

Nile R.

EGYPT

Cyrene

Barca

Mediterranean Sea

Persian Empire

ROYAL HIGHWAY
About 1600 miles

Liam Dunne

*Persian treat-
ment of con-
quered peoples*

that neither Cyrus nor any of his successors imitated the terrorism of the Assyrians, the policies of the Persian despots were not free from oppression. Otherwise it would be difficult to account for the frequency of insurrections against them. After all, they did levy tribute upon conquered nations—to the extent of 700 talents of silver annually from Egypt and 1000 talents from Chaldea [1]—to say nothing of forcing their citizens to serve in the army and excluding them from offices of government. Disadvantages like these were scarcely counterbalanced by the privilege of retaining local customs, laws, and religions, which the Persians accorded to the peoples they subjugated.

*Persian govern-
ment*

In theory the Persian king was an absolute monarch ruling by the grace of the god of light. No constitution or principles of justice limited his sovereign authority. In practice he was required to defer to the chief nobles of the realm and to pay some regard to ancient customs, to the traditional laws of the Medes and Persians. For purposes of local government the empire was divided into twenty-one provinces, each under a satrap or civil governor. Although supreme in all matters of civil jurisdiction, the satrap had no military authority. Military powers were entrusted to the commander of the garrisons throughout the province. As an additional safeguard, a secretary for each province was appointed to examine the mail of the satrap and to report any evidences of disloyalty. And, finally, to make assurance doubly sure, the king sent out special inspectors once a year with a powerful guard to visit each province and investigate the conduct of the government. These officials, known as the "Eyes and Ears of the King," were generally members of the royal family or others whom the monarch could especially trust. Elaborate and costly though this system was, it worked so ineffectively that rebellions of the satraps were among the principal causes of Persia's downfall.

*Achievements
of the
Persian kings*

Nearly all the activities of the imperial government were directed to the ends of military efficiency and political security. Darius I, in particular, made efforts to train the young men of Persian birth in habits which would fit them for the soldierly life. He sought to instill in the upper classes the virtues of austerity, loyalty, and honor and to keep them from succumbing to luxury and vice. In the end all his efforts were in vain, for the Persians no more than the Assyrians could withstand the temptations of sudden power and wealth. Another of the conspicuous activities of the government was the construction of a marvelous system of roads, the best ever built before the time of the Romans. Most famous was the Royal Road, some 1600 miles in length, which connected Susa near the Persian Gulf

---

[1] A talent was a unit of weight rather than coinage, and varied from country to country and from time to time. The Persians, if they used the Hebrew-Babylonian talent, were levying about 1.6 million ounces of silver from Chaldea and about 1.1 million ounces from Egypt. Silver in 1961 was selling at about 91 cents per ounce.

with Sardis in Asia Minor. So well kept was this highway that the king's messengers, traveling day and night, could cover its entire length in less than a week. Nearly every province was linked with one or another of the four Persian capitals: Susa, Persepolis, Babylon, and Ecbatana. Although they naturally contributed to ease of trade, the highways were all built primarily to facilitate control over the outlying sections of the empire.

2. Persian Culture

The culture of the Persians, in the narrower sense of intellectual and artistic achievements, was largely derived from that of previous civilizations. Much of it came from Mesopotamia, but a great deal *The eclectic* of it from Egypt, and some from Lydia and northern Palestine. *culture of* Their system of writing was originally the Babylonian cuneiform, *Persia* but in time they devised an alphabet of thirty-nine letters, based upon the alphabet of the Arameans who traded within their borders. In science they accomplished nothing, except to adopt with some slight modifications the solar calendar of the Egyptians and to encourage exploration as an aid to commerce. They deserve credit also for diffusing a knowledge of the Lydian coinage throughout many parts of western Asia.

It was the architecture of the Persians, however, which gave the most positive expression of the eclectic character of their culture. They copied the raised platform and the terraced building style *The eclectic* which had been so common in Babylonia and Assyria. They imitated *character* also the winged bulls, the brilliantly colored glazed bricks, and *of Persian art*

The Great Palace of Darius and Xerxes at Persepolis. Shown here is the Eastern Stairway with the Gate of Xerxes on the left. Persian archi- tects made use of fluted columns, probably copied from the Greeks, and reliefs resembling those of the Assyrians.

91

other decorative motifs of Mesopotamian architecture. But at least two of the leading features of Mesopotamian construction were not used by the Persians at all—the arch and the vault. In place of them they adopted the column and the colonnade from Egypt. Such matters as interior arrangement and the use of palm and lotus designs at the base of columns also point very distinctly toward Egyptian influence. On the other hand, the fluting of the columns and the volutes or scrolls beneath the capitals were not Egyptian but Greek, adopted not from the mainland of Greece itself but from the Ionian cities of Asia Minor. If there was anything unique about Persian architecture, it was the fact that it was purely secular. The great Persian structures were not temples but palaces. The most famous were the magnificent residences of Darius and Xerxes at

Reliefs from the Staircase at Persepolis. Pictured here are conquered peoples bringing tribute to the Persian king. The various nationalities differ only in styles of dress.

Persepolis. The latter, built in imitation of the temple at Karnak, had an enormous central audience-hall containing a hundred columns and surrounded by innumerable rooms which served as offices and as quarters for the eunuchs and members of the royal harem.

3. The Zoroastrian Religion

The religion of the Persians

By far the most enduring influence left by the ancient Persians was that of their religion. Their system of faith was of ancient origin. It was already highly developed when they began their conquests. And so strong was its appeal, and so ripe were the conditions for its acceptance, that it spread through most of western Asia. Its doctrines turned other religions inside out, displacing beliefs which had been held for ages. The world outlook of nations to this day has been both uplifted and perverted by it.

Although the roots of this religion can be traced as far back as the fifteenth century B.C., its real founder was Zoroaster,[2] who ap-

[2] "Zoroaster" is the corrupt Greek form of the Persian name Zarathustra.

pears to have lived about one hundred years before the Persians established their empire. From him the religion derives its name of Zoroastrianism. He seems to have conceived it to be his mission to purify the traditional beliefs of his people—to eradicate polytheism, animal sacrifice, and magic and to establish their worship on a more spiritual and ethical plane. That the movement he led was the natural accompaniment of the transition to a more civilized agricultural existence is revealed in his teaching of reverence for the cow and in his prescription of cultivation of the soil as a sacred duty. In spite of his reforming efforts many of the old superstitions survived (as they usually do), and were gradually fused with the new ideals.

In many respects Zoroastrianism had a character unique among the religions of the world up to that time. First of all, it was dualistic —not monistic like the Sumerian and Babylonian religions, in which the same gods were capable of both good and evil; nor did it make any pretensions to monotheism, or belief in a single divinity, as did the late Egyptian and Hebrew religions. Two great deities ruled over the universe: one, Ahura-Mazda,[3] supremely good and incapable of any wickedness, embodied the principles of light, truth, and righteousness; the other, Ahriman, treacherous and malignant, presided over the forces of darkness and evil. The two were engaged in a desperate struggle for supremacy. Although they were about evenly matched in strength, the god of light would eventually triumph, and the world would be saved from the powers of darkness.

In the second place, Zoroastrianism was an eschatological religion. "Eschatology" is the doctrine of last or final things. It includes such ideas as the coming of a messiah, the resurrection of the dead, a last judgment, and the translation of the redeemed into a paradise eternal. According to the Zoroastrian belief the world would endure for twelve thousand years. At the end of nine thousand years the second coming of Zoroaster would occur as a sign and a promise of the ultimate redemption of the good. This would be followed in due course by the miraculous birth of Saoshyant, the messiah, whose work would be the perfection of the good as a preparation for the end of the world. Finally the last great day would arrive when Ahura-Mazda would overpower Ahriman and cast him down into the abyss. The dead would then be raised from their graves to be judged according to their deserts. The righteous would enter into immediate bliss, while the wicked would be sentenced to the flames of hell. Ultimately, though, all would be saved; for the Persian hell, unlike the Christian, did not last forever.

From what has been said already, the inference will readily be drawn that the Zoroastrian religion was definitely an ethical one. Although it contained suggestions of predestination, of the election

[3] The name was frequently abbreviated to Mazda.

of some from all eternity to be saved, in the main it rested upon the assumption that men possessed free will, that they were free to sin or not to sin, and that they would be rewarded or punished in the after-life in accordance with their conduct on earth. The virtues commended by the religion made an imposing list. Some were obviously of economic or political origin: diligence, the keeping of contracts, obedience to rulers, the begetting of numerous offspring, and tilling the soil ("He who sows corn sows holiness"). Others had a broader significance: Ahura-Mazda commanded that men should be truthful, that they should love and help one another to the best of their power, that they should befriend the poor and practice hospitality. The essence of these broader virtues was perhaps expressed in another of the god's decrees: "Whosoever shall give meat to one of the faithful . . . he shall go to Paradise."

The principal sins

The forms of conduct forbidden were sufficiently numerous and varied to cover the whole list of the Seven Cardinal Sins of medieval Christianity and a great many more. Pride, gluttony, sloth, covetousness, wrathfulness, lust, adultery, abortion, slander, and waste were among the more typical. The taking of interest on loans to others of the same faith was described as the "worst of sins," and the accumulation of riches was strongly discountenanced. The restraints which men were to practice included also a kind of negative Golden Rule: "That nature alone is good which shall not do unto another whatever is not good for its own self." It is pertinent to add that the original Zoroastrianism condemned the ascetic way of life. Self-inflicted suffering, fasting, and even excessive grief were prohibited on the ground that they injured both mind and body and rendered human beings unfit for the duties of agriculture and the begetting of children. Temperance rather than complete abstinence was the traditional Persian ideal.[4]

(4) a revealed religion

Zoroastrianism is especially significant because it was a revealed religion—apparently the first of its type in the history of the Western world. Its followers were believed to be the exclusive possessors of truth; not because they were wiser than other men, but because they shared the secrets of the god. As members of his substance they automatically partook of his wisdom; not in its entirety, of course, but certain portions of it. The truth which they possessed was therefore occult. It could not be deduced by logic or discovered by investigation. Part of it was in the form of sacred writings—the *Avesta*, believed to have been sent down from heaven —but much of it consisted of an oral revelation received by Zoroaster from Mazda and transmitted to his disciples. Contrary to the general opinion, revealed religions have not been so common in the Western world. The Egyptians had no bible or any other Word of God, and neither did the Mesopotamian nations. Likewise, the re-

[4] The quotations in the last two paragraphs are taken from J. O. Hertzler, *The Social Thought of the Ancient Civilizations,* pp. 149–158.

ligions of Greece and Rome rested upon no Truth vouchsafed by the gods. Zoroastrianism, Judaism, Christianity, and Islam are the only faiths, with the possible exception of Hinduism, which have had divine revelation as one of their essential elements. Without doubt this has been a factor augmenting their strength, but it has accounted in some measure also for their dogmatism and intolerance.

4. The Mystical and Otherworldly Heritage from Persia

The religion of the Persians as taught by Zoroaster did not long continue in its original state. It was corrupted, first of all, by the persistence of primitive superstitions, of magic and priestcraft. The farther the religion spread, the more of these relics of barbarism were engrafted upon it. As the years passed, additional modification resulted from the influence of alien faiths, particularly that of the Chaldeans. The outcome in the end was the growth of a powerful synthesis in which the primitive priestliness, messianism, and dualism of the Persians were combined with the pessimism and fatalism of the Neo-Babylonians.

The fusion of Zoroastrianism with alien faiths

Out of this synthesis gradually emerged a profusion of cults, alike in their basic dogmas but according them different emphasis. The oldest of these cults was Mithraism, deriving its name from Mithras, the chief lieutenant of Mazda in the struggle against the powers of evil. At first only a minor deity in the religion of Zoroastrianism, Mithras finally won recognition in the hearts of many of the Persians as the god most deserving of worship. The reason for this change was probably the emotional appeal made by the incidents of his career. He was believed to have been born of a rock in the presence of a small group of shepherds, who brought him gifts in token of their reverence for his great mission on earth. He then proceeded to subdue all the living creatures around him, taming many of them and rendering them useful to man. The better to accomplish his purpose, he entered into a compact with the sun, obtaining warmth and light that agriculture might flourish. But the most important of his exploits was the capture of the divine bull. Seizing the animal by the horns, he struggled desperately until he had forced him into a cave, where in obedience to a command from the sun he slew him. From the blood and flesh of the bull came all manner of herbs, grain, and other plants valuable to man. No sooner had these things been accomplished than Ahriman produced a drought on the earth; but Mithras thrust his spear into a rock and the waters gushed forth. Next the god of evil sent a flood, but Mithras caused an ark to be built to permit the escape of one man with his flocks. Finally, his work accomplished, Mithras ate a sacramental meal with the sun and ascended into heaven. In due time he would return and bestow immortality upon all of the faithful.

Mithraism

*The ritual and
observances of
Mithraism*

The ritual of Mithraism was both elaborate and significant. It included a complicated initiation ceremony of seven stages or degrees, the last of which cemented a mystic fellowship with the god. Prolonged self-denial and laceration of the flesh were necessary accompaniments of the initiation process. Admission to full membership in the cult entitled one to participate in the sacraments, the most important of which were baptism and a sacred meal of bread, water, and possibly wine. Still other observances included lustration (ceremonial cleansing with holy water), the burning of incense, chanting sacred music, and the keeping of sacred days. Of the last, Sunday and the twenty-fifth of December were the specific examples. In imitation of the Chaldean astral religion each day of the week was dedicated to a celestial body. Since the sun as the giver of light and the faithful ally of Mithras was the most important of these bodies, his day was naturally the most sacred. The twenty-fifth of December also possessed its solar significance: as the approximate date of the winter solstice it marked the return of the sun from his long journey south of the Equator. It was in a sense the "birthday" of the sun, since it connoted the revival of his life-giving powers for the benefit of man.

*The spread
and influence of
Mithraism*

Exactly when the worship of Mithras became a definite cult is unknown, but it was certainly not later than the fourth century B.C. Its characteristics became firmly established during the period of social ferment which followed the collapse of Alexander's empire, and its spread at that time was exceedingly rapid. In the last century B.C. it was introduced into Rome, although it was of little importance in Italy itself until after 100 A.D. It drew its converts especially from the lower classes, from the ranks of soldiers, foreigners, and slaves. Ultimately it rose to the status of one of the most popular religions of the Empire, the chief competitor of Christianity and of the old Roman paganism itself. After 275, however, its strength rapidly waned. How much influence this astonishing cult exerted is impossible to say. Its superficial resemblance to Christianity is certainly not hard to perceive, but this does not mean, of course, that the two were identical, or that one was an offshoot of the other. Nevertheless, it is probably true that Christianity as the younger of the two rivals borrowed a good many of its externals from Mithraism, at the same time preserving its own philosophy virtually untouched.

Manicheism

One of the principal successors of Mithraism in transmitting the legacy from Persia was Manicheism, founded by Mani, a high-born priest of Ecbatana, about 250 A.D. Like Zoroaster he conceived it to be his mission to reform the prevailing religion, but he received scant sympathy in his own country and had to be content with missionary ventures in India and western China. About 276 A.D. he was condemned and crucified by his Persian opponents. Following his death his teachings were carried by his disciples into practically every country of western Asia and finally into Italy about 330 A.D.

Large numbers of western Manicheans, the great Augustine among them, eventually became Christians.

Of all the Zoroastrian teachings, the one which made the deepest impression upon the mind of Mani was dualism. It was therefore natural that it should have become the central doctrine of the new faith. But Mani gave to this doctrine a broader interpretation than it had ever received in the earlier religion. He conceived not merely of two deities engaged in a relentless struggle for supremacy, but of a whole universe divided into two kingdoms, each the antithesis of the other. The first was the kingdom of spirit ruled over by a God eternally good. The second was the kingdom of matter under the dominion of Satan. Only "spiritual" substances like fire, light, and the souls of men were created by God. Darkness, sin, desire, and all things bodily and material owed their origin to Satan. Human nature itself was evil, for the first parents of the race had received their physical bodies from the prince of darkness.

The strict dualism of the Manicheans

The moral implications of this rigorous dualism were readily apparent. Since everything connected with sensation or desire was the work of Satan, man should strive to free himself as completely as possible from enslavement to his physical nature. He should refrain from all forms of sensual enjoyment, the eating of meat, the drinking of wine, the gratification of sexual desire. Even marriage was prohibited, for this would result in the begetting of more physical bodies to people the kingdom of Satan. In addition, man should subdue the flesh by prolonged fasting and the infliction of pain. Recognizing that this program of austerities would be too difficult for ordinary mortals, Mani divided the race of mankind into the "perfect" and the "secular." Only the former would be obliged to adhere to the full program as the ideal of what all should hope to attain. The latter were merely required to eschew idolatry, avarice, fornication, falsehood, and the eating of meat. To aid the children of men in their struggle against the powers of darkness, God had sent prophets and redeemers from time to time to comfort and inspire them. Noah, Abraham, Zoroaster, Jesus, and Paul were all numbered among these divine emissaries; but the last and greatest of them was Mani.

The moral implications of dualism

The influence of Manicheism is very difficult to estimate, but it was undoubtedly considerable. People of all classes in the Roman Empire, including some members of the Christian clergy, embraced its doctrines. In its Christianized form it became one of the principal sects of the early church,[5] and it exerted some influence upon the development of the Albigensian heresy as late as the twelfth and thirteenth centuries. It inspired extravagant Christian speculations upon the dualism between God and the devil and between spirit and matter. Not only did it contribute to the asceticism of Christianity, but it strengthened also the doctrines of original sin and the total depravity of man, as taught by some theologians. Finally, it was a

The influence of Manicheism

[5] See pp. 255, 258.

sovereign source of the famous duality of ethical standards set up by St. Augustine and other Church Fathers: (1) a standard of perfection for the few (the monks and nuns), who would withdraw from the world and lead saintly lives as an example for the rest; and (2) a socially possible standard for the ordinary Christians.

Gnosticism

The third most important cult which developed as an element in the Persian heritage was Gnosticism (from the Greek *gnosis*, meaning knowledge). The name of its founder is unknown, and likewise the date of its origin, but it was certainly in existence as early as the first century A.D. It reached the height of its popularity in the latter half of the second century. Although it gained some followers in Italy, its influence was confined primarily to the Near East.

The mysticism of the Gnostics

The feature which most sharply distinguished this cult from the others was mysticism. The Gnostics denied that the truths of religion could be discovered by reason or could even be made intelligible. They regarded themselves as the exclusive possessors of a secret spiritual knowledge revealed to them directly by God. This knowledge was alone important as a guide to faith and conduct. In like manner, their religious observances were highly esoteric, that is, fraught with hidden meaning known only to the initiated. Sacraments in great profusion, innumerable baptisms, mystic rites, and the use of holy formulas and sacred numbers made up the leading examples.

The combined influence of the several offshoots of Zoroastrianism

The combined influence of these several Persian religions was enormous. Most of them were launched at a time when political and social conditions were particularly conducive to their spread. The breakup of Alexander's empire about 300 B.C. inaugurated a peculiar period in the history of the ancient world. International barriers were broken down; there was an extensive migration and intermingling of peoples; and the collapse of the old social order gave rise to profound disillusionment and a vague yearning for individual salvation. Men's attentions were centered as never before since the downfall of Egypt upon compensations in a life to come. Under such circumstances religions of the kind described were bound to flourish like the green bay tree. Otherworldly, mystical, and messianic, they offered the very escape that men were seeking from a world of anxiety and confusion.

Other elements in the heritage from Persia

Although not exclusively religious, the heritage left by the Persians contained few elements of a secular nature. Their form of government was adopted by the later Roman monarchs, not in its purely political aspect, but in its character of a divine-right despotism. When such emperors as Diocletian and Constantine I invoked divine authority as a basis for their absolutism and required their subjects to prostrate themselves in their presence, they were really submerging the state in the religion as the Persians had done from the time of Darius. Traces of Persian influence upon certain

Hellenistic philosophies are also discernible; but here again it was essentially religious, for it was confined almost entirely to the mystical theories of the Neo-Platonists and their philosophical allies.

Selected Readings

· Items so designated are available in paperbound editions.

Cambridge Ancient History, Vol. IV.
· Cumont, Franz, *The Mysteries of Mithra*, Chicago, 1903. (Dover) A thorough analysis, interestingly presented.
Dhalla, M. N., *History of Zoroastrianism*, New York, 1938. A scholarly and balanced account.
Hogarth, D. G., *The Ancient East*, New York, 1915.
Huart, C. I., *Ancient Persian and Iranian Civilization*, New York, 1927. A standard work, but limited in coverage.
Jackson, A. W. W., *Zoroaster, the Prophet of Ancient Iran*, New York, 1928.
Moore, G. F., *The History of Religions*, New York, 1913, Vol. I.
· Olmstead, A. T. E., *History of the Persian Empire (Achaemenid Period)*, Chicago, 1948. (Phoenix) Detailed and complete but somewhat uncritical.
Pavry, J. D. C., *The Zoroastrian Doctrine of a Future Life*, New York, 1929.
Rogers, R. W. A., *A History of Ancient Persia from Its Earliest Beginnings to the Death of Alexander*, New York, 1929. Good for political history.
Ross, Sir E. D., *The Persians*, New York, 1931.
Sykes, Sir P. M., *A History of Persia*, New York, 1921, Vol. I.

Source Materials

Darmesteter, James, tr., "The Zend-Avesta," *Sacred Books of the East*, Vol. III.
Hertzler, J. O., *The Social Thought of the Ancient Civilizations*, pp. 149–68.

CHAPTER 6

The Hebrew Civilization

I am the Lord thy God, which brought thee out of the land of
Egypt from the house of bondage.
Thou shalt have none other Gods before me.
Thou shalt not make thee any graven image, or any likeness of
any thing that is in heaven above, or that is in the earth beneath,
or that is in the waters beneath the earth:
Thou shalt not bow down thyself unto them, nor serve them: for
I the Lord thy God am a jealous God, visiting the iniquity of the
fathers upon the children unto the third and fourth generation of
them that hate me . . .

—*Deuteronomy* v. 6–9

*Importance of
the Hebrew
civilization*

Of all the peoples of the ancient Orient, none with the possible exception of the Egyptians has been of greater importance to the
modern world than the Hebrews. It was the Hebrews, of course,
who provided much of the background of the Christian religion—
its Commandments, its stories of the Creation and the Flood, its concept of God as lawgiver and judge, and more than two-thirds of its
Bible. Hebrew conceptions of morality and political theory have
also profoundly influenced modern nations, especially those in which
the Calvinist faith has been strong. On the other hand, it is necessary to remember that the Hebrews themselves did not develop their
culture in a vacuum. No more than any other people were they able
to escape the influence of nations around them. Hebrew religion,
as a consequence, contained numerous elements which were quite
clearly derived from Egyptian and Mesopotamian sources. Despite
all the efforts of prophets to purge the Hebraic faith of foreign corruptions, many of them still remained, and others were added later.
As we shall soon discover, Hebrew law was based very largely upon
Old Babylonian origins, though of course with modifications. Hebrew philosophy was partly Egyptian and partly Greek; while long
before the Book of Job was ever written, there was an Old Babylonian drama of similar character. No one can deny, of course, that
the Hebrews were capable of original achievement; at the same time,
we cannot overlook the fact that they were influenced greatly by
the older civilizations around them.

1. Hebrew Origins and Relations with Other Peoples

The origin of the Hebrew people is still a puzzling problem. Certainly they were not a separate race, nor did they have any physical
characteristics sufficient to distinguish them clearly from other na-

tions around them. The origin of their name is in doubt. According to one account, it was derived from Khabiru or Habiru, a name invented by their enemies and meaning the equivalent of "alien," "outcast," or "nomad." [1] According to other authorities, it is related to the word "Ever" or "Eber," referring to those who came from the other side of the Euphrates. Whatever its origin, it seems to have been applied originally to various immigrant peoples, and was restricted later to the Israelites.

ORIGINS AND
RELATIONS
WITH OTHER
PEOPLES

*Ethnic character
of the Hebrews*

Most scholars agree that the original home of the Hebrews was the Arabian Desert. The first definite appearance of the founders of the nation of Israel, however, was in northwestern Mesopotamia. Apparently as early as 1800 B.C. a group of Hebrews under the leadership of Abraham had settled there. Later Abraham's grandson Jacob led a migration westward and began the occupation of Palestine. It was from Jacob, subsequently called Israel, that the Israelites derived their name. Sometime after 1600 B.C. certain tribes of the Israelites, together with other Hebrews, went down into Egypt to escape the consequences of famine. They appear to have settled in the vicinity of the Delta and to have been enslaved by the Pharaoh's government. Around 1300–1250 B.C. their descendants found a new leader in the indomitable Moses, who freed them from bondage, led them to the Sinai Peninsula, and persuaded them to become worshipers of Yahweh, a god whose name is sometimes written erroneously as Jehovah. Hitherto Yahweh had been the deity of Hebrew shepherd folk in the general locality of Sinai. Making use of a Yahwist cult as a nucleus, Moses welded the various tribes of his followers into a confederation, sometimes called the Yahweh Amphictyony. It was this confederation which played the dominant role in the conquest of Palestine, or the Land of Canaan.

With its scanty rainfall and rugged topography, Palestine as a haven for the Children of Israel left much to be desired. For the most part it was a barren and inhospitable place. But compared with the arid wastes of Arabia it was a veritable paradise, and it is not surprising that the leaders should have pictured it as a "land flowing with milk and honey." Most of it was already occupied by the Canaanites, another people of Semitic speech who had lived there for centuries. Through contact with the Babylonians, Hittites, and Egyptians they had built up a culture which was no longer primitive. They practiced agriculture and carried on trade. They knew the use of iron and the art of writing, and they had adapted the laws of Hammurabi's code to the needs of their simpler existence. Their religion, which was also derived in large part from Babylonia, was cruel and sensual, including human sacrifice and temple prostitution.

The Hebrew conquest of the land of Canaan was a slow and difficult process. Seldom did the tribes unite in a combined attack, and even when they did, the enemy cities were well enough fortified to

[1] A. T. E. Olmstead, *History of Palestine and Syria*, p. 196.

resist capture. After several generations of sporadic fighting the Hebrews had succeeded in taking only the limestone hills and a few of the less fertile valleys. In the intervals between wars they mingled freely with the Canaanites and adopted no small amount of their culture. Before they had a chance to complete the conquest, they found themselves confronted by a new and more formidable enemy, the Philistines, who had come into Palestine from Asia Minor and from the islands of the Aegean Sea. Stronger than either the Hebrews or Canaanites, the new invaders rapidly overran the country and forced the Hebrews to surrender much of the territory they had already gained. It is from the Philistines that Palestine derives its name.

2. The Record of Political Hopes and Frustrations

The crisis produced by the Philistine conquests served not to discourage the Hebrews but to unite them and to intensify their ardor for battle. Moreover, it led directly to the founding of the Hebrew monarchy about 1025 B.C. Up to this time the nation had been ruled by "judges," who possessed little more than the authority of religious leaders. But now with a greater need for organization and discipline, the people demanded a king to rule them and to go out before them and fight their battles. The man selected as the first incumbent of the office was Saul, "a choice young man and a goodly," a member of the tribe of Benjamin.

In spite of his popularity at the start, the reign of King Saul was not a happy one, either for the nation or for the ruler himself. Only a few suggestions of the reasons are given in the Old Testament account. Evidently Saul incurred the displeasure of Samuel, the last of the great judges, who had expected to remain the power behind the throne. Before long there appeared on the scene the ambitious David, who, with the encouragement of Samuel, carried on skillful maneuvers to draw popular support from the king. Waging his own military campaigns, he achieved one bloody triumph after another. By contrast, the armies of Saul met disastrous reverses. Finally the king himself, being critically wounded, requested his armor-bearer to kill him. When the latter would not, he drew his own sword, fell upon it, and died.

David now became king and ruled for forty years. His reign was one of the most glorious periods in Hebrew history. He smote the Philistines hip and thigh and reduced their territory to a narrow strip of coast in the south. He united the Twelve Tribes into a consolidated state under an absolute monarch, and he began the construction of a magnificent capital at Jerusalem. But strong government, military glory, and material splendor were not unmixed blessings for the people. Their inevitable accompaniments were high taxation and conscription. As a consequence, before David died,

Entrance to King David's Tomb on Mt. Zion. King David ruled in the tenth century B.C. The entrance to his tomb is obviously of later construction, but the tomb itself is reputed to date from David's death.

rumblings of discontent were plainly to be heard in certain parts of his kingdom.

David was succeeded by his son Solomon, the last of the kings of the united monarchy. As a result of the nationalist aspirations of later times, Solomon has been pictured in Hebrew lore as one of the wisest, justest, and most enlightened rulers in all history. The facts of his career furnish little support for such a belief. About all that can be said in his favor is that he was a shrewd diplomat and an active patron of trade. Most of his policies were oppressive, although of course not deliberately so. Ambitious to copy the luxury and magnificence of other Oriental despots, he established a harem of 700 wives and 300 concubines and completed the construction of sumptuous palaces, stables for 4000 horses, and a costly temple in Jerusalem. Since Palestine was poor in resources, most of the materials for the building projects had to be imported. Gold, silver, bronze, and cedar were brought in in such quantities that the revenues from taxation and from the tolls levied upon trade were insufficient to pay for them. To make up the deficit Solomon ceded twenty towns and resorted to the corvée, or the system of conscripting labor. Every three months 30,000 Hebrews were drafted and sent into Phoenicia to work in the forests and mines of King Hiram of Tyre, from whom the most expensive materials had been purchased.

Solomon aspires to Oriental magnificence

Solomon's extravagance and oppression produced acute discontent among his subjects. His death in 935 B.C. was the signal for open revolt. The ten northern tribes, refusing to submit to his son Rehoboam, seceded and set up their own kingdom. Sectional differences played their part also in the disruption of the nation. The northern Hebrews were sophisticated, accustomed to urban living, and steeped in foreign influences. By contrast, the two southern tribes were composed very largely of pastoral and agricultural folk, loyal to the religion of their fathers, and hating the ways of the foreigner.

The secession of the Ten Tribes

103

Perhaps these differences alone would have been sufficient in time to break the nation asunder.

The fate of Israel and Judah

After the secession the ten northern tribes came to be known as the Kingdom of Israel,[2] while the two southern tribes were called henceforth the Kingdom of Judah. For more than two centuries the two little states maintained their separate existences. But in 722 B.C. the Kingdom of Israel was conquered by the Assyrians. Its inhabitants were scattered throughout the vast empire of their conquerors and were eventually absorbed by the more numerous population around them. They have ever since been referred to as the Lost Ten Tribes of Israel. The Kingdom of Judah managed to survive for more than a hundred years longer, successfully defying the Assyrian menace. But in 586 B.C., as we have already learned, it was overthrown by the Chaldeans under Nebuchadnezzar. Jerusalem was plundered and burned, and its leading citizens were carried off into captivity in Babylon. When Cyrus the Persian conquered the Chaldeans, he freed the Jews and permitted them to return to their native land. Few were willing to go, and considerable time elapsed before it was possible to rebuild the temple. From 539 to 332 B.C. Palestine was a vassal state of Persia. In 332 B.C. it was conquered by Alexander and after his death was placed under the rule of the Ptolemies of Egypt. In 63 B.C. it became a Roman protectorate. Its political history as a Jewish commonwealth was ended in 70 A.D. after a desperate revolt which the Romans punished by destroying Jerusalem and annexing the country as a province. The inhabitants were gradually diffused through other parts of the Empire.

The Diaspora

The destruction of Jerusalem and annexation of the country by the Romans were the principal factors in the so-called *Diaspora,* or dispersion of the Jews from Palestine. Even earlier large numbers of them had fled into various parts of the Greco-Roman world on account of difficulties in their homeland. In their new environment they rapidly succumbed to foreign influences, a fact which was of tremendous importance in promoting a fusion of Greek and Oriental ideas. It was a Hellenized Jew, St. Paul, who was mainly responsible for remolding Christianity in accordance with Greek philosophical doctrines.

3. *The Hebrew Religious Evolution*

Reasons for the varied evolution of Hebrew religion

Few peoples in history have gone through a religious evolution comparable to that of the Hebrews. Its cycle of development ranged all the way from the crudest superstitions to the loftiest spiritual and ethical conceptions. Part of the explanation is doubtless to be found in the peculiar geographic position occupied by the Hebrew people. Located as they were after their conquest of Canaan on the highroad between Egypt and the major civilizations of Asia,

104   [2] Or the kingdom of Samaria, from the name of its capital city.

they were bound to be affected by an extraordinary variety of influences.

At least five different stages can be distinguished in the growth of the Hebrew religion. The first we can call the pre-Mosaic stage, from the earliest beginnings of the people to approximately 1100 B.C. *The pre-Mosaic* This stage was characterized at first by animism, the worship of *stage* spirits that dwelt in trees, mountains, sacred wells and springs, and even in stones of peculiar shape. Diverse forms of magic were practiced also at this time—necromancy, imitative magic, scapegoat sacrifices, and so on. Numerous relics of these early beliefs and practices are preserved in the Old Testament. For example, the reference in Deuteronomy 33:16 to the Lord as "Him that dwelt in the bush." See also II Kings 6:5–7, in which the story is related of how Elisha made an axehead float by throwing a piece of wood into the water. Under the principle of imitative magic, the floating of the wood on the water brought the axehead to the surface.

Gradually animism gave way to anthropomorphic gods. It would appear that few of the new deities were as yet given names; each was usually referred to merely by the generic name of "El," that *Anthropomor-* is, "God." They were guardian deities of particular places and *phic gods* possibly of separate tribes. No national worship of Yahweh was known at this time.

The second stage, which lasted from the twelfth century B.C. to the ninth, is frequently designated the stage of national monolatry. The term may be defined as the exclusive worship of one god but *The stage of* without any denial that other gods exist. Due chiefly to the in- *national* fluence of Moses, the Hebrews gradually adopted as their national *monolatry* deity during this period a god whose name appears to have been written "Jhwh" or "Yhwh." How it was pronounced no one knows, but scholars generally agree that it was probably uttered as if spelled "Yahweh." The meaning is also a mystery. When Moses inquired of Yahweh what he should tell the people when they demanded to know what god had sent him, Yahweh replied: "I AM THAT I AM: and he said, Thus shalt thou say unto the children of Israel, I AM hath sent me unto you."[3] Neither at this time nor in any other period of ancient history did the Hebrews refer to their god as "Jehovah." The latter name was the result of a blunder committed by Christian Hebraists of the thirteenth century A.D.[4]

During the time of Moses and for two or three centuries thereafter Yahweh was a somewhat peculiar deity. He was conceived almost exclusively in anthropomorphic terms. He possessed a physi- *Characteristics* cal body and the emotional qualities of men. He was capricious, on *of Yahweh* occasions, and somewhat irascible—as capable of evil and wrathful judgments as he was of good. His decrees were often quite arbitrary,

[3] Exodus 3:13-14.
[4] Adolphe Lods, *Israel from Its Beginnings to the Middle of the Eighth Century*, p. 321.

and he would punish the man who sinned unwittingly just about as readily as him whose guilt was real.[5] Omnipotence was scarcely an attribute that Yahweh could claim, for his power was limited to the territory occupied by the Hebrews themselves. When Naaman the Syrian decided to become a follower of Yahweh, he could solve the problem of territorial dominion only by taking two mules' burden of good Palestinian earth with him.[6] But in spite of these limitations the Hebrews revered their God as their only guide and deliverer, the protector of widows and orphans, and the swift avenger of the nation's wrongs.

The supremacy of law and ritual

The religion of this stage was neither primarily ethical nor profoundly spiritual. Yahweh was revered as a supreme lawgiver and as the stern upholder of the moral order of the universe. According to Biblical account, he issued the Ten Commandments to Moses on top of Mt. Sinai. Old Testament scholars, however, do not generally accept this tradition. They admit that a primitive Decalogue may have existed in Mosaic times, but they doubt that the Ten Commandments in the form in which they are preserved in the Book of Exodus go back any farther than the seventh century. In any event, it is clear that Moses' God was interested just about as much in sacrifice and in ritualistic observances as he was in good conduct or in purity of heart. Moreover, the religion was not vitally concerned with spiritual matters. It offered naught but material rewards in this life and none at all in a life to come. Finally, the belief in monolatry was corrupted by certain elements of fetishism, magic, and even grosser superstitions that lingered from more primitive times or that were gradually acquired from neighboring peoples. These varied all the way from serpent worship to bloody sacrifices and licentious fertility orgies.

The need for reform

By the ninth century the Hebrew faith was badly in need of reform from within. Superstition and idolatry had steadily increased with the passing of the years until the worship of Yahweh was scarcely distinguishable from the worship of the Phoenician and Canaanite Ba'als. First to sense the need for drastic changes were the leaders of ascetic sects like the Nazirites and Rechabites, who denounced the foreign corruptions and clamored for a return to what they thought was the simple piety of their fathers. To emphasize their hatred of everything foreign, they condemned the refinements of civilized life and urged that the people should dwell in tents. Their work was followed by that of the vehement preacher Elijah, who dragged the priests of the Ba'al cults from their altars and slew them with his own hands. Notwithstanding his crusade against the foreign cults, Elijah did not deny the existence of their

---

[5] By way of illustration, he struck Uzza dead merely because that unfortunate individual placed his hand upon the Ark of the Covenant to steady it while it was being transported to Jerusalem. 1 Chronicles 13:9–10.

[6] II Kings 5:17.

gods; but he insisted that Yahweh was a god of righteousness and the only deity whom the Hebrews should worship.

The really important work of religious reform, however, was accomplished by the great prophets—Amos, Hosea, Isaiah,[7] and Micah. And their achievements represented the third stage in the development of the Hebrew religion, the stage of the prophetic revolution, which occupied the eighth and seventh centuries B.C. The great prophets were men of much broader vision than Elijah or the leaders of the ascetic sects. Their outlook was progressive; they did not demand a return to some age of simplicity in the past but taught that the religion should be infused with a new philosophy and a new conception of the ends it was supposed to serve. Three basic doctrines made up the substance of their teachings: (1) monotheism—Yahweh is the lord of the universe; the gods of other nations do not exist; (2) Yahweh is a god of righteousness exclusively; He is not really omnipotent, but His power is limited by justice and goodness; the evil in the world comes from man not from God; (3) the purposes of religion are chiefly ethical; Yahweh cares nothing for ritual and sacrifice, but that men should "seek justice, relieve the oppressed, judge the fatherless, plead for the widow." Or as Micah expressed it: "What doth the Lord require of thee, but to do justly, and to love mercy, and to walk humbly with thy God?" [8]

The stage of the prophetic revolution

In these doctrines was contained a definite repudiation of nearly everything that the older religion had stood for. Such, however, was apparently not the intention of the prophets. They conceived it rather as their mission to restore the religion to its ancient purity. The crudities within it they regarded as foreign corruptions. But like many such leaders, they builded better than they knew. Their actual accomplishments went so far beyond their original objectives that they amounted to a religious revolution. To a considerable extent this revolution also had its social and political aspects. Wealth had become concentrated in the hands of a few. Thousands of small farmers had lost their freedom and had passed under subjection to rich proprietors. If we can believe the testimony of Amos, bribery was so rife in the law courts that the plaintiff in a suit for debt had merely to give the judge a pair of shoes and the defendant would be handed over as a slave.[9] Overshadowing all was the threat of Assyrian domination. To enable the nation to cope with that threat, the prophets believed that social abuses should be

Contrasts with the older religion; political and social aspects

---

[7] Many Old Testament authorities consider the Book of Isaiah the work of two authors. They ascribe the first part to Isaiah, and the second part, beginning with Chapter 40, to Deutero-Isaiah, or the Second Isaiah. The Second Isaiah is more emphatic than the first in denying the existence of the gods of other peoples.

[8] Micah 6:8.

[9] Amos 2:6. This, of course, was poetic propaganda and may have been slightly exaggerated.

Remains of an Ancient Synagogue at Capernaum. Capernaum was supposed to have been the scene of many of the miracles attributed to Jesus. Here also he called out Peter, Andrew, and Matthew to be his disciples.

Mount Zion, Jerusalem, Israel. Tradition has it that this is where the Last Supper took place. It is also the burial place of King David.

HEBREW
CIVILIZATION:
ITS SETTING
AND MONUMENTS

Model of King Solomon's Temple. Significant details are: A, Royal Gates; B, Treasury; C, Royal Palace; D, People's Gate; E, Western ("Wailing") Wall; F, Priests' Quarters; G, Court House; H, Solomon's Porch.

King Solomon's Mines in the Negev, the most desolate portion of Israel. The mines were principally copper and silver mines, and much of the ore was exported to Phoenicia.

stamped out and the people united under a religion purged of its alien corruptions.

The religion not yet otherworld-ly or mystical

The results of this revolution must not be misinterpreted. It did eradicate some of the most flagrant forms of oppression, and it rooted out permanently most of the barbarities which had crept into the religion from foreign sources. But the Hebrew faith was not yet a religion which bore much resemblance to modern orthodox Judaism. It contained little of a spiritual character and hardly a trace of the mystical. Instead of being otherworldly, it was oriented toward this life. Its purposes were social and ethical—to promote a just and harmonious society and to abate man's inhumanity to man—not to confer individual salvation in an afterlife. As yet there was no belief in heaven and hell or in Satan as a powerful opponent of God. The shades of the dead went down into Sheol to linger there for a time in the dust and gloom and then disappear.

The stage of the Exile or Babylonian Captivity

Nevertheless, the ideals of the prophetic revolution probably represented the highest perfection of the Hebrew religion. After that time it shifted its emphases, responding again to outside influences. The first of these influences made themselves felt during the period of the Babylonian Captivity from 586 to 539 B.C., which constitutes a fourth stage in the evolution of the religion. As a result of association with the Neo-Babylonians, the Jews adopted ideas of pessimism, fatalism, and the transcendence of God. No longer did they conceive of Yahweh as intimately concerned with the social problems of His people, but as an omnipotent, unapproachable being whose essential characteristic was holiness. His thoughts were not men's thoughts nor His ways the ways of mortals. Man's chief duty was to submit absolutely to His inscrutable will.[10] The forms of the religion were also profoundly changed. In a desperate attempt to preserve the identity of the Jews as a nation, their leaders adopted or revived customs and observances which would serve to distinguish them as a peculiar people. The institution of the Sabbath, the forms of synagogal worship, the practice of circumcision, and elaborate distinctions between clean and unclean foods were now given places of fundamental importance. While it is true that most of these observances were of pre-Exilic origin, they had not been regarded as religious essentials for many years. The prophets, moreover, had emphatically denied their importance. The growth of extensive regulations for the conduct of ritual inevitably increased the power of the priests, with the result that Judaism was gradually transformed into an ecclesiastical religion.

The final significant stage in Hebrew religious evolution was the post-Exilic stage or the period of Persian influence. This period may be considered to have covered the years from 539 to about

[10] These ideas are to be found in the Book of Ezekiel and in the writings of Deutero-Isaiah (Isaiah 40–55) which date from the period of the Captivity; also in the Book of Job, written a century or more later.

300 B.C. Perhaps enough has been said already to indicate the character of the influence from Persia. It will be recalled from the preceding chapter that Zoroastrianism was a dualistic, messianic, otherworldly, and esoteric religion. In the period following the Exile these very ideas gained wide acceptance among the Jews. They adopted a belief in Satan as the Great Adversary and the author of evil. They developed an eschatology, including such notions as the coming of a spiritual savior, the resurrection of the dead, and a last judgment. They turned their attention to salvation in an after-world as more important than enjoyment of this life. Lastly, they embraced the conception of a revealed religion. The Book of Ezekiel, for example, was asserted to have been prepared by God in heaven and given to the man whose name it bears with instruction to "eat" it.[11] In time the idea grew that many other books had been dictated directly by Yahweh to certain of His followers. With the adoption of beliefs such as these the Hebrew faith had evolved far from the strict monotheism and the simple ethical religion of the days of the prophets.

The post-Exilic stage

4. Hebrew Culture

In certain respects the Hebrew genius was inferior to that of some other great nations of antiquity. In the first place, it revealed no talent for science. Not a single important discovery in any scientific field has ever been traced to the ancient Hebrews. Nor were they particularly adept in appropriating the knowledge of others. They could not build a bridge or a tunnel except of the crudest sort. Whether it was from lack of interest in these things or whether it was because of too deep an absorption in religious affairs is not clear. In the second place, they seem to have been almost entirely devoid of artistic skill. Their only examples of the glyptic arts were engraved seals similar to those made by the Sumerians and Hittites and used for the purpose of affixing signatures. They had no architecture, sculpture, or painting worthy of mention. The famous temple at Jerusalem was not a Hebrew building at all but a product of Phoenician skill, for Solomon imported artisans from Tyre to finish the more complicated tasks.

The limitations of the Hebrew genius

It was rather in law, literature, and philosophy that the Hebrew genius was most perfectly expressed. Although all of these subjects were closely allied with religion, they did have their secular aspects. The finest example of Jewish law was the Deuteronomic Code, which forms the core of the Book of Deuteronomy. Despite claims of its great antiquity, it was probably an outgrowth of the prophetic revolution. It was based in part upon an older Code of the Covenant, which was derived in considerable measure from the laws of the

Hebrew law

[11] Ezekiel 3:1-4.

Canaanites and the Old Babylonians.[12] In general, its provisions were more enlightened than those of Hammurabi's code. One of them enjoined liberality to the poor and the stranger. Another commanded that the Hebrew slave who had served six years should be freed; and insisted that he must not be sent away empty. A third provided that judges and other officers should be chosen by the people and forbade them to accept gifts or to show partiality in any form. A fourth condemned witchcraft, divination, and necromancy. A fifth denounced the punishment of children for the guilt of their fathers and affirmed the principle of individual responsibility for sin. A sixth prohibited the taking of interest on any kind of loan made

The Shekel of Ancient Israel. Depicted are the two sides of the silver shekel of 141–137 B.C. This coin weighs 220 grains; a United States silver dollar weighs 412.5 grains. The Chaldeans and Phoenicians also had coins called shekels.

by one Jew to another. A seventh required that at the end of every seven years there should be a "release" of debts. "Every creditor that lendeth aught unto his neighbour shall release it; he shall not exact it of his neighbour, or of his brother . . . save when there shall be no poor among you." [13]

As one would expect from the circumstances out of which it grew, a cardinal purpose of the Deuteronomic Code was to infuse into Jewish society a more democratic and equalitarian character. Its authors were not interested in abstract principles. For example, they did not condemn slavery as wrong in itself; they sought merely to prevent the permanent enslavement of Jews. Nevertheless, it is undeniably true that this code did provide for more political and social democracy than the laws of any other Oriental nation except Egypt. Even the king himself was forbidden to accumulate great wealth or to indulge in ostentatious luxury. No military despotism of the Assyrian or Babylonian type was to be tolerated. The king was not above the law but very definitely subject to it; he was

Democratic and equalitarian ideals

[12] C. F. Kent, *The Message of Israel's Lawgivers*, p. 24.
[13] Deuteronomy 15:1–4.

required to have constantly with him a copy of the code and to "read therein all the days of his life . . . that his heart be not lifted up above his brethren, and that he turn not aside from the commandment." [14] Moreover, his power and that of his officers was strictly limited. The administration of justice was left almost entirely in the hands of the people. In cases of disputed guilt the elders of the city would decide, but the punishment provided in the code would be inflicted by the family of the victim or by the community at large. The conscription of labor for foreign service was also prohibited, and exemption from military duty was required to be granted to the man who had built a new house, planted a new vineyard, or married a new wife; and even to the man who was "fearful and faint-hearted . . . lest his brethren's heart faint as well as his heart." [15]

The literature of the Hebrews was by far the best that the ancient Orient ever produced. Nearly all of it now extant is preserved in the Old Testament and in the books of the so-called Apocrypha. Except for a few fragments like the Song of Deborah in Judges 5 it is not really so ancient as is commonly supposed. Scholars now recognize that the Old Testament was built up mainly through a series of collections and revisions (redactions) in which the old and new fragments were merged and generally assigned to an ancient author, Moses, for example. But the oldest of these redactions was not prepared any earlier than 850 B.C. The majority of the books of the Old Testament were of even more recent origin, with the exception, of course, of certain of the chronicles. As one would logically expect, the philosophical books were of late authorship. Although the bulk of the Psalms were ascribed to King David, a good many of them actually refer to events of the Captivity. It seems certain that the collection as a whole was the work of several centuries. Most recent of all were the books of Ecclesiastes, Esther, and Daniel, composed no earlier than the third century. Likewise, the Apocrypha, or books of doubtful religious authority, did not see the light of day until Hebrew civilization was almost extinct. Some, like Maccabees I and II, relate events of the second century B.C. Others including the Wisdom of Solomon and the Book of Enoch were written under the influence of Greco-Oriental philosophy.

Hebrew literature

Not all of the writings of the Hebrews had high literary merit. A considerable number were dull, repetitious chronicles. Nevertheless, most of them, whether in the form of battle song, prophecy, love lyric, or drama, were rich in rhythm, concrete images, and emotional vigor. Few passages in any language can surpass the scornful indictment of social abuses voiced by the prophet Amos:

Amos' indictment of social abuses

[14] Deuteronomy 17:18–20.
[15] Deuteronomy 20:5–8. It is necessary to remember, however, that there was a strong utopian element in this code. We cannot be sure that all its provisions were actually accepted by the government.

Hear this, O ye that swallow up the needy, even to make the poor
    of the land to fail,
Saying, when will the new moon be gone, that we may sell corn?
And the sabbath that we may set forth wheat,
Making the ephah small, and the shekel great,
And falsifying the balances by deceit?
That we may buy the poor for silver, and the needy for a pair of
    shoes;
Yea, and sell the refuse of the wheat?

*The Song of
Songs*

The most beautiful of Hebrew love lyrics was the Song of Songs,
or the Song of Solomon. Its theme was quite probably derived from
an old Canaanite hymn of spring, celebrating the passionate affection of the Shulamith or fertility goddess for her lover, but it had
long since lost its original meaning. The following verses are typical
of its sensuous beauty:

I am the rose of Sharon
and the lily of the valleys.
As the lily among thorns,
so is my love among the daughters.

     .   .   .   .

My beloved is white and ruddy,
the chiefest among ten thousand.
His head is as the most fine gold;
his locks are bushy and black as a raven:
His eyes are as the eyes of doves by the rivers of waters,
washed with milk and fitly set.
His cheeks are as a bed of spices, as sweet flowers;
his lips like lilies, dropping sweet smelling myrrh.

     .   .   .   .

How beautiful are thy feet with shoes, O prince's daughter!
The joints of thy thighs are like jewels,
the work of the hands of a cunning workman.

*The Book of
Job*

Few authorities would deny that the supreme achievement of the
Hebrew literary genius was the Book of Job. In form the work is a
drama of the tragic struggle between man and fate. Its central theme
is the problem of evil: how it can be that the righteous suffer while
the eyes of the wicked stand out with fatness. The story was an
old one, adapted very probably from a Babylonian writing of similar
content, but the Hebrews introduced into it a much deeper realization of philosophical possibilities. The main character, Job, a man
of unimpeachable virtue, is suddenly overtaken by a series of disasters: he is despoiled of his property, his children are killed, and
his body is afflicted with a painful disease. His attitude at first is

one of stoic resignation; the evil must be accepted along with the good. But as his sufferings increase he is plunged into despair. He curses the day of his birth and delivers an apostrophe to death, where "the wicked cease from troubling and the weary be at rest."

Then follows a lengthy debate between Job and his friends over the meaning of evil. The latter take the traditional Hebraic view that all suffering is a punishment for sin, and that those who repent are forgiven and strengthened in character. But Job is not satisfied with any of their arguments. Torn between hope and despair, he strives to review the problem from every angle. He even considers the possibility that death may not be the end, that there may be some adjustment of the balance hereafter. But the mood of despair returns, and he decides that God is an omnipotent demon, destroying without mercy wherever His caprice or anger directs. Finally, in his anguish he appeals to the Almighty to reveal Himself and make known His ways to man. God answers him out of the whirlwind with a magnificent exposition of the tremendous works of nature. Convinced of his own insignificance and the unutterable majesty of God, Job despises himself and repents in dust and ashes. In the end no solution is given of the problem of individual suffering. No promise is made of recompense in a life hereafter, nor does God make any effort to refute the hopeless pessimism of Job. Man must take comfort in the philosophic reflection that the universe is greater than himself, and that God in the pursuit of His sublime purposes cannot really be limited by human standards of equity and goodness.

The problem of evil

As philosophers the Hebrews surpassed every other people before the Greeks with the possible exception of the Egyptians. While they were not brilliant metaphysicians and constructed no great theories of the universe, they did concern themselves with most of the problems relating to the life and destiny of man. Their thought was essentially personal rather than abstract. Probably the earliest of their writings of a distinctly philosophical character were the Old Testament Book of Proverbs and the Apocryphal Book of Ecclesiasticus. In their final form both were of late composition, but much of the material they contain was doubtless quite ancient. Not all of it was original, for a considerable portion had been taken from Egyptian sources, especially from the writings of Amenemope, who lived about 1000 B.C. The philosophy of Proverbs and Ecclesiasticus is not very profound and may be considered as representing the mental adolescence of the Hebrew nation. It is almost entirely ethical, but its appeal is primarily to prudential considerations, not to the will of God or to any absolute standards of right and wrong. It has as its essential teaching: be temperate, diligent, wise, and honest, and you will surely be rewarded with prosperity, long life, and a good name among men. Only in such isolated passages as the following is any recognition given to higher motives of sympathy

Hebrew philosophy: early examples

or respect for the rights of others: "Whoso mocketh the poor reproacheth his Maker; and he that is glad at calamities shall not be unpunished." [16]

Ecclesiastes

A much more profound and critical philosophy is contained in Ecclesiastes, an Old Testament book, not to be confused with the Apocryphal Ecclesiasticus mentioned above. The author of Ecclesiastes is unknown. In some way it came to be attributed to Solomon, but he certainly did not write it, for it includes doctrines and forms of expression unknown to the Hebrews for hundreds of years after his death. Modern critics date it no earlier than the third century B.C. The basic ideas of its philosophy may be summarized as follows:

(1) Mechanism. The universe is a machine that rolls on forever without evidence of any purpose or goal. There is nothing new under the sun, no progress, merely endless repetition of the past. Sunrise and sunset, birth and death are but separate phases of constantly recurring cycles.

(2) Fatalism. Man is a victim of the whims of fate. There is no necessary relation between effort and success: "The race is not to the swift, nor the battle to the strong, neither yet bread to the wise . . . but time and chance happeneth to them all."

(3) Skepticism. Knowledge of ultimate things is impossible. There is no evidence of any soul or any life after death. Men and beasts are alike: "all are of the dust, and all turn to dust again."

(4) Pessimism. All is vanity and vexation of spirit. Fame, riches, extravagant pleasure are snares and delusions in the end. Although wisdom is better than folly, even it is not a sure key to happiness, for an increase in knowledge brings a keener awareness of suffering. Only a good name and joy in the work of one's hands are much to be prized.

(5) Moderation. Extremes of asceticism and extremes of indulgence are both to be avoided. "Be not righteous over much . . . be not over much wicked: why shouldest thou die before thy time?" [17]

5. The Magnitude of the Hebrew Influence

The nature of the Hebrew influence

The influence of the Hebrews, like that of most other Oriental nations, has been chiefly religious and ethical. While it is true that the Old Testament has served as a source of inspiration for much of the literature and art of the Renaissance and early modern civilizations, this has resulted largely because the Bible was already familiar material as a part of the religious heritage. The same explanation can be applied to the use of the Old Testament as a

[16] Proverbs 17:5.
[17] For a more complete analysis of the philosophy of Ecclesiastes see Morris Jastrow, *A Gentle Cynic.*

116

source of law and political theory by the Calvinists in the sixteenth century, and by many other Christians both before and since.

But these facts do not mean that the Hebrew influence has been slight. On the contrary, the history of nearly every Western civilization during the past two thousand years would have been radically different without the heritage from Israel. For it must be remembered that Hebrew beliefs were among the principal foundations of Christianity. The relationship between the two religions is frequently misunderstood. The movement inaugurated by Jesus of Nazareth is commonly represented as a revolt against Judaism; but such was only partly the case. On the eve of the Christian era the Jewish nation had come to be divided into three main sects: a majority sect of Pharisees, and two minority sects of Sadducees and Essenes. The Pharisees represented the middle classes and some of the better educated common folk. They believed in the resurrection, in rewards and punishments after death, and in the coming of a political messiah. Intensely nationalistic, they advocated participation in government and faithful observance of the ancient ritual. They regarded all parts of the law as of virtually equal importance, whether they applied to matters of ceremony or to obligations of social ethics.

Representing altogether different strata of society, the minority sects disagreed with the Pharisees on both religious and political issues. The Sadducees, including the priests and the wealthier classes, were most famous for their denial of the resurrection and of rewards and punishments in an afterlife. Although temporarily at least they favored the acceptance of Roman rule, their attitude toward the ancient law was even more inflexible than that of the Pharisees. The sect of Essenes, the smallest of them all, was possibly the most influential. Its members, who were drawn from the lower classes, practiced asceticism and preached otherworldliness as means of protest against the wealth and power of priests and rulers. They ate and drank only enough to keep themselves alive, held all their goods in common, and looked upon marriage as a necessary evil. Far from being fanatical patriots, they regarded government with indifference and refused to take oaths under any conditions. They emphasized the spiritual aspects of religion rather than the ceremonial and stressed particularly the immortality of the soul, the coming of a religious messiah, and the early destruction of the world. Their most noted member appears to have been John the Baptist, though he later repudiated the sect on the ground that it was preparing only its own followers and not the nation as a whole for the coming of the messiah. It was he who provided an apparent link between the Essenes and the earliest Christians.

Until recently scholars were dependent for their knowledge of the Essenes almost entirely upon secondary sources. But in 1947 an Arab shepherd unwittingly opened the way to one of the most spectacular discoveries of documentary evidence in world history.

Hebrew foundations of Christianity: the beliefs of the Pharisees

The Sadducees and the Essenes

The Dead Sea scrolls

117

Searching for a lost sheep on the western shore of the Dead Sea, he threw a stone that entered a hole in the rocks and made such a peculiar noise that he ran away in fright. He returned, however, with a friend to investigate and discovered a cave in which were stored about fifty cylindrical earthen jars stuffed with writings on leather scrolls. Studied by scholars, the scrolls revealed the existence of a monastic community which flourished from about 130 B.C. to 67 A.D. Its members lived a life of humility and self-denial, holding their goods in common, and devoting their time to prayer and sacraments and to studying and copying Biblical texts. They looked forward confidently to the coming of a messiah, the overthrow of evil, and the establishment of God's kingdom on earth. That they belonged to the sect of Essenes seems almost beyond question.

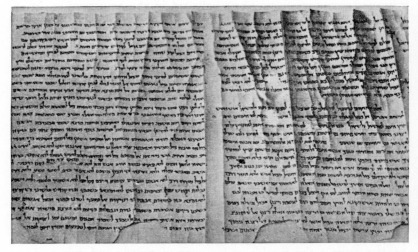

The Dead Sea Scrolls, Now on Display in an Underground Vault at the Hebrew University in Jerusalem. The oldest extant examples of Hebrew religious literature, they furnish us with evidence of the activities of the Essenes, and perhaps other mystical and otherworldly sects, about the beginning of the Christian era.

Hebrew influence upon Christianity

All branches of Judaism except the Sadducees strongly influenced the development of Christianity. Indeed, many Christians regard their religion as the completion and fulfillment of the religion of the Jews. From Jewish sources Christianity obtained its cosmogony, or theory of the origin of the universe; the Ten Commandments; and a large portion of its theology. Jesus himself, although he condemned the Pharisees for their legalism and hypocrisy, did not repudiate all of their tenets. Like them he revered the prophets, believed in rewards and punishments after death, and considered the Jewish people the chosen of God. Instead of abolishing the ancient law, as he is popularly supposed to have done, he demanded its

118

fulfillment, insisting, however, that it should not be made the essential part of religion. To what extent the beliefs and practices of the Christian religion were molded by the more radical Judaism of the Essenes is a question whose answer must await further research. Perhaps the fundamental influence was slight. Nonetheless, we know that many early Christians practiced asceticism, regarded government with indifference, held all their goods in common, and believed in the imminent end of the world. These parallels do not mean, of course, that Christianity was a mere adaptation of beliefs and practices emanating from Judaism. On account of various factors there was much in it that was unique; but that is a subject which can be discussed more conveniently in another connection.[18]

The ethical and political influence of the Hebrews has also been substantial. Their moral conceptions have been a leading factor in the development of the negative approach toward ethics which has prevailed for so long in Western countries. For the early Hebrews "righteousness" consisted primarily in the observance of taboos. Although a positive morality of charity and social justice made rapid headway during the time of the prophets, this in turn was partly obscured by the revival of priestly influence in the period that followed. As a result, the Torah or Pentateuch (the first five books of the Old Testament), which embraced the code of personal behavior for the Jew, came to be crammed with ritualistic prohibitions. With respect to political influence, the record is more impressive. Hebrew ideals of limited government, the sovereignty of law, and regard for the dignity and worth of the individual have been among the major formative influences which have shaped the growth of modern democracy. It is now almost universally recognized that the traditions of Judaism contributed equally with the influence of Christianity and the Stoic philosophy in fostering recognition of the rights of man and in promoting the development of the free society.

Ethical and political influence of the Hebrews

Selected Readings

· *Items so designated are available in paperbound editions.*

· Albright, W. F., *From the Stone Age to Christianity*, Baltimore, 1940. (Anchor)
———, *Archaeology and the Religion of Israel*, Baltimore, 1942.
Anderson, B. W., *Rediscovering the Bible*, New York, 1951.
Baron, S. W., *A Social and Religious History of the Jews*, New York, 1937, 3 vols. Complete and scholarly.
Bertholet, Alfred, *A History of Hebrew Civilization*, London, 1926.
· De Burgh, *The Legacy of the Ancient World*. (Penguin) A good survey of the influence of Hebrew thought.
Burrows, Millar, *Outline of Biblical Theology*, Philadelphia, 1946.

[18] See chapter on The Civilization of Early Medieval Europe.

Finegan, Jack, *Light from the Ancient Past*, Princeton, 1946.
Fowler, H. T., *A History of the Literature of Ancient Israel*, New York, 1914.
Fritsch, C. T., *The Qumrān Community*, New York, 1956. Relates the importance of the Dead Sea Scrolls.
Kent, C. F., *The Message of Israel's Lawgivers*, New York, 1902.
Klausner, Joseph, *The Messianic Idea in Israel*, New York, 1955.
Lods, Adolphe, *Israel from Its Beginnings to the Middle of the Eighth Century*, New York, 1932. Excellent on religious, intellectual and social history.
———, *The Prophets and the Rise of Judaism*, New York, 1951.
Meek, T. J., *Hebrew Origins*, rev., New York, 1951. (Torchbooks)
Oesterley, W. O. E., and Robinson, T. H., *Hebrew Religion, Its Origin and Development*, New York, 1932. One of the best interpretations.
Olmstead, A. T. E., *History of Palestine and Syria*, New York, 1931.
· Orlinsky, H. M., *Ancient Israel*, Ithaca, 1956. (Cornell) Brief but good.
Smith, J. M. P., *The Moral Life of the Hebrews*, Chicago, 1923.
———, *The Origin and History of Hebrew Law*, Chicago, 1931.
Vaux, Roland de, *Ancient Israel: Its Life and Institutions*, New York, 1962. Especially valuable for archaeological data.
Wright, G. E., *The Challenge of Israel's Faith*, Chicago, 1944.

Source Materials

The Old Testament, especially the following books and portions of books: Deuteronomy 5, 12–21; Ecclesiastes; Amos; I Samuel 8–31; II Samuel; I Kings 1–12; Job; Proverbs; Isaiah 1–12, 40–66; Micah; Psalms.

The Hittite, Aegean, and Lesser Cultures

But for them among these gods will be bled for annual food:
to the god Karnua one steer and one sheep;
to the goddess Kupapa one steer and one sheep;
to the divinity Sarku one sheep;
and a Kutupalis sheep to the male divinities.
            —Hittite sacrifice formula, translated from
            a hieroglyph by H. T. Bossert

A few other ancient cultures of the Near Orient require more than passing attention. Chief among them are the Hittite, Aegean, Phoenician, and Lydian cultures. The Hittites are important primarily as intermediaries between East and West. They were one of the main connecting links between the civilizations of Egypt, the Tigris-Euphrates valley, and the region of the Aegean Sea. It appears certain also that they were the original discoverers of iron. They introduced that metal to the surrounding peoples, who rapidly adopted it in place of bronze. The Aegean civilization is significant for its remarkable achievements in the arts and for its quality of freedom and courage for experimentation. Though many of its achievements perished, there is evidence that the Greeks owed to the Aegean peoples a considerable debt. The Greek religion, for example, contained numerous Aegean elements. Likewise of Aegean origin were probably such things as the devotion of the Greeks to athletics, their system of weights and measures, their knowledge of navigation, and perhaps also a great many of their artistic traditions. As for the Phoenicians, no one could overlook the importance of their distribution of a knowledge of the alphabet to the surrounding civilized world. The Lydians have gone down in history as the originators of the first system of coinage.

Importance of these cultures

1. The Hittites and the Phrygians

Until about eighty years ago little was known of the Hittites except their name. They were commonly assumed to have played no role of any significance in the drama of history. The slighting references to them in the Bible give the impression that they were **121**

The discovery of remains of the Hittite civilization

The Hittite empire

The mystery of the race and language of the Hittites

The economic life of the Hittites

little more than a half-barbarian tribe. But in 1870 some curiously inscribed stones were found at Hamath in Syria. This was the beginning of an extensive inquiry which has continued with a few interruptions to the present day. It was not long until scores of other monuments and clay tablets were discovered over most of Asia Minor and through the Near East as far as the Tigris-Euphrates valley. In 1907 certain evidences of an ancient city were unearthed near the village of Boghaz-Keui in the province of Anatolia. Further excavation eventually revealed the ruins of a great fortified capital which was known as Hattusas or Hittite City. Within its walls were discovered more than 20,000 documents and fragments, most of them laws and decrees, of which a good number have since been deciphered.

On the basis of these finds and other evidences gradually accumulated, it was soon made clear that the Hittites were once the rulers of a mighty empire covering most of Asia Minor and extending to the upper reaches of the Euphrates. Part of the time it included Syria as well and even portions of Phoenicia and Palestine. The Hittites reached the zenith of their power during the years from 2000 to 1200 B.C. In the last century of this period they waged a long and exhausting war with Egypt which had much to do with the downfall of both empires. Neither was able to regain its strength. After 1200 B.C. Carchemish on the Euphrates River became for a time the leading Hittite city, but as a commercial center rather than as the capital of a great empire. The days of imperial glory were over. Finally, after 717 B.C., all the remaining Hittite territories were conquered and absorbed by the Assyrians, Lydians, and Phrygians.

Where the Hittites came from and what were their relationships to other peoples are problems which still defy a perfect solution. As depicted by the Egyptians, some of them appear to have been of a Mongoloid type. All had enormous hooked noses, receding foreheads, and slanting eyes. Most modern scholars trace their place of origin to Turkestan and consider them related to the Greeks. Their language was Indo-European. Its secret was unlocked during World War I by the Czech scholar Hrozny. Since then thousands of clay tablets making up the laws and official records of the emperors have been deciphered. They reveal a civilization resembling more closely the Old Babylonian than any other.

Hardly enough evidence has yet been collected to make possible an accurate appraisal of Hittite civilization. Some modern historians refer to it as if it were on a level with the Mesopotamian or even with the Egyptian civilization. Such may have been the case from the material standpoint, for the Hittites undoubtedly had an extensive knowledge of agriculture and a highly developed economic life in general. They mined great quantities of silver, copper, and lead, which they sold to surrounding nations. They discovered the mining and use of iron and made that material available for the rest

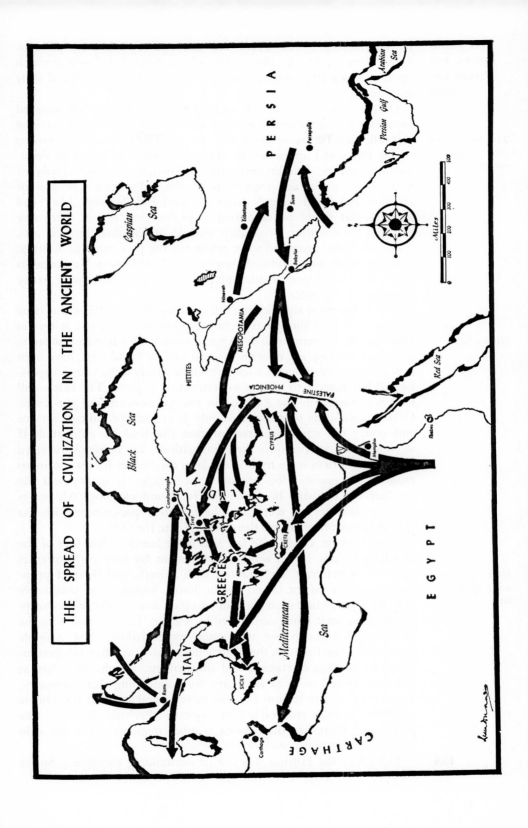

THE SPREAD OF CIVILIZATION IN THE ANCIENT WORLD

of the civilized world. Trade was also one of their principal economic pursuits. In fact, they seem to have depended almost as much upon commercial penetration as upon war for the expansion of their empire.

The intellectual level of Hittite culture

On the other hand, there is nothing as yet to indicate any marked superiority in intellectual attainments, although of course no one can tell what future research may reveal. The thousands of tablets so far recovered appear to be business, legal, and religious documents primarily. The literature of the Hittites consisted chiefly of mythology, including adaptations of the Gilgamesh epic and of creation and flood legends from the Old Babylonians. They had nothing that could be described as philosophy, nor is there any evidence of scientific originality outside of the metallurgical arts. They evidently possessed some talent for the perfection of writing, for in addition to a modified cuneiform adapted from Mesopotamia they also developed a hieroglyphic system which was partly phonetic in character.

Hittite law

One of the most significant achievements of the Hittites was their system of law. Although reflecting Babylonian influence, it was in considerable measure unique. Approximately two hundred separate paragraphs or decrees, covering a great variety of subjects, have been translated. They reflect a society comparatively urbane and sophisticated but subject to minute governmental control. The title to all land was vested in the king or in the governments of the cities. Grants were made to individuals only in return for military service and under the strict requirement that the land be cultivated. If anyone failed to perform these obligations, his holdings reverted to the state. Prices were fixed in the laws themselves for an enormous number of commodities; not only for articles of luxury and the products of industry but even for food and clothing. All wages and fees for services were likewise minutely prescribed, with the pay of women fixed at less than half the rate for men.

Humane character of Hittite law

On the whole, the Hittite law was more humane than that of the Old Babylonians. Death was the punishment for only eight offenses —such as witchcraft, sex relations with animals, and theft of property from the palace. Even premeditated murder was punishable only by a fine. Mutilation was not specified as a penalty at all except for arson or theft when committed by a slave. The contrast with the cruelties of Assyrian law was much more striking. Not a single example is to be found in the Hittite decrees of such fiendish punishments as flaying, castration, and impalement, which the rulers at Nineveh seemed to think necessary for maintaining their authority. Unfortunately the reasons for this more liberal spirit of the Hittite lawgivers remain enshrouded in mystery. Perhaps they had the good sense to realize that justice is more important than force in preserving an orderly society.

124   The art of the Hittites was not of outstanding excellence. So far as we know, it included only sculpture and architecture. The former was generally crude and naïve, but at the same time it revealed a freshness and vigor all too uncommon in the work of Oriental peoples. Most of it was in the form of reliefs depicting scenes of war and mythology. Architecture was ponderous and huge. Temples and palaces were squat, unadorned structures with small, two-columned porches and great stone lions guarding the entrance.

Hittite Sculpture. Perhaps the most highly conventionalized sculpture of the ancient world was that of the Hittite reliefs. Noteworthy are the animal legs and tails with human torsos and heads, the Mesopotamian treatment of the hair and beard, the fingers of even length, and the huge noses. Curious also is the facing position of the king's feet.

Not a great deal is known about the Hittite religion except that it had an elaborate mythology, innumerable deities, and forms of worship of Mesopotamian origin. The name of the chief male deity seems to have been Addu, a god of the storm, who was always represented with a bolt of lightning issuing from his hand. But the chief place in the pantheon was given to a mother goddess of fertility, whose name is unknown. A sun god was also worshiped and a great host of other deities, some of whom appear to have had no particular function at all. The Hittites seem to have welcomed into the divine company practically all of the gods of the peoples they conquered and even of the nations that bought their wares. The practices of the religion included divination, sacrifice, purification ceremonies, and the offering of prayers. Nothing can be found in the records to indicate that the religion was in any sense ethical.

Hittite religion

The chief historical importance of the Hittites probably lies in the role which they played as intermediaries between the Tigris-Euphrates valley and the westernmost portions of the Near East. Doubtless in this way certain culture elements from Mesopotamia were transmitted to such nations as the Canaanites and Hyksos and perhaps to the peoples of the Aegean islands. But the Hittite culture itself appears not to have been without direct influence. It seems to have been reflected in the social customs of the Phrygians, who flourished from about 900 to 300 B.C. Their territory occupied the west central portion of Asia Minor, extending as far east as the Halys River. In language and literature they appear to have been

The Hittites as intermediaries

The Phrygians

The Goddess Kybele (Cybele), or Great Mother, on a Processional Car Drawn by Lions. Although this statue was produced by the Romans in the Second Century A.D., the goddess herself was of Phrygian origin. She became one of the most popular deities of the ancient world.

related to the Greeks, and they constituted an important channel for the transmission of culture elements to the Greeks and Romans. Their most widely copied institution was the cult of Cybele, the Great Mother, which spread rapidly and influenced the mystery religions of both Greece and Italy. The chief deities of the cult were Cybele, the Earth Mother, and Sabazius, the Son, who died and rose from the dead each year with the death and rebirth of vegetation. Its ceremonies were characterized by ecstatic frenzy, bloody sacrifices, and wild, orgiastic dances. The Phrygians were conquered by the Lydians about 610 B.C. but recovered their power and enjoyed a semi-independent and relatively prosperous status for another two centuries. Their early kings were all named either Gordius or Midas. The tomb of one of them was discovered in 1957 by a University of Pennsylvania archaeological expedition near Ankara, the capital of modern Turkey.

The Hittites and the Aegean civilization

Some authorities maintain that the Trojans who were attacked by the Greeks in the twelfth century B.C. were allies of the Hittites. If this is true, it would almost certainly follow that Trojan culture would bear the stamp of Hittite influence. And inasmuch as the Trojans maintained close relations with the Cretans, if they were not indeed of the same race, it would be reasonable to assume some cultural interchange between the Hittites and the principal centers of the Aegean civilization.

2. The Aegean Civilization

A long-forgotten civilization

By a strange coincidence the discovery of the existence of the Hittite and Aegean civilizations was made at just about the same time. Before 1870 scarcely anyone dreamed that a great civilization had flourished on the Aegean islands and on the shores of Asia Minor for hundreds of years prior to the rise of the Greeks. Students of the *Iliad* knew of course of the references to a strange people who were supposed to have dwelt in Troy, to have kidnaped the fair Helen, and to have been punished by the Greeks for this act by the siege and destruction of their city; but it was commonly supposed that these accounts were mere figments of a poetical imagination.

The first discovery of an Aegean culture center was made not by a professional archaeologist but by a retired German business-man, Heinrich Schliemann. Fascinated from early youth by the stories of the Homeric epics, he determined to dedicate his life to archaeological research as soon as he had sufficient income to enable him to do so. Luckily for him and for the world he accumulated a fortune in Russian petroleum and then retired from business to spend both time and money in the pursuit of his boyhood dreams. In 1870 he began excavating at Troy. Within a few years he had uncovered portions of nine different cities, each built upon the ruins of its predecessor. The second of these cities he identified as the Troy of the *Iliad*, although it has been proved since that Troy was the sixth. After fulfilling his first great ambition, he started excavations on the mainland of Greece and eventually discovered two other Aegean cities, Mycenae and Tiryns. The work of Schliemann was soon followed by that of other investigators, notably the Eng-lishman, Sir Arthur Evans, who discovered Knossos, the resplendent capital of the kings of Crete. Up to the present time more than half of the ancient Aegean sites have been carefully searched, and a wealth of knowledge has been accumulated about various aspects of the culture.

The discoveries by Schliemann and others

The Aegean civilization appears to have originated on the island of Crete, the settlements on the mainland of Greece and in Asia Minor being evidently due to expansion. In few other cases in his-tory does the geographic interpretation of culture origins fit so neatly. Crete has a benign and equable climate, neither so hot as to make men lazy nor so cold as to require a life of unceasing struggle. While the soil is fertile, it is not of unlimited area; consequently, as the population increased, men were impelled to sharpen their wits and to contrive new means of earning a living. Some emigrated; others took to the sea; but a larger number remained at home and developed articles for export. The latter included, especially, wine and olive oil, pottery, gems and seals, knives and daggers, and ob-jects of skilled craftsmanship. The chief imports were foodstuffs and metals. As a result of such trade, the country became an in-dustrial and commercial nation with prosperous cities and extensive contacts with the surrounding civilized world. Added to these fac-tors of a favorable environment were the beauties of nature, which abounded almost everywhere, stimulating the development of a marvelous art.

Geographic factors in Aegean history

The Aegean civilization was one of the earliest in the history of the world. As far back as 3000 B.C. the natives of Crete had made the transition from the Neolithic stage to the age of metals and probably to the age of writing. The first peak of advancement was attained under the leadership of the cities of Knossos and Phaistos about 1800

The Aegean civilization one of the oldest in the world

127

B.C. About a hundred years later a frightful calamity occurred. The great palace at Knossos was demolished and the chief buildings in several other cities as well. Exactly what happened has not been determined, but there is evidence that an earthquake followed by revolution accounted for the disaster. At any rate a new dynasty came to the throne, a new system of writing was adopted, and other elements in the life of the past were changed.

The glory and the downfall of the Aegean civilization

After about fifty years of uncertainty the Aegean civilization rose to new heights of brilliance and strength. Troy and the cities of Crete were rebuilt, and other great centers were established at Mycenae and Tiryns. Soon afterward Cretan hegemony was extended over the remaining portions of the Aegean world. But the new age of power and splendor was not destined for long duration. In the sixteenth century B.C. a group of barbarian Greeks known as Achaeans expanded from their original home Achaia in the northern Peloponnesus and eventually conquered Mycenae. Gradually absorbing the material culture of the vanquished, they became rich and powerful sea lords. About 1400 B.C. they overwhelmed the city of Knossos, and soon the whole island of Crete passed under their sway. Although they were no longer a primitive people, they seem never to have appreciated the finer aspects of Aegean culture. As a result this period of Mycenaean supremacy was marked by a decline in Aegean art and probably in intellect as well. In the twelfth century the Achaeans waged their successful war with the Trojans, but less than two hundred years later they fell themselves the victims of barbarian invasion. The new hordes that came in were also Greeks, but they belonged to the group known as Dorians (from Doris in central Greece). Their culture was relatively primitive, except for the fact that they had iron weapons. For centuries they had lived on the mainland of Greece, gradually penetrating farther southward. About 1200 B.C. they began their conquest of the Mycenaean cities. Two hundred years later the Aegean civilization had passed into the limbo of history.

The racial character of the Aegean people

The racial character of the Aegean people has been determined with substantial accuracy. Archaeological data from Crete, at least, have been found in sufficient profusion to leave little doubt that its ancient inhabitants were a composite nation. Their ancestors appear to have come from Syria and Anatolia and were closely related to the Hittites and to the earliest invaders of India. At the same time there is evidence—from the fact that their artists depicted them with long heads, short, slender bodies, and dark, wavy hair—that they bore a relationship to the Egyptians. Although they occupied Greek territory, they were not Greeks at all in the historic meaning of that name. The true Greeks, as we shall presently see, were of altogether different ethnic origin.

The Aegean civilization was probably one of the freest and most progressive in all the Near Orient. The ruler was known by the title of Minos, which was roughly the equivalent of Pharaoh (hence the name *Minoan* which is sometimes applied to the civilization). That it was a title of divinity is shown by the fact that it was occasionally used as if it referred to a god. But the Minos was no bristling war lord like the Assyrian and Persian kings. His professional army was small; he had no great fortified cities; nor is there any indication of his use of conscription. He did have a large and efficient navy; but this was for defense against external attack and for the protection of trade, not to overawe the citizens at home.

The liberal character of Aegean government

On the other hand, there was some regimentation of industry; whether benevolent or not is unknown. The king was the chief capitalist and entrepreneur in the country. The factories in connection with his palace turned out great quantities of fine pottery, textiles, and metal goods. Some of their products were intended to supply the needs of the court, but plenty were sold at home and abroad for profit. Although private enterprise was not prohibited, the owners of smaller establishments were naturally at some disadvantage in competing with the king. Nevertheless, numerous privately owned factories did flourish, especially in cities other than the capital, and agriculture and trade were also in private hands. Gournia, for example, had its foundries for the manufacture of bronze, Therasia its olive-oil refineries, and Phaistos its potteries. It must be understood that these establishments, both royal and private, were factories in nearly every modern sense of the word. While they did not use power-driven machinery, they were engaged in large-scale production, and there was division of labor and centralized control and supervision of workers. The hundreds of women employed in the royal textile factory worked under the supervision of the queen.

Industry partly state controlled

The Aegean people of nearly all classes appear to have led happy and fairly prosperous lives. If slavery existed at all, it certainly occupied an unimportant place. The dwellings in the poorest quarters of great industrial towns such as Gournia were substantially built and commodious, often with as many as six or eight rooms, but we do not know how many families resided in them. If we can judge from the number of inscriptions found in the homes of the common people, literacy was well-nigh universal. Women enjoyed complete equality with men. Regardless of class there was no public activity from which they were debarred, and no occupation which they could not enter. Crete had its female bull fighters and even female pugilists. Ladies of the upper strata devoted much time to fashion. Dressed in their tight-fitting bodices and bell-shaped skirts with flounces which would not have been much out of style in nineteenth-century Europe, they vied with each other for attention in the theaters and at public entertainments of numerous kinds.

Evidences of social equality

The natives of the Aegean area delighted in games and sports of

129

*The love
of sports and
games*

every description. Chess, dancing, running matches, and boxing rivaled each other in their attraction for the people. The Cretans were the first to build stone theaters where processions and music entertained large audiences. But the most popular of all the diversions, as a spectacle at least, was the rodeo or bull-leaping exhibition. This sport was not so cruel as modern bullfighting, since there was no picador to torture the bull or matador to kill him. As soon as the animal was sufficiently infuriated to charge head down, an athlete would seize him by the horns, leap upon his back, turn a few somersaults, and then jump to the ground. No doubt these exhibitions were somewhat lacking in the tragic beauty which Ernest Hemingway saw in the Spanish bullfight, but they were decidedly more humane.

*The Aegean
religion*

The religion of the subjects of Minos was a medley of strange characteristics. First of all it was matriarchal. The chief deity was not a god but a goddess, who was the ruler of the entire universe —the sea and the sky as well as the earth. All existing things were emanations from her. But it was especially as the embodiment of fecundity, and therefore as the source of all life, that she attained her chief significance. In this capacity she was often represented as a madonna with bared breasts, carrying the holy child or tenderly watching over him. The serpent and the dove were her constant companions, possibly as active symbols of her generative power or of her qualities of wisdom and mercy. Originally no male deity appears to have been worshiped, but later a god was associated with the goddess as her son and lover. Although, like the divine sons in several other religions, he died and rose from the dead, he was never regarded by the Cretans as of particular importance.

*The mother
goddess*

In the second place, the Aegean religion was thoroughly monistic. The mother goddess was the source of evil as well as good; but not in any morbid or terrifying sense. Though she brought the storm and spread destruction in her path, these served for the replenishment of nature. Death itself was interpreted as the condition prerequisite for life. Whether the religion had any ethical purposes is unknown. Its followers undoubtedly looked forward to a happy survival in another world, although not necessarily as a reward for good deeds done on earth. The dead were buried with solicitous care and provided with nearly every accessory that would enhance their comfort and pleasure. Food and drink, toilet articles, lamps, razors, mirrors, and games were the principal articles furnished for the deceased of all classes and ages. In addition, the hunter was given his spear, the sailor a miniature of his favorite boat, children their toys, and rich men their servants in effigy. No signs of any belief in a place of future punishment have ever been found.

Other rather curious features included the worship of animals (the bull, the stag, and the minotaur, which was half bull and half man); the worship of sacred trees; the veneration of sacred objects

130

which were probably reproductive symbols (the double-axe, the
pillar, and the cross); and the employment of priestesses instead of
priests to administer the rites of the cult. By far the most important
act of worship was sacrifice. At the great religious festivals hundreds
of animals and large quantities of grain and fruit were brought as
grateful offerings to the goddess and her son. It is doubtful, however, that these sacrifices represented in any sense an atonement for
sin. They were intended rather to provide sustenance for the deities
and to bring man into sacramental fellowship with them. The
common Oriental idea of the scapegoat sacrifice, or the shedding
of blood for the remission of sins, would appear to have been foreign
to the Aegean temperament.

*Symbols
and sacrifices*

For nearly eighty years after the discovery of the Aegean civilization, its system of writing remained one of the enigmas of history.
About 1950, however, the Czech scholar Bedrich Hrozny, who had
already deciphered Hittite writing, succeeded in unlocking the
mystery of Cretan inscriptions. He showed that this dominant
Aegean people produced not only one system of writing but three—
a hieroglyphic script and two linear scripts, which were used in
successive periods. In 1953 an English scholar, Michael Ventris, announced that he had discovered a method which would enable him to
decipher the second of these scripts, Linear Script B. In 1962 Dr.
Cyrus H. Gordon, of Brandeis University, concluded that Linear
Script A was Phoenician, written with a Cretan variation. But all of
the inscriptions found thus far are records of business transactions, in-
ventories, and the like. No literary texts have yet been unearthed. It is
impossible therefore to tell whether any literature or philosophy had
been written. The problem of scientific achievements is easier of
solution, since we have material remains for our guidance. Archaeological discoveries on the island of Crete indicate that the ancient
inhabitants were gifted inventors and engineers. They built excellent
roads of concrete about eleven feet wide. Nearly all the basic principles of modern sanitary engineering were known to the designers of
the palace of Knossos, with the result that the royal family of Crete in
the seventeenth century B.C. enjoyed comforts and conveniences
which were not available for the wealthiest rulers of Western countries in the seventeenth century A.D.

*Cretan writing
and scientific
achievements*

If there was any one achievement of the Aegean people which
appears more than others to emphasize the vitality and freedom of
their culture, it was their art. With the exception of the Greek, no
other art of the ancient world was quite its equal. Its distinguishing
features were delicacy, spontaneity, and naturalism. It served not to
glorify the ambitions of an arrogant ruling class or to inculcate the
doctrines of a religion, but to express the delight of the ordinary
man in the world of beauty around him. As a result, it was remarkably free from the retarding influence of ancient tradition. It was
unique, moreover, in the universality of its application, for it ex-

Aegean art

131

Architecture

Painting

tended not merely to paintings and statues but even to the humblest objects of ordinary use.

Of the major arts, architecture was the least developed. The great palaces were not remarkably beautiful buildings but rambling structures designed primarily for capaciousness and comfort. As more and more functions were absorbed by the state, the palaces were enlarged to accommodate them. New quarters were annexed to those already built or piled on top of them without regard for order or symmetry. The interiors, however, were decorated with beautiful paintings and furnishings. The architecture of Crete may be said to have resembled the modern international style in its subordination of form to utility and in its emphasis upon a pleasing and livable interior as more important than external beauty.

Painting was the art supreme of the Aegean world. Nearly all of it consisted of murals done in fresco, although painted reliefs were occasionally to be found. The murals in the palaces of Crete were by all odds the best that have survived from ancient times. They re-

Throne Room in the Palace of Minos. The throne and bench are original; the fresco has been restored in accordance with fragments found on the site which are now in the Candia Museum on the island of Crete. A remarkable grace characterizes the lilies and the body and head of the mythical animal.

vealed almost perfectly the remarkable gifts of the Minoan artist—his instinct for the dramatic, his sense of rhythm, his feeling for nature in her most characteristic moods. He loved to depict the furious gallop of the frightened deer, the stealthy tread of the cat

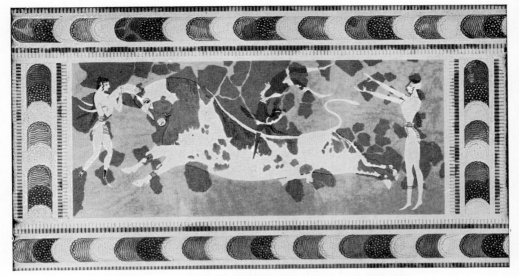

Scenes from the Bull Ring. Cretan painting, about 1500 B.C. Evident are the Cretans' devotion to sport and the skill and agility of their athletes. The body and horns of the bull, however, are exaggerated as are the slenderness of the athletes and their full-face eyes in profile heads.

stalking its prey in the weeds, or the graceful bending of the lily on its slender stem.

Sculpture and the ceramic and gem-carving arts were also developed to a high stage of perfection. The sculpture of the Cretans differed from that of any other people in the ancient Orient. It never relied upon size as a device to convey the idea of power. The Cretans produced no colossi like those of Egypt or reliefs like those of Babylonia depicting a king of gigantic proportions smiting his puny enemies. Instead, they preferred sculpture in miniature. Nearly all of the statues of human beings or of deities that the archaeologists have found are smaller than life-size. Neither was the plastic art of the Aegean essentially propagandistic. Its dominant purpose, as in the case of painting, was to express the individual's delight in the color and drama of his environment. Likewise, the delicately painted pottery, thin as eggshell, the skillfully engraved and inlaid daggers and knives, and the gems and seals of infinitely varied design revealed an almost incredible mastery of materials and respect for the form and beauty of nature.

Sculpture, pottery, and engraving

Much has been written about the significance of the Aegean civilization and its relation to the surrounding cultures. By some historians it is regarded as a mere offshoot of the civilization of Egypt. A number of facts can be adduced to support this view. Both nations were ethnically similar. Their governments were alike in their theocratic character. Both societies contained elements of

Was the Aegean civilization an offshoot of the Egyptian?

matriarchy and economic collectivism. But that is about as far as the comparison can be carried. The differences were just as marked. The Aegean people built no great pyramids or magnificent temples. Only in painting did their art resemble that of Egypt very closely. The systems of writing of the two civilizations appear to have been of entirely independent origin, as is evidenced by the fact that a knowledge of Egyptian helps very little in deciphering Cretan. Whereas the Egyptian religion was an elaborate ethical system based upon the worship of a sun god of righteousness and justice, the religion of the Aegean venerated a goddess of nature with no evidence of a concept of ethical purpose. Finally, the two peoples differed in their basic philosophies of life. The Egyptians believed in the sacrifice of personal interests to the glory and eternity of the state and looked to rewards in an after-existence as a just compensation for good deeds on earth. The people of the Aegean were individualists, intent upon living their own lives of pleasurable activity and concerned with the hereafter merely as an extension of their pleasant and satisfying earthly careers.

*The influence
of the Aegean
civilization*

The influence of the Aegean civilization is not easy to estimate. The Philistines, who came from some part of the Aegean world, introduced certain aspects of the culture into Palestine and Syria. There is reason to believe that various elements of Phoenician art and the Samson legends of the Old Testament were really acquired from the Philistines. It is probable also that the religious and aesthetic traditions of the Cretans and perhaps something of their spirit of freedom influenced the Greeks. But a considerable part of the Aegean civilization was lost or destroyed. Following the downfall of Knossos a dark age began which lasted for nearly four hundred years. The conquerors were barbarians who were unable to appreciate much of the culture of the people they conquered and consequently allowed it to perish.

*Importance of
the Aegean civ-
ilization for the
modern world*

Despite its limited influence the Aegean civilization is not without importance for the student of history; for it was one of the few in ancient times which assured to even its humblest citizens a reasonable share of happiness and prosperity, free from the tyranny of a despotic state and a crafty priesthood. The apparent absence of slavery, brutal punishments, forced labor, and conscription, together with the substantial equality of classes and the dignified status accorded to women, all point to a social regime in striking contrast with those of the Asiatic empires. If additional evidence of this contrast is needed, it can be found in the art of the various nations. The Aegean sculptor or painter gloried not in portraying the slaughter of armies or the sacking of cities but in picturing flowery landscapes, joyous festivals, thrilling exhibitions of athletic prowess, and similar scenes of a free and peaceful existence. Last of all, the Aegean civilization is significant for its kinship with what we often think of as the modern spirit. This is clearly exemplified in the devotion of the people to comfort and opulence, in their love of amusement, in their individualism, zest for life, and courage for experimentation.

3. The Lydians and the Phoenicians

When the Hittite empire fell in the eighth century B.C., its successor in its main areas of power was the kingdom of Lydia. The Lydians established their rule in what is now the territory of the Turkish Republic in Anatolia. They quickly secured control of the Greek cities on the coast of Asia Minor and of the entire plateau west of the Halys River. But their power was short-lived. In 550 B.C. their fabulous king, Croesus, fancied he saw a good opportunity to add to his domain the territory of the Medes east of the Halys. The Median king had just been deposed by Cyrus the Persian. Thinking this meant an easy triumph for his own armies, Croesus set out to capture the territory beyond the river. After an indecisive battle with Cyrus, he returned to his own capital (Sardis) for reinforcements. Here Cyrus caught him unprepared in a surprise attack and captured and burned the city. The Lydians never recovered from the blow, and soon afterward all of their territory, including the Greek cities on the coast, passed under the dominion of Cyrus the Great.

The kingdom of Lydia

The Lydians were a people of Indo-European speech, who were probably a mixture of native peoples of Asia Minor with migrant stocks from eastern Europe. Benefiting from the advantages of favorable location and abundance of resources, they enjoyed one of the highest standards of living of ancient times. They were famous for the splendor of their armored chariots and the quantities of gold and articles of luxury possessed by the citizens. The wealth of their kings was legendary, as attested by the simile "rich as Croesus." The chief sources of this prosperity were gold from the streams, wool from the thousands of sheep on the hills, and the profits of the extensive commerce which passed overland from the Tigris-Euphrates valley to the Aegean Sea. But with all their wealth and opportunities for leisure, they succeeded in making only one original contribution to civilization. This was the coinage of money from electrum or "white gold," a natural mixture of gold and silver found in the sands of one of their rivers. Hitherto all systems of money had consisted of weighed rings or bars of metal. The new coins, of varying sizes, were stamped with a definite value more or less arbitrarily given by the ruler who issued them.

The Lydian people and their culture

In contrast with the Lydians, who gained their ascendancy as a result of the downfall of the Hittites, were the Phoenicians, who benefited from the break-up of Aegean supremacy. But the Phoe-

*The Phoenician
cities and con-
federation*

nicians were neither conquerors nor the builders of an empire. They exerted their influence through the arts of peace, especially through commerce. During most of their history their political system was a loose confederation of city-states, which frequently bought their security by paying tribute to foreign powers. The territory they occupied was the narrow strip between the Lebanon Mountains and the Mediterranean Sea. With good harbors and a central location, it was admirably situated for trade. The great centers of commerce included Tyre, Sidon, and Beirut. Under the leadership of the first, Phoenicia reached the zenith of her cultural brilliance, from the tenth to the eighth century B.C. During the sixth century she passed under the domination of the Chaldeans and then of the Persians. In 332 B.C. Tyre was destroyed by Alexander the Great after a siege of seven months.

*Achievements
of the Phoe-
nicians*

The Phoenicians were a people of Semitic language, closely related to the Canaanites. They displayed very little creative genius, but were remarkable adapters of the achievements of others. They produced no original art worthy of the name, and they made but slight contributions to literature. Their religion, like that of the Canaanites, was characterized by human sacrifice to the god Moloch and by licentious fertility rites. They excelled, however, in specialized manufactures and in geography and navigation. They were renowned throughout the ancient world for their glass and metal industries and for their purple dye obtained from a mollusk in the adjacent seas. They developed the art of navigation to such a stage that they could sail by the stars at night. To less venturesome peoples, the North Star was known for some time as the Phoenicians' star. A company of Phoenicians is believed to have circumnavigated Africa. The most lasting achievement of the Phoenicians, however, was the completion and diffusion of an alphabet based upon principles discovered by the Egyptians. The Phoenician contribution was the adoption of a system of signs representing the sounds of the human voice, and the elimination of all pictographic and syllabic characters. The Egyptians, as we have seen, had accomplished the first of these steps but not the second.

4. Lessons from the History of the Near Orient Empires

*Defects of the
Near Orient
empires*

Like most other periods in world history, the period of the empires we have studied thus far was an era of contention and strife. Nearly all of the great empires, and the majority of the smaller states as well, devoted their energies most of the time to policies of expansion and aggression. The only notable exceptions were the Aegean and Egyptian, but even the Egyptians, in the later period of their history, yielded to no one in their addiction to imperialism. The causes were largely geographic in nature. Each nation grew

136

accustomed to the pursuit of its own interests in some fertile river valley or on some easily defended plateau. Isolation bred fear of foreigners and an incapacity to think of one's own people as members of a common humanity. The feelings of insecurity that resulted seemed to justify aggressive foreign policies, the waging of preventive wars, and the annexation of neighboring states to serve as buffers against a hostile world. Of course, greed played a part also, especially when conquest came to be regarded as equivalent to opportunity for plunder.

It seems possible to trace nearly all of the woes of the Near Orient nations to wars of aggression and imperialist greed. The great British historian Arnold J. Toynbee has shown this in devastating fashion in *Results of* the case of the Assyrians. He contends that it was no less true of such *Near Orient* later peoples as the Spartans, the Carthaginians, the Macedonians, *imperialism* and the Ottoman Turks. Each made militarism and conquest its gods and wrought such destruction upon itself that when it made its last heroic stand against its enemies, it was a mere "corpse in armor." Not death by foreign conquest but national suicide was the fate which befell it.[1] The way of the warrior brought race intolerance, a love of ease and luxury, crime and racketeering, and crushing burdens of taxation. Expansion of empire promoted a fictitious prosperity, at least for the upper classes, and aroused enough envy among poorer nations to make them willing conspirators against a rich neighbor who could easily be portrayed as an oppressor. The current revolt of underdeveloped nations, which Adlai Stevenson has called the "revolution of rising expectations," had its parallels far back in ancient history.

Selected Readings

· *Items so designated are available in paperbound editions.*

Burn, A. R., *Minoans, Philistines and Greeks,* New York, 1930.
Ceram, C. W., *The Secret of the Hittites,* New York, 1956. The best of recent works.
Childe, V. G., *The Bronze Age,* New York, 1930.
Cowley, A. E., *The Hittites,* New York, 1926.
Evans, Sir A. J., *The Palace of Minos,* New York, 1921–23, Vols. I–IV. Excellent as archaeology.
Garstang, John, *The Hittite Empire,* New York, 1929.
Glotz, Gustave, *The Aegean Civilization,* New York, 1927. Still the best account, though some of the details are doubtful.
Hall, H. R., *The Civilization of Greece in the Bronze Age,* London, 1928.
Hrozny, Bedrich, *Ancient History of Western Asia, India and Crete,* Prague, 1953.
Nilsson, M. P., *The Minoan-Mycenaean Religion and Its Survival in Greek Religion,* New York, 1927. A good study of Aegean influence.
Willetts, R. F., *Aristocratic Society in Ancient Crete,* London, 1955.

Source Materials

Evans, Sir Arthur, *Scripta Minoa; the Written Documents of Minoan Crete.*
Hertzler, J. O., *The Social Thought of the Ancient Civilizations,* pp. 135–44.

[1] *A Study of History* (D. C. Somervell, ed.), Vol. I, pp. 338–43.

THE CLASSICAL CIVILIZATIONS

OF GREECE AND ROME

PART
2

THE CLASSICAL CIVILIZATIONS OF GREECE AND ROME

After 600 B.C. the centers of civilization in the Western world were no longer confined to the Near Orient. By that time new cultures were already growing to maturity in Greece and in Italy. Both had started their evolution considerably earlier, but the civilization of Greece did not begin to ripen until about 600 B.C., while the Romans showed little promise of original achievement before 500. About 300 B.C. Greek civilization, properly speaking, came to an end and was superseded by a new culture representing a fusion of elements derived from Greece and from the Near Orient. This was the Hellenistic civilization, which lasted until about the

A CHRONOLOGICAL TABLE

Dates are B.C. unless given as A.D.

	Politics	Arts and Letters
	Homeric Age, 1200–800	
1000— B.C.	Rome founded, *ca.* 1000 Beginning of city-states in Greece, *ca.* 800	*Iliad* and *Odyssey, ca.* 800
500— B.C.	Age of the Tyrants in Greece, 650–500 Reforms of Solon, 594–560 Reforms of Cleisthenes, 508–502 Overthrow of monarchy in Rome and establishment of republic, *ca.* 500 Patrician-plebeian struggle in Rome, 500–287 Greco-Persian War, 493–479 Delian League, 479–404 Perfection of Athenian democracy, 461–429 Law of the Twelve Tables (Rome), *ca.* 450 Peloponnesian War, 431–404	Doric architecture, 650–500 Aeschylus, 525–456 Phidias, 500?–432 Ionic architecture, *ca.* 500–400 Sophocles, 496–406 Herodotus, 484–425 Euripides, 480–406 Thucydides, 471?–400? Parthenon, *ca.* 460 Aristophanes, 448?–380?
400— B.C.	Decline of democracy in Greece, 400 Theban supremacy in Greece, 371–362 Macedonian conquest of Greece, 338–337 Conquests of Alexander the Great, 336–323 Division of Alexander's empire, 323	Corinthian architecture, *ca.* 400–300 Praxiteles, 370?–310?
300— B.C.	Hortensian Law (Rome), 287 Punic Wars, 264–146	

beginning of the Christian era and included not only the Greek peninsula but Egypt and most of Asia west of the Indus River. The outstanding characteristic which serves to distinguish these three civilizations from the ones that had gone before is secularism. No longer does religion absorb the interests of man to the extent that it did in ancient Egypt or in the nations of Mesopotamia. The state is now above the church, and the power of the priests to determine the direction of cultural evolution has been thoroughly shattered. Furthermore, ideals of human freedom and an emphasis upon the welfare of man as an individual have largely superseded the despotism and collectivism of the ancient Near Orient.

Philosophy and Science	Economics	Religion
		Development of worldly, non-ethical religion of the Greeks, 1200–800
	Economic Revolution and colonization in Greece, 750–600 Rise of middle class in Greece, 750–600	
Thales of Miletus, 640–546 Pythagoras, 582?–507		
		Orphic and Eleusinian mystery cults, 500–100
Protagoras, 481?–411 Socrates, 469–399 Hippocrates, 460–377? Democritus, 460?–362? Sophists, ca. 450–400 Plato, 427–347		
Aristotle, 384–322 Epicurus, 342–270 Zeno (the Stoic), 336–264 Euclid, 323?–285 Aristarchus, 310–230	Growth of advertising and insurance, 300 B.C.–100 A.D. Hellenistic world trade, 300 B.C.–100A.D. International money economy, 300 B.C.–100 A.D.	

	Politics	Arts and Letters
200— **B.C.**		
	Revolt of the Gracchi, 133–121	
100— **B.C.**		Vergil, 70 B.C.–19 A.D. Horace, 65 B.C.–8 A.D.
	Dictatorship of Julius Caesar, 46–44 Principate of Augustus Caesar, 27 B.C.–14 A.D.	
		Tacitus, 55?–117 A.D. Colosseum, *ca.* 80 A.D.
100— **A.D.**	Barbarian invasions of Rome, *ca.* 100–476 A.D. Completion of Roman law by the great jurists, *ca.* 200 A.D.	
300— **A.D.**	Diocletian, 284–305 A.D. Constantine I, 306–337 A.D.	
476— **A.D.**	Theodosius I, 378–395 A.D. Deposition of last of Roman emperors, 476 A.D.	

Philosophy and Science	Economics	Religion
	Growth of serfdom in Hellenistic empires, 300 B.C.–100 A.D.	
Archimedes, 287?–212 Eratosthenes, 276?–195?	Growth of metropolitan cities, 300 B.C.–400 A.D.	
	Growth of slavery in Rome, 250–100	Oriental mystery cults in Rome, 250–50
	Rise of middle class in Rome, 250–100	
Herophilus, 220?–150 Polybius, 205?–123?	Decline of small farmer in Rome, 250–100	
	Depressions and unemployment in Hellenistic world, 200 B.C.–100 A.D.	
Skeptics, 200–100	Decline of slavery in Hellenistic world, 200 B.C.–100 A.D.	Development of mysticism and otherworldliness, 200
Introduction of Stoicism into Rome, *ca.* 140 Cicero, 106–43 Lucretius, 98–55		
Seneca, 3 B.C.–65 A.D.	Decline of slavery in Rome, 27 B.C.–476 A.D.	Spread of Mithraism in Rome, 27 B.C.–270 A.D. First persecution of Christians in Rome, *ca.* 65 A.D.
Marcus Aurelius, 121–180 A.D. Galen, 130–200? A.D. Neo-Platonism, 250–600 A.D.		
	Growth of serfdom and extralegal feudalism in Rome, 300–500 A.D.	Beginning of toleration of Christians in Rome, 311 A.D. Christianity made official religion of Roman Empire, 380 A.D.

The Hellenic Civilization

There Lawfulness dwells and her sisters,
Safe foundation of cities,
Justice and Peace, who was bred with her
Dispensers of wealth to men
Golden daughters of wise-counselling Right.
—Pindar, on the city of Corinth, *Olympian Ode XIII*

Now, what is characteristic of any nature is that which is best for it and gives most joy. Such to man is the life according to reason, since it is this that makes him man.
—Aristotle, *Nichomachean Ethics*

The character of Hellenic civilization

Among all the peoples of the ancient world, the one whose culture most clearly exemplified the spirit of Western man was the Hellenic or Greek. No other of these nations had so strong a devotion to liberty or so firm a belief in the nobility of human achievement. The Greeks glorified man as the most important creature in the universe and refused to submit to the dictation of priests or despots or even to humble themselves before their gods. Their attitude was essentially secular and rationalistic; they exalted the spirit of free inquiry and made knowledge supreme over faith. It was largely for these reasons that they advanced their culture to the highest stage which the ancient world was destined to reach. But the Greeks did not begin without foundations. It is necessary to remember that the groundwork for many of their achievements had already been laid by certain of the Oriental peoples. The rudiments of their philosophy and science had been prepared by the Egyptians. The Greek alphabet was derived from Phoenicia. And probably to a larger extent than we shall ever realize the Hellenic appreciation of beauty and freedom was a product of Aegean influence.

1. The Homeric Age

The foundations of Greek civilization

In order to understand the evolution of the Hellenic civilization it is necessary to go back to the first period of its history, the Homeric Age, which extended from approximately 1200 to 800 B.C. It was then that the Greek nation was formed and the foundations laid for many of the social and political developments of subsequent centuries. Not all of the glory that was Greece can be traced to the Homeric Age, but it is nonetheless true that several of the most typical institutions and attitudes of the Greeks in their prime were modifications of forms which had survived from the earliest days.

Probably the original home of the Greeks was somewhere in the
Danube valley. When they began their migrations into the Greek
peninsula about 2000 B.C., they appear to have been a mixture of
Alpine and Nordic stocks, predominantly the former. Later they
mingled with the Mediterranean natives who were already established in Greece, especially in the southern portions and on the
islands of the Aegean Sea. It is therefore patently absurd to attempt
any explanation of the genius of the Greeks on the basis of purity
of race, for no one really knows which of the principal admixtures
finally came to predominate. About all that it is possible to say is
that the Hellenes were a mixed race who spoke a language of Indo-
European relationship.

Racial origins of the Greeks

By 1200 B.C. the Greeks had occupied most of the northern sections of the peninsula and a few scattered locations along the coast.
At first they filtered in slowly, bringing their herds and flocks with
them and settling in the more sparsely populated areas. Many of
these early immigrants seem to have belonged to the group which
later came to be known as Ionians. Another division, the Achaeans,
pushed farther south, conquered Mycenae and Troy, and ultimately
gained dominion over Crete. Soon after 1200 the great Dorian invasions began and reached their climax about two centuries later.
Some of the Dorians settled in central Greece, but most of them
took to the sea, conquering the eastern sections of the Peloponnesus
and the southern islands of the Aegean. About 1000 B.C. they captured Knossos, the chief center of the Minoan civilization on the
island of Crete.

*The early mi-
grations*

Whether Achaeans, Ionians, or Dorians, all of the Greeks in the
Homeric Age had essentially the same culture, which was comparatively primitive. Not until the very last century of the period
was there any general knowledge of writing. Although evidence
exists that the Achaeans had a system of writing as early as 1200 B.C.,
their case was exceptional. We must therefore envisage the Homeric
Greeks as a preliterate people during the greater part of their history, with intellectual accomplishments that extended no farther
than the development of folk songs, ballads, and short epics sung
and embellished by bards as they wandered from one village to
another. A large part of this material was finally woven into a great
epic cycle by one or more poets and put into written form in the
ninth century B.C. Though not all of the poems of this cycle have
come down to us, the two most important, the *Iliad* and the *Odyssey*,
provide us with our richest store of information about the ideals and
customs of the Homeric Age.

*The primitive
character of
Homeric cul-
ture*

The political institutions of the Homeric Greeks were exceedingly primitive. Each little community of villages was independent
of external control, but political authority was so tenuous that it
would not be too much to say that the state scarcely existed at all.
The king could not make or enforce laws or administer justice. He

*Government in
the Homeric
Age*

received no remuneration of any kind, but had to cultivate his farm for a living the same as any other citizen. Practically his only functions were military and priestly. He commanded the army in time of war and offered sacrifices to keep the gods on the good side of the community. Although each little group of villages had its council of nobles and assembly of warriors, neither of these bodies had any definite membership or status as an organ of government. The duties of the former were to advise and assist the king and prevent him from usurping despotic powers. The functions of the latter were to ratify declarations of war and assent to the conclusion of peace. Almost without exception custom took the place of law, and the administration of justice was private. Even willful murder was punishable only by the family of the victim. While it is true that disputes were sometimes submitted to the king for settlement, he acted in such cases merely as an arbitrator, not as a judge. As a matter of fact, the political consciousness of the Greeks of this time was so poorly developed that they had no conception of government as an indispensable agency for the preservation of social order. When Odysseus, king of Ithaca, was absent for twenty years, no regent was appointed in his place, and no session of the council or assembly was held. No one seemed to think that the complete suspension of government, even for so long a time, was a matter of any critical importance.

The rudimentary pattern of social and economic life

The pattern of social and economic life was amazingly simple. Though the general tone of the society portrayed in the epics is aristocratic, there was actually no rigid stratification of classes. Any warrior who displayed unusual bravery in battle could become a noble. Manual labor was not looked upon as degrading, and there were apparently no idle rich. That there were dependent laborers of some kind who worked on the lands of the nobles and served them as faithful warriors seems clear from the Homeric epics, but it is doubtful that they were really slaves, for they were treated as members of the noble's family and could not be sold away from their homes. Agriculture and herding were the basic occupations. Except for a few skilled crafts like those of wagonmaker, swordsmith, goldsmith, and potter, there was no specialization of labor. For the most part every household made its own tools, wove its own clothing, and raised its own food. So far were the Greeks of this time from being a trading people that they had no word in their language for "merchant," and barter was the only method of exchange that was practiced.

Religious conceptions in the Homeric Age

To the Greeks of the Homeric Age religion meant chiefly a system for: (1) explaining the physical world in such a way as to remove its awesome mysteries and give man a feeling of intimate relationship with it; (2) accounting for the tempestuous passions which seized man's nature and made him lose that self-control which the Greeks considered essential for success as a warrior; and (3) obtaining such material benefits as good fortune, long life, skill in craftsmanship, and abundant harvests. Neither at this time nor at any other period of their history did the Greeks expect that their religion would save them from sin or endow them with spiritual blessings. As they conceived it, piety was neither a matter of conduct nor of faith. Their religion, accordingly, had no commandments and no dogmas, no complicated ritual and no sacraments. Every man was at liberty to believe what he pleased and to conduct his own life as he chose without fear of the wrath of the gods. Probably it is no exaggeration to say that this freedom from dogmatism and from fear of the supernatural was one of the most important factors contributing to the intellectual and artistic progress of the Greeks.

As is commonly known, the deities of the Homeric religion were merely human beings writ large. It was really necessary that this should be so if the Greek was to feel at home in the world over which they ruled. Remote, omnipotent beings like the gods of most Oriental religions would have inspired fear rather than a sense of security. What the Greek wanted was not necessarily gods of great power, but deities he could bargain with on equal terms. Consequently he endowed his gods with attributes similar to his own—with human bodies and human weaknesses and wants. He imagined the great company of divinities as frequently quarreling with one another, needing food and sleep, mingling freely with men, and even procreating children occasionally by mortal women. They differed from men only in the fact that they subsisted on ambrosia and nectar, which made them immortal. They dwelt not in the sky or in the stars but on the summit of Mount Olympus, a peak in northern Greece with an altitude of about 10,000 feet.

The deities of the Homeric religion

The religion was thoroughly polytheistic, and no one deity was elevated very high above any of the others. Zeus, the sky god and wielder of the thunderbolt, who was sometimes referred to as the father of the gods and of men, frequently received less attention than did Poseidon, the sea god, Aphrodite, goddess of love, or Athena, the goddess of war and patroness of handicrafts. Since the Greeks had no Satan, their religion cannot be described as dualistic. Nearly all of the deities were capable of malevolence as well as good, for they sometimes deceived men and caused them to commit wrongs. The nearest approach to a god of evil was Hades, who presided over the nether world. Although he is referred to in the Homeric poems as "implacable and unyielding" and the most hateful of gods to mortals, he was never assumed to have played an active role in affairs on earth. He was not considered as the source of pestilence, earthquake, or famine. He did not tempt men or work to defeat the benevolent designs of other gods. In short, he was really not regarded as anything more than the guardian of the realm of the dead.

Nature of the gods and goddesses

The Greeks of the Homeric Age were almost completely indif-

*Indifference to
a life hereafter*

ferent to what happened to them after death. Not only did they bestow no care upon the bodies of the dead, but they frequently cremated them. They did assume, however, that the shades or ghosts of men survived for a time after the death of their bodies. All, with a few exceptions, went to the same abode—to the murky realm of Hades situated beneath the earth. This was neither a paradise nor a hell: no one was rewarded for his good deeds, and no one was punished for his sins. Each of the shades appeared to continue the same kind of life its human embodiment had lived on earth. The Homeric poems make casual mention of two other realms, the Elysian Plain and the realm of Tartarus, which seem at first glance to contradict the idea of no rewards and punishments in the hereafter. But the few individuals who enjoyed the ease and comfort of the Elysian Plain had done nothing to deserve such blessings; they were simply persons whom the gods had chosen to favor. The realm of Tartarus was not really an abode of the dead but a place of imprisonment for rebellious deities.

*The external
and mechanical
character of
worship*

Worship in the Homeric religion consisted primarily of sacrifice. The offerings were made, however, not as an atonement for sin, but merely in order to please the gods and induce them to grant favors. In other words, religious practice was external and mechanical and not far removed from magic. Reverence, humility, and purity of heart were not essentials in it. The worshiper had only to carry out his part of the bargain by making the proper sacrifice, and the gods would fulfill theirs. For a religion such as this no elaborate institutions were required. Even a professional priesthood was unnecessary. Since there were no mysteries and no sacraments, one man could perform the simple rites about as well as another. As a general rule, each head of a family implored the favor of the gods for his own household, and the king performed the same function for the community at large. Although it is true that seers or prophets were frequently consulted because of the belief that they were directly inspired by the gods and could therefore foretell the future, these were not of a priestly class. Furthermore, the Homeric religion included no cult or sacred relics, no holy days, and no system of temple worship. The Greek temple was not a church or place of religious assemblage, and no ceremonies were performed within it. Instead it was a shrine which the god might visit occasionally and use as a temporary house.

*Conceptions of
virtue and evil*

As intimated already, the morality of the Greeks in the Homeric period had only the vaguest connection with their religion. While it is true that the gods were generally disposed to support the right, they did not consider it their duty to combat evil and make righteousness prevail. In meting out rewards to men, they appear to have been influenced more by their own whims and by gratitude for sacrifices offered than by any consideration for moral character. The only crime they punished was perjury, and that none too consistently. The conclusion seems justified, then, that Homeric morality rested upon no basis of supernatural sanctions. Perhaps its true foundation was military. Nearly all the virtues extolled in the epics were those which would make the individual a better soldier— bravery, self-control, patriotism, wisdom (in the sense of cunning), love of one's friends, and hatred of one's enemies. There was no conception of sin in the Christian sense of wrongful acts to be repented of or atoned for.

At the end of the Homeric Age the Greek was already well started along the road of social ideals that he was destined to follow in later centuries. He was an optimist, convinced that life was worth living for its own sake, and he could see no reason for looking forward to death as a glad release. He was an egoist, striving for the fulfillment of self. As a consequence, he rejected mortification of the flesh and all forms of denial which would imply the frustration of life. He could see no merit in humility or in turning the other cheek. He was a humanist, who worshiped the finite and the natural rather than the otherworldly or sublime. For this reason he refused to invest his gods with awe-inspiring qualities, or to invent any conception of man as a depraved and sinful creature. Finally, he was devoted to liberty in an even more extreme form than most of his descendants in the classical period were willing to accept.

The basic Greek ideals

2. *The Evolution of the City-States*

About 800 B.C. the village communities of the Homeric Age, which had been founded mainly upon clan organization, began to give way to larger political units. As the need for defense increased, an acropolis or citadel was built on a high location, and a city grew up around it as the seat of government for a whole community. Thus emerged the city-state, the most famous unit of political society developed by the Greeks. Examples were to be found in almost every section of the Hellenic world. Athens, Thebes, and Megara on the mainland; Sparta and Corinth on the Peloponnesus; Miletus on the shore of Asia Minor; and Mitylene and Chalcis on the islands of the Aegean Sea were among the best known. They varied enormously in both area and population. Sparta with more than three thousand square miles and Athens with 1060 had by far the greatest extent; the others averaged less than a hundred. At the peak of their power Athens and Sparta, each with a population of about 400,000, had approximately three times the numerical strength of most of their neighboring states.

The origin and nature of the city-states

With a few exceptions the Greek city-states went through a similar political evolution. They began their histories as monarchies. During the eighth century they were changed into oligarchies. About a hundred years later, on the average, the oligarchies were overthrown by dictators, or "tyrants," as the Greeks called them,

The evolution of the city-states

meaning usurpers who ruled without legal right whether op-
pressively or not. Finally, in the sixth and fifth centuries, democracies were set up; or in some cases "timocracies," that is, governments
based upon a property qualification for the exercise of political
rights, or in which love of honor and glory was the ruling principle.

On the whole, it is not difficult to determine the causes of this
political evolution. The first change came about as a result of the
concentration of landed wealth. As the owners of great estates
waxed in economic power, they determined to wrest political authority from the king and vest it in the council, which they generally controlled. In the end they abolished the kingship entirely.
Then followed a period of sweeping economic changes and political
turmoil. The increasing scarcity of land forced many of the Greeks
to emigrate and seek new homes for themselves in unoccupied regions. As a result, numerous colonies were founded, mostly along
the shores of the Aegean and Ionian Seas, but some as far east as
the Black Sea and as far west as Italy and Spain. The demand for
new outlets for trade also prompted some of this expansion. The
consequence was a veritable economic revolution in the Greek
world. Commerce and industry grew to be leading pursuits, the
urban population increased, and wealth assumed new forms. The
rising middle class now joined with dispossessed farmers in an attack
upon the landholding oligarchy. The natural fruit of the bitter class
conflicts that ensued was dictatorship. By encouraging extravagant
hopes and promising relief from chaos, ambitious demagogues attracted enough popular support to enable them to ride into power
in defiance of constitutions and laws. Ultimately, however, dis-
satisfaction with tyrannical rule and the increasing economic power
and political consciousness of the common citizens led to the establishment of democracies or liberal oligarchies.

*The causes
of the political
cycle*

Unfortunately space does not permit an analysis of the political
history of each of the Greek city-states. Except in the more backward sections of Thessaly and the Peloponnesus, it is safe to conclude that the internal development of all of them paralleled the
account given above, although minor variations due to local conditions doubtless occurred. The two most important of the Hellenic
states, Sparta and Athens, deserve more detailed study.

*The similar
development of
the city-states*

3. The Armed Camp of Sparta

*The peculiar
development of
Sparta*

The history of Sparta [1] was the great exception to the political
evolution of the city-states. Despite the fact that her citizens were
of the purest Dorian strain, she failed to make any progress in the
direction of democratic rule. Instead, her government rapidly de-

[1] Sparta was the leading city of a district called Laconia or Lacedaemonia;
sometimes the *state* was referred to by one or the other of these names. The
people, also, were frequently called Laconians or Lacedaemonians.

generated into a form more closely resembling a modern élite dictatorship. Culturally, also, the nation stagnated. The causes were due
partly to isolation. Hemmed in by mountains on the northeast and
west and lacking good harbors, the Spartan people had little opportunity to profit from the advances made in the outside world. Besides, no middle class arose to aid the masses in the struggle for
freedom.

The real explanation is to be found, however, in militarism. The
Spartans had come into the eastern Peloponnesus as an invading
army. For centuries they had struggled to subdue the Mycenaean
natives they found there. By 800 B.C., when they finally succeeded
in gaining dominion over all of Laconia, military habits were so
firmly fixed that they could not be thrown off. As a consequence,
while the other Greek states sated their land hunger through col-
onization, Sparta, as her population increased, inevitably chose to
live by the sword. West of the Taygetus Mountains lay the fertile
plain of Messenia. In the late eighth century the Spartans determined to conquer it. The venture was successful, and the Messenian
territory was annexed to Laconia. About fifty years later the Messenians enlisted the aid of Argos and launched a revolt. The war that
followed was desperately fought, Laconia itself was invaded, and apparently it was only the death of the Argive commander and the
patriotic pleas of the fire-eating poet Tyrtaeus that saved the day for
the Spartans. This time the victors took no chances. They confiscated the lands of the Messenians, murdered or expelled their leaders,
and forced the masses into serfdom.

*The origins of
Spartan milita-
rism*

There was scarcely a feature of the life of the Spartans which was
not the result of their martial enterprises. In subduing and despoil-
ing their enemies they unwittingly enslaved themselves; for they
lived through the remaining centuries of their history in deadly
fear of insurrections. It was this fear which explains their conservatism, their stubborn resistance to change, lest any innovation
result in a fatal weakening of the system. Their provincialism can
also be attributed to the same cause. Frightened by the prospect that
dangerous ideas might be brought into their country, they discouraged travel and prohibited trade with the outside world. The necessity of maintaining the absolute supremacy of the citizen class over
an enormous population of serfs required an iron discipline and a
strict subordination of the individual; hence the Spartan collectivism,
which extended into every branch of the social and economic life.
Finally, much of the cultural backwardness of Sparta grew out of the
atmosphere of coarseness and hate which inevitably resulted from
the bitter struggle to conquer the Messenians and hold them under
stern repression.

*The results of
Spartan milita-
rism*

The Spartan constitution, which tradition ascribed to an ancient
lawgiver, Lycurgus, provided for a government preserving the
forms of the old Homeric system. Instead of one king, however,

there were two, representing separate families of exalted rank. The Spartan sovereigns enjoyed but few powers and those chiefly of a military and priestly character. A second and more authoritative branch of the government was the council, composed of the two kings and twenty-eight nobles sixty years of age and over. This body supervised the work of administration, prepared measures for submission to the assembly, and served as the highest court for criminal trials. The third organ of government, the assembly, approved or rejected the proposals of the council and elected all public officials except the kings. But the highest authority under the Spartan constitution was vested in a board of five men known as the ephorate. The ephors virtually were the government. They presided over the council and the assembly, controlled the educational system and the distribution of property, censored the lives of the citizens, and exercised a veto power over all legislation. They had power also to determine the fate of newborn infants, to conduct prosecutions before the council, and even to depose the kings if the religious omens appeared unfavorable. The Spartan government was thus very decidedly an oligarchy. In spite of the fact that the ephors were chosen for one-year terms by the assembly, they were indefinitely re-eligible, and their authority was so vast that there was hardly any ramification of the system which they could not control. Moreover, it should be borne in mind that the assembly itself was not a democratic body. Not even the whole citizen class, which was a small minority of the total population, was entitled to membership in it, but only those males of full political status who had incomes sufficient to qualify them for enrollment in the heavy infantry.

The population of Sparta, which numbered at its peak about 400,-000, was divided into three main classes. The ruling element was made up of the Spartiates, or descendants of the original conquerors. Though never exceeding one-twentieth of the total population, the Spartiates alone had political privileges. Next in order of rank were the perioeci, or "dwellers around." The origin of this class is uncertain, but it was probably composed of peoples that had at one time been allies of the Spartans or had submitted voluntarily to Spartan domination. In return for service as a buffer population between the ruling class and the serfs, the perioeci were allowed to carry on trade and to engage in manufacturing. At the bottom of the scale were the helots, or serfs, bound to the soil and despised and persecuted by their masters.

Among these classes only the perioeci enjoyed any appreciable measure of comfort and freedom. While it is true that the economic condition of the helots cannot be described in terms of absolute misery, since they were permitted to keep for themselves a good share of what they produced on the estates of their masters, they were personally subjected to such shameful treatment that they were constantly wretched and rebellious. On occasions they were compelled to give exhibitions of drunkenness and lascivious dances as an example to the Spartan youth of the effects of such practices. At the beginning of each year, if we can believe the testimony of Aristotle, the ephors declared war upon the helots, presumably for the purpose of giving a gloss of legality to the murder of any by the secret police upon suspicion of disloyalty.

Those who were born into the Spartiate class were doomed to a respectable slavery for the major part of their lives. Forced to submit to the severest discipline and to sacrifice individual interests, they were nothing but cogs in a vast machine. Their education was limited almost entirely to military training, supplemented by exposure and merciless floggings to harden them for the duties of war. Between the ages of twenty and sixty they gave all their time to service to the state. Although marriage was practically compulsory, no family life was permitted. Husbands carried off their wives on the wedding night by a show of force. But they did not live with them. Instead, they were supposed to contrive means of escaping at night to visit them secretly. According to Plutarch, it thus sometimes happened that men "had children by their wives before ever they saw their faces by daylight." [2] No jealousy between marital partners was allowed. The production of vigorous offspring was all-important. Whether they were born within the limits of strict monogamy was a secondary consideration. In any case, children were the property not of their parents but of the state. *Discipline for the benefit of the state*

The economic organization of Sparta was designed almost solely for the ends of military efficiency and the supremacy of the citizen class. The best land was owned by the state and was originally divided into equal plots which were assigned to the Spartiate class as inalienable estates. Later these holdings as well as the inferior lands were permitted to be sold and exchanged, with the result that some of the citizens became richer than others. The helots, who did all the work of cultivating the soil, also belonged to the state and were assigned to their masters along with the land. Their masters were forbidden to emancipate them or to sell them outside of the country. The labor of the helots provided for the support of the whole citizen class, whose members were not allowed to be associated with any economic enterprise other than agriculture. Trade and industry were reserved exclusively for the perioeci. *Economic regulations*

The Spartan economic system is frequently described by modern historians as communistic. It is true that some of the means of production (the helots and the land) were collectively owned, in theory at least, and that the Spartiate males contributed from their incomes to provide for a common mess in the clubs to which they belonged. But with these rather doubtful exceptions the system was as far removed from communism as it was from anarchy. Essentials of the communist ideal include the doctrines that all the instruments of *Was the Spartan system communistic?*

[2] Plutarch, "Lycurgus," *Lives of Illustrious Men* (Dryden ed.), Vol. I, p. 81.

production shall be owned by the community, that no one shall live by exploiting the labor of others, and that all shall work for the benefit of the community and share the wealth in proportion to need. In Sparta commerce and industry were in private hands; the helots were forced to contribute a portion of what they produced to provide for the subsistence of their masters; and political privileges were restricted to an hereditary aristocracy, most of whose members performed no socially useful labor whatever. With its militarism, its secret police, its minority rule, and its closed economy, the Spartan system would seem to have resembled fascism more nearly than true communism.

4. The Athenian Triumph and Tragedy

Athens began her history under conditions quite different from those which prevailed in Sparta. The district of Attica had not been the scene of an armed invasion or of bitter conflict between opposing races. The Ionian penetration of that area was gradual and largely peaceful. As a result, no military caste imposed its rule upon a vanquished people. Furthermore, the wealth of Attica consisted of mineral deposits and splendid harbors rather than agricultural resources. Athens, consequently, never remained a predominantly agrarian state but rapidly developed a prosperous trade and a culture essentially urban.

Advantages enjoyed by the Athenians

Until the middle of the eighth century B.C. Athens, like the other Greek states, had a monarchical form of government. During the century that followed, the council of nobles, or Council of the Areopagus, as it came to be called, gradually divested the king of his powers. The transition to rule by the few was both the cause and the result of an increasing concentration of wealth. The introduction of vine and olive culture about this time led to the growth of agriculture as a great capitalistic enterprise. Since vineyards and olive orchards require considerable time to become profitable, only those farmers with abundant resources were able to survive in the business. Their poorer and less thrifty neighbors sank rapidly into debt, especially since grain was now coming to be imported at ruinous prices. The small farmer had no alternative but to mortgage his land, and then his family and himself, in the vain hope that some day a way of escape would be found. Ultimately many of his class became serfs when the mortgages could not be paid.

From monarchy to oligarchy in Athens

Bitter cries of distress now arose and threats of revolution were heard. The middle classes in the towns espoused the cause of the peasants in demanding liberalization of the government. Finally, in 594 B.C., all parties agreed upon the appointment of Solon as a magistrate with absolute power to carry out reforms. The measures which Solon enacted provided for both political and economic adjustments. The former included: (1) the establishment of a new council, the

Threats of revolution and the reforms of Solon

Council of Four Hundred, and the admission of the middle classes
to membership in it; (2) the enfranchisement of the lower classes
by making them eligible for service in the assembly; and (3) the
organization of a supreme court, open to all citizens and elected
by universal manhood suffrage, with power to hear appeals from the
decisions of the magistrates. The economic reforms benefited the
poor farmers by canceling existing mortgages, prohibiting enslavement for debt in the future, and limiting the amount of land any one
individual could own. Nor did Solon neglect the middle classes. He
introduced a new system of coinage designed to give Athens an advantage in foreign trade, imposed heavy penalties for idleness, ordered every man to teach his son a trade, and offered full privileges
of citizenship to alien craftsmen who would become permanent
residents of the country.

Significant though these reforms were, they did not allay the discontent. The nobles were disgruntled because some of their privileges
had been taken away. The middle and lower classes were dissatisfied *The rise*
because they were still excluded from the offices of magistracy, and *of dictatorship*
because the Council of the Areopagus was left with its powers in-
tact. Worse still was the fact that Solon, like certain rulers of modern
times, attempted to divert the people from their domestic troubles
by persuading them to embark upon military adventures abroad. An
old quarrel with Megara was revived, and Athens committed her
fate to the uncertainties of war. The chaos and disillusionment that
followed paved the way in 560 B.C. for the triumph of Peisistratus,
the first of the Athenian tyrants. Although he proved to be a benevolent despot, he nevertheless destroyed many of the liberties the
people had previously gained, and Hippias, one of his two sons who
succeeded him, was a ruthless and spiteful oppressor.

In 510 B.C. Hippias was overthrown by a group of nobles with aid
from Sparta. Factional conflict raged anew until Cleisthenes, an intelligent aristocrat, enlisted the support of the masses to eliminate *The reforms of*
his rivals from the scene. Having promised concessions to the peo- *Cleisthenes*
ple as a reward for their help, he proceeded to reform the government in so sweeping a fashion that he has since been known as the
father of Athenian democracy. He greatly enlarged the citizen population by granting full rights to all freemen who resided in the
country at that time. He established a new Council of Five Hundred
and made it the chief organ of government with power to prepare
measures for submission to the assembly and with supreme control
over executive and administrative functions. Members of this body
were to be chosen by lot from lists of candidates submitted by the
demes or townships. Any male citizen over thirty years of age was
eligible. Since the Council was so large, it was to be divided into
ten committees of fifty, each to manage the affairs of government for
a month. Cleisthenes also expanded the authority of the assembly,
giving it power to debate and pass or reject the measures submitted **155**

by the Council, to declare war, to appropriate money, and to audit the accounts of retiring magistrates. Lastly, Cleisthenes is believed to have instituted the device of ostracism, whereby any citizen who might be dangerous to the state could be sent into honorable exile for a ten-year period. The device was quite obviously intended to eliminate men who were suspected of cherishing dictatorial ambitions.

The perfection of Athenian democracy

The Athenian democracy attained its full perfection in the Age of Pericles (461–429 B.C.). It was during this period that the assembly acquired the authority to initiate legislation in addition to its power to ratify or reject proposals of the Council. It was during this time also that the famous Board of Ten Generals rose to a position roughly comparable to that of the British cabinet. The Generals were chosen by the assembly for one-year terms and were eligible for re-election indefinitely. Pericles held the position of Chief Strategus or president of the Board of Generals for more than thirty years. The Generals were not simply commanders of the army but the chief legislative and executive officials in the state, gradually assuming most of the prerogatives which Cleisthenes had given to the Council of Five Hundred. Though wielding enormous power, they could not become tyrants, for their policies were subject to review by the assembly, and they could easily be recalled at the end of their one-year terms or indicted for malfeasance at any time. Finally, it was in the Age of Pericles that the Athenian system of courts was developed to completion. No longer was there merely a supreme court to hear appeals from the decisions of magistrates, but an array of popular courts with authority to try all kinds of cases. At the beginning of each year a list of 6000 citizens was chosen by lot from the various sections of the country. From this list separate juries, varying in size from 201 to 1001, were made up for particular trials. Each of these juries constituted a court with power to decide by majority vote every question involved in the case. Although one of the magistrates presided, he had none of the prerogatives of a judge; the jury itself was the judge, and from its decision there was no appeal. It would be difficult to imagine a system more thoroughly democratic.

Athenian democracy compared with modern democracy

The Athenian democracy differed from the modern form in various ways. First of all, it did not extend to the whole population, but only to the citizen class. While it is true that in the time of Cleisthenes (508–502 B.C.) the citizens probably included a majority of the inhabitants because of his enfranchisement of resident aliens, in the Age of Pericles they were distinctly a minority. It may be well to observe, however, that within its limits Athenian democracy was more thoroughly applied than is the modern form. The choice by lot of nearly all magistrates except the Ten Generals, the restriction of all terms of public officials to one year, and the uncompromising adherence to the principle of majority rule even in judicial trials were

Geometric Horse, VIII cent. B.C. Greek art of this early period was angular, formal, and conventionalized.

Geometric Jar, VIII cent. B.C. Another example of the stylized decorative patterns of early Greek art.

Sphinx, *ca.* 540–530 B.C. Though doubtless of Oriental derivation, Greek sphinxes had a softer and more human aspect than the Oriental.

Statue of an Amazon, one of the fabled tribe of women warriors, V cent. B.C. (Roman copy)

Departure of a Warrior. Gravestone, *ca.* 530 B.C., a period when naturalism was the dominant note of Greek art.

Athena, *ca.* 460 B.C. The young, graceful patron-goddess of Athens is about to send forth an owl as a sign of victory.

Jar, 500–490 B.C. The figures depicted in a fine black glaze on the natural red clay show athletes in the Panathenaic games.

Chorus of Satyrs, *ca.* 420 B.C. The background is black with the figures in red clay. The satyrs, dressed in fleecy white, with flowing tails, are the chorus of a play.

Toilet Box, 465–460 B.C., showing the Judgment of Paris, an early incident in the Trojan War.

All pictures courtesy MMA.

Bronze Mirror Case, V cent. B.C. Greek articles of everyday use were commonly finished with the same delicacy and precision as major works of art.

Diadoumenos, after Polykleitos, V cent. B.C. An idealized statue of a Greek athlete tying the "diadem," or band of victory, around his head.

Statuette of a Horse, 480–470 B.C. Though an idealized type rather than an individual animal, the detail is almost perfect.

Bracelet Pendant, IV–III cent. B.C. This tiny figure of the god Pan is a masterpiece of detail and expression.

Woman Arranging Her Hair, 400–300 B.C. Sculptors of antiquity took pride in these statuettes of ordinary people in ordinary activities, which were usually made of terra cotta painted soft blue, pink, or yellow.

Head of an Athlete, *ca.* 440–420 B.C. The sculptor aimed to express manly beauty in perfect harmony with physical and intellectual excellence.

Comic Actor, 200–100 B.C. Hellenistic realism often included portrayal of ugly and even deformed individuals.

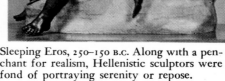

Sleeping Eros, 250–150 B.C. Along with a penchant for realism, Hellenistic sculptors were fond of portraying serenity or repose.

Statuette of Hermarchos, III cent. B.C. An example of the realism of Hellenistic sculpture.

All pictures courtesy MMA.

examples of a serene confidence in the political capacity of the average man which few modern nations would be willing to accept. The democracy of Athens differed from the contemporary ideal also in the fact that it was direct, not representative. Contrary to the traditional view, the Athenians understood the principle of representation, but they never applied it except in a limited way in the selection of members of the Council of Five Hundred. They were not interested in being governed by men of reputation and ability; what vitally concerned them was the assurance to every citizen of an actual voice in the control of all public affairs. In a word, their ideal was not efficiency in government but democracy.

In the last century of her existence as an independent state Athens fought two great wars. The first, the war with Persia, was an outgrowth of the expansion of that empire into the eastern Mediterranean area. The Athenians resented the conquest of their Ionian kinsmen in Asia Minor and aided them in their struggle for freedom. The Persians retaliated by sending a powerful army and fleet to attack the Greeks. Although all Greece was in danger of conquest, Athens bore the chief burden of repelling the invader. Sparta, especially, rendered but little assistance until the struggle was almost over. The war, which began in 493 B.C. and lasted with interludes of peace for about fourteen years, is commonly regarded as one of the most significant in the history of the world. The decisive victory of the Greeks put an end to the menace of Persian conquest and forestalled at least for a time the submergence of Hellenic ideals of freedom in Oriental despotism. The war also had the effect of strengthening democracy in Athens and making that state the leading power in Greece.

The Persian War and its results

The other of the great struggles, the Peloponnesian War with Sparta, had results of a quite different character. Instead of being another milestone in the Athenian march to power, it ended in tragedy. Athens was so completely humbled that she never again played an eminent role in Greek politics. The causes of this war are of particular interest to the student of the downfall of civilizations. First and most important was the growth of Athenian imperialism. In the last year of the war with Persia, Athens had joined with a number of other Greek states in the formation of an offensive and defensive alliance known as the Delian League. When peace was concluded the League was not dissolved, for many of the Greeks feared that the Persians might come back. As time went on, Athens gradually transformed the League into a naval empire for the advancement of her own interests. She used some of the funds in the common treasury for her own purposes. She tried to reduce all the other members to a condition of vassalage, and when one of them rebelled, she overwhelmed it by force, seized its navy, and imposed tribute upon it as if it were a conquered state. Such high-handed methods aroused the

Athenian imperialism and the Peloponnesian War

suspicions of the Spartans, who feared that an Athenian hegemony
would soon be extended over all of Greece.

A second major cause was to be found in the social and cultural
differences between Athens and Sparta. Athens was democratic, progressive, urban, imperialistic, and intellectually and artistically advanced. Sparta was aristocratic, conservative, agrarian, provincial,
and culturally backward. Where such sharply contrasting systems
exist side by side, conflicts are almost bound to occur. The attitude
of the Athenians and Spartans had been hostile for some time. The
former looked upon the latter as uncouth barbarians. The Spartans
accused the Athenians of attempting to gain control over the northern Peloponnesian states and of encouraging the helots to rebel. Economic factors also played a large part in bringing the conflict to a
head. Athens was ambitious to dominate the Corinthian Gulf, the
principal avenue of trade with Sicily and southern Italy. This made
her the deadly enemy of Corinth, the chief ally of Sparta.

The war, which broke out in 431 B.C. and lasted until 404, was a
record of frightful calamities for Athens. Her trade was destroyed,
her democracy overthrown, and her population decimated by a terrible pestilence. Quite as bad was the moral degradation which followed in the wake of the military reverses. Treason, corruption, and
brutality were among the hastening ills of the last few years of the
conflict. On one occasion the Athenians even slaughtered the whole
male population of the state of Melos, and enslaved the women and
children, for no other crime than refusing to abandon neutrality.
Ultimately, deserted by all her allies except Samos and with her food
supply cut off, Athens was left with no alternative but to surrender
or starve. The terms imposed upon her were drastic enough: destruction of her fortifications, surrender of all foreign possessions
and practically her entire navy, and submission to Sparta as a subject state.

5. *Political Debacle—the Last Days*

Not only did the Peloponnesian War put an end to the supremacy
of Athens; it annihilated freedom throughout the Greek world and
sealed the doom of the Hellenic political genius. Following the war
Sparta asserted her power over all of Hellas. Oligarchies supported
by Spartan troops replaced democracies wherever they existed.
Confiscation of property and assassination were the methods regularly employed to combat opposition. Although in Athens the tyrants were overthrown after a time and free government restored
temporarily, Sparta was able to dominate the remainder of Greece
for more than thirty years. In 371 B.C., however, Epaminondas of
Thebes defeated the Spartan army at Leuctra and thereby inaugurated a period of Theban supremacy. Unfortunately Thebes

showed little more wisdom and tolerance in governing than Sparta, and nine years later a combination was formed to free the Greek cities from their new oppressor. Failing to break up the alliance, the Thebans gave battle on the field of Mantinea. Both sides claimed the victory, but Epaminondas was slain, and the power of his empire soon afterward collapsed.

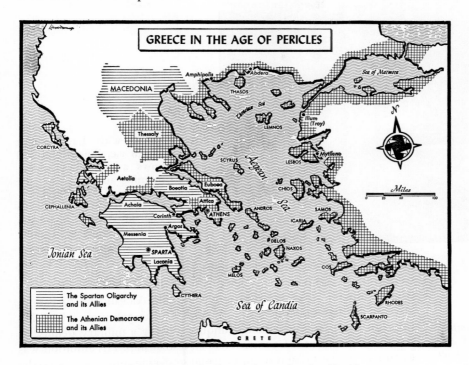

The long succession of wars had now brought the Greek states to the point of exhaustion. Though the glory of their culture was yet undimmed, politically they were prostrate and helpless. Their fate *The Macedo-* was soon decided for them by the rise of Philip of Macedon. Except *nian conquest* for a thin veneer of Hellenic culture, the Macedonians were barbarians; but Philip, before becoming their king, had learned how to lead an army while a hostage at Thebes. Perceiving the weakness of the states to the south, he determined to conquer them. A series of early successes led to the decisive victory at Chaeronea in 338 B.C. and soon afterward to dominion over all of Greece except Sparta. Two years later Philip was murdered as the sequel to a family brawl.

Rule over Hellas now passed into the hands of his son Alexander, a youth of twenty years. After putting to death all possible aspirants to the throne and quelling some feeble revolts of the Greeks, Alex- *Alexander the* ander conceived the grandiose scheme of conquering Persia. One *Great* victory followed another until in the short space of twelve years the whole ancient Near Orient from the Indus River to the Nile had been annexed to Greece as the personal domain of one man. Alex-

Marble Stele with Law against Tyranny, 338 B.C. The sculptured relief shows a woman (Democracy) crowning an aged man (the People of Athens). The law provides that if anyone establishes a dictatorship in Athens, a person who kills him shall be held guiltless.

ander did not live to enjoy it long. In 323 B.C. he fell ill of Babylonian swamp fever and died at the age of thirty-three.

The significance of Alexander's career

It is difficult to gauge the significance of Alexander's career. A slave of his emotions, he scarcely deserves the greatness which has been thrust upon him. Though unquestionably a military genius, he left few monuments of constructive statesmanship. His ambition was to rule after the fashion of an Oriental god-king, not to advance the Hellenic ideals of freedom and justice. Moreover, his influence in spreading Greek culture appears to have been exaggerated considerably. Persia adopted no large number of Hellenic institutions and customs as a result of the Alexandrian conquest. Except for her cities at the mouth of the Nile, Egypt remained Egyptian. The influence of Alexander's conquests was rather in the opposite direction: they opened the way for a stronger infusion of Orientalism into Europe than had ever occurred before—so strong in fact that the days of Hellenic civilization as such were now practically over.

6. Hellenic Thought and Culture

The antecedents of Greek philosophy

I. PHILOSOPHY From what has been said in preceding chapters it should be clear that the popular notion that all philosophy originated with the Greeks is fallacious. Centuries earlier the Egyptians had given much thought to the nature of the universe and to the social and ethical problems of man. The achievement of the Greeks was rather the development of philosophy in a more inclusive mean-

160

ing than it had ever possessed before. They attempted to find answers to every conceivable question about the nature of the universe, the problem of truth, and the meaning and purpose of life. The magnitude of their accomplishment is attested by the fact that philosophy ever since has been largely a debate over the validity of their several conclusions.

Greek philosophy had its origins in the sixth century B.C. in the work of the so-called Milesian school, whose members were natives of the great commercial city of Miletus on the shore of Asia Minor. Their philosophy was fundamentally scientific and materialistic. The problem which chiefly engaged their attention was to discover the nature of the physical world. They believed that all things could be reduced to some primary substance or original matter which was the source of worlds, stars, animals, plants, and men, and to which all would ultimately return. Thales, the founder of the school, perceiving that all things contained moisture, taught that the primary substance is water. Anaximander insisted that it could not be any particular thing such as water or fire but some substance "ungendered and imperishable" which "contains and directs all things." He called this substance the Infinite or the Boundless. Evidently what he had in mind was an indeterminate material mass out of which individual things are formed. The third member of the school, Anaximenes, declared that the original material of the universe is air. At first thought this appears to have been a step backward to the idea that some one of the elements is the source from which everything comes. But this is not so, for Anaximenes really chose air as the germinal substance because it made possible a quantitative interpretation of the universe. In other words, he maintained that the essential difference between things consists merely in the *amount* of the basic substance they contain. Air when rarefied becomes fire; when condensed it turns successively to wind, vapor, water, earth, and stone.

The philosophy of the Milesian school

Although seemingly naïve in its conclusions the philosophy of the Milesian school was of real significance. It broke through the mythological beliefs of the Greeks about the origin of the world and substituted a purely rational explanation. It revived and expanded the Egyptian ideas of the eternity of the universe and the indestructibility of matter. It suggested very clearly, especially in the teachings of Anaximander, the concept of evolution in the sense of rhythmic change, of continuing creation and decay. And the conclusion would seem logical that Anaximenes' quantitative interpretation of the universe helped to prepare the way for the atomic conception of matter.

Significance of the teachings of the Milesian school

Before the end of the sixth century Greek philosophy developed a metaphysical turn; that is, it ceased to be occupied solely with problems of the physical world and shifted its attention to abstruse questions about the nature of being, the meaning of truth, and the position of the divine in the scheme of things. First to exemplify the new

The Pythagoreans

161

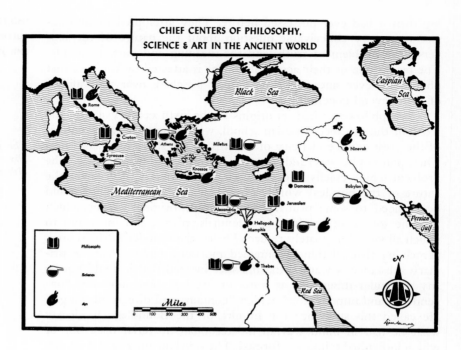

tendency were the Pythagoreans, who interpreted philosophy largely in terms of religion. Little is known about them except that their leader, Pythagoras, migrated from the island of Samos to southern Italy and founded a religious community at Croton. He and his followers apparently taught that the speculative life is the highest good, but that in order to pursue it, man must purify himself from the evil desires of the flesh. They held that the essence of things is not a material substance but an abstract principle, number. Their chief significance lies in the sharp distinctions they drew between spirit and matter, harmony and discord, good and evil. Perhaps it is not inaccurate to regard them as the real founders of dualism in Greek thought.

A consequence of the work of the Pythagoreans was to intensify the debate over the nature of the universe. Some of their contemporaries, notably Parmenides, argued that stability or permanence is the real nature of things; change and diversity are simply illusions of the senses. Parmenides meant by this that underneath all of the surface changes which go on around us there are things which really endure. We cannot perceive them with our senses, but we can discover their existence by reason. Directly opposed to this was the position taken by Heracleitus, who argued that permanence is an illusion, that change alone is real. The universe, he maintained, is in a condition of constant flux, so that it is impossible to step twice into the same stream. Creation and destruction, life and death, are but the obverse and reverse sides of the same picture. In affirming

Renewal of the debate over the nature of the universe

162

such views Heracleitus was really contending that the things we see and hear and feel are all that there is to reality. Evolution or constant change is the law of the universe. The tree or the stone that is here today is gone tomorrow; no underlying substance exists immutable through all eternity.

The eventual answer to the question of the nature of the universe was provided by the atomists. The founder of the atomic theory was Leucippus, but the philosopher chiefly responsible for its development was Democritus, who lived in Abdera on the Thracian coast in the second half of the fifth century. As their name implies, the atomists held that the ultimate constituents of the universe are atoms, infinite in number, indestructible, and indivisible. Although these differ in size and shape, they are exactly alike in composition. Because of the motion inherent in them, they are eternally uniting, separating, and reuniting in different arrangements. Every individual object or organism in the universe is thus the product of a fortuitous concourse of atoms. The only difference between a man and a tree is the difference in the number and arrangement of their atoms. Here was a philosophy which represented the final fruition of the materialistic tendencies of early Greek thought. Democritus denied the immortality of the soul and the existence of any spiritual world. Strange as it may appear to the minds of some people, he was a moral idealist, affirming that "Good means not merely not to do wrong, but rather not to desire to do wrong." [3]

Solution of the problem by the atomists

About the middle of the fifth century B.C. an intellectual revolution began in Greece. The rise of the common man, the growth of individualism, and the demand for the solution of practical problems produced a reaction against the old ways of thinking. As a result philosophers abandoned the study of the physical universe and turned to consideration of subjects more intimately related to man himself. The first exponents of the new intellectual trend were the Sophists. Originally the term meant "those who are wise," but later it came to be used in the derogatory sense of men who employ specious reasoning. Since most of our knowledge of the Sophists was derived, until comparatively recently, from Plato, one of their severest critics, they were commonly considered to have been the enemies of all that was best in Hellenic culture. Modern research has exposed the fallacy of so extreme a conclusion, even though some members of the group lacked a sense of social responsibility and were quite unscrupulous in "making the worse appear the better cause."

The intellectual revolution begun by the Sophists

The greatest of the Sophists was undoubtedly Protagoras, a native of Abdera who did most of his teaching in Athens. His famous dictum, "Man is the measure of all things," comprehends the essence of the Sophist philosophy. By this he meant that goodness, truth, justice, and beauty are relative to the needs and interests of man himself. There are no absolute truths or eternal standards of right and

The doctrines of Protagoras

[3] Quoted by Frank Thilly, *History of Philosophy*, p. 40.

justice. Since sense perception is the exclusive source of knowledge, there can be only particular truths valid for a given time and place. Morality likewise varies from one people to another. The Spartans encourage adultery in certain cases on the part of wives as well as husbands; the Athenians seclude their women and refuse even to allow them a normal social life. Which of these standards is right? Neither is right in any absolute sense, for there are no absolute canons of right and wrong eternally decreed in the heavens to fit all cases; yet both are right in the relative sense that the judgment of man alone determines what is good.

The extremist doctrines of the later Sophists

Some of the later Sophists went far beyond the teachings of their great master. Gorgias, for example, perverted the skepticism of Protagoras into the doctrine that the human mind can never know anything except its own subjective impressions. "Nothing exists," he declared; "if anything did exist it could not be known; if a man should chance to apprehend it, it would still be a secret; he would be unable to communicate it to his fellows." [4] The individualism which was necessarily implicit in the teachings of Protagoras was twisted by Thrasymachus into the doctrine that all laws and customs are merely expressions of the will of the strongest and shrewdest for their own advantage, and that therefore the wise man is the "perfectly unjust man" who is above the law and concerned with the gratification of his own desires.

The valuable contributions of the Sophists

Yet there was much that was admirable in the teachings of all the Sophists, even of those who were the most extreme. Without exception they condemned slavery and the racial exclusiveness of the Greeks. They were champions of liberty, the rights of the common man, and the practical and progressive point of view. They perceived the folly of war and ridiculed the silly chauvinism of many of the Athenians. Perhaps their most important work was the extension of philosophy to include not only physics and metaphysics, but ethics, politics, and epistemology, or the science of knowledge, as well. As Cicero expressed it, they "brought philosophy down from heaven to the dwellings of men."

The reaction against Sophism

It was inevitable that the relativism, skepticism, and individualism of the Sophists should have aroused strenuous opposition. In the judgment of the more conservative Greeks these doctrines appeared to lead straight to atheism and anarchy. If there is no final truth, and if goodness and justice are merely relative to the whims of the individual, then neither religion, morality, the state, nor society itself can long be maintained. The result of this conviction was the growth of a new philosophic movement grounded upon the theory that truth is real and that absolute standards do exist. The leaders of this movement were perhaps the three most famous individuals in the history of thought—Socrates, Plato, and Aristotle.

Socrates was born in Athens in 469 B.C. of humble parentage, his

[4] Quoted by A. A. Trever, *History of Ancient Civilization*, Vol. I, p. 348.

father being a sculptor, his mother a midwife. How he obtained an education no one knows, but he was certainly familiar with the teachings of earlier Greek thinkers, presumably from extensive reading. The impression that he was a mere gabbler in the market place is quite unfounded. He became a philosopher on his own account chiefly to combat the doctrines of the Sophists, and he soon gathered around him a circle of admirers, which included the two young aristocrats, Plato and Alcibiades. In 399 B.C. he was condemned to death on a charge of "corrupting the youth and introducing new gods." The real reason for the unjust sentence was the tragic outcome for Athens of the Peloponnesian War. Overwhelmed by resentment and despair, the people turned against Socrates because of his associations with aristocrats, including the traitor Alcibiades, and because of his criticism of popular beliefs.

For the reason that Socrates wrote nothing himself, historians have been faced with a problem in determining the scope of his teachings. He is generally regarded as primarily a teacher of ethics with no interest in abstract philosophy or any desire to found a new school of thought. Certain admissions made by Plato, however, indicate that a large part of the famous doctrine of Ideas was really of Socratic origin. At any rate we can be reasonably sure that Socrates believed in a stable and universally valid knowledge, which man could possess if he would only pursue the right method. This method would consist in the exchange and analysis of opinions, in the setting up and testing of provisional definitions, until finally an essence of truth recognizable by all could be distilled from them. Socrates argued that in similar fashion man could discover enduring principles of right and justice independent of the selfish desires of human beings. He believed, moreover, that the discovery of such rational principles of conduct would prove an infallible guide to virtuous living, for he denied that anyone who truly knows the good can ever choose the evil.

By far the most distinguished of Socrates' pupils was Plato, who was born in Athens in 427 B.C., the son of noble parents. His real name was Aristocles, "Plato" being a nickname supposedly given to him by one of his teachers because of his broad frame. When he was twenty years old he joined the Socratic circle, remaining a member until the tragic death of his teacher. He seems to have drawn inspiration from other sources also, notably from the teachings of Parmenides and the Pythagoreans. Unlike his great master he was a prolific writer, though some of the works attributed to him are of doubtful authorship. The most noted of his writings are such dialogues as the *Apology*, the *Protagoras*, the *Phaedrus*, the *Timaeus*, and the *Republic*. He was engaged in the completion of another great work, the *Laws*, when death overtook him in his eighty-first year.

Plato's objectives in developing his philosophy were similar to those of Socrates although somewhat broader: (1) to combat the

*Plato's philoso-
phy of Ideas*

theory of reality as a disordered flux and to substitute an interpretation of the universe as essentially spiritual and purposeful; (2) to refute the Sophist doctrines of relativism and skepticism; and (3) to provide a secure foundation for ethics. In order to realize these objectives he developed his celebrated doctrine of Ideas. He admitted that relativity and constant change are characteristics of the world of physical things, of the world we perceive with our senses. But he denied that this world is the complete universe. There is a higher, spiritual realm composed of eternal forms or Ideas which only the mind can conceive. These are not, however, mere abstractions invented by the mind of man, but spiritual things. Each is the archetype or pattern of some particular class of objects or relation between objects on earth. Thus there are Ideas of man, tree, shape, size, color, proportion, beauty, and justice. Highest of them all is the Idea of the Good, which is the active cause and guiding purpose of the whole universe. The things we perceive with our senses are merely imperfect copies of the supreme realities, Ideas.

*Plato's ethical
and religious
philosophy*

Plato's ethical and religious philosophy was closely related to his doctrine of Ideas. Like Socrates he believed that true virtue has its basis in knowledge. But the knowledge derived from the senses is limited and variable; hence true virtue must consist in rational apprehension of the eternal Ideas of goodness and justice. By relegating the physical to an inferior place, he gave to his ethics a mildly ascetic tinge. He regarded the body as a hindrance to the mind and taught that only the rational part of man's nature is noble and good. In contrast with some of his later followers, he did not demand that appetites and emotions should be denied altogether, but urged that they should be strictly subordinated to the reason. Plato never made his conception of God entirely clear. Sometimes he referred to the Idea of the Good as if it were a divine power of subordinate rank; at other times as if it were the supreme creator and ruler of the universe. Probably the latter is what he really meant. At any rate it is certain that he conceived of the universe as spiritual in nature and governed by intelligent purpose. He rejected both materialism and mechanism. As for the soul, he regarded it not only as immortal but as pre-existing from all eternity.

*Plato
as a political
philosopher*

As a political philosopher Plato was motivated by the ideal of constructing a state which would be free from turbulence and self-seeking on the part of individuals and classes. Neither democracy nor liberty but harmony and efficiency were the ends he desired to achieve. Accordingly, he proposed in his *Republic* a famous plan for society which would have divided the population into three principal classes corresponding to the functions of the soul. The lowest class, representing the appetitive function, would include the farmers, artisans, and merchants. The second class, representing the spirited element or will, would consist of the soldiers; while the highest class, representing the reason, would include the intellectual aristocracy. Each of these classes would be supposed to perform those tasks for which it was best fitted. The function of the lowest class would be the production and distribution of goods for the benefit of the whole community; that of the soldiers, defense; while the aristocracy by reason of special aptitude for philosophy would enjoy a monopoly of political power. The division of the people into these several ranks would not be made on the basis of birth or wealth, but through a sifting process which would take into account the ability of each individual to profit from education. Thus the farmers, artisans, and merchants would be those who had shown the least intellectual capacity, whereas the philosopher-kings would be those who had shown the greatest.

The last of the great champions of the Socratic tradition was Aristotle, a native of Stagira, born in 384 B.C. At the age of seventeen he entered Plato's Academy,[5] continuing as student and teacher there for twenty years. In 343 he was invited by King Philip of Macedon to serve as tutor to the young Alexander. Perhaps history affords few more conspicuous examples of wasted talent. Seven years later he returned to Athens, where he conducted a school of his own, known as the Lyceum, until his death in 322 B.C. Aristotle wrote even more voluminously than Plato and on a greater variety of subjects. His principal works include treatises on logic, metaphysics, rhetoric, ethics, natural sciences, and politics. A considerable number of the writings credited to him have never been found.

Aristotle

Though Aristotle was as much interested as Plato and Socrates in absolute knowledge and eternal standards, his philosophy differed from theirs in several outstanding respects. To begin with, he had a higher regard for the concrete and the practical. In contrast with Plato, the aesthete, and Socrates, who declared he could learn nothing from trees and stones, Aristotle was a scientist with a compelling interest in biology, medicine, and astronomy. Moreover, he was less inclined than his predecessors to a spiritual outlook. And lastly, he did not share their strong aristocratic sympathies.

Aristotle compared with Plato and Socrates

Aristotle agreed with Plato that universals, Ideas (or forms as he called them), are real, and that knowledge derived from the senses is limited and inaccurate. But he refused to go along with his master in ascribing an independent existence to universals and in reducing material things to pale reflections of their spiritual patterns. On the contrary, he asserted that form and matter are of equal importance; both are eternal, and neither can exist inseparable from the other. It is the union of the two which gives to the universe its essential character. Forms are the causes of all things; they are the purposive forces which shape the world of matter into the infinitely varied objects and organisms around us. All evolution, both cosmic and organic, results from the interaction of form and matter upon each

Aristotle's conception of the universe

[5] So called from the grove of Academus, where Plato and his disciples met to discuss philosophic problems.

other. Thus the presence of the form *man* in the human embryo molds and directs the development of the latter until it ultimately evolves as a human being. While the mechanical motion of the matter itself plays some part in the process also, the determining factor is the purposive action of the form. Aristotle's philosophy may therefore be regarded as a halfway house between the spiritualism and transcendentalism of Plato, on the one hand, and the mechanistic materialism of the atomists on the other. His conception of the universe was *teleological*—that is, governed by purpose; but he refused to regard the spiritual as completely overshadowing its material embodiment.

Aristotle's religious doctrines

That Aristotle should have conceived of God primarily as a First Cause is no more than we should expect from the dominance of the scientific attitude in his philosophy. Unlike Plato's Idea of the Good, Aristotle's God did not fulfill an ethical purpose. His character was that of a Prime Mover, the original source of the purposive motion contained in the forms. In no sense was he a personal God, for his nature was pure intelligence, devoid of all feelings, will, or desire. Aristotle seems to have left no place in his religious scheme for individual immortality: all the functions of the soul, except the creative reason which is not individual at all, are dependent upon the body and perish with it.

Aristotle's ethical philosophy of the golden mean

Aristotle's ethical philosophy was less ascetic than Plato's. He did not regard the body as the prison of the soul, nor did he believe that physical appetites are necessarily evil in themselves. He taught that the highest good for man consists in self-realization, that is, in the exercise of that part of man's nature which most truly distinguishes him as a human being. Self-realization would therefore be identical with the life of reason. But the life of reason is dependent upon the proper combination of physical and mental conditions. The body must be kept in good health and the emotions under adequate control. The solution is to be found in the *golden mean*, in preserving a balance between excessive indulgence on the one hand and ascetic denial on the other. This was simply a reaffirmation of the characteristic Hellenic ideal of *sophrosyne* ("nothing too much").

The golden mean applied to politics

Although Aristotle included in his *Politics* much descriptive and analytical material on the structure and functions of government, he dealt primarily with the broader aspects of political theory. He considered the state as the supreme institution for the promotion of the good life among men, and he was therefore vitally interested in its origin and development and in the best forms it could be made to assume. Declaring that man is by nature a political animal, he denied that the state is an artificial product of the ambitions of the few or of the desires of the many. On the contrary, he asserted that it is rooted in the instincts of man himself, and that civilized life outside of its limits is impossible. He considered the best state to be neither

a monarchy, an aristocracy, nor a democracy, but a *polity*—which he defined as a commonwealth intermediate between oligarchy and democracy. Essentially it would be a state under the control of the middle class, but Aristotle intended to make sure that the members of that class would be fairly numerous, for he advocated measures to prevent the concentration of wealth. He defended the institution of private property, but he opposed the heaping up of riches beyond what is necessary for intelligent living. He recommended that the government should provide the poor with money to buy small farms or to "make a beginning in trade and husbandry" and thus promote their prosperity and self-respect.[6]

II. SCIENCE Contrary to a popular belief, the period of Hellenic civilization, strictly speaking, was not a great age of science. The vast majority of the scientific achievements commonly thought of as Greek were made during the Hellenistic period, when the culture was no longer predominantly Hellenic but a mixture of Hellenic and Oriental.[7] The interests of the Greeks in the Periclean age and in the century that followed were chiefly speculative and artistic; they were not deeply concerned with material comforts or with mastery of the physical universe. Consequently, with the exception of some important developments in mathematics, biology, and medicine, scientific progress was relatively slight.

Hellenic science

The founder of Greek mathematics was apparently Thales of Miletus, who is supposed to have originated several theorems which were later included in the geometry of Euclid. Among them were the following: (1) a circle is bisected by any diameter; (2) the angles at the base of an isosceles triangle are equal; (3) if two straight lines cut one another, the vertically opposite angles are equal. Perhaps more significant was the work of the Pythagoreans, who developed an elaborate theory of numbers, classifying them into various categories, such as odd, even, prime, composite, even-times-even, perfect, and so forth. They are also supposed to have discovered the theory of proportion and to have proved for the first time that the sum of the three angles of any triangle is equal to two right angles. But the most famous of their achievements was the discovery of the theorem attributed to Pythagoras himself: the square of the hypotenuse of any right-angled triangle is equal to the sum of the squares on the other two sides. The Greek who first developed geometry as a science is now considered to have been Hippocrates of Chios, not to be confused with the physician, Hippocrates of Cos.[8]

Mathematics

The first of the Greeks to manifest an interest in biology was the philosopher Anaximander, who developed a crude theory of organic evolution based upon the principle of survival through progressive adaptations to the environment. The earliest ancestral animals, he asserted, lived in the sea, which originally covered the whole face of

Biology

[6] *Politics*, Maurice Francis Egan, ed., pp. 158–59.
[7] See the chapter on The Hellenistic Civilization.
[8] George Sarton, *An Introduction to the History of Science*, Vol. I, p. 92.

the earth. As the waters receded, some organisms were able to adjust themselves to their new environment and became land animals. The final product of this evolutionary process was man himself. The real founder of the science of biology, however, was Aristotle. Devoting many years of his life to painstaking study of the structure, habits, and growth of animals, he revealed many facts which were not destined to be discovered anew until the seventeenth century or later. The metamorphoses of various insects, the reproductive habits of the eel, the embryological development of the dog-fish (how the embryo is nourished in the womb by means of a placenta after the fashion of unborn mammals)—these are only samples of the amazing extent of his knowledge. Unfortunately he committed some errors. He denied the sexuality of plants, and he accepted uncritically some ancient myths about goats breathing through their ears and vultures being impregnated by the wind. Although he subscribed to the general theory of evolution, he believed in the spontaneous generation of certain species of worms and insects.

Medicine

Greek medicine also had its origin with the philosophers. The pioneers were Empedocles, exponent of the theory of the four elements (earth, air, fire, and water), and Alcmeon, a member of the Pythagorean school. The former discovered that blood flows to and from the heart, and that the pores of the skin supplement the work of the respiratory passages in breathing. Alcmeon originated the practice of dissecting animal bodies, discovered the optic nerve and the Eustachian tubes, and learned that the brain is the center of the nervous system. More important still was the work of Hippocrates of Cos in the fifth and fourth centuries. If this great physician had made no other contribution than his overthrow of the supernatural explanation of disease, he would still deserve to be called the father of medicine. He dinned into the ears of his pupils the doctrine that "Every disease has a natural cause, and without natural causes, nothing ever happens." In addition, by his methods of careful study and comparison of symptoms he laid the foundations for clinical medicine. He discovered the phenomenon of crisis in disease and improved the practice of surgery. Though he had a wide knowledge of drugs, his chief reliances in treatment were diet and rest. The main fact to his discredit was his development of the theory of the four humors—the notion that illness is due to excesssive amounts of yellow bile, black bile, blood, and phlegm in the system. The practice of bleeding the patient was the regrettable outgrowth of this theory.

III. LITERATURE Generally the most common medium of literary expression in the formative age of a people is the epic of heroic deeds.

*The epic
of heroic deeds*

It is a form well adapted to the pioneering days of battle and lusty adventure when men have not yet had time to be awed by the mystery of things. The most famous of the Greek epics, the *Iliad* and the *Odyssey*, were put into written form just at the end of the Homeric Age. The first has its theme in the love and wrath of

Achilles; the second describes the wanderings and return of Odysseus. Both have supreme literary merit in their carefully woven plots, in the music of their poetry, in the sensuous appeal of their imagery, in the realism of their character portrayals, and in their mastery of the full range of emotional intensity. They exerted an almost incalculable influence upon later writers. Their style and language inspired the fervid emotional poetry of the sixth century, and they were an unfailing source of plots and themes for the great tragedians of the Golden Age.

The three centuries which followed the Homeric Age were distinguished, as we have already seen, by tremendous social changes. The rural pattern of life gave way to an urban society of steadily increasing complexity. The founding of colonies and the growth of commerce provided new interests and new habits of living. Individuals hitherto submerged rose to a consciousness of their power and importance. It was inevitable that these changes should be reflected in new forms of literature, especially of a more personal type. The first to be developed was the elegy, which was probably intended to be declaimed rather than sung to the accompaniment of music. Elegies varied in theme from individual reactions toward love to the idealism of patriots and reformers. Generally, however, they were devoted to melancholy reflection on the disillusionments of life or to bitter lament over loss of prestige. Outstanding among the authors of elegiac verse were Solon the legislator, Mimnermus, and Theognis.

Development of the elegy

In the sixth century and the early part of the fifth, the elegy was gradually displaced by the lyric, which derives its name from the fact that it was sung to the music of the lyre. The new type of poetry was particularly well adapted to the expression of passionate feelings, the violent loves and hates engendered by the strife of classes. It was employed for other purposes also. Both Alcaeus and Sappho used it to describe the poignant beauty of love, the delicate grace of spring, and the starlit splendor of a summer night. Meanwhile other poets developed the choral lyric, intended to express the feelings of the community rather than the sentiments of any one individual. Greatest of all the writers of this group was Pindar of Thebes, who wrote during the first half of the fifth century. The lyrics of Pindar took the form of odes celebrating the victories of athletes and the glories of Hellenic civilization. They are significant also for their religious and moral conceptions. Pindar had accepted the idea that Zeus is a god of righteousness, and that he will punish the wicked with the "direst doom" and reward the good with a life "that knows no tears."

Lyric poetry

The supreme literary achievement of the Greeks was the tragic drama. Like so many of their other great works, it had its roots in religion. At the festivals dedicated to the worship of Dionysus, the god of spring and of wine, a chorus of men dressed as satyrs or goat-men sang and danced around an altar, enacting the various

The origins of tragic drama

Greek Theater in Syracuse on the Island of Sicily. Syracuse was one of the largest and most prosperous of Greek colonial cities. The construction, to take advantage of the slope of the hill, and the arrangement of the stage are of particular interest in this picture. Greek dramas were invariably presented in the open air.

parts of a dithyramb or choral lyric which related the story of the god's career. In time a leader came to be separated from the chorus to recite the main parts of the story. The true drama was born about the beginning of the fifth century when Aeschylus introduced a second "actor" and relegated the chorus to the background. The name "tragedy" which came to be applied to this drama was probably derived from the Greek word *tragos* meaning "goat."

Greek tragedy compared with modern tragedy

Greek tragedy stands out in marked contrast to the tragedies of Shakespeare or Arthur Miller. There was, first of all, little action presented on the stage; the main business of the actors was to recite the incidents of a plot which was already familiar to the audience, for the story was drawn from popular legends. Secondly, Greek tragedy devoted little attention to the study of complicated individual personality. There was no unfoldment of personal character as shaped by the vicissitudes of a long career. Those involved in the plot were scarcely individuals at all, but types. On the stage they wore masks to disguise any characteristics which might serve to distinguish them too sharply from the rest of humanity. In addition, Greek tragedies differed from the modern variety in having as their theme the conflict between man and the universe, not the clash of individual personalities, or the conflict of man with himself. The

172

tragic fate which befell the main characters in these plays was external to man himself. It was brought on by the fact that someone had committed a crime against society, thereby offending the moral scheme of the universe. Punishment must follow in order to balance the scale of justice. Finally, the purpose of Greek tragedies was not merely to depict suffering and to interpret human actions, but to portray "the ideal conduct of the ideal Hellene in a painful situation," and to purify the emotions of the audience by representing the triumph of justice.

As already indicated, the founder of Greek tragedy was Aeschylus (525–456 B.C.). Though he is supposed to have written about eighty plays, only seven have survived in complete form, among them *The Persians, Seven against Thebes, Prometheus Bound,* and a trilogy known as *Oresteia.* Guilt and punishment is the recurrent theme of nearly all of them. The second of the dramatists, Sophocles (496–406), is often considered to have been the greatest. His style was more polished and his philosophy more profound than that of his predecessor. He was the author of over a hundred plays, eighteen of which won first or second prize. More than any other writer in Greek history, he personified the Hellenic ideal of "nothing too much." His attitude was distinguished by love of harmony and peace, intelligent respect for democracy, and profound sympathy for human weakness. The most famous of his plays now extant are *Oedipus Rex, Antigone,* and *Electra.*

The work of the last of the tragedians, Euripides (480–406), reflects a far different spirit. He was a skeptic, an individualist, a humanist, who took delight in ridiculing the ancient myths and the "sacred cows" of his time. An embittered pessimist who suffered from the barbs of his conservative critics, he loved to humble the proud in his plays and to exalt the lowly. He was the first to give the ordinary man, even the beggar and the peasant, a place in the drama. Euripides is also noted for his sympathy for the slave, for his condemnation of war, and for his protests against the exclusion of women from social and intellectual life. Because of his humanism, his tendency to portray men as they actually were (or even a little worse), and his introduction of the love *motif* into drama, he is often considered a modernist. It must be remembered, however, that in other respects his plays were perfectly consistent with the Hellenic model. They did not exhibit violent action, the evolution of individual character, or the conflict of egos to any more notable extent than did the works of Sophocles or Aeschylus. Among the best-known tragedies of Euripides are *Alcestis, Medea,* and *The Trojan Women.*

Hellenic comedy was definitely inferior to tragedy. In common with tragedy it appears to have grown out of the Dionysiac festivals, but it did not attain full development until late in the fifth century B.C. Its only outstanding representative was Aristophanes (448?–

380?), a somewhat coarse and belligerent aristocrat who lived in Athens. Most of his plays were written to satirize the political and intellectual ideals of the radical democracy of his time. In *The Knights* he pilloried the incompetent and greedy politicians for their reckless adventures in imperialism. In *The Frogs* he lampooned Euripides for the innovations the latter had made in the drama. *The Clouds* he reserved for ridicule of the Sophists, ignorantly or maliciously classifying Socrates as one of them. While he was undoubtedly a clever poet with a mastery of subtle humor and imaginative skill, his ideas were founded largely upon prejudice.[9]

No account of Greek literature would be complete without some mention of the two great historians of the Golden Age. Herodotus, the "father of history" (484–425), was a native of Halicarnassus in *The Greek historians: Herodotus* Asia Minor. He traveled extensively through the Persian empire, Egypt, Greece, and Italy, collecting a multitude of interesting data about various peoples. His famous account of the great war between the Greeks and the Persians included so much background that the work seems almost a history of the world. He regarded that war as an epic struggle between East and West, with Zeus giving victory to the Greeks against a mighty host of barbarians.

Thucydides

If Herodotus deserves to be called the father of history, much more does his younger contemporary, Thucydides, deserve to be considered the founder of scientific history. Influenced by the skepticism and practicality of the Sophists, Thucydides chose to work on the basis of carefully sifted evidence, rejecting opinions, legends, and hearsay. The subject of his *History* was the war between Sparta and Athens, which he described scientifically and dispassionately, emphasizing the complexity of causes which led to the fateful clash. His aim was to present an accurate record which could be studied with profit by statesmen and generals of all time, and it must be said that he was in full measure successful. If there was any defect in his historical method, it consisted in overemphasizing political factors to the neglect of the social and economic.

See color plates at pages 156, 157

7. The Meaning of Greek Art

Probably art even more than literature reflected the true character of Hellenic civilization. The Greek was essentially a materialist who conceived his world in physical terms. Plato and the followers of the *The importance of Greek art* mystic religions were, of course, exceptions, but very few other Greeks had much interest in a universe of spiritual realities. It would be natural therefore to find that the material emblems of architecture and sculpture should exemplify best the ideals which the Greek held before him.

What did Greek art express? Above all, it symbolized humanism

---

[9] He is deserving of much credit, however, for his sharp criticisms of the stupid policies of the war-hawks of Athens during the struggle with Sparta.

—the glorification of man as the most important creature in the universe. Though much of the sculpture depicted gods, this did not detract in the slightest from its humanistic quality. The Greek deities existed for the benefit of man, so that in glorifying them he glorified himself. Certainly there was nothing mystical or otherworldly in the religious aspects of Greek art. Both architecture and sculpture embodied the ideals of balance, harmony, order, and moderation. Anarchy and excess were abhorrent to the mind of the Greek, but so was absolute repression. Consequently, his art exhibited qualities of simplicity and dignified restraint—free from decorative extravagance, on the one hand, and from restrictive conventions on the other. Moreover, Greek art was an expression of the national life. Its purpose was not merely aesthetic but political: to symbolize the pride of the people in their city and to enhance their consciousness of unity. The Parthenon at Athens, for example, was the temple of Athena, the protecting goddess who presided over the corporate life of the state. In providing her with a beautiful shrine which she might frequently visit, the Athenians were giving evidence of their love for their city and their hope for its continuing welfare.

The art of the Hellenes differed from that of nearly every people

*The ideals
embodied
in Greek art*

The Parthenon. The largest and most famous of Athenian temples, the Parthenon is considered the classic example of Doric architecture. Its columns were made more graceful by tapering them in a slight curve toward the top. Its friezes and pediments were decorated with lifelike sculptures of prancing horses, fighting giants, and benign and confident deities.

*Greek art
compared with
that of later
peoples*

since their time in an interesting variety of ways. Like most of the tragedies of Aeschylus and Sophocles, it was universal. It included few portraits of personalities either in sculpture or in painting.[10] The human beings depicted were generally types, not individuals. Again, Greek art differed from that of most later peoples in its ethical purpose. It was not art for the sake of mere decoration or for the expression of the artist's individual philosophy, but it was a medium for the ennoblement of man. This does not mean that it was didactic in the sense that its merit was determined by the moral lesson it taught; but rather that it was supposed to exemplify qualities of living essentially artistic in themselves. The Athenian, at least, drew no sharp distinction between the ethical and aesthetic spheres; the beautiful and the good were really identical. True morality therefore consisted in rational living, in the avoidance of grossness, disgusting excesses, and other forms of conduct aesthetically offensive. Finally, Greek art may be contrasted with most later forms in the fact that it was not "naturalistic." Although the utmost attention was given to the depiction of beautiful bodies, this had nothing to do with fidelity to nature. The Greek was not interested in interpreting nature for its own sake, but in expressing *human* ideals.

Marble Statue of the Apollo Type. Probably end of Seventh Century B.C. At this time Greek sculpture was still under Egyptian influence, as can be seen in the headdress, the imperturbable face, and the arms and feet of this statue.

[10] Most of the portraits in sculpture commonly considered Greek really belong to the Hellenistic Age, although a few were produced at the end of the fourth century B.C.

Details of the Three Famous Orders of Greek Architecture. A, Doric;
B, Ionic; C, Corinthian.

The history of Greek art divides itself naturally into three great periods. The first, which can be called the archaic period, covered the seventh and sixth centuries. During the greater part of this age sculpture was dominated by Egyptian influence, as can be seen in the *frontality and rigidity of the statues*, with their square shoulders and one foot slightly advanced. Toward the end, however, these conventions were thrown aside. The chief architectural styles also had their origin in this period, and several crude temples were built. The second period, which occupied the fifth century, witnessed the full perfection of both architecture and sculpture. The art of this time was completely idealistic. During the fourth century, which was the last period of Hellenic art, architecture declined and sculpture assumed new characteristics. It came to reflect more clearly the reactions of the individual artist, to incorporate traces of realism, and to lose some of its quality as an expression of civic pride.

Periods in the evolution of Greek art

For all its artistic excellence, Greek temple architecture was one of the simplest of structural forms. Its essential elements were really only five in number: (1) the cella or nucleus of the building, which was a rectangular chamber to house the statue of the god; (2) the columns, which formed the porch and surrounded the cella; (3) the entablature or lintel, which rested upon the columns and supported the roof; (4) the gabled roof itself; and (5) the pediment or triangular section under the gable of the roof. Two different architectural styles were developed, representing modifications of certain of these elements. The more popular was the Doric, which made use of a rather heavy, sharply fluted column surmounted by a plain capital. The other, the Ionic, had more slender and more graceful columns with flat flutings, a triple base, and a scroll or volute capital. The so-called Corinthian style, which was chiefly Hellenistic, differed from the Ionic primarily in being more ornate. The Parthenon, the best example of Greek architecture, was essentially a Doric build-

Architecture

177

ing, but it reflected some of the grace and subtlety of Ionic influence.

According to the prevailing opinion among critics, Greek sculpture attained its acme of development in the work of Phidias (500?–432?). His masterpieces were the statue of Athena in the Parthenon and the statue of Zeus in the Temple of Olympian Zeus. In addition, he designed and supervised the execution of the Parthenon reliefs. The main qualities of his work are grandeur of conception, patriotism,

Reconstruction of the Interior of the Parthenon. The statue was a resplendent gold and ivory figure of Athena, protecting goddess of the city state. Like most of the rest of Parthenon sculpture, it was the work of Phidias.

Temple of Athena Nike. This temple, in Athens, is one of the most graceful specimens of the Ionic style. Planned by Pericles in 450 B.C., it was probably not completed until nearly the end of the Fifth Century.

proportion, dignity, and restraint. Nearly all of his figures are idealized representations of deities and mythological creatures in human form. The second most important fifth-century sculptor was Myron, famous for his statue of the discus thrower and for his glorification of other athletic types. The names of three great sculptors in the fourth century have come down to us. The most gifted of them was Praxiteles, renowned for his portrayal of humanized deities with slender, graceful bodies and countenances of philosophic repose. The best known of his works is the statue of Hermes with the infant Dionysus. His older contemporary, Scopas, gained distinction as an emotional sculptor. One of his most successful creations was the statue of a religious ecstatic, a worshiper of Dionysus, in a condition of mystic frenzy. At the end of the century Lysippus introduced even stronger qualities of realism and individualism into sculpture. He was the first great master of the realistic portrait as a study of personal character.

Hermes with the Infant Dionysus, by Praxiteles, Fourth Century B.C. The god Hermes is represented as a slender, graceful youth, reflecting the humanism of Greek religion. The countenance suggests an attitude of repose and philosophic contentment. Original in the Olympia Museum, Greece.

The *Discobolus,* or Discus Thrower, of Myron. This statue reflects the glorification of the human body characteristic of Athens in the Golden Age. The proportions of the figure, the development and co-ordination of the muscles, and the repose and confidence of the face are perfect. *The Discobolus* is now in the Vatican Museum. **179**

8. *Athenian Life in the Golden Age*

The population of Athens in the fifth and fourth centuries was divided into three distinct groups: the citizens, the metics, and the slaves. The citizens, who numbered at the most about 160,000, included only those born of citizen parents, except for the few who were occasionally enfranchised by special law. The metics, who probably did not exceed a total of 100,000, were resident aliens, chiefly non-Athenian Greeks, although some were Phoenicians and Jews. Save for the fact that they had no political privileges and generally were not permitted to own land, the metics had equal opportunities with citizens. They could engage in any occupation they desired and participate in any social or intellectual activities. Contrary to a popular tradition, the slaves in Athens were never a majority of the population. Their maximum number does not seem to have exceeded 140,000. On the whole, they were very well treated and were often rewarded for faithful service by being set free. They could work for wages and own property, and some of them held responsible positions as minor public officials and as managers of banks.

The amazing degree of social and economic equality

Life in Athens stands out in rather sharp contrast to that in most other civilizations. One of its leading features was the amazing degree of social and economic equality which prevailed among all the inhabitants. Although there were many who were poor, there were few who were very rich. The average wage was the same for practically all classes of workers, skilled and unskilled alike. Nearly everyone, whether citizen, metic, or slave, ate the same kind of food, wore the same kind of clothing, and participated in the same kind of amusement. This substantial equality was enforced in part by the system of *liturgies*, which were services to the state rendered by wealthy men, chiefly in the form of contributions to support the drama, equip the navy, or provide for the poor.

The poverty of Athenian life

A second outstanding characteristic of Athenian life was its poverty in comforts and luxuries. Part of this was due to the low income of the mass of the people. Teachers, sculptors, masons, carpenters, and common laborers all received the same standard wage of one drachma (about 30 cents) per day. Part of it may have been due also to the mild climate, which made possible a life of simplicity. But whatever the cause, the fact remains that, in comparison with modern standards, the Athenians endured an exceedingly impoverished existence. They knew nothing of such common things as watches, soap, newspapers, cotton cloth, sugar, tea, or coffee. Their beds had no springs, their houses had no drains, and their food consisted chiefly of barley cakes, onions, and fish, washed down with diluted wine. From the standpoint of clothing they were no better off. A rectangular piece of cloth wrapped around the body and fastened with pins at the shoulders and with a rope around the waist served as the main garment. A larger piece was draped around the body as an extra garment for outdoor wear. No one wore either stockings or socks, and few had any footgear except sandals.

But lack of comforts and luxuries was a matter of little consequence to the Athenian citizen. He was totally unable to regard these as the most important things in life. His aim was to live as interestingly and contentedly as possible without spending all his days in grinding toil for the sake of a little more comfort for his family. Nor was he interested in piling up riches as a source of power or prestige. What each citizen really wanted was a small farm or business which would provide him with a reasonable income and at the same time allow him an abundance of leisure for politics, for gossip in the market place, and for intellectual or artistic activities if he had the talent to enjoy them.

Indifference toward the business of making a living

It is frequently supposed that the Athenian was too lazy or too snobbish to work hard for luxury and security. But such was not quite the case. It is true that there were some occupations in which he would not engage, because he considered them degrading or destructive of moral freedom. He would not break his back digging silver or copper out of a mine; such work was fit only for slaves of the lowest intellectual level. On the other hand, there is plenty of evidence to show that the great majority of Athenian citizens did not look with disdain upon manual labor. Most of them worked on their farms or in their shops as independent craftsmen. Hundreds of others earned their living as hired laborers employed either by the state or by their fellow Athenians. Cases are on record of citizens, metics, and slaves working side by side, all for the same wage, in the construction of public buildings; and in at least one instance the foreman of the crew was a slave.[11]

Attitudes toward work

In spite of expansion of trade and increase in population, the economic organization of Athenian society remained comparatively simple. Agriculture and commerce were by far the most important enterprises. Even in Pericles' day the majority of the citizens still lived in the country. Industry was not highly developed. Very few examples of large-scale production are on record, and those chiefly in the manufacture of pottery and implements of war. The largest establishment that ever existed was apparently a shield factory owned by a metic and employing 120 slaves. There was no other more than half as large. The enterprises which absorbed the most labor were the mines, but they were owned by the state and were leased in sections to petty contractors to be worked by slaves. The bulk of industry was carried on in small shops owned by individual craftsmen who produced their wares directly to the order of the consumer.

The basic economic activities

Religion underwent some notable changes in the Golden Age. The primitive polytheism and anthropomorphism of the Homeric myths were largely supplanted, among intellectuals at least, by a belief in one God as the creator and sustainer of the moral law. Such

Changes in religion

[11] A. E. Zimmern, *The Greek Commonwealth*, p. 258.

a doctrine was taught by many of the philosophers, by the poet Pindar, and by the dramatists Aeschylus and Sophocles. Other significant consequences flowed from the mystery cults. These new forms of religion first became popular in the sixth century because of the craving for an emotional faith to make up for the disappointments of life. The more important of them was the Orphic cult, which revolved around the myth of the death and resurrection of Dionysus. The other, the Eleusinian cult, had as its central theme the abduction of Persephone by Pluto, god of the nether world, and her ultimate redemption by Demeter, the great Earth Mother. Both of these cults had as their original purpose the promotion of the life-giving powers of nature, but in time they came to be fraught with a much deeper significance. They expressed to their followers the ideas of vicarious atonement, salvation in an afterlife, and ecstatic union with the divine. Although entirely inconsistent with the spirit of the ancient religion, they made a powerful appeal to certain classes of Greeks and were largely responsible for the spread of the belief in personal immortality. The majority of the people, however, seem to have persisted in their adherence to the worldly, optimistic, and mechanical faith of their ancestors and to have shown little concern about a conviction of sin or a desire for salvation in a life to come.

The family in Athens in the Golden Age

It remains to consider briefly the position of the family in Athens in the fifth and fourth centuries. Though marriage was still an important institution for the procreation of children who would become citizens of the state, there is reason to believe that family life had declined. Men of the more prosperous classes, at least, now spent the greater part of their time away from their families. Wives were relegated to an inferior position and required to remain secluded in their homes. Their place as social and intellectual companions for their husbands was taken by alien women, the famous *hetaerae*, many of whom were highly cultured natives of the Ionian cities. Marriage itself assumed the character of a political and economic arrangement, devoid of romantic elements. Men married wives so as to ensure that at least some of their children would be legitimate and in order to obtain property in the form of a dowry. It was important also, of course, to have someone to care for the household. But husbands did not consider their wives as their equals and did not appear in public with them or encourage their participation in any form of social or intellectual activity.

9. The Greek Achievement and Its Significance for Us

The magnitude of the Greek achievement

No careful historian would deny that the achievement of the Greeks was one of the most remarkable in the history of the world. With no great expanse of fertile soil or abundance of mineral resources, they succeeded in developing a higher and more varied civilization than any of the most richly favored nations of the

The Parthenon, Detail. Frieze of carved panels (metopes) and grooved blocks (triglyphs). Reclining figures fitted pediment angles.

Orient had ever brought forth. With only a limited cultural inheritance from the past to build upon as a foundation, they produced intellectual and artistic achievements which have served ever since as the chief inspiration to man in his quest for wisdom and beauty. It seems reasonable to conclude also that they achieved a more normal and more rational mode of living than most other peoples who have strutted and fretted their hour upon this planet. The absence of violent revolution except in the earlier period, the infrequency of brutal crimes, and the contentment with simple amusements and modest wealth all point to a comparatively happy and satisfied existence. Moreover, the sane moral attitude of the Greek helped to keep him almost entirely free from the nervous instability and emotional conflicts which wreak so much havoc in modern society. Suicide, for example, was exceedingly rare in Greece.[12]

It is necessary to be on our guard, however, against certain un-

[12] For a discussion of this point see E. A. Westermarck, *The Origin and Development of Moral Ideas*, pp. 247 ff.

183

*Undesirable
features
of Greek life*

*Hellenic influ-
ence sometimes
exaggerated*

*The influence
of the Greeks
on the West*

critical judgments which are sometimes expressed in reference to the achievement of the Greeks. We must not assume that all of the natives of Hellas were as cultured, wise, and free as the citizens of Athens and of the Ionian states across the Aegean. The Spartans, the Arcadians, the Thessalians, and probably the majority of the Boeotians remained untutored and benighted from the beginning to the end of their history. Furthermore, the Athenian civilization itself was not without its defects. It permitted some exploitation of the weak, especially of the ignorant slaves who toiled in the mines. It was based upon a principle of racial exclusiveness which reckoned every man a foreigner whose parents were not both Athenians and consequently denied political rights to the majority of the inhabitants of the country. Its statecraft was not sufficiently enlightened to avoid the pitfalls of imperialism and even of aggressive war. Finally, the attitude of its citizens was not always tolerant and just. Socrates was put to death for his opinions, and two other philosophers, Anaxagoras and Protagoras, were forced to leave the country.[13]

Nor is it true that the Hellenic influence has really been as great as is commonly supposed. No intelligent student could accept the sentimental verdict of Shelley: "We are all Greeks; our laws, our literature, our religion, our arts have their roots in Greece." Our laws do not really have their roots in Greece but chiefly in Hellenistic and Roman sources. Much of our poetry is undoubtedly Greek in inspiration, but such is not the case with most of our prose literature. Our religion is no more than partly Greek; except as it was influenced by Plato, Aristotle, and the Romans, it reflects primarily the spirit of the Orient. Even our arts take their form and meaning from Rome as much as from Greece. Actually, modern civilization has been the result of the convergence of several influences coming from a variety of sources. The influence from Greece has been partly overshadowed by heritages from the Near Orient and from the Romans and the Germans. Philosophy appears to have been the only important segment of Greek civilization which has been incorporated into modern culture virtually intact.

In spite of all this, the Hellenic adventure was of profound significance for the history of the world. For the Greeks were the founders of nearly all those ideals which we commonly think of as peculiar to the West. The civilizations of the ancient Orient, with the exception, to a certain extent, of the Hebrew, Egyptian, and Chinese, were dominated by absolutism, supernaturalism, ecclesiasticism, the denial of both body and mind, and the subjection of the individual to the group. Their political regime was the reign of force

[13] It must be conceded, however, that the record of the Athenians for tolerance was better than that of most other nations, both ancient and modern. There was probably more freedom of expression in Athens during the war with Sparta than there was in the United States during the war of 1917–1918 with Germany.

The Acropolis Today. Occupying the commanding position is the Parthenon. To the left is the Erech- theum with its Porch of the Maidens facing the Parthenon.

as expressed in an absolute monarch supported by a powerful priesthood. Their religion was the worship of omnipotent gods who demanded that man should humble and despise himself for the purpose of their greater glory. Culture in these mighty empires served mainly as an instrument to magnify the power of the state and to enhance the prestige of rulers and priests.

By contrast, the civilization of Greece, notably in its Athenian form, was founded upon ideals of freedom, optimism, secularism, rationalism, the glorification of both body and mind, and a high regard for the dignity and worth of the individual man. In so far as the individual was subjected at all, his subjection was to the rule of the majority. Religion was worldly and practical, serving the interests of human beings. Worship of the gods was a means for the ennoblement of man. As opposed to the ecclesiasticism of the Orient, the Greeks had no organized priesthood at all. They kept their priests in the background and refused under any circumstances to allow them to define dogma or to govern the realm of intellect. In addition, they excluded them from control over the sphere of morality. The culture of the Greeks was the first to be based upon the primacy of intellect—upon the supremacy of the spirit of free inquiry. There was no subject they feared to investigate, or any question they regarded as excluded from the province of reason. To an extent never before realized, mind was supreme over faith; logic and science over superstition.[14]

Contrast of Greek and Oriental ideals

[14] For further discussion of the contrast between Hellas and the Orient see the admirable study by Edith Hamilton, *The Greek Way.*

185

*The tragedy of
Hellenic history*

The supreme tragedy of the Greeks was, of course, their failure to solve the problem of political conflict. To a large degree, this conflict was the product of social and cultural dissimilarities. Because of different geographic and economic conditions the Greek city-states developed at an uneven pace. Some went forward rapidly to high levels of cultural superiority, while others lagged behind and made little or no intellectual progress. The consequences were discord and suspicion, which gave rise eventually to hatred and fear. Though some of the more advanced thinkers made efforts to propagate the notion that the Hellenes were one people who should reserve their contempt for non-Hellenes, or "barbarians," the conception never became part of a national ethos. Athenians hated Spartans, and *vice versa*, just as vehemently as they hated Lydians or Persians. Not even the danger of Asiatic conquest was sufficient to dispel the distrust and antagonism of Greeks for one another. The war that finally broke out between Athenians and Spartans sealed the doom of Hellenic civilization just as effectively as could ever have resulted from foreign conquest. For a time it appeared as if a new world, largely devoid of ethnic distinctions, might emerge from the ruins of the Greek city-states, as a result of the conquests of Alexander the Great. Alexander dreamed of such a world, in which there would be neither Athenian nor Spartan, Greek nor Egyptian, but unfortunately neither he nor his generals knew any means of achieving it except to impose it by force. The parallels between the last phases of Hellenic history and the developments in our own time are at least interesting, if not conclusive.

Selected Readings

· *Items so designated are available in paperbound editions.*

Abbot, Evelyn, *Pericles and the Golden Age of Athens*, New York, 1925.
· Agard, Walter, *What Democracy Meant to the Greeks*, Chapel Hill, 1942. (Wisconsin)
· Barker, Ernest, *Greek Political Theory: Plato and His Predecessors*, New York, 1919, 2 vols. (Barnes & Noble) One of the best of the commentaries.
· Burnet, John, *Early Greek Philosophy*, New York, 1930. (Meridian)
Burn, A. R., *Pericles and Athens*, New York, 1949.
Cooper, Lane, ed., *The Greek Genius and Its Influence*, New Haven, 1917.
· Dickinson, G. L., *The Greek View of Life*, New York, 1927. (Ann Arbor, Collier) An excellent interpretation.
Ehrenberg, Victor, *The Greek State*, New York, 1960.
Ferguson, W. S., *Greek Imperialism*, Boston, 1913.
Fowler, H. N., *A History of Ancient Greek Literature*, New York, 1923.
Gardner, Percy, *The Principles of Greek Art*, New York, 1926.
Glotz, Gustave, *Ancient Greece at Work*, New York, 1926. A good account of Greek economic conditions.
Glover, T. R., *Democracy in the Ancient World*, New York, 1927.
Grant, A. J., *Greece in the Age of Pericles*, New York, 1897.
· Hamilton, Edith, *The Greek Way*, New York, 1930. (New American Library) Thoughtful and stimulating.

Larsen, J. A. O., *Representative Government in Greek and Roman History*,
Berkeley, 1955.
Livingstone, R. W., ed., *The Legacy of Greece*, New York, 1928.
Mahaffy, J. P., *Social Life in Greece from Homer to Menander*, New York, 1907.
——, *What Have the Greeks Done for Modern Civilization?* New York, 1909.
Mitchell, H., *Sparta*, New York, 1952.
Moore, C. H., *The Religious Thought of the Greeks*, Cambridge, Mass., 1925.
Oakeley, H. D., *Greek Ethical Thought from Homer to the Stoics*, Boston, 1950.
Ridder, A. H. P. de, and Deonna, Waldemar, *Art in Greece*, New York, 1927.
Perhaps the best one-volume account.
Robin, Leon, *Greek Thought and the Origins of the Scientific Spirit*, New York, 1928.
· Ross, W. D., *Aristotle*, New York, 1924. (Meridian)
Sarton, George, *A History of Science: Ancient Science through the Golden Age of Greece*, Cambridge, Mass., 1952.
——, *An Introduction to the History of Science*, Baltimore, 1927, Vol. I. The most complete and comprehensive account.
Sedgwick, W. T., and Tyler, H. W., *A Short History of Science*, New York, 1925.
Seymour, T. D., *Life in the Homeric Age*, New York, 1907. An excellent survey of political, social and religious life in the archaic period.
Smith, Morton, *The Ancient Greeks*, Ithaca, 1960. A volume in the Development of Western Civilization Series.
Trever, A. A., *History of Ancient Civilization*, New York, 1939, Vol. I.
Tucker, T. G., *Life in Ancient Athens*, New York, 1907.
Westermann, W. L., *The Slave Systems of Greek and Roman Antiquity*, Philadelphia, 1955.
· Zimmern, A. E., *The Greek Commonwealth*, New York, 1911. (Galaxy) Good, though perhaps a bit too laudatory of the Athenians.

Source Materials

Adams, Francis, *The Genuine Works of Hippocrates.*
Aristotle, *Politics; Ethics; History of Animals.*
Herodotus, *History.*
Hesiod, *Works and Days.*
Homer, *The Iliad; The Odyssey.*
Plato, *Dialogues*, especially "The Republic," "Phaedo," "The Apology," and "The Sophist." See especially improved translation by D. J. Allan and H. E. Dale, Oxford, 1953.
Plutarch, *Lives of Illustrious Men*, especially "Lycurgus," "Solon," "Pericles," "Aristides," "Themistocles."
Thucydides, *History of the Peloponnesian War.*
Xenophon, *Memorabilia.*

The Hellenistic Civilization

Beauty and virtue and the like are to be honored, if they give
pleasure, but if they do not give pleasure, we must bid them
farewell.

—Epicurus, "On the End of Life"

I agree that Alexander was carried away so far as to copy oriental
luxury. I hold that no mighty deeds, not even conquering the
whole world, is of any good unless the man has learned mastery
of himself.

—Arrian, *Anabasis of Alexander*

A new stage in world history

The death of Alexander the Great in 323 B.C. marked the beginning
of a new stage in world history. Hellenic civilization, properly defined, was now at an end. The fusion of cultures and intermingling
of peoples resulting from Alexander's conquests had accomplished
the overthrow of most of the ideals represented by the Greeks in
their prime. Gradually a new pattern of civilization emerged based
upon a mixture of Greek and Oriental elements. To this new civilization, which lasted until about the beginning of the Christian era,
the name Hellenistic is the one most commonly applied.

Comparison of the Hellenistic Age with the Golden Age of Greece

While the Hellenistic Age is sometimes regarded as simply a final
chapter in the history of Greece, this is by no means correct. The
centuries which followed the death of Alexander were so markedly
different from the Golden Age of Greece that they cannot be accurately regarded as a continuation of it. Though the language of the
new era was Greek, and though persons of Greek nationality continued to play an active role in many affairs, the spirit of the culture
was largely the spirit of the Orient. The classical ideal of democracy
was now superseded by despotism perhaps as rigorous as any that
Egypt or Persia had ever produced. The Hellenic devotion to simplicity and the golden mean gave way to extravagance in art and to
a love of luxury and riotous excess. The Athenian economic system
of small-scale production was supplanted by the growth of big business and ruthless competition for profits. Though progress in science continued, the sublime confidence in the power of the mind
which had characterized the teachings of most of the philosophers
from Thales to Aristotle was swallowed up in defeatism and ultimately in the sacrifice of logic to faith. In view of these changes it
seems justifiable to conclude that the Hellenistic Age was really
the era of a new civilization as distinct from the Greek as modern
civilization is from the culture of the Middle Ages.

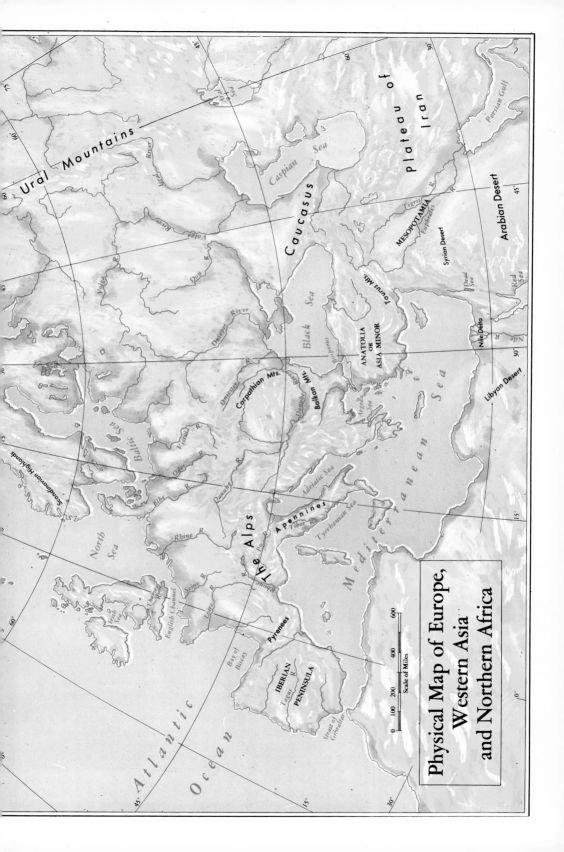

Physical Map of Europe,
Western Asia
and Northern Africa

Scale of Miles
0   100   200   400   600

Unidentified Man, I cent. B.C. The Romans excelled in portraits of sharp individuality.

Augustus, Reigned 31 B.C.–14 A.D. This portrait suggests the contradictory nature of the genius who gave Rome peace after years of strife.

Constantine, Reign 306–337 A.D. The head from a statue sixteen f in height. Such colo marked the decline Roman sculpture.

Wall Painting, I cent. B.C. From a villa near Pompeii.

Mosaic, I cent. A.D. A floor design composed of small pieces of colored marble fitted together to form a picture.

Wall Painting of a Satyr Mask, I cent. B.C. The belief in satyrs, thought to inhabit forests and pastures, was taken over from the Greeks.

Mummy Portrait, II cent. A.D. A Roman woman buried in Egypt.

Architectural Wall Painting fr a Pompeiian Villa, I cent. B suggesting the Greek origin Roman forms of architecture.

1. Political History and Institutions

When Alexander died in 323 B.C., he left no legitimate heir to succeed him. His nearest male relative was a feeble-minded half-brother. Tradition relates that when his friends requested him on his deathbed to designate a successor, he replied vaguely, "To the best man." After his death his highest ranking generals proceeded to divide the empire among them. Some of the younger commanders contested this arrangement, and a series of wars followed which culminated in the decisive battle of Ipsus in 301 B.C. The result of this battle was a new division among the victors. Seleucus took possession of Persia, Mesopotamia, and Syria; Lysimachus assumed control over Asia Minor and Thrace; Cassander established himself in Macedonia; and Ptolemy added Phoenicia and Palestine to his original domain of Egypt. Twenty years later these four states were reduced to three when Seleucus defeated and killed Lysimachus in battle and appropriated his kingdom. In the meantime most of the Greek states had revolted against the attempts of the Macedonian king to extend his power over them. By banding together in defensive leagues several of them succeeded in maintaining their independence for nearly a century. Finally, between 146 and 30 B.C. nearly all of the Hellenistic territory passed under Roman rule.

The Hellenistic states

The dominant form of government in the Hellenistic Age was the despotism of kings who represented themselves as at least semi-divine. Alexander himself was hailed as divine in Egypt. His most powerful successors, the Seleucid kings in Western Asia and the Ptolemies in Egypt, made more systematic attempts to deify themselves. A Seleucid monarch, Antiochus IV, adopted the title "Epiphanes" or "God Manifest." The later members of the dynasty of the Ptolemies signed their decrees "Theos" (God) and revived the practice of sister marriage which had been followed by the Pharaohs as a means of preserving the divine blood of the royal family from contamination. Only in the kingdom of Macedonia was despotism tempered by a modicum of respect for the liberties of the citizens.

Divine monarchy the dominant form of government

Two other political institutions developed as by-products of Hellenistic civilization: the Achaean and Aetolian Leagues. We have already seen that most of the Greek states rebelled against Macedonian rule following the division of Alexander's empire. The better to preserve their independence, several of these states formed alliances among themselves, which were gradually expanded to become confederate leagues. The states of the Peloponnesus, with the exception of Sparta and Elis, were united in the Achaean League, while the Aetolian federation included nearly all of central Greece with the exception of Athens. The organization of these leagues was essentially the same in both cases. Each had a federal council composed of representatives of the member cities with power to enact laws on subjects of general concern. An assembly which all of the

The Achaean and Aetolian Leagues

citizens in the federated states could attend decided questions of war and peace and elected officials. Executive and military authority was vested in the hands of a general, elected for one year and eligible for re-election only in alternate years. Although these leagues are frequently described as federal states, they were scarcely more than confederacies. The central authority, like the government of the American States under the Articles of Confederation, was dependent upon the local governments for contributions of revenue and troops. Furthermore, the powers delegated to the central government were limited primarily to matters of war and peace, coinage, and weights and measures. The chief significance of these Leagues is to be found in the fact that they embodied the principle of representative government and constituted the nearest approach ever made in Greece to voluntary national union.

2. Significant Economic and Social Developments

The economic revolution and its causes

The history of the Hellenistic civilization was marked by economic developments second only in magnitude to the Commercial and Industrial Revolutions of the modern era. Several important causes can be distinguished: (1) the opening up of a vast area of trade from the Indus River to the Nile as a result of the Alexandrian conquests; (2) the rise in prices as a consequence of the release of the enormous Persian hoard of gold and silver into the channels of circulation, resulting in an increase in investment and speculation; and (3) the promotion of trade and industry by governments as a means of augmenting the revenues of the state. The net result of these factors was the growth of a system of large-scale production, trade, and finance, with the state as the principal capitalist and entrepreneur.

Developments in agriculture

Agriculture was as profoundly affected by the new developments as any other branch of the economic life. The most striking phenomena were the concentration of holdings of land and the degradation of the agricultural population. One of the first things which the successors of Alexander did was to confiscate the estates of the chief landowners and add them to the royal domain. The lands thus acquired were either granted to the favorites of the king or leased to tenants under an arrangement calculated to ensure an abundant income for the crown. The tenants were generally forbidden to leave the lands they cultivated until after the harvest and were not allowed to dispose of their grain until after the king had had a chance to sell the share which he received as rent at the highest price the market would bring. When some of the tenants went on strike or attempted to run away, they were all bound to the soil as hereditary serfs. Many of the small independent farmers also became serfs when they got into debt as a result of inability to compete with large-scale production.

190   In an effort to make all of the resources of the state contribute to

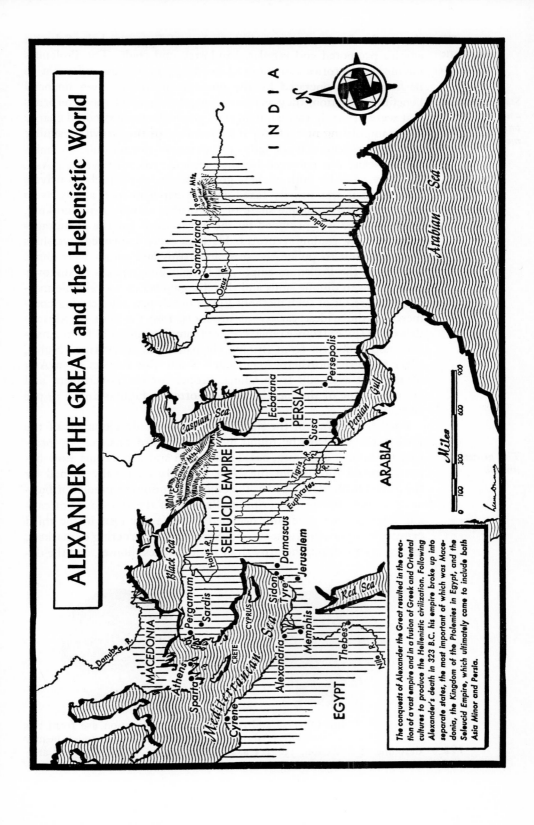

ALEXANDER THE GREAT and the Hellenistic World

INDIA

Arabian Sea

Pamir Mts.

Samarkand

Oxus R.

Indus R.

Caspian Sea

Ecbatana

PERSIA

Persepolis

Susa

SELEUCID EMPIRE

Caucasus Mts.

Persian Gulf

Halys R.

Tigris R.

Euphrates R.

ARABIA

Black Sea

Pergamum

Sardis

Damascus

Jerusalem

Sidon

Tyre

CYPRUS

Mediterranean Sea

CRETE

Memphis

Red Sea

Alexandria

MACEDONIA

Athens

Sparta

Cyrene

Thebes

Nile R.

EGYPT

Danube R.

Miles

0   100   300   600   900

The conquests of Alexander the Great resulted in the creation of a vast empire and in a fusion of Greek and Oriental
cultures to produce the Hellenistic civilization. Following
Alexander's death in 323 B.C. his empire broke up into
separate states, the most important of which was Macedonia, the Kingdom of the Ptolemies in Egypt, and the
Seleucid Empire, which ultimately came to include both
Asia Minor and Persia.

**THE
HELLENISTIC
CIVILIZATION**

*State capitalism
and regimen-
tation of com-
merce*

the profit of the government, the rulers of Egypt and the Seleucid empire promoted and regulated industry and trade. The Ptolemies established factories and shops in nearly every village and town to be owned and operated by the government for its own financial benefit. In addition, they assumed control over all of the enterprises that were privately owned, fixing the prices the owners could charge and manipulating markets for the advantage of the crown. A similar plan of regimentation for industry, although not on quite so ambitious a scale, was enforced by the Seleucid rulers of western Asia. Trade was left by both of these governments very largely in private hands, but it was heavily taxed and regulated in such a way as to make sure that an ample share of the profits would go to the king. Every facility was provided by the government for the encouragement of new trading ventures. Harbors were improved, warships were sent out to police the seas, and roads and canals were built. Moreover, the Ptolemies employed famous geographers to discover new routes to distant lands and thereby gain access to valuable markets. As a result of such methods Egypt developed a flourishing commerce in the widest variety of products. Into the port of Alexandria came spices from Arabia, copper from Cyprus, gold from Abyssinia and India, tin from Britain, elephants and ivory from Nubia, silver from the northern Aegean and Spain, fine carpets from Asia Minor, and even silk from China. Profits for the government and even for some of the merchants were often as high as 20 or 30 per cent.

Further evidence of the significant economic development of the Hellenistic Age is to be found in the growth of finance. An international money economy, based upon gold and silver coins, now became general throughout the Near East. Banks, usually owned by the government, developed as the chief institutions of credit for business ventures of every description. Because of the abundance of capital, interest rates gradually declined from 12 per cent in the third century to 7 per cent in the second. Speculation, cornering of markets, intense competition, the growth of large business houses, and the de-

Hellenistic Coins. Obverse and reverse sides of the silver tetradrachma of Macedon, 336–323 B.C.

Objects of common use from this period often show as much beauty of design as formal works of art.

velopment of insurance and advertising were other significant phenomena of this remarkable age.

According to the available evidence, the Hellenistic Age, during the first two centuries at least, was a period of prosperity. Although serious crises frequently followed the collapse of speculative booms, they appear to have been of short duration. But the prosperity that existed seems to have been limited chiefly to the rulers, the upper classes, and the merchants. It certainly did not extend to the peasants or even to the workers in the towns. The daily wages of both skilled and unskilled workers in Athens in the third century had dropped to less than half of what they had been in the Age of Pericles. The cost of living, on the other hand, had risen considerably. To make matters worse, unemployment in the large cities was so serious a problem that the government had to provide free grain for many of the inhabitants. Slavery declined in the Hellenistic world, partly because of the influence of the Stoic philosophy, but mainly for the reason that wages were now so low that it was cheaper to hire a free laborer than to purchase and maintain a slave.

Prosperity for the rich, slums and unemployment for the poor

An interesting result of social and economic conditions in the Hellenistic Age was the growth of metropolitan cities. Despite the fact that a majority of the people still dwelt in the country, there was an increasing tendency for men to become dissatisfied with the dullness of rural living and to flock into the cities, where life if not easier was at least more exciting. But the chief reasons are to be found in the expansion of industry and commerce, in the enlargement of governmental functions, and in the desire of former independent farmers to escape the hardships of serfdom. Cities multiplied and grew in the Hellenistic empires almost as rapidly as in nineteenth-century America. Some of them attained metropolitan size virtually overnight. Antioch in Syria quadrupled its population during a single century. Seleucia on the Tigris grew from nothing to a metropolis of several hundred thousand in less than two centuries. The largest and most famous of all the Hellenistic cities was Alexandria in Egypt with over 500,000 inhabitants and possibly as many as 1,000,000. No other city in ancient times, not even Rome, surpassed it in size or in magnificence. Its streets were well paved and laid out in regular order. It had splendid public buildings and parks, a museum, and a library of 750,000 volumes. It was the most brilliant center of Hellenistic cultural achievement, especially in the field of scientific research. The masses of its people, however, were a helpless mob without any share in the brilliant and luxurious life around them, although it was paid for in part out of the fruits of their labor.

The growth of metropolitan cities

3. Hellenistic Culture: Philosophy, Literature, and Art

Hellenistic philosophy went through a peculiar evolution—or retrogression, it might almost be better to say. During the first stage it was still under the influence of Greek thought and consequently

Gradual retrogression in philosophy

showed an elemental regard for reason as the key to the solution of man's problems. During what may be considered a second stage, skepticism concerning all truth and all values resulted in the rejection of reason entirely. Toward the end of the civilization philosophy degenerated into a barren mysticism, with the consequence that the whole intellectual approach, whether based upon reason or experience, was thrown into the discard. Despite the fundamental differences in their teachings, the philosophers of the Hellenistic Age were all agreed upon one thing: the necessity of finding some way of salvation for man from the hardships and evils of his existence.

Epicureanism and Stoicism

The first and most important of the Hellenistic philosophies were Epicureanism and Stoicism, both of which originated about 300 B.C. The founders were, respectively, Epicurus and Zeno, who were residents of Athens, though the former was born on the island of Samos, while the latter was a native of Cyprus, probably of Phoenician descent. Epicureanism and Stoicism had several features in common. Both were individualistic, concerned not with the welfare of society primarily, but with the good of the individual. Both were materialistic, denying categorically the existence of any spiritual substances; even divine beings and the soul were declared to be formed of matter. In Stoicism and Epicureanism alike there were definite traces of defeatism, since both of them implied that the efforts of man are futile and suggested a retreat into Oriental quietism as an aim for the wise to pursue. Lastly, the two philosophies were similar in their doctrines that concepts and abstractions are nothing but names, that only particular things are real, and that all knowledge has its basis in sense perception.

The Stoics pursue tranquillity of mind through fatalism

But in many ways the two systems were quite different. Zeno and his principal disciples taught that the cosmos is an ordered whole in which all contradictions are resolved for ultimate good. Evil is, therefore, relative; the particular misfortunes which befall human beings are but necessary incidents to the final perfection of the universe. Everything that happens is rigidly determined in accordance with rational purpose. Man is not master of his fate; his destiny is a link in an unbroken chain. He is free only in the sense that he can accept his fate or rebel against it. But whether he accepts or rebels, he cannot overcome it. The supreme duty of man is to submit to the order of the universe in the knowledge that that order is good; in other words, to resign himself as graciously as possible to his fate. Through such an act of resignation he will attain to the highest happiness, which consists in tranquillity of mind. The individual who is most truly happy is therefore the man who by the assertion of his rational nature has accomplished a perfect adjustment of his life to the cosmic purpose and has purged his soul of all bitterness and whining protest against evil turns of fortune.

The Stoics developed an ethical and social theory which accorded well with their general philosophy described above. Believing that the highest good consists in serenity of mind, they naturally emphasized duty and self-discipline as cardinal virtues. Recognizing the prevalence of particular evil, they taught that men should be tolerant and forgiving in their attitudes toward one another. They denied racial exclusiveness and held that all men are brothers under the fatherhood of one God. Unlike their contemporaries, the Cynics, they did not recommend that man should withdraw from society but urged participation in public affairs as a duty for the citizen of rational mind. They condemned slavery and war, but it was far from their purpose to preach any crusade against these evils. They were disposed to think that the results which would flow from violent measures of social change would be worse than the diseases they were supposed to cure. Besides, what difference did it make that the body should be in bondage so long as the mind was free? Despite its negative character the Stoic philosophy was the noblest product of the Hellenistic Age. Its equalitarianism, pacifism, and humanitarianism were important factors in mitigating the harshness not only of that time but of later centuries as well.

Whereas the Stoics went back to Heracleitus for much of their conception of the universe, the Epicureans derived their metaphysics chiefly from Democritus. Epicurus taught that the basic ingredients of all things are minute, indivisible atoms, and that change and growth are the results of the combination and separation of these particles. Nevertheless, while accepting the materialism of the atomists, Epicurus rejected their absolute mechanism. He denied that an automatic, mechanical motion of the atoms can be the cause of all things in the universe. Though he admitted that the atoms move downward in perpendicular lines because of their weight, he insisted upon endowing them with a spontaneous ability to swerve from the perpendicular and thereby to combine with one another. The chief reason for this peculiar modification of the atomic theory was to make possible a belief in human freedom. If the atoms were capable only of mechanical motion, then man, who is made up of atoms, would be reduced to the status of an automaton; and fatalism would be the law of the universe. In this repudiation of the mechanistic interpretation of life, Epicurus was probably closer to the Hellenic spirit than either Democritus or the Stoics.

The ethical philosophy of the Epicureans was based upon the doctrine that the highest good for man is pleasure. But they did not include all forms of indulgence in the category of genuine pleasure. The so-called pleasures of the debauched man should be avoided, since every excess of carnality must be balanced by its portion of pain. On the other hand, a moderate satisfaction of bodily appetites is permissible and may be regarded as a good in itself. Better than this is mental pleasure, sober contemplation of the reasons for the choice of some things and the avoidance of others, and mature reflection upon satisfactions previously enjoyed. The highest of all

The ethical and social teachings of the Stoics

Epicurus revives atomism but rules out determinism

The Epicureans pursue tranquillity of mind through overcoming fear of the supernatural

pleasures, however, consists in serenity of soul, in the complete absence of both mental and physical pain. This end can be best achieved through the elimination of fear, especially fear of the supernatural, since that is the sovereign source of mental pain. Man must recognize from the study of philosophy that the soul is material and therefore cannot survive the body, that the universe operates of itself, and that the gods do not intervene in human affairs. The gods live remote from the world and are too intent upon their own happiness to bother about what takes place on earth. Since they do not reward or punish men either in this life or in a life to come, there is no reason why they should be feared. The Epicureans thus came by a different route to the same general conclusion as the Stoics—the supreme good is tranquillity of mind.

The ethical and political theories of the Epicureans

The ethics of the Epicureans as well as their political theory rested squarely upon a utilitarian basis. In contrast with the Stoics, they did not insist upon virtue as an end in itself but taught that the only reason why man should be good is to increase his own happiness. In like manner, they denied that there is any such thing as absolute justice; laws and institutions are just only in so far as they contribute to the welfare of the individual. Certain rules have been found necessary in every complex society for the maintenance of security and order. Men obey these rules solely because it is to their advantage to do so. Thus the origin and existence of the state are rooted directly in self-interest. Generally speaking, Epicurus held no high regard for either political or social life. He considered the state as a mere convenience and taught that the wise man should take no active part in public life. Unlike the Cynics, he did not propose that man should abandon civilization and return to nature; yet his conception of the happiest life was essentially passive and defeatist. The wise man will recognize that he cannot eradicate the evils in the world no matter how strenuous and intelligent his efforts; he will therefore withdraw to "cultivate his garden," study philosophy, and enjoy the fellowship of a few congenial friends.

The defeatist philosophy of the Skeptics

A more radically defeatist philosophy was that propounded by the Skeptics. Although Skepticism was founded by Pyrrho, a contemporary of Zeno and Epicurus, it did not reach the zenith of its popularity until about a century later under the influence of Carneades (214–129 B.C.). The chief source of inspiration of the Skeptics was the Sophist teaching that all knowledge is derived from sense perception and therefore must be limited and relative. From this they deduced the conclusion that we cannot prove anything. Since the impressions of our senses deceive us, no truth can be certain. All we can say is that things *appear* to be such and such; we do not know what they really *are*. We have no definite knowledge of the supernatural, of the meaning of life, or even of right and wrong. It follows that the sensible course to pursue is suspension of judgment; this alone can lead to happiness. If man will abandon the fruitless quest for absolute truth and cease worrying about good and evil, he will attain that equanimity of mind which is the highest satisfaction that life affords. The Skeptics were even less concerned than the Epicureans with political and social problems. Their ideal was the typically Hellenistic one of escape for the individual from a world he could neither understand nor reform.

Hellenistic thought reached its lowest point in the philosophies of Philo Judaeus and the Neo-Pythagoreans in the last century B.C. and the first century A.D. The proponents of the two systems were in general agreement as to their basic teachings, especially in their predominantly religious viewpoint. They believed in a transcendent God so far removed from the world as to be utterly unknowable to mortal minds. They conceived the universe as being sharply divided between spirit and matter. They considered everything physical and material as evil; man's soul is imprisoned in his body, from which an escape can be effected only through rigorous denial and mortification of the flesh. Their attitude was mystical and anti-intellectual: truth comes neither from science nor from reason but from revelation; the feeble deductions of the human mind are worthy of nothing but contempt; the ultimate aim in life is to accomplish a mystic union with God, to lose one's self in the divine. *The new religious philosophies*

Hellenistic literature is significant mainly for the light which it throws upon the character of the civilization. Most of the writings showed little originality or depth of thought. But they poured forth from the hands of the copyists in a profusion that is almost incredible when we consider that the art of printing by movable type was unknown. The names of at least 1100 authors have been discovered already, and more are being added from year to year. Much of what they wrote was trash, comparable to the Sunday supplements and cheap novels of our own day. Nevertheless, there were several works of more than mediocre quality and a few which met the highest standards ever set by the Greeks. *The profusion of ephemeral literature*

The leading types of Hellenistic poetry were the drama, the pastoral, and the mime. Drama was almost exclusively comedy, represented mainly by the plays of Menander. His plays were entirely different from the comedy of Aristophanes. They were distinguished by naturalism rather than by satire, by preoccupation with the seamy side of life rather than with political or intellectual issues. Their dominant theme was romantic love, with its pains and pleasures, its intrigues and seductions, and its culmination in happy marriage. The greatest author of pastorals and mimes was Theocritus of Syracuse, who wrote in the first half of the third century B.C. His pastorals, as the name implies, celebrate the charm of life in the country and idealize the simple pleasures of rustic folk. The mimes, on the other hand, portray in colorful dialogue the squabbles, ambitions, and varied activities of the bourgeoisie in the great metropolitan cities. *Hellenistic poetry*

The field of prose literature was dominated by the historians, the

*Historians, bi-
ographers, and
authors of uto-
pias*

biographers, and the authors of utopias. By far the ablest of the writers of history was Polybius of Megalopolis, who lived during the second century B.C. From the standpoint of his scientific approach and his zeal for truth, he probably deserves to be ranked second only to Thucydides among all the historians in ancient times; but he excelled Thucydides in his grasp of the importance of social and economic forces. Although most of the biographies were of a light and gossipy character, their tremendous popularity bears eloquent testimony to the literary tastes of the time. Even more significant was the popularity of the utopias, or descriptive accounts of ideal states. Virtually all of them depicted a life of social and economic equality, free from greed, oppression, and strife, on an imaginary island or in some distant, unfamiliar region. Generally in these paradises money was considered to be unknown, trade was prohibited, all property was held in common, and all men were required to work with their hands in producing the necessaries of life. We are probably justified in assuming that the profusion of this utopian literature was a direct result of the rottenness and injustice of Hellenistic society and a consciousness of the need for reform.

Hellenistic art

*See color
plates at
page 157*

Hellenistic art preserved only a few of the superior qualities of the art of the Greeks. In place of the humanism, balance, and restraint which had characterized the architecture and sculpture of the Golden Age, qualities of exaggerated realism, sensationalism, and voluptuousness now became dominant. The simple and dignified Doric and Ionic temples gave way to luxurious palaces, costly mansions, and elaborate public buildings and monuments symbolical of power and wealth. A typical example was the great lighthouse of Alexandria, which rose to a height of nearly 400 feet, with three diminishing stories and eight columns to support the light at the top. Sculpture likewise exhibited tendencies in the direction of extravagance and sentimentality. Many of the statues and figures in relief were huge and some of them almost grotesque. Violent emotionalism and sordid realism were features common to the majority. Among the examples of this type of sculpture may be mentioned the *Laocoön* and the frieze of the Great Altar of Zeus at Pergamum with its giant gods, ferocious animals, and hybrid monsters mingled in desperate combat to symbolize the struggle of Greeks with Gauls. But by no means all of Hellenistic sculpture was overwrought and grotesque. Some of it was distinguished by a calmness and poise and compassion for human suffering reminiscent of the best work of the great fourth-century artists. Statues which exemplify these superior qualities include the *Aphrodite of Melos* (*Venus de Milo*) and the *Winged Victory of Samothrace*.

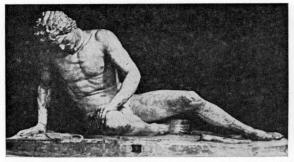

The Dying Gaul. A good example of Hellenistic realism in sculpture, which often reflected a preoccupation with the morbid and sensational. Every detail of the warrior's agony is dramatically portrayed. Now in the Capitoline Museum, Rome.

The Winged Victory of Samothrace. In this figure and in the *Venus de Milo,* Hellenistic sculptors preserved some of the calmness and devotion to grace and proportion characteristic of Hellenic art in the Golden Age. Now in the Louvre.

4. The First Great Age of Science

The most brilliant age in the history of science prior to the seventeenth century A.D. was the period of the Hellenistic civilization. Indeed, many of the achievements of the modern age would scarcely have been possible without the discoveries of the scientists of Alexandria, Syracuse, Pergamum, and other great cities of the Hellenistic world. The reasons for the phenomenal development of science in the centuries after the downfall of Alexander's empire are not far to seek. Alexander himself had given some financial encouragement to the progress of research. More important was the stimulus provided for intellectual inquiry by the fusion of Chaldean and Egyptian science with the learning of the Greeks. Possibly a third factor was the new interest in luxury and comfort and the demand for practical knowledge which would enable man to solve the problems of a disordered and unsatisfying existence.

Factors responsible for the remarkable progress of science

The sciences which received the major attention in the Hellenistic Age were astronomy, mathematics, geography, medicine, and physics. Chemistry as a pure science was practically unknown. Except for the work of Theophrastus, who was the first to recognize the sexuality of plants, the biological sciences were also largely neglected. Neither chemistry nor biology bore any definite relationship to trade or to the forms of industry then in existence and apparently they were not regarded as having much practical value.

The most popular sciences

The most famous of the earlier astronomers of this time was **199**

Aristarchus of Samos (310–230 B.C.), who is sometimes called the "Hellenistic Copernicus." As a result of his discovery that the apparent immobility of the "fixed" stars is due to their vast distance from the earth, he was the first to have any adequate conception of the enormous size of the universe. But his chief title to fame comes from his deduction that the earth and the other planets revolve around the sun. Unfortunately this deduction was not accepted by his successors. It conflicted with the teachings of Aristotle and with the anthropocentric ideas of the Greeks. Besides, it was not in harmony with the beliefs of the Jews and other Orientals who made up so large a percentage of the Hellenistic population. The only other astronomer of much importance in the Hellenistic Age was Hipparchus, who did his most valuable work in Alexandria in the latter half of the second century B.C. His chief contributions were the invention of the astrolabe, the preparation of the best chart of the heavens known to antiquity, the approximately correct calculation of the diameter of the moon and its distance from the earth, and the discovery of the precession of the equinoxes. His fame was eventually overshadowed, however, by the reputation of Ptolemy of Alexandria, the last of the Hellenistic astronomers. Although Ptolemy made few original discoveries, he systematized the work of others. His principal writing, the *Almagest*, based upon the geocentric theory, was handed down to medieval Europe as the classic summary of ancient astronomy.

Closely allied with astronomy were two other sciences, mathematics and geography. The Hellenistic mathematician of greatest renown was of course Euclid (*ca.* 323–*ca.* 285 B.C.), erroneously considered the founder of geometry. Until the middle of the nineteenth century his *Elements of Geometry* remained the accepted basis for the study of that branch of mathematics. Much of the material in this work was not original but was compiled as a synthesis of the discoveries of others. The most original of the Hellenistic mathematicians was probably Hipparchus, who laid the foundations of both plane and spherical trigonometry. Hellenistic geography owed most of its development to Eratosthenes (*ca.* 276–*ca.* 194 B.C.), astronomer, poet, philologist, and librarian of Alexandria. By means of sun dials placed some hundreds of miles apart, he calculated the circumference of the earth with an error of less than 200 miles. He produced the most accurate map that had yet been devised, with the surface of the earth divided into degrees of latitude and longitude. He propounded the theory that all of the oceans are really one, and he was the first to suggest the possibility of reaching India by sailing west. One of his successors divided the earth into the five climatic zones which are still recognized and explained the ebb and flow of the tides as due to the influence of the moon.

Perhaps none of the Hellenistic advances in science surpassed in importance the progress in medicine. Especially significant was the work of Herophilus of Chalcedon, who conducted his researches in Alexandria about the beginning of the third century. Without question he was the greatest anatomist of antiquity and, according to Galen, the first to practice human dissection. Among his most important achievements were a detailed description of the brain, with an attempt to distinguish between the functions of its various parts; the discovery of the significance of the pulse and its use in diagnosing illness; and the discovery that the arteries contain blood alone, not a mixture of blood and air as Aristotle had taught, and that their function is to carry blood from the heart to all parts of the body. The value of this last discovery in laying the basis for a knowledge of the circulation of the blood can hardly be overestimated.

The ablest of the successors of Herophilus was Erasistratus, who flourished in Alexandria about the middle of the third century. He is considered the founder of physiology as a separate science. Not only did he practice dissection, but he is believed to have gained a great deal of his knowledge of bodily functions from vivisection. He discovered the valves of the heart, distinguished between motor and sensory nerves, and taught that the ultimate branches of the arteries and veins are connected. He was the first to reject absolutely the humoral theory of disease and to condemn excessive blood-letting as a method of cure. Unfortunately this theory was revived by Galen, the great encyclopedist of medicine who lived in the Roman Empire in the second century A.D.

Prior to the third century B.C. physics had been a branch of philosophy. It was made a separate experimental science by Archimedes of Syracuse. Archimedes discovered the law of floating bodies or specific gravity and formulated with scientific exactness the principles of the lever, the pulley, and the screw. Among his memorable inventions were the compound pulley, the tubular screw for pumping water, the screw propeller for ships, and the burning lens. Although he has been called the "technical Yankee of antiquity," there is evidence that he set no high value upon his ingenious mechanical contraptions and preferred to devote his time to pure scientific research.

Certain other individuals in the Hellenistic Age were quite willing to give all their attention to applied science. Pre-eminent among them was Hero or Heron of Alexandria, who lived in the last century B.C. The record of inventions credited to him almost passes belief. The list includes a fire engine, a siphon, a force pump, a hydraulic organ, a slot machine, a catapult operated by compressed air, a thermoscope, and even a steam engine. How many of these inventions were really his own is impossible to say, but there appears to be no question that such contrivances were actually in existence in his time or soon thereafter. Nevertheless, the total progress in applied science was comparatively slight, probably for the reason that human labor continued to be so abundant and cheap that it was not worth while to substitute the labor of machines.

5. Religion in the Hellenistic Age

The new trend in religion

If there was one aspect of the Hellenistic civilization which served more than others to accent the contrast with Hellenic culture, it was the new trend in religion. The civic religion of the Greeks as it was in the age of the city-states had now almost entirely disappeared. For the majority of the intellectuals its place was taken by the philosophies of Stoicism, Epicureanism, and Skepticism. Some who were less philosophically inclined turned to the worship of Fortune or became followers of dogmatic atheism.

The popularity of mystic religions

Among the masses a tendency to embrace the emotional religions of Oriental origin was even more clearly manifest. The Orphic and Eleusinian mystery cults attracted more votaries than ever before. The worship of the Egyptian mother-goddess Isis threatened for a time to reach the proportions of a world religion. The astral religion of the Chaldeans likewise spread rapidly, with the result that its chief product, astrology, was received with fanatical enthusiasm throughout the Hellenistic world. So strong was its appeal that it had much to do with the eclipse of science and reason in the second and first centuries B.C. But the most powerful influence of all came from the offshoots of Zoroastrianism, especially from Mithraism and Gnosticism. While all of the cults of Oriental origin resembled each other in their promises of salvation in a life to come, Mithraism and Gnosticism had a more ethically significant mythology, a deeper contempt for this world, and a more clearly defined doctrine of redemption through a personal savior. These were the ideas which satisfied the emotional cravings of the common people, convinced as they were of the worthlessness of this life and ready to be lured by extravagant promises of better things in a world to come. If we can judge by conditions in our own time, some of the doctrines of these cults must have exerted their influence upon members of the upper classes also. Even the most casual observer of modern society knows that pessimism, mysticism, and otherworldliness are not confined to the downtrodden. In some cases the keenest disgust with this life and the deepest mystical yearnings are to be found among those whose pockets bulge with plenty.

The influence of the Jews

A factor by no means unimportant in the religious developments of the Hellenistic Age was the dispersion of the Jews. As a result of Alexander's conquest of Palestine in 332 B.C. and the Roman conquest about three centuries later, thousands of Jews migrated to various sections of the Mediterranean world. It has been estimated that 1,000,000 of them lived in Egypt in the first century A.D. and 200,000 in Asia Minor. They mingled freely with other peoples, adopting the Greek language and no small amount of the Hellenic culture which still survived from earlier days. At the same time they played a major part in the diffusion of Oriental beliefs. Their religion had already taken on a spiritual and messianic character as a result of Persian influence. Their leading philosopher of this time, Philo Judaeus of Alexandria, developed a body of doctrine representing the farthest extreme which mysticism had yet attained. Many of the Hellenistic Jews eventually became converts to Christianity and were largely instrumental in the spread of that religion outside of Palestine.

6. A Foretaste of Modernity?

With the possible exception of the Roman, no great culture of ancient times appears to suggest the spirit of the modern age quite so emphatically as does the Hellenistic civilization. Here as in the modern world were to be found a considerable variety of forms of government, the growth of militarism, a decline of respect for democracy, and a trend in the direction of authoritarian rule. Many of the characteristic economic and social developments of the Hel-

Hellenistic civilization compared with that of the modern age

Statue of an Old Market Woman. In the Hellenistic Age the idealism and restraint of Hellenic art were succeeded by a tendency to portray the humble aspects of life and to express compassion for human suffering. Original in the Metropolitan Museum of Art, New York.

lenistic Age are equally suggestive of contemporary experience: the growth of big business, the expansion of trade, the zeal for exploration and discovery, the interest in mechanical inventions, ruthless competition among merchants, the devotion to comfort and the craze for material prosperity, the growth of metropolitan cities

203

with congested slums, and the widening gulf between rich and poor. In the realms of intellect and art the Hellenistic civilization also bore a distinctly modern flavor. This was exemplified by the exaggerated emphasis upon science, the narrow specialization of learning, the penchant for realism and naturalism, the vast production of mediocre literature, and the popularity of mysticism side by side with extreme skepticism and dogmatic unbelief.

Basic differences

Because of these resemblances there has been a tendency among certain writers to regard our own civilization as decadent. But this is based partly upon the false assumption that the Hellenistic culture was merely a degenerate phase of Greek civilization. Instead, it was a new social and cultural organism born of a fusion of Greek and Oriental elements. Moreover, the differences between the Hellenistic civilization and that of the contemporary world are perhaps just as important as the resemblances. The Hellenistic political outlook was essentially cosmopolitan; nothing comparable to the national patriotism of modern times really prevailed. Despite the remarkable expansion of trade in the Hellenistic Age, no industrial revolution ever took place, for reasons which have already been noted. Finally, Hellenistic science was somewhat more limited than that of the present day. Modern pure science is to a very large extent a species of philosophy—an adventure of the mind in the realm of the unknown. Notwithstanding frequent assertions to the contrary, much of it is gloriously impractical and will probably remain so.

Selected Readings

· *Items so designated are available in paperbound editions.*

Bevan, E. R., *Stoics and Skeptics,* New York, 1913. A standard work.
Bury, J. B., and others, *The Hellenistic Age,* New York, 1923.
Cary, Max, *The Legacy of Alexander: A History of the Greek World from 323 to 146 B.C.,* New York, 1932.
Dudley, Donald R., *A History of Cynicism,* London, 1937.
Hicks, R. D., *Stoic and Epicurean,* New York, 1910. A good summary.
Larsen, J. A. O., *Representative Government in Greek and Roman History,* Berkeley, 1955.
Reymond, Arnold, *History of the Sciences in Greco-Roman Antiquity,* New York, 1927.
Robinson, C. A., Jr., *Alexander the Great,* New York, 1947.
Rostovstzev, M. I., *Social and Economic History of the Hellenistic World,* Oxford, 1941, 3 vols. Detailed but well written.
Sarton, George, *An Introduction to the History of Science,* Baltimore, 1927.
· Tarn, W. W., *Alexander the Great,* Boston, 1956. (Beacon)
· ———, *Hellenistic Civilization,* New York, 1952. (Meridian)
Trever, A. A., *History of Ancient Civilization,* New York, 1939, Vol. I.

Source Materials

Heath, T. L., *The Works of Archimedes.*
Hicks, R. D., ed., *Diogenes Laërtius; Lives of Eminent Philosophers,* Vol. II.
Oates, W. J., ed., *The Stoic and Epicurean Philosophers,* New York, 1940.
Plutarch, *Lives of Illustrious Men,* "Alexander."
Polybius, *Histories.*

Roman Civilization

Like Hercules, citizens, they said just now
He had sought the laurel at the cost of death:
Returning from Spain, seeking his household gods,
      Caesar has conquered.

After sacrifice to the just gods, let his
wife come forth, happy for her matchless husband,
And the sister of our famous leader, and,
      Wearing the bands of

Suppliants, mothers of young men and maidens
Who are now safe . . .
                              —Horace, *Odes*, III.xiv

Long before the glory of Greece had begun to fade, another civilization, derived in large measure from that of the Greeks, had started its growth on the banks of the Tiber in Italy. In fact, by the time the Greeks had entered their Golden Age, Rome was already a dominant power on the Italian peninsula. For more than six centuries thereafter her might increased, and she still maintained her supremacy over the civilized world when the glory of Greece was no more than a memory.

The rise of Rome

But the Romans never equaled the Greeks in intellectual or artistic accomplishments. The reasons may have been partly geographic. Except for some excellent marble and small quantities of copper, gold, and iron, Italy has no mineral resources. Her extensive coast line is broken by only two good harbors, Tarentum and Naples. On the other hand, the amount of her fertile land is much larger than that of Greece. As a consequence, the Romans were practically destined to remain a predominantly agrarian people through the greater part of their history. They never enjoyed the intellectual stimulus which comes from extensive trading with other nations. In addition, the topography of Italy is such that the peninsula was more easily accessible to invasion than was Greece. The Alps opposed no effectual barrier to the influx of peoples from central Europe, while the low-lying coast in many places invited conquest by sea. As a result, domination of the country by force was more common than peaceful intermingling of immigrants with original settlers. For this reason the Romans became absorbed in military pursuits almost from the moment of their settlement on Italian soil, since they were forced to defend their own conquests against other invaders.

Why Roman civilization was generally inferior to that of the Greeks

205

1. From the Beginning to the Overthrow of the Monarchy

The earliest inhabitants of Italy

Archaeological evidence indicates that Italy was inhabited at least as far back as the Upper Paleolithic age. At this time the territory was occupied by a people closely related to the Cro-Magnon race of southern France. In the Neolithic period people of Mediterranean stock entered the land, some coming in from northern Africa and others from Spain and Gaul. The beginning of the Bronze Age witnessed several new invasions. From the lake country north of the Alps came the first of the immigrants of the Indo-European language group. They were herdsmen and farmers, who brought the horse and the wheeled cart into Italy. Their culture was based upon the use of bronze, although after 1000 B.C. they appear to have acquired a knowledge of iron. These Indo-European invaders seem to have been the ancestors of most of the so-called Italic peoples, including the Romans. Racially they were probably related to the Hellenic invaders of Greece.

The Etruscans and the Greeks

Between the twelfth and sixth centuries B.C. two other nations of immigrants occupied different portions of the Italian peninsula: the Etruscans and the Greeks. Where the Etruscans came from is a question which has never been satisfactorily answered. Most authorities believe that they were natives of some part of the Near Orient, probably Asia Minor. Although their writing has never been completely deciphered, enough materials survive to indicate the nature of their culture. They had an alphabet based upon the Greek, a high degree of skill in the metallurgical arts, a flourishing trade with the East, and a gloomy religion concerned with the worship of malignant spirits. They bequeathed to the Romans a knowledge of the arch and the vault, the practice of divination, and the cruel amusement of gladiatorial combats. The Etruscans established no great empire but contented themselves with dominating the Italic peoples north and west of the Tiber and exploiting their wealth and labor. The Greeks located mainly along the southern and southwestern shores of Italy and on the island of Sicily. Their most important settlements were Tarentum, Syracuse, and Naples, each of which was an entirely independent city-state. From the Greeks the Romans derived their alphabet, a number of their religious concepts, and much of their art and mythology.

The founding of Rome

The actual founders of Rome were Italic peoples who lived in the district of Latium south of the Tiber River. Though the date of the founding of the city is unknown, the event was probably no later than 1000 B.C. The traditional date, 753 B.C., was the invention of later Roman writers. Latium included a number of towns, but Rome by reason of its strategic location soon came to exercise an effective suzerainty over several of the most important of them. One conquest followed another until by the end of the sixth century B.C. the ter-

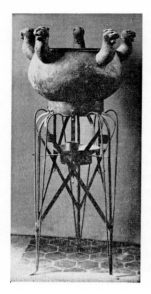

Bronze Cauldron on Iron Tripod. Found in Regalini-Galassi tomb, Cerveteri.

Busts of Jove. Etruscan art is often considered independent, but influences from Greece and the Near East are clearly discernible. Roman art, in turn, received much from the earlier influence of Etruria.

Votive Chariot. Chariot racing, like horse-riding, boxing, and wrestling, was much the vogue among the Etruscans.

ETRUSCAN ART
AND ARTIFACTS

Etruscan Art. Typical scene on sarcophagus shows preparations for funeral. Etruscans often depicted social events, sports, funeral banquets, and processions, either in painting or relief, on their tombs.

ritory dominated by the Roman state was probably coextensive with the whole Latin plain from the slopes of the Apennines to the Mediterranean Sea.

The political evolution of Rome in this early period resembled in some ways the governmental development of the Greek communities in the formative stage of their history. But it was far from being the same. The Romans appear from the first to have had a much stronger interest in authority and stability than in liberty or democracy. Their state was essentially an application of the idea of the patriarchal family to the whole community, with the king exercising a jurisdiction over his subjects comparable to that of the head of the family over the members of his household. But just as the authority of the father was limited by custom and by the requirement that he respect the wishes of his adult sons, the sovereignty of the king was limited by the ancient constitution, which he was powerless to change without the consent of the chief men of the realm. His prerogatives were not primarily legislative but executive and judicial. He punished men for infractions of order, usually by infliction of the death penalty or by flogging. He judged all civil and criminal cases, but he had no authority to pardon without the consent of the assembly. Although his accession to office had to be confirmed by the people, he could not be deposed, and there was no one who could really challenge the exercise of his regal powers.

In addition to the kingship the Roman government of this time included an assembly and a Senate. The former was composed of all the male citizens of military age. As one of the chief sources of sovereign power, according to the theory, this body had an absolute veto on any proposal for a change in the law which the king might make. Besides, it determined whether pardons should be granted and whether aggressive war should be declared. But it was essentially a ratifying body with no right to initiate legislation or recommend changes of policy. Its members could not even speak except when invited to do so by the king. The Senate, or council of elders, comprised in its membership the heads of the various clans which formed the community. Even more than the common citizens, the rulers of the clans embodied the sovereign power of the state. The king was only one of their number to whom they had delegated the active exercise of their authority. When the royal office became vacant, the powers of the king immediately reverted to the Senate until the succession of a new monarch had been confirmed by the people. In ordinary times the chief function of the Senate was to examine proposals of the king which had been ratified by the assembly and to veto them if they violated rights established by ancient custom. It was thus almost impossible for fundamental changes to be made in the law even when the majority of the citizens were ready to sanction them. This extremely conservative attitude of the ruling classes persisted until the end of Roman history.

Toward the end of the sixth century B.C. senatorial jealousy of the kings increased to such a point that the monarchy was overthrown and an oligarchic republic set up. While the real nature of this revolution was doubtless a movement of the aristocracy to gain supreme power for itself, factors of nationalism may have played some part in it also. Tradition relates that the last of the Roman kings was an Etruscan, whose family, the Tarquins, had usurped the royal office some years before. The Romans of later centuries described in lurid fashion the wicked deeds of these rulers and implied that the overthrow of the monarchy was due primarily to a revolt against alien oppressors. It was probably inevitable, however, that the senatorial class would sooner or later develop ambitions for a monopoly of power, as the nobles in the Greek city-states had done a few centuries before.

The overthrow of the monarchy

2. The Early Republic

The history of the Roman Republic for more than two centuries after its establishment was occupied by almost constant warfare. The causes which led to the series of conflicts are not easy to untangle. It is possible that the overthrow of the Tarquins resulted in acts of reprisal by their kinsmen in neighboring countries. It is conceivable also that other nations on the borders took advantage of the confusion accompanying the revolution to slice off portions of Roman territory. But doubtless the compelling reason was greed for more land. The Romans were already a proud and aggressive people with a rapidly growing population. As the number of the inhabitants increased, the need for outlets into new territory became ever more urgent. Such was the cause which apparently led to the wars with the Volsci and the Aequi at the beginning of the fifth century. Roman expansion at the expense of these peoples aroused the jealousy of other strong nations. First the Republic had to fight the powerful Etruscan city of Veii, located a short distance to the north across the Tiber. After years of siege the city was destroyed, its people sold into slavery, and its territory annexed to the Roman domain. About 390 B.C. ferocious tribes of Gauls took advantage of the temporary exhaustion of Rome to invade the Republic. They captured and sacked the city but were finally bought off with 1000 pounds of gold. Next the Romans had to deal with revolts of some of the peoples previously conquered: the Aequi, the Volsci, and several of the Latin nations. The suppression of these revolts awakened the suspicions of surrounding states and sharpened the appetite of the victors for further triumphs. New wars followed each other in what seemed an unending succession, until by 265 B.C. Rome had conquered the entire Italian peninsula.

The origins of Roman imperialism

See color plates at page 189

This long series of military conflicts had profound effects upon the subsequent history of Rome. It affected adversely the interests

Effects of the early military conflicts

of the poorer citizens and furthered the concentration of land in the possession of wealthy proprietors. Long service in the army forced the ordinary farmers to neglect the cultivation of the soil, with the result that they fell into debt and frequently lost their farms. Many of them took refuge in the city, until they were settled later as tenants on great estates in the conquered territories. The wars had the effect also of confirming the agrarian character of the Roman nation. The repeated acquisition of new lands made it possible to absorb the entire population into agricultural pursuits. As a consequence there was no need for the development of industry and commerce as means of earning a livelihood. Lastly, as in the case of Sparta, the Roman wars of conquest enslaved the nation to the military ideal and thereby retarded cultural growth.

Political changes following the overthrow of the monarchy

During this same period of the early Republic, Rome underwent some significant political changes. These were not due so much to the revolution of the sixth century as to the developments of later years. The revolution which overthrew the monarchy was about as conservative as it is possible for a revolution to be. Its chief effect was to substitute two elected consuls for the king and to exalt the position of the Senate by vesting it with control over the public funds and with a veto on all actions of the assembly. The consuls themselves were usually senators and acted as the agents of their class. They did not rule jointly, but each was supposed to possess the full executive and judicial authority which had previously been wielded by the king. If a conflict arose between them, the Senate might be called upon to decide; or, in time of grave emergency, a dictator might be appointed for a term not greater than six months. In other respects the government remained the same as in the days of the monarchy.

The struggle between patricians and plebeians

It was not long after the establishment of the Republic until a struggle began by the common citizens for a larger share of political power. Before the end of the monarchy the Roman population had come to be divided into two great classes—the patricians and the plebeians. The former were the aristocracy, wealthy landowners, who were apparently the descendants of the old clan leaders. They monopolized the seats in the Senate and the offices of magistracy. The plebeians were the common people—small farmers, craftsmen, and tradesmen. Many were clients or dependents of the patricians, obliged to fight for them, to render them political support, and to cultivate their estates in return for protection. The grievances of the plebeians were numerous. Compelled to pay heavy taxes and forced to serve in the army in time of war, they were nevertheless excluded from all part in the government except membership in the assembly. Moreover, they felt themselves the victims of discriminatory decisions in judicial trials. They did not even know what legal rights they were supposed to enjoy, for the laws were unwritten, and no one but the consuls had the power to interpret them. In suits for debt the creditor was frequently allowed to sell the debtor into slavery. It was in order to obtain a redress of these grievances that the plebeians rebelled soon after the beginning of the fifth century B.C.

The first victory of the plebeians was gained about 470 B.C., when they forced the patricians to agree to the election of a number of tribunes with power to protect the citizens by means of a veto over unlawful acts of the magistrates. This victory was followed by a successful demand for codification of the laws about 450 B.C. The result was the publication of the famous Law of the Twelve Tables, so called from the fact that it was written on tablets of wood. Although the Twelve Tables came to be revered by the Romans of later times as a kind of charter of the people's liberties, they were really nothing of the sort. For the most part they merely perpetuated ancient custom without even abolishing enslavement for debt. They did, however, enable the people to know where they stood in relation to the law, and they permitted an appeal to the assembly against a magistrate's sentence of capital punishment. About a generation later the plebeians won eligibility to positions as lesser magistrates, and in 362 B.C. the first plebeian consul was elected. Since ancient custom provided that consuls upon completing their term of office should automatically enter the Senate, the patrician monopoly of seats in that body was broken. The final plebeian victory came in 287 B.C. with the passage of the Hortensian Law (named for the dictator Quintus Hortensius), which provided that measures enacted by the assembly should become binding upon the state whether the Senate approved them or not.

The victories of the plebeians

The significance of these changes must not be misinterpreted. They did not constitute a revolution to gain more liberty for the individual but merely to curb the power of the magistrates and to win for the common man a larger share in government. The state as a whole remained as despotic as ever, for its authority over the citizens was not even challenged. As Theodor Mommsen says, the Romans from the time of the Tarquins to that of the Gracchi "never really abandoned the principle that the people were not to govern but to be governed." [1] Because of this attitude the grant of full legislative powers to the assembly seems to have meant little more than a formality; the Senate continued to rule as before. Nor did the admission of plebeians to membership in the Senate have any effect in liberalizing that body. So high was its prestige and so deep was the veneration of the Roman for authority, that the new members were soon swallowed up in the conservatism of the old. Moreover, the fact that the magistrates received no salaries prevented most of the poorer citizens from seeking public office.

Significance of the Plebeian victories

Intellectually and socially the Romans appear to have made but slow advancement as yet. The times were still harsh and crude. Though

[1] *The History of Rome*, Vol. I, p. 313.

writing had been adopted as early as the sixth century, little use was made of it except for the copying of laws, treaties, and funerary inscriptions and orations. Inasmuch as education was limited to instruction imparted by the father in manly sports, practical arts, and soldierly virtues, probably the great majority of the people were still illiterate. War and agriculture continued as the chief occupations for the bulk of the citizens. A few craftsmen were to be found in the cities, and a minor development of trade had occurred, evidenced by the founding of a maritime colony at Ostia on the coast in the fourth century. But the comparative insignificance of Roman commerce at this time is pretty clearly revealed by the fact that the country had no standard system of coinage until 269 B.C.

*The religion
of the Romans
compared with
that of the
Greeks*

The period of the early Republic was the period when the Roman religion assumed the character it was destined to retain through the greater part of the nation's history. In several ways this religion resembled the religion of the Greeks, probably for the reason that the original cultural heritage of both peoples came from the same source. Both religions were worldly and practical with neither spiritual nor ethical content. The relation of man to the gods was external and mechanical, partaking of the nature of a bargain or contract between two parties for their mutual advantage. The deities in both religions performed similar functions: Jupiter corresponded roughly to Zeus as god of the sky, Minerva to Athena as patroness of craftsmen, Venus to Aphrodite as goddess of love, Neptune to Poseidon as god of the sea, and so on. The Roman religion no more than the Greek had any dogmas or sacraments or belief in rewards and punishments in an afterlife.

*Contrasts
with Greek
religion*

But there were significant differences also. The Roman religion was distinctly more political and less humanistic in purpose. It served not to glorify man or to make him feel at home in his world but to protect the state from its enemies and to augment its power and prosperity. The gods were less anthropomorphic; indeed, it was only as a result of Greek and Etruscan influences that they were made personal deities at all, having previously been worshiped as *numina* or animistic spirits. The Romans never conceived of their deities as quarreling among themselves or mingling with human beings after the fashion of the Homeric divinities. Finally, the Roman religion contained a much stronger element of priestliness than the Greek. The priests, or pontiffs as they were called, formed an organized class, a branch of the government itself. They not only supervised the offering of sacrifices, but they were guardians of an elaborate body of sacred traditions and laws which they alone could interpret. It must be clearly understood, however, that these pontiffs were not priests in the sense of intermediaries between the individual Roman and his gods; they heard no confessions, forgave no sins, and administered no sacraments.

The morality of the Romans in this as in later periods had almost no connection with religion. The Roman did not ask his gods to make him good but to bestow upon the community and upon his family material blessings. Morality was a matter of patriotism and of respect for authority and tradition. The chief virtues were bravery, honor, self-discipline, reverence for the gods and for one's ancestors, and duty to country and family. Loyalty to the state took precedence over everything else. For the good of the state the citizen must be ready to sacrifice not only his own life but, if necessary, the lives of his family and friends. The courage of certain consuls who dutifully put their sons to death for breaches of military discipline was a subject of profound admiration. Few peoples in European history with the exception of the Spartans and perhaps the modern Germans have ever taken the problems of national interest so seriously or subordinated the individual so completely to the good of the state.

Morality in the early Republic

3. The Fateful Wars with Carthage

By 265 B.C., as we have already learned, Rome had conquered and annexed the whole of Italy. Proud and confident of her strength, she was almost certain to strike out into new fields of empire. The prosperous island of Sicily was not yet within her grasp, nor could she regard with indifference the situation in other parts of the Mediterranean world. She was now prone to interpret almost any change in the *status quo* as a threat to her own power and security. It was for such reasons that Rome after 264 B.C. became involved in a series of wars with other great nations which decidedly altered the course of her history.

The beginning of imperialism on a major scale

The first and most important of these wars was the struggle with Carthage, a great maritime empire which stretched along the northern coast of Africa from Numidia to the Strait of Gibraltar. Carthage had originally been founded in the ninth century B.C. as a Phoenician colony. In the sixth century it severed its ties with the homeland and gradually developed into a rich and powerful nation. The prosperity of its upper classes was founded upon commerce and upon exploitation of the silver and tin resources of Spain and Britain and the tropical products of north central Africa. Conditions within the country were far from ideal. The Carthaginians appear to have had no conception of free and orderly government. Shameless bribery and cynical oppression of the masses were methods regularly employed by the plutocracy to maintain its dominant position. The form of government itself can best be described as an oligarchy. At the head of the system were two magistrates, or *suffetes*, who exercised powers approximating those of the Roman consuls. The real governors, however, were thirty merchant princes who constituted an inner council of the Senate. By methods constitutional and otherwise these men controlled elections and dominated every other

Carthage

branch of the government. The remaining 270 members of the Senate appear to have been summoned to meet only on special occasions. In spite of these political deficiencies, Carthage had a civilization superior in luxury and scientific attainment to that of Rome when the struggle between the two countries began.

*Causes of the
First Punic War*

The initial clash with Carthage began in 264 B.C.[2] The primary cause was Roman jealousy over Carthaginian expansion in Sicily. Carthage already controlled the western portion of the island and was threatening the Greek cities of Syracuse and Messana on the eastern coast. If these cities should be captured, all chances of Roman occupation of Sicily would be cut off. Faced with this danger, Rome declared war upon Carthage with the hope of forcing her back into her African domain. Twenty-three years of fighting finally brought victory to the Roman generals. Carthage was compelled to surrender her possessions in Sicily and to pay an indemnity of 3200 talents, or about 2 million dollars at 1957 silver prices.

*The Second
Punic War*

But the Romans were unable to stand the strain of this triumph. They had had to put forth such heroic efforts to win that when victory was finally secured it made them more arrogant and greedy than ever. As a result, the struggle with Carthage was renewed on two different occasions thereafter. In 218 B.C. the Romans interpreted the Carthaginian attempt to rebuild an empire in Spain as a threat to their interests and responded with a declaration of war. This struggle raged through a period of sixteen years. Italy was ravaged by the armies of Hannibal, the famous Carthaginian commander, whose tactics have been copied by military experts to the present day. Although Rome escaped defeat by the narrowest of margins, the patriotism of her citizens and the leadership of her brilliant general Scipio ultimately saved the day. Carthage was more completely humbled than before. She was compelled to abandon all her possessions except the capital city and its surrounding territory in Africa, and to pay an indemnity of 10,000 talents.

*The Third
Punic War and
the destruction
of Carthage*

Roman vindictiveness and avarice reached their maximum level about the middle of the second century B.C. By this time Carthage had recovered a modicum of her former prosperity—enough to excite the envy and fear of her conquerors. Nothing would now satisfy the senatorial magnates but the complete destruction of Carthage and the expropriation of her land. In 149 B.C. the Senate dispatched an ultimatum demanding that the Carthaginians abandon their city and settle at least ten miles from the coast. Since this demand was tantamount to a death sentence for a nation dependent upon commerce, it was refused—as the Romans probably hoped it would be. The result was the Third Punic War, which was fought between 149 and 146 B.C. Seldom has the world witnessed a more desperate and

[2] The wars with Carthage are known as the Punic Wars. The Romans called the Carthaginians *Poeni,* i.e., Phoenicians, whence is derived the adjective "Punic."

more barbarous struggle. The final assault upon the city was carried into the houses of the natives themselves, and a frightful butchery took place. When the resistance of the Carthaginians was finally broken, the few citizens who were left to surrender were sold into slavery, and their once magnificent city was razed to the ground. The land was organized into a Roman province with the best areas parceled out as senatorial estates.

The wars with Carthage had momentous effects upon Rome. First, they brought her into conflict with eastern Mediterranean powers and thereby paved the way for world dominion. During the Second Punic War, Philip V of Macedon had entered into an alliance with Carthage and had plotted with the king of Syria to divide Egypt between them. In order to punish Philip and to forestall the execution of his plans, Rome sent an army into the East. The result was the conquest of Greece and Asia Minor and the establishment of a protectorate over Egypt. Thus before the end of the second century B.C. virtually the entire Mediterranean area had been brought under Roman dominion. The conquest of the Hellenistic East led to the introduction of semi-Oriental ideas and customs into Rome, changing the whole aspect of cultural life.

Results of the wars with Carthage: (1) conquest of the Hellenistic East

By far the most important effect of the Punic Wars was a great social and economic revolution which swept over Rome in the third and second centuries B.C. The incidents of this revolution may be enumerated as follows: (1) a marked increase in slavery due to the capture and sale of prisoners of war; (2) the decline of the small farmer as a result of the establishment of the plantation system in conquered areas and the influx of cheap grain from the provinces; (3) the growth of a helpless city mob composed of impoverished farmers and workers displaced by slave labor; (4) the appearance of a middle class comprising merchants, moneylenders, and "publicans" or men who held government contracts to operate mines, build roads, or collect taxes; and (5) an increase in luxury and vulgar display, particularly among the *parvenus* who fattened on the profits of war.

(2) a social and economic revolution

As a consequence of this social and economic revolution, Rome was changed from a republic of yeoman farmers into a nation composed very largely of parasites and slaves. Though property had never been evenly distributed, the gulf which separated rich and poor now yawned more widely than before. The old-fashioned ideals of discipline and devotion to the service of the state were sadly weakened, and men began to make pleasure and wealth their gods. A few members of the senatorial aristocracy exerted efforts to check the evil tendencies and to restore the homely virtues of the past. The eminent leader of this movement was Cato the Elder, who inveighed against the new rich for their soft living and strove to set an example to his countrymen by performing hard labor on his farm and dwelling in a house with a dirt floor and no plaster on the walls. But his

Rome transformed into a nation of parasites and slaves

efforts had little effect. The rich continued to indulge their expensive tastes and to rival each other in vulgar consumption of wealth. At the same time public morality decayed. Tax gatherers plundered the provinces and used their illicit gains to purchase the votes of the poor. The helpless masses in the city came to expect that politicians would feed them and provide for their amusement with ever more brutal shows. The total effect was so serious that some authorities date the beginning of Rome's decline from this period.[3]

4. The Storm and Stress of the Late Republic

The new period of turbulence

The period from the end of the Punic Wars in 146 B.C. to the accession of Julius Caesar in 46 B.C. was one of the most turbulent in the history of Rome. It was between these years that the nation reaped the full harvest of the seeds of violence sown during the wars of conquest. Bitter class conflicts, assassinations, desperate struggles between rival dictators, wars, and insurrections were the all too common occurrences of this time. Even the slaves contributed their part to the general disorder: first, in 104 B.C. when they ravaged Sicily; and again in 73 B.C. when 70,000 of them under the leadership of Spartacus held the consuls at bay for more than a year. Spartacus was finally slain in battle and six thousand of his followers were captured and crucified.

The revolt of the Gracchi

The first stage in the conflict between classes of citizens began with the revolt of the Gracchi. The Gracchi were mainly spokesmen for the landless farmers against the senatorial aristocracy, but they recruited some support from the middle classes also. In 133 B.C. Tiberius Gracchus, having been elected tribune, persuaded the assembly to enact a law limiting the amount of land which any person might hold to about 310 acres and providing that the excess should be surrendered to the state for lease to poor citizens at a nominal rental. Before the law could be put into effect, Tiberius' term as tribune expired. He thereupon determined to stand for re-election, in defiance of the constitutional provision limiting magistrates' terms to one year. This illegal move gave the senators an excuse for a resort to violence. The elections were accompanied by riots in which Tiberius and three hundred of his followers were slaughtered by clients and slaves of the aristocracy.

Significance of the Gracchan affair

Nine years later Gaius Gracchus, the younger brother of Tiberius, renewed the struggle for the underprivileged orders. Elected tribune for 123 B.C., he procured the enactment of a law providing for a monthly distribution of grain to the people of the city at one-half the market price. Next he prepared an attack upon the powers of the Senate, but he was defeated for re-election as tribune in 121 and was branded as an enemy of the state. When he refused to stand trial be-

[3] See A. J. Toynbee, *A Study of History* (D. C. Somervell ed.), Vol. I, p. 258.

fore the Senate, a state of war was proclaimed against him. After his followers had been routed, Gaius persuaded a faithful slave to kill him. Subsequently three thousand of his adherents were condemned to death. The chief significance of the Gracchan affair is to be found in the extent to which it illustrates the political incapacity of the Romans and the dangers of their narrow conservatism. It is important also for the vicious precedents which were established for the future. The Senate, by its resort to violence, set the example of an appeal to force which the demagogues of later years were not slow to follow.

In spite of all this, the decay of constitutional government was not necessarily inevitable because of the downfall of the Gracchi. The Romans might yet have succeeded in working out a compromise solution of their problems if only they could have kept out of war. But this they were unable to do, for the creation of so vast an empire meant frequent conflicts with bordering nations. In 111 B.C. a great struggle began with Jugurtha, the king of Numidia in northern Africa. This was followed by campaigns to punish the invading Gauls and by a war against Mithradates of Pontus, who was taking advantage of Roman misrule in the East to extend his dominion over Asia Minor. The heroes of these wars invariably returned to Italy to become leaders of one or the other of the great political factions.

The renewal of foreign wars

The first of the conquering heroes to make capital out of his military reputation was Marius, who was elevated to the consulship by the masses in 107 B.C. and re-elected five times thereafter. Unfortunately Marius was no statesman and accomplished nothing for his followers beyond demonstrating the ease with which a military leader with an army at his back could override opposition. Following the death of Marius in 86 B.C. the aristocrats took a turn at government by force. Their champion was Sulla, victor in the war with Mithradates. Appointed dictator in 82 B.C. for an unlimited term, Sulla proceeded to exterminate his opponents and to restore to the Senate its original powers. Even the senatorial veto over acts of the assembly was revived, while the authority of the tribunes was sharply curtailed. After three years of rule Sulla decided to exchange the pomp of power for the pleasures of sense and retired to a life of luxury and ease on his Campanian estate.

The rise of military dictatorships: Marius and Sulla

It was not to be expected that the "reforms" of Sulla would stand unchallenged after he had relinquished his office; for the effect of his decrees was to give control to a bigoted and selfish aristocracy. Several new leaders now emerged to espouse the cause of the people. The most famous of them were Pompey and Julius Caesar. For a time they pooled their energies and resources in a plot to gain control of the government, but later they became rivals and sought to outdo each other in bids for popular support. Pompey won fame as the conqueror of Syria and Palestine, while Caesar devoted his talents to a series of brilliant forays against the Gauls, adding to the Roman state the territory of modern Belgium and France. In 52 B.C.,

The struggle between Pompey and Caesar

Head of Julius Caesar, showing individuality of Roman portrait sculpture. In the British Museum.

after a series of mob disorders in Rome, the Senate turned to Pompey and caused his election as sole consul. Caesar was branded an enemy of the state, and Pompey conspired with the senatorial faction to deprive him of political power. The result was a deadly war between the two men. With the famous pronouncement, "The die is cast," Caesar crossed the Rubicon (49 B.C.) and began a march on Rome. Pompey fled to the East in the hope of gathering a large enough army to regain control of Italy. In 48 B.C. the forces of the two rivals met at Pharsalus in Thessaly. Pompey was defeated and soon afterward was murdered by agents of the king of Egypt.

Caesar's triumph and his downfall

After dallying for a season at the court of Cleopatra in Egypt, Caesar returned to Rome. There was now no one who dared to challenge his power. With the aid of his veterans he cowed the Senate into granting his every desire. In 46 B.C. he became dictator for ten years, and in the following year for life. In addition, he assumed nearly every other magisterial title that would augment his power. He was consul, tribune, censor, and supreme pontiff. He obtained from the Senate full authority to make war and peace and to control the revenues of the state. For all practical purposes he was above the law, and the other agents of the government were merely his servants. There seems to be little doubt that he intended to make himself king; at any rate, it was on such a charge that he was assassinated in 44 B.C. by a group of conspirators, under the leadership of Brutus and Cassius, representing the old aristocracy.[4]

Through the centuries ever since, students of history have been

[4] During the last few months of his life Caesar became more ill-tempered and domineering than ever. Perhaps this change was due to the fact that he was really a sick man, his old affliction of epilepsy having returned. W. E. Heitland, *The Roman Republic*, Vol. III, p. 355.

blinded by hero worship in estimating Caesar's political career. It is undoubtedly erroneous to acclaim him as the savior of his country or to praise him as the greatest statesman of all time. For he destroyed the essential features of the Republic and made the problem of governing more difficult for those who came after him. What Rome needed at this time was not the rule of force, however efficiently it might be exercised; but an enlightened attempt to correct the inequities of her political and economic regime. Though it is true that Caesar carried out numerous reforms, not all of them were really fundamental. With the aid of a Greek astronomer he revised the official calendar so as to bring it into harmony with the Egyptian solar calendar of 365 days, with an extra day added every fourth year. He investigated extravagance in the distribution of public grain and reduced the number of recipients by more than 50 per cent. He made plans for codification of the law and increased the penalty for criminal offenses. By conferring citizenship upon thousands of Spaniards and Gauls he took an important step toward eliminating the distinction between Italians and provincials. He settled a great many of his veterans and a considerable proportion of the urban poor on unused lands not only in Italy but throughout the empire, and he ordered the proprietors of large estates to employ at least one free citizen to every two slaves. On the other hand, he did nothing to reduce the most glaring inequalities in the distribution of wealth or to enlarge the political rights of the discontented masses. Perhaps if he had lived longer, his record might have been better; but there is nothing to prove that he really had the qualities of statesmanship which the times demanded.

Atrium of an Upper-class House in Pompeii, seen from the Interior. Around the atrium or central court were grouped suites of living rooms. The marble columns and decorated walls still give an idea of the luxury and refinement enjoyed by the privileged minority.

5. *Rome Becomes Sophisticated*

Rome under the influence of Hellenistic civilization

During the last two centuries of republican history Rome came under the influence of Hellenistic civilization. The result was a modest flowering of intellectual activity and a further impetus to social change beyond what the Punic Wars had produced. The fact must be noted, however, that several of the components of the Hellenistic pattern of culture were never adopted by the Romans at all. The science of the Hellenistic Age, for example, was largely ignored, and the same was true of some of its art.

Roman Epicureanism: Lucretius

One of the most notable effects of Hellenistic influence was the adoption of Epicureanism and Stoicism by numerous Romans of the upper classes. The most renowned of the Roman exponents of the Epicurean philosophy was Lucretius (98–55 B.C.), author of a didactic poem entitled *On the Nature of Things*. In writing this work Lucretius was animated by the desire to explain the universe in such a way as to liberate man from all fear of the supernatural, which he regarded as the chief obstacle to peace of soul. Worlds and all things in them, he taught, are the results of fortuitous combinations of atoms. Though he admitted the existence of the gods, he conceived of them as living in eternal peace, neither creating nor governing the universe. Everything is a product of a mechanical evolution, including man himself and his habits, institutions, and beliefs. Since mind is indissolubly linked with matter, death means utter extinction; consequently, no part of the human personality can survive to be rewarded or punished in an after-existence. Lucretius' conception of the good life was perhaps even more negative than that of Epicurus: what man needs, he asserted, is not enjoyment but "peace and a pure heart."

The Stoic philosophy of Cicero

Stoicism was introduced into Rome by Panaetius of Rhodes about 140 B.C. Although it soon came to include among its converts numerous influential leaders of public life, its most distinguished representative was Cicero (106–43 B.C.), the famous orator and statesman. While Cicero adopted doctrines from a number of philosophers, including both Plato and Aristotle, the fact remains that he derived far more of his ideas from the Stoics than from any other source. Certainly his chief ethical writings, *On Duty* and the *Tusculan Disputations*, reflect substantially the doctrines of Zeno and his school. The basis of Cicero's ethical philosophy was the premise that virtue is sufficient for happiness, and that tranquillity of mind is the highest good. He conceived of the ideal man as one who has been guided by reason to an indifference toward sorrow and pain. In political philosophy Cicero went considerably beyond the earlier Stoics. He was one of the first to deny that the state is superior to the individual and taught that government had its origin in a compact among men for their mutual protection. In his *Republic* he set forth the idea of a higher law of eternal justice which is superior to the statutes and decrees of governments. This law is not made by man but is a product of the natural order of things and is discoverable by reason. It is the source of those rights to which all men are entitled as human beings and which governments must not assail. As we shall see presently, this doctrine influenced considerably the development of the Roman law by the great jurists of the second and third centuries A.D. By reason of his contributions to political thought, and by virtue of his urbanity and tolerance, Cicero deserves to be ranked as one of the greatest men Rome ever produced. He typified the genius of the nation at its best.

Hellenistic influence was in large measure responsible for Roman literary progress in the last two centuries of the Republic. It now became the fashion among the upper classes to learn the Greek language and to strive to reproduce in Latin some of the more popular forms of Hellenistic literature. The most noteworthy results were the comedies of Plautus and Terence, written in imitation of the New Comedy of Menander; the passionate lyrics of Catullus; the histories of Sallust, which in spite of their Caesarist bias are among the most scientific ever produced in Rome; and the letters, essays, and orations of Cicero, which are generally regarded as the finest examples of Latin prose. *Roman literary progress*

Several of the early Roman writers showed promise at times of equaling the originality and artistry of the Greeks in the classical age. Plautus, for instance, occasionally displayed a freshness of approach, a perception of philosophic implications, and a capacity for social satire. Of humble origin himself, he delighted in ridiculing the mores and institutions which the respectable classes esteemed so highly. He allowed his genius to be thwarted, however, by too slavish a dependence upon the stock characters and themes of Hellenistic comedy. After his time Latin drama degenerated into lifeless formalism. The other of the most original writers of this period was Catullus (84–54 B.C.), one of the greatest lyric poets of all time. He is best known for his passionate love poems written to describe his tortured feelings while infatuated with the dissolute wife of a prominent politician. For years he was unable to free himself from his ardor, though maddened by jealousy of his rivals. But not all of his poetry dealt with the expression of personal emotion. Apparently he was an ardent republican, and in the latter part of his life he wrote coarse lampoons attacking Pompey and Caesar for their demagogic ambitions. *Plautus and Catullus*

The conquest of the Hellenistic world accelerated the process of social change which the Punic Wars had begun. The effects were most clearly evident in the growth of luxury, in a widened cleavage between classes, and in a further increase in slavery. The Italian people, numbering about two million at the end of the Republic, had come to be divided into four main castes: the aristocracy, the eques- *Social conditions in the late Republic*

221

trians, the common citizens, and the slaves.[5] The aristocracy included the senatorial class with a total membership of three hundred citizens and their families. The majority of them inherited their status, although occasionally a plebeian would gain admission to the Senate through serving a term as consul. Most of the aristocrats gained their living as office holders and as owners of great landed estates. The equestrian order was made up of government contractors, bankers, and the wealthier merchants. Originally this class had been composed of those citizens with incomes sufficient to enable them to serve in the cavalry at their own expense, but the term *equites* had now come to be applied to all outside of the senatorial class who possessed property in substantial amount. The equestrians were the chief offenders in the indulgence of vulgar tastes and in the exploitation of the poor and the provincials. As bankers they regularly charged interest rates of 12 per cent and three or four times that much when they could get it. By far the largest number of the citizens were mere commoners or plebeians. Some of these were independent farmers, a few were industrial workers, but the majority were members of the city mob. When Julius Caesar became dictator, 320,000 citizens were actually being supported by the state.

The status of the slaves

The Roman slaves were scarcely considered people at all but instruments of production like cattle or horses to be worked for the profit of their masters. Notwithstanding the fact that some of them were refined and intelligent foreigners, they had none of the privileges granted to slaves in Athens. The policy of their owners was to get as much work out of them as possible during the years of their prime and then to turn them loose to be fed by the state when they became old and useless. It is a sad commentary on Roman civilization that nearly all of the productive labor in the country was done by slaves. They produced practically all of the nation's food supply, for the amount contributed by the few surviving independent farmers was quite insignificant. At least 80 per cent of the workers employed in factories and shops were slaves or former slaves. But many of the members of the servile population were engaged in nonproductive activities. A lucrative form of investment for the business classes was ownership of slaves trained as gladiators, who could be rented to the government or to aspiring politicians for the amusement of the people. The growth of luxury also required the employment of thousands of slaves in domestic service. The man of great wealth must have his doorkeepers, his litter-bearers, his couriers (for the government of the Republic had no postal service), his valets, and his pedagogues or tutors for his children. In some great mansions there were special servants with no other duties than to rub the master down after his bath or to care for his sandals.

[5] In addition, of course, there were numerous aliens, who really did not constitute a separate class. Many were on about the same level as the common citizens. Others were slaves.

The religious beliefs of the Romans were altered in various ways in the last two centuries of the Republic—again due mainly to the extension of Roman power over most of the Hellenistic states. There was, first of all, a tendency of the upper classes to abandon the traditional religion for the philosophies of Stoicism and Epicureanism. But many of the common people also found worship of the ancient gods no longer satisfying. It was too formal and mechanical and demanded too much in the way of duty and self-sacrifice to meet the needs of the masses, whose lives were now empty and meaningless. Furthermore, Italy had attracted a stream of immigrants from the East, most of whom had a religious background totally different from that of the Romans. The result was the rapid spread of Oriental mystery cults, which satisfied the craving for a more emotional religion and offered the reward of a blessed immortality to the wretched and downtrodden of earth. From Egypt came the cult of Isis and Osiris (or Sarapis, as the god was now more commonly called), while from Phrygia was introduced the worship of the Great Mother, with her eunuch priests and wild, symbolic orgies. So strong was the appeal of these cults that the decrees of the Senate against them proved almost impossible to enforce. In the last century B.C. the Persian cult of Mithraism, which came to surpass all the others in popularity, gained a foothold in Italy.

Changes in religion

6. The Principate or Early Empire (27 B.C.–284 A.D.)

Shortly before his death in 44 B.C., Julius Caesar had adopted as his sole heir his grandnephew Octavian, then a young man of eighteen quietly pursuing his studies in Illyria across the Adriatic Sea. Upon learning of his uncle's death, Octavian hastened to Rome to take over control of the government. He soon found that he must share his ambition with two of Caesar's powerful friends, Mark Antony and Lepidus. The following year the three men formed an alliance for the purpose of crushing the power of the aristocratic clique responsible for Caesar's murder. The methods employed were not to the new leaders' credit. Prominent members of the aristocracy were hunted down and slain and their property confiscated. The most noted of the victims was Cicero, brutally slain by Mark Antony's soldiers. Though Cicero had taken no part in the conspiracy against Caesar's life, he was feared as the most brilliant defender of the old constitution. The real murderers, Brutus and Cassius, escaped and organized an army of 80,000 republicans, but were finally defeated by Octavian and his colleagues in 42 B.C. About eight years later a quarrel developed among the members of the alliance themselves, inspired primarily by Antony's jealousy of Octavian. The ultimate outcome in 31 B.C. was the triumphant emergence of Caesar's heir as the most powerful man in the Roman state.

The victory of Octavian ushered in a new period in Roman history,

The triumph of Octavian or Augustus Caesar

*The revival of
constitutional
government*

*The reforms of
Augustus*

*See color
plates at
page 189*

*The successors
of Augustus*

the most glorious and the most prosperous that the nation experienced. Although problems of peace and order were still far from being completely solved, the deadly civil strife was ended, and the people now had their first decent opportunity to show what their talents could achieve. Unlike his great uncle, Octavian seems to have entertained no monarchical ambitions. He was determined, at any rate, to preserve the forms if not the substance of constitutional government. He accepted the titles of Augustus and Imperator conferred upon him by the Senate and the army.[6] He held the positions of proconsul and tribune permanently; but he refused to make himself dictator or even consul for life, despite the pleas of the populace that he do so. The title by which he preferred to have his authority designated was Princeps, or First Citizen of the State. For this reason the period of his rule and that of his successors is properly called the Principate, or early Empire, to distinguish it from the period of the Republic (sixth century B.C. to 27 B.C.) and from the period of the late Empire (284 A.D. to 476 A.D.).

Octavian, or Augustus as he was now more commonly called, ruled over Italy and the provinces for forty-four years (31 B.C.–14 A.D.). At the beginning of the period he governed by military power and by common consent, but in 27 B.C. the Senate bestowed upon him the series of offices and titles described above. His work as a statesman at least equaled in importance that of his more famous predecessor. Among the reforms of Augustus were the establishment of new forms of taxation, the creation of a centralized system of courts under his own supervision, and the bestowal of a large measure of local self-government upon cities and provinces. For the nation as a whole he laid the foundations for an elaborate postal service. He insisted upon experience and intelligence as qualifications for appointment to administrative office. By virtue of his proconsular authority he assumed direct control over the provincial governors and punished them severely for graft and extortion. He abolished the old system of farming out the collection of taxes in the provinces, which had led to such flagrant abuses, and appointed his own personal representatives as collectors at regular salaries. But he did not stop with political reforms. He procured the enactment of laws designed to check the more glaring social and moral evils of the time —divorce, race suicide, and adultery. By his own example of temperate living he sought to discourage luxurious habits and to set the precedent for a return to the ancient virtues.

After the death of Augustus in 14 A.D. Rome had few enlightened and capable rulers. Several of his successors were brutal tyrants who squandered the resources of the state and kept the country in an uproar by their deeds of bloody violence. As early as 68 A.D. the army began to take a hand in the selection of the Princeps, with the result

[6] The title Augustus signified "consecrated" and implied the idea that its bearer was specially favored of the gods. Imperator meant "victorious general."

that on several occasions thereafter the head of the government was little more than a military dictator. Between 235 and 284 A.D. sheer anarchy prevailed: of the twenty-six men who were elevated to power in that time only one escaped violent death. As a matter of fact, in the 270 years which followed the demise of Augustus, Rome had scarcely more than four or five rulers of whom much good could be said. The list would include Nerva (96–98 A.D.), Trajan (98–117), Antoninus Pius (138–161), Marcus Aurelius (161–180), and possibly Vespasian (70–79) and Hadrian (117–138).

How can this comparative failure of the political genius of the Romans in the very best period of their history be accounted for? The assertion is frequently made that it was due to the absence of any definite rule of hereditary succession to the office of Princeps. But this answer rests upon a misconception of the nature of the Roman constitution at this time. The government which Augustus established was not intended to be a monarchy. Although the Princeps was virtually an autocrat, the authority he possessed was supposed to be derived exclusively from the Senate and the people of Rome; he could have no inherent right to rule by virtue of royal descent. The explanation must therefore be sought in other factors. The Romans were now reaping the whirlwind which had been sown in the civil strife of the late Republic. They had grown accustomed to violence as the way out when problems did not admit of an easy solution. Furthermore, the long wars of conquest and the suppression of barbarian revolts had cheapened human life in the estimation of the people themselves and had fostered the growth of crime. As a consequence it was practically inevitable that men of vicious character should push their way into the highest political office.

Reasons for the political troubles in Rome

7. Culture and Life in the Period of the Principate

From the standpoint of variety of intellectual and artistic interests the period of the Principate outshone all other ages in the history of Rome. Most of the progress took place, however, in the years from 27 B.C. to 200 A.D. It was between these years that Roman philosophy attained its characteristic form. This period witnessed also the feeble awakening of an interest in science, the growth of a distinctive art, and the production of the best literary works. After 200 A.D. economic and political decay stifled all further cultural growth.

Cultural progress under the Principate

Stoicism was now the prevailing philosophy of the Romans. Much of the influence of Epicureanism lingered and found occasional expression in the writings of the poets, but as a system it had ceased to be popular. The reasons for the triumph of Stoicism are not hard to discover. With its emphasis upon duty, self-discipline, and subjection to the natural order of things, it accorded well with the ancient virtues of the Romans and with their habits of conservatism.

Roman Stoicism

225

Moreover, its insistence upon civic obligations and its doctrine of cosmopolitanism appealed to the Roman political-mindedness and pride in world empire. Epicureanism, on the other hand, was a little too negative and individualistic to agree with the collectivist traditions of Roman history. It seemed not only to repudiate the idea of any purpose in the universe, but even to deny the value of human effort. Since the Romans were men of action rather than speculative thinkers, the Epicurean ideal of the solitary philosopher immersed in the problem of his own salvation could have no permanent attraction for them. It is necessary to observe, however, that the Stoicism developed in the days of the Principate was somewhat different from that of Zeno and his school. The old physical theories borrowed from Heracleitus were now discarded, and in their place was substituted a broader interest in politics and ethics. There was a tendency also for Roman Stoicism to assume a more distinctly religious flavor than that which had characterized the original philosophy.

Seneca, Epic-
tetus, and Mar-
cus Aurelius

Three eminent apostles of Stoicism lived and taught in Rome in the two centuries which followed the rule of Augustus: Seneca (3 B.C.–65 A.D.), millionaire adviser for a time to Nero; Epictetus, the slave (60?–120 A.D.); and the Emperor Marcus Aurelius (121–180 A.D.). All of them agreed that inner serenity is the ultimate goal to be sought, that true happiness can be found only in surrender to the benevolent order of the universe. They preached the ideal of virtue for virtue's sake, deplored the sinfulness of man's nature, and urged obedience to conscience as the voice of duty. Seneca and Epictetus adulterated their philosophy with such deep mystical yearnings as to make it almost a religion. They worshiped the cosmos as divine, governed by an all-powerful Providence who ordains all that happens for ultimate good. Submission to the order of nature is thus equivalent to placing oneself in harmony with the will of God, and is therefore conceived as a religious duty. The last of the Roman Stoics, Marcus Aurelius, was more fatalistic and less hopeful. Although he did not reject the conception of an ordered and rational universe, he shared neither the faith nor the dogmatism of the earlier Stoics. He was confident of no blessed immortality to balance the sufferings of one's earthly career. Living in a melancholy time, he was inclined to think of man as a creature buffeted by evil fortune for which no distant perfection of the whole could fully atone. He urged, nevertheless, that men should continue to live nobly, that they should neither abandon themselves to gross indulgence nor break down in angry protest, but that they should derive what contentment they can from dignified resignation to suffering and tranquil submission to death.

The literary achievements of the Romans bore a definite relation to their philosophy. This was especially true of the works of the most distinguished writers of the Augustan Age. Horace, for ex-

Marcus Aurelius. This mounted figure of the great emperor-philosopher is one of the few equestrian statues produced in the ancient world. It was originally entirely gilded. Now on the Piazza del Campidoglio, Rome.

ample, in his famous *Odes* drew copiously from the teachings of both Epicureans and Stoics. He confined his attention, however, to their doctrines of a way of life, for like most of the Romans he had little curiosity about the nature of the world. He developed a philosophy which combined the Epicurean justification of pleasure with the Stoic bravery in the face of trouble. While he never reduced pleasure to the mere absence of pain, he was sophisticated enough to know that the highest enjoyment is possible only through the exercise of rational control. Perhaps the following lines express about as well as any others the essence of his view of life:

Roman literature: Horace

> Be brave in trouble; meet distress
> With dauntless front; but when the gale
> Too prosperous blows, be wise no less
> And shorten sail.[7]

Vergil likewise reflects a measure of the philosophical temper of his age. Though his *Eclogues* convey something of the Epicurean ideal of quiet pleasure, Vergil was much more of a Stoic. His utopian vision of an age of peace and abundance, his brooding sense of the tragedy of human fate, and his idealization of a life in harmony with nature indicate an intellectual heritage similar to that of Seneca and Epictetus. Vergil's most noted work, the *Aeneid*, like several of the *Odes* of Horace, was a purposeful glorification of Roman imperialism. The *Aeneid* in fact was an epic of empire recounting the toils and triumphs of the founding of the state, its glorious traditions, and

Vergil, Ovid, and Livy

[7] *Odes* (S. Conington trans.), Vol. II, p. 10.

The Baths of Caracalla, Rome. The gigantic scale is typical of Late Empire buildings. Elaborate and luxurious public baths like these were often presented to the people by the emperor or rich citizens. Shown is the *caldarium*, one of several types of chambers, for hot tub baths.

its magnificent destiny. The only other major writers of the Augustan Age were Ovid and Livy. The former, the greatest of Roman elegiac poets, was the chief representative of the cynical and individualist tendencies of his day. His writings, although brilliant and witty, often reflected the dissolute tastes of the time, and their popularity gives evidence of the failure of the efforts of Augustus to regenerate Roman society. The chief title of Livy to fame rests upon his skill as a prose stylist. As a historian he was woefully deficient. His main work, a history of Rome, is replete with dramatic and picturesque narrative, designed to appeal to the patriotic emotions rather than to present the impartial truth.

The literature of the period which followed the death of Augustus also exemplified conflicting social and intellectual tendencies. The *Petronius, Apuleius, Martial, Juvenal, and Tacitus* novels of Petronius and Apuleius and the epigrams of Martial are specimens of individualist writing generally descriptive of the meaner aspects of life. The attitude of the authors is unmoral; their purpose is not to instruct or uplift but chiefly to tell an entertaining story or turn a witty phrase. An entirely different viewpoint is presented in the works of the other most important writers of this age: Juvenal, the satirist, and Tacitus, the historian. Juvenal wrote under the influence of the Stoics but with little intelligence and narrow vision. Laboring under the delusion that the troubles of the nation were due to moral degeneracy, he lashed the vices of his countrymen with the fury of an evangelist. A somewhat similar attitude characterized the writing of his younger contemporary, Tacitus. The best-known of Roman historians, Tacitus described the events of his age not entirely with a view to scientific analysis but largely for the purpose of moral indictment. In his *Annals* and *Histories* he painted a lurid picture of political chaos and social corruption. His description of the customs of the ancient Germans in his *Germania* served to heighten the contrast between the manly virtues of an unspoiled race and the effeminate vices of the decadent Romans. Whatever his failings as a historian, he was a master of ironic wit and brilliant

228

aphorism. Referring to the boasted *Pax Romana*, he makes a barbarian chieftain say: "They create a wilderness and call it peace." [8]

The period of the Principate was the period when Roman art first assumed its distinctive character as an expression of the national life. Before this time what passed for an art of Rome was really an importation from the Hellenistic East. Conquering armies brought back to Italy wagonloads of statues, reliefs, and marble columns as part of the plunder from Greece and Asia Minor. These became the property of wealthy publicans and bankers and were used to embellish their sumptuous mansions. As the demand increased, hundreds of copies were made, with the result that Rome came to have by the end of the Republic a profusion of objects of art which had no more cultural significance than the Rembrandts or Botticellis in the home of some modern broker. The aura of national glory which surrounded the early Principate stimulated the growth of an art more nearly indigenous. Augustus himself boasted that he found Rome a city of brick and left it a city of marble. Nevertheless, much of the old Hellenistic influence remained until the talent of the Romans themselves was exhausted.

The arts most truly expressive of the Roman character were archi-

[8] Tacitus, *Agricola*, p. 30.

The Colosseum. The Colosseum was built by the Roman emperors as a place of entertainment and public exhibition. It was the scene of gladiatorial combats and of the throwing of Christians to the lions.

229

THE ARCHITECTURE OF ROME AND HER PROVINCES

The Arch of Titus with the Colosseum in the Background. Triumphal arches celebrating the military victories of individual emperors were among the most conspicuous examples of Roman architecture.

Arch of Hadrian, Athens.

Roman Aqueduct at Segovia, Spain. Aqueducts for conveying water from the mountains to the larger cities of the empire were among the most splendid engineering accomplishments of the Romans. The picture shows the skill with which large blocks of stone were fitted together to form arches.

The Maison Carrée at Nîmes, France. The most perfect example of Roman temple extant. Reflecting possibly Etruscan influence, it was built on a high base, or *podium*, with great steps leading to the entrance. The interior was larger and more lavish than that of a Greek temple. It dates from about the beginning of the Christian era.

The Pantheon, in Rome. Built by the Emperor Hadrian and dedicated to the deities of the seven planets, the Pantheon is a witness to the cosmopolitan religious attitude of the Romans. The distinctive feature of the interior is the dome, 140 feet in diameter, which still stands virtually unimpaired. For upwards of 16 centuries the building has been used as a Christian church.

A Street in Ostia, the Ancient Seaport of Rome. The round arches and masonry columns form the balcony of a rich man's house.

tecture and sculpture. Both were monumental, designed to symbolize power and grandeur rather than freedom of mind or contentment with life. Architecture contained as its leading elements the round arch, the vault, and the dome, although at times the Corinthian column was employed, especially in the construction of temples. The materials most commonly used were brick, squared stone blocks, and concrete, the last generally concealed with a marble facing. As a further adornment of public buildings, sculptured entablatures and façades, built up of tiers of colonnades or arcades, were frequently added. Copied from Hellenistic sources and bearing little relation to the rest of the structure, many of these decorative devices were showy and unseemly. Roman architecture was devoted primarily to utilitarian purposes. The foremost examples were government buildings, amphitheaters, baths, race courses, and private houses. Nearly all were of massive proportions and solid construction. Among the largest and most famous were the Pantheon, with its dome having a diameter of 142 feet, and the Colosseum, which could accommodate 65,000 spectators at the gladiatorial combats. Roman sculpture included as its main forms triumphal arches and columns, narrative reliefs, altars, and portrait busts and statues. Its distinguishing characteristics were individuality and naturalism. Even more than architecture it served to express the vanity and love of power of the Roman aristocracy, although some of it was marked by unusual qualities of harmony and grace.[9]

As scientists the Romans accomplished comparatively little either in this period or in any other. Scarcely an original discovery of fundamental importance was made by a man of Latin blood. This fact seems strange when we consider that the Romans had the advantage of Hellenistic science as a foundation upon which to build. But they neglected their opportunity almost completely. Why should this have been so? It was due, first of all, to the circumstance that the Romans were absorbed in problems of government and military conquest. Forced to specialize in law, politics, and military strategy, they had very little time for investigation of nature. A reason of more vital importance was the fact that the Romans were too practical-minded. They had none of that divine fire which impels man to lose himself in the quest for unlimited knowledge. They had no vigorous intellectual curiosity about the world in which they lived. In short, they were not philosophers. Contrary to the popular notion, practical-mindedness is not of itself sufficient to carry scientific progress very far. Modern science would probably have died of undernourishment long ago if it had had to depend solely upon the work of inventors and technologists.

Mainly because of this lack of talent for pure science, the achievements of the Romans were limited almost entirely to engineering and

[9] A great many of the best examples of both architecture and sculpture were produced not by Romans at all but by Greeks resident in Italy.

to the organization of public services. They built marvelous roads, bridges, and aqueducts. They provided the city of Rome with a water supply of 300,000,000 gallons daily. They established the first hospitals in the Western world and the first system of state medicine for the benefit of the poor. But their own writers on scientific subjects were hopelessly devoid of critical intelligence. The most renowned and the most typical of them was Pliny the Elder, who completed about 77 A.D. a voluminous encyclopedia of "science" which he called *Natural History*. This work was admittedly a compilation supposed to have been based upon the writings of nearly 500 different authors. The subjects discussed varied from cosmology to economics. Despite the wealth of material it contains, the work is of limited value. Pliny was totally unable to distinguish between fact and fable. In his estimation, the weirdest tales of wonders and portents were to be accepted as of equal value with the most solidly established facts. He described the marvels of a primitive people whose feet all turned backward, of a country where females conceived at the age of five and died at the age of eight, and of a tiny Mediterranean fish which could cause ships to stand still merely by clinging to them. The other best-known author of an encyclopedia of science was Seneca, the Stoic philosopher, who took his own life at Nero's command in 65 A.D. Seneca was less credulous than Pliny but no more original. Besides, he maintained that the purpose of all scientific study should be to divulge the moral secrets of nature. If there was any Latin who could be considered an original scientist, the title would have to be given to Celsus, who flourished during the reign of Tiberius. Celsus wrote a comprehensive treatise on medicine, including an excellent manual of surgery, but there is a strong suspicion that the entire work was compiled, if not actually translated, from the Greek. Among the operations he described were tonsillectomy, operations for cataracts and goiter, and plastic surgery.

No account of the scientific aspects of Roman civilization would be complete without some mention of the work of Hellenistic scientists who lived in Italy or in the provinces during the period of the Principate. Nearly all of them were physicians. The most distinguished, although apparently not the most original, was Galen of Pergamum, who was active in Rome at various times during the latter half of the second century. While his fame rests primarily upon his medical encyclopedia, systematizing the learning of others, he is deserving of more credit for his own experiments which brought him close to a discovery of the circulation of the blood. He not only taught but proved that the arteries carry blood, and that severance of even a small one is sufficient to drain away all of the blood of the body in little more than half an hour. But Galen was not the only Hellenistic physician who made important contributions in this time. At least two others are entitled to more recognition than is commonly given to them: Soranus of Ephesus, the greatest gynecologist

Hellenistic scientists in Italy

233

of antiquity and inventor of the speculum, and Rufus of Ephesus, who wrote the first accurate description of the liver and of the rhythm of the pulse, and was the first to recommend boiling of suspicious water before drinking it.

Roman society exhibited the same general tendencies under the Principate as in the last days of the Republic. A few significant differences, however, can be noted. Owing in part to the influence of the Stoic philosophy and in part to the abundance of free labor, slavery began to decline. Despite the efforts of Augustus to limit the manumission of slaves, the number of freedmen steadily increased. They crowded into every field of employment, including the civil service. Many succeeded in becoming proprietors of small shops, and some even became rich. Not entirely unconnected with these developments was the growth of the institution of clientage. Members of the citizen class who had lost their property or who had been driven out of business by the competition of enterprising freedmen now frequently became "clients" or dependents of wealthy aristocrats. In return for pittances of food and money these "shabby genteel" served the great magnates by applauding their speeches and fawning before them when they appeared in public. Custom made it practically obligatory for every man of great wealth to maintain a retinue of these miserable flatterers.

Social tendencies under the Principate

Although the evidence has frequently been exaggerated, the period of the Principate was apparently marked by moral decay. Divorce among the upper classes was now so common as to be scarcely a matter of remark. According to the records there were 32,000 prostitutes in Rome during the reign of Trajan, and, if we can judge from the testimony of some of the most noted writers, homosexuality was exceedingly common and even fashionable. While political corruption had been subjected to more stringent control, crimes of violence appear to have increased. But the most serious moral indictment which can be brought against the age would seem to have been a further growth of the passion for cruelty. The great games and spectacles became bloodier and more disgusting than ever. The Romans could no longer obtain a sufficient thrill from mere exhibitions of athletic prowess; pugilists were now required to have their hands wrapped with thongs of leather loaded with iron or lead. The most popular amusement of all was watching the gladiatorial combats in the Colosseum or in other amphitheaters capable of accommodating thousands of spectators. Fights between gladiators were nothing new, but they were now presented on a much more elaborate scale. Not only the ignorant rabble attended them, but wealthy aristocrats also, and frequently the head of the government himself. The gladiators fought to the accompaniment of savage cries and curses from the audience. When one went down with a disabling wound, it was the privilege of the crowd to decide whether his life should be spared or whether the weapon of his op-

Signs of moral decay

ponent should be plunged into his heart. One contest after another was staged in the course of a single exhibition. Should the arena become too sodden with blood, it was covered over with a fresh layer of sand, and the revolting performance went on. Most of the gladiators were condemned criminals or slaves, but some were volunteers even from the respectable classes. The Princeps Commodus, the worthless son of Marcus Aurelius, entered the arena several times for the sake of the plaudits of the mob.

Notwithstanding its low moral tone, the age of the Principate was characterized by an even deeper interest in salvationist religions than that which had prevailed under the Republic. Mithraism now gained adherents by the thousands, absorbing most of the followers of the cults of the Great Mother and of Isis and Sarapis. About 40 A.D. the first Christians appeared in Rome. The new sect grew rapidly and eventually succeeded in displacing Mithraism as the most popular of the mystery cults. For some time the Roman government was no more hostile toward Christianity than it was toward the other mystery religions. While it is a fact that some members of the sect were put to death by Nero in response to the demand for a scapegoat for the disastrous fire of 64 A.D., there was no systematic persecution of Christians as such until the reign of Decius nearly two hundred years later. Even then the persecution was inspired by political and social considerations more than by religious motives. Because of their otherworldliness and their refusal to take the customary oaths in the courts or participate in the civic religion, the Christians were regarded as disloyal citizens and dangerous characters. Moreover, their ideals of meekness and non-resistance, their preaching against the rich, and their practice of holding what appeared to be secret meetings made the Romans suspect them as enemies of the established order. In the end, persecution defeated its own purpose. It intensified the zeal of those who survived, with the result that the new faith spread more rapidly than ever.

The spread of Mithraism and Christianity

The establishment of stable government by Augustus ushered in a period of prosperity for Italy which lasted for more than two centuries. Trade was now extended to all parts of the known world, even to Arabia, India, and China. Manufacturing reached more than insignificant proportions, especially in the production of pottery, textiles, and articles of metal and glass. As a result of the development of rotation of crops and the technique of soil fertilization, agriculture flourished as never before. In spite of all this, the economic order was far from healthy. The prosperity was not evenly distributed but was confined primarily to the upper classes. Since the stigma attached to manual labor persisted as strong as ever, production was bound to decline as the supply of slaves diminished. Worse still was the fact that Italy had a decidedly unfavorable balance of trade. The meager industrial development which had occurred was by no means sufficient to provide enough articles of export to meet the demand

Economic prosperity during the first two centuries

for luxuries imported from the provinces and from the outside world. As a consequence, Italy was gradually drained of her supply of precious metals. By the third century signs of economic collapse were already abundant.

8. Roman Law

The early development of Roman law

There is general agreement that the most important legacy which the Romans left to succeeding cultures was their system of law. This system was the result of a gradual evolution which may be considered to have begun with the publication of the Twelve Tables about 450 B.C. In the later centuries of the Republic the law of the Twelve Tables was modified and practically superseded by the growth of new precedents and principles. These emanated from different sources: from changes in custom, from the teachings of the Stoics, from the decisions of judges, but especially from the edicts of the praetors. The Roman praetors were magistrates who had authority to define and interpret the law in a particular suit and issue instructions to the jury for the decision of the case. The jury merely decided questions of fact; all issues of law were settled by the praetor, and generally his interpretations became precedents for the decision of similar cases in the future. Thus a system of judicial practice was built up in somewhat the same fashion as the English common law.

Roman law under the Principate; the great jurists

It was under the Principate, however, that the Roman law attained its highest stage of development. This later progress was due in part to the extension of the law over a wider field of jurisdiction, over the lives and properties of aliens in strange environments as well as over the citizens of Italy. But the major reason was the fact that Augustus and his successors gave to certain eminent jurists the right to deliver opinions, or *responsa* as they were called, on the legal issues of cases under trial in the courts. The most prominent of the men thus designated from time to time were Gaius, Ulpian, Papinian, and Paulus. Although most of them held high judicial office, they had gained their reputations primarily as lawyers and writers on legal subjects. The responses of these jurists came to embody a science and philosophy of law and were accepted as the basis of Roman jurisprudence. It was typical of the Roman respect for authority that the ideas of these men should have been adopted so readily even when they upset, as they occasionally did, time-honored beliefs.

The three divisions of the Roman law

The Roman law as it was developed under the influence of the jurists comprised three great branches or divisions: the *jus civile*, the *jus gentium*, and the *jus naturale*. The *jus civile*, or civil law, was essentially the law of Rome and her citizens. As such it existed in both written and unwritten forms. It included the statutes of the Senate, the decrees of the Princeps, the edicts of the praetors, and also certain ancient customs operating with the force of law. The

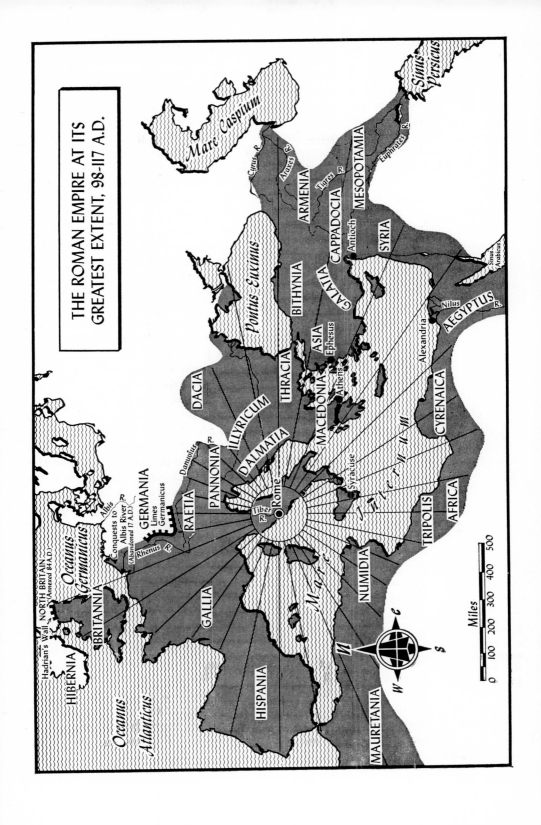

THE ROMAN EMPIRE AT ITS
GREATEST EXTENT, 98-117 A.D.

Mare Caspium

Sinus Persicus

Cyrus R.
Araxes R.
ARMENIA
Tigres R.
Euphrates R.
MESOPOTAMIA
CAPPADOCIA
BITHYNIA
Antioch
GALATIA
SYRIA
Pontus Euxinus
ASIA
Ephesus
Sinus Arabicus
Nilus
AEGYPTUS
Alexandria
THRACIA
DACIA
MACEDONIA
Athens
ILLYRICUM
Syracuse
CYRENAICA
DALMATIA
PANNONIA
Danubius R.
Rome
Mare Internum
RAETIA
Tiber R.
GERMANIA
Limes Germanicus
AFRICA
Albis
Albis River
(Abandoned 17 A.D.)
Conquests to
TRIPOLIS
Rhenus R.
Albis R.
NUMIDIA
Oceanus Germanicus
Hadrian's Wall NORTH BRITAIN
(Annexed 84 A.D.)
BRITANNIA
GALLIA
Mare
HIBERNIA
HISPANIA
Oceanus
Atlanticus
MAURETANIA

N
W E
S

Miles
0   100 200 300 400 500

jus gentium, or law of peoples, was the law which was held to be common to all men regardless of nationality. It was the law which authorized the institutions of slavery and private ownership of property and defined the principles of purchase and sale, partnership, and contract. It was not superior to the civil law but supplemented it as especially applicable to the alien inhabitants of the empire.

The jus naturale

The most interesting and in many ways the most important branch of the Roman law was the *jus naturale*, or natural law. This was not a product of judicial practice at all but of philosophy. The Stoics had developed the idea of a rational order of nature which is the embodiment of justice and right. They had affirmed that all men are by nature equal, and that they are entitled to certain basic rights which governments have no authority to transgress. The father of the law of nature as a legal principle, however, was none of the Hellenistic Stoics, but Cicero. "True law," he declared, "is right reason consonant with nature, diffused among all men, constant, eternal. To make enactments infringing this law, religion forbids, neither may it be repealed even in part, nor have we power through Senate or people to free ourselves from it." [10] This law is prior to the state itself, and any ruler who defies it automatically becomes a tyrant. Some of the later Stoics—Seneca in particular—elaborated the doctrine of a primordial state of nature in which all men were equal, and no one was exploited by another. In time, the wickedness and greed of some brought slavery and private property into existence; government therefore became necessary for the protection of the weak. With the exception of Gaius, who identified the *jus naturale* with the *jus gentium*, all of the great jurists subscribed to conceptions of the law of nature very similar to those of the philosophers. While the jurists did not regard this law as an automatic limitation upon the *jus civile*, they thought of it nevertheless as a great ideal to which the statutes and decrees of men ought to conform. This development of the concept of abstract justice as a legal principle was one of the noblest achievements of the Roman civilization.

9. The Late Empire (284–476 A.D.)

*Rome becomes
a despotic
empire during
the reign of
Diocletian*

The last period of Roman history, from 284 to 476 A.D., is properly called the period of the late Empire. With the accession of Diocletian in 284, the government of Rome finally became an undisguised autocracy. It is true, of course, that constitutional government had been little more than a fiction for some time before this, but now all pretense of maintaining the Republic was thrown aside. Both in theory and in practice the change was complete. No longer was the doctrine advanced that the ruler was the mere agent of the Senate and the people; he was now held to be absolutely sovereign on the assumption that the people had surrendered all power to him. Diocletian

[10] *The Republic*, Vol. III, p. 22.

adopted the regalia and ceremony of an Oriental despot. In place of the simple military garb of the Princeps he substituted a purple robe of silk interwoven with gold. He required all his subjects who were admitted to an audience with him to prostrate themselves before him. Needless to say, the Senate was now completely excluded from participation in the government. It was not formally abolished, but it was reduced to the status of a municipal council and a social club for the plutocracy. The chief reason for these political changes is undoubtedly to be found in the economic decline of the third century. The people had lost confidence in themselves, as they frequently do under such circumstances, and were ready to sacrifice all of their rights for the faint hope of security.

Diocletian's successors continued his system of absolutism. The most famous of them were Constantine I (306–337), Julian (361–363), and Theodosius I (379–395). Constantine is best known for his establishment of a new capital, called Constantinople, on the site of ancient Byzantium, and for his policy of religious toleration toward Christians. Contrary to a common belief, he did not make Christianity the official religion of the Empire; his various edicts issued in 313 simply gave Christianity an equality of status with the pagan cults, thereby terminating the policy of persecution. Later in his reign he bestowed upon the Christian clergy certain special privileges and caused his sons to be brought up in the new faith, but he continued to maintain the imperial cult. Although he was acclaimed by historians of the church as Constantine the Great, his practice of favoring Christianity was dictated primarily by political motives. A generation after Constantine's death the Emperor Julian attempted to stimulate a pagan reaction. He had come under the influence of the Neo-Platonist philosophy and regarded Christianity as a product of Jewish superstition. The last of the noted pagan emperors, he has been branded by Christian historians as Julian the Apostate. The other most prominent of the rulers of Rome in its dying stage was Theodosius I, who, in spite of his butchery of thousands of innocent citizens on imaginary charges of conspiracy, is also known as "the Great." The chief importance of his reign comes from his decree of 380 commanding all of his subjects to become orthodox Christians. A few years later he classified participation in any of the pagan cults as an act of treason.

Diocletian's successors

See color plates at page 189

From the standpoint of cultural achievement the period of the Empire is of little significance. With the establishment of a despotic state and the degradation of intellect by mystical and otherworldly religions, creative talent was destroyed. The few literary works produced were characterized by an overemphasis upon form and a neglect of content. A barren and artificial rhetoric took the place of the study of the classics in the schools, while science died out completely. Aside from the teachings of the Christian Fathers, which will be discussed later, the prevailing philosophy of the age was Neo-

Cultural stagnation and the adoption of mystical philosophy

Platonism. This philosophy, purporting to be a continuation of the system of Plato, was really an outgrowth of the doctrines of the Neo-Pythagoreans and of Philo Judaeus.[11] The first of its basic teachings was emanationism: everything that exists proceeds from God in a continuing stream of emanations. The initial stage in the process is the emanation of the world-soul. From this come the divine Ideas or spiritual patterns, and then the souls of particular things. The final emanation is matter. But matter has no form or quality of its own; it is simply the privation of spirit, the residue which is left after the spiritual rays from God have burned themselves out. It follows that matter is to be despised as the symbol of evil and darkness. The second major doctrine was mysticism. The soul of man was originally a part of God, but it has become separated from him through its union with matter. The highest goal of life should be mystic reunion with the divine, which can be accomplished through contemplation and through emancipation of the soul from bondage to matter. Man should be ashamed of the fact that he possesses a physical body and should seek to subjugate it in every way possible. Asceticism was therefore the third main teaching of this philosophy.

Neo-Platonism

The real founder of Neo-Platonism was Plotinus, who was born in Egypt about 204 A.D. In the later years of his life he taught in Rome and won many followers among the upper classes. His principal successors diluted the philosophy with more and more bizarre superstitions. In spite of its anti-intellectual viewpoint and its utter indifference to the state, Neo-Platonism became so popular in Rome in the third and fourth centuries A.D. that it almost completely supplanted Stoicism. No fact could have expressed more eloquently the extent of the social and intellectual decline which the Roman nation had experienced.

Plotinus

10. Decay and Decline

In 476 A.D. the last of the emperors in the West, the insignificant Romulus Augustulus, was deposed, and a barbarian chieftain assumed the title of King of Rome. Though this event is commonly taken to have marked the end of Roman history, it was really only the final incident in a long process of disintegration. The fall of Rome did not occur with dramatic suddenness, but extended over a period of approximately two centuries. A large part of the civilization was already dead before the Empire collapsed. Indeed, for all practical purposes the pagan culture of Rome from the middle of the third century on could be considered as belonging to the Dark Ages.

The decline and fall of Rome

More has been written on the fall of Rome than on the death of any other civilization. The theories offered to account for the tragedy have been many and various. Moralist historians have found the explanation in the evidences of lechery unearthed at Pompeii or re-

Alleged causes of the decline

[11] See above, p. 197.

vealed in the satires of Juvenal and Martial. They overlook the fact, however, that nearly all of this evidence comes from the early Principate, and that in the centuries preceding the collapse of the Empire, morality became much more austere, due to the influence of ascetic religions. Historians of a sociological bent have attributed the downfall to a declining birth rate, a factor which is often alleged to hold ominous significance for the modern world. But there is little to indicate that Rome could have been saved by greater numbers. The Athenian civilization reached the height of its glory during the very centuries when growth of population was most strictly limited.

If there was one primary factor which operated more than others to accomplish the downfall of Roman civilization it was imperialism. Nearly all of the troubles which beset the country were traceable in some measure to the conquest of a great empire. It was this which was largely responsible for the creation of the city mob, for the growth of slavery, for the strife between classes and the widespread political corruption. It was imperialism also which was partly responsible for the barbarian invasions, for the exhaustion of the resources of the state to maintain a huge military machine, and for the influx of alien ideas which the Romans could not readily assimilate. The idea that Rome became a civilized nation as a result of her conquests is undoubtedly a fallacy. Instead, her repeated victories caused her ruling population to become greedy and domineering. It is true that she appropriated much of the Hellenistic culture after her conquest of the Near East; but the really valuable elements of this culture would eventually have been acquired anyway through the normal expansion of trade, while the evil consequences of domination of vast areas by force would have been avoided.

Actual causes:
(1) imperialism

Another important cause, closely related to imperialism, deserves analysis: namely, the revolution in economic and social conditions which swept over Italy in the third and fourth centuries A.D. This revolution, which differed radically from the one that had occupied the third and second centuries B.C., had the following features: (1) the disappearance of money from circulation and the return to a natural economy; (2) the decline of industry and commerce; (3) the growth of serfdom and the rise of an extralegal feudalism; (4) the extension of government control over a large portion of the economic sphere; and (5) the transition from a regime of individual initiative to a regime of hereditary status. The primary cause of this revolution seems to have been the unfavorable balance of trade which Italy suffered in her commerce with the provinces. In order to check the withdrawal of precious metals from the country, the government, instead of encouraging manufactures for export, resorted to the hazardous expedient of debasing the coinage. Nero began the practice, and his successors continued it until the proportion of baser metal in the Roman coins had increased to 98.5 per cent.

(2) economic decay

The inevitable result was disappearance of money from circulation. Commerce could no longer be carried on, salaries had to be paid in food and clothing, and taxes collected in produce. The scarcity of money in turn led to a decline in production, until the government intervened with a series of decrees binding peasants to the soil and compelling every townsman to follow the occupation of his father. The great landlords, now that they had control over a body of serfs, entrenched themselves on their estates, defied the central government, and ruled as feudal magnates. So close were the peasants to the margin of starvation that many of them sold their newborn children in order to escape from the burden of supporting them.

Other causes

No one can present an exhaustive list of causes of Rome's decline. Among others of at least minor significance were the following: (1) the unjust policy of taxation, which rested most heavily on business and farming classes and resulted in the discouragement of productive enterprise; (2) the social stigma attached to work, resulting in the deliberate choice by thousands of the debasing relationship of clientage in preference to useful labor; (3) exhaustion of the soil, resulting in part from unscientific farming and in part from the attempt of too many people to make a living from the land; and (4) the disastrous plagues of Asiatic origin which broke out in 166 and 252 A.D., resulting in depopulating whole sections of Italy and thereby opening the way for barbarian incursions. To the last of these causes should be appended the fact that as lands along the low-lying coast were withdrawn from cultivation, due to the competition of grain from the provinces, malaria spread. The effect of this disease in undermining the vigor of the Italian population is impossible to estimate, but it must have been considerable.

11. The Roman Heritage

Comparison of Rome and the modern world

It is tempting to believe that the modern world owes a vast debt to the Romans: first of all, because Rome is nearer to us in time than any of the other civilizations of antiquity; and secondly, because Rome seems to bear such a close kinship to the modern temper. The resemblances between Roman history and the history of Great Britain or the United States in the nineteenth and twentieth centuries have often been noted. The Roman economic evolution progressed all the way from a simple agrarianism to a complex urban system with problems of unemployment, monopoly, gross disparities of wealth, and financial crises. Roman society likewise exhibited its "modern" phenomena of divorce, declining birth rates, and love of spectacular amusements. The Roman Empire, in common with the British and the American, was founded upon conquest and upon visions of Manifest Destiny. It must not be forgotten, however, that the spirit of Rome was the spirit of classical man, and that, consequently, the similarities between the Roman and modern civilizations are not so important as they seem. As we have noted already, the Romans despised industrial activities, and they were incredibly naïve in matters of science. Neither did they have any idea of the modern national state; the provinces were mere appendages, not integral parts of a body politic. It was largely for this reason that the Romans never developed an adequate system of representative government. Finally, the Roman conception of religion was vastly different from our own. Their system of worship, like that of the Greeks, was external and mechanical, not inward or spiritual in any sense. What Christians consider the highest ideal of piety—an emotional attitude of love for the divine—the Romans regarded as gross superstition.

Nevertheless, the civilization of Rome was not without a definite influence upon later cultures. The form, if not the spirit, of Roman architecture was preserved in the ecclesiastical architecture of the Middle Ages and survives to this day in the design of most of our government buildings. The sculpture of the Augustan Age also lives on in the equestrian statues, the memorial arches and columns, and the portraits in stone of statesmen and generals which adorn our boulevards and parks. Although subjected to new interpretations, the law of the great jurists became an important part of the Code of Justinian and was thus handed down to the later Middle Ages. Mod-

The influence of Roman civilization

The Forum, the civic center of ancient Rome. In addition to public squares, the Forum included triumphal arches, magnificent temples, and government buildings. In the foreground is the Temple of Saturn. Behind it is the Temple of Antoninus and Faustina. The three columns at the extreme right are what is left of the Temple of Castor and Pollux, and in the farthest background is the Arch of Titus.

243

ern lawyers and especially American judges frequently cite maxims originally invented by Gaius or Ulpian. Furthermore, the legal systems of nearly all Continental European countries today incorporate much of the Roman law. This law has had notable effects in strengthening the right of private ownership of property. It should not be forgotten either that Roman literary achievements furnished much of the inspiration for the revival of learning which spread over Europe in the twelfth century and reached its zenith in the Renaissance. Perhaps not so well known is the fact that the organization of the Catholic Church, to say nothing of part of its ritual, was adapted from the structure of the Roman state and the complex of the Roman religion. For example, the Pope still bears the title of Supreme Pontiff (*Pontifex Maximus*), which was used to designate the authority of the emperor as head of the civic religion. But the most important element in the Roman influence has probably been the idea of the absolute authority of the state. In the judgment of nearly all Romans, with the exception of philosophers like Cicero and Seneca, the state was legally omnipotent. However much the Roman may have detested tyranny, it was really only *personal* tyranny that he feared; the despotism of the Senate as the organ of popular sovereignty was perfectly proper. This conception survives to our own day in the popular conviction that the state can do no wrong, and especially in the doctrines of absolutist political philosophers that the individual has no rights except those which the state confers upon him.

The Roman conception of a world empire

One other political conception, emanating from the Romans, has had lasting significance. This is the conception of a world empire established and maintained by a single people by virtue of its martial prowess and its superior civilization. The Romans brought to a temporary end the regime of national independence that had prevailed during most of previous history except during the brief rule of the Hellenistic empires. Under the *Pax Romana* none of the smaller nations was really master of its own fate. All were mere appendages of Rome, in theory if not in actuality. They had not chosen this fate for themselves but had been obliged to accept it because of the overwhelming power of their mighty neighbor. As a consequence, the Mediterranean Sea, which washed the shores of most of what was then the civilized Western world, had become a Roman lake. This same *Pax Romana* provided much of the inspiration for the *Pax Britannica* of the nineteenth century. Controlling a population amounting to three-fourths of the world's total and maintaining a navy equal in strength to the combined navies of any two other powers, Great Britain molded the destinies of most of the Western world. In this way she succeeded in preventing major wars and in acquiring cultural and economic supremacy. At the end of the nineteenth century many Americans also fell under the spell of the *Pax Romana*. Politicians and propagandists like Albert J. Beveridge,

William Allen White, and Theodore Roosevelt proclaimed it the mission of the American people to become the "master organizers" of the world, to enforce peace, and to advance the cause of human welfare. They insisted that their country had been given a divine appointment as "trustee of the civilization of the world." [12]

Selected Readings

· *Items so designated are available in paperbound editions.*

Arnold, E. V., *Roman Stoicism,* Cambridge, 1911.
Bailey, Cyril, ed., *The Legacy of Rome,* New York, 1924.
Baker, G. P., *Hannibal,* New York, 1929.
Boak, A. E. R., *A History of Rome to 565 A.D.,* New York, 1929. Clear and concise.
· Cowell, F. R., *Cicero and the Roman Republic,* New York, 1948. (Penguin) A good account of the fall of the Republic.
Declareuil, J., *Rome, the Law-Giver,* New York, 1927. A masterly explanation.
——, *Roman Society in the Last Century of the Western Empire,* London, 1899. A vivid portrayal of decay.
· Dill, Samuel, *Roman Society from Nero to Marcus Aurelius,* New York, 1905. (Meridian) Old but still highly regarded.
Fowler, W. W., *Social Life at Rome in the Age of Cicero,* New York, 1915.
——, *The Religious Experience of the Roman People,* London, 1911.
Frank, Tenney, *Economic History of Rome,* Baltimore, 1927. Perhaps the best economic history.
Greene, W. C., *The Achievement of Rome,* Cambridge, Mass., 1933.
Haskell, H. J., *This Was Cicero,* New York, 1942.
Heitland, W. E., *The Roman Republic,* Cambridge, 1909, 3 vols.
· Lot, Ferdinand, *The End of the Ancient World,* New York, 1931. (Torchbooks)
Louis, Paul, *Ancient Rome at Work,* New York, 1927.
Marsh, F. D., *The Foundation of the Roman Empire,* London, 1927. Balanced and scholarly.
· Mommsen, Theodor, *The History of Rome,* Chicago, 1957. (Meridian, Wisdom Library) A reprint of a great masterpiece.
Rostovtzev, M. I., *Social and Economic History of the Roman Empire,* New York, 1926. Has become almost a classic.
——, *History of the Ancient World,* New York, 1927, Vol. II.
Thorndike, Lynn, *A History of Magic and Experimental Science in the First Thirteen Centuries of Our Era,* New York, 1923, 2 vols. Detailed but excellent.
Tucker, T. G., *Life in the Roman World of Nero and St. Paul,* New York, 1915. A good study of social life when Rome was at its zenith.
Westermann, W. L., *The Slave Systems of Greek and Roman Antiquity,* Philadelphia, 1955.

Source Materials

Caesar, *Commentaries on the Gallic War.*
Cicero, *On the Republic; On the Laws.*
Epictetus, *Discourses.*
Horace, *Odes; Epodes.*
Juvenal, *Satires.*
Lucretius, *On the Nature of Things.*
Marcus Aurelius, *Meditations.*
Tacitus, *Agricola; Germania.*
Vergil, *Aeneid.*

[12] For an extended discussion of this subject see E. M. Burns, *The American Idea of Mission,* pp. 206–10.

THE EARLY MIDDLE AGES

PART

3

THE EARLY MIDDLE AGES

During the period from 284 to 476 A.D. Roman civilization was strongly influenced by a revival of Oriental ideals of despotism, otherworldliness, pessimism, and fatalism. In the midst of economic distress and cultural decay men lost interest in earthly achievement and began to yearn for spiritual blessings in a life after death. This change in attitude was due primarily to the spread of Oriental religions, especially Christianity. When the Roman Empire finally collapsed, the victory of Orientalism was almost complete. The result was the evolution of new civilizations, compounded in part of elements taken from Greece and from Rome but with religion as a dominant factor behind most of their achievements. Altogether three new cultures finally emerged: the civilization of western Europe in the early Middle Ages, the Byzantine civilization, and the Saracenic civilization. The periods covered by the history of all three overlapped. The civilization of western Europe in the early Middle Ages extended from about 400 to 800. Although Constantine established his capital on the site of ancient Byzantium in the fourth century A.D., Byzantine civilization did not begin its independent evolution until after 500. It survived until the capture of Constantinople by the Turks in 1453. The Saracenic civilization flourished from the seventh century to the end of the thirteenth.

A CHRONOLOGICAL TABLE

	Western Europe	Byzantine Empire	The Saracens
	Rise of the Papacy, 50–300 Germanic migrations and invasions, 100–600 Growth of the colonate, *ca.* 200–500		
300—		Rise of monasticism, *ca.* 300 Council of Nicaea, 325 Constantinople established as capital, 330	
	Invasions of England by Angles and Saxons, 400–600 Decline of industry and commerce, 400–800 Capture of Rome by Visigoths, 410 St. Augustine's *City of God*, 413–426 Origin of Seven Liberal Arts, *ca.* 450 Merovingian dynasty in France, 481–751	Monophysite movement, 450–565	

	Western Europe	Byzantine Empire	The Saracens
500—	Ostrogothic rule in Italy, 493–552 Boethius' *Consolation of Philosophy*, 523		
		Justinian's empire, 527–565 Revision and codification of Roman law, 527–535 Construction of church of Santa Sophia, 532–537 Byzantine conquest of Italy, 535–552	
	Lombard invasion of Italy, 568		Mohammed, 570?–632
			The Hegira, 622 Capture of Mecca, 630 Conquest of Persia, Egypt, Palestine, Syria, North Africa, Spain, 632–732 Division of Islam into sects—Sunnites, Shiites, and Sufis, *ca.* 640
		Iconoclastic movement, 725–850	
800—	Battle of Tours, 732 Carolingian dynasty, 751–887 Development of feudalism, 800–1300 Charlemagne's empire, 800–814 Treaty of Verdun, 843 Holy Roman Empire, 962–		Development of steel manufacturing, textile manufacturing, leather tooling, and paper making, *ca.* 800-1400
			Hindu-Arabic system of numerals, *ca.* 1000 Saracenic world trade, *ca.* 1000–1500
		Separation of Eastern and Western churches, 1054 Battle of Manzikert, 1071	
1100—	The Crusades, 1096–1204		Cultivation of cotton, sugar, oranges, lemons, bananas, coffee, *ca.* 1100 Transmission of complete works of Aristotle to Europe, *ca.* 1150
		Capture of Constantinople by Crusaders of Fourth Crusade, 1204	
	Black Death, 1347–1349		Transmission of compass and astrolabe to Europe, *ca.* 1400
1453—		Capture of Constantinople by Ottoman Turks, 1453	

The Civilization of Early
Medieval Europe

Think not that I am come to destroy the law, or the prophets:
I am not come to destroy, but to fulfill.
  —Jesus of Nazareth, The Sermon on the Mount, *Matthew* v.17

Although checked for the time, this pernicious superstition [Christianity] broke out again . . . throughout the City, in which the atrocities and shame from all parts of the world center and flourish. Therefore those who confessed were first seized, then on their information a great multitude were convicted, not so much of the crime of incendiarism, as of hatred of the human race.
  —Tacitus on Nero's persecution of Christians

Misinterpretation of the word "medieval"

Sometime during the Renaissance the practice arose of dividing the history of the world into three great epochs: ancient, medieval, and modern. This classification has come to be accepted with almost dogmatic finality. It ties in with the average man's belief that this planet of ours has witnessed only two great periods of progress: the time of the Greeks and the Romans and the age of modern invention. Between these two periods were the Middle Ages, popularly regarded as an interlude of abysmal ignorance and superstition when man lived enveloped in a cowl, oblivious of the wonders of knowledge, and concerned only with escape from the miseries of this world and the torments of hell. The very word "medieval" has an odious meaning in the average mind of today. It has come to be a synonym for reactionary or unprogressive. Thus when a modern reformer wishes to cast reproach upon the ideas of his conservative opponent, all he has to do is to brand them as "medieval." No doubt he would be very much surprised if he should learn that the social and economic doctrines of some medieval thinkers were really quite similar to his own.

Only the period from 400 to 800 A.D. really dark

The reason for such erroneous judgments lies in the conventional notion that the entire medieval period from the fall of Rome to the beginning of the Renaissance was a cultural unit, that the ideals and institutions of the sixth century, for example, were the same as those of the thirteenth. Nothing could be farther from the truth. The medieval period, in western Europe, really encompassed two civilizations, as different from each other as Greece from Rome or the Renaissance from the nineteenth and twentieth centuries. The first of these civilizations, beginning about 400 A.D., when the process of Roman decay was virtually complete, and extending until 800, was that of the early Middle Ages. It was this period alone which was really distinguished by most of those attributes commonly referred to as "medieval." The culture of the early Middle Ages undoubtedly represented in certain respects a reversion to barbarism. Intellect did not merely stagnate but sank to very low depths of ignorance and credulity. Economic activity declined to primitive levels of barter and ruralism, while morbid asceticism and contempt for this world superseded more normal social attitudes. With the Carolingian Renaissance of the ninth century, however, a new life began in Europe. The human spirit soared to magnificent heights in literature, philosophy, and art. The result was another of the world's great cultures, distinguished alike by intellectual progress and a high degree of prosperity and freedom. Indeed, this later medieval civilization, which endured until the end of the thirteenth century, was more nearly similar to the modern age than most people realize.

1. The Christian Foundation of Early Medieval Culture

Three main factors combined to produce the civilization of early medieval Europe: the Christian religion, the influence of the Germanic barbarians, and the heritage from the classical cultures. The effect of the third was probably less than that of the others. Outside the realm of philosophy the influence of the Greek and Hellenistic civilizations was comparatively slight. While the Roman heritage was still powerful, the men of the early Middle Ages rejected some portions of it as inconsistent with Christianity and barbarized much of the remainder.

Factors influencing early medieval culture

The chief foundation of the new culture was the Christian religion, whose founder, Jesus of Nazareth, was born in a small town of

Nazareth. A modern view of the small town in Judea where Jesus spent his early life, where he worked for a time as a carpenter and began his career of preaching. **251**

*The career of
Jesus of
Nazareth*

Judea some time near the beginning of the Christian era. Judea was then under Roman rule, though the Jews themselves recognized only their own king, Herod I, as their rightful sovereign. The atmosphere of the country was charged with religious emotionalism and political discontent. Some of the people, notably the Pharisees, looked forward to the coming of a political messiah, a son of David, who would rescue the country from foreign rule. Others, for example the Essenes, thought in terms of spiritual deliverance through asceticism, repentance, and mystical union with God. It was this latter sect which prepared the way for the ministry of Jesus. When he was about twenty-eight years old, he was acclaimed by an Essene evangelist, John the Baptist, as one "mightier than I, whose shoes I am not worthy to bear." [1] Thenceforth for about three years the career of Jesus, according to the New Testament accounts, was a continuous course of preaching and teaching and of healing the sick, "casting out devils," restoring sight to the blind, and raising the dead. He not only denounced shame, greed, and licentious living but set the example himself by a life of humility and self-denial. Though the conception he held of himself is somewhat obscure, he apparently believed that he had a divine mission to save mankind from error and sin. His preaching and other activities eventually aroused the antagonism of some of the chief priests and conservative rabbis. They disliked his caustic references to the legalism of the Pharisees, his contempt for form and ceremony, and his scorn for pomp and luxury. They feared also that his claims to being the Messiah would cause trouble with the Romans. Accordingly, they brought him into the highest court in Jerusalem, where he was solemnly condemned for blasphemy and for setting himself up as "King of the Jews" and turned over to Pontius Pilate, the Roman governor, for execution of the sentence. After hours of agony he died on the cross between two thieves on the hill of Golgotha outside Jerusalem.

The crucifixion

The crucifixion of Jesus marked a great climax in Christian history. At first his death was viewed by his followers as the end of their hopes. Their despair soon vanished, however, for rumors began to spread that the Master was alive, and that he had been seen by certain of his faithful disciples. The remainder of his followers were quickly convinced that he had risen from the dead, and that he was truly a divine being. With their courage restored, they reorganized their little band and began preaching and testifying in the name of their martyred leader. In such lowly fashion another of the world's great religions was launched on a career that would ultimately shake the foundations of no less an empire than mighty Rome.

There has never been perfect agreement among Christians as to the precise teachings of Jesus of Nazareth. The only dependable records

[1] Matthew 3:11.

are the four Gospels, but the oldest of these was not written until at
least a generation after Jesus' death. According to the beliefs of his
orthodox followers, the founder of Christianity revealed himself as
the Christ, the divine Son of God, who was sent on this earth to
suffer and die for the sins of mankind. They were convinced that
after three days in the tomb, he had risen from the dead and ascended
into heaven, whence he would come again to judge the world. The
Gospels at least make it clear that he included the following among
his basic teachings: (1) the fatherhood of God and the brotherhood
of man; (2) the Golden Rule; (3) forgiveness and love of one's enemies; (4) repayment of evil with good; (5) self-denial; (6) condemnation of hypocrisy and greed; (7) opposition to ceremonialism
as the essence of religion; (8) the imminent approach of the end of
the world; and (9) the resurrection of the dead and the establishment of the Kingdom of Heaven.

Christianity was broadened and invested with a more elaborate
theology by some of the successors of Jesus. Chief among them was
the Apostle Paul, originally known as Saul of Tarsus. Although of
Jewish nationality, Paul was not a native of Palestine but a Jew of
the Dispersion, born in the city of Tarsus in southeastern Asia
Minor. Here he came into contact with the Stoic philosophy, but he
was possibly more deeply influenced by Gnosticism. Eventually converted to Christianity, he devoted his limitless energy to propagat-
ing that faith throughout the Near East. It would be almost impossible to overestimate the significance of his work. Denying that Jesus
was sent merely as the redeemer of the Jews, he proclaimed Christianity to be a universal religion. But this was not all. He gave major
emphasis to the idea of Jesus as the Christ, as the God-man who existed from the foundation of the world and whose death on the
cross was a propitiation for the sins of mankind. Not only did he
reject the works of the Law (i.e., Jewish ritualism) as of primary
importance in religion, but he declared them to be utterly worthless
in procuring salvation. Man is a sinner by nature, and he can therefore be saved only by faith and by the grace of God "through the
redemption that is in Christ Jesus." It follows, according to Paul,
that man's fate in the life to come is almost entirely dependent upon
the will of God; for "Hath not the potter power over the clay, of the
same lump to make one vessel unto honour, and another unto dis-
honour?" [2] He has mercy "on whom he will have mercy, and whom
he will he hardeneth." [3]

By the beginning of the Middle Ages the triumph of Christianity
over all its rivals was almost complete. The Emperor Galerius' edict
of toleration in 311 was already an admission that the religion was
too strong to be stamped out by persecution. By a series of decrees
between 380 and 392 Christianity was recognized as the only lawful

[2] Romans 9:21.
[3] Romans 9:18.

faith of the Roman Empire. How is this triumph to be explained? Perhaps as much as anything else it was due to the composite character of Christianity. Here was a religion which ultimately came to embody elements from a wide variety of sources. A large number of them were taken from Judaism: the name of the deity, the cosmogony, the world history, the Ten Commandments, and such doctrines as original sin and the providence of God. In addition, several of the ethical doctrines were really of Jewish origin. Although many of these elements were modified by Jesus and his followers, there can be no doubt that the Hebrew contributions to Christianity were of great importance.

*Persian
and Hellenistic
elements*

But obviously Christianity derived much from other than Jewish sources. Some idea of the debt which it owed to the various religions of Persian origin has been indicated in a preceding chapter.[4] Zoroastrianism had already made the ancient world familiar with such concepts as otherworldliness and an eternal conflict between good and evil. Gnosticism had developed the belief in secret revelation and had taught the notion of a primal man or God-man becoming incarnate in human form. Mithraism had fixed men's attention upon forms of ritual, such as baptism and the use of holy water, and upon the celebration of Sunday and the twenty-fifth of December as sacred days. Supplementing these influences was that of the philosophy of Stoicism which had familiarized the educated classes with ideals of cosmopolitanism and the brotherhood of man. In short, mystery religions and Hellenistic philosophy had already brought into existence a large deposit of doctrines and practices upon which Christianity could draw, at the same time preserving its distinctive character. The early church was an organism that fed upon the whole pagan world, selecting and incorporating a wide variety of ideas and practices which were not inconsistent with its own nature. The appeal of Christianity was therefore more nearly universal than that of any other of the ancient religions.

*Other reasons
for the Christian triumph*

The other main reasons for the triumph of Christianity may be summarized briefly. It admitted women to full rights of participation in worship, whereas Mithraism, the strongest of its early competitors, excluded them. It enjoyed the advantage for about fifty years of systematic persecution by the Roman government—a factor which enormously strengthened the cohesiveness of the movement, since those who remained in the faith had to be ready to die for their convictions. While most of the other religions revolved around imaginary figures, the creatures of grotesque legends, Christianity possessed as its founder a historic individual of clearly defined personality. Lastly, the triumph of Christianity is partly explained by the fact that it made a stronger appeal to the poor and oppressed than did any of the other mystery religions. Although it included the ideal of the equality of all men in the sight of God, its founder and

[4] See the chapter on The Civilization of Ancient Persia.

some of his followers had condemned the rich and exalted the lowly. It propagated a new and exceedingly democratic morality, with meekness, self-effacement, and love of one's enemies as primary virtues. Perhaps these were the qualities most likely to find ready acceptance among the helpless masses who had long since abandoned all hope of bettering their material condition.

Hardly had Christianity emerged victorious over its rivals than disaffection developed within its own ranks. This was due partly to the heterogeneous elements out of which the religion had been formed, and partly also to the compromising attitudes displayed by the leaders as the success of the movement increased. A more fundamental reason seems to have been the conflict between the intellectual and emotional tendencies within the religion. Representing the former were the two most important sects of *subordinationist* Christians [5]—the Arians and the Nestorians. Both of them agreed in their refusal to accept what has since become the orthodox doctrine of the Trinity. Under the influence of Greek philosophy they rejected the idea that the Christ could be the equal of God. The Arians maintained that the Son was created by the Father and therefore was not co-eternal with him or formed of the same substance. Their chief opponents were the Athanasians, who held that Father, Son, and Holy Ghost were all absolutely equal and composed of identical substance. The Nestorians broke away from the rest of the church with the contention that Mary should be called the mother of Christ but not the mother of God, implying of course that they considered the Christ something less than divine.

The division of Christians into rival sects: Arians, Athanasians, and Nestorians

The most important of the sects that emphasized the emotional character of Christianity were the Gnostics and the Manicheans. Both were extreme ascetics and mystics. Believing that genuine religious truth was a product of revelation exclusively, they were inclined to be strongly suspicious of any attempt to rationalize the Christian faith. They were opposed also to the tendency toward worldliness which was making itself evident among many of the clergy. The Gnostics and the Manicheans were not originally sects of Christianity at all, but eventually many of them went over to that faith. Those who became Christians retained their old doctrines of exaggerated spiritualism and contempt for matter as evil. Naturally along with these went an abiding distrust of every variety of human knowledge. The doctrines of all these sects, with the exception of the Athanasian, were eventually condemned by church councils as heresies.

Gnostics and Manicheans

Notwithstanding the condemnation of many beliefs as heresies, the body of Christian doctrine was never very firmly fixed during the early Middle Ages. Of course, all Christians believed in a God who was the creator and governor of the universe, in salvation from

The persistence of doctrinal disputes

[5] Called "subordinationist" because they insisted upon subordinating Christ to God the Father.

sin, and in rewards and punishments after death. But as regards many other questions of dogma there was confusion and uncertainty. Even the concept of the Trinity continued to be an issue of debate for several centuries. Many of the Eastern Christians never accepted the extreme Athanasian view of the relation of the Father and the Son adopted by the Council of Nicaea (325). Furthermore, there was no clearly formulated theory at this time of the number and the precise nature of the sacraments, nor was the doctrine of the powers of the priesthood definitely established. In general, there were two main points of disagreement affecting all of these issues. Some very devout believers clung to an ideal of Christianity similar to that of the Apostolic age, when the church was a community of mystics, each of them guided by the Inner Light in matters of faith and conduct. Others envisaged the Christian church as an organized society prescribing its own rules for the government of its members in accordance with the practical requirements of the time.

The importance of Christian organization

The growth of Christian organization was one of the most important developments of the whole medieval era. Even during the first few centuries of that period the church and its related institutions evolved into an elaborate structure which ultimately became the principal framework of society itself. As the Roman Empire in the West decayed, the church took over many of its functions and helped to preserve order amid the deepening chaos. That anything at all was saved out of the wreckage was due in large part to the stabilizing influence of the organized church. It aided in civilizing the barbarians, in promoting ideals of social justice, and in preserving and transmitting the antique learning.

The evolution of church organization

The organization of the church was at first very simple. The early Christian congregations met in the homes of their members and listened to the spiritual testimony of various of the brethren who were believed to have been in direct communication with the Holy Ghost. No distinction between laymen and clergy was recognized. Each independent church had a number of officers, generally known as bishops and elders, whose functions were to preside at the services, discipline members, and dispense charity. Gradually, under the influence of the pagan mystery religions, the ritual of Christianity increased to such a stage of complexity that a professional priesthood seemed to become necessary. The need for defense against persecution and the desire to attain uniformity of belief also favored the development of ecclesiastical organization. The consequence was that about the beginning of the second century one bishop in each important city came to be recognized as supreme over all the clergy in that vicinity. The sphere of his jurisdiction corresponded to the *civitas*, the smallest administrative unit of the Roman state. As the number of congregations multiplied, and as the influence of the church increased due to the adoption of Christianity as the official religion of Rome, distinctions of rank among the bishops themselves began to appear. Those who had their headquarters in the larger cities came to be called metropolitans, with authority over the clergy of an entire province. In the fourth century the still higher dignity of patriarch was established to designate those bishops who ruled over the oldest and largest of Christian communities—such cities as Rome, Constantinople, Antioch, and Alexandria with their surrounding districts. Thus the Christian clergy by 400 A.D. had come to embrace a definite hierarchy of patriarchs, metropolitans, bishops, and priests.

The climax of all this development was the growth of the primacy of the bishop of Rome, or in other words the rise of the papacy. For several reasons the bishop of Rome enjoyed a pre-eminence over *The rise of the* the other patriarchs of the church. The city in which he ruled was *papacy* venerated by the faithful as a scene of the missionary activities of the Apostles Peter and Paul. The tradition was widely accepted that Peter had founded the bishopric of Rome, and that therefore all of his successors were heirs of his authority and prestige. This tradition was supplemented by the theory that Peter had been commissioned by the Christ as his vicar on earth and had been given the keys of the kingdom of heaven with power to punish men for their sins and even to absolve them from guilt.[6] This theory, known as the doctrine of the Petrine Succession, has been used by Popes ever since as a basis for their claims to authority over the church. The bishops of Rome had an advantage also in the fact that after the transfer of the imperial capital to Constantinople there was seldom any emperor with effective sovereignty in the West. Finally, in 455 the Emperor Valentinian III issued a decree commanding all Western bishops to submit to the jurisdiction of the Pope. It must not be supposed, however, that the church was yet under a monarchical form of government. The patriarchs in the East regarded the extreme assertions of the papal claims as a brazen effrontery, and even many bishops in the West continued to ignore them for some time.

The organization of the church was by no means confined to an ecclesiastical hierarchy. In any study of Christian institutions a prominent place must be given to monasticism. Since monasticism was *Reasons for the* originally an outgrowth of asceticism, it becomes necessary, first of *popularity* all, to examine the relationship between that ideal and the Christian *of asceticism* religion. Original Christianity was only mildly ascetic. Neither Jesus nor his immediate followers practiced any extremes of self-torture. To be sure, Jesus did not marry; he declared that he had no place to lay his head; and he was supposed to have fasted for forty days in the wilderness; but these examples could scarcely have encouraged the pathological excesses of mortification of the flesh indulged in by the hermits of the third and fourth centuries. We must therefore look for additional causes of the growth of this later asceticism. Perhaps the following may be considered fundamental:

[6] See Matthew 16:18-19.

(1) The desire of many pious Christians to protest against the increasing worldliness of the church. The farther they might go to the opposite extreme of the luxurious lives of some of the clergy, for example, the more effective that protest would become.

(2) The choice of morbid self-torture as a substitute for martyrdom. With the abandonment of persecution by the Romans all chances of winning a crown of glory in heaven by undergoing death for the faith were eliminated. But the desire to give evidence of one's religious ardor by self-abasement and suffering was still present and demanded an outlet.

(3) The desire of some Christians who were sincerely devoted to the faith to set an example of exalted piety and unselfishness as an inspiration to their weaker brethren. Even though most men should fail to attain the ideal, the general level of morality and piety would be raised.

(4) The influence of other Oriental religions, especially Gnosticism and Manicheism, with their exaggerated spiritualism, contempt for this world, and degradation of the body.

The asceticism of Christian hermits

The earliest Christian ascetics were hermits, who withdrew from the world to live in seclusion in some wilderness or desert. This form of asceticism seems to have originated in Egypt in the third century. From there it spread into other provinces of the eastern section of the Empire and continued to be popular for more than one hundred years. It developed into a kind of religious mania characterized by morbid excesses. We read of hermits or anchorites grazing in the fields after the manner of animals, rolling naked in thorn bushes, or living in swamps infested with snakes. The famous St. Simeon Stylites passed a whole summer "as a rooted vegetable in a garden" and then began the construction of his celebrated pillar. He built it to a height of sixty feet and spent the remaining thirty years of his life on the top. Such absurdities as these, while certainly not typical of the attitude of the majority of Christians at this time, were probably the natural fruit of too strong an emphasis upon the spiritual way of life.

The rise of monasticism

In time the force of the anchorite hysteria subsided. Certain of the more practical Christian ascetics came to the conclusion that the solitary life of the hermit was not good for the soul, since it sometimes drove men insane. The result of this conclusion was the origin of monasticism. Credit for founding the earliest monastery is commonly assigned to Pachomius, who lived in Egypt in the middle fourth century. The movement he initiated was continued by St. Basil, a bishop of Cappadocia, who was the first to issue a set of rules for the government of a monastic order. Disapproving of extreme self-torture, St. Basil required his monks to discipline themselves by useful labor. They were not to engage in prolonged fasting or in degrading laceration of the flesh, but they were compelled to submit to obligations of poverty and humility and to spend many

A Monastery of the Basilian Order on Mt. Athos. The asceticism of the Basilian monks caused them to build their monasteries in almost inaccessible places on lofty crags or on the steep sides of rugged mountains.

hours of the day in silent religious meditation. The Basilian type of monasticism came to be adopted universally in the eastern division of Christendom. Many of its units are still to be seen perched on lofty crags to which access can be gained only by climbing long rope ladders or being hauled up in a basket. The history of monasticism in western Europe also began in the fourth century, when ascetic communities on the Egyptian model were established in Rome. There was really no important monasticism in the West, however, until the sixth century, when St. Benedict drafted his famous rule which ultimately became the standard for nearly all the monks of Latin Christendom. The Benedictine rule imposed obligations similar to those of the rule of St. Basil—poverty, obedience, labor, and religious devotion. If there was any essential difference, it probably lay in the stronger emphasis of the Benedictine system upon organized control. The abbot of each monastery had practically unlimited authority to discipline the monks under him. The Basilian rule was predicated more upon the assumption that each monk would discipline himself.

The influence of monasticism upon the society of the early Middle Ages would be difficult to exaggerate. The monks were generally the best farmers in Europe; they reclaimed waste lands, drained swamps, and made numerous discoveries relating to the improvement of the soil. They preserved some of the building skill of the Romans and achieved noteworthy progress in many of the industrial arts, especially in wood carving, metal-working, weaving, glass-making, and brewing. Indeed, some modern writers maintain that the foundations of the Industrial Revolution were actually laid in the medieval monasteries. It was monks, furthermore, who wrote most of the

The results of monasticism

books, copied the ancient manuscripts, and maintained the majority of the schools and libraries and nearly all of the hospitals that existed during the early Middle Ages. The growth of monasticism also profoundly affected the history of the church. It led to a division in the ranks of the clergy. Living according to a definite rule or *regula*, the monks came to be called the *regular* clergy; while the priests, bishops, and archbishops, who carried on their activities in the midst of the affairs of the world (*saeculum*), were henceforth known as the *secular* clergy. Between the two groups intense rivalry developed, with the monks sometimes organizing reform movements against the worldliness of the priests. The Benedictine monks enjoyed the special favor of the Popes, and it was partly on account of an alliance between the papacy and monasticism that the former was able to extend its power over the church.

2. The Germanic Foundations of the New Culture

The second most important of the factors which combined to produce the civilization of early medieval Europe was the influence of the Germanic barbarians. They were not the only northern peoples who helped to mold the pattern of early medieval society; the contributions of the Celts in Brittany and Ireland and of the Slavs in central and eastern Europe were by no means insignificant. Nevertheless, the Germanic influence appears to have been the most extensive. The ancient Germans were a long-headed people of predominantly Nordic stock and of Indo-European tongue. Where they came from originally is a problem upon which scholars disagree, but they seem to have migrated into northern Europe from western Asia. By the beginning of the Christian era they had come to be divided into several nations: Scandinavians, Vandals, Goths, Franks, Alemanni, Burgundians, Frisians, Anglo-Saxons, Dutch, and so on. Both in language and in race they originally bore some affinity to the Greeks and the Romans.

The ancient Germans

For centuries different nations of Germanic barbarians had been making incursions into Roman territory. At times they came as invading armies, but generally they filtered in slowly, bringing their families and belongings with them and occupying depopulated or abandoned areas. Many were brought in by Roman commanders and rulers. Julius Caesar was impressed by their value as warriors and enrolled thousands of them in his armies. They were to be found in the bodyguard of nearly every Princeps and emperor. Finally, by the time of Constantine, they formed the bulk of the soldiers in the entire Roman army. Many were also drawn into the civil service and thousands were settled by the government as *coloni* or serfs on the great estates. In view of these conditions it is not surprising that Rome should eventually have been conquered by the Germans. They were a virile and energetic race, constantly in-

The Germanic invasions of the Roman Empire

creasing in numbers; and as more and more of them gained a foothold in Italy, others were bound to be tempted by the opportunities for plunder. In addition, the Romans frequently exploited those who were already in the Empire and thereby provided their kinsmen with an excuse for making an attack. Although armed invasions of Italy began as early as the second century B.C., and were repeated several times thereafter, there were no really disastrous incursions until the fourth and fifth centuries A.D. In 378 the Visigoths, angered by the oppression of imperial governors, raised the standard of revolt. They overwhelmed a Roman army at Adrianople and then marched westward into Italy. In 410 under Alaric they captured and plundered Rome, later moving on into southern Gaul. In 455 Rome was sacked by the Vandals, who had migrated from their original home between the Oder and Vistula rivers and established a kingdom in the province of Carthage. Other Germanic nations also made their way into Italy, and before the end of the fifth century the Roman Empire in the West had passed completely under the domination of the barbarians.

For our knowledge of ancient Germanic society we are dependent primarily upon the *Germania* of Tacitus, written in 98 A.D. The literature and the laws of the Germans themselves also contain much information, but these were not put into written form until after Roman and Christian influences had begun to exert their effect. When Tacitus wrote, the Germanic barbarians had attained a cultural level about equal to that of the Homeric Greeks. They were illiterate and ignorant of any knowledge of the arts. Their houses were built of rough timber plastered over with mud. While they had achieved some development of agriculture, they preferred the risks of plundering expeditions to the prosaic labor of tilling the soil. Nearly all of the work was done by the women and old men and other dependents. When not fighting or hunting, the warriors spent most of their time sleeping and carousing. Gambling and drunkenness were glaring vices, but, if we can believe the testimony of Tacitus, sex morality was singularly pure. Monogamous marriage prevailed, except in those cases where a chief might be permitted to take more than one wife for political reasons. Adultery was rare and was severely punished, while divorce was almost unknown. In some tribes even widows were forbidden to remarry.

Ancient German society

The economic and political institutions of the Germans were such as befitted a people who were just emerging into a settled existence. The tiny proportion of trade carried on rested solely upon a basis of barter, while cattle were still the main article of wealth. Whether the agricultural land was individually or collectively owned is still a debated question, but there seems little doubt that the forests and pastures were held and used in common. Possibly the community controlled the distribution of new lands as they were acquired, allotting the arable portions as individual farms. There is

Economic and political institutions

evidence that a class of wealthy proprietors had grown up as an aristocracy in certain of the tribes. Although Tacitus states that the Germans had slaves, it seems probable that most of their dependents were serfs, since they had houses of their own and paid their masters only a portion of what they produced. Their servitude was a result not only of capture in war but also of indebtedness and especially reckless gambling, in which men staked their own liberty when everything else had been lost. The state scarcely existed at all. Law was a product of custom, and the administration of justice remained very largely in private hands. While the Germans had their tribal courts, the function of these bodies was chiefly to mediate between plaintiff and defendant. It was left to the former to bring the accused to trial and to carry out the penalty prescribed by the customary law. The court merely decided what proofs should be required of each litigant to determine the validity of his plea. Usually these consisted of oaths and ordeals, both of which were considered as appeals to the judgment of the gods. The most important of the remaining political institutions was the primary assembly of the warriors. But this body had no lawmaking powers beyond those involved in the interpretation of custom. Its main function was to decide questions of war and peace and whether the tribe should migrate to some new locality. Originally the German tribes had no kings. They had chiefs elected by the freemen, but these were little more than ceremonial officials. In time of war a military leader was elected and endowed with considerable power, but as soon as the campaign was over his authority lapsed. Nevertheless, as wars increased in frequency and duration, some of the military leaders actually became kings. The formality of election, however, was generally retained.

*The Germanic
influence*

The influence of the Germans upon medieval history, while not so important as is sometimes imagined, was extensive enough to deserve consideration. Above all, they were largely responsible for several of the elements of feudalism: (1) the conception of law as an outgrowth of custom and not as the expression of the will of a sovereign; (2) the idea of law as a personal possession of the individual which he could take with him wherever he went, in contrast to the Roman conception of law as limited to a definite territory; (3) the notion of a contractual relationship between rulers and subjects, involving reciprocal obligations of protection and obedience; (4) the theory of an honorable relationship between lord and vassal, growing out of the Germanic institution of the *comitatus* or military band, in which the warriors were bound by pledges of honor and loyalty to fight for and serve their leader; (5) trial by ordeal as a prevailing mode of procedure in the feudal courts; and (6) the idea of elective kingship.

3. Political and Economic Developments in Early Medieval Europe

POLITICAL AND ECONOMIC DEVELOPMENTS

The political history of western Europe from 476 to 800 has comparatively little interest except for the specialist. A few of the major developments, however, deserve some attention. Following the deposition of the last of the Roman emperors in the West, a Germanic chieftain by the name of Odovacar proclaimed himself king of Italy. But in 493 Italy was conquered by the Ostrogoths under Theodoric, one of the ablest and most intelligent of barbarian leaders. Until nearly the end of his reign of thirty-three years, Theodoric gave Italy a more enlightened rule than the country had known under many of the Caesars. He fostered agriculture and commerce, repaired public buildings and roads, patronized learning, and enforced religious toleration. But in his last years he became querulous and suspicious, accusing some of his faithful subordinates of plotting with the Roman aristocracy to overthrow him. Several of them were put to death, including the philosopher Boethius. Soon after Justinian became emperor at Constantinople in 527 he determined to reconquer Italy and the provinces in the West. Not until 552 was the power of the Ostrogoths finally broken. The long war utterly ruined Italy and opened the way for the Lombard invasion in 568. The Lombards succeeded in holding most of the peninsula under the rule of semi-independent dukes until the conquest of Charlemagne in the late eighth century.

The political history of Italy

The strongest western European state in the early Middle Ages was not established in Italy but in France. In 481 a youth by the name of Clovis became king of an important tribe of the Salian Franks, who dwelt on the left bank of the Rhine. In less than twenty years Clovis conquered nearly all of what is now France and a portion of Germany besides. His adoption of orthodox Christianity won for him the support of the clergy and made possible the subsequent alliance between the Frankish kings and the Popes. The Merovingian dynasty,[7] which he really founded, occupied the throne of the Frankish state until 751. For more than a century the successors of Clovis continued his policy of rigorous despotism, annexing the territory of their enemies, dominating the church, and exploiting the lands of the kingdom as if they were their private possessions. By 639, however, the royal line had begun to degenerate. A series of short-lived weaklings, the so-called do-nothing kings, inherited the crown of their lusty forebears. Absorbed in the pursuit of pleasure, these worthless youths delegated most of their authority to their chief subordinates, the mayors of the palace. Nothing more natural could have happened than the eventual displacement of the Merovingian kings by these very officials to whom they had en-

The kingdom of the Franks

See color plates at page 284

[7] So called from Meroveus, supposedly the original founder of the family to which Clovis belonged.

263

trusted their powers. The most capable and aggressive of the mayors of the palace was Charles Martel ("the Hammer"), who may be considered a second founder of the Frankish state. He won fame in 732 by defeating the Moors at Tours, a town only a little more than a hundred miles from Paris. Although his opponents were merely a marauding band, the Battle of Tours is nevertheless important as the high-water mark of Moorish invasion of France. Yet, even after his victory, Charles was content with the substance of power and did not bother to assume the royal title. It was left for his son, Pepin the Short, to have himself elected king of the Franks in 751 and thereby to put an end to Merovingian rule. The new dynasty came to be known as the Carolingian from the name of its most famous representative, Carolus Magnus or Charlemagne.

*The rule
of Charlemagne*

In the minds of most students of history Charlemagne stands out as one of the two or three most important individuals in the whole medieval period. By some of his contemporaries he was acclaimed as a new Augustus who would bring peace and prosperity to western Europe. There can be no question that he established efficient gov-

The Emperor Charlemagne. From a painting by Albrecht Dürer.

ernment, and that he did much to combat the centrifugal tendencies which had gathered momentum during the reigns of the later Merovingians. Not only did he abolish the office of mayor of the palace, but he eliminated the tribal dukes and bestowed all the powers of local government upon his own appointees, the counts. To prevent abuses of authority by the latter he appointed *missi dominici*, or royal messengers, to visit the counties and to report to the king any acts of official injustice. He authorized the *missi* to hold their own courts for the purpose of hearing complaints of oppression and even in extreme cases to remove local officers. He modified the old system of private administration of justice by authorizing the counts to summon accused persons to court and by vesting the magistrates with more control over judicial procedure. He revived the Roman institution of the sworn inquest, in which a number of persons were summoned by agents of the king and bound by oath to tell what they knew of any crimes committed in their locality. This institution survived the downfall of the Carolingian state and was carried by the Normans to England, where it eventually became an important factor in the origin of the grand-jury system. While much of the remainder of the political structure which Charlemagne established perished with the end of his dynasty, the precedent which he set for strong government undoubtedly influenced many of the French kings in the later Middle Ages and the German emperors as well. It should be noted, however, that the glory of Charlemagne's empire rested in large part upon a foundation of slaughter. During the forty-six years of his reign from 768 to 814, he conducted no fewer than fifty-four wars. There was scarcely a people of western Europe against whom he did not fight, except the English. Since most of his campaigns were successful, he annexed to the Frankish domain the greater part of central Europe and northern and central Italy. But some of these conquests were made possible only by a fearful sacrifice of blood and a resort to measures of the harshest cruelty. The campaign against the Saxons met with such stubborn opposition that Charlemagne finally ordered the beheading of forty-five hundred of them. It is typical of the spirit of the times that all of this was done under the pretext of inducing the pagans to adopt Christianity.

As a matter of fact, it was Charlemagne's constant intervention in religious affairs which led to the climax of his whole career—his coronation as Roman Emperor by Pope Leo III. Leo had been in trouble for some time. Accused of being a tyrant and a rake, he so aroused the indignation of the people of Rome that in 799 they gave him a severe beating and forced him to flee from the city. Struggling over the mountains to Germany, he implored the aid of Charlemagne. The great king sent him back to Italy and was instrumental in restoring him to the papal throne. On Christmas day, 800, as Charles knelt in prayer in St. Peter's church the grateful Pope placed a crown on his head while the assembled multitude hailed him as "Augustus, crowned of God, great and pacific Emperor of the Romans." The significance of this event is rather hard to appraise. Charles has been represented as surprised and embarrassed by the honor. But the real cause of his irritation was probably his being made to accept a crown from the Pope. There is evidence that he had already developed some ambitious scheme of his own for reviving imperial power in the

Charlemagne becomes emperor

West. Moreover, he regarded his own authority as in no wise limited by any higher sovereignty of the church. He legislated freely on religious matters, controlled all appointments to ecclesiastical offices, and lectured priests and bishops alike on their morals and on what they should preach. Nevertheless, the fact that the coronation was acclaimed by so many of Charlemagne's contemporaries as marking the return to a golden age bears witness to its more than trivial importance. The Carolingian empire thus established was not conceived as the beginning of a new state, but as a revival of the Empire of the Caesars. The grandeur of Rome was now held to be reborn. It would have been more nearly in harmony with the truth if the event had been interpreted as an expression of the cultural and po-

*See color
plates at
pages 284, 285*

litical awakening of the West. Theoretically the Empire with its capital at Constantinople still included Italy and the surrounding areas of Europe. The establishment of an empire in the West was a symbol of the widening gulf between Latin Christendom and Byzantium. Finally, the fact that Charlemagne was crowned by Leo III gave the Popes of the later Middle Ages a bulwark for their claims to supremacy. They could argue that it was they who had really created the empire, acting of course as the vicegerents of God.

*The Saxon
kingdoms in
England*

At the beginning of the early Middle Ages a large part of what is now England was still under Roman rule. But in the fifth century the Romans were forced to withdraw on account of increasing trouble with Germanic invasions into Italy. Soon afterward England was overrun by hordes of Saxons, Angles, and Jutes from the Continent. They brought with them the customs and institutions of their homeland, which were similar to those of the other Germanic barbarians. Driving the original Celtic natives into the mountains of Wales and Cornwall, they quickly established their own kingdoms. At one time there were seven—Northumbria, East Anglia, Kent, Essex, Sussex, Wessex, and Mercia—mutually suspicious and hostile. In the ninth century tribes of Danes took advantage of the strife among the Saxon kingdoms and attempted their conquest. Efforts to defeat the new enemy brought the seven kingdoms into a strong confederation under the leadership of Wessex and its celebrated ruler, Alfred the Great. King Alfred reorganized the army, infused new vigor into local government, and revised and broadened the laws. In addition, he founded schools and fostered an interest in literature and other elements of a national culture.

*The Norman
conquest*

King Alfred's successors were men of weaker fiber. One of them, Ethelred the Unready, surrendered his kingdom to the powerful Danish King Canute. For eighteen years England was ruled as part of a North Sea empire which also included Norway and Denmark. But in 1035 Canute died, and the Saxon dynasty regained control of England. It was not for long. Ethelred's son, Edward the Confessor, was more interested in cultivating a reputation for piety than he was in statecraft, and allowed affairs of his country to be regulated

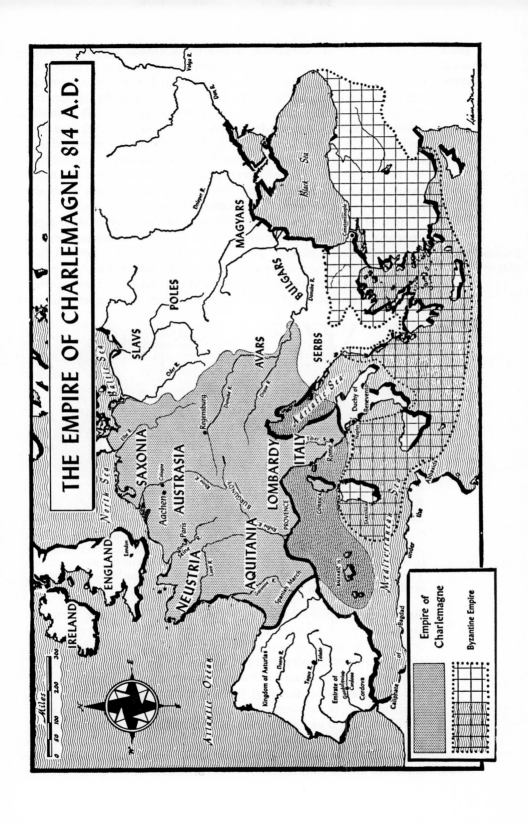

THE EMPIRE OF CHARLEMAGNE, 814 A.D.

Miles
0 50 100 200 300

IRELAND

ENGLAND
London

North Sea

Baltic Sea

SLAVS

POLES

Volga R.

Don R.

Dnieper R.

MAGYARS

BULGARS

SERBS

AVARS

Black Sea

Constantinople

Oder R.

Elbe R.

Danube R.

Regensburg

SAXONIA

AUSTRASIA

Aachen
Cologne

NEUSTRIA

Seine R.
Paris

Loire R.

AQUITANIA

Burgundy

Rhone R.

Garonne R.

Spanish March

PROVENCE

LOMBARDY

ITALY

Tiber R.
Rome

Naples

Duchy of
Benevento

Adriatic Sea

CORSICA

SARDINIA

BALEARIC IS.

Mediterranean Sea

under the

Atlantic Ocean

Kingdom of Asturias

Duero R.

Tagus R.
Toledo

Emirate of
Guadalquivir R.
Cordova
Cordova

Caliphate of Bagdad

Empire of Charlemagne

Byzantine Empire

by the Duchy of Normandy, across the Channel. Upon Edward's death the Duke of Normandy, subsequently known as William the Conqueror, laid claim to the crown of England. Landing an army in Sussex in 1066, he caught the English monarch Harold unprepared and defeated him in the Battle of Hastings. Harold fell mortally wounded, and his forces disintegrated. Apparently regarding discretion as the better part of valor, the surviving magnates offered the crown to Duke William. The Battle of Hastings is considered as a turning point in English history, for it ended the period of Anglo-Saxon supremacy and prepared the way for the ultimate establishment of a nation state under William the Norman's successors.

Most of the records of economic life in the early Middle Ages present a mournful picture of return to primitive conditions and in some cases actual misery. The decline of Italy in the second half of the fifth century was especially swift. The forces which were set in motion by the economic revolution of the preceding two hundred years had now attained their full momentum. Commerce and in-

Economic decline in Italy

Duke William of Normandy Crossing the Channel to Conquer England, from the Bayeux Tapestry. The Bayeux Tapestry depicts, in needlework on linen, 72 scenes of the Norman Conquest. It was probably completed under the direction of Bishop Odo of Bayeux, the Conqueror's half-brother.

dustry were rapidly becoming extinct, lands that were formerly productive were growing up in briars and brambles, and the population was declining so noticeably that a law was enacted forbidding any woman under forty years of age to enter a convent. While the proprietors of the great landed estates extended their control over agriculture and over many of the functions of government as well, larger and larger numbers of the masses of the people became serfs. During the reign of Theodoric this process of economic decline was arrested in some measure as a result of the benefits he extended to agriculture and commerce and his reduction of taxes. But Theodoric was unable to eliminate serfdom or to reverse the concentration

of landed wealth, for he felt that he needed the support of the aristocracy. After his death the forces of decay again became operative;
yet if it had not been for Justinian's war of reconquest, Italy might
still have preserved a degree of the prosperity she had gained under
the Ostrogothic king. The long military conflict brought the country to the verge of stark barbarism. Pestilence and famine completed
the havoc wrought by the contending armies. Fields were left un-
tilled, and most of the activities in the towns were suspended. Wolves
penetrated into the heart of the country and fattened on the corpses
that remained unburied. So great was the danger of starvation that
cannibalism appeared in some areas.[8] Only in the larger cities were
the normal functions of civilization continued to any appreciable
extent.

Economic change in what is now France followed a pattern very
similar to that in Italy, but it proceeded at a slower rate. In Roman
times southern Gaul had had a flourishing commerce and considerable industry. By the end of the ninth century, however, stagnation
was almost complete. The streets of the city of Marseille were grown
over with grass and weeds, while the port itself was deserted for
over two hundred years. In some other Mediterranean towns and in
the interior of the country, trade on a petty scale continued to be
carried on, mostly by Jews and Syrians and later by Lombards; but
even the activities of these men became steadily more difficult as
brigandage increased, the roads deteriorated, and money disappeared
from general circulation. The economic history of France was also
characterized by the growth of an irregular feudalism similar to that
which had sprung up in Italy. Several of the causes were closely
related to the policies of the Merovingian and Carolingian kings.
Nearly all of these rulers compensated their officials by grants of
land. Both Pepin the Short and Charlemagne adhered to the example of Charles Martel in expropriating lands of the church and
turning them over to their chief followers as rewards for military
services. More serious was the practice of granting *immunities*, or
exemptions from the jurisdiction of the king's agents. Originally
immunities were given only as favors to bishops and abbots to protect them from unscrupulous officials, but later they were granted
to secular nobles as well. Their legal effect was to make the holder
subject to the exclusive jurisdiction of the king; but as the king was
far away and generally preoccupied with other matters, the nobles
took advantage of the opportunity to increase their own independence. Wars, brigandage, and oppression also contributed to the
growth of a largely feudal structure of society by forcing the weaker
citizens to seek the protection of their more powerful neighbors.
The result was a tendency toward a division of the population into
two distinct classes: a landed aristocracy and serfs.

*Economic
conditions
in France; the
foundations of
feudalism*

[8] J. W. Thompson, *Economic and Social History of the Middle Ages*,
p. 124.

4. *Intellectual Attainments of Early Medieval Europe*

The low intellectual level

Generally speaking, the intellectual culture of early medieval Europe was not of a very high order. Superstition and credulity frequently characterized the work even of many of the outstanding writers. A fondness for compilation rather than for original achievement was also a distinguishing feature of much of the intellectual endeavor. Few men any longer had much interest in philosophy or science, except in so far as those subjects could be made to serve religious purposes. Such an attitude naturally led to mystical interpretations of knowledge and to the acceptance of fables as fact when they appeared to be freighted with symbolical significance for the sphere of religion. In spite of all this, the mind of the times was not hopelessly submerged in darkness. The light of antique learning was never entirely extinguished; even some of the most pious of Church Fathers recognized the value of classical literature. Moreover, there were a few men in the period who, if not creative geniuses, at least had abilities of scholarship which would not have been rated inferior in the best days of Greece.

The authoritarian Christian philosophers: Tertullian

Nearly all of the philosophers of the early Middle Ages may be classified as either Christians or pagans, although a few seem to have been nominal adherents of the church who wrote in the spirit of pagan thought. The Christian philosophers tended to divide into two different schools: (1) those who emphasized the primacy of authority; and (2) those who believed that the doctrines of the faith should be illumined by the light of reason and brought into harmony with the finest products of pagan thinking. The authoritarian tradition in Christian philosophy stemmed originally from Tertullian, a priest of Carthage who lived about the beginning of the third century. For him, Christianity was a system of sacred law to be accepted entirely upon faith. God was an absolute sovereign, whose decrees no mortal had any right to question. Human knowledge was of no value for religion; indeed, now that the Christ had come, and men had the Gospels, there was no need for any further curiosity. As Tertullian would have it, the wisdom of men was mere foolishness with God, and the more a tenet of the faith contradicted reason the greater was the merit in accepting it.

St. Ambrose, St. Jerome, and Gregory

While few of the Christian Fathers went as far as Tertullian in despising intellectual effort, there were several who adhered to his general principle that the dogmas of the faith were not to be tested by reason. St. Ambrose, the great bishop of Milan in the fourth century, was one of them, in spite of his well-trained mind and his liberal social philosophy. His contemporary, St. Jerome, was another. But the most influential of them all was Pope Gregory I (540–604), known in church history as Gregory the Great. The scion of a rich senatorial family, Gregory scorned the seductions of wealth and power in order that he might dedicate his life to the church.

He turned his father's palace into a convent and gave all of the re- mainder of the wealth he had inherited to the poor. In his work as a theologian he laid great stress upon the idea of penance as essential to the remission of sins and strengthened the notion of purgatory as a place where even the righteous must suffer for minor offenses in order to be purified for admission to heaven. Perhaps more than anyone else he was responsible for developing the doctrine that the priest in celebrating the mass co-operates with God in performing a miracle which has the effect of repeating and renewing the sacrifice of Christ on the cross.

The most eminent of the Christian philosophers who may be de- scribed as representatives of a rationalist tradition were Clement of Alexandria and Origen. Both of them lived in the third century and *The rationalist* were deeply influenced by Neo-Platonism and Gnosticism, although *Christian phi-* they adhered to neither one of those systems very closely. Far from *losophers:* despising all human knowledge, they taught that the best of the *Clement and* Greek thinkers had really anticipated the teachings of Jesus, and *Origen* that Christianity is improved by being brought into harmony with pagan learning. While Clement and Origen would not qualify as rationalists in the modern sense, inasmuch as they took a great many of their beliefs on faith, they nevertheless recognized the importance of reason as a fundamental basis of knowledge whether religious or secular. They denied the omnipotence of God and taught that God's power is limited by His goodness and wisdom. They rejected the fatalism of many of their opponents and insisted that man by his own free will molds his course of action while on earth. Neither the universe nor anything in it, they declared, was ever created in time; instead, the process of creation is eternal, new things supplant- ing the old in unending succession. Both Clement and Origen con- demned the extreme asceticism of some of their more zealous breth- ren; in particular, they deplored the tendency of such men as Ter- tullian to speak of marriage as simply a legalized form of carnality. They avowed, on the contrary, that wedlock and the begetting of children are necessary not only for the good of society but for the perfection of man himself. Finally, they maintained that the purpose of all future punishment is purification and not revenge. Conse- quently, punishment in hell cannot be eternal, for even the blackest of sinners must eventually be redeemed. If it were not so, God would not be a God of goodness and mercy.

The most erudite and perhaps the most original of all the early Christian philosophers was St. Augustine. In so far as it is possible to classify him at all, he occupied an intermediate position between *The career of* Clement and Origen, on the one hand, and Tertullian and Gregory *St. Augustine* on the other. Though contending that truths of revelation were above natural reason, he perceived the need for an intellectual understand- ing of what he believed. Born in 354, the son of a pagan father and a Christian mother, Augustine was torn by conflicting impulses throughout the greater part of his life. As a young man he was addicted to sensual pleasures, from which he tried vainly to escape, though he admits in his *Confessions* that his efforts were not wholly sincere. Even after his engagement to marry he could not resist the temptation to take a new mistress. Meanwhile, when he was about eighteen years old, he was attracted to philosophy by reading Cicero's *Hortensius*. He passed from one system of thought to another, unable to find spiritual satisfaction in any. For a brief period he considered the possibilities of Christianity, but it impressed him as too crude and superstitious. Then for nine years he was a Manichean, but ultimately he became convinced that that faith was decadent. Next he was attracted to Neo-Platonism, and then, finally, after listening to the preaching of Ambrose, he returned to Christianity. Though already in his thirty-third year when he was baptized, Augustine advanced rapidly in ecclesiastical positions. In 395 he became Bishop of Hippo in northern Africa, an office which he held until his death in 430.

The philosophy of St. Augustine

As a philosopher Augustine derived a great many of his theories from the Neo-Platonists. He believed in absolute and eternal truth and in instinctive knowledge which God implants in the minds of men. The supremely important knowledge, however, is knowledge of God and His plan of redemption for mankind. Though most of this knowledge must be derived from the revelation contained in the Scriptures, it is nevertheless the duty of man to understand as much of it as possible in order to strengthen his belief. On the basis of this conclusion St. Augustine developed his famous conception of human history as the unfoldment of the will of God. Everything that has happened or ever will happen represents but an episode in the fulfillment of the divine plan. The whole race of human beings comprises two great divisions: those whom God has predestined to eternal salvation constitute the City of God; all others belong to the Earthly City. The end of the drama of history will come with the Day of Judgment, when the blessed few who compose the City of God will put on the garment of immortality, while the vast multitude in the earthly kingdom will be cast into the fires of hell. This, according to St. Augustine, is the whole meaning of human existence.

St. Augustine's theology

St. Augustine's theology was an integral part of his philosophy. Believing as he did in a deity who controls the operation of the universe down to the smallest detail, he naturally emphasized the omnipotence of God and set limits to the freedom of the will. Since man is sinful by nature, the will has to struggle against an inclination to commit evil. Although man has the power to choose between good and bad, it is God who provides the motive or "inspiration" for the choice. Therefore the virtuous man must thank God for having been able to choose the path of virtue. God created the world in the knowledge that some men would respond to the divine "invitation" to lead holy lives, and that others would resist or refuse to cooperate. In this way God *predestined* a portion of the human race

272

to be saved and left the remainder to perish; or, in other words, He fixed for all time the number of inhabitants of the heavenly city. It was not that He elected some for salvation and denied to all others the opportunity to be saved. Rather, He knew infallibly from all eternity that some would not *wish* to be saved. The influence of St. Augustine was enormous. In spite of the fact that his teachings were modified slightly by the Council of Orange in 529, and still more by the theologians of the later Middle Ages, he is revered to this day as one of the most important Fathers of the Roman Catholic religion. Luther and other Protestant Reformers also held him in the highest esteem, although the interpretations they gave to his teachings frequently differed from those of the Catholics.

Practically the only pagan school of philosophy in early medieval Europe was that of the Neo-Platonists, whose doctrines were discussed in a preceding chapter. There was one other individual *The Neo-* thinker, however, who cannot be positively classified as either a *Platonists and* pagan or a Christian. It is quite probable that he was a Christian, *Boethius* though he makes no reference to the church or to the name of Christ in his chief work. The name of this man was Boethius. Born about 480 of aristocratic parentage, Boethius eventually became principal adviser to Theodoric, the Ostrogothic king. Later he fell out with that monarch, was accused of treason, and thrown into prison. In 524 he was put to death. The chief philosophical work of Boethius, which he wrote while languishing in prison, is entitled *The Consolation of Philosophy*. Its dominant theme is the relation of man to the universe. The author considers such problems as fate, the divine government of the world, and individual suffering. After carefully weighing the various conceptions of fortune, he comes to the conclusion that true happiness is synonymous with philosophic understanding that the universe is really good, and that evil is only apparent. Pointing out that men who yield to violent impulses either suffer pangs of remorse or find themselves slaves of their passions, he endeavors to show that vice never goes unpunished nor virtue unrewarded. Although he apparently assumes the immortality of the soul, he refers to no definitely Christian belief as a source of consolation. His attitude is essentially that of the Stoics, colored by a trace of Neo-Platonist mysticism. Few treatises on philosophy were more popular in medieval Europe than Boethius' *Consolation of Philosophy*. Not only was it ultimately translated into nearly every vernacular language, but numerous imitations of it also were written.

The history of literature in the early Middle Ages was marked, first of all, by a decline of interest in the classical writings and later *Literature in* by the growth of a crude originality which ultimately paved the way *the early Mid-* for the development of new literary traditions. By the fifth century *dle Ages* the taste for good Latin literature had already begun to decay. Some of the Christian Fathers who had been educated in pagan schools were inclined to apologize for their attachment to the ancient writings; others expressly denounced them; but the attitude which generally prevailed was that of St. Augustine. The great bishop of Hippo declared that men should continue to study the pagan classics, not for their aesthetic value or their human appeal, but "with a view to making the wit more keen and better suited to penetrate the mystery of the Divine Word." [9] The Latin language also suffered from the effects of the gradual barbarization of culture. Many theologians appeared to feel that it was almost impious for a Christian to write too well. In composing his commentaries on the Scriptures, Pope Gregory I avowed that he considered it exceedingly inappropriate to "fetter the Heavenly Oracle" to the rules of grammar. As a result, medieval Latin was eventually corrupted by a hopeless confusion of changes in syntax and spelling and by the introduction of new words from colloquial usage. Toward the close of the period, however, the vernacular languages, which had been slowly evolving from a fusion of barbarian dialects, with some admixture of Latin elements, began to be employed for crude poetic expression. The consequence was a new and vigorous literary growth which attained its full momentum about the thirteenth century.

Beowulf and other examples of vernacular literature

The best-known example of this literature in the vernacular is the Anglo-Saxon epic poem *Beowulf*. First put into written form about the eighth century, this poem incorporates ancient legends of the Germanic peoples of northwestern Europe. It is a story of fighting and seafaring and of heroic adventure against deadly dragons and the forces of nature. The background of the epic is heathen, but the author of the work introduced into it some qualities of Christian idealism. *Beowulf* is important, not only as one of the earliest specimens of Anglo-Saxon or Old English poetry, but also for the picture which it gives of the society of the English and their ancestors in the early Middle Ages. Many of the remaining examples of the popular literature of this time were also written in Old English. They include the hymns of Caedmon and numerous elegies describing the rude virtues of early barbarian culture. But no account of the vernacular literature of this time would be complete without some mention of the achievements of the Irish. Ireland in the late sixth and early seventh centuries experienced a brilliant renaissance which made that country one of the brightest spots in the so-called Dark Ages. Without the benefit of any influence from Latin culture, Irish monks and bards wrote stories of fantastic adventure on land and sea and hundreds of poems of gorgeous color and sympathetic understanding of human nature.

The historians

Aside from theological works the leading productions of authors who wrote in Latin during the early Middle Ages were the histories of Orosius, Gregory of Tours, and Bede. At the request of St. Augustine, a Spanish priest by the name of Orosius wrote his *Seven Books against the Pagans*. Distinguished neither by accuracy nor by literary charm, this work was intended to be a history of the world

[9] Quoted by Thompson and Johnson, *An Introduction to Medieval Europe*, p. 221.

showing that the calamities which had befallen ancient nations were the result of wickedness. Bishop Gregory of Tours, a near-contemporary of Clovis, also wrote with a view to defense of the faith. In his *History of the Franks* he condoned the murders of Clovis on the ground that they were committed in the service of the church. Although his work contains interesting information about the events of his time, it is marred by his accounts of the miraculous powers of sacred relics and his tendency to give a supernatural interpretation to every occurrence. By far the best of the historical writings of the early medieval period was the Venerable Bede's *Ecclesiastical History of the English Nation.* Bede, an English monk, lived between 673 and 735. Apparently more interested in scholarship than in pious meditation, he pursued his studies so assiduously that he gained a reputation as one of the most learned men of his time. In collecting material for his history he devoted careful attention to sources. He did not hesitate to reject the statements of some of the most respectable authorities when he found them to be in error; and when the evidence was a matter of mere oral tradition, he was honest enough to say so.

No account of intellectual attainments in the early Middle Ages would be complete without some reference to developments in education. After the reign of Theodoric the old Roman system of state schools rapidly disappeared. In some of the Italian cities municipal schools survived even as late as the Renaissance, but throughout the remainder of western Europe the monasteries had a practical monopoly of education. The man who did most to establish the monasteries as institutions of learning was Cassiodorus, formerly chief secretary to Theodoric. Following his retirement from official service, Cassiodorus founded a monastery on his ancestral estate in Apulia and set the monks to work copying manuscripts. The precedent he established was gradually adopted in nearly all the Benedictine institutions. Cassiodorus also insisted that his monks should be trained as scholars, and for this purpose he prepared a curriculum based upon seven subjects, which came to be called the Seven Liberal Arts. These subjects were divided, apparently by Boethius, into the *trivium* and the *quadrivium.* The former included grammar, rhetoric, and logic, which were supposed to be the keys to knowledge; while the *quadrivium* embraced the subjects of more definite content—arithmetic, geometry, astronomy, and music.

Developments in education; the Seven Liberal Arts

The textbooks used in the monastic schools were for the most part elementary. In some of the best schools, however, translations of Aristotle's logical works were studied. But nowhere was any attention given to laboratory science, and history was largely neglected. No professional training of any kind was provided, except for careers in the church. Learning was, of course, a privilege for the few; the masses as a rule received no education, save what they acquired incidentally, and even most members of the secular aristocracy were illiterate. Yet, with all of its shortcomings, this system of education

The value of monastic education

did help to save European culture from complete eclipse. And it is worth remembering that the best of the monastic and cathedral schools—notably those at Yarrow and York in England—provided the main impetus for the first of the revivals of learning which occurred in the later Middle Ages.

Selected Readings

· *Items so designated are available in paperbound editions.*

Artz, F. B., *The Mind of the Middle Ages,* New York, 1954.

Case, S. J., *The Social Origins of Christianity,* Chicago, 1923.

Coulton, G. G., *Five Centuries of Religion,* New York, 1926.

· Dawson, C. H., *The Making of Europe,* New York, 1932. (Meridian)

· Dill, Samuel, *Roman Society in the Last Century of the Western Empire,* London, 1921. (Meridian) Valuable for excerpts from the writers of the fifth century.

· Duckett, E. S., *The Gateway to the Middle Ages,* New York, 1938. (Ann Arbor)

Edman, Irwin, *The Mind of Paul,* New York, 1935.

Fisher, G. P., *The History of Christian Doctrine,* New York, 1923. One of the best, but it must be studied and not merely read.

· Glover, T. R., The Conflict of Religions in the Early Roman Empire, New York, 1909. (Beacon)

Hearnshaw, F. J. C., *The Social and Political Ideas of Some Great Medieval Thinkers,* New York, 1923.

Laistner, M. L. W., *Thought and Letters in Western Europe, A.D. 500–900,* New York, 1931.

Lamonte, J. L., *The World of the Middle Ages,* New York, 1949.

Latourette, K. S., *A History of Christianity,* New York, 1953.

· Lot, Ferdinand, *The End of the Ancient World and the Beginnings of the Middle Ages,* New York, 1931. (Torchbooks) An excellent account of the decline of Rome and the transition to the Middle Ages.

McGiffert, A. C., *History of Christian Thought,* New York, 1932, 2 vols.

Moss, H. St. L. B., *The Birth of the Middle Ages,* 395–814, New York, 1935. Clear and concise.

Patch, R. R., *The Tradition of Boethius,* New York, 1935.

· Rand, E. K., *Founders of the Middle Ages,* Cambridge, Mass., 1928. (Dover) A very good presentation of the contributions of individuals.

Rops, Daniel, *Jesus and His Times,* New York, 1954.

· Taylor, H. O., *The Classical Heritage of the Middle Ages,* New York, 1925. (Torchbooks)

————, *The Medieval Mind,* New York, 1927, 2 vols.

Thompson, J. W., *Economic and Social History of the Middle Ages,* New York, 1928. An interesting summary, no longer considered entirely reliable.

————, and Johnson, E. N., *An Introduction to Medieval Europe,* New York, 1937. One of the best surveys of medieval history.

Source Materials

Boethius, *The Consolation of Philosophy.*

Gregory of Tours, *History of the Franks.*

King, J. E., ed., *The Historical Works of Bede,* 2 vols.

St. Augustine, *The City of God,* especially Books IV, VII, X, XII, XIV, XV, XVII.

————, *Confessions.*

————, *Enchiridion,* especially Chs. XXVI, XXVII, XXX–XXXIII, XLI, L, LI, XCVIII, XCIX.

Shotwell, J. T., and Loomis, L. R., eds., *The See of Peter,* New York, 1927.

The Byzantine and Saracenic Civilizations

What is there greater, what more sacred than imperial majesty? Who so arrogant as to scorn the judgment of the Prince, when lawgivers themselves have precisely and clearly laid down that imperial decisions have the force of law?

—Justinian

Muhammad is the messenger of Allah. And those with him are hard against the disbelievers and merciful among themselves. Allah hath promised, unto such of them as believe and do good works, forgiveness and immense reward.

—*The Koran*, Sûrah XLVIII

The so-called medieval period of history does not concern Europe alone. In addition to the cultures of the early European Middle Ages and of the Feudal Age which followed, medieval history includes two other civilizations, the Byzantine and the Saracenic. Although each occupied territory on the European continent, the larger portions of their empires were located in Africa and in Asia. Of greater significance is the fact that the features of both civilizations were largely those of the Orient. While the Saracens were Moslems and the Byzantine people Christians, religion was the dominant factor in the lives of both. The two states were so closely linked with the religious organizations that their governments were mainly theocratic. Moreover, both civilizations were characterized by attitudes of pessimism and fatalism and by a tendency for the mystical point of view to gain supremacy over the rational. It should be noted, however, that the Saracens, especially, made distinctive contributions to philosophy and science, while the Byzantine Empire was exceedingly important for its art and for its work in preserving innumerable achievements of the Greeks and Romans.

The semi-Oriental character of the Byzantine and Saracenic civilizations

1. The Byzantine Empire and Its Culture

In the fourth century the Emperor Constantine established a new capital for the Roman Empire on the site of the old Greek colony of Byzantium. When the western division of the Empire collapsed, Byzantium (or Constantinople as the city was now more commonly called) survived as the capital of a powerful state which included the Near Eastern provinces of the Caesars. Gradually this state came to be known as the Byzantine Empire, although the existence of a

The founding of the Byzantine Empire

277

Byzantine civilization was not clearly recognized before the sixth century. Even after that there were many who believed that Rome had merely shifted its center of gravity to the East.

Although Byzantine history covered a period similar to that of the Middle Ages, the cultural pattern was far different from the one which prevailed in western Europe. Byzantine civilization had a much more pronounced Oriental character. Not only did Constantinople face the Orient, but most of the territories of the Empire actually lay outside of Europe. The most important among them were Syria, Asia Minor, Palestine, and Egypt. Furthermore, Greek and Hellenistic elements entered into the formation of Byzantine culture to a greater extent than was ever true in western Europe. The language of the eastern state was predominantly Greek, while the traditions in literature, art, and science were largely Hellenistic. Lastly, the Christianity of the Byzantine Empire differed from that of Latin Europe in being more mystical, abstract, and pessimistic and more completely subject to political control.

Byzantine culture more distinctly Oriental than that of Latin Europe

The population of the territories under Byzantine rule comprised a great number of nationalities. The majority of the inhabitants were Greeks and Hellenized Orientals—Syrians, Jews, Armenians, Egyptians, and Persians. In addition, the European sections of the Empire included numerous barbarians, especially Slavs and Mongols. There were some Germans also, but the emperors at Constantinople were generally able to divert the German invasions to the west. The encroachments of the Slavs and the Mongols, on the other hand, proved to be much more difficult to deal with. The original home of the Slavs, a round-headed people of Alpine stock, was apparently the region northeast of the Carpathian Mountains, principally in what is now southwestern Russia. A peaceful agricultural folk, they seldom resorted to armed invasion but gradually expanded into thinly settled territories whenever the opportunity arose. Not only did they move into the vast empty spaces of central Russia, but they occupied many of the regions vacated by the Germans and then slowly filtered through the frontiers of the Eastern Empire. By the seventh century they were the most numerous people in the entire Balkan peninsula, as well as in the whole region of Europe east of the Germans. The Mongolian inhabitants of the Empire included Bulgars and Avars, who had come into Europe from the steppes of what is now Asiatic Russia. Both of these nations were herdsmen, with the furious energy and warlike habits characteristic of that mode of existence. After entering the valley of the Danube, many of them forced their way into Byzantine territory. It was a fusion of some of these Mongolian peoples with Slavs which gave rise to such modern nations as the Bulgarians and the Serbs.

Nationalities in the Byzantine Empire

The details of Byzantine political development have little significance for the modern age. The early history of the Empire was marked by struggles to repel the Germanic barbarians. The con-

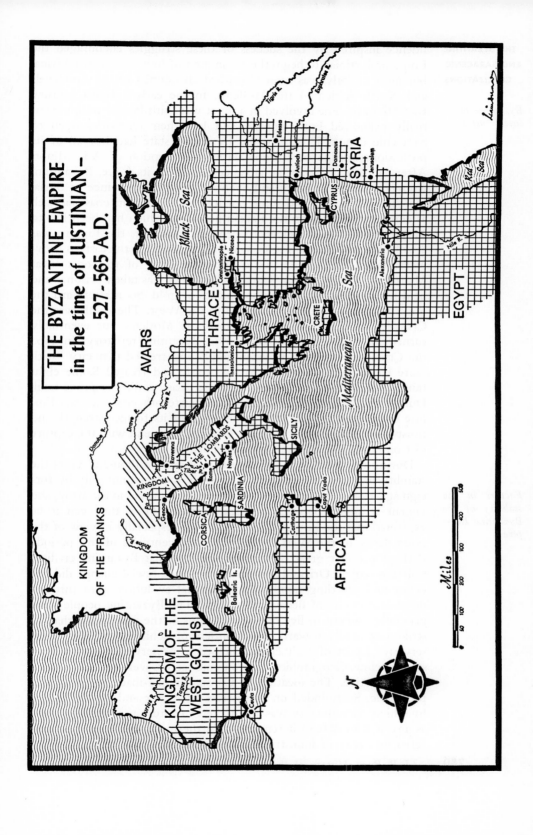

THE BYZANTINE EMPIRE
in the time of JUSTINIAN—
527-565 A.D.

*Byzantine po-
litical history*

fidence inspired by the success of these struggles encouraged the Emperor Justinian to begin the reconquest of Italy and North Africa, but most of Italy was soon afterward abandoned to the Lombards and North Africa to the Moslems. In the early seventh century Byzantium became involved in a great war with Persia, which eventually exhausted both empires and laid their territories open to Saracenic conquest. By 750 the Byzantine state had lost all of its possessions outside of Europe with the exception of Asia Minor. After the tide of Saracenic advance had spent its force, Byzantium enjoyed a brief recovery and even regained the province of Syria, the island of Crete, and some portions of the Italian coast, as well as certain territories on the Balkan peninsula which had been lost to the barbarians. In the eleventh century, however, the Empire was attacked by the Seljuk Turks, who rapidly overran the eastern provinces and in 1071 annihilated a Byzantine army of 100,000 men at Manzikert. The Emperor Romanus Diogenes was taken prisoner and held for a ransom of one million pieces of gold. Soon afterward the government sent an appeal for aid to the West. The result was the Crusades, launched originally against the Moslems but eventually turned into plundering attacks upon Byzantine territory. In 1204 the Crusaders captured Constantinople and treated that city "with more barbarity than the barbarian Alaric had treated Rome eight hundred years before." [1] But even these disasters did not prove fatal. During the late thirteenth and early fourteenth centuries the Empire once again recovered some measure of its former strength and prosperity. Its history was finally brought to an end with the capture of Constantinople by the Ottoman Turks in 1453.

*Factors in the
stability of the
Byzantine Em-
pire*

During this long period of approximately one thousand years the stability of Byzantine rule was frequently menaced not only by foreign aggression but also by palace intrigues, mutinies in the army, and violent struggles between political factions. How then can it be explained that the Empire survived so long, especially in view of the rapid decay of the West during the early centuries of this period? Perhaps the first great reason was the fact that Byzantine civilization was largely Oriental and relatively static. Social change did not occur with startling rapidity, and cultural evolution went through no violent cycles of decay and rebirth. The Byzantine people were generally content to live on the traditions of the past rather than to strike out boldly toward new frontiers of achievement. This conservative aspect of their culture helped to preserve the nation from swift decline. Geographic and economic factors were probably much more effective. The location of Constantinople made it almost impregnable. Surrounded on three sides by water and on the fourth by a high wall, the city was able to resist capture practically as long as any will to defend it remained. Furthermore, the Near East suffered no decay of industry and commerce like that which had oc-

[1] J. B. Bury, *History of the Later Roman Empire* (1931 ed.), Vol. I, p. 3.

curred in Italy at the beginning of the Dark Ages. Last of all, the Byzantine government had a well-filled treasury which could always be drawn upon for purposes of defense. The annual revenues of the state have been estimated as high as $106 million (1957 dollars).

The government of the Byzantine Empire was similar to that of Rome after the time of Diocletian, except that it was even more despotic and theocratic. The emperor was an absolute sovereign with *The government of the By-* unlimited power over every department of national life. His sub- *zantine Empire* jects not only fell prostrate before him, but in petitioning his grace they customarily referred to themselves as his slaves. Moreover, the spiritual dignity of the emperor was in no sense inferior to his temporal power. He was the vicar of God with a religious authority supposed to be equal to that of the Apostles. Although some of the emperors were able and hard-working officials, most of the actual functions of the government were performed by an extensive bureaucracy, many of whose members were highly trained. A great army of clerks, inspectors, and spies maintained the closest scrutiny over the life and possessions of every inhabitant.

The economic system was as strictly regulated as in Hellenistic Egypt. In fact, the Byzantine Empire has been described as a "paradise of monopoly, of privilege, and of paternalism." [2] The state ex- *State control of* ercised a thorough control over virtually every activity. The wage of *the economic* every workman and the price of every product were fixed by gov- *system* ernment decree. In many cases it was not even possible for the individual to choose his own occupation, since the system of guilds which had been established in the late Roman Empire was still maintained. Each worker inherited his status as a member of one guild or another, and the walls which surrounded these organizations were hermetically sealed. Neither did the manufacturer enjoy much greater freedom. He could not choose for himself what quantity or quality of raw materials he would purchase, nor was he permitted to buy them directly. He could not determine how much he would produce or under what conditions he would sell his product. All of these matters were regulated by the trade association to which he belonged, and it in turn was subject to supervision by the government. To provide for cheap administration of the system, the emperors encouraged competing businessmen and workers to act as informers against each other. A number of large industrial enterprises were owned and operated by the state. Chief among them were the murex or purple fisheries, the mines, the armament factories, and the establishments for the weaving of cloth. An attempt was made at one time to extend monopolistic control over the silk industry, but the government factories were unable to supply the demand, and permission had to be given to private manufacturers to resume production.

The agricultural regime developed under the late Roman Empire

[2] J. W. Thompson, *Economic and Social History of the Middle Ages*, p. 336. **281**

*The agricultur-
al regime*

was also perpetuated and extended in the Byzantine territories. Most of the land was divided into great estates comparable to the *latifundia* in Italy. Except in the hilly and mountainous regions, there were few independent farmers left. In the richest areas the agricultural population was made up almost entirely of tenant farmers and serfs. The number of the latter was increased in the fifth century when the Emperor Anastasius issued a decree forbidding all peasants who had lived on a particular farm for thirty years ever to remove therefrom. The purpose of the decree was to insure a minimum of agricultural production, but its natural effect was to bind the peasants to the soil and make them actual serfs of their landlords. Another of the significant agricultural developments in the Byzantine Empire was the concentration of landed wealth in the hands of the church. The monasteries, especially, came to be included among the richest proprietors in the country. With the increasing difficulty of making a living from the soil and the growing popularity of asceticism, more and more farmers sought refuge in the cloister and made gifts of their lands to the institutions which admitted them. The estates acquired by the church were cultivated not by the monks or the priests but by serfs. During the seventh and eighth centuries an economic transformation occurred. Many of the serfs gained their freedom and became owners of the lands they cultivated. But by the eleventh century the great estates had reappeared, and the independent peasantry virtually ceased to exist.

*The absorbing
interest in reli-
gion*

No subject appears to have absorbed the interest of the Byzantine people more completely than religion. They fought over religious questions as vehemently as citizens of the modern world quarrel over issues of government control versus private ownership or democracy versus totalitarianism. They took great delight in theological subtleties which would impress most people in our time as barren and trivial. Gregory of Nyssa, one of their own Church Fathers, thus described Constantinople in the fourth century: "Everything is full of those who are speaking of unintelligible things—streets, markets, squares, crossroads. I ask how many oboli I have to pay; in answer they are philosophizing on the born or unborn; I wish to know the price of bread; one answers: 'The Father is greater than the Son'; I inquire whether my bath is ready; one says, 'The Son has been made out of nothing.' "[3]

*Religious con-
troversies; the
Monophysite
movement*

The most crucial of the religious issues, however, were those which grew out of the Monophysite and Iconoclastic movements, although neither of these movements was exclusively religious in character. The Monophysites derived their name from their contention that the Christ was composed of only one nature, and that that nature was divine. This doctrine, which was probably a reflection of the Neo-Platonist contempt for everything physical or material, flatly contradicted the official theology of Christianity. Having begun as early

[3] A. A. Vasiliev, *History of the Byzantine Empire*, Vol. I, pp. 99 f.

as the fifth century, the Monophysite movement reached its height during the reign of Justinian (527–565). Its strength lay chiefly in Syria and in Egypt, where it served as an expression of nationalist resentment against subjection to Constantinople. In dealing with the sect Justinian was caught between two fires. Not only was he ambitious to unite his subjects in allegiance to a single faith, but he was anxious to win the support of Rome. On the other hand, he was reluctant to take any steps for the suppression of the Monophysites partly because of their strength and also because his wife, the popular actress Theodora, was a member of the sect. It was her will that finally prevailed. During the seventh century the Monophysites broke away from the Eastern church. The sect survives to this day as an important branch of Christendom in Egypt, Syria, and Armenia.

The Iconoclastic movement was launched about 725 by a decree of the Emperor Leo III forbidding the use of images in the church. In the Eastern church any image of God, the Christ, or a saint was called an icon. Those who condemned the use of icons in worship were known as Iconoclasts, or image-breakers. The Iconoclastic movement was a product of several factors. First of all, it had a certain affinity with the Monophysite movement in its opposition to anything sensuous or material in religion. Secondly, it was a protest against paganism and worldliness in the church. But perhaps more than anything else it represented a revolt of certain of the emperors against the increasing power of the ecclesiastical system. The monasteries in particular were absorbing so large a proportion of the national wealth and enticing so many men away from service in the army and from useful occupations that they were rapidly undermining the economic vitality of the Empire. Since the monks derived a large part of their income from the manufacture and sale of icons, it was logical that the reforming emperors should center their attacks upon the use of images in the church. Naturally they had the support of many of their pious subjects, who resented what they considered a corruption of their religion by idolatrous practices.

The Iconoclasts

Although the struggle against the worship of images was continued until well into the ninth century, it really accomplished no more than the elimination of sculptured representations; the flat or painted icons were eventually restored. Nevertheless, the Iconoclastic controversy had more than a trivial significance. It may be said to have represented an important stage in the irrepressible conflict between Roman and Oriental traditions, which occupied so large a place in Byzantine history. Those who upheld the use of images generally believed in an ecclesiastical religion in which symbols and ceremony were regarded as indispensable aids to worship. Most of their opponents were mystics and ascetics who condemned any form of institutionalism or veneration of material objects and advocated a return to the spiritualism of primitive Christianity. Many of the ideals

Significance of the Iconoclastic controversy

of the Iconoclasts were similar to those of the Protestant Reformers of the sixteenth century, and the movement itself may be said to have foreshadowed the great revolt of Luther and Calvin against what were considered pagan elements in the Roman Catholic religion. Finally, the Iconoclastic controversy was a potent cause of the separation of the Greek and Roman branches of the church in 1054. Even though the attack upon the use of images was not entirely successful, it went far enough to arouse much antagonism between Eastern and Western Christians. The Pope excommunicated the Iconoclasts and turned from the Byzantine emperors to the Frankish kings for support. From this point on the East and the West drew farther apart.

Social conditions in the Byzantine Empire

Social conditions in the Byzantine Empire presented a marked contrast with western Europe during the early Middle Ages. Whereas large sections of Italy and southern France had sunk to almost primitive levels of ruralism, Byzantine society continued to maintain its essentially urban and luxurious character. Approximately a million people lived in the city of Constantinople alone, to say nothing of

Silver Plate Portraying David and Goliath, and Plaque, in Gold and Enamel, Portraying the Christ. Such objects were among the most appealing examples of Byzantine minor arts.

the thousands who dwelt in Tarsus, Nicaea, Edessa, Thessalonica, and other great urban centers. Merchants, bankers, and manufacturers ranked with the great landlords as members of the aristocracy, for there was no tendency in Byzantium as there had been in Rome to despise the man who derived his income from industry or trade. The rich lived in elegance and ease, cultivating the indulgence of opulent tastes as a fine art. A large part of the industrial activity of the nation was absorbed in the production of articles of luxury to meet the demand of the wealthier classes. Magnificent garments of wool and silk interwoven with gold and silver thread, gorgeously colored tapestries of brocaded or damasked stuffs, exquisite glass and porcelain ware, illuminated gospels, and rare and costly jeweled orna-

284

Gold Cup, Byzantine, VI–IX cent. The figure is a personification of Constantinople, a queen or goddess holding the scepter and orb of imperial rule. (MMA)

Saint John Writing His Gospel. From an Anglo-Frankish illuminated manuscript, *ca.* 850, produced in a Carolingian monastery. The unknown artist knew nothing of perspective, but excelled in coloring and conveying a sense of vitality and energy. (Morgan Library)

Merovingian Fibula or Brooch, VII cent. A fabulous gold-plated animal set with garnets and colored paste reveals the lively imagination of the early Middle Ages. (MMA)

Enthroned Madonna and Child, Byzantine School, XIII cent. The painters of Siena followed the opulent and brilliant style of Byzantine art. Their madonnas were not earthly mothers, but celestial queens reigning in dignified splendor. (National Gallery)

The Young King, Louis IX, XIII cent. Though Louis was widely revered as a saint, the artist has endowed him with distinctively human features. (Morgan Library)

Kings in Battle, French, *ca.* 1250. A scene depicting, with the trappings of knighthood, Joshua's fight against the five kings of Canaan. In the center Joshua raises his hand, commanding the sun and moon to stand still to enable him to complete his victory. (Morgan Library)

Aquamanile, German, XII–XIII cent. Aquamaniles were water jugs used for hand-washing during church ritual, or at meal times. (MMA)

Ivory Plaque, German, X cent. The plaque shows Otto the Great presenting a church to Christ while St. Peter watches, a reference to Otto's building an empire by co-operating with the Church. (MMA)

Chalice, German, XIII cent. A beautifully embellished wine cup used in the sacrament of the Eucharist. (MMA)

ments composed only a small part of the sumptuous output of factories and shops, both public and private.

The life of the lower classes was poor and mean by comparison. And yet the common man in the Byzantine Empire was probably better off than the average citizen in most other parts of the Christian world at that time. The extensive industrial and commercial development and the high degree of economic stability provided opportunities for employment for thousands of urban workers, except during the period of Moslem invasions, when Constantinople was filled with refugees who could not be absorbed into the economic system. Even the lot of the serf who was attached to the estate of some one of the great secular proprietors was probably superior to that of the peasants in western Europe, since the landlord's powers of exploitation were at least regulated by law. Nevertheless, the serf's condition was bad enough, for he was doomed to a life of ignorance and dull routine within the narrow horizon of the village in which he was born. His status was unalterably fixed by the mere accident of his having been born of parents who were serfs. The Byzantine population also included a considerable percentage of slaves, but most of them were employed in domestic service and doubtless enjoyed a fairly comfortable existence.

The tone of morality in the Empire exhibited sharp contrasts. The Byzantine people in spite of their Greek antecedents apparently had no aptitude for the typical Hellenic virtues of balance and restraint. In place of the golden mean they seemed always to prefer the extremes. Consequently the most extravagant self-indulgence was frequently to be found side by side with the humblest self-denial or laceration of the flesh. The contradictory qualities of sensuality and piety, charity and heartless cruelty, were commonly evident in the same stratum of society or even in the same individuals. For example, the great reform Emperor, Leo III, tried to improve the lot of the peasants, but he also introduced mutilation as a punishment for crime. Life at the imperial court and among some members of the higher clergy appears to have been characterized by indolence, luxurious vice, effeminacy, and intrigue. As a consequence, the very word "Byzantine" has come to be suggestive of elegant sensuality and refinements of cruelty.

In the intellectual realm the Byzantine people won little distinction for originality. Comparatively few discoveries or contributions in any of the fields of knowledge can actually be credited to them. Probably their most noteworthy achievement was the revision and codification of the ancient Roman law. After the time of the great jurists (second and third centuries A.D.) the creative genius of the Roman lawyers decayed, and nothing new was added to the philosophy or the science of law. The volume of statutory enactments, however, continued to grow. By the sixth century the Roman law had come to contain numerous contradictory and obsolete provisions. Moreover, conditions had changed so radically that many of the old legal principles could no longer be applied, particularly on account of the establishment of an Oriental despotism and the adoption of Christianity as the official religion. When Justinian came to the throne in 527, he immediately decided upon a revision and codification of the existing law to bring it into harmony with the new conditions and to establish it as an authoritative basis of his rule. To carry out the actual work he appointed a commission of lawyers under the supervision of his minister, Tribonian. Within two years the commission published the first result of its labors. This was the Code, a systematic revision of all of the statutory laws which had been issued from the reign of Hadrian to the reign of Justinian. The Code was later supplemented by the Novels, which contained the legislation of Justinian and his immediate successors. By 532 the commission had completed the Digest, representing a summary of all of the writings of the great jurists. The final product of the work of revision was the Institutes, a textbook of the legal principles which were reflected in both the Digest and the Code. The combination of all four of these results of the program of revision constitutes the *Corpus Juris Civilis,* or the body of the civil law.

*The Institutes
and the Digest*

From the historical standpoint the two most important sections of the *Corpus Juris* were unquestionably the Institutes and the Digest. It was these which contained the philosophy of law and of government which had come to prevail in Justinian's time. There is a popular but somewhat inaccurate belief that this philosophy was the same as that of Ulpian, Papinian, and the other great jurists of three hundred years before. While it is true that most of the old theory was preserved, a few fundamental changes were introduced. First, the *jus civile* was more completely denationalized than it had ever been during Roman times and was now made applicable to citizens of a great many divergent nationalities. The *jus naturale* was now declared to be divine and consequently superior to all of the enactments of men—a conception which was destined to become exceedingly popular in later medieval philosophy. There was a tendency also for Justinian's jurists to speak of the emperor as the sole legislator, on the assumption that the people had surrendered all of their power to him. In other words, the classical Roman law was being revised to make it fit the needs of an Oriental monarch whose sovereignty was limited only by the law of God.

*Other Byzan-
tine intellectual
achievements*

As to the remainder of Byzantine intellectual achievements, comparatively little needs to be said. The nation produced no philosophers of more than secondary rank. But several of them made important contributions to the development of Scholasticism, which emerged as the most popular philosophy of the later Middle Ages. They emphasized the value of reason and attempted to reconcile the teachings of Aristotle with those of the Scriptures and the Christian Fathers. Byzantine literature consisted for the most part of compilations and religious writings, especially encyclopedias, commentaries, hymns, and biographies of saints. Some epic and lyric poetry was also written and numerous histories. By far the most famous of the historians was Procopius, a contemporary of Justinian. Despite his penchant for scandal-mongering in his celebrated *Secret History*, others of his works contain valuable information about the events of his time.

The Byzantine record in science was possibly somewhat better than in most other branches of learning. Most of the progress was made in the early years of the Empire, perhaps on account of the survival of Hellenistic influence. This first golden age was followed by a long period of stagnation until the middle of the tenth century, when a revival began due in large part to Moslem influence and to the patronage of the Emperor Constantine VII. But neither of these eras of progress lasted for more than two centuries. The leading scientists of the early period were John the Grammarian, Aetius, and Alexander of Tralles, all of whom lived in the sixth century. John the Grammarian is far more deserving of credit for his work in physics than for any contributions to grammar. He is especially worthy of attention for having been the first to challenge the traditional theories of motion and gravity. Not only did he anticipate the concept of inertia, but he rejected the notion that the speed of falling bodies is directly proportional to their weight, and he denied the impossibility of creating a vacuum. The other two scientists of the early period were encyclopedists of medicine. Although the influence of Alexander of Tralles surpassed that of Aetius, the work of the latter was more original. Aetius wrote not only the first description of diphtheria but also the best account of diseases of the eye which had been published thus far. The only outstanding scientist of the later period was Symeon Seth, who was also a physician. His chief work was a medical dictionary defining the curative properties of numerous drugs lately discovered by the Hindus and the Saracens.

The record in science

The tastes of the Byzantine people, with their fondness for luxury and splendor, were signally expressed in their art. However, it was not a mere emblem of sensuous delight. It was profoundly conditioned by the peculiar ideals of the civilization itself. For one thing, the strong undercurrent of asceticism prohibited the glorification of man; as a consequence, sculpture was not permitted to develop very far. The art which held the position of pre-eminence was architecture, and it had to be mystical and otherworldly. Furthermore, since the Byzantine civilization was a compound of elements both Roman and Oriental, it was inevitable that its art should combine the love of grandeur and the engineering talent of Rome with the gorgeous coloring and richness of detail characteristic of the Orient.

Byzantine art

The supreme artistic achievement of the Byzantine civilization was the church of Santa Sophia (Holy Wisdom), built at enormous cost by the Emperor Justinian. Although designed by architects of Hel-

*The church of
Santa Sophia*

lenic descent, it was vastly different from any Greek temple. Its purpose was not to express man's pride in himself or his satisfaction with this life, but to symbolize the inward and spiritual character of the Christian religion. It was for this reason that the architects gave little attention to the external appearance of the building. Nothing but plain brick covered with plaster was used for the exterior walls; no marble facings, graceful columns, or sculptured entablatures. The interior, however, was decorated with richly colored mosaics, gold leaf, colored marble columns, and bits of tinted glass set on edge to refract the rays of sunlight after the fashion of sparkling gems.

Mosaic, from the Church of Santa Sophia. The mosaic represents the Emperor Leo VI adoring the Christ seated on the throne.

It was for this reason also that the building was constructed in such a way that no light appeared to come from the outside at all but to be manufactured within.

The structural design of Santa Sophia was something altogether new in the history of architecture. Its central feature was the application of the principle of the dome to a building of square shape. The church was designed, first of all, in the form of a cross, and then over the central square was to be erected a magnificent dome, which would dominate the entire structure. The main problem was how to fit the round circumference of the dome to the square area it was supposed to cover. The solution consisted in having four great arches spring from pillars at the four corners of the central square. The rim of the dome was then made to rest on the keystones of the arches, with the curved triangular spaces between the arches filled in with masonry. The result was an architectural framework of marvelous strength, which at the same time made possible a style of im-

*Advantages
of structural
design*

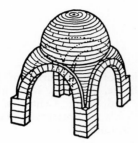

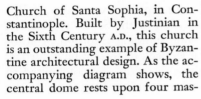

Church of Santa Sophia, in Constantinople. Built by Justinian in the Sixth Century A.D., this church is an outstanding example of Byzantine architectural design. As the accompanying diagram shows, the central dome rests upon four massive arches. The tremendous downward thrust of the dome necessitates the buttressing seen in the photograph in the two enormous masonry piles and half domes. The minarets were added later by the Moslems.

posing grandeur and even some delicacy of treatment. The great dome of Santa Sophia has a diameter of 107 feet and rises to a height of nearly 180 feet from the floor. So many windows are placed around its rim that the dome appears to have no support at all but to be suspended in mid-air.

The other arts of Byzantium included ivory-carving, the making of embossed glassware and brocaded textiles, the illumination of manuscripts, the goldsmith's and jeweler's arts, and considerable painting. The last, however, was not so highly developed as some of the others. In place of painting the Byzantine artist generally preferred mosaics. These were designs produced by fitting together small pieces of colored glass or stone to form a geometric pattern, symbolical figures of plants and animals, or even an elaborate scene of theological significance. Representations of saints and of the Christ were commonly distorted to create the impression of extreme piety.

Other Byzantine arts

See color plates at pages 284, 285

The importance of the Byzantine civilization is usually underestimated. It was undoubtedly the most powerful factor in determining the course of development of eastern Europe. To a very large extent the civilization of imperial Russia was founded upon the institutions and achievements of Byzantium. The Russian church was an offshoot of the so-called Greek Orthodox or Eastern church, which broke away from Rome in 1054. The Tsar as the head of the religion as well as the state occupied a position analogous to that of the emperor at Constantinople. The architecture of the Russians,

The Byzantine influence in eastern Europe

Interior of the Church of Sant' Apollinare, Ravenna. Built in the Fifth and Sixth Centuries, this church is a well preserved example of Byzantine influence.

their calendar, and a large part of their alphabet were also of Byzantine origin. Perhaps even the despotism of the Soviet regime can be traced in some measure to the long-standing tradition of absolute rule in Russia which ultimately goes back to Byzantine influence.

The Byzantine influence in the West

But the influence of the Byzantine civilization was not limited to eastern Europe. It would be hard to overestimate the debt of the West to scholars in Constantinople and the surrounding territory who copied and preserved manuscripts, prepared anthologies of Greek literature, and wrote encyclopedias embodying the learning of the ancient world. Moreover, Byzantine scholars exerted a notable influence upon the Italian Renaissance. In spite of the fact that the Eastern emperors eventually lost control of Italy, many of their former subjects continued to live there, and some others fled to the Italian cities after the overthrow of the Iconoclastic movement. The extensive trade between Venice and Constantinople in the late Middle Ages also fostered cultural relations between East and West. Consequently, long before the fifteenth century when eminent Greek scholars arrived in Italy, a foundation for the revival of interest in the Greek classics had already been laid. Likewise, Byzantine art exerted its effect upon the art of western Europe. Some authorities regard the stained glass windows of the Gothic cathedrals as an adaptation of the mosaics in Eastern churches. Several of the most famous churches in Italy, for example St. Mark's in Venice, were built in close imitation of the Byzantine style. Byzantine painting also influenced the painting of the Renaissance, especially of the Venetian school and of El Greco. Finally, it was the *Corpus Juris* of Justinian which really made possible the transmission of the Roman law to the late Middle Ages and to the modern world.

2. Islam and the Saracenic Civilization

The history of the Saracenic civilization began a little later than the history of Byzantium and ended a short time earlier. The dates were roughly 630 A.D. to 1300. In many ways the Saracenic civilization was one of the most important in the Western world—not only because it was the orbit of a new religion, which has attracted converts by the hundreds of millions, but mainly because its impact upon Christian Europe was responsible for social and intellectual changes which can only be described as revolutionary. The term "Saracen" originally meant an Arab, but later it came to be applied to any member of the Moslem faith, regardless of his nationality. Some of the Saracens were Jews, some were Persians, some were Syrians. Nevertheless, the founders of the civilization were Arabs, and it therefore becomes necessary to examine the culture of that people on the eve of their expansion beyond the borders of their homeland.

ISLAM AND
THE SARACENIC
CIVILIZATION

*The Saracenic
empire
not exclusively
Arabian*

Toward the end of the sixth century the people of Arabia had come to be divided into two main groups: the urban Arabs and the Bedouins. The former, who dwelt in such cities as Mecca and Yathrib, were traders and petty craftsmen. Many of them were literate, and some were comparatively wealthy. The Bedouins were mostly nomads, subsisting on dates and the flesh and milk of their animals. Ignorant and superstitious, they practiced infanticide and occasional human sacrifice. They were frequently involved in bloody warfare over possession of wells and oases. Neither Bedouins nor urban Arabs had any organized government. The clan and the tribe took the place of the state. When a member of one clan committed a crime against a member of another, the issue was settled by means of the blood feud, which sometimes raged until scores had been killed on each side. The religion was generally polytheistic, although some of the better educated townsmen had adopted a belief in Allah as the only God. From time immemorial Mecca had been a sacred city. Here was the shrine known as the Kaaba, which was supposed to contain a sacred black stone miraculously sent down from heaven. The men who controlled this shrine formed the tribe of the Kuraish, the nearest approach to an Arabian aristocracy that ever existed before the migrations.

*Conditions in
Arabia before
Mohammed*

Whether the Saracenic civilization would ever have originated without the development of the Moslem religion is a question almost impossible to answer. It is commonly assumed that a new religion was necessary to unite the people and to imbue them with ardor in a common cause. Yet other nations had expanded before this and had accomplished great things without the influence of any particularly inspiring system of belief. Nevertheless, in the case of the Arabs it was a new religion which undoubtedly provided much of the driving force behind the development of their civilization. The origin and nature of that religion must therefore be given careful attention.

The Moslem religion as a driving force in the civilization

The founder of the new faith was born in Mecca about the year 570. The child of parents who belonged to one of the poorest clans of the Kuraish tribe, he was given the common Arabic name of Muhammad or Mohammed. Nothing is known about his early life,

*The early life
of Mohammed*

except that he was left an orphan while still very young and was reared by his grandfather and his uncle. Whether he ever learned to read and write is uncertain, but it is probable that as a member of the leading tribe he would be given some education. When he was about twenty-five years old, he entered the employment of a rich widow and accompanied her caravans perhaps as far north as Syria. Soon afterward he became her husband, thereby acquiring leisure and security to devote all of his time to religious interests.

Mohammed as-
sumes the role
of social critic

Exactly what influences led Mohammed to become the founder of a new religion, no one knows. He was apparently of a highly emotional nature and may have been an epileptic. At any rate he was subject to fits or convulsive seizures of some kind, during the course of which he believed he heard voices from heaven. Very early in his life he became acquainted with numerous Jews and Christians who lived in the cities of northern Arabia, and he appears to have been deeply impressed by their religious beliefs. In addition, he seems to have developed the idea that social and moral conditions in his country were badly in need of reform. He began to denounce the plutocrats of Mecca for their greed and to reproach his people for their bloody feuds and their practice of infanticide. Gradually he came to conceive of himself as the appointed instrument of God to rescue the Arabian people from the path of destruction.

Founding the
new religion

Mohammed's preaching was not at first particularly successful. After almost nine years of communicating the revelations of Allah to all who would listen, he had managed to win very few converts outside of his immediate family. The wealthy Kuraish were naturally against him, and even the common people of Mecca were generally indifferent. As yet he had made no attempt to carry his message to the Bedouins. In 619 he decided to seek a more promising field for the propagation of his teachings. He had learned that the city of Yathrib on the caravan route to the north had been torn for some time by bitter factional strife, and that there might be some chance for a neutral leader to step in and assume control. He sent a number of agents to explore the ground very carefully, and finally in September, 622, he and the remainder of his followers decided to abandon the sacred city of Mecca entirely and to risk their future in the new location. This migration to Yathrib is known to Mohammedans as the Hegira, from the Arabic word meaning "flight," and is considered by them so important that they regard it as the beginning of their era and date all their records from it.

The conquest of
Mecca

Mohammed changed the name of Yathrib to Medina (the "city of the Prophet"), and quickly succeeded in establishing himself as ruler of the city. But to obtain means of support for his followers was a somewhat more difficult matter. Besides, the Jews in Medina rejected his leadership. Under these circumstances Mohammed began to enlist the support of the Bedouins for a holy war against his enemies. In a single year approximately six hundred Jews were

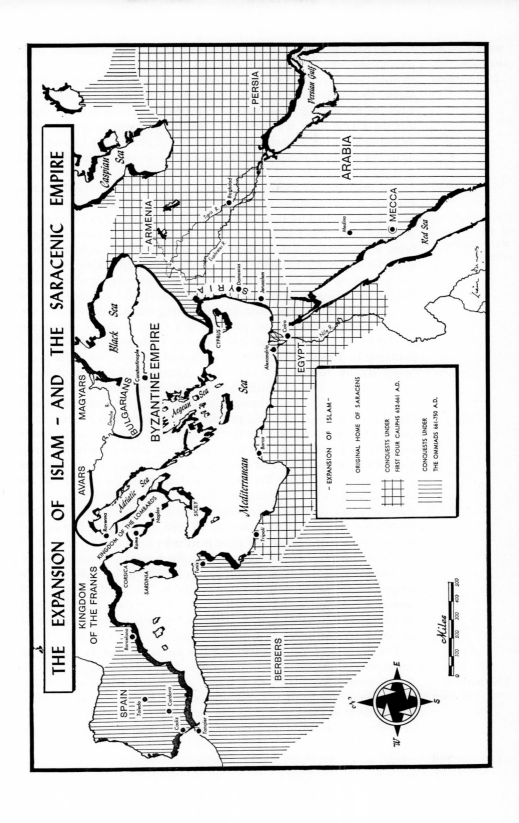

THE EXPANSION OF ISLAM – AND THE SARACENIC EMPIRE

ICELAND

Caspian Sea

PERSIA

Persian Gulf

ARMENIA

Baghdad

Tigris R.

Euphrates R.

ARABIA

Medina

MECCA

Red Sea

Black Sea

MAGYARS

AVARS

Danube R.

BULGARIANS

Constantinople

BYZANTINE EMPIRE

Aegean Sea

CYPRUS

Damascus

S Y R I A

Jerusalem

Cairo

EGYPT

Nile R.

Alexandria

Adriatic Sea

Ravenna

KINGDOM OF THE LOMBARDS

Rome

Naples

SICILY

KINGDOM OF THE FRANKS

CORSICA

SARDINIA

Mediterranean Sea

Barca

Tripoli

Tunis

BERBERS

SPAIN

Toledo

Cordova

Cadiz

Tangier

Barcelona

– EXPANSION OF ISLAM –

ORIGINAL HOME OF SARACENS

CONQUESTS UNDER
FIRST FOUR CALIPHS 632-661 A.D.

CONQUESTS UNDER
THE OMMIADS 661-750 A.D.

Miles

0   100   200   300   400   500

N   E   S   W

massacred, and then the followers of the Prophet launched their plundering attacks upon the caravans of the merchants of Mecca. When the latter took up arms to resist, they were badly defeated in battle. In 630 Mohammed entered Mecca in triumph. He murdered a few of his leading opponents and smashed the idols in the temple, but the Kaaba itself was preserved, and Mecca was established as a sacred city of the Mohammedan faith. Two years later Mohammed died, but he lived to see the religion he had founded a militant and successful enterprise.

The doctrines of the Mohammedan religion

The doctrines of the Mohammedan religion as developed by the Prophet are really quite simple. They revolve around a belief in one God, who is called by the old Arabic name Allah, and in Mohammed as his prophet. This God desires that men shall be kind to their neighbors, lenient toward debtors, honest, and forgiving; and that they shall refrain from infanticide, eating swine's flesh, drinking intoxicating beverages, and waging the blood feud. The religion also enjoins the faithful observance of certain obligations. Chief among these are the giving of alms to the poor, fasting during the day throughout the sacred month of Ramadan, praying five times a day, and making a pilgrimage, if possible, at least once in a lifetime to Mecca. But contrary to a general belief, the religion of the Prophet is far from being rigidly formal or mechanical. Almost as much emphasis is placed upon purity of heart and practical benevolence as in Christianity or Judaism. Several passages in the Koran, which constitutes the Mohammedan Scriptures, provide ample warrant for such a conclusion. One of them declares that "There is no piety in turning your faces toward the east or the west, but he is pious who believeth in God, and the last day, and the angels, and the Scriptures, and the prophets; who for the love of God disburseth his wealth to his kindred, and to the orphans, and the needy, and the wayfarer and those who ask, and for ransoming." [4] Another affirms that the highest merit is "to free the captive; or to feed, in a day of famine, the orphan who is of kin, or the poor man who lieth on the ground." [5] Furthermore, there are no sacraments in the system of worship taught by Mohammed, and there are no priests in the Moslem religion. The religion itself is officially known as "Islam," a word meaning "to submit, or to surrender oneself absolutely to God." The official designation of a believer is a "Moslem," which is the participle of the same verb of which "Islam" is the infinitive.

The probable sources of Islam

The sources of the religion of Islam are somewhat in doubt. Judaism was unquestionably one of them. Mohammed taught that the Arabs were descendants of Ishmael, Abraham's oldest son. Moreover, a good many of the teachings of the Koran are quite similar to doctrines in the Old Testament: strict monotheism, the sanction of polygamy, and the prohibition of usury, the worship of images,

---

[4] Sura 2:v. 172.
[5] Sura 90:v. 12.

and the eating of pork. Christianity was also an exceedingly important source. Mohammed considered the New Testament as well as the Old to be a divinely inspired book, and he regarded Jesus as one of the greatest of a long line of prophets. Besides, the Mohammedan doctrines of the resurrection of the body, the last judgment, rewards and punishments after death, and the belief in angels were more probably derived from Christianity than from any other system of belief. On the other hand, it is necessary to remember that the Christianity with which Mohammed was acquainted was far from being the orthodox variety. Nearly all of the Christians who lived in Syria as well as those in Arabia itself were Ebionites or Nestorians. It is perhaps for this reason that Mohammed always thought of Jesus as human, the son of Joseph and Mary, and not as a god.

It was not long after the origin of Islam until its followers split into a number of sects not entirely dissimilar to some of the offshoots of Christianity. The three most important of the Moslem sects were the Sunnites, the Shiites, and the Sufis. The first two had a political as well as a religious character. The Sunnites maintained that the head of the Islamic state and successor to the Prophet should be elected by representatives of the whole body of believers, in accordance with the ancient Arabian custom of election of tribal chiefs. In matters of religion they contended that the *sunna*, or traditions which had grown up outside of the Koran, should be accepted as a valid source of belief. The Shiites were opposed to the elevation of anyone to the highest political and religious office who was not related to the Prophet himself, either by blood or by marriage. In general, they represented the absolutist ideal in Islam as distinct from the democratic ideal of the Sunnites. What is more, the Shiites were against the acceptance of anything but the Koran as a source of religious belief. The Sufis adhered to a mystical and ascetic ideal. Denying absolutely the validity of rational judgment, they maintained that the only truth worth anything is that which proceeds from divine revelation. They believed that it is possible for man to partake of this divine revelation through torturing his body and thereby releasing the soul for a mystic union with God. Many of the fakirs and dervishes in India and Persia today are members of the Sufi sect.

The principal Mohammedan sects

The political history of the Saracenic civilization is closely interwoven with the growth of the religion. As we have already seen, Mohammed became the founder not merely of a religion but also of an Arabic state with its capital at Medina. Following his death in 632 his companions chose as his successor Abu-Bekr, one of the earliest converts to the faith and the father-in-law of Mohammed. The new ruler was given the title of *caliph*, that is, successor to the Prophet. After Abu-Bekr's death two other caliphs were chosen in succession from among the earlier disciples of Mohammed. In 656, however, a long struggle began for possession of the supreme power

Political history of the Islamic state: the caliphs

in Islam. First the Shiites succeeded in deposing a member of the Ommiad family and in electing Ali, the husband of Mohammed's daughter Fatima, as caliph. Five years later Ali was murdered, and the Ommiads came back into power. Soon afterward they transferred the capital to Damascus and established their family as a reigning dynasty with a luxurious court in imitation of the Byzantine model. In 750 the Shiites revolted again, this time under the leadership of a member of the Abbasid family who was a distant relative of the Prophet. The Abbasids seized the throne and moved the capital to the city of Baghdad on the Tigris River, where they ruled as Oriental despots for more than three centuries. A few of them were enlightened patrons of learning, especially Harun-al-Raschid (786–809) and Al-Mamun (813–33).

The Saracenic conquests

In the meantime, a great wave of Saracenic expansion had swept over Asia, Africa, and Europe. When Mohammed died in 632, the authority of his little state probably did not extend over more than one-third of the Arabian peninsula. A hundred years later nearly half of the civilized world was under Moslem domination. The Saracenic empire extended from the borders of India to the Strait of Gibraltar and the Pyrenees Mountains. One after another with startling rapidity, Persia, Syria, Egypt, North Africa, and Spain had been conquered. How can this prodigious expansion be explained? Contrary to common belief, it was not the result primarily of religious ardor. The Saracens were not engaged in a great crusade to impose their beliefs upon the rest of the world. Naturally there were outbreaks of fanaticism from time to time, but as a general rule the Moslems of this period did not really care very much whether the nations they conquered accepted their religion or not. Subject peoples were usually quite leniently treated. As long as they refrained from the possession of arms and paid the tribute levied upon them, they were permitted to retain their own beliefs and customs. Jews and Christians lived unmolested in the Moslem empire for centuries, and some of them rose to positions of prominence in political and intellectual circles.

Reasons for the success of the Saracens as conquerors

In truth, economic and political factors were much more important than religion in causing the Saracenic expansion. First of all, it must be borne in mind that the majority of the Arabs were a prolific race of nomads. Since the men were polygamists, the occasional practice of infanticide was far from sufficient to prevent a rapid increase in population. Arabia, moreover, was suffering from a serious drought, which extended over a number of years shortly after the beginning of the seventh century. Oases which had formerly provided good crops of dates and good pasturage for flocks and herds were gradually being absorbed by the surrounding desert. Discontent among the famished tribes increased to such a point that they would probably have seized upon almost any excuse to plunder neighboring countries. The initial attacks upon Byzantine territory appear to have grown out of a revolt of Arab mercenaries in Syria. The leaders of the rebellion appealed to the followers of the Prophet in Medina, who already had some reputation for military prowess as a result of their conquest of Mecca. The outcome of this appeal was a great wave of military invasion which soon made the Arabs masters not merely of Syria, but also of Persia, Palestine, and Egypt. Finally, it should be noted that the conquests of the Moslems were facilitated by the fact that the Byzantine and Persian empires had fought each other to the point of exhaustion in the previous century, and their governments were now attempting to replenish their treasuries by heavier taxation. As a consequence, many of the inhabitants of these empires were disposed to welcome the Arabs as deliverers.

The decline of the Saracenic empire was almost as swift as its rise. The Arabs themselves lacked political experience, and, besides, the empire they conquered was too vast in extent and composed of too heterogeneous a mixture of peoples ever to be welded into a strong and cohesive political unit. But a more powerful reason for its downfall was sectarian and factional strife. Sunnites and Shiites were never able to reconcile their differences, and widening cleavages between the mystics and rationalists also helped to weaken the religion, which was the basis of the state. In 929 members of the Ommiad family succeeded in establishing an independent caliphate at Cordova in Spain. Soon afterward descendants of Ali and Fatima proclaimed themselves independent rulers of Morocco and Egypt. Meanwhile the caliphs at Baghdad were gradually succumbing to the debilitating effects of Oriental customs. Aping the practices of Eastern monarchs, they retired more and more into the seclusion of the palace and soon became the puppets of their Persian viziers and later of their Turkish mercenary troops. In 1057 they surrendered all of their temporal power to the Sultan of the Seljuk Turks, who two years before had taken possession of Bagdad. For all practical purposes this marked the extinction of the Saracenic empire, although much of the territory continued to be ruled by peoples who had adopted the Moslem faith—the Seljuk Turks until the middle of the twelfth century and the Ottoman Turks from the fifteenth century to 1918.

The decline of the Islamic empire

The intellectual achievements of the Saracens were far superior to any of which Christian Europe could boast before the twelfth century. The explanation can be found partly in the energy and confidence of the Saracens themselves, but it is related also to the fact that in conquering Persia and Syria they came into possession of a brilliant intellectual heritage. In both of these countries traditions of Greek learning had survived. Numerous physicians of Greek nationality had been attracted to the court of the Persian kings, while in Syria there were excellent schools of philosophy and rhetoric and several libraries filled with copies of writings of the Hellenic philosophers, scientists, and poets. Of course, it would be foolish to suppose that very many of the Arabs themselves were able to appreciate

The intellectual achievements of the Saracens

297

*Saracenic phi-
losophy*

this cultural heritage; their mission was rather to provide the encouragement and the facilities for others to make use of it.

Saracenic philosophy was essentially a compound of Aristotelianism and Neo-Platonism. Its basic teachings may be set forth as follows: Reason is superior to faith as a source of knowledge; the doctrines of religion are not to be discarded entirely, but should be interpreted by the enlightened mind in a figurative or allegorical sense; when thus interpreted they can be made to yield a pure philosophical knowledge which is not in conflict with reason but supplementary to it. The universe never had a beginning in time but is created eternally; it is a series of emanations from God. Everything that happens is predetermined by God; every event is a link in an unbroken chain of cause and effect; both miracles and divine providence are therefore impossible. Although God is the First Cause of all things, He is not omnipotent; His power is limited by justice and goodness. There is no immortality for the individual soul, for no spiritual substance can exist apart from its material embodiment; only the soul of the universe goes on forever, since its primal substance is eternal.

*Periods
of development*

The development of Saracenic philosophy was limited to two brief periods of brilliance: the ninth and tenth centuries in the Baghdad caliphate and the twelfth century in Spain. Among the philosophers in the East three great names stand out—Al Kindi, Al Farabi, and Avicenna. The first of them died about 870, and the last was born in 980. All of them seem to have been of Turkish or Persian nationality. In the eleventh century, under the leadership of Algazel, Saracenic philosophy in the East degenerated into religious fundamentalism and mysticism. Like the Sufis, from whom he derived a great many of his doctrines, Algazel denied the competence of reason and urged a reliance upon faith and revelation. After his time philosophy died out in the Bagdad caliphate. The most renowned of the philosophers in the West, and probably the greatest of all the Saracenic thinkers, was Averroës of Cordova (1126–98). His influence upon the Christian Scholastics of the thirteenth century was especially profound.

*Astronomy,
mathematics,
physics,
and chemistry*

In no subject were the Saracens farther advanced than in science. In fact, their achievements in this field were the best the world had seen since the end of the Hellenistic civilization. The Saracens were brilliant astronomers, mathematicians, physicists, chemists, and physicians. Despite their reverence for Aristotle, they did not hesitate to criticize his notion of a universe of concentric spheres with the earth at the center, and they admitted the possibility that the earth rotates on its axis and revolves around the sun. Their celebrated poet, Omar Khayyám, developed one of the most accurate calendars ever devised by the mind of man. The Saracens were also capable mathematicians and developed algebra and trigonometry considerably beyond the stage they had reached in Hellenistic times. While they did not invent the celebrated "Arabic" system of numerals, they were nevertheless responsible for adapting it from the Indian system and making it available to the West. Saracenic physicists founded the science of optics and drew a number of significant conclusions regarding the theory of magnifying lenses and the velocity, transmission, and refraction of light. As is commonly known, the chemistry of the Moslems was an outgrowth of alchemy, that famous pseudo-science which was based upon the principle that all the metals were the same in essence, and that baser metals could therefore be transmuted into gold if only the right instrument, the philosopher's stone, could be found. But the efforts of scientists in this field were by no means confined to this fruitless quest. Some even denied the whole theory of transmutation of metals. As a result of innumerable experiments by chemists and alchemists alike, various new substances and compounds were discovered; among them carbonate of soda, alum, borax, bichloride of mercury, nitrate of silver, saltpeter, and nitric and sulphuric acids. In addition, Moslem scientists were the first to describe the chemical processes of distillation, filtration, and sublimation.

The accomplishments in medicine were just as remarkable. Saracenic physicians appropriated the knowledge contained in the medical writings of the Hellenistic Age; but some of them at least were not content with that. Avicenna discovered the contagious nature of tuberculosis, described pleurisy and several varieties of nervous ailments, and pointed out that disease can be spread through contamination of water and soil. His chief medical writing, the *Canon*, was venerated in Europe as an authoritative work until late in the seventeenth century. Avicenna's older contemporary, Rhazes, was the greatest clinical physician of the medieval world. His supreme achievement was the discovery of the true nature of smallpox. Other Moslem physicians discovered the value of cauterization and of styptic agents, diagnosed cancer of the stomach, prescribed antidotes for cases of poisoning, and made notable progress in treatment of diseases of the eyes. In addition, they recognized the highly infectious character of the plague, pointing out that it could be transmitted by garments, by eating utensils and drinking cups, as well as by personal contact. Finally, the Saracens excelled all other medieval peoples in the organization of hospitals and in the control of medical practice. Authentic information is on record of at least thirty-four great hospitals located in the principal cities of Persia, Syria, and Egypt. They appear to have been organized in a strikingly modern fashion. Each had its wards for particular cases, its dispensary, and its library. The chief physicians and surgeons lectured to the students and graduates, examined them, and issued diplomas or licenses to practice. Even the owners of leeches, who in most cases were also barbers, had to submit them for inspection at regular intervals.

So far as literature was concerned, the Saracens derived their inspiration almost entirely from Persia. If they knew anything about the classic poetry of the Greeks, they evidently found it of little in-

Saracenic contributions to medicine

*Saracenic liter-
ature*

terest. As a result, their own writings are colorful, imaginative, sensuous, and romantic; but with a few exceptions they make no very strong appeal to the intellect. The best-known examples of their poetry are the *Book of Kings* by Al-Firdausi (935–1020) and the *Rubáiyát* by Omar Khayyám (*ca.* 1048–*ca.* 1124). The *Book of Kings* is not a work dealing with any theme of Moslem civilization, but is an epic celebrating the glories of the medieval Persian empire. Nevertheless, its 60,000 verses were written under the patronage of Moslem rulers. The *Rubáiyát*, as it is preserved for us in the translation by Edward Fitzgerald, also appears to reflect the qualities of an effete Persian culture much more than the ideals of the Arabs themselves. Its philosophy of mechanism, skepticism, and hedonism is quite similar to that of the Book of Ecclesiastes in the Old Testament. The most famous example of Saracenic literature in prose is the so-called *Arabian Nights*, or *Book of the 1001 Nights*, written mainly during the eighth and ninth centuries. The material of the collection includes fables, anecdotes, household tales, and stories of erotic adventures derived from the literatures of various nations from China to Egypt. The chief significance of the collection of tales is to be found in the picture they present of the sophisticated life of the Moslems in the best days of the Baghdad caliphate.

*The eclectic art
of the Saracens*

Since the Arabs themselves had scarcely any more of an artistic background than the Hebrews, it was necessary that the art of the Moslem civilization should be an eclectic product. Its primary sources were Byzantium and Persia. From the former came many of the structural features of the architecture, especially the dome, the column, and the arch. Persian influence was probably responsible for the intricate, non-naturalistic designs which were used as decorative *motifs* in practically all of the arts. From both Persia and Byzantium came the tendency to subordinate form to rich and sensuous color. Architecture is generally considered the most important of the Saracenic arts, inasmuch as the development of both painting and sculpture was inhibited by religious prejudice against representation

The Court of the Lions in the Alhambra, Granada, Spain. The palace-fortress of the Alhambra is one of the finest monuments to Moslem artistic talent. Notable are the graceful columns, the horseshoe arches, and the delicate tracery in stone which surmounts the arches.

of the human form. By no means all of the examples of this architecture were mosques or churches; many were palaces, schools, libraries, private mansions, and hospitals. Indeed, Saracenic architecture had a much more decidedly secular character than any in medieval Europe. Among its principal elements were bulbous domes, minarets, horseshoe arches, and twisted columns, together with the use of tracery in stone, alternating stripes of black and white, mosaics, and Arabic script as decorative devices. As in the Byzantine style, comparatively little attention was given to exterior ornamentation. The so-called minor arts of the Moslems included the weaving of gorgeous pile carpets and rugs, magnificent leather tooling, and the making of brocaded silks and tapestries, inlaid metal work, enameled glassware, and painted pottery. Most of the products of these arts were embellished with complicated patterns of interlacing geometric designs, plants and fruits and flowers, Arabic script, and fantastic animal creatures. The richness and variety of these works of art, produced in defiance of a religion which often displayed a puritanical trend, afford most convincing proof of the vitality of Moslem civilization.

The economic development of the Saracenic civilization remains to this day one of the marvels of history. In areas which had produced practically nothing for centuries, the Moslems literally made the desert to blossom as the rose. Where only squalid villages encumbered the landscape, they built magnificent cities. The products of their industries were known from China to France and from the interior of Africa to the shores of the Baltic. As the builders of a vast commercial empire, they excelled the Carthaginians. The reasons for this astounding economic development do not lend themselves to easy explanation. Perhaps it was due in some measure to the long experience with trade which many of the Arabs had had in their homeland. When a wider field opened up, they made the most of their skill. The diffusion of the Arabic language over a vast expanse of territory also helped to extend the avenues of trade. In addition, the great variety of resources in the various sections of the empire served to stimulate exchange of the products of one region for those of another. The principal reason, however, was probably the energy of the conquerors themselves, together with their spirit of adventure, which led them to explore every possibility of increasing their wealth and power. They did not hesitate to take risks or to penetrate into unknown regions. They were among the boldest mariners and explorers who had yet appeared on the scene of history.

The economic development of the Islamic empire

Commerce and manufacturing were the main foundations of the national wealth. Both were developed in extraordinary degree. The Saracens made use of a great many of the instruments of commerce familiar to the modern world: checks, receipts, bills of lading, letters of credit, trade associations, joint-stock companies, and various others. Moslem merchants penetrated into southern Russia and even

Commerce and industry

into the equatorial regions of Africa. Caravans of thousands of camels traveled overland to the gates of India and China. Moslem ships furrowed new paths across the Indian Ocean, the Persian Gulf, and the Caspian Sea. Except for the Aegean Sea and the route from Venice to Constantinople, the Saracens dominated the Mediterranean almost as if it were a private lake. But so vast an expansion of commerce would scarcely have been possible without a corresponding development of industry; for it was the ability of the people of one region to turn their natural resources into finished products for sale to other regions which provided a basis for a large part of the trade. Nearly every one of the great cities specialized in some particular variety of manufactures. Mosul was a center of the manufacture of cotton cloth; Baghdad specialized in glassware, jewelry, pottery, and silks; Damascus was famous for its fine steel and for its "damask," or woven-figured silk; Morocco was noted for the manufacture of leather; and Toledo for its excellent swords. The products of these cities, of course, did not exhaust the list of Saracenic manufactures. Drugs, perfumes, carpets, tapestries, brocades, woolens, satins, metal products, and a host of others were turned out by the craftsmen of many cities. From the Chinese the Moslems learned the art of paper-making, and the products of that industry were in great demand, not only in the empire itself but in Europe as well. The men engaged in the various industries were organized into guilds, over which the government exercised only a general supervision for the prevention of fraudulent practices. For the most part, the guilds themselves regulated the conduct of business by their own members. Control by the state over economic affairs was much less rigid than in the Byzantine Empire.

Agriculture

From what has been said about commerce and industry, it must not be assumed that agriculture was neglected in the Moslem empire. On the contrary, the Saracens developed farming to as high a level as did any other people of the medieval world. They repaired and extended the irrigation systems originally built by the Egyptians, the Sumerians, and the Babylonians. They terraced the slopes of the mountains in Spain in order to plant them with vineyards, and here as elsewhere they converted many barren wastes into highly productive lands by means of irrigation. Experts attached to the imperial palaces and the mansions of the rich devoted much attention to ornamental gardening, to the cultivation of shrubs and flowers of rare beauty and delightful fragrance. The variety of products of the Moslem farms and orchards almost passes belief. Cotton, sugar, flax, rice, wheat, spinach, asparagus, apricots, peaches, lemons, and olives were cultivated as standard crops almost everywhere, while bananas, coffee, and oranges were grown in the warmer regions. Some of the farms were great estates, worked in part by serfs and slaves and in part by free peasants as tenants, but the major portion of the land was divided into small holdings cultivated by the owners themselves.

The influence of the Saracenic civilization upon medieval Europe and upon the Renaissance was almost incalculable; and some of that influence has, of course, persisted until the present time. The philosophy of the Saracens was almost as important as Christianity in providing a basis for the Scholastic thought of the thirteenth century; for it was the Moslems who made available to the West most of the works of Aristotle and indicated more thoroughly than ever before the use to which those writings could be put as a support for religious doctrine. The scientific achievements of the Moslems furnished even more enduring contributions. The list of these contributions includes the Hindu-Arabic system of numerals, the science of algebra, such medical discoveries as the fact of contagion and the nature of smallpox and measles, innumerable drugs and compounds, and the chemical processes of sublimation and filtration. Though the activity of the Saracens in literature was hardly as extensive as in science, their literary influence has been decidedly important. The songs of the troubadours and some other examples of the love poetry of medieval France were directly inspired by Sara-

The intellectual and artistic influence of the Saracenic civilization

Interior of the Great Mosque at Cordoba, Spain. This splendid specimen of Moorish architecture gives an excellent view of the cusped arches and alternating stripes of black and white so commonly used by Moslem architects.

cenic writings. Some of the stories in the *Book of the 1001 Nights* found their way into Boccaccio's *Decameron* and Chaucer's *Canterbury Tales*, while Firdausi's *Book of Kings* furnished the nineteenth-century English writer, Matthew Arnold, with the material for his story of *Sohrab and Rustum*. The art of the Saracens has likewise had an influence of deep significance, especially upon Gothic architecture. A surprisingly large number of the elements in the design of Gothic cathedrals were apparently derived from the mosques and palaces of the Moslems. A partial list would include the cusped arches, the traceried windows, the pointed arch, the use of script and arabesques as decorative devices, and possibly ribbed vaulting. The architecture of late medieval castles was even more closely copied from the design of Moslem buildings, especially the fortresses of Syria.[6]

Economic contributions

Finally, the Saracens exerted a profound influence upon the economic development of late medieval and early modern Europe. The revival of trade which took place in western Europe in the eleventh, twelfth, and thirteenth centuries would scarcely have been possible without the development of Moslem industry and agriculture to stimulate the demand for new products in the West. From the Moslems, western Europeans acquired a knowledge of the compass, the astrolabe, the art of making paper, and possibly the production of silk, although knowledge of the last may have been obtained somewhat earlier from the Byzantine Empire. Furthermore, it seems probable that the development by the Moslems of the joint-stock company, checks, letters of credit, and other aids to business transactions had much to do with the beginning of the Commercial Revolution in Europe about 1400. Perhaps the extent of Saracenic economic influence is most clearly revealed in the enormous number of words now in common usage which were originally of Arabic or Persian origin. Among them are "traffic," "tariff," "risk," "check," "magazine," "alcohol," "cipher," "zero," "algebra," "muslin," and "bazaar."

International significance of the Saracenic civilization

The Saracenic civilization has significance also for the modern world from the standpoint of international relations. The Islamic empire was itself an international state. Though loosely organized, it united peoples as diverse as Persians, Arabs, Turks, and Berbers. Its binding cement was a great religion. The spread of this empire and religion constituted the first threat from the Orient that the Western world had faced since the destruction of Carthage. But this threat was quite different from those that had loomed so dangerous in ancient history; for it was essentially ideological rather than political. The long conflict between East and West, which extended at least from the Battle of Tours to the end of the Crusades, was commonly represented as a struggle of ideals. The rise and expansion of Islam anticipated in several respects the dynamism of such twentieth-

[6] For a more complete discussion of the influence of Saracenic literature and art, see Arnold and Guillaume, eds., *The Legacy of Islam*.

century movements as Nazism and communism. There was one outstanding difference, however. Despite their fanaticism at times, the
Saracens devoted only part of their energies to military objectives.
They adopted the cultures of the peoples they conquered, built a
civilization that surpassed in magnificence any that then existed, and
left a splendid legacy of original discoveries and achievements.

Selected Readings

· *Items so designated are available in paperbound editions.*

Ameer Ali, Syed, *The Spirit of Islam*, London, 1922.
Arnold, Thomas, and Guillaume, Alfred, eds., *The Legacy of Islam*, New
York, 1931. Excellent as a study of Saracenic influence.
Baynes, N. H., *The Byzantine Empire*, London, 1925. Compact and interest-
ingly written.
Byron, Robert, *The Byzantine Achievement*, New York, 1929.
· Dawson, C. H., *The Making of Europe*, New York, 1932. (Meridian)
De Boer, T. J., *History of Philosophy in Islam*, London, 1903. The best ac-
count. Concise and clear.
Diehl, Charles, *History of the Byzantine Empire*, New Brunswick, N. J., 1956.
Perhaps the definitive work.
Goldziher, Ignaz, *Mohammed and Islam*, New Haven, 1917. Good on the early
history of Islam.
· Hitti, P. K., *The Arabs, A Short History*, Princeton, 1946. (new edn., Gate-
way)
Margoliouth, D. S., *Mohammed and the Rise of Islam*, New York, 1927. Com-
plete and interesting.
· Pirenne, Henri, *Mohammed and Charlemagne*, New York, 1939. (Meridian)
· Runciman, Steven, *Byzantine Civilization*, New York, 1933. (Meridian) Com-
plete and thorough but easily readable.
Sarton, George, *An Introduction to the History of Science*, Baltimore, 1927,
Vol. I. Detailed and thorough. A valuable reference.
Scott, S. P., *History of the Moorish Empire in Europe*, Philadelphia, 1904, 3
vols. The most complete account in English of Moslem rule in Spain.
Thompson, J. W., *Economic and Social History of the Middle Ages*, New
York, 1928, Chs VI, VII, XIV, XV. Interesting but no longer considered
entirely reliable.
· Vasiliev, A. A., *History of the Byzantine Empire*, Madison, Wis., 1928-29,
2 vols. (Wisconsin, 2 vols.) One of the most dependable works.

Source Materials

Dewing, H. B., tr., *Procopius: History of the Wars*, 5 vols.
Poole, Lane, ed., *Speeches and Table Talk of the Prophet Mohammed*.
Sanders, T. C., tr., *The Institutes of Justinian*.
The Koran.

AND THE TRANSITION
TO THE MODERN WORLD

PART
4

THE LATER MIDDLE AGES AND THE TRANSITION TO THE MODERN WORLD

By no means all of medieval history in western Europe was characterized by stagnation and barbarism. It cannot be too strongly emphasized
that the period which used to be called the Dark Ages did not really
extend beyond 800. Soon after that date there were several movements of
intellectual awakening which culminated finally in a brilliant flowering of
culture in the twelfth and thirteenth centuries. In fact, so remarkable was
the progress in western Europe from the ninth century to the end of the
thirteenth that the achievements of that period can justifiably be called a
new civilization. While some of these achievements were discarded during
the subsequent period of the Renaissance, quite a few were preserved and
have exerted their influence to the present day. Indeed, the civilization of
the later Middle Ages, or the Feudal Age, and that of the Renaissance had
more in common than is usually suspected. Both were distinguished by
humanism, by a new interest in man as the most important creature in the
universe. Both were concerned very largely with affairs of this world as
opposed to the otherworldliness of the early Middle Ages. In the Feudal
Age and the Renaissance alike there was a tendency to glorify the life of
adventure and of conquest in place of the early Christian ideals of humility
and self-effacement. It should be noted, however, that before the end of
the Renaissance a religious revolution known as the Reformation began,
which in some respects attempted to turn the clock back to the very
beginning of the Middle Ages.

A CHRONOLOGICAL TABLE

	Europe as a Whole	Southern Europe	Northern Europe
800—	Feudalism develops, 800–1300		Unification of England under Saxon kings, 802–
	Treaty of Verdun, 843		
	Rise of papal monarchy, 850–1000		
	Scholasticism, 850–1300		Founding of national monarchy in France, 987
	Cluny movement, 950–1100		
	Romanesque architecture, 1000–1150		
	Revival of trade with the East, 1050–1150		
	Struggle between secular and spiritual powers, 1050–1350		
	Separation between Eastern and Western churches, 1054		
	Establishment of the College of Cardinals, 1059		Norman Conquest of England, 1066
	The Crusades, 1096–1204		

Europe as a Whole	Southern Europe	Northern Europe
Rise of merchant and craft guilds, 1100–1300 Growth of cities, 1100–1300 Development of the sacramental system of the church, 1100–1300 First universities, *ca.* 1150 Gothic architecture, 1150–1300 Orders of friars, 1200– Fourth Lateran Council, 1215	St. Francis of Assisi, 1182–1226 Dante, 1265–1321	Romances of chivalry, 1100–1300 Holy Roman (Hohenstaufen) Empire, 1152–1254 Roger Bacon, 1214?–1294 Magna Charta, 1215 St. Thomas Aquinas, 1225?–1274? Origin of Parliament in England, 1265–1295 Hanseatic League, 1300–1500
Feudalism declines, 1300–1500 Rise of capitalism, 1300–1500 Growth of banking and development of money economy, 1300–1600 Black Death, 1347–1349	Boccaccio, 1313–1375 Savonarola, 1452–1498 Leonardo da Vinci, 1452–1519 Machiavelli, 1469–1527 Michelangelo, 1475–1564 Unification of Spain, 1492 Cervantes, 1547–1616 Galileo, 1564–1642	Establishment of Estates-General in France, 1302 Hundred Years' War, 1337–1453 Christian Renaissance, 1400–1500 War of the Roses in England, 1455–1485 Erasmus, 1466?–1536 Copernicus, 1473–1543 Tudor dynasty in England, 1485–1603 Montaigne, 1533–1592 Sir Francis Bacon, 1561–1626 Shakespeare, 1564–1616 Sir William Harvey, 1578–1657

1200—

1600—

The Civilization of the Feudal Age: Political and Economic Institutions

The count asked if he was willing to become completely his man, and the other replied "I am willing," and with clasped hands, surrounded by the hands of the count, they were bound together by a kiss. Secondly, he who had done homage gave his fealty to the representative of the count in these words, "I promise on my faith that I will in future be faithful to count William and will observe my homage to him completely against all persons in good faith and without deceit," and thirdly, he took his oath to this upon the relics of the saints.
—Description of Ceremony of Homage and Fealty at court of Count of Flanders, Twelfth Century

Long before the famous Renaissance of the fourteenth and succeeding centuries, western Europe began slowly to emerge from the ignorance and barbarism of the Dark Ages. The start of this gradual awakening can be dated as far back as 800 A.D. During the five or six centuries that followed, the people of Latin Christendom cast off at least some of their winter garments of repentance and otherworldliness and put on the less restrictive attire of the man who is determined to live in this world and mold his environment to his own advantage. The causes of this change in attitude were many and various: the influence of contact with the Saracenic and Byzantine civilizations, the increase in economic security, the revitalizing effects of the Norse invasions, and the influence of monastic education. Later on, the revival of trade in the eleventh and twelfth centuries and the growth of cities led to an increase in prosperity and sophistication which greatly stimulated the progress of enlightenment. The results of these several causes were reflected in a brilliant intellectual and artistic civilization which reached the zenith of its development in the thirteenth century. Probably the most distinctive element in the social and political structure of this civilization was the feudal regime; hence we can justifiably speak of this culture as the civilization of the Feudal Age. We must not overlook the fact, however, that from the twelfth century on the role of the commercial and industrial classes in the cities was an exceedingly important one.

The cultural revival of the Feudal Age

311

1. The Origins of the Feudal Regime

Feudalism may be defined as a decentralized structure of society in which the powers of government are exercised by private barons over persons economically dependent upon them. It is a system of overlordship and vassalage in which the right to govern is conceived as a property right belonging to anyone who is the holder of a fief. The relationship between the overlord and his vassals is a contractual relationship involving reciprocal obligations. In return for the protection and economic assistance they receive, the vassals are bound to obey their lord or suzerain, to serve him faithfully, and generally to compensate him by dues or taxes for the services he renders in their interest. Defined in this fashion, feudalism was not limited to the late Middle Ages. Examples of it had existed in several other periods of world history—in many parts of the Roman Empire, for instance, and throughout the early Middle Ages. Late medieval feudalism, however, differed from the earlier specimens in being a legally recognized framework of society. Men did not apologize for it as a crude substitute for centralized government but glorified it as an ideal system, much as we idealize democracy and the national state at the present time.

How did late medieval feudalism originate? To some extent it was the outgrowth of ancient Roman institutions. One of these was *clientage*. From very early times Roman citizens who had fallen upon evil days had sought the protection of wealthy patrons, becoming their clients or personal dependents. During the confusion that accompanied the decline of the Empire, clientage was greatly extended. A second of these Roman institutions was the *colonate*. In a desperate attempt to check the decline of agricultural production during the economic revolution of the third and fourth centuries, the government of the Empire bound many of the agricultural laborers and tenants to the soil as *coloni* or serfs, and in effect placed them under the control of the proprietors of large estates. Another institution which developed in the declining stage of the Roman Empire was *precarium*. Originally the *precarium* was a lease of land to a tenant who would cultivate it and pay rent to the owner. If at any time the tenant failed to pay his rent, the owner had the right to evict him. Later the *precarium* frequently assumed the form of the surrender of land by a small owner to a powerful magnate because of indebtedness or need of protection. At the same time the small farmer would bind himself to cultivate the land and to pay rent for its use. The last two of these institutions, the *colonate* and the *precarium*, had much to do with the growth of an extralegal feudalism in late Roman history, since they increased the wealth and importance of the great landed proprietors. As time went on, the tendency of these men was to ignore or defy the central government and to arrogate to themselves the powers of sovereign rulers over their estates. They levied taxes upon their dependents, made laws for the regulation of their affairs, and administered what passed for justice.

Late medieval feudalism was also derived in large part from significant economic and political developments of the early Middle Ages. One of these was the growth of the institution of *beneficium*, which seems to have been developed by the church as a modification of *precarium*. *Beneficium* consisted in the grant of a *benefice*, or the right to use land in return for rent or services. In the seventh century the Merovingian kings adopted the practice of rewarding their counts and dukes with benefices, thereby cementing a bond between public office and landholding. Not long afterward Charles Martel and the Carolingian kings resorted to the granting of benefices to local nobles in return for furnishing mounted troops to fight against the Moors. The result was to increase the dependence of the central government upon the principal landowners throughout the country. The bestowal of *immunities* by the Frankish kings upon some of the holders of benefices also accelerated the growth of a feudal regime. The immunities were exemptions of the lands of a secular or ecclesiastical noble from the jurisdiction of the king's agents. The natural outcome was the exercise of public authority by the noble himself as a virtually independent sovereign, subject only to the nominal overlordship of the king. The other most important development in the early Middle Ages which hastened the growth of a feudal organization of society was the invasions of the Norsemen, the Magyars, and the Moslems. In the eighth and ninth centuries these peoples began making swift incursions into the settled portions of western Europe, plundering the richer areas and occasionally massacring the inhabitants. The attacks of the Norsemen in particular were widely feared. As a consequence, many small farmers who had hitherto maintained their independence now sought the protection of their more powerful neighbors, who frequently had armed retainers and strongholds in which men could take refuge.

Church institutions

Carolingian institutions

The need for defense

But feudalism would never have acquired the special character which it came to possess in the later Middle Ages if it had not been for the Germanic influence. For it was the Germans who provided the ideals of honor, loyalty, and freedom which came to occupy a place of considerable importance in the system. Mention has already been made of the Germanic institution of the *comitatus* as a source of feudal theory and practice. The *comitatus* was a band of warriors and their chief united by mutual obligations of service and loyalty. Though the warriors took a personal oath to protect and defend their chief, and he in return agreed to provide them with horses and weapons, the relationship between the two parties was altogether different from that which existed between the Roman clients and their patron. No element of servility was present in it at all; the warriors were practically the equals of their chief, since all were engaged in the same activities of fighting for glory and plunder.

Germanic institutions

This ideal of a relationship of honor and loyalty in the *comitatus* later found its way into feudalism, so far as the relation between lords and vassals was concerned. The feudal practice of *commendation*, by which vassals swore fealty in a ceremony of homage to their suzerain, was also probably an outgrowth of the *comitatus*. Finally, the feudal conception of law as a product of custom instead of authority, and as the personal possession of the individual which he could take with him wherever he went, is likewise traceable to Germanic influence.

2. *Feudalism as a Political and Economic Structure*

Feudalism as a system of government

As a system of government, feudalism embodied a number of basic conceptions. First of all, as we have seen, it included the notion that the right to govern was a privilege belonging to any man who was the holder of a fief; but it was a privilege entailing very definite obligations, the violation of which might be followed by loss of the fief. Secondly, it included the notion that all government rests upon contract. Rulers must agree to govern justly in accordance with the laws, both human and divine. Subjects must pledge themselves to obey so long as their rulers govern justly. If either party violates the contract, the other is absolved from his obligations and has the right to take action for redress. In the third place, feudalism was based upon the ideal of limited sovereignty, upon opposition to absolute authority no matter by whom it might be exercised. Feudal government was supposed to be a government of laws and not of men. No ruler, regardless of his rank, had any right to impose his personal will upon his subjects in accordance with the dictates of his own whims. Indeed, under feudal theory, no ruler had the right to make law at all; law was the product of custom or of the will of God. The authority of the king or the baron was limited to the issuance of what might be called administrative decrees to carry the law into effect. Whether the ideals of feudalism were carried out any less successfully in practice than the ideals of political systems generally is a question very hard to answer. Doubtless most people, with their prejudices against everything medieval, would answer it in the affirmative. Yet revolts against oppression were not of very frequent occurrence in the late Middle Ages, notwithstanding the fact that the existence of the *right* to revolt against a ruler who had made himself a tyrant was commonly taught.

Fiefs, vassals, and overlords

Not only in theory but in practice the feudal regime was a system of overlordship and vassalage based upon the granting and holding of fiefs. In the main, a fief was a benefice which had become hereditary. It was not always an area of land, however; it might also be an office or position or the right to collect tolls at a bridge or even the right to coin money or to establish markets and enjoy the profits therefrom. The man who granted the fief was a lord or suzerain,

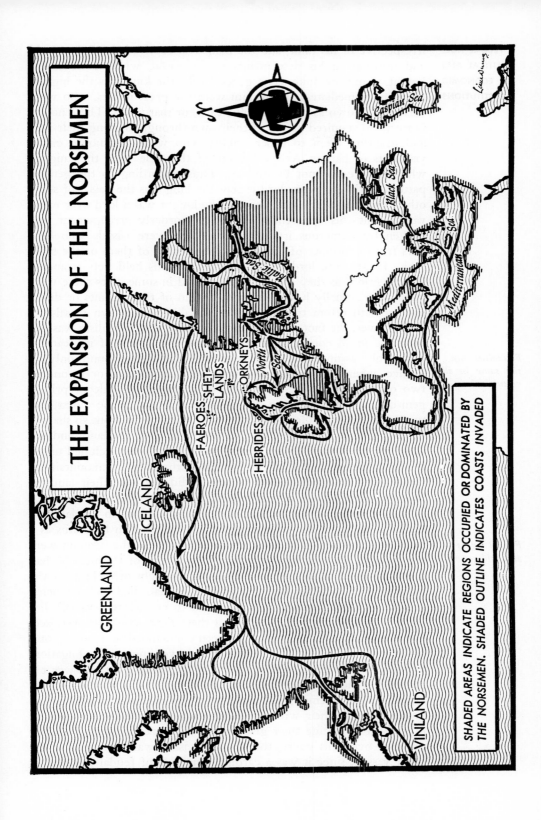

THE EXPANSION OF THE NORSEMEN

GREENLAND

ICELAND

FAEROES
SHET-
LANDS
ORKNEYS
HEBRIDES

VINLAND

Caspian Sea

Black Sea

Mediterranean Sea

Baltic Sea

North Sea

SHADED AREAS INDICATE REGIONS OCCUPIED OR DOMINATED BY
THE NORSEMEN. SHADED OUTLINE INDICATES COASTS INVADED

irrespective of his rank; and the man who received the fief to hold and transmit to his descendants was a vassal, whether he was a knight, count, or duke. As a general rule, the king was the highest suzerain. Immediately below him were the great nobles, who were variously known as dukes, counts, earls, or margraves. These nobles in turn had acquired vassals of their own through dividing their fiefs and granting them to lesser nobles, who were commonly called viscounts or barons. At the bottom of the scale were the knights, whose fiefs could not be divided. Thus, according to the general pattern of things, every lord except the king was the vassal of some other lord, and every vassal except the knight was a lord over other vassals. But this apparently logical and orderly arrangement was broken by numerous irregularities. There were vassals who held fiefs from a number of different lords, not all of them of the same rank. There were lords some of whose vassals held fiefs from the same overlord as they themselves did. And in some cases there were kings who actually held fiefs from certain of their counts or dukes and were therefore to some extent vassals of their own vassals.

Moreover, the fact must be borne in mind that feudalism was not the same in all countries of western Europe. Many of its features commonly assumed to have been universal were found only in France, where the system was most fully developed, or in one or two other countries at the most. For example, the rule of primogeniture, under which the fief descended intact to the oldest son, was not in force in Germany; nor were social distinctions so sharply defined there as in France. Furthermore, not all of the lands and not all of the inhabitants of any European country were included under the feudal regime. Most of the farmers in the hilly and mountainous regions of France, Italy, and Germany did not hold their lands as fiefs but owned them outright, as their ancestors had for centuries.

Feudalism not the same in all countries

Each member of the feudal nobility was involved in an elaborate network of rights and obligations which varied with his status as a suzerain or a vassal. The most important rights of the suzerain were the right to serve as legal guardian in case any of the fiefs he had granted should be inherited by a minor; the right of escheat, or the right to take back the fief of a vassal who had died without heirs; and the right of forfeiture, or the right to confiscate a vassal's fief for violation of contract. The last of these rights could be exercised, however, only after the vassal had been condemned by a court composed of his own equals. There were two important obligations which every suzerain was supposed to perform. First, he was expected to render military assistance to his vassals in warding off attacks by their enemies; and second, he was required to aid his vassals in righting their wrongs, which usually meant the summoning of a court to decide their grievances. The suzerain himself merely presided over this court; the actual decision was rendered by the other vassals, since it was a cardinal principle of feudal justice that

Feudal rights and obligations

Stained Glass, German, *ca.* 1300. Some stained-glass windows were purely decorative; others told a story. (MMA)

Building Operations. From a French picture Bible, *ca.* 1250. Note the treadmill, with wheel, ropes, and pulley, by means of which a basket of stones is brought to the construction level. (Morgan Library)

Gothic Virgin, French, XIII cent. The Queen of Heaven here is a gentle, understanding mother. (MMA)

Siege of a City. From the *Universal Chronicle* by Jean de Courcy, Flemish, *ca.* 1470. The cannon meant the end of feudal knights and medieval towered fortresses. (Morgan Library)

Vespers of the Holy Ghost, with a View of Paris, Jean Fouquet. From the *Book of Hours* of Etienne Chevalier, 1461. Demons in the sky are sent flying by the divine light from Heaven. The cathedral is Notre Dame. (Robert Lehman)

A Scholar at Work. From the Flemish manuscript *The Golden Legend*, 1445–1460. This beautiful book came at the end of the era of costly handwritten, hand-decorated manuscripts. (Morgan Library)

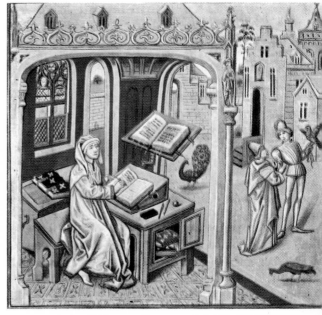

no noble could be tried except by his peers. Aside from this privilege of being judged only by his equals, the noble in his capacity as a vassal had only one other important right. That was the right to repudiate his lord for acts of injustice or failure to provide adequate protection. But the obligations of the vassal were more numerous. He must render military service for a certain number of days each year, attend the lord's court, ransom his lord if he were captured, and pay a heavy tax if he inherited or sold a fief.

Feudal society was, of course, highly aristocratic. It was a regime of status, not of individual initiative. In almost all cases the members of the various ranks of the nobility owed their positions to heredity, although occasionally noble rank would be conferred upon a commoner for his services to the king. Seldom was it possible for a man to win advancement under the system by his own efforts or intelligence. Nevertheless, an important exception was to be found in the case of the *ministeriales* in Germany and in the Low Countries. The *ministeriales*, as their name implies, formed a class of administrative officials under feudal rule. They had charge of castles, toll gates, bridges, market places, and so on. Some of the most capable of them rose to be bailiffs or administrators of towns or districts, serving under a great prince or bishop or even under the Emperor himself. Their position was of such high advantage that ultimately they invaded the ranks of the lesser nobility and came to form a subordinate class of knights.

A regime of status, with a few exceptions

The life of the feudal nobility was scarcely the idyllic existence frequently described in romantic novels. While there was undoubtedly plenty of excitement, there was also much hardship, and death took its toll at an early age. From a careful study of medieval skeletons a modern scientist has estimated that the peak of the mortality rate in feudal times came at the age of forty-two,[1] whereas at the present time it occurs at about seventy-five. Moreover, conditions of living even for the richest nobles were comparatively poor. Until almost the end of the eleventh century the feudal castle was nothing but a crude blockhouse of timber. And even the great stone castles of later date were far from being models of comfort and convenience. Rooms were dark and damp, and the bare stone walls were cold and cheerless. Until after the revival of trade with the Orient, which led to the introduction of carpets and rugs, floors were generally covered with rushes or straw, a new layer being put down from time to time as the old became vile from the filth of hunting dogs. The food of the noble and his family, though plentiful and substantial, was neither particularly varied nor appetizing. Meat and fish, cheese, cabbages, turnips, carrots, onions, beans, and peas were the staple articles of diet. The only fruits obtainable in abundance were apples and pears. Coffee and tea were unknown, and so were

The life of the feudal nobles

[1] J. W. Thompson, *An Economic and Social History of the Middle Ages,* p. 718.

Tournament with Lances. Engraving by Lucas Cranach. Tournaments, imitating the conditions of medieval warfare but with blunted spears and lances, were among the principal recreational pursuits of the feudal aristocracy.

spices until after trade with the Orient had continued for some time. Sugar was also eventually introduced, but for a long while it remained so rare and costly that it was often sold as a drug.

Although the nobles did not work for a living, their time was not spent in idleness. The conventions of their society dictated an active *Feudal warfare* life of war, high adventure, and sport. Not only did they wage war on flimsy pretexts for the conquest of neighboring fiefs, but they fought for the sheer love of fighting as an exciting adventure. So much violence resulted that the church intervened with the Peace of God in the tenth century and supplemented this with the Truce of God in the eleventh. The Peace of God pronounced the solemn anathemas of the church against any who did violence to places of worship, robbed the poor, or injured members of the clergy. Later the same protection was extended to merchants. The Truce of God prohibited fighting entirely from "vespers on Wednesday to sunrise on Monday" and also from Christmas to Epiphany (January 6) and throughout the greater part of the spring, late summer, and early fall. The purpose of the last regulation was obviously to protect the peasants during the seasons of planting and harvesting. The penalty against any noble who violated this truce was excommunication. Perhaps if rules such as these could have been maintained for a few centuries longer, human beings would eventually have abandoned war as senseless and unprofitable. But the church itself, in launching the Crusades, was really responsible for making the rules a dead letter. And the holy wars against the infidel were fought with a great deal more barbarity than had ever resulted from the petty squabbles of feudal nobles among themselves.

Until comparatively late in the Middle Ages the manners of the feudal aristocracy were anything but refined and gentle. Gluttony was a common vice, and the quantities of wine and beer consumed at a medieval castle brawl would stagger the imagination of a modern toper. At dinner everyone carved his meat with his own dagger and ate it with his fingers. Bones and scraps were thrown on the floor for the omnipresent dogs to fight over. Women were treated with indifference and sometimes with contempt and brutality, for this was a masculine world. In the twelfth and thirteenth centuries, however, the manners of the aristocratic classes were softened and improved considerably by the growth of what is known as chivalry. Chivalry was the social and moral code of feudalism, the embodiment of its highest ideals and the expression of its virtues. The origins of this code were mainly Germanic and Christian, but Saracenic influence played some part in its development also. Chivalry set forth the ideal of a knight who is not only brave and loyal but generous, truthful, reverent, kind to the poor and defenseless, and disdainful of unfair advantage or sordid gain. But perhaps above all, the perfect knight must be the perfect lover. The chivalric ideal made the high love of ladies a veritable cult with an elaborate ceremonial which the hot-blooded young noble must be careful to follow. As a result, women in the late Middle Ages were elevated to a much higher status than they had enjoyed in early medieval Europe. Chivalry also imposed upon the knight the obligation of fighting in defense of noble causes. It was especially his duty to serve as the champion of the church and to further its interests with sword and spear.

Manners of the feudal aristocracy

Chivalry

The main economic unit of the feudal regime was the manorial estate, although manorialism itself had a political as well as an economic aspect. The manor, or manorial estate, was generally the fief of an individual knight. Lords of higher rank held many manors, the number frequently running into the hundreds or thousands. No one knows even the average size of these economic units, but the smallest appear to have included at least three hundred or four hundred acres. Each manorial estate comprised one or more villages, the lands cultivated by the peasants, the common forest and pasture lands, the land belonging to the parish church, and the lord's demesne, which included the best farm land on the manor. With minor exceptions, all of the arable land was divided into three main blocks: the spring planting ground, the autumn planting ground, and the fallow. These were rotated from year to year, so that the spring planting ground one year would become the autumn planting ground the next, and so on. Such was the famous *three-field system*,

The manorial estate

The three-field system and the open-field system

which seems to have originated in western Europe toward the end of the eighth century. Manorial agriculture was also conducted very largely under the *open-field system*. The holding allotted to each peasant was not a compact area of the manor, but consisted of a number of strips located in each of the three main blocks of arable land. These strips, averaging about an acre in size, were generally separated only by a narrow band of unplowed turf. The main object of the system was apparently to give to each serf his fair share of the three different kinds of land. In cultivating these strips the peasants worked co-operatively, chiefly because their holdings were scattered, and it was therefore logical for a number of men to combine their efforts in farming all the strips in a particular area. Besides, no one peasant had enough oxen to draw the crude wooden plows through the stubborn soil.

The servile classes

Except for the noble and his family, the parish priest, and possibly a few administrative officials, the entire population of the manor consisted of persons of servile status. These might be embraced in as many as four different classes: villeins, serfs, crofters and cotters, and slaves. Though villeins and serfs eventually came to be almost indistinguishable, there were at one time several important differences between them. Villeins were originally small farmers who had surrendered their lands as individuals to some powerful neighbor. The ancestors of the serfs had frequently been subjected *en masse*, whole villages of them at once. The villeins were perpetual tenants, not bound in person to the soil; whereas the serfs were bought and sold with the land to which they were attached. As another difference, the villein was liable to obligations only within the definite terms of his customary contract, while the labor of the serf could be exploited virtually as his owner saw fit. Finally, the villein could be taxed only within limits fixed by custom, but the serf was taxable at the lord's mercy. By the thirteenth century, however, most of these differences had disappeared. And it is a notable fact that the villeins were not degraded to the level of serfs; instead, the serfs rose to the level of villeins. While the other dependent classes on the manor were much less numerous than the villeins and serfs, a word or two must be said about them. The crofters and cotters were wretchedly poor men who had no definite status under the feudal regime at all. Unlike even the meanest of the serfs, they had no strips of land which they could cultivate for their living. They occupied small cottages or shanties and hired themselves out to the richer villeins or did odd jobs for the lord of the manor. A few slaves continued to be held throughout the Feudal Age, but in steadily diminishing numbers. They did not fit in well with the manorial type of economy, for the manor was not a plantation but an aggregate of petty farms cultivated under perpetual lease. The few slaves who were to be found were employed mainly as household servants. After the year 1000 slavery as an institution became prac-

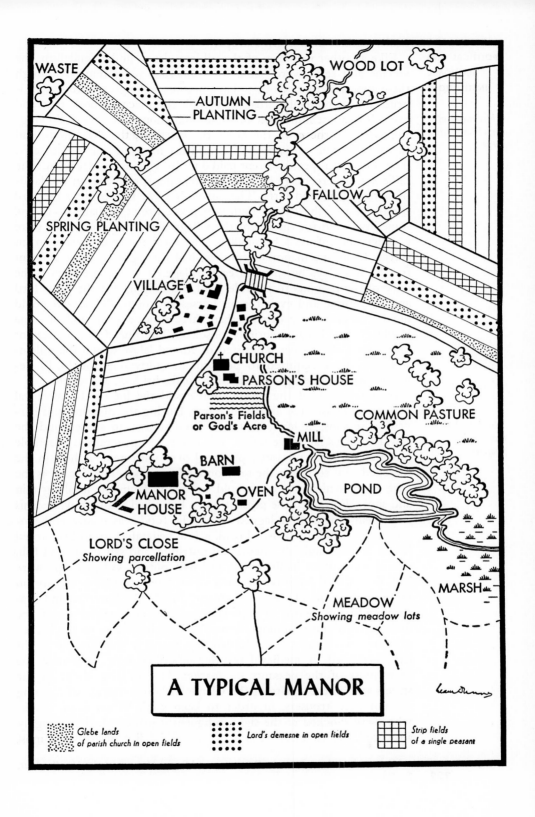

WASTE

WOOD LOT

AUTUMN
PLANTING

SPRING PLANTING

FALLOW

VILLAGE

✝ CHURCH
PARSON'S HOUSE

Parson's Fields
or God's Acre

MILL

COMMON PASTURE

BARN

OVEN

POND

MANOR
HOUSE

LORD'S CLOSE
Showing parcellation

MARSH

MEADOW
Showing meadow lots

A TYPICAL MANOR

Glebe lands
of parish church in open fields

Lord's demesne in open fields

Strip fields
of a single peasant

tically extinct in western Europe.

Like all other members of the subject classes under feudalism, the villeins and serfs were liable for numerous obligations. Although these appear at first glance to have been exceedingly oppressive, it is necessary to remember that they took the place of both rent and taxes. The most important of these obligations were the following: the *capitatio*, the *cens*, the *taille*, the *banalités*, the *prestations*, and the *corvée*. The *capitatio* was a head tax imposed only upon serfs. The *cens* was a species of rent paid only by villeins and freemen. The *taille* was a percentage of nearly everything produced on the lands of both villeins and serfs. The *banalités* were fees paid to the lord for the use of the village mill, winepress, brewery, bake-oven, and sometimes even for the use of the village well. The *prestations* were a variety of enforced hospitality. The local count or baron, in his travels from one manor to another, had the right to entertainment for the few days he spent in each village. It was consequently the duty of the peasants to provide food and lodging for the great lord and his retinue and even for his horses and dogs. *Prestations* could not be enforced any oftener than three times a year, and in some localities they became entirely obsolete. The final form of peasant obligations, the *corvée*, consisted of forced labor which the villeins and serfs were required to perform in cultivating the lord's demesne and in building and repairing roads, bridges, and dams.

By no stretch of the imagination could the lot of the medieval peasant be considered an enviable one. During the planting and harvesting seasons, at least, he toiled from sunrise to sunset, and the rewards of his labor were few. His home was generally a miserable hovel constructed of wattle plastered over with mud. A hole in the thatched roof served as the only outlet for smoke. The floor was the bare earth, which was often cold and damp from the infalling rain and snow. For a bed the peasant had a box filled with straw, and his easy chair was a three-legged stool. His food was coarse and monotonous—black or brown bread, a few vegetables from his garden in the summer and fall, cheese and porridge, and salt meats and fish, which were often badly cured and half putrid. When crops were bad, he suffered from famine, and death from starvation was by no means unknown. He was, of course, invariably illiterate and was commonly the victim of superstitious fears and sometimes of the dishonesty of unscrupulous stewards. The hardships of his barren existence were such as to deaden any moral sensibilities he might have possessed. A medieval traveler described how in summer he "saw most of the peasants on market day walking about in the streets and on the square of the village without a vestige of clothing on, not even trousers, in order to keep cool. When some monks who were shocked at the sight indignantly protested, they roughly answered: 'What business is it of yours?' " [2] But perhaps the most

[2] Quoted by Thompson, *An Economic and Social History of the Middle Ages,* p. 742.

lamentable aspect of the peasant's life was the fact that he was a despised and degraded creature. Spokesmen for the nobles and townsmen alike seldom referred to him except in the most scornful and odious terms. It was said that all peasants were shifty, dull-witted, mean, squint-eyed, and ugly; that they were "born of ass's dung," and that "the devil did not want them in hell because they smelled too badly." [3]

Yet the medieval peasant enjoyed some advantages which undoubtedly helped to redress the balance of his miseries. Many of the fears and uncertainties that plague the lowly in modern times meant nothing to him. He was in very little danger of loss of employment or of insecurity in old age. It was an established principle of feudal law that the peasant could not be deprived of his land. If the land was sold, the serf went with it and retained the right to cultivate his holdings as before. When he became too old or too feeble to work, it was the duty of the lord to care for him through the remainder of his days. Although he worked very hard during the busiest seasons, he had at least as many holidays as are allowed to the laborer today. In some parts of Europe these amounted to

The medieval peasant and the modern worker

Medieval Peasant at Work in the Fields. From Jean Mielot's *Miracles de Notre Dame.*

about sixty out of the year, not counting Sundays. Moreover, it was customary for the lord of the manor to feast his peasants after the spring planting was completed and after the harvest was gathered, as well as during the principal religious holidays. Last of all, the peasant was under no obligation to render military service. His crops might be trampled and his cattle driven off by the armies of warring nobles, but at least he could not be compelled to sacrifice his life for the benefit of some swashbuckling dictator or capitalists greedy for profits.

No sooner had feudalism reached the height of its development than it began to show signs of decay. The decline was well along

[3] See illustrations from medieval literature in G. G. Coulton, *The Medieval Village.*

The decline of feudalism: economic causes

on its way in France and Italy by the end of the thirteenth century. The system continued longer in Germany and England, but by 1500 it was almost extinct in all countries of western Europe. Many relics of it, of course, survived until much later—some till the middle of the nineteenth century in central and eastern Europe. The causes of the decline of the feudal regime are not far to seek. Many of them were closely associated with the revolutionary economic changes of the eleventh and succeeding centuries. The revival of trade with the Near East and the growth of cities led to an increased demand for products of the farms. Prices rose, and as a consequence some peasants were able to buy their freedom. Moreover, the expansion of commerce and industry created new opportunities for employment and tempted many serfs to flee to the towns. Once they had made good their escape, it was almost impossible to bring them back. Still another economic cause was the opening up of new lands to agricultural production, mainly on account of the higher prices for products of the soil. In order to get peasants to clear forests and drain swamps, it was frequently necessary to promise them their freedom. The Black Death, which swept over Europe in the fourteenth century, while not exactly an economic factor, had results very similar to those of the causes already mentioned. In other words, it produced a scarcity of labor and thereby enabled the serfs who survived to enforce their demands for freedom. With the peasant a free man, the manorial system was practically impossible, and one of the chief props of the feudal regime had been broken.

Political causes

The political causes of the downfall of feudalism were also of major significance. One was the establishment of professional armies and the inducements offered to the peasants to become mercenary soldiers. Another was the adoption of new methods of warfare which rendered the knights somewhat less indispensable as a military class. A third was the condition of chaos produced by the Hundred Years' War and the peasant insurrections resulting therefrom. A fourth was the influence of the Crusades in eliminating powerful nobles, in promoting the adoption of direct taxation, and in compelling the sale of privileges to communities of serfs as a means of raising money to equip armies. But probably the most important political cause was the rise of strong national monarchies, especially in France and England. By various means the ambitious kings of these countries in the late Feudal Age gradually deprived the nobles of all of their political authority.

3. The Rise of National Monarchies

The division of Charlemagne's Empire

Soon after the death of Charlemagne in 814 the strong government which he had built up in western Europe collapsed. In 843, by the Treaty of Verdun, his grandsons agreed to divide the Carolingian Empire into three separate parts. The two largest portions

became the kingdoms of East Francia and West Francia, corresponding roughly to the modern states of Germany and France. A wide
belt of land between the two was formed into a middle kingdom
including the territories of modern Belgium, Holland, Alsace, and
Lorraine. Such was the beginning of some of the most important
political divisions in the map of Europe today.

Meanwhile all three of these kingdoms passed rapidly and completely under feudal domination. The real rulers were not the
descendants of the great Carolingian king, but a host of petty
princes, counts, and dukes. The kings themselves sank to the level of
mere feudal overlords, dependent upon the local nobles for their
soldiers and their revenues. While as kings their moral preponderance was still very great, their actual authority over the people was
practically non-existent. Toward the end of the twelfth century,
however, signs of a change in this condition began to appear in
France. In 987 the last of the weak Carolingian monarchs was displaced by the Count of Paris, Hugh Capet. The direct descendants
of this man were to occupy the throne of France for more than
three hundred years. Although neither Hugh nor any of his immediate successors exercised the degree of sovereignty commonly associated with the royal office, several of the later Capetians were
powerful rulers. A number of factors aided these kings in establishing their dominant position. First of all, they were fortunate enough
for hundreds of years to have sons to succeed them, and often an
only son. Consequently there were no deadly quarrels over the
right of succession, nor was there any necessity of dividing the
royal property among disgruntled relatives who might be able to
defend a claim to the throne. In the second place, most of these kings
lived to an advanced age, with the result that their sons were already
mature men when they came to the throne. There were therefore
no regencies to haggle the royal power away during the minority of
a prince. Another factor was the growth of trade, which afforded
the kings new sources of revenue and enabled them to find powerful
allies among the bourgeoisie for their struggle against the nobles.
Finally, considerable credit must be given to the shrewdness and
vigor of several of the kings themselves.

*The rise of a
national mon-
archy in France*

The first of the Capetian kings who may be considered as the
founders of a national monarchy in France was Philip Augustus
(1180-1223). Although Philip may never have conceived of himself
as other than the highest feudal overlord, most of his policies had
the effect of seriously weakening the feudal structure. When he
granted fiefs to his vassals he required them to agree that their own
vassals would owe first allegiance to him. Greedy for revenue, he
commuted as many as possible of the feudal reliefs into money payments, sold charters to cities, and levied special taxes on Jews and on
all persons who declined to go on a crusade to reconquer the Kingdom of Jerusalem from the Moslems. He appointed bailiffs and

*Founders
of the French
monarchy:
Philip Augustus*

seneschals to supervise the administration of justice in the feudal courts and to enforce the king's rights as an overlord. While he continued to depend upon his vassals for contributions of troops, he took steps toward the founding of a national army subject to his own control. He hired mercenary soldiers by the thousands and compelled the towns to furnish recruits from among their own citizens. So aggressively did he crowd the nobles into the background that he actually quadrupled the royal domain and transferred many of the functions of the feudality into his own hands.

Enlargement of the kingdom

When the first Capetian monarch ascended the throne, France consisted of only a small territory surrounding the town of Paris. Most of the remainder of the country was held by such powerful nobles as the Duke of Normandy, the Count of Champagne, the Duke of Brittany, the Duke of Burgundy, and the Duke of Aquitaine. Although all of these rulers were technically vassals of the French king, they had become so domineering or acquired so much power that they seldom made more than a pretense of fulfilling their feudal obligations. For example, William the Conqueror and his immediate successors were still dukes of Normandy and therefore vassals of the king of France, but actually as kings of England they were his powerful rivals and scarcely made even a formal acknowledgment of his overlordship. When Philip Augustus came to the throne of France in 1180 he determined to put an end to such conditions. Taking advantage of the absence of the English kings, he managed by a series of bold strokes to acquire the Duchy of Normandy and a number of adjoining counties, thereby extending the royal domain to the English Channel. By participating in a papal crusade against the Albigenses he also acquired territory in the south. The Albigenses were heretics, and by the standards of the time the lands they inhabited were legitimate plunder. King Philip seized as his share of the booty the County of Toulouse.

Louis IX

The second of the kings most active in consolidating monarchical power in France was Louis IX (1226–1270). Probably few rulers in history have had more interesting personalities. For Louis was a strange mixture of exaggerated piety, shrewd benevolence, and ambitious practicality. At times he imitated the life of a monk, wearing a haircloth shirt next to his skin, fasting punctiliously, and having himself whipped with small chains. He often entertained paupers at his table, considered it his duty to wash the feet of the poor, and sometimes even waited on lepers. Because of his wide reputation for piety and his martyrdom for the faith on a crusade to Tunis, he was canonized only twenty-seven years after his death. But Louis was not merely a saintly ascetic. He found time to establish hospitals, to abolish trial by combat, and to emancipate thousands of serfs on the royal domain, being careful to make each one pay a fee for his freedom. So zealously did he patronize learning and the arts that his reign has been called "the Golden Age of Medieval France." In addition, he labored to increase the power of the monarchy by every shrewd device he could think of. He extended the right of appeal from decisions in the feudal courts to his own court and encouraged his lawyers to draw up a category of cases which would be subject only to the king's jurisdiction. This category was made broad enough to include cases of treason and practically all breaches of the peace. He commanded that his own currency should be accepted in all parts of the kingdom. He made an earnest but not altogether successful attempt to curb the power of the nobles by prohibiting their right of private warfare. Perhaps most significant of all, he assumed for himself the authority to issue ordinances for the entire country without the previous consent of his vassals. Probably nothing could have expressed a more emphatic disavowal of feudal principles than this, since under feudal theory the king could make no departures from customary law without the approval of the chief men of the realm.

The evolution of a national monarchy in medieval France was carried still farther during the reign of Philip IV (1285–1314), or Philip the Fair as he is more commonly called. The policies of this king were determined very largely by an increasing need for revenue, but they partially resulted from the growing popularity of the Roman law with its basic doctrine of the absolute sovereignty of the state. Philip's ambition to raise money led not only to his expulsion of the Jews and the Italian bankers and the confiscation of their property, but prompted him also to change nearly all of the remaining feudal dues into direct taxes. In addition, he devised new levies upon incomes and upon the goods and property of the merchants. But it was Philip's attempt to tax the possessions of the church that was fraught with the deepest significance. This precipitated an angry quarrel with the Pope which had two momentous results: (1) the subjection of the French Catholic church to the king; and (2) the summoning of what has come to be considered the first parliament in the history of France. In order to determine the attitude of his subjects toward his quarrel with the Pope, Philip in 1302 convoked an assembly of the clergy, the lay nobles, and representatives of the towns. Since these were the principal estates or classes of all of his subjects, the assembly came to be known as the Estates-General. It was summoned on two other occasions by Philip to approve new modes of taxation. His successors continued the precedent of convoking it more or less regularly thereafter until 1614. The Estates-General, of course, was not really intended to be an independent legislative assembly but a body of advisers to the king. It was only under the influence of eighteenth-century liberalism that men came to look back upon it as a true parliament. On the other hand, since it included representatives from outside the

Philip the Fair

327

nobility, its establishment may be considered as another stage in the transformation of the French government from a feudal to a national character.

Causes of the Hundred Years' War

Monarchical power in France underwent still further consolidation as a result of the Hundred Years' War (1337–1453). This war grew out of a number of causes. The primary one was probably the long-standing conflict between the French and English kings over territory in France. At the end of the thirteenth century, English monarchs still held part of Guienne and Gascony in southwestern France as vassals of the French crown. The French monarchs resented the presence of a foreign power on their soil. Moreover, they feared that the English interest in the woolen trade of Flanders might lead to an alliance with the Flemish burghers against their sovereign, the King of France. To add fuel to the flames, Edward III, who succeeded to the throne of England in 1327, had a claim to the French crown through his mother, who was a daughter of Philip the Fair. Sensing that war was inevitable, he determined to press this claim in the hope that by so doing he might find a convenient pretext for conquering the Flemish cities.

The course and climax of the conflict

The Hundred Years' War actually covered more than a century, although the fighting was by no means continuous. Hostilities between the royal armies were interrupted by several truces and were accompanied by a number of bloody uprisings of townsmen and peasants. During the greater part of the conflict the English armies were generally victorious. They were better organized, better disciplined, and better equipped. Besides, England did not suffer from the extremes of internal discord which plagued the French. By 1420 the Duke of Burgundy had deserted the French cause, and all of the northern half of France had been occupied by English soldiers. Soon afterward occurred the most dramatic incident of the war, which infused new confidence into the French armies and paved the way for their ultimate victory. A devout but simple peasant girl, Jeanne

Jeanne d'Arc

d'Arc or Joan of Arc, came forward with the declaration that she had been commissioned by God to "drive the English out of the whole kingdom of France." Though she was completely uneducated, "knowing neither A nor B," her piety and sincerity made such a strong impression upon the French soldiers that they firmly believed they were being led by an angel from heaven. In a few months she had liberated most of central France and had brought the dauphin Charles VII to Reims, where he was crowned King of France. But in May, 1430, she was captured by the Burgundians and turned over to the English. The latter regarded her as a witch and set up a special court of the clergy to try her for heresy. Found guilty, she was given over to the secular government on May 30, 1431, and burned in the public square of Rouen.

As is often true of martyrs, Jeanne d'Arc was more powerful dead than alive. Her memory lingers in France to this day as the spiritual embodiment of a patriotic cause. The years that followed her death witnessed a series of uninterrupted triumphs for the French armies. In 1453 the capture of Bordeaux, the last of the English strongholds, brought the war to an end. Only the port of Calais remained of the once extensive English holdings in France. But the Hundred Years' War did more than expel the English from French territory. It added the capstone to the consolidation of royal power in the kingdom of France. The attempts of both the Estates-General and the great nobles to control the government had proved abortive. In spite of the confusion and sufferings of the greater part of the war, France had emerged with enough of a national consciousness to enable her kings to centralize their power in accordance with a pattern of absolute monarchy. The completion of this process marked the final transition from feudalism to something resembling a modern state.

Effects of the Hundred Years' War

The development of a national monarchy in England goes back to the reign of William the Conqueror. His conquest of the island in 1066 resulted in the establishment of a stronger monarchy than had previously existed under the Saxon rulers. The enlargement of power thus effected was not necessarily deliberate. King William made few sweeping changes. For the most part he preserved Anglo-Saxon laws and institutions. He brought over certain elements of feudalism from the Continent, but he took care to prevent too great a degree of decentralization. By the Salisbury Oath he required his vassals to swear allegiance to him directly instead of to their immediate overlords. He prohibited private warfare and retained the right to coin money as a royal prerogative. When he granted lands to his followers, he rarely gave any of them large estates composed of compact territory. He transformed the old *witan*, or advisory council of the Anglo-Saxon kings, into a *curia regis*, or court of the king, composed primarily of his own retainers and administrative subordinates. By the end of his reign the constitution of England had been markedly changed, but the alterations had been so gradual that few were aware of their significance.

Foundations of national monarchy in England

William the Conqueror's immediate successors continued their father's policies, but after the death of Henry I in 1135 a violent quarrel broke out between rival claimants for the throne, and the country was plunged into the depths of anarchy. When Henry II became king in 1154, he found the treasury depleted and the barons entrenched in power. His first objectives, therefore, were to increase the royal revenues and to reduce the power of the nobles. In pursuance of the first, he made a regular practice of commuting the feudal obligation of military service into a money payment known as *scutage*, and levied the first English taxes on personal property and on incomes. In his war against the nobles he demolished hundreds of castles that had been built without authorization and curtailed the jurisdiction of the feudal courts. But he apparently realized that the

The reforms of Henry II

power of the barons could not be permanently restricted without thoroughgoing changes in the law and in judicial procedure. Accordingly, he gathered around him a staff of eminent lawyers to advise him regarding the laws which ought to be in force. In addition, he followed a practice already established of appointing itinerant judges to administer justice in the various parts of the realm. These judges, traveling from one region to another, applied a uniform law throughout the kingdom. The precedents laid down by their decisions gradually supplanted local customs and came to be recognized as the Common Law of England. Henry also issued writs commanding the sheriffs to bring before the judges as they went from shire to shire groups of men who were familiar with local conditions. Under oath these men were required to report every case of murder, arson, robbery, or similar crime they knew to have occurred since the judges' last visit. This was the origin of the grand jury. Another of Henry's reforms made it possible for either party to a civil dispute to purchase a writ which would order the sheriff to bring both plaintiff and defendant, together with twelve citizens who knew the facts, before the judge. The twelve were then asked under oath if the plaintiff's statements were true, and the judge rendered his decision in accordance with the answer. Out of this practice grew the institution of the trial jury.

The Common Law and jury system

There was one branch of the administration of justice which Henry failed to bring under royal control, though he made strenuous efforts to do so. This was the judging and punishing of members of the clergy. Priests and other members of the ecclesiastical hierarchy were not tried in ordinary courts but in church courts under the rules of the canon law. Punishment was notoriously lax. A priest, for instance, convicted of murder, was deprived of his clerical status but was rarely given any further penalty. Not only this, but appeals could be taken to the papal court in Rome from decisions in any English courts on ecclesiastical matters. In an effort to eradicate these practices Henry issued the Constitutions of Clarendon in 1164. The Constitutions provided that any clergyman accused of crime must be taken into a royal court first. If the royal court found that a crime had been committed, the defendant would be sent to a church court for trial. If found guilty he would be sent back to the royal court to be sentenced. From such judgments no appeal could be taken to Rome without the king's consent. In attempting to enforce the Constitutions, Henry ran afoul of the Archbishop of Canterbury. The latter, Thomas à Becket, was as devoted to the interests of the church as Henry was to the strengthening of the monarchy. The quarrel reached a tragic climax when the Archbishop was murdered by a band of Henry's knights after the king, in an outburst of anger, had rebuked his followers for doing nothing to rid him of "a turbulent priest." The crime so shocked the English public that the whole program of bringing the ecclesiastical

Henry's quarrel with Thomas à Becket

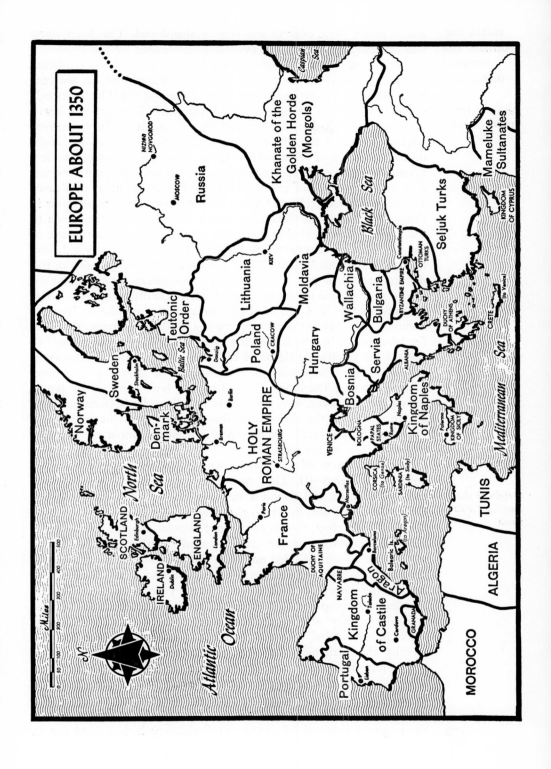

EUROPE ABOUT 1350

courts under royal control was largely abandoned. The Archbishop was revered as a martyr and eventually canonized by the Pope.

Revolt of the barons against King John

During the reigns of Henry's sons, Richard I and John, feudalism enjoyed a partial recovery. For all but six months of his ten-year reign Richard was absent from England waging the Third Crusade or defending his possessions on the Continent. Moreover, the heavy taxation which had to be imposed to defray his military expenses angered many of the barons. The feudal revolt reached its height during the reign of King John, who was perhaps not much worse a tyrant than some of his predecessors. But John had the misfortune to have two powerful enemies in King Philip Augustus of France and Pope Innocent III; and when he lost most of his possessions in France to Philip and suffered a humiliating defeat at the hands of the Pope, it was inevitable that the barons would take advantage of the opportunity to regain their power. In 1215 they compelled John to sign the famous Magna Charta, a document which remains to this day an important part of the British constitution. The popular interpretation placed upon the Magna Charta is really erroneous. It was not intended to be a Bill of Rights or a charter of liberties for the common man. On the contrary, it was a feudal document, a written feudal contract in which the king as an overlord pledged himself to respect the traditional rights of his vassals. It was chiefly important at the time as an expression of the principle of limited government, of the idea that the king is bound by the law. Some of its feudal provisions, however, lent themselves to a broader application later on; for example, the declaration that no man could be imprisoned or otherwise punished "except by the legal judgment of his peers or by the law of the land."

Origin of the English Parliament

The opposition of the barons continued during the reign of John's son, Henry III. They now drew considerable support from the middle class and found a new leader in Simon de Montfort. Civil war broke out, in which the king was taken prisoner. In 1265 Simon de Montfort, wishing to secure popular support for his plans to limit the powers of the crown, called together an assembly or parliament which included not only the higher nobles and churchmen but also two knights from each shire and two citizens from each of the more important towns. Thirty years later this device of a parliament composed of members of the three great classes became a regular agency of the government when Edward I in 1295 convoked the so-called Model Parliament. Edward's purpose in summoning this parliament was not to inaugurate democratic reform but merely to broaden the political structure and thereby make the king less dependent upon the nobles. Nevertheless, a precedent was established that representatives of the commons should always meet with the two higher classes to advise the king. By the end of the reign of Edward III (1327–77) Parliament had divided for all practical purposes into two houses, and they had increased their control over taxation and were assuming lawmaking authority. The subsequent evolution of the English Parliament into the sovereign power in the country will be discussed in later chapters.

During the fourteenth century England was profoundly affected by economic changes which had begun somewhat earlier on the Continent. The development of commerce and industry, the growth of cities, the greater use of money, the scarcity of labor—all of these seriously weakened the manorial system and consequently undermined feudal power. In addition, the Hundred Years' War increased the military and financial powers of the kings and tended to make them more independent of baronial support. Feudalism in England was finally extinguished in a great struggle among rival factions for control of the crown. This struggle, known as the War of the Roses, lasted from 1455 to 1485. The death of a great many of the nobles in this war and the disgust of the people with continual disorder enabled the new king, Henry Tudor, or Henry VII, to establish a more highly consolidated rule than the country had known up to this time.

*The extinction
of feudalism in
England*

Although the feudal regime became extinct in Germany by the fifteenth century and in Italy somewhat earlier, in neither of these countries was a national monarchy set up until long after the close of the Middle Ages. The power of the dukes in Germany and the power of the Pope always proved too strong to be overcome. Some of the German Emperors might have succeeded in building up centralized rule if they had been content to remain in their own country, but they persisted in interfering in Italy, thereby antagonizing the Popes and encouraging revolts at home.

*The failure of
Germany and
Italy to form
national states*

When the eastern branch of the Carolingian dynasty died out in 911, the Germans returned to their ancient practice of electing a king. Their first choice was Conrad of Franconia. He, in turn, was succeeded by Henry I, the founder of the Saxon dynasty. The most famous member of this dynasty was Henry's son, Otto the Great, who became king in 936. From the beginning of his reign Otto apparently entertained ambitions of becoming something more than a mere king of Germany. He had himself crowned at Aachen, probably to convey the idea that he was the rightful successor of Charlemagne. Soon afterward he intervened in Italian affairs and assumed the title of King of the Lombards. From this it was only a step to becoming involved with the papacy. In 961 Otto responded to an appeal from Pope John XII for protection against his enemies, and in January of the following year he was rewarded by being crowned Roman Emperor. Although the empire of Otto the Great was confined to Germany and Italy, there was doubtless the belief in the mind of its founder that it would eventually be enlarged, perhaps to embrace all of Latin Christendom. It was, of course, not

*The empire of
Otto the Great*

*See color
plates at
page 285*

333

conceived as a new state at all but as a continuation of the Carolingian Empire and the Empire of the Caesars.

In the twelfth century the crown of Otto the Great came into possession of the Hohenstaufen family, whose most distinguished representatives were Frederick Barbarossa and Frederick II. Both of these rulers were outspoken in asserting their claims to imperial dignity. Frederick Barbarossa called the empire of Germany and Italy the Holy Roman Empire on the theory that it was a universal empire established directly by God and co-ordinate in rank with the church. Frederick II, who was king of Sicily and southern Italy as well as Holy Roman Emperor, was much more interested in his southern kingdom than he was in Germany. Nevertheless, he be-

The Emperor Frederick Barbarossa (Frederick I) and His Two Sons. A miniature dating from about 1180.

lieved just as firmly as did his grandfather Barbarossa in a universal empire as the highest secular power in western Europe. But he considered that the only possible way to make the claims of the Emperor a reality was to build a strong state in Sicily and southern Italy and then extend its power northward. Accordingly, he proceeded to reorganize his southern kingdom into a divine-right despotism. He swept away the vestiges of feudalism almost at a single stroke. Like William the Conqueror he required all nobles, regardless of rank, to swear allegiance to him directly. He established a professional army, introduced direct taxation, and abolished trial by ordeal and by combat. He appointed traveling judges to promote the development of a uniform law and judicial procedure. He decreed it to be an act of sacrilege even to discuss the Emperor's statutes or judgments. He set up a rigid control over commerce and industry and founded government monopolies of the grain trade, the exchange of money, and the manufacture of textiles and other commodities. He even anticipated modern dictators in a campaign for racial purity; for he declared that "When the men of Sicily ally themselves with the daughters of foreigners, the purity of the race becomes besmirched." He seemed to forget the fact that the blood of most of his people was already mixed with Saracenic, Greek, Italian, and Norman infusions, and that he himself was half German and half Norman.

Frederick II was no more successful than any of his predecessors in increasing the power of the Holy Roman Empire. His great mistake was his failure to enlist the support of the middle class in the cities as the Capetian monarchs in France had done. Without this it was impossible to break through the wall of papal opposition. After Frederick died in 1250 the Popes proceeded to annihilate the remaining members of the Hohenstaufen line. In 1273 Rudolf of Hapsburg was elected to the imperial throne, but the Holy Roman Empire over which he and his descendants ruled was seldom very powerful. When finally abolished in 1806 by Napoleon, it was little more than a political fiction.

The crown of the Holy Roman Emperor passes to the Hapsburgs

4. Urban Life in the Feudal Age

By no means all of the inhabitants of western Europe in the Feudal Age lived in castles, manor houses, or peasant villages. Thousands of others dwelt in cities and towns; and from the eleventh century on, at least, the activities of the urban classes were just as important as the fighting and love-making of nobles or the toiling and roistering of peasants. Indeed, the cities were the real centers of most of the intellectual and artistic progress of the late Middle Ages.

Importance of the cities

The oldest of the medieval cities in western Europe were undoubtedly those which had survived from Roman times. But outside of Italy these were few indeed. Others came into being from a variety of causes. A great many were towns which had increased in size and importance because of the establishment of bishoprics there. Some had grown out of the expansion of monasteries into centers of trade and industry. Still others had developed from castles or strongholds where people congregated because of the need for protection. But by far the greatest number originated as a result of the revival of trade which began in the eleventh century. The leaders in this revival were the Italian towns of Venice, Genoa, and Pisa. Their merchants rapidly built up a flourishing commerce with the Byzantine Empire and with the great Moslem cities of Baghdad, Damascus, and Cairo. The products brought in by these merchants stimulated a brisk demand not only in Italy but also in Germany, France, and England. As a result, new markets were opened up, and many people turned to manufacturing to imitate products imported from the Near East. Cities and towns multiplied so rapidly that in some regions half the population had been drawn from agriculture into commercial and industrial pursuits by the fourteenth century. As one would expect, the largest cities of feudal Europe were

The origins of the medieval cities

A Medieval Bridge. Pont Valentre on the Lot River (tributary of the Garonne in southwest France). The town in the background is Cahors.

Relic of a Medieval City Gate, the Eastgate of Chester, England. The Eastgate is the principal entrance to the city of Chester. Its present archway, built in 1769, replaced a narrow medieval gateway. The keepers of the gate had the duty of inspecting weights and measures, and they levied a toll on all merchandise entering the city from the east. The clock tower above the present gateway was erected in 1897 to commemorate Queen Victoria's Jubilee.

A Section of the Medieval Town of Nordlingen, Germany. The need for protection against invaders led to congested housing conditions inside the walls.

THE MEDIEVAL CITY

The Palazzo Communale, or City Hall, in Siena (1288–1309). Built of brick, with a tower 334 feet high, it was a fine example of painted Gothic. The chapel at the foot of the tower was built as a public thankoffering after the plague of 1348.

Scene in a Medieval Village. Among the activities shown are plowing, grinding grain, and slaughtering a boar for meat. In the lower right two friars are dispensing bread and soup to the poor.

Medieval cities were generally surrounded by fortified walls. Shown above are the massive walls of Avila, a city in central Spain. The apse of the cathedral built into the walls is the supposed birthplace of St. Teresa (1515–1582).

located in the south. Palermo on the island of Sicily with possibly 300,000 inhabitants surpassed all the others in size and probably in magnificence also. The metropolis of northern Europe was Paris, with a population of about 240,000 in the thirteenth century. The only other cities with a population of 100,000 or over were Venice, Florence, and Milan. Although England doubled the number of her inhabitants between the eleventh century and the fourteenth, only about 45,000 of them lived in London in the thirteenth century. By the end of the Middle Ages nearly all of the cities of western Europe had gained some degree of exemption from feudal control. Their citizens had complete freedom to dispose of their property as they saw fit, to marry whom they pleased, and to go and come as they liked. All feudal dues were either abolished or commuted to monetary payments; and provision was made for cases involving townsmen to be tried in the municipal courts. Some of the largest and wealthiest towns were almost entirely free, having organized governments with elected officials to administer their affairs. This was especially true in northern Italy, Provence, northern France, and Germany. This freedom was secured in a variety of ways—frequently by purchase, occasionally by violence, and sometimes by taking advantage of the weakness of the nobles or their preoccupation with quarrels of their own. The governments of these cities were generally dominated by an oligarchy of merchants, but in some cases democracy prevailed. Annual elections of magistrates were relatively common; universal suffrage was occasionally employed; while in a few towns the rich were disfranchised entirely, and the government was controlled by the masses.

Most of the medieval cities grew so rapidly that it would have been almost impossible to provide optimum standards of healthfulness and comfort for the inhabitants even if there had been sufficient knowledge and inclination to do so. Overcrowding was so bad that sometimes as many as sixteen people lived in three rooms. Part of this congestion was due to the need of the cities for protection against nobles and brigands. To fulfill this need, fortified walls had to be built around each city with gates that could be securely barred to shut out marauders. Naturally it was too much trouble to tear down these walls and build new ones with every substantial increase in the population, although eventually this had to be done several times in a great many of the principal towns. Land values within these walls rose to fantastic heights and brought into existence a wealthy rent-collecting class, usually composed of the leading members of the merchant guilds. Because of the high cost of land, houses were built with upper stories that projected over the street, and even space on the walls was utilized for cottages and gardens. Streets were narrow and crooked and generally remained unpaved for centuries. The practice of paving began in Italy in the eleventh century and then gradually spread northward, but no thoroughfare in Paris had a hard surface until 1184 when Philip Augustus paved a single roadway in front of the Louvre. With space in the cities so limited, the streets served as the common playgrounds for boys and young men. Many were the protests voiced by their elders and by the clergy against wrestling, bowling, and pitching of quoits in the streets. "Football was constantly denounced, with good reason, as it was not an orderly game with a fixed number of players . . . but a wild struggle between opposing parties to force the ball through the streets from one end of the town to the other, frequently resulting in broken legs." [4]

Standards of sanitation in most of the medieval cities were distinctly inferior to those of ancient Rome. The great majority of the towns depended upon wells or rivers for their water supply, with the result that outbreaks of typhoid fever were of common occurrence. Although a few cities had underground sewers, none appears to have made provision for the collection of garbage. Refuse was generally thrown into the streets to be removed eventually by the rain or by the pigs and dogs that roamed at large. Conditions in Paris in the twelfth century may be illustrated by the fact that a son of Louis VI was killed when a hog rooting in the offal in the Rue St. Jacques charged between the legs of his horse and threw him to the ground.[5]

Standards of sanitation

The basic economic institutions in the medieval cities were the guilds. Of the two, the merchant and the craft guilds, the merchant organizations were the older, having developed as far back as the eleventh century. At first these included both traders and artisans, and then as industry became more specialized, the original guilds were split up into separate organizations of craftsmen and merchants. The main functions of the merchant guild were to maintain a monopoly of the local market for its own members and to preserve a stable, non-competitive economic system. To accomplish these ends the guild severely restricted trading by foreign merchants in the city, guaranteed to every member the right to participate in every purchase of goods made by any other member, required all of its members to charge uniform prices for the things they sold, drastically punished cornering of the market, and prohibited many forms of advertising. In some cases these rules were enforced by municipal ordinances, since the leading members of the guild were frequently the most powerful officials of the town corporation; but in other instances the methods used were more direct. An English herring merchant complained that "because he sold his merchandise at a less price than other merchants of the town of Yaxley . . . they assaulted him, beat him and ill-treated him and left him there for dead, so that he despaired of his life." [6]

The merchant guilds

[4] L. F. Salzman, *English Life in the Middle Ages*, pp. 82–83.
[5] Thompson, *An Economic and Social History of the Middle Ages*, p. 787.
[6] Quoted by Ephraim Lipson, *Economic History of England*, Vol. I, p. 246.

Each of the craft guilds had three different classes of members—the master craftsmen, the journeymen, and the apprentices. But only the first two had any voice in the management of guild affairs, and toward the close of the Middle Ages even the journeymen lost most of their privileges. The master craftsmen were always the aristocrats of medieval industry; they owned their shops, employed other workers, and were responsible for the training of apprentices. The whole craft guild system operated very largely for their benefit. The journeymen (from the French *journée,* meaning "day" or "day's work") were craftsmen who worked in the masters' shops for wages. In some parts of Germany it was customary for the young journeyman to spend a year wandering about the country picking up casual employment, the so-called *Wanderjahr,* before settling down in any particular place. But in most other sections of Europe he seems to have lived with the master's family. The industrious and intelligent journeyman could eventually become a master craftsman by accumulating enough money to set up his own shop and by passing an examination, which sometimes included the submission of a masterpiece. As in many specialized trades today, entrance into the medieval craft could be accomplished only through serving an apprenticeship, varying in length from two to seven years, the longer period being more common. The apprentice was entirely under the control of the master craftsman, who was commonly held responsible for the boy's education in elementary subjects, and for the development of his character as well as for teaching him his trade. Usually the apprentice received no compensation except his food, lodging, and clothing. When the period of training was over, he became a journeyman. During the waning of the Middle Ages the craft guilds grew more and more exclusive. Terms of apprenticeship were lengthened, and it was made increasingly difficult for journeymen ever to become masters. The guilds themselves came to be dominated by the richer members, who endeavored to restrict their particular crafts to their own families. As a result, the great mass of the workers were reduced to the level of proletarians, doomed to remain wage earners as long as they lived. Many of the owners of shops now ceased to work with their hands and became capitalists and employers exclusively.

The functions of the craft guilds were similar to those of the related organizations of merchants, except for the additional responsibility of maintaining standards of quality. The craftsmen were just as ambitious as the merchants to preserve monopolies in their particular fields and to prevent any real competition among those producing the same article. Consequently they required uniformity of prices and wages, prohibited working after hours, and set up elaborate regulations governing methods of production and the quality of materials used. They even went to the extreme of discouraging new inventions and discoveries unless they were made

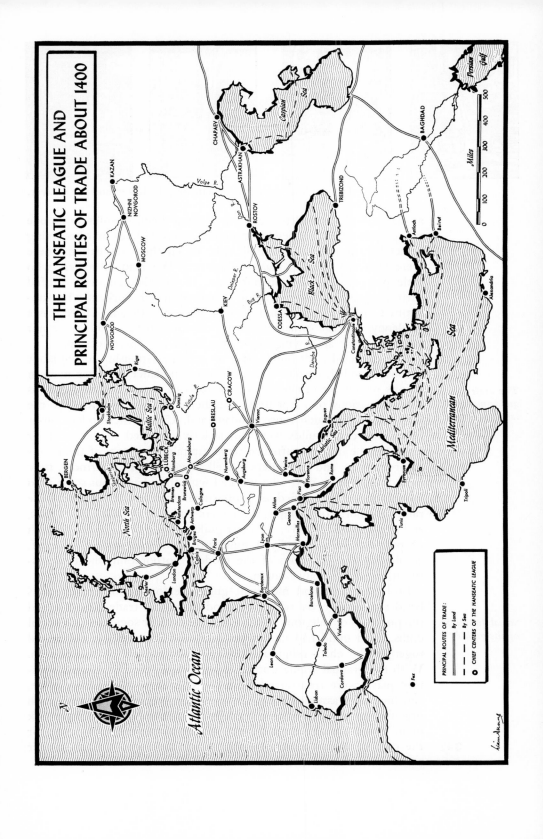

THE HANSEATIC LEAGUE AND
PRINCIPAL ROUTES OF TRADE ABOUT 1400

PRINCIPAL ROUTES OF TRADE:
——— By Land
– – – By Sea
○ CHIEF CENTERS OF THE HANSEATIC LEAGUE

Miles
0   100   200   300   400   500

Atlantic Ocean

North Sea

Baltic Sea

Mediterranean Sea

Black Sea

Caspian Sea

Adriatic Sea

Persian Gulf

Chester
London
Calais
Bruges
Antwerp
Amsterdam
Bremen
Brunswick
Cologne
Hamburg
LÜBECK
Magdeburg
Nuremberg
Augsburg
BERGEN
Stockholm
Riga
NOVGOROD
Danzig
Visula R.
BRESLAU
CRACOW
Vienna
Venice
Ragusa
Florence
Pisa
Rome
Milan
Genoa
Marseilles
Lyon
Paris
Bordeaux
Barcelona
Valencia
Toledo
Leon
Cordova
Lisbon
Fez
Tunis
Tripoli
Syracuse
Alexandria
Beirut
Antioch
BAGHDAD
Constantinople
ODESSA
KIEV
Danube
Bug R.
Dnieper R.
Don R.
ROSTOV
TREBIZOND
ASTRAKHAN
CHAPAEV
KAZAN
NIZHNI NOVGOROD
MOSCOW
Volga R.
Skagerrak

N

Medieval Craftsmen: The tailor, the shoemaker, the baker, and the weaver.

available to all and unless everyone adopted them. Absolutely no one was permitted to practice his trade in a town without first becoming a member of the guild. But in spite of all these regulations there were evidently a good many "chiselers." We read of millers who stole part of their customers' grain, of upholsterers who stuffed their mattresses with thistledown, and of metal-workers who substituted iron for copper and covered it over with gilt. There was a tendency also for some masters to employ workers who were not journeymen at all, having never completed an apprenticeship.

The craft guilds not really labor unions

The medieval craft guilds bore no actual relationship to the labor unions of today, despite a superficial resemblance to those modern unions which are organized on the basis of separate crafts, such as the associations of carpenters, plumbers, and electricians. But the differences are much more fundamental. Unlike the modern labor union, the craft guilds were not strictly confined to the working class; for the master craftsmen were capitalists, owners of the means of production, and employers as well as workers. Furthermore, they included not only men who worked with their hands but some who would now be classified as professional men entirely outside the ranks of labor. For example, there were guilds of notaries, physicians, and pharmacists. Finally, the craft guild had a much greater breadth of purpose. It was really a miniature industrial system in itself, combining the functions of the modern corporation, the trade association, and the labor union.

Social functions of the guilds

Both the craft and merchant guilds performed other functions besides those directly related to production and trade. They served the purposes of religious associations, benevolent societies, and social clubs. Each guild had its patron saint, and its members celebrated together the chief religious holidays and festivals of the church. With the gradual secularization of the drama, the miracle and mystery plays were transferred from the church to the market place, and the guilds assumed charge of presenting them. In addition, each organization ministered to the needs of its members who were sick or in distress of any kind. Money was appropriated to provide for the care of widows and orphans. A member who was no longer

342

able to work or who had been thrown into jail by his enemies could look to his colleagues for assistance. Even an unfortunate brother's debts might be assumed by the guild if his financial plight was serious.

The economic theory upon which the guild system rested was vastly different from that which prevails in capitalist society. It reflected, first of all, some of the ascetic flavor of Christianity. In the eyes of the church the vitally important aim in life should be the salvation of one's soul. Everything else should be kept in a subordinate place. It was not proper that men should expend their energies in the pursuit of luxury, or even that they should strive to become too comfortable. Moreover, the religion had been founded upon the idea that riches are a hindrance to the welfare of the soul. St. Ambrose, one of the most influential of the Christian Fathers, had even referred to private property as "a damnable usurpation." However, the economic theory of the late Middle Ages was influenced not only by Christianity but by Aristotle's doctrines of the golden mean and the just price and by his condemnation of usury. This theory included the following basic assumptions:

The economic theory of the guild system

(1) The purpose of economic activity is to provide goods and services for the community and to enable each member of society to live in security and freedom from want. Its purpose is not to furnish opportunities for the few to get rich at the expense of the many. Men who engage in business with the object of making as much money as possible are no better than pirates or robbers. The only legitimate objects of trade or other business are to provide for the upkeep of a household, for the assistance of the needy, or for some public advantage, lest one's country lack the necessaries of life.[7]

Basic doctrines

(2) Every commodity has its "just price," which is equal to its cost of production. No merchant has a right to sell any article for more than this price plus a small charge for the service he renders in making goods available to the community. To take advantage of scarcity to boost the price or to charge all that the traffic will bear is to commit a mortal sin.

(3) No man is entitled to any larger share of this world's goods than is necessary for his reasonable needs. Any surplus that may come into his possession is not rightfully his but belongs to society. St. Thomas Aquinas, the greatest of all the medieval philosophers, taught that if a rich man refuses to share his wealth with the poor, it is entirely justifiable that his surplus should be taken from him.

(4) No man has a right to financial reward unless he engages in socially useful labor or incurs some actual risk in an economic venture. The taking of interest on loans where no genuine risk is involved constitutes the sin of usury. Medieval economic theory would

[7] Thomas Aquinas, *Summa Theologica*, Fourth Article.

*Exceptions to
the ideal*

therefore conflict with the socially reputable practice today of making investments in high-grade bonds for a safe return, but it would approve a modest return from common stocks.

It would be foolish, of course, to suppose that these lofty ideals of an economic system largely devoid of the profit motive were ever carried out to perfection. As we have seen, manifestations of greed were not lacking among many members of the guilds. But more than this, the non-capitalistic guild system did not extend into every sphere of medieval economic activity. For example, it was never successfully applied to international trade. Seldom would an individual merchant or craftsman have sufficient resources to engage in importing or exporting goods. Consequently, companies or associations of merchants had to be formed. The most famous of these associations in the Middle Ages were the Merchants of the Staple and the Teutonic Hanse. The former, organized in the thirteenth century, controlled the exporting of wool from England and the importing of goods from Flemish manufacturing towns such as Bruges and Antwerp. Apparently of somewhat earlier origin, the Teutonic Hanse was an association of German merchants engaged in exchanging the furs, fish, amber, leather, salt, and grain from the Baltic region for the wines, spices, textiles, fruits, and other products of the west and the south. By the fourteenth century this association had developed into the powerful Hanseatic League with a membership of about eighty towns under the leadership of Lübeck, Hamburg, and Bremen. Both the Merchants of the Staple and the Hanse were essentially profit-making organizations, and the activities of their members foreshadowed the growth of a capitalist economy in the Commercial Revolution that was soon to begin.

Selected Readings

· *Items so designated are available in paperbound editions.*

Adams, G. B., *Civilization during the Middle Ages*, New York, 1914. Valuable for interpretation.
Bateson, Mary, *Medieval England*, London, 1904.
Boissonnade, Prosper, *Life and Work in Medieval Europe*, New York, 1927. Interesting and dependable.
· Bryce, James, *The Holy Roman Empire*, New York, 1919. (Schocken)
Buchan, Alice, *Joan of Arc and the Recovery of France*, New York, 1948.
Clough, S. B., and Cole, C. W., *Economic History of Europe*, Boston, 1947. Contains excellent chapters on medieval economy.
Davis, H. W. C., *Medieval Europe*, London, 1948. Brief and interesting.
· Ganshof, F. L., *Feudalism*, New York, 1952. (Torchbooks) A high-level and somewhat technical account. Valuable for a clear understanding of feudal theory and institutions.
Henderson, E. F., *A Short History of Germany*, New York, 1931, 2 vols.
Lindsay, P., and Groves, R., *The Peasants' Revolt of 1381*, London, n.d.
Lipson, Ephraim, *Economic History of England*, New York, 5th edn., 1929, Vol. I.

Luchaire, A., *Social France in the Time of Philip Augustus*, New York, 1912.   **READINGS**
· Myers, A. R., *England in the Late Middle Ages*, London, 1952. (Penguin)
· Painter, Sidney, *The Rise of Feudal Monarchies*, Ithaca, 1951. (Cornell)
· ———, *Medieval Society*. (Cornell) A brief but scholarly survey.
Perroy, Edouard, *The Hundred Years War*, New York, 1951.
· Pirenne, Henri, *Economic and Social History of Medieval Europe*, New York, 1956. (Harvest) Stimulating and authoritative.
· ———, *Medieval Cities*, Princeton, 1925. (Anchor) The most highly regarded book on the subject.
· Power, Eileen, *Medieval People*, London, 1924. (Anchor)
Runciman, Steven, *A History of the Crusades, The First Crusade and the Foundation of the Kingdom of Jerusalem*, New York, 1951, Vol. I.
Salzman, L. F., *English Life in the Middle Ages*, Oxford, 1926.
· Sayles, G. O., *The Medieval Foundations of England*, London, 1952. (Perpetua)
Seignobos, Charles, *The Feudal Regime*, New York, 1902.
Stearns, W. S., *Life on a Medieval Barony*, New York, 1923. Gives a good impression of the actualities of feudalism.
· Stephenson, Carl, *Medieval Feudalism*, New York, 1935. (Cornell)
· Tawney, R. H., *Religion and the Rise of Capitalism*, New York, 1947. (Mentor) Interesting for the light it throws on medieval economic theory under the influence of the Church.
Thompson, J. W., *An Economic and Social History of the Middle Ages*, New York, 1928.
Tilley, A., *Medieval France*, Cambridge, 1922.
Vickers, K. H., *England in the Later Middle Ages*, London, 1913.

Source Materials

Coulton, G. G., *Life in the Middle Ages*, 4 vols.
———, *The Medieval Village*.
Dante, *De Monarchia (On Monarchy)*.
John of Salisbury, *Policraticus*.
Johnes, Thomas, *Froissart's Chronicles of England, France, Spain, and the Adjoining Countries*, Vol. I, 240–41; Vol. II, 94–95.
McKechnie, W. S., *Magna Carta*.
Marsiglio of Padua, *Defensor Pacis (Defender of the Peace)*, especially Book I, Chs. IV, XII, XV.
Riley, H. T., *Memorials of London and London Life*.
Thatcher, O. J., and McNeal, E. H., *A Source Book for Medieval History*, pp. 283–306, "The Golden Bull of Charles IV"; also documents of feudalism, pp. 341–87.
Webster, Hutton, *Historical Selections*, pp. 467–500, documents of the Feudal Regime.

CHAPTER 14

The Civilization of the Feudal Age:
Religious and Intellectual Developments

Now in those things which we hold about God there is truth in
two ways. For certain things that are true about God wholly surpass the capability of human reason, for instance that God is three
and one; while there are certain things to which even natural religion can attain, for instance that God is, that God is one, and
others like these, which even the philosophers proved demonstra-
tively of God, being guided by the light of natural reason.
—St. Thomas Aquinas, *Summa Contra Gentiles*, Book I

*The change in
religious and
intellectual at-
titudes*

It has been mentioned more than once already that the civilization
of western Europe between 800 and 1300 was vastly different from
that which had existed at the beginning of the medieval period. Nowhere was the contrast more striking than in the spheres of religion
and the intellect. The religious and intellectual attitudes of the early
Middle Ages were products of a time of transition and of considerable chaos. The Roman political and social structure had disintegrated, and no new regime had yet emerged to take its place. As a
consequence, the thinking of this time was directed toward pessimism
and otherworldly concerns. In the midst of conditions of barbarism
and decadence, there did not seem to be much hope for man's
earthly future or much reason for confidence in the powers of the
mind. But after the ninth century these attitudes gradually gave
way to more optimistic sentiments and to an increasing interest in
worldly affairs. The original causes were directly related to the
progress of monastic education, to the rise of more stable government, and to an increase in economic security. Later such factors
as the influence of the Saracen and Byzantine civilizations and the
growth of prosperity in the cities and towns brought the culture of
the Feudal Age to a magnificent climax of intellectual achievement
in the twelfth and thirteenth centuries. At the same time religion
took on a less otherworldly aspect and evolved into an institution
more deeply concerned with the affairs of this life.

1. The New Christianity

During the Feudal Age, Christianity underwent so many significant developments from its early medieval character that it seemed in some respects to be almost a new religion. To be sure, such cardinal features as faith in one God, the belief in the Trinity, and the hope for salvation in a world to come continued to be accepted in their original form; but certain other elements in the religion of St. Augustine and Gregory the Great were modified or eliminated and different ones substituted for them. The transformation began about 850 and reached its zenith in the thirteenth century under the influence of such leaders as St. Thomas Aquinas, St. Francis, and Innocent III.

*Late medieval
Christianity*

Perhaps the most important developments were in matters of doctrine and religious attitudes. The religion of the early Middle Ages had been pessimistic, fatalistic, and, theoretically at least, opposed to everything worldly as a compromise with the devil. Man was considered to be inherently wicked and incapable of any good works except as the beneficiary of God's grace. God Himself was omnipotent, selecting for reasons of His own those human beings who would enter His paradise, and leaving the rest to follow the path to destruction. By the thirteenth century, however, quite different religious conceptions had come to prevail. Life in this world was now held to be exceedingly important, not only as a preparation for eternity but for its own sake as well. No longer was human nature regarded as totally evil. Man could therefore co-operate with God in achieving the salvation of his soul. Instead of emphasizing the omnipotence of God, philosophers and theologians now stressed the divine justice and mercy.

*New doctrines
and new attitudes*

The first great summary of late medieval theology was the *Sentences* of Peter Lombard, written during the second half of the twelfth century. More inclusive statements of doctrine were contained in the *Summary of Theology* of St. Thomas Aquinas and in the pronouncements issued by church councils, especially the Fourth Lateran Council of 1215. Probably the most important of the new elements in this theology were the theory of the priesthood and the theory of the sacraments. There had, of course, been priests and sacraments in the church long before the late Feudal Age, but neither the exact functions of the priests nor the precise nature of the sacraments had ever been clearly formulated. The theory now came to be held that the priest, by virtue of his ordination by a bishop and the latter's confirmation by the Pope, was the inheritor of a portion of the authority conferred by the Christ upon the Apostle Peter. In effect, this meant that the priest had the power to co-operate with God in performing certain miracles and in releasing sinners from the temporal consequences of their wickedness.

*The new theology: (1) the
theory of the
priesthood*

It was primarily a result of Peter Lombard's influence that the

(2) the theory of the sacraments

number of sacraments came to be accepted as seven. The seven were and still are: baptism; confirmation; penance; the Eucharist, or Lord's Supper; marriage; ordination; and extreme unction, or the last rites administered to the dying. The Roman church defines a sacrament as an instrumentality whereby divine grace is communicated to men. The sacramental theory as it came to be accepted during the last centuries of the Feudal Age included a number of separate doctrines. First, there was the doctrine that the sacraments were indispensable means of procuring God's grace, that no individual could be saved without them. Second, there was the principle that the sacraments were automatic in their effects. In other words, it was held that the efficacy of the sacraments did not depend upon the character of the priest who administered them. The priest might be a very unworthy man, but the sacraments in his hands would remain as unpolluted as if they were administered by a saint. Finally, at the Fourth Lateran Council, the doctrine of transubstantiation was made an integral part of the sacramental theory. This doctrine means that the priest, at a given moment in the Eucharistic ceremony, actually co-operates with God in the performance of a miracle whereby the bread and wine of the sacrament are changed or transubstantiated into the body and blood of Christ. The change, of course, is considered a change in essence only; the "accidents" of taste and appearance remain the same.

Mechanical religion modified by rationalism and humanism

The adoption of these two fundamental theories, the theory of the priesthood and the theory of the sacraments, had potent effects in exalting the power of the clergy and in strengthening the formal and mechanical elements in the Latin church. However, medieval Catholicism was revitalized and made into a civilizing influence by two other developments which marked the late Feudal Age. One of these was the adoption of a rationalist philosophy by the leading theologians, and the other was the growth of a humanistic attitude. The influence of rationalist philosophy will be discussed farther on in this chapter. The humanizing element in religion expressed itself in a variety of ways—in the revolt against the selfish asceticism of monks and hermits, in the naturalism of St. Francis, but perhaps most of all in the veneration of saints and the Virgin Mary. All through the later medieval period, the veneration or "invocation" of saints was an exceedingly popular practice, especially among the common people. For the average person God and Christ were remote and sublime beings who could hardly be bothered with the petty problems of men. But the saints were human; one could ask them for favors which one would hesitate to request of God. For example, a woman could implore the aid of St. Agnes in helping her find a husband. Even more popular than the invocation of saints was reverence for the Virgin Mary, which came to be almost a religion in itself during the twelfth and thirteenth centuries. Devotion to

348 Mary as the beautiful and compassionate Mother undoubtedly served as one of the strongest expressions of the humanist tendency in medieval religion. For she was venerated not only as the ideal woman but also as Our Lady of Sorrows. The grief that she experienced over the tragic death of her Son was believed to endow her with a special sympathy for the sorrows of mankind. Though revered as the Queen of Heaven, she was, above all, the goddess of this life.

Significant developments in ecclesiastical organization and the adoption of new forms of religious discipline also occurred during the Feudal Age. In 1059 the College of Cardinals was established as a papal electoral college. Originally the members of this body were the deacons, priests, and bishops of certain churches in the city of Rome. Later high ranking clergy from nearly all countries of the Western world were appointed to membership, although the College included a majority of Italians until 1946. At present there are ninety seats, and a two-thirds vote is necessary to elect the Pope, who is invariably a cardinal himself. Prior to 1059 Popes were chosen in a variety of ways. In the early days they had been elected by the clergy of the diocese of Rome, but later they were often appointed by powerful nobles and frequently by the German emperors. The vesting of the sole right of election in the College of Cardinals was part of a great reform movement to free the church from political control. The other main development in religious organization was the growth of the papal monarchy. The first of the Popes to achieve much success in extending his supremacy over the whole ecclesiastical hierarchy was Nicholas I (858–867). Intervening in disputes between bishops and archbishops, he forced all of them to submit to his own direct authority. Nicholas was followed, however, by a series of weak successors, and the papal monarchy was not revived until the reign of Gregory VII (1073–1085). It reached the highest stage of its medieval development during the pontificate of Innocent III (1198–1216).

Changes in the organization of the church

During the later centuries of the Feudal Age the church made systematic attempts to extend its moral authority over all of its lay members, whether of high or of low degree. The chief methods adopted were excommunication and the requirement of oral confession. Excommunication was not used to any extent before the eleventh century. Its effect was to expel an individual from the church and to deprive him of all the privileges of a Christian. His body could not be buried in consecrated ground, and his soul was temporarily consigned to hell. All other Christians were forbidden to associate with him, under penalty of sharing his fate. Sometimes a decree of excommunication against a king or a powerful noble was fortified by placing an *interdict* upon the area over which he ruled. The interdict, by withholding most of the benefits of religion from a ruler's subjects, was intended to kindle their resentment against him and force him to submit to the church. Both excom-

New methods of discipline

349

munication and the interdict proved to be powerful weapons until about the end of the thirteenth century; after that their effectiveness waned. By a decree of the Fourth Lateran Council in 1215 the church adopted the requirement that every individual must make an oral confession of his sins to a priest at least once a year, and then undergo the punishment imposed before becoming eligible to partake of the Eucharist. The result of this decree was to give the priest the authority of a moral guardian over every individual in his parish.

*Medieval
reform move-
ments: (1) the
Cluniac revival*

Long before the great Reformation of the sixteenth century, medieval Catholicism went through a series of reformations calculated to restore the institutions of the church to some earlier state of purity or to make them more useful to society. The first of these reform movements was the Cluny movement or the Cluniac revival, which derived its name from the monastery of Cluny, founded in 910. The original purpose of the Cluny movement was simply to reform monasticism. The Benedictine monasteries, which were practically the only ones in existence by the tenth century in western Europe, had grown corrupt and were rapidly passing under the control of feudal nobles. Consequently the Cluniac leaders took as their objectives the enforcement of the rules of piety and chastity upon the monks and the liberation of the monasteries themselves from feudal domination. But by the eleventh century the movement had gained a much broader significance. In fact, its purposes were now so different from the original ones that it is often referred to as the New Cluny movement. No longer were the reformers content merely to purify monasticism and free it from the clutches of the lay feudality; their primary aims were now to eliminate corruption and worldliness from the entire church, to abolish feudal control over the secular clergy as well as over monks, and to establish the absolute supremacy of the Pope in ecclesiastical matters. They centered their attacks, first of all, upon *simony*, which was interpreted to include the buying and selling of church offices, any form of appointment to church offices contrary to the canon law, and the investing of bishops and abbots with the symbols of their spiritual power by secular authorities. In addition, the reformers demanded celibacy for all grades of the clergy. Nearly all of these elements in their program were directed toward making the church entirely independent of the great nobles, especially by depriving them of their power to dictate the appointment of bishops, abbots, and priests. The movement aroused bitter opposition, since it struck at the very basis of the feudal relationship which had been established between secular rulers and the clergy. But most of the program was eventually put into effect, due in large part to the fanatical zeal of such leaders as Hildebrand, the "holy Satan" who in 1073 became Pope Gregory VII.

By the end of the eleventh century the Cluniac monks had begun to sink into the same morass of worldliness as did their older Benedictine brothers whom they had set out to reform. The result was the launching of new movements to set an even stronger example of purity and austerity for the regular clergy. In 1084 the Carthusian order was established with a set of rules more rigorous than any hitherto adopted in the West. The Carthusian monks were required to live in cells, to fast three days each week on bread and water, to wear hair shirts, and to spend all their time in prayer, meditation, and manual labor. A few years later the Cistercian order was founded at Citeaux in Burgundy and soon proved to be one of the most popular of them all. By the middle of the twelfth century more than three hundred Cistercian monasteries were receiving converts from all over western Europe. Although not so strict in their requirements of individual asceticism as the Carthusians, the founders of the Cistercian order saw to it that the rules would be puritanical enough to constitute an emphatic protest against the luxury and idleness of the Cluniac monks. Only a vegetarian diet was allowed, and manual labor was strictly enforced. Both the Cistercian and Carthusian orders ultimately went down the same road to decline as their predecessors, partly as a result of the accumulation of wealth, but also because monasticism of the old-fashioned type was by the thirteenth century no longer consistent with the ideals of the time.

Undoubtedly the most significant reform movement of the Feudal Age was the rise of the friars in the thirteenth century. Though the friars are often regarded as simply another species of monks, they were really quite different. Originally they were not members of the clergy at all but laymen. Instead of shutting themselves up in monasteries, they devoted all of their time to social welfare work and to preaching and teaching. The growth of the new orders was symptomatic of an attempt to bring religion into harmony with the needs of a world which had completely outgrown the Dark Ages. Men were now coming to realize that the main business of religion was not to enable a few selfish monks to save their own souls at the expense of society, but to help make this world a happier place in which to live and to rescue the great mass of mankind from the slough of ignorance and sin.

The founder of the original order of friars was St. Francis of Assisi (1182–1226). The son of a rich merchant, the young Francis became dissatisfied with the useless life of vanity and pleasure he was expected to lead and determined to become a servant of the poor. Giving away all of his property and donning the rags of a beggar, he set out on his great mission of preaching salvation in the darkest corners of the Italian cities and ministering to the needs of poor, diseased, and helpless outcasts. The philosophy of St. Francis, if such it can be called, was different from that of many other Christian leaders. The major portion of it was founded almost literally upon the teachings of Jesus. St. Francis followed Jesus in his selflessness,

(2) the Carthusian and Cistercian movements

(3) the rise of the orders of friars: the Franciscan order

St. Francis of Assisi

351

in his devotion to poverty as an ideal, in his indifference to doctrine, and in his contempt for form and ceremony. In addition he had a profound love not merely for man but for every creature around him, and even for the objects of inanimate nature. He found God revealed in the sun, the wind, the flowers, and everything that existed for the use or delight of man. His disciples related how he would never put out a fire, but "treated it reverently," and how "he directed the brother who cut and fetched the fire wood never to cut a whole tree, so that some part of it might remain untouched for the love of Him who was willing to work out our salvation upon the wood of the cross." [1] Finally, it should be made clear that St. Francis was not an ascetic in the accurate meaning of that term. Although he denied himself comforts and pleasures, he did not despise the body or practice laceration of the flesh to achieve the salvation of his soul. His abandonment of earthly possessions was done primarily to conquer pride and bring himself down to the level of the people whom he wished to help.

The Dominican order

The second of the orders of friars was the Dominican order, founded about 1215 by St. Dominic, a Castilian noble who lived in southern France. The Dominicans adopted as their principal task the combating of heresy. Believing that the best means to this end was education, they prepared themselves by diligent study to refute the arguments of pagans and skeptics. Many members of the order gained teaching positions in the universities and contributed much to the development of philosophy and theology. By the fourteenth century both the Dominican and Franciscan orders had departed widely from the teachings of their founders, but they continued to exert a strong influence upon late medieval civilization. The majority of the philosophers and scientists of the thirteenth and fourteenth centuries were either Dominicans or Franciscans.

2. The Struggle between the Secular and Spiritual Authorities

The scope of the conflict

As it happened, the growth of the church in the Feudal Age was accompanied by the rise of ambitious political leaders. A conflict between secular and spiritual authorities was practically unavoidable, since the jurisdictions claimed by each frequently overlapped. The struggle began in 1075 and continued with varying intensity until well into the fourteenth century. Two separate stages in the conflict can be distinguished, the first ending in 1122, and the second beginning about twenty years later.

The two great opponents in the first stage were Pope Gregory VII and the German emperor, Henry IV. The quarrel between these powerful rivals was a direct outgrowth of the New Cluny movement, of which Gregory had been the leader for some time before

[1] Quoted by H. O. Taylor, *The Medieval Mind*, Vol. I, pp. 454–55.

he became Pope. As noted previously, one of the fundamental aims of this movement was to free the church from secular control. During a period of many years the practice had been established that a bishop, abbot, or priest who held his position as a fief should be invested with the symbols of his office by the king or noble who granted the fief. This practice, known as lay investiture, was a thorn in the side of such zealous reformers as Gregory; for they feared that as long as the clergy owed allegiance in any degree to secular overlords, papal supremacy would be impossible. But this was not the only issue involved; there was also the question of the Pope's right to exercise temporal authority. Just how much temporal jurisdiction Gregory intended to claim is not quite clear. Sometimes it appears from his decrees that he regarded himself as the supreme ruler of the world and thought of all princes and kings as merely his vassals. But leading scholars of medieval political theory have denied that this was the case. They contend that Gregory's conception of his authority was merely that of *pastor of the Christian flock*, and that he never claimed an unlimited right to create and depose secular rulers or annul their decrees. He would intervene only to protect the interests of the church and the religious rights of Christians.[2] Naturally, this was a rather extensive authority, but it would still fall short of the right to rule as an autocrat over the whole world.

SECULAR vs. SPIRITUAL AUTHORITIES

The struggle between Gregory VII and Henry IV

The quarrel between Henry and Gregory was one of the most bitter in the Middle Ages. When Henry refused to obey decrees of the Pope prohibiting lay investiture, Gregory threatened to excommunicate him. The king retaliated by denouncing the Pope as a false monk and ordering him to descend from the throne "to be damned throughout the ages." Whereupon Gregory not only excommunicated Henry but declared his throne vacant and released all his subjects from allegiance to him. Faced with revolt by his vassals, Henry had no alternative but to make peace with the Pope. How he journeyed over the Alps in the depth of winter to Canossa in northern Italy and implored the Pope's forgiveness is a familiar story and need not be recounted here. Later on, Henry had his revenge when he led an army into Italy, set up an anti-pope, and compelled Gregory to flee from Rome. The great apostle of reform died in exile in 1085.

Outcome of the struggle

The first stage of the conflict was brought to an end by the Concordat of Worms, an agreement ratified by a meeting of German princes and clergy and papal legates in 1122. The settlement was a compromise providing that in the future bishops should be invested with the symbols of their political authority by the king and should take an oath of fealty to him as his vassals, but the archbishop was to have the right to invest them with the symbols of their spiritual functions. It was not long, however, until the struggle was re-

The compromise of 1122 and the beginning of the second stage of the struggle

[2] *Cf.* C. H. McIlwain, *The Growth of Political Thought in the West*, pp. 208 ff.

Shrine of the Three Kings, Cologne Cathedral. Richly decorated shrines are one of the principal forms of interior ornamentation in Gothic cathedrals. The cathedral of Cologne (Köln) in western Germany contains the Shrine of the Three Kings, or the Three Wise Men of the East, who are supposed to have brought gifts to the infant Jesus. According to legend, the bones of the Three Kings were brought from Italy in the Twelfth Century by Frederick Barbarossa and buried in Cologne.

newed, this time on a much larger scale. Before it ended in the fourteenth century, nearly all of the monarchs of western Europe had been involved. Among them were the Holy Roman Emperors, Frederick Barbarossa and Frederick II; the French kings, Philip Augustus and Philip the Fair; and the English king, John. The leading contenders on the papal side were Innocent III, Innocent IV, and Boniface VIII. The issues in this second stage of the struggle were more numerous than in the first. They included localism versus centralization in Germany, the right of the Holy Roman Emperors to rule over Italy, the freedom of Italian towns from German domination, and the right of kings to tax the property of the church. Furthermore, the Popes were now extending their claims to temporal authority a degree or two beyond what had been asserted by Gregory VII. Innocent III declared that "It is the business of the pope to look after the interests of the Roman empire, since the empire derives its origin, and its final authority from the papacy." [3] Innocent IV appears to have gone a step further and to have claimed jurisdiction over all temporal affairs and over all human beings, whether Christians or not. Nevertheless, it must be borne in mind that none of these Popes was really demanding absolute power. What they were insisting upon was not a legislative but a judicial authority; in other words, an authority to judge and punish rulers for their sins. The fundamental issue was whether rulers were directly responsible to God for their official acts or indirectly through the Pope.

The second stage of the conflict had momentous results not only for medieval Europe but for subsequent ages as well. For a time the Popes were almost uniformly successful. With the aid of the Lom-

Results of the second stage

[3] O. J. Thatcher and E. H. McNeal, *A Source Book for Medieval History*, p. 220.

bard cities and the rebellious dukes in Germany, they checked the ambitions of the Holy Roman Emperors and finally broke the power of the Empire entirely. By means of interdicts Innocent III compelled Philip Augustus to take back the wife he had repudiated and forced King John to recognize England and Ireland as fiefs of the papacy. At the beginning of the fourteenth century, however, Boniface VIII went down to humiliating defeat at the hands of King Philip the Fair of France. As the outcome of a quarrel over Philip's attempt to tax the property of the church, Boniface was taken prisoner by the king's soldiers, and a month later he died. The Archbishop of Bordeaux was chosen to succeed him, and the papal capital was transferred to Avignon in France, where it remained for seventy years. But there were other results also. Many pious Christians now came to believe that the Popes were carrying their ambitions for political power too far and were forgetting their spiritual functions. As a consequence, the papacy lost prestige, and the way was opened for repudiation of its leadership even in religious affairs. In like manner, papal meddling in the internal politics of different countries tended to strengthen the growth of nationalism, particularly in England and France. Finally, the struggle led to a quickening of intellectual activity. As each side attempted to justify its position, interest was awakened in ancient writings, an incentive was provided for the study of the Roman law, and many valuable contributions were made to political theory.

3. The Crusades

It is probably not inaccurate to regard the Crusades as the chief expression of medieval imperialism. Unfortunately it appears to be true that nearly every civilization sooner or later develops expansionist tendencies. Certain ones, of course, have been much worse offenders than others, but imperialism in some degree has been characteristic of nearly all of them. It seems to be the natural fruit of the increasing complexity of economic life and of the growth of pride in the real or fancied superiority of a system.

The Crusades an expression of medieval imperialism

Although the Crusades were by no means a religious movement exclusively, there can be no denying the importance of the religious factor in producing them. The century in which they were launched was an age when religion occupied a predominant place in men's thinking. The medieval Christian had a deep conviction of sin. He feared its consequences in the form of eternal damnation and was anxious to avert them by acts of penance. For hundreds of years the most popular type of penance had been the making of pilgrimages to sacred places. A trip to the Holy Land, if at all possible, had been the cherished ambition of every Christian. By the eleventh century the religious revivalism generated by the Cluniac reform movement, combined with the opening up of trade with the Near

The religious causes of the Crusades: (1) mass pilgrimages

East, had made pilgrimages to Palestine especially appealing. Hundreds of people now joined the roving bands that trailed across central and eastern Europe on their way to the Levant. In 1065 the Bishop of Bamberg led a horde of seven thousand Germans to visit the holy places in and around Jerusalem. Of course, not everyone who joined these mass migrations was inspired by religious ardor. Pilgrimages afforded an opportunity for adventure and sometimes even for profit. Besides, what better chance need one want to escape the responsibilities of life for a season and have a good time in the bargain? Every pilgrim who returned brought back stories of the wonderful sights he had seen and thereby aroused the desire of others to follow his example. Without these mass pilgrimages interest in conquest of the Holy Land would probably never have developed.

(2) religious wars as means of promoting unity

Other religious causes must also be mentioned. For a time during the late eleventh century, prospects for papal supremacy did not look too bright. Gregory VII had been driven from the throne and had died in exile in 1085. His successor was an aged friend who went to his grave after a year of failure. The cardinals then chose a younger and more vigorous man, who adopted the name of Urban II. Urban had been a French noble who had renounced the world to become a monk at Cluny. Subsequently he became the talented assistant of Gregory VII. Elected Pope himself in 1088, he turned his attention to the glorious dream of uniting all classes of Christians in support of the church. Perhaps he might even force a reunion of the Eastern and Western branches of Christendom. At any rate, a war against the infidel, for the rescue of the Holy Places from desecration, would enable Latin Christians to forget their differences and to rally behind the Pope. Already the papacy had inspired or given its blessing to wars on behalf of religion. Predecessors of Urban II had blessed the Norman conquest of England, the campaigns of Robert Guiscard against heretical Greeks in Italy, and the wars of Christians against Moors in Spain. To merge these efforts in a grand enterprise against the whole unbelieving world must have seemed but a logical climax to what had already occurred.

(3) other religious causes

For more than a century the religious leaders in Europe had been disturbed by the prevalence of fighting among the feudal nobles. Despite the Peace of God and the Truce of God, the warfare of barons and knights continued to be a menace to the security of the church. The rights of clergy, peasants, and other noncombatants were often trampled upon, merchants were robbed, and religious edifices pillaged and burned. Against these depredations the penalty of excommunication was of little avail. Small wonder, therefore, that Popes should have turned to the idea of protecting the church and its members by diverting the military ardor of the nobles into a holy war against the heathen. Still another religious cause was surplus idealism left over from the New Cluny movement. Move-

356

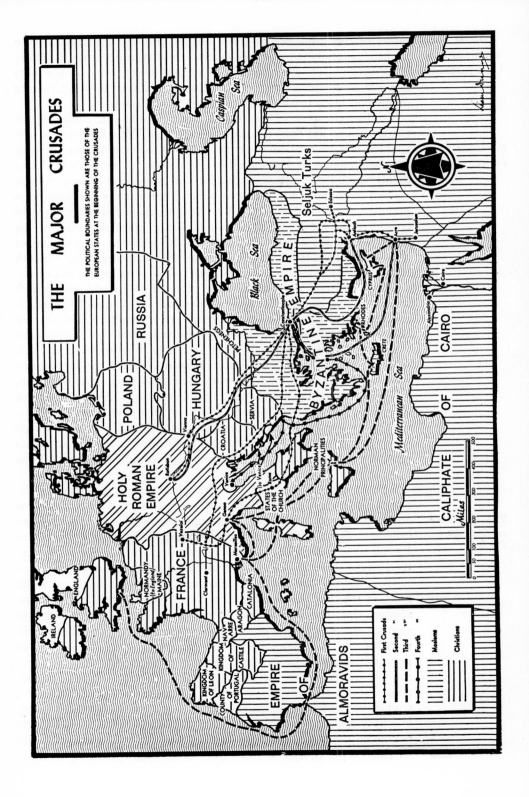

ments of this kind, which strike deeply into the emotional nature of man, generally stir up more enthusiasm than is necessary for their immediate objectives. Some of this surplus must then find new outlets, just as in later years the fanaticism engendered by the Crusades themselves burst forth into persecution of the Jews.

Economic causes

To discover some of the most important economic causes of the Crusades, one has only to read the speech of Pope Urban II at the Council of Clermont inviting the nobles of France to take up arms for the conquest of Palestine. He urged them to let nothing detain them, "since this land which you inhabit, shut in on all sides by the sea and surrounded by mountain peaks, is too narrow for your large population; nor does it abound in wealth; and it furnishes scarcely enough food for its cultivators. . . . Enter upon the road to the Holy Sepulchre; wrest that land from the wicked race and subject it to yourselves. That land which, as the Scripture says, 'floweth with milk and honey,' was given by God into the possession of the children of Israel. Jerusalem is the navel of the world; the land is fruitful above others, like another paradise of delights." [4] There is evidence also that the manorial system of agriculture was already beginning to impair the fertility of the soil, with the consequence that a good many nobles had fallen into debt. Furthermore, the rule of primogeniture in France and in England created the problem of what to do with the younger sons. New fiefs were hard to obtain, and positions in the church were becoming scarce. As a result, these surplus offspring of the nobles tended to form a rebellious and disorderly class, alert for any opportunity to despoil a weak neighbor of his property. Confronted by such problems as these, the nobles of western Europe needed no second invitation to respond to Pope Urban's plea.

The immediate cause of the Crusades

The immediate cause of the Crusades was the advance of the Seljuk Turks in the Near East. In about 1050 these people had come down into western Asia and had gained control over the Baghdad caliphate. Soon afterward they conquered Syria, Palestine, and Egypt. In 1071 they slaughtered a Byzantine army at Manzikert and then swept through Asia Minor and captured Nicaea, within a few miles of Constantinople. After the death of the great Sultan, Malik Shah, in 1092 the Seljuk empire began to disintegrate. The time now seemed ripe for the Byzantine emperor, Alexius Comnenus, to attempt the reconquest of his lost possessions. Realizing the difficulty of this task, since his own government was exhausted from previous struggles, he sent an appeal in 1095 to the Pope, probably for aid in recruiting mercenary soldiers. Urban II, the reigning pontiff, took full advantage of this opportunity. He summoned a council of French nobles and clergy at Clermont and exhorted them in a fiery speech to make war upon the accursed race of Turks. He employed every artful device of eloquence to arouse the fury and

[4] Thatcher and McNeal, *A Source Book for Medieval History*, pp. 519–20.

cupidity of his hearers, emphasizing especially the horrible atrocities which he declared the Turks were committing upon Christians. When he had finished, it is reported that all who were present cried out with one accord, "It is the will of God," and rushed forward to take the crusader's oath. The appeal of Urban II was supplemented soon after the Council of Clermont by the impassioned preaching of Peter the Hermit, who went among the peasants rousing them to a frenzied enthusiasm for the holy cause. In the spring of 1096 he led a great mob of them from France and Germany to Constantinople. Most of his followers were ignorant, poorly equipped, and totally untrained for war. When they began looting in the Byzantine capital, the emperor promptly shipped them across the Bosporus into Asia Minor where the Turks made short work of them.

The first of the organized Crusades was not actually started until late in 1096. The majority of those who participated in it were Frenchmen and Normans, under the leadership of Godfrey of Bouillon, Count Raymond of Toulouse, and Bohemund from the Norman kingdom of Sicily. Altogether, between 1096 and 1244, three other major Crusades and a number of minor ones were launched. Only the first achieved much success in destroying Turkish control over Christian territory. By 1098 most of Syria had been captured, and a year later Jerusalem was taken. But these gains were only temporary. In 1187 Jerusalem was recaptured by the Moslems under Saladin, Sultan of Egypt. Before the end of the thirteenth century every one of the petty states established by the crusaders in the Near East had been wiped out.

The major Crusades

The ultimate failure of the Crusades resulted from several causes. To begin with, the expeditions were frequently badly managed; there was seldom any unified command, and rival leaders quarreled among themselves. Further, the victorious armies were always surrounded by an enormous alien population, a fact which increased the difficulty of holding conquered territory. In some of the later expeditions the original purpose of conquering the Holy Land from the Turks was lost sight of altogether. The Fourth Crusade, for example, turned out to be a gigantic plundering foray against Constantinople. But there was also another cause which cannot be overlooked, and that was the conflicting ambitions of the East and the West. According to the evidence, Alexius Comnenus, in appealing to the Pope for aid, professed a desire to protect the Christian churches of the Orient. But this was not his primary objective. He had come to the conclusion that the time was ripe for a major offensive against the Turks. He was not interested simply or even primarily in driving them out of the Holy Land but in reconquering all of the Asiatic provinces of his empire. By contrast, Pope Urban II had the grandiose dream of a holy war of all of Latin Christendom to expel the infidel from Palestine. His underlying purpose was not to rescue the Byzantine Empire but to strengthen Latin

Reasons for the failure of the Crusades

Christianity, to exalt the papacy, and perhaps to restore the union of the Eastern and Western churches. An additional cause of friction between East and West was the ambition of Italian merchants to extend their commercial empire. They coveted the trade that passed through Constantinople and were ready to capture or destroy the city for their own advantage.

*The importance
of the Crusades
not to
be exaggerated*

In line with a common tendency to overestimate the importance of wars, the Crusades were at one time considered as the primary cause of nearly all of European progress in the late Feudal Age. It was assumed that they led to the growth of cities, to the overthrow of feudalism, and to the introduction of Moslem philosophy and science into Latin Europe. Most historians now regard this assumption as of limited validity, for several reasons. First, the progress of civilization in the Feudal Age was already well under way before the Crusades began. Second, the educated classes in Europe did not generally take part in the military expeditions; as a result, the soldiers who actually went were totally devoid of the intellectual background necessary for an appreciation of Moslem learning. Third, very few of the armies ever reached the real centers of Moslem civilization, which were not Jerusalem or Antioch, but Baghdad, Damascus, Toledo, and Cordova. European intellectual progress in the twelfth and thirteenth centuries was due far more to the revival of trade with the Near East and to the work of scholars and translators in Spain and Sicily than to any influence of holy wars against the Turks. Nor were the Crusades primarily responsible for the political and economic changes at the end of the Middle Ages. The decline of feudalism, for instance, occurred chiefly because of the Black Death, the growth of an urban economy, and the rise of national monarchies; and these in turn were only in minor degree the results of the Crusades.

*The actual
results of
the Crusades*

What effects, then, is it possible to ascribe to the great holy wars against Islam? To some extent they hastened the emancipation of the common people. Nobles who were hard pressed for money sold privileges to townsmen and to communities of serfs somewhat earlier than they would otherwise have done. Furthermore, many peasants took advantage of the absence of the nobles to break away from bondage to the soil. Among other economic effects were an increased demand for products of the East, the growth of banking, and the elimination of Constantinople as the middleman in the trade between East and West. Venice, Genoa, and Pisa now gained a virtual monopoly of commerce in the Mediterranean area. In addition, the Crusades had some influence in strengthening the monarchies of France and England by eliminating powerful nobles and providing a pretext for direct taxation; but the political consequences were relatively slight. In the domain of religion, where we would normally expect the most profound results, few except negative effects can be discovered. It is impossible to prove that the Popes

French Knights about to Depart on a Crusade. Their chief weapons are the long bow and the spear.

enjoyed any increase in power or repute as a result of having launched the Crusades. On the contrary, as the true character of the expeditions became more and more transparent, the papacy seems rather to have suffered a loss of prestige. There was, however, an increase in religious fanaticism, which expressed itself particularly in savage persecution of the Jews. These unfortunate people suffered nearly everywhere. They were cruelly beaten and sometimes killed in mob attacks. Naturally, the fury against them was partly economic in origin, since they were the chief moneylenders of the time; nevertheless, it is a significant fact that hostility to Jews had one of its chief sources in the holy wars against Islam. Finally, it is doubtless true that the Crusades had some effect in widening geographic knowledge and in encouraging travel and exploration; but these developments were the result even more of the gradual expansion of trade.

4. The Late Medieval Mind

The beginning of intellectual progress in the Feudal Age dates from the so-called Carolingian Renaissance of the ninth century. This was a movement initiated by Charles the Great when he brought to his court at Aachen the most distinguished scholars he could find. In doing this the emperor was prompted partly by his own interest in learning but also by his desire to find uniform standards of orthodoxy which could be imposed upon all of his subjects. Fortunately he seems to have allowed the scholars he imported a generous freedom to pursue their own inclinations. The

The revival of learning in western Europe

361

result was a revival of learning which gathered sufficient momentum to carry over into the reigns of several of Charlemagne's successors. Among the leaders in the movement were Alcuin, director of the palace school; John Scotus Erigena, the rationalist philosopher; and Walafrid Strabo, the poet. After the Carolingian Renaissance intellectual progress in western Europe was comparatively slow for some time. A brief revival under the patronage of the Ottos in Germany in the tenth century was followed by a more virile growth of classical studies in Italy and France after the year 1000. But the climax of intellectual achievement in the Feudal Age was not reached until the twelfth and thirteenth centuries.

Scholasticism

I. PHILOSOPHY The outstanding philosophic achievement of the late Middle Ages was the famous system of thought known as Scholasticism. This system is usually defined as the attempt to harmonize reason and faith or to make philosophy serve the interests of theology. But no such definition is sufficient to convey an adequate conception of the Scholastic mind. The great thinkers of the Middle Ages did not limit their interests to problems of religion. On the contrary, they were just as anxious as philosophers in any period to answer the great questions of life, whether they pertained to religion, politics, economics, or metaphysics. Perhaps the best way to explain the true nature of Scholasticism is to define it in terms of its characteristics. In the first place, it was rationalistic, not empirical; in other words, it was based primarily upon logic rather than upon science or experience. The Scholastic philosophers, like the Greek thinkers of the Socratic school, did not believe that the highest truth could be derived from sense perception. They admitted that the senses could provide man with a knowledge of the appearances of things, but they maintained that reality or the essential nature of the universe is discoverable mainly by reason. In the second place, Scholastic philosophy was authoritarian. Even reason was not considered a sufficient instrument for the discovery of all knowledge, but the deductions of logic needed to be buttressed by the authority of the Scriptures, of the Church Fathers, and especially of Plato and Aristotle. Third, Scholastic philosophy had a predominantly ethical approach. Its cardinal aim was to discover how man could improve this life and insure salvation in the life to come. The Scholastic philosopher was a humanist to the extent that he was interested primarily in man. His universe was a compact and ordered whole created for the benefit of the human race. Fourth, Scholastic thought, unlike modern philosophy, was not mainly concerned with causes and underlying relationships; its purpose was rather to discover the attributes of things; the universe was assumed to be static, and therefore it was only necessary to explain the meaning of things and what they were good for, not to account for their origin and evolution.

The primary development of the Scholastic philosophy began

with the teachings of Peter Abelard (1079–1142), one of the most significant figures in the history of thought. This handsome and talented Frenchman was educated in the best schools of Paris and gained a wide reputation for dialectical skill before he was out of his twenties. For a number of years he taught in Paris, drawing great crowds to his lectures on philosophy and theology. Despite the fact that he was a monk, his habits of life were far from ascetic. He was proud, belligerent, and egotistical—boastful of his intellectual triumphs and even of his prowess in love. He avowed that he possessed such advantages of comeliness and youth that "he feared no repulse from whatever woman he might deign to honor with his love." His tragic affair with Heloïse, which he poignantly describes in his autobiography, *The Story of My Misfortunes*, finally brought his downfall. But as a philosopher Abelard had accomplishments to his credit for which he had a right to be proud. He was probably the most critical of all the medieval thinkers. In his most famous philosophical work, *Sic et Non* (*Yes and No*), he exposed many of the shabby arguments from authority that were commonly accepted in his time. The preface to this work contains a statement which expresses clearly his conviction of the vital importance of critical reasoning: "For the first key to wisdom is called interrogation, diligent and unceasing. . . . By doubting we are led to inquiry; and from inquiry we perceive the truth."

The heyday of Scholasticism came in the thirteenth century, as a result mainly of the labors of Albertus Magnus and his renowned pupil, St. Thomas Aquinas. These men had the advantage of being able to study most of the works of Aristotle, recently translated from copies in the possession of the Saracens. Albertus Magnus, the only scholar ever to be honored with the title of Great, was born in Germany in 1193. During a long and active career he served as a teacher, especially at Cologne and at the University of Paris. A profound admirer of Aristotle, he strove to emulate the example of that ancient master by taking the whole field of knowledge as his province. His writings included more than twenty volumes on subjects ranging from botany and physiology to the soul and the creation of the universe. He was often skeptical of ancient authorities, and he attempted to found his conclusions upon reason and experience. In referring to hoary myths, such as the one about ostriches eating iron, he would frequently say: "but this is not proved by experience." He defined natural science "as not simply receiving what one is told, but the investigation of causes in natural phenomena." [5]

Thomas Aquinas, the most noted of all the Scholastic philosophers, was born in southern Italy about 1225. Following the example of the great Albert, he entered the Dominican order and devoted his life

[5] Lynn Thorndike, *A History of Magic and Experimental Science*, Vol. II, ch. 59.

to teaching. He was a professor at the University of Paris by the time he was twenty-five. His most famous work was his *Summary of Theology*, but he wrote on many other subjects as well, including politics and economics. The fundamental aims of St. Thomas were, first, to demonstrate the rationality of the universe, and second, to establish the primacy of reason. He believed that the universe is an ordered whole governed by intelligent purpose. All things were created in order to make possible the fulfillment of the great Christian plan for the promotion of justice and peace on earth and the salva-

St. Thomas Aquinas (*ca.* 1225-1274).

tion of mankind in a world to come. The philosophy of St. Thomas implied a serene confidence in the ability of man to know and understand his world. The great *Summaries* he wrote were attempts to build up out of logic and the wisdom of the past comprehensive systems of knowledge which would leave no mysteries unsolved. Though he leaned very heavily upon the authority of Aristotle, he regarded reason as the primary key to truth. Even his attitude toward religion was essentially intellectual rather than emotional; piety to him was a matter of knowledge much more than of faith. He admitted that a few doctrines of Christianity, such as the belief in the Trinity and the creation of the world in time, could not be proved by the intellect; but he denied that they were contrary to reason, for God Himself is a rational being. As a disciple of Aristotle, St. Thomas taught that the highest good for man is the realization of his true nature; this, he maintained, consists in the knowledge of God, which can be attained in large measure by reason in this life, but will be perfectly realized only in the hereafter. The influence

of St. Thomas was not only of cardinal importance in his own time, but it survives to this day. In the late nineteenth century Pope Leo XIII exhorted the bishops of the church "to restore the golden wisdom of St. Thomas and to spread it far and wide for the defense of the faith, for the good of society, and for the advantage of all the sciences." He recommended St. Thomas as a master and guide for everyone interested in scholarly studies.

By the end of the thirteenth century Scholasticism had begun to decline. Its decay was due partly to the teachings of the last of the Scholastics, John Duns Scotus. A member of the Franciscan order, *The decay of* Duns Scotus was inclined to emphasize the emotional and practical *Scholasticism* side of religion in place of the intellectual. He conceived of piety as an act of will rather than an act of intellect. Less confident of the powers of reason than St. Thomas, he excluded a large number of the doctrines of religion from the sphere of philosophy altogether. From this it was only a step to denial that any religious beliefs were capable of rational demonstration; all would have to be accepted on faith or rejected entirely. When this step was finally taken by Duns Scotus' successors, the overthrow of Scholasticism was speedily accomplished.

The other main reason for the decline of Scholasticism was the growing popularity of nominalism. Although nominalism is often considered a branch of Scholasticism, actually the nominalists were *The growth of* fundamentally opposed to nearly everything the Scholastics taught. *nominalism* They denied that concepts or class names have any reality, insisting that they are nothing but abstractions invented by the mind to express the qualities common to a number of objects or organisms. Only individual things are real. Far from accepting the Scholastic confidence in reason, the nominalists contended that all knowledge has its source in experience. Anything beyond the realm of concrete experience must be taken on faith, if it is to be accepted at all; the truths of religion cannot be demonstrated by logic. Although some of the earlier nominalists inclined toward religious skepticism, the majority became mystics. Nominalism flourished in the fourteenth century and for some time was the most popular philosophy in western Europe. Its ablest exponent was the English Franciscan, William of Occam. Nominalism is especially important for having laid the foundations for the scientific progress of the Renaissance and for the mystical religious movements which helped to bring on the Protestant Revolution.

A good many medieval philosophers devoted earnest attention to questions of political authority; a few, in fact, were primarily concerned with such questions. The political theorists of the Feudal *The political* Age were in substantial agreement on a large part of their philosophy. *theory of the* phy. Practically all of them had abandoned the idea of the Church Fathers *Feudal Age* thers that the state was established by God as a remedy for sin, and that men must therefore render faithful obedience even to the tyrant. It was now commonly held that the state is a product of man's social nature, and that when justice is the guiding principle of the ruler, government is a positive good, not a necessary evil. In the second place, it was generally agreed by the philosophers of the Feudal Age that all of western Europe should constitute a single commonwealth under one supreme ruler. There might be many subordinate kings or princes in the different parts of the continent, but one supreme overlord, either the Pope or the Holy Roman Emperor, should have the highest jurisdiction. The most noted of those who defended the supremacy of the Emperor was Dante in his *De Monarchia*. On the papal side were the Englishman John of Salisbury (*ca.* 1115–1180) and Thomas Aquinas. Virtually without exception the political theorists of the Feudal Age believed in limited government. They had no use for absolutism in any form. John of Salisbury even went so far as to defend the right of the subjects of a tyrant to put him to death. Practically all of late medieval theory was based upon the assumption that the authority of every ruler, whether Pope, Emperor, or king, was essentially judicial in character. His function was merely to apply the law, not to make or alter it in accordance with his will. Indeed, the medievalists did not conceive of law as the command of a sovereign at all, but as the product of custom or of the divine order of nature. On the other hand, the medieval political theorists were not democrats, for not one of them believed in the doctrine of majority rule. The man who came closest to an exposition of the democratic ideal was Marsiglio of Padua in the fourteenth century. He advocated that the people should have the right to elect the monarch and even to depose him if necessary. He believed also in a representative body with power to make laws. But Marsiglio was no champion of unlimited popular sovereignty. In fact, he defined democracy as a degraded form of government. His idea of representative government was representation of the citizens according to quality rather than mere numbers, and the law-making powers of his representative body would be confined to the enactment of statutes regulating the structure of the government.

Opposition to absolutism

II. SCIENCE The record of scientific achievements in the Feudal Age can scarcely be considered an imposing one. Yet it was probably about all we should expect in view of the absorption of interest in other fields. The names of only a few individual scientists need to be mentioned. One of the most original was Adelard of Bath, who lived in the early years of the twelfth century. Not only did he condemn reliance upon authority, but he devoted many years of his life to direct investigation of nature. He discovered some important facts about the causes of earthquakes, the functions of different parts of the brain, and the processes of breathing and digestion. He was probably the first scientist since the Hellenistic Age to affirm the indestructibility of matter.

The Feudal Age not a great age of science

The toughest-minded of all the medieval scientists was the notori-

Alchemists in Their Laboratory. Note the great variety of instruments used and the spectacles worn by the experimenter.

ous Holy Roman Emperor, Frederick II, whose reign occupied the first part of the thirteenth century. Frederick was skeptical of almost everything. He denied the immortality of the soul, and he was accused of having written a brochure entitled *Jesus, Moses and Mohammed: The Three Great Impostors*. But he was not satisfied merely to scoff. He performed various experiments of his own to gratify his boundless curiosity, testing the artificial incubation of eggs, for example, and sealing the eyes of vultures to determine whether they found their food by sight or by smell. He was even alleged to have shut a man up in a wine-cask in an effort to prove that the soul dies with the body. His most important scientific contributions were made, however, as a patron of learning. An ardent admirer of Moslem culture, he brought distinguished scholars to Palermo to translate the writings of the Saracens into Latin. He subsidized leading scientists, especially Leonard of Pisa, the most brilliant mathematician of the thirteenth century. In addition, Frederick instituted measures for the improvement of medical practice. He legalized the practice of dissection, established a system of examining and licensing physicians, and founded the University of Naples with one of the best medical schools in Europe.

Frederick II as a scientist

By far the best known of medieval scientists was Roger Bacon (*ca.* 1214–1294), possibly because he predicted certain modern inventions such as horseless carriages and flying machines. In reality, Bacon was much less critical than Frederick II; for he believed that all knowledge must enhance the glory of theology, the queen of the sciences. Moreover, Adelard of Bath preceded him by more than a century in advocating and using the experimental method. Nevertheless, Bacon, by virtue of his strong insistence upon accurate investigation, deserves a high place among medieval scientists. He

Roger Bacon

367

denied that either reason or authority could furnish valid knowledge unless supported by experimental research. Besides, he himself did some practical work of great value. His writings on optics remained authoritative for several centuries. He discovered much about magnifying lenses, and it seems more than probable that he invented the simple microscope. Not only was he the best geographer of the Feudal Age, but he was also apparently the first scientist to perceive the inaccuracy of the Julian calendar and to advocate its revision.

III. EDUCATION Much of the advancement in philosophy and science in the late Middle Ages would have been quite impossible without the educational progress which marked the centuries from the ninth to the fourteenth. The Carolingian Renaissance resulted in the establishment of better schools and libraries in several of the monasteries of western Europe. As a consequence of the religious reform movements of the eleventh century, however, the monasteries tended to neglect education, with the result that the monastic educational institutions were gradually overshadowed by the cathedral schools. Some of the latter developed into what would now be considered the equivalent of colleges, providing excellent instruction in the so-called liberal arts. This was notably true of the cathedral schools located at Canterbury, Chartres, and Paris. But by far the most important educational development of the Middle Ages was the rise of the universities.

The transfer of education from the monasteries to the cathedral schools

The term university (from the Latin, *universitas*) originally meant a corporation or guild. In fact, many of the medieval universities were very much like craft guilds, organized for the purpose of training and licensing teachers. Gradually the word came to have the meaning of an educational institution with a school of liberal arts and one or more faculties in the professional subjects of law, medicine, and theology. No one knows which of the universities was the oldest. It may have been Salerno, which was a center of medical study as far back as the tenth century. The universities of Bologna and Paris are also very ancient, the former having been established about 1150 and the latter before the end of the twelfth century. The next oldest included such famous institutions as the universities of Oxford, Cambridge, Montpellier, Salamanca, Rome, and Naples. There were no universities in Germany until the end of the fourteenth century, when schools of this type were organized at Prague, Vienna, Heidelberg, and Cologne. By the end of the Middle Ages some eighty universities had been set up in western Europe.

The rise of the universities

Practically every university in medieval Europe was patterned after one or the other of two different models. Throughout Italy, Spain, and southern France the standard was generally the University of Bologna, in which the students themselves constituted the guild or corporation. They hired the teachers, paid their salaries, and fined or discharged them for neglect of duty or inefficient

Organization of the medieval universities

368

A Noted Teacher, Henricus de Alemania, Lecturing in a Medieval University. Some interesting comparisons and contrasts may be observed between his students and those in a modern classroom.

instruction. Nearly all of these southern institutions were secular in character, specializing in law or medicine. The universities of northern Europe were modeled after the one at Paris, which was not a guild of students but of teachers. It included the four faculties of arts, theology, law, and medicine, each headed by an elected dean. In the great majority of the northern universities arts and theology were the leading branches of study. Before the end of the thirteenth century separate colleges came to be established within the University of Paris. The original college was nothing more than an endowed home for poor students, but the discovery was soon made that discipline could best be preserved by having all of the students live in colleges. Eventually the colleges became centers of instruction as well as residences. While on the Continent of Europe most of these colleges have ceased to exist, in England the universities of Oxford and Cambridge still retain the pattern of federal organization copied from Paris. The colleges of which they are composed are practically independent educational units.

Though modern universities have borrowed much of their organization from their medieval prototypes, the course of study has been radically changed. No curriculum in the Middle Ages included much history or natural science, nor any great amount of mathematics or classical literature. The conservative educator of today who believes that mathematics and the classics should form the backbone of university training can find no support for his argument in the history of the medieval universities. The student in the Middle Ages was required, first of all, to spend four or five years in studying the *trivium*—grammar, rhetoric, and logic, or dialectic. If he passed his examinations he received the preliminary

The course of study

degree of bachelor of arts, which conferred no particular distinction. To assure himself a place in professional life he must devote some additional years to the pursuit of an advanced degree, such as master of arts, doctor of laws, or doctor of medicine. For the master's degree three or four years had to be given to study of the *quadrivium*—arithmetic, geometry, astronomy, and music. These subjects were not quite what their names imply now. Their content was highly philosophical; arithmetic, for example, included primarily a study of the theory of numbers, while music was concerned largely with the properties of sound. The requirements for the doctor's degree were generally more severe and included more specialized training. By the end of the Middle Ages the course for the doctorate of theology at Paris had been extended to fourteen years, and the degree could not be conferred unless the candidate was at least thirty-five years of age. Both the master's and doctor's degrees were teaching degrees; even the title of doctor of medicine meant a teacher of medicine, not a practicing physician.

The university students

The life of medieval students differed in many ways from that of their modern descendants. The student body in any one university was not a homogeneous group but was composed of diverse nationalities. The young Frenchman or German who wanted to study law would almost certainly go to Bologna or Padua, just as the young Italian with an interest in theology would probably enroll at Paris. The entire university was usually an independent community, so that the students were exempt from the jurisdiction of the political authorities. A relic of this ancient autonomy is to be found in the fact that some of the German universities still have their own jails. Very few of the medieval students had books, and there was seldom any library from which they could borrow them. As a consequence, the learning process consisted primarily in taking down copious notes on wax tablets from the master's lecture and then analyzing and discussing them afterwards. The young man's education was supposed to be acquired through logic and memory rather than from extensive reading or research. In other respects, however, student life in the Middle Ages was not so far different from what it is now. If the medieval student knew nothing of intercollegiate sports, he at least had his violent fights with the hoodlums of the town to absorb his surplus energy. In the medieval universities as in those of today there were the sharply contrasting types of sincere, intelligent scholars and frank and frivolous loafers. We hear much about radicalism and irreverence in modern colleges, but these tendencies were certainly not absent in the universities of the Middle Ages. Many of these institutions were roundly denounced as breeding places of heresy, paganism, and worldliness. It was said that young men "seek theology at Paris, law at Bologna, and medicine at Montpellier, but nowhere a life that is pleasing to God." The students at Paris even had to be admonished to stop playing dice on the altar of Notre Dame after one of their holiday celebrations.

IV. LITERATURE No one who has more than a casual acquaintance with the literature of the Feudal Age could ever imagine the whole medieval period to have been an era of darkness and otherworldliness. For much of this literature expresses a humanism, a zest for living, as spontaneous, joyous, and gay as any attitude revealed in the writings of the Renaissance of the fourteenth and succeeding centuries. Indeed, the spirit of late medieval literature was even closer to that of the modern age than most people realize. Probably the actual amount of religious literature in the Feudal Age did not bear a much larger ratio to the total quantity of writings produced than would be true at the present time.

Late medieval writings can be classified, first of all, as either Latin or vernacular literature. The revival of classical studies in the cathedral schools and in the earliest universities led to the production of some excellent Latin poetry. The best examples of this were the secular lyrics, especially those written by a group of poets known as the Goliards or Goliardi. The Goliards derived their name from the fact that they commonly referred to themselves as disciples of Golias. Who Golias was, no one knows, but Professor Haskins thinks that he was probably the devil.[6] Such a choice of a master would undoubtedly have been appropriate enough, for most of the Goliard poets were regarded by the church as lewd fellows of the baser sort for whom nothing was too sacred to be ridiculed. They wrote parodies of the creeds, travesties of the mass, and even burlesques of the Gospels. Their lyrics were purely pagan in spirit, celebrating the beauties of the changing seasons, the carefree life of the open road, the pleasures of drinking and gambling, and especially the joys of love. The authors of these rollicking and satirical songs were mostly wandering students, although some appear to have been men more advanced in years. The names of nearly all of them are unknown. Their poetry is particularly significant as the first emphatic protest against the ascetic ideal of Christianity. The following stanzas taken from *The Confession of Golias* may be considered typical of what they wrote:

> Prelate, most discreet of priests,
> Grant me absolution!
> Dear's the death whereof I die,
> Sweet my dissolution;
> For my heart is wounded by
> Beauty's soft suffusion;
> All the girls I come not nigh
> Mine are in illusion.
>
> 'Tis most arduous to make

[6] C. H. Haskins, *The Renaissance of the Twelfth Century*, p. 177.

Nature's self-surrender;
Seeing girls, to blush and be
Purity's defender!
We young men our longings ne'er
Shall to stern law render,
Or preserve our fancies from
Bodies smooth and tender.[7]

The growth of vernacular literature

By no means all of medieval literature was written in Latin. As the Feudal Age advanced, the vernacular languages of French, German, Spanish, English, and Italian became increasingly popular as media of literary expression. Until the beginning of the twelfth century nearly all of the literature in the vernacular languages assumed the form of the heroic epic. Among the leading examples were the French *Song of Roland,* the German *Song of the Nibelungs,* the eddas and sagas of the Norsemen, and the Spanish *Poem of My Cid.* These epics picture a virile but unpolished feudal society in its earlier stage of evolution, when valorous deeds in battle on behalf of one's suzerain represented the fulfillment of the highest knightly ideal. Heroism, honor, and loyalty were practically the exclusive themes. The tone of the epics was almost entirely masculine. If women were mentioned at all, it was generally in a condescending fashion. The hero must show the utmost devotion to his superior, but it was not considered inappropriate that he should beat his wife.

The literature of chivalry: (1) the songs of the troubadours

During the twelfth and thirteenth centuries feudal society in western Europe attained the full flower of its growth. As a result of the progress of learning and of contact with the higher civilization of the Moslems the feudal aristocracy adopted new attitudes and interests. Chivalry, with its glorification of woman and its emphasis upon kindness and refinement of manners, tended to displace the older conception of a feudal ideal limited to the virtues of the battlefield. The first literary works to reflect and in part to inspire this change in ideals were the songs of the troubadours. The original home of the troubadours was southern France, especially the region known as Provence. Here was one of the most highly civilized areas of feudal Europe. It received the full impact of Saracenic influence from Spain, and it seems to have preserved an extensive inheritance from ancient Rome. The prevailing religion of Provence was an outgrowth of Manicheism, embodied in the teachings of an heretical Christian sect called the Albigenses. Perhaps the spirit of religious independence had something to do with the vigor and originality of the culture. Whatever the reasons, there can be no doubt that the troubadours of Provence initiated a movement of profound importance in late medieval literature. The central theme of their songs was romantic love. Woman was idealized now as never

[7] J. A. Symonds, *Wine, Women and Song,* p. 66.

before. The virtues of her who had once been condemned by monks and church fathers as the very incarnation of evil were extolled to the skies. But the love of the troubadours for the ladies of the feudal courts was not supposed to be sensual; it was a rarefied, almost mystical emotion which could be satisfied by a smile or some trifling memento from the haughty goddesses who were the objects of the singers' affection. The fact must be emphasized also that romantic love was not the only topic in which the troubadours were interested. Many of them wrote acrid satires against the rapacity and hypocrisy of the clergy, and one even addressed a powerful "poem of blame" to God. The literary tradition originated by the troubadours was continued by the *trouvères* in northern France and by the *minne-singers* in Germany.

The most important of all the writings which expressed the ideals of the feudal aristocracy were the romances of the Arthurian cycle. The material of these romances consisted of legends woven about the career of a Celtic chieftain by the name of Arthur, who had *(2) the ro-* been the hero of the struggle against the Anglo-Saxon invaders of *mances of the* Britain. In the twelfth century certain Norman and French writers, *Arthurian cycle* especially Marie de France and Chrétien de Troyes, became interested in these legends as a background for the chivalric ideal. The result was the composition of a number of romances of love and adventure, famous alike for their colorful narrative and their poetic beauty. Later the best known of these romances were adapted and completed by German poets. Wolfram von Eschenbach developed what is usually considered the most perfect version of the Parzival legend, while Gottfried von Strassburg gave to the story of Tristram and Iseult its classic medieval form. Although these romances differed in form and in substance, they may yet be said to have had certain features in common. All of them glorified adventure for its own sake, and taught that experience of the deepest and most varied kind is the only sure road to wisdom. All of them strove to inculcate gentleness, protection of the weak, and rescue of those in distress as knightly obligations, in addition to honor, truthfulness, and bravery. The redeeming power of love was another universal element, although not all of the authors agreed as to the form which this love should assume. Some maintained that it ought to be the faithful affection between husband and wife, but others insisted that it must be love unsustained by wedlock. In the minds of the latter group true love was possible only between knight and mistress, never between husband and wife. Finally, in the best of these romances an element of tragedy was nearly always present. Indeed, such a work as Gottfried von Strassburg's *Tristan* might almost be regarded as the prototype of modern tragic literature. He was certainly one of the first to develop the idea of individual suffering as a literary theme and to point out the indistinct dividing line which separates pleasure from pain. For him, to love is to yearn, and suffering and death are integral chapters of the book of life.

By the thirteenth century the merchants and craftsmen of the towns had risen to a position of power and influence equal if not superior to that of the feudal nobles. We can therefore logically expect that some literature would be written to appeal to burgher tastes. Among the foremost examples of such writings were the romance of *Aucassin and Nicolette* and the short stories in verse known as the *fabliaux*. The romance of *Aucassin and Nicolette* resembles in some ways the romances of chivalry. The hero Aucassin is a young noble, and the main theme of the romance is the imperious demands of love; but the plot is frequently turned into channels distinctly at variance with the chivalric ideal. Aucassin has fallen desperately in love, not with the high-born wife of some noble, but with Nicolette, a Saracen slave girl. Warned that he will suffer in hell if he does not give up his beloved, the hero replies that he does not mind, for in hell he will enjoy the company of all who have really lived. The story is also quite different from the romances of chivalry in its occasional expression of sympathy for the peasant. But the writings which undoubtedly made the strongest appeal to the urban classes were the *fabliaux*. These were stories written not to edify or instruct but chiefly to amuse. Often richly spiced with indecency, they reveal a contempt for the trappings of chivalry, with its romanticized love and idiotic pursuit of adventure. Most of them are also strongly anti-clerical and indicate no high regard for the religious spirit. Nearly always it is monks and priests who are made the butts of the jokes. The *fabliaux* are significant as expressions of the growing worldliness of the urban classes and as forerunners of the robust realism which was later to appear in the works of such writers as Chaucer and Boccaccio.

The supreme achievements of medieval literary talent were two great masterpieces written in the thirteenth and fourteenth centuries. The first was the *Romance of the Rose* of William of Lorris and John of Meun, and the second was Dante's *Divine Comedy*. Each in its own way is a kind of summary of late medieval civilization. The *Romance of the Rose* consists of two parts: the first four thousand lines were begun by William of Lorris about 1230; the other part, nearly three times as long, was finished by John of Meun about 1265. The two parts are entirely different, the first being an allegory dealing with the cult of chivalric love, while the second is a eulogy of reason. John of Meun was quite skeptical of the value of the feudal aristocracy to medieval society; he hated superstition; and he satirized the monastic orders, the papacy, and many other established institutions of his time. He embodied the mocking, realistic attitude of the bourgeoisie, as his predecessor, William of Lorris, symbolized the romantic, mystical spirit of chivalry. The work of the two men taken together furnishes a kind of guidebook to the late Middle Ages.

Without doubt the most profound of the medieval summaries was the *Divine Comedy* of Dante Alighieri (1265–1321). Not a great deal is known about the life of Dante except that he was the son of a Florentine lawyer and was active during the early part of his career in the political affairs of his city. Despite his absorption in politics he managed to acquire a full mastery of the philosophic and literary knowledge of his time. In 1302 the party to which he belonged was ousted from power in Florence, and he was compelled to live the remainder of his years outside of his native city. Most of his writings were apparently produced during this period of exile. Dante called his chief work simply the *Comedy*, but his admirers during the Italian Renaissance always spoke of it as the *Divine Comedy*, and that is the title which has come down to us. In form the work may be considered a drama of the struggles, temptations, and ultimate redemption of the soul. But of course it is much more than this; for it embraces a complete summation of medieval culture, a magnificent synthesis of the Scholastic philosophy, the science, the religion, and the economic and ethical ideals of the high Feudal Age. Its dominant theme is the salvation of mankind through reason and divine grace, but it includes many other ideas as well. The universe is conceived as a finite world of which the earth is the center and in which everything exists for the benefit of man. All natural phenomena have their meaning in relation to the divine scheme for peace and justice on earth and salvation in the life beyond. Human beings possess free will to choose the good and avoid the evil. The worst of the sins which man can commit is treason or betrayal of trust; the least serious are those which proceed from weakness of the flesh. In many ways Dante was a humanist. He took earnest pleasure in the classical authors, almost worshiping Aristotle, Seneca, and Vergil. He chose Vergil rather than some Christian theologian to personify philosophy, and he admitted certain other distinguished pagans to very comfortable places in purgatory. Furthermore, he did not hesitate to place a number of prominent Popes in hell. By reason of his imaginative power and the warmth and vigor of his style, Dante deserves to be ranked as one of the greatest poets of all time, but he is especially important to the historian for the well-rounded picture he presents of the late medieval mind.

The Divine Comedy

5. Art and Music in the Feudal Age

If there was one tendency which medieval man strove to avoid, it was the tendency to specialize in any particular branch of achievement. He conceived of the whole field of knowledge as one, dominated by logic as the key to wisdom. Not only the universe but everything in it was created for a single purpose, the welfare of man. Unity in philosophy, in religion, in government was the pre-

The unity of the arts in the Feudal Age

Chapel of Le Grand Palais in Paris. Built in the thirteenth century, it exemplifies interior pointed arches and ribbed vaulting.

MEDIEVAL CATHEDRALS: ROMANESQUE AND GOTHIC

Worms Cathedral, Eleventh Century, Romanesque. It still stands, though most of the city was destroyed in World War II.

The Cathedral of Chartres, France. Regarded by some as the purest and most beautiful example of Gothic design, the Cathedral of Chartres is renowned for the grace and perfect proportions of its towers. The one on the right was built in the Thirteenth Century and reflects the simpler Gothic style of that period. The one on the left was finished in the Sixteenth Century and reveals some of the influence of flamboyant Gothic.

vailing ideal. The same passion for unity carried over into the domain of art, with the result that sculpture and painting were both subordinated to architecture.

The Feudal Age produced two great styles of architecture, the Romanesque and the Gothic. The Romanesque was mainly a product of the monastic revival and attained its full development in the century and a half following the year 1000. Fundamentally it was an ecclesiastical architecture, symbolizing the pride of the monastic orders at the height of their power. Naturally, since the Cluniac revival affected the entire church, the Romanesque style was not confined to monasteries. Nevertheless, it is significant that some of the most impressive Romanesque buildings were houses of the Cluniac order. The essential features of this building style were the round arch, massive walls, enormous piers, small windows, gloomy interiors, and the predominance of horizontal lines. The plainness of interiors was sometimes relieved by mosaics or by frescoing in bright colors, but the style of construction was not such

Architecture: the Romanesque style

Evolution of the Floor Plan of the Medieval Cathedral. *A* is the plan of the Early Christian basilica, the church of Santa Maria Maggiore in Rome, built in the Fourth Century. It is a simple plan of rectangular building with nave flanked by colonnades and side aisles. *B* is the church of San Michele at Pavia, Twelfth Century, Romanesque, with the apse elongated and transepts added, giving the church the form of a Latin cross. *C* is the cathedral at Amiens, Thirteenth Century Gothic. Here the typical Gothic plan shows up—the side aisles continue around the elongated choir and apse, forming the ambulatory, off which radiate the chapels, and the transepts are fully developed with side aisles.

A   B   C

as to encourage elaborate ornamentation. Moreover, the strong religious spirit in which this architecture was conceived did not foster any appeal to the senses. Churches and monasteries should be plain and dark within in order to create the proper atmosphere of piety and of otherworldliness. Some of the architects of southern Europe, however, succeeded in breaking away from this somber monastic tradition and often decorated their churches with an elaborate symbolic sculpture.

In the late twelfth and thirteenth centuries the Romanesque architecture was superseded in popularity by the Gothic. The increase in wealth, the advancement of learning, the growth of secular interests, and the pride of the cities in their newly acquired free-

*The Roman-
esque architec-
ture gives way
to the Gothic*

*The Gothic
style*

*See color
plates at
pages 285, 316,
37*

dom and prosperity led to a demand for a more elaborate architectural style to express the ideals of the new age. Besides, the monastic revival had now spent its force. Gothic architecture was almost exclusively urban. Its monuments were not monasteries situated on lonely crags but cathedrals, bishops' churches, located in the largest cities and towns. It must be understood, though, that the medieval cathedral was not simply a church but a center of the community life. It generally housed a school and a library and was sometimes used as a town hall. The people of the entire community participated in erecting it, and they rightfully regarded it as civic property. Indeed, many of the Gothic cathedrals were the outcome of town rivalry. For example, the people of Siena became dissatisfied with their modest church after the cathedral at Florence was completed and determined to build a new one on a much more pretentious scale. Frequently the citizens' ambitions got far out of bounds, with the result that many of the buildings were left unfinished. The architects of the cathedral of Chartres, for instance, planned for several more lofty towers than were ever completed.

Gothic architecture was one of the most intricate of building styles. Its basic elements were the pointed arch, groined and ribbed vaulting, and the flying buttress. These devices made possible a much lighter and loftier construction than could ever have been achieved with the round arch and the engaged pier of the Romanesque. In fact, the Gothic cathedral could be described as a skeletal framework of stone enclosed by enormous windows. Other features included lofty spires, rose windows, delicate tracery in stone, elaborately carved façades, multiple columns, and the use of gargoyles, or representations of mythical monsters, as decorative devices. Ornamentation in the best of the cathedrals was generally concentrated on the exterior. Except for the stained glass windows and the intricate carving on woodwork and altars, interiors were kept rather simple and occasionally almost severe. But the inside of the Gothic cathedral was never somber or gloomy. The stained glass windows served not to exclude the light but to glorify it, to catch the rays

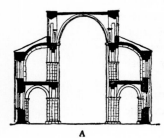

Cross Sections of Medieval Cathedrals: *A,* Romanesque Abbaye-aux-hommes; *B,* French Gothic cathedral of Amiens. Note the round Romanesque arches in *A* as well as the method of buttressing the nave vaulting by the half barrel vault over the triforium gallery. In *B* the pointed Gothic arch makes for a higher nave vaulting and, in all, the frame of the structure is lighter. Here can be seen the typical flying buttresses which take the thrust of the nave vaulting clear of the main structure to the great masonry buttress piers.

A   B

of sunlight and suffuse them with a richness and warmth of color which nature herself could hardly produce even in her gayest moods.

The significance of Gothic architecture is frequently misunderstood. As a matter of fact, its very name, implying that the art was of barbarian origin, was originally a term of reproach given to it by the men of the Renaissance, who wanted to express their contempt for everything medieval. Many people still think of the Gothic cathedral as a product of an ascetic and otherworldly civilization. Nothing could be more inaccurate. In so far as Gothic architecture was spiritual at all, it was the symbol of a religion which had come to recognize the importance of this life. But as we have already seen, the cathedral was more than a church. It was in large part an expression of the new secular spirit which had grown out of the rise of cities and the progress of enlightenment. Many of the scenes depicted on the stained glass windows—a medieval bakeshop in operation, for instance—had no direct religious significance whatever. Moreover, Gothic architecture was in no small degree humanistic. The definite appeal to the senses revealed in the sparkling radiance of colored glass and in the naturalistic sculpture of saints and the Virgin gives positive proof that man's interest in his human self and in the world of natural beauty was no longer considered a sin. Last of all, Gothic architecture was an expression of the medieval intellectual genius. The complicated design, the perfect balance of thrust and counterthrust, and the soaring height of the buildings represented not only the triumph of reasoning skill, but also a desire to burst the confines of limited knowledge and push upward into the highest realms of truth. Each cathedral itself, with its detailed mass of carvings of plant and animal life and symbolic figures, was a kind of encyclopedia of medieval knowledge—a culture epic in stone.

Music in the Feudal Age was the product of an evolution extending far back into the early history of medieval Europe. The beginning of this evolution was the development of the plain chant, ascribed by tradition to Pope Gregory the Great. The Gregorian chant was a single unaccompanied melody sung by a solo voice or by a choir in unison. This simple art form provided the basis for nearly all of medieval music. By the tenth century the first signs of a harmonic system had begun to appear, although the original tone combinations chosen were somewhat austere, including most typically successions of fourths and fifths. As time went on, other intervals were added, gradually enriching the color content. It is significant, however, that the modern concept of a *harmony* subordinate to a *melody* was entirely lacking. Each new voice that was added was expected to be interesting in itself and not merely part of a tonal background. Thus the new development was along contrapuntal rather than strictly harmonic lines; it was polyphonic

*Music in
the Feudal Age*

379

rather than monophonic. By the thirteenth century considerable skill had been attained in weaving together two, three, and even four independent voices into a pleasing pattern. As a part of the quadrivium taught in the universities, music was a dryly theoretical and formalized subject, primarily a branch of physics. But as utilized for practical needs by church composers it was a vital, growing thing. Some of the composers in their zeal for freshness and experimentation even chose popular tavern songs, words and all, as the base around which to weave contrapuntally the sacred words of the Mass. In this connection it may be observed that a secular music existed quite apart from that of the church. It too was chiefly vocal, but in contrast to sacred music was emphatically rhythmical, was sung to an instrumental accompaniment, and employed the vernacular languages. It included both folk music of anonymous origin and also, in the late Feudal Age, the songs of the troubadours, trouvères, and minnesingers, some of whom were gifted composers. Ultimately secular music added its influence to the more significant and serious art produced by the church.

Illuminated Manuscript from *Les Belles Heures de Jean, Duc de Berry*, a book of hours. Monks reading prayers at the bier of their deceased brother, St. Anthony. Illuminated manuscripts have value not merely as works of art but for their portrayals of medieval life and culture.

The Nativity, Fra Angelico (1387–1455). A Dominican friar, Fra Angelico is noted for his serenely happy religious paintings. (MMA)

The Flight into Egypt, Giotto (1276–1337). Giotto is regarded as the founder of the modern tradition in painting. This is one of the frescoes in the Arena Chapel, Padua, depicting scenes from the life of Christ.

St. Lawrence Enthroned, Fra Lippo Lippi (1406–1469). One of the first of the psychological painters, Fra Lippo Lippi exhibited in this work his gift for portraying pensive melancholy. (MMA)

Spring, Sandro Botticelli (1444–1510). Despite the pagan symbolism, the faces are thoughtful and sober, for Botticelli was a mystic as well as a lover of classical beauty. (Uffizi)

Mona Lisa, Leonardo da Vinci (1452–1519). Unlike most other Renaissance painters who sought to convey an understandable message, Leonardo created questions to which he gave no answer. Nowhere is this more evident than in the enigmatic countenance of Mona Lisa. (Louvre)

The Virgin of the Rocks, Leonardo da Vinci. This painting reveals not only Leonardo's interest in human character, but also his absorption in the phenomena of nature. (Louvre)

The Last Supper, Leonardo da Vinci. This great fresco depicts the varying reactions of Jesus' disciples when he announces that one of them will betray Him. (Santa Maria della Grazie, Milan)

Selected Readings

· Items so designated are available in paperbound editions.

· Adams, Henry, *Mont-Saint-Michel and Chartres*, New York, 1913. (Mentor)
Stimulating and provocative.

Artz, F. B., *The Mind of the Middle Ages*, New York, 1954. Brief but scholarly
and interesting.

Barker, Ernest, *The Crusades*, London, 1923.

Chaytor, H. J., *The Troubadours*, Cambridge, Mass., 1912.

· Cheyney, E. P., *The Dawn of a New Era, 1250-1453*, New York, 1936.
(Torchbooks) Written in a clear and interesting style.

Compayre, Gabriel, *Abelard and the Origin and Early History of Universities*,
New York, 1901.

Crump, C. G., and Jacob, E. F., *The Legacy of the Middle Ages*, New York,
1926. Especially good on medieval arts and crafts.

Easton, Stewart C., *Roger Bacon and His Search for a Universal Science*, New
York, 1952.

Evans, Joan, *Art in Medieval France*, London, 1948.

Flick, A. C., *The Decline of the Medieval Church*, New York, 1930, 2 vols.
A mine of information.

Gardner, Helen, *Art through the Ages*, New York, 1948. Comprehensive and
valuable.

Gilson, E. H., *The Philosophy of St. Thomas Aquinas*, Cambridge, Mass., 1924.

——, *Dante the Philosopher*, London, 1948.

Haskins, C. H., *Studies in Medieval Culture*, New York, 1929.

——, *Studies in the History of Medieval Science*, Cambridge, Mass., 1924.

· ——, *The Renaissance of the Twelfth Century*, Cambridge, Mass., 1928.
(Meridian) Excellent.

Hearnshaw, F. J. C., *The Social and Political Ideas of Some Great Medieval
Thinkers*, New York, 1923.

——, *Medieval Contributions to Modern Civilization*, New York, 1922.

· Huizinga, J., *The Waning of the Middle Ages*, New York, 1954. (Anchor)
A provocative interpretation.

Jackson, T. G., *Gothic Architecture*, Cambridge, Mass., 1915, 2 vols.

Jones, Charles W., ed., *Medieval Literature in Translation*, New York, 1950.

Krey, A. C., *The First Crusade*, Princeton, 1921.

Lang, Paul, *Music in Western Civilization*, New York, 1941.

Latourette, K. S., *A History of Christianity*, New York, 1953.

Mazzeo, J. A., *The Medieval Cultural Tradition in Dante's Comedy*, Ithaca,
N.Y., 1960.

McCabe, Joseph, *Peter Abelard*, New York, 1901.

McGiffert, A. C., *History of Christian Thought*, New York, 1932, Vol. II.

McIlwain, C. H., *The Growth of Political Thought in the West*, New York,
1932. Perhaps the best interpretation.

Morey, C. R., *Medieval Art*, New York, 1942.

Newhall, R. S., *The Crusades*, New York, 1927. The best short history.

Packard, Sidney, *Europe and the Church under Innocent III*, New York, 1927.
Contains much excellent material.

Rait, R. S., *Life in the Medieval University*, Cambridge, 1912.

Rashdall, Hastings, *The Universities of Europe in the Middle Ages*, New
York, 1895, 2 vols. The standard work.

Reese, Gustave, *Music in the Middle Ages*, New York, 1940.

Runciman, Stephen, *A History of the Crusades*, Cambridge, 1952, 2 vols. Complete and authoritative.

Setton, K. M., ed., *A History of the Crusades*, Philadelphia, 1955, Vol. I.

Taylor, H. O., *The Medieval Mind*, New York, 1927, 2 vols. Good for interpretation.

Thorndike, Lynn, *A History of Magic and Experimental Science during the
First Thirteen Centuries of Our Era*, New York, 1923, Vol. II. Thorough
and complete.

381

FEUDAL AGE:
RELIGIOUS AND
INTELLECTUAL

Tout, T. F., *The Empire and the Papacy, 918–1273*, London, 1941. A standard work.

Ueberweg, Friedrich, *History of Philosophy*, New York, 1876, Vol. I.

Vossler, Karl, *Medieval Culture: An Introduction to Dante and His Times*, New York, 1929, 2 vols. Profound and very valuable for the student with a good background of medieval knowledge.

· Waddell, Helen, *The Wandering Scholars*, London, 1927. (Anchor) A vivid and sympathetic account.

· ———, *Peter Abelard*, New York, 1933. (Compass) Valuable not only as biography but for its grasp of the spirit of medieval culture.

Source Materials

Abelard, Peter, *The Story of My Misfortunes.*

Baumer, F. L. V., *Main Currents of Western Thought*, New York, 1952.

Coulton, G. G., *A Medieval Garner.*

Jones, C. W., ed., *Medieval Literature in Translation*, New York, 1950.

Krey, A. C., *The First Crusade; The Accounts of Eyewitnesses and Participants.*

Marzialis, F. T., tr., *Memoirs of the Crusades*, for *Villehardouin's Chronicle of the Fourth Crusade* and *Joinville's Chronicle of the Crusade of St. Louis.*

Norton, A. O., *Readings in the History of Education: Medieval Universities.*

Pegis, A. C., ed., *Basic Writings of St. Thomas Aquinas*, 2 vols.

Polo, Marco, *Travels.*

Poole, R. L., *Illustrations of the History of Medieval Thought and Learning.*

Robinson, Paschal, tr., *The Writings of St. Francis of Assisi.*

Shackford, M. H., *Legends and Satires from Medieval Literature.*

Thatcher, O. J., and McNeal, E. H., *A Source Book for Medieval History*, pp. 513–21, Speech of Urban at Council of Clermont.

The Civilization of the Renaissance:
In Italy

Soon after 1300 the majority of the characteristic institutions and
ideals of the Feudal Age had begun to decay. Chivalry, feudalism
itself, the Holy Roman Empire, the universal authority of the
papacy, the guild system of trade and industry were all gradually
being weakened and would eventually disappear. The great age
of the Gothic cathedrals was practically over, the Scholastic philosophy was beginning to be ridiculed and despised, and the supremacy of the religious and ethical interpretations of life was being
slowly but effectively undermined. In place of all these there gradually emerged new institutions and ways of thinking of sufficient importance to stamp the centuries that followed with the character of a
different civilization. The traditional name applied to this civilization, which extended from 1300 to approximately 1650, is the Renaissance.

*The transition
from the
Feudal Age to
the Renaissance*

The term Renaissance leaves much to be desired from the standpoint of historical accuracy. Literally it means rebirth, and it is commonly taken to imply that in the fourteenth century there was a
sudden revival of interest in the classical learning of Greece and
Rome. But this implication is far from being strictly true. Interest in
the classics was by no means rare in the Feudal Age. Such writers as
John of Salisbury, Dante, and the Goliard poets were just as en-
thusiastic admirers of Greek and Latin literature as any who lived
in the fourteenth century. Indeed, the so-called Renaissance was in
considerable measure simply the culmination of a series of revivals
which began as far back as the ninth century. All of these movements were characterized by a reverence for the ancient authors.
Even in the cathedral and monastic schools Cicero, Vergil, Seneca,

*Meaning of
the term
Renaissance*

*The Renais-
sance more than
a revival of
pagan learning*

and, later on, Aristotle frequently received as much worshipful adoration as was given to any of the saints.

The Renaissance was a great deal more than a mere revival of pagan learning. It embraced, first of all, an impressive record of new achievements in art, literature, science, philosophy, politics, education, and religion. While the foundation of many of these was classical, they soon expanded beyond the measure of Greek and Roman influence. Indeed, most of the achievements in painting, science, politics, and religion bore little relation to the classical heritage. Secondly, the Renaissance incorporated a number of dominant ideals and attitudes which are commonly assumed to have set the standard for the modern world. Conspicuous among them were optimism, worldliness, hedonism, naturalism, and individualism; but the most significant of them all was humanism. In its broadest sense humanism may be defined as the glorification of the human and the natural as opposed to the divine or otherworldly. Conceived in this fashion, it was the heart and soul of the Renaissance; for it included practically all of the other ideals already mentioned. Humanism also has the more restricted meaning of enthusiasm for the classical writings because of their human interest. This is the sense in which it was frequently used by the men of the early Renaissance.

Not only was the Renaissance much more than a revival of pagan learning; in some ways it was closely related to the spirit of the late Middle Ages. The pride in human achievement reflected in Gothic architecture, the naturalism of the *fabliaux* and of *Aucassin and Nicolette*, the secularism of the orders of friars, and the striving after knowledge and understanding in the universities all clearly foreshadowed the prevailing ideals of the fourteenth and succeeding centuries. On the other hand, it is hardly correct to think of the Renaissance as only a final chapter in medieval civilization. Many of the new attitudes and achievements were distinctly at variance with the medieval world perspective. No longer did men conceive of the universe as a finite system of concentric spheres revolving around the earth and existing for the glory and salvation of man. The revival of the heliocentric theory as early as the fifteenth century suggested a cosmos of infinitely greater extent, with the earth only one of a number of worlds. The goal of human knowledge was thus pushed much farther into the distance, since the universe according to the new conception could not be so easily reduced to a simple explanation in terms of the Christian epic.

In other ways also the civilization of the Renaissance contrasted sharply with the Middle Ages. Chivalry was now quite generally treated with contempt. The Scholastic philosophy was despised as a stupid mixture of logic and religious dogma. The medieval condemnation of business for the sake of profit no longer received even lip service from the grasping merchants and bankers in every European city. The collectivism of the Middle Ages—the submer-

gence of the individual in the guild, in the church, and in the social
order to which he belonged—now gave way to a rabid egoism which
glorified almost every form of self-assertiveness and elevated pride
from a deadly sin to a cardinal virtue. Perhaps the most striking contrasts were those to be found in the realm of politics. The medieval
ideal of a universal commonwealth under the sovereign authority of
the Holy Roman Emperor or the Pope had no meaning at all for the
political philosophers of the Renaissance. Instead, they maintained
that every individual state regardless of its size should be absolutely
free from external control. Unfortunately they also rejected the
medieval doctrines of limited government and the ethical basis of
politics. It was now commonly held that the authority of the ruler
was subject to no limitations whatever, and some even asserted that
the prince in the exercise of his official functions was not bound by
the canons of morality; whatever was necessary to maintain his own
power or the power of the state over which he ruled provided its
own justification. Scarcely any philosopher in the Middle Ages
would have tolerated such doctrines.

1. The Causes of the Renaissance

Most of the causes of the Renaissance have already been indicated.
In general they were the very same factors that had stimulated the
intellectual and artistic revival of the twelfth and thirteenth centuries: (1) the influence of the Saracenic and Byzantine civilizations;
(2) the development of a flourishing commerce; (3) the growth of
cities; (4) the revival of an interest in classical studies in the cathedral and monastic schools; (5) the growth of a critical and skeptical
attitude exemplified in the philosophies of such men as Abelard; and
(6) the gradual escape from the otherworldly and ascetic atmosphere
of the early Middle Ages. To these should be added certain other
causes which were really elements in the medieval renaissance of the
twelfth and thirteenth centuries: first, the revival of the study of the
Roman law, with the impetus it gave to the growth of secular interests; second, the expansion of intellectual interests made possible by
the rise of the universities; third, the Aristotelianism of the Scholastic
philosophy, with its appeal to the authority of a pagan thinker;
fourth, the growth of naturalism in literature and art; and fifth, the
development of a spirit of scientific inquiry, exemplified in the work
of Adelard of Bath, Roger Bacon, and Frederick II. Soon after the
Renaissance got under way, its progress was greatly accelerated by
the influence of secular and ecclesiastical patrons of learning. Outstanding among the former were the Medici family in Florence, the
Sforza family in Milan, the Este lords of Ferrara, and Alfonso the
Magnanimous of Naples. Most of these patrons were wealthy merchants who had become despots of the city republics in which they
lived. The ecclesiastical patrons included such Popes as Nicholas V,

*The real causes
of the Renais-
sance*

*Patronage of
learning*

385

Pius II, Julius II, and Leo X. The attitude of these men was singularly
at variance with what is normally expected of occupants of the
fisherman's throne. They displayed no interest in theology or in the
conversion of the ungodly. They kept on the payroll of the church
men who openly attacked fundamental Christian doctrines. Nicholas V, for example, employed as a papal secretary the celebrated
Lorenzo Valla, who exposed an important document of the church
as a forgery and preached a philosophy of carnal pleasure. Whatever the incongruity of their attitude, the work of these Popes was
of inestimable value to cultural progress, for they bestowed their
patronage upon some of the most brilliant artists and literary men of
the Italian Renaissance.

*Alleged causes
of the Renais-
sance: (1) the
Crusades*

Before leaving this subject of factors responsible for the Renaissance, it will be desirable to dispose of two alleged causes commonly
believed to have been of decisive importance. One of these is the
Crusades, and the other is the invention of printing. In a preceding chapter we observed that the intellectual influence of the Crusades was slight. The introduction of Moslem learning into Europe
came about as a result of the work of scholars in the libraries of
Toledo and Cordova and as a consequence of the deliberate attempts
of Frederick II to undermine the power of the church by diffusing
a pagan culture throughout his domains. Only to the extent that the
Crusades weakened feudalism, diminished the prestige of the papacy,
and helped to give the Italian cities a monopoly of Mediterranean
trade may they be considered as in any way responsible for the
beginning of Renaissance civilization. And even these results can be
ascribed in large part to other factors.

*(2) the inven-
tion of printing
by movable
type*

While the invention of printing was an achievement of the utmost
importance, it was perhaps even less than the Crusades a direct cause
of the Renaissance. For one thing, it came too late. So far as the evidence shows, no printing press was in operation much before the
middle of the fifteenth century. The earliest work known to have
been printed from movable type actually dates from 1454.[1] By
this time the Renaissance in Italy was already well under way,
having started about a century and a half before. Furthermore,
many of the early humanists were decidedly hostile toward the
new invention. They regarded it as a barbarous German contraption
and refused to allow their works to be printed lest they obtain too
wide a circulation and be misunderstood by the common people. The
fact should also be noted that the earliest publishing firms were
far more interested in turning out religious books and popular
stories than in printing the writings of the new learning. Devo-
tional tracts, service books for the church, writings of the theo-

---

[1] This was an indulgence issued from the press of Johann Gutenberg at
Mainz, who is commonly credited with the invention of printing, though it is
somewhat doubtful that he did more than perfect the technique developed by
others.

logians, and collections of ancient legends were the types of reading matter which really appealed to the public of that day, and were accordingly more profitable to the printers than any of the recondite works of the humanists. The conclusion seems amply justified that the influence of the invention of printing upon the Renaissance extended no farther than to aid slightly in spreading and accelerating the movement in its later stages, particularly in northern Europe. Most of the great benefits of the invention came after the Renaissance had ended.

2. *The Renaissance in Italy*

Reference has already been made to the fact that the Renaissance had its beginning in Italy. Why should this have been so? As one reason, Italy had a stronger classical tradition than any other country of western Europe. All through the medieval period the Italians had managed to preserve the belief that they were descendants of the ancient Romans. They looked back upon their ancestry with pride, ignoring of course the infiltrations of Lombard, Byzantine, Saracenic, and Norman blood that had been poured into their nation from time to time. In some of the Italian cities traces of the old Roman system of education still survived in the municipal schools. Relics of the ancient pagan spirit were also to be found in the essentially unmoral attitude of the Italians. Ethical considerations did not generally weigh with them so heavily as with northern Europeans. Few Italians appear to have been shocked by the fact that Pope Alexander VI had illegitimate children or that Julius II was a crafty politician and a hard-swearing leader of papal armies. It is likewise true that Italy had a more thoroughly secular culture than most other regions of Latin Christendom. The Italian universities were founded primarily for the study of law or medicine rather than theology, and, with the exception of the University of Rome, few of them had any ecclesiastical connections whatever. In addition to all this, Italy received the full impact of cultural influences from the Byzantine and Saracenic civilizations. Finally, and perhaps most important of all, the Italian cities were the main beneficiaries of the revival of trade with the East. For years the seaport towns of Venice, Naples, Genoa, and Pisa enjoyed a virtual monopoly of the Mediterranean trade, while the merchants of Florence, Bologna, Piacenza, and other cities of the Lombard plain served as the chief middlemen in the commerce between northern and southern Europe. The economic prosperity thus acquired was the principal foundation of the intellectual and artistic progress.

Why the Renaissance began in Italy

I. THE POLITICAL BACKGROUND It is generally assumed that orderly and efficient government is a necessary condition for the development of a superior culture; but such was not the case with the civilization we are now considering. The Renaissance was born

Statue of a *Condottiere* by Verrocchio. In front of the Church of S. Giovanni e Paolo, Venice.

The turbulent political life of Renaissance Italy

in the midst of political turmoil. Not only was Italy not a unified state when the Renaissance began, but throughout the history of the movement the country remained in a turbulent condition. Factional revolts and bitter feuds between petty states followed each other in rapid succession. The reasons for this chaos were several. In the revolt against medieval collectivism, with its condemnation of pride and emphasis upon self-effacement, men went to the opposite extreme and glorified the aggrandizement of self. Almost any form of egoism was now considered justifiable—the pursuit of power or wealth, the quest of physical or artistic pleasure, or the ruthless suppression of one's rivals. It was perhaps inevitable that this change in social attitude should lead to political racketeering, to the rise of adventurers eager to turn every factional difference into angry discord in order to pave the highroad to a seizure of power. Another cause was the fact that the leading citizens were too deeply absorbed in making money to bother very much with affairs of government. Since they were especially reluctant to waste their time in military service, they insisted that their governments should employ mercenary troops. The result was the appearance of bands

The condottieri

of professional soldiers, under leaders known as *condottieri*, who sold their services to the highest bidder. As almost anyone could have predicted, some of these *condottieri* eventually became strong enough to seize control of the governments for which they fought. Much of the turbulence of Italian politics in this period was due also to the intense commercial rivalry among the principal cities. In fact, nearly all of the major wars grew out of attempts by one city or another to gain control of trade routes or to destroy the commerce of a competing city.

At the beginning of the Renaissance, Italy was divided into a host

388 of petty states. Nearly all were independent city republics that had succeeded during the late Middle Ages in throwing off the domination of the Holy Roman Emperor. In the course of their struggle for freedom many of them had adopted some degree of democratic government. In the midst of the turmoil of the Renaissance, however, practically all traces of this democracy disappeared. One city after another fell under the sway of powerful usurpers. As early as 1311 the government of Milan was transformed into a dictatorship under the head of the Visconti family. When the Visconti died out in 1450, their authority was taken over by one of the most famous of the *condottieri,* Francesco Sforza. In 1434 the republic of Florence passed under the control of the enlightened plutocrat, Cosimo de' Medici. Although Cosimo had no official title, he was accepted by the people of the city as a virtual dictator, mainly because they longed for relief from partisan strife. The Medici family dominated the political life of Florence for sixty years. After the great Cosimo the leading representative of the family was his grandson Lorenzo, styled the "Magnificent." To these two men must be given a large

POLITICAL
BACKGROUND

*The evolution
of government
in the city-
states*

THE STATES OF ITALY DURING THE RENAISSANCE (about 1494)

part of the credit for the fact that Florence remained for so long a time the most brilliant center of the Italian Renaissance. The republic of Venice also underwent a similar change from modified democracy to despotism. But here the despotic authority was exercised by an oligarchy instead of by a single individual. A small number of the wealthiest families controlled absolutely the elections to the Senate, to the Grand Council, and to the office of Doge, or life president. Even the States of the Church, which included a broad belt stretching across the central portion of the Italian peninsula, presented no contrast to the general pattern of Renaissance government. Except for their greater wealth, the Popes of this time were scarcely distinguishable from the rest of the Italian potentates. They made and broke treaties, hired *condottieri* for wars of conquest, and dealt questionably with troublesome opponents.

The expansion of the city-states

Not only was the history of the Italian Renaissance marked by the growth of despotic government; there was also a definite tendency for the larger and more powerful states to absorb the smaller. Under the rule of Gian Galeazzo Visconti (1378–1402) the city-state of Milan reached out and annexed nearly the whole of the Lombard plain. This expansion aroused the apprehension of Venice. As a consequence, the merchants of that city determined to conquer an inland empire which would protect the avenues of trade with central Europe. By 1454 Venice had succeeded in annexing nearly all of northeastern Italy, including the wealthy city of Padua and considerable territory formerly conquered by Milan. Nor did the republic of Florence lag behind in the development of expansionist ambitions. Before the end of the fourteenth century practically all of the district of Tuscany had been taken, and in 1406 the great mercantile city of Pisa succumbed to Florentine domination. The papacy also took part in the general movement of territorial aggrandizement. Under such worldly and aggressive Popes as Alexander VI (1492–1503) and Julius II (1503–1513) the dominion of the Papal States was extended over nearly all of the petty lords of central Italy. Alexander's son, Cesare Borgia, dreamed of nothing less than the unification of all Italy. But he was treacherous and his conduct unscrupulous; moreover, Italian nationalism was too weak to permit more than a reduction of the number of petty sovereignties. By the early 1500's nearly all Italian territory had been brought under the five most powerful states: the duchy of Milan, the republics of Venice and Florence, the kingdom of Naples, and the Church States.

II. THE LITERARY AND ARTISTIC CULTURE No wide gulf separated Italian Renaissance literature from the literature of the late Middle Ages. The vast majority of the literary achievements between 1300 and 1550 were already foreshadowed in one or another of the different trends initiated in the twelfth and thirteenth centuries. The so-called father of Italian Renaissance literature, Francesco Petrarca or Petrarch (1304–1374), was himself very close to the medieval

Petrarch, the father of Italian Renaissance literature

temper. He employed the same Tuscan dialect which Dante had chosen as the basis of an Italian literary language. Moreover, he believed quite firmly in Christianity as the way of salvation for man, and he was addicted at times to a monkish asceticism. His best-known writings, the sonnets he addressed to his beloved Laura, partook of the same flavor as the chivalrous love poetry of the thirteenth-century troubadours. Although Petrarch has been widely acclaimed as the father of humanism, the humanism he founded differed but slightly from that of many a medieval poet. About all that was new in Petrarch was his intense absorption in his own personality and his passionate devotion to the Greek as well as to the Latin classics.[2] Even here the novelty was primarily a matter of degree. It is not quite accurate to think of Petrarch as "the first modern man."

The second of the great figures in the Italian literary Renaissance, Giovanni Boccaccio (1313–1375), was scarcely much more of an original genius. Like Petrarch, Boccaccio was a Florentine, the *The more ro-* illegitimate son of a prosperous merchant. His father having planned *bust humanism* for him a business career, he was sent to Naples to serve an ap- *of Boccaccio* prenticeship in a branch of the great Florentine banking house of the Bardi. But the young Boccaccio soon displayed more ardor in worshiping in the temple of the Muses than in computing the interest on loans. It was perhaps natural that this should be so, for Naples was a center of gracious living under languorous skies and of strong poetic traditions emanating from the lands of the Saracens and the troubadours. It was an environment especially fitted to stimulate the poetic fancies of youth. Boccaccio was also inspired by a passionate love for the beautiful wife of a Neapolitan citizen. Nearly all of his earlier works were poems and romances dealing with the triumphs and tortures of this love. Gradually his skill in the story-telling art attained perfection, and he eventually found prose a more suitable medium for his purposes. His first work of merit in the new style was *Fiammetta*, a forerunner of the psychological novel. But by far the most notable of Boccaccio's writings was his *De-cameron*, which he wrote after his return to Florence about 1348. The *Decameron* consists of one hundred stories which the author *The* Decameron puts into the mouths of seven young women and three young men. The stories do not form a novel revolving about a continuous theme but are united by the artificial plot of having been told by a group of people who are concerned merely with passing the time during their sojourn at a villa outside of Florence to escape the ravages of the Black Death. Though some of the tales were probably invented by Boccaccio, most of them were drawn from the *fabliaux*,

[2] Curiously enough, Petrarch could not read Greek. His knowledge of Hellenic culture was acquired entirely from what the Romans said about it. His earnest attempts to learn the language resulted in failure, for he could find no competent tutor. He therefore contented himself to the end of his life with gazing admiringly at the pages of Homer but with no more than a vague understanding of what they contained.

from the *Book of the 1001 Nights,* and from other medieval sources. In general they differ from their medieval prototypes in being slightly more ribald, egoistic, and anti-clerical and more deeply concerned with a frank justification of the carnal life; but the *Decameron* certainly does not represent, as many people think, the first emphatic protest against the ascetic and impersonal ideals of the early Middle Ages. Its real significance lies in the fact that it set the pattern for Italian prose and exerted considerable influence upon Renaissance writers in other countries.

The character of literature in the Quattro- cento

The death of Boccaccio in 1375 marks the end of the first period in the Italian Renaissance in literature, a period which is often called the Trecento.[3] The age which followed, known as the Quattrocento, was distinguished by a revival of the Latin language. Enthusiasm for the classics had now attained such force that men could not bear to write in any other language than that of the great masters of ancient Rome. The Italian of Dante and Boccaccio was scorned as the uncouth tongue of butchers and bakers. Naturally such an attitude did not foster the development of the highest talent, for it tended to set as the supreme goal of literary effort the faithful imitation of Latin models. It is therefore not strange that the majority of the writers of this time—such men as Poggio, Beccadelli, Filelfo, and Pontano—should be remembered merely as second-rate figures whose chief claim to distinction is their militant paganism and their delight in erotic themes. Their work represents one of the farthest extremes to which the reaction against Christian belief and morality was destined to go. The Quattrocento was also the period when the passion for Greek studies was at its zenith. Prior to this time the Italian humanists had achieved but indifferent success in their attempts to learn the Greek language and to discover the treasures of Hellenic culture. But in 1393 a famous scholar of Constantinople, Manuel Chrysaloras, arrived in Venice on a mission from the Byzantine emperor to implore the aid of the West in a war against the Turks. Almost immediately acclaimed by the Italians as an apostle of the glorious Hellenic past, he was eventually persuaded to accept a professorship of the Greek classics at the University of Florence. About the beginning of the fifteenth century several other Byzantine scholars, notably Platonist philosophers, migrated to Italy. The influence of these men in providing information about the achievements of the ancient Greeks seems to have been considerable. At any rate, it was not long until Italian scholars began to make trips to Constantinople and other Byzantine cities in search of manuscripts. Between 1413 and 1423 a certain Giovanni Aurispa, for example, brought back nearly two hundred and fifty

---

[3] So called from the Italian word for three hundred, *trecento,* used to designate the century which followed 1300. Quattrocento, from the word for four hundred, is applied to the period of the fifteenth century and Cinquecento to the sixteenth.

manuscript books, including works of Sophocles, Euripides, and Thucydides. It was in this way that many of the Hellenic classics, particularly the writings of the dramatists, historians, and earlier philosophers, were first made available to the modern world.

The last great age in the development of Italian Renaissance litera- ture was the Cinquecento, or the period from 1500 to about 1550. Italian was now raised to a full equality with Greek and Latin, classi- cal and modern influences were more perfectly blended, and a deeper originality of both form and content was achieved. But the literary capital of the Renaissance was no longer Florence. In 1494 that city came under the rule of the fanatical reformer Savonarola; and, while the Medici were restored to power about eighteen years later, the brilliant Tuscan metropolis soon afterward fell a victim of factional disputes and foreign invasion. During the first half of the sixteenth century the city of Rome gradually rose to a position of cultural leadership, mainly because of the patronage of the church, especially during the reign of Pope Leo X (Giovanni de' Medici). This gorgeous prelate was the son of Lorenzo the Magnificent. When he was only fourteen years old, his father's in- fluence had been sufficient to procure his appointment as a cardinal. Elevated to St. Peter's throne in 1513, he is reported to have said, "Let us enjoy the papacy since God has given it to us." There can be little doubt that he did enjoy it, for he was a magnificent spend- thrift, lavishing rewards upon artists and writers and financing the construction of beautiful churches.

The chief forms of literature developed in the Cinquecento were epic and pastoral poetry, drama, and history. The most eminent of the writers of epics was Ludovico Ariosto (1474–1533), author of a lengthy poem entitled *Orlando Furioso.* Although woven largely of materials taken from the romances of adventure and the legends of the Arthurian cycle, this work differed radically from any of the medieval epics. It incorporated much that was derived from classical sources; it lacked the impersonal quality of the medieval romances; and it was totally devoid of idealism. Ariosto wrote to make men laugh and to charm them with felicitous descriptions of the quiet splendor of nature and the passionate beauty of love. His work represents the disillusionment of the late Rennaissance, the loss of hope and of faith, and the tendency to seek consolation in the pursuit of aesthetic pleasure. The development of pastoral poetry at this time probably reflects a similar attitude of disenchantment and loss of confidence. As the name implies, the pastoral romance glorifies the simple life amid rustic surroundings and expresses the yearning for a golden age of unspoiled pleasures and freedom from the worries and frustrations of artificial urban society. The chief author of this type of literature in the Italian Renaissance was Jacopo Sannazaro (1458–1530), who gave to his main work the title of *Arcadia.*

In the field of the drama the Italians never achieved more than moderate success. Their failure as writers of tragedy was particularly noticeable, despite the fact that they had considerable knowledge of classical models from which to profit. The Italian was apparently too much of an individualist to be influenced profoundly by the Greek conception of a tragic conflict between man and society and too much of an optimist to brood over personal suffering. His mind was fixed upon the compensations of life rather than upon its grim and terrifying aspects. His real talents lay in naturalistic description, in the development of light and joyous themes, and in the expression of personal egotism. It was natural, therefore, that the best of his dramas should have been comedies, especially satirical comedies, rather than tragedies. The first and the greatest of the Italian comedians was a man who is far better known as a political philosopher—Niccolo Machiavelli (1469–1527). The finest product of his dramatic skill was a work entitled *Mandragola*, which has been called "the ripest and most powerful play in the Italian language." [4] Sparkling with salacious wit and based upon incidents typical of life in the author's native city of Florence, it is a lurid satire of Renaissance society. In this as in his other writings Machiavelli reveals his cynical views of human nature. He appears to believe that all human beings are knaves and fools at heart, with their meanness and stupidity only partly concealed by a thin veneer of refinement and learning.

History

The historians of the High Renaissance in Italy displayed a critical spirit and a degree of objectivity which had not been seen since the end of the ancient world. First among them in order of time although not in order of greatness was Machiavelli. In his main historical work, an account of the evolution of the Florentine republic to the death of Lorenzo de' Medici, he rigidly excluded all theological interpretations and sought to discover the natural laws which govern the life of a people. More scientific in his methods of analysis was Machiavelli's younger contemporary, Francesco Guicciardini (1483–1540). Having served many years as an ambassador of Florence and as a governor of papal territories, Guicciardini enjoyed a unique advantage in acquiring familiarity with the cynical and tortuous political life of his day. His special gifts as a historian were a capacity for minute and realistic analysis and an uncanny ability in disclosing the springs of human action. His masterpiece was his *History of Italy*, a detailed and dispassionate account of the varying fortunes of that country from 1492 to 1534. No study of Renaissance historians would be complete without some mention of Lorenzo Valla (1406–1457), who may properly be regarded as the father of historical criticism. By careful scrutiny of their literary style he challenged the authenticity of a number of

[4] J. A. Symonds, "Machiavelli," *Encyclopedia Britannica* (14th edition), Vol. XIV, p. 577.

accepted documents. He proved the famous "Donation of Constantine" to be a forgery, thereby demolishing one of the principal bases of papal supremacy, since this document purported to have been a grant by the Emperor Constantine of the highest spiritual and temporal power in the West to the Pope. In addition, Valla denied that the so-called Apostles' Creed had ever been written by the Apostles, and he pointed out numerous corruptions in the Vulgate edition of the New Testament as compared with the earlier Greek texts. His critical methods served later on to stimulate a much broader attack by the northern humanists upon the doctrines and practices of the organized church.

LITERARY AND ARTISTIC CULTURE

Despite the wealth of brilliant accomplishments in literature, the proudest achievements of the Italian Renaissance were made in the realm of art. Of all the arts, painting was undoubtedly supreme. The evolution of Italian painting followed a course of development which roughly paralleled the history of literature. During the initial period of the Trecento, however, there was only one artist of distinction worthy to be compared to Petrarch and Boccaccio in literature. His name was Giotto (1276–1337). With him, painting definitely took on the status of an independent art, although his master Cimabue had already made some beginnings in this direction. Giotto was pre-eminently a naturalist. So skillful was he in depicting the semblance of life that, according to the story, one of his drawings of a fly so completely deceived Cimabue that he attempted to brush the creature away with his hand. Giotto also displayed more than ordinary talent in the portrayal of action, especially in such frescoes as *Saint Francis Preaching to the Birds*, *The Massacre of the Innocents*, and his scenes from the life of Christ.

Italian painting in the Trecento: Giotto the naturalist

See color plates at page 380

It was not till the Quattrocento, however, that Italian Renaissance painting really attained its majority. By this time the increase in wealth and the partial triumph of the secular spirit had freed the domain of art to a large extent from the service of religion. The church was no longer the only patron of artists. While subject matter from Biblical history was still commonly employed, it was frequently infused with nonreligious themes. The painting of portraits for the purpose of revealing the hidden mysteries of the soul now became popular. Paintings intended to appeal primarily to the intellect were paralleled by others whose only purpose was to delight the eye with gorgeous color and beauty of form. The Quattrocento was characterized also by the introduction of painting in oil, probably from Flanders. The use of the new technique doubtless had much to do with the artistic advance of this period. Since oil does not dry so quickly as water, the painter could now work more leisurely, taking his time with the more difficult parts of the picture and making corrections if necessary as he went along.

Painting in the Quattrocento

The majority of the painters of the Quattrocento were Florentines. First among them was a precocious youth by the name of

Masaccio, *The Expulsion of Adam
and Eve from the Garden of Eden*.
As the first of the realists, Masaccio
departed from the tradition of Giotto and introduced emotion and
psychological study into his paintings. In the Church of Santa Maria
del Carmine, Florence.

*The Floren-
tine painters:
Masaccio*

*See color
plates at
page 380*

396

Masaccio. Although he died at the age of twenty-seven, Masaccio
inspired the work of Italian painters for a hundred years. He is
commonly considered the first of the realists in Renaissance art.
Besides, he introduced an element of universality into his work
which profoundly influenced many of his successors. The greatest
of his paintings, *The Expulsion of Adam and Eve from the Garden*
and *The Tribute Money*, dealt not with specific themes but with
the simple emotions common to mankind in all ages. Masaccio was
also the first to achieve any notable success in imparting unity of
action to groups of figures and in giving the effect of thickness to
objects by the use of light and shade.

The best known of the painters who followed directly the
paths marked out by Masaccio were Fra Lippo Lippi and Botticelli.
As his name indicates, Fra Lippo Lippi was a member of a religious
brotherhood. But that did not prevent him from giving his paint-

ings an intensely human appeal. For his portraits of saints and madonnas he chose as models the ordinary men and women of the city of Florence. He was accustomed to depict the Christ child as a lusty infant whom one might expect to pull his mother's hair or fly into an unspiritual tantrum at any minute. Probably his chief contribution to painting was a tradition of psychological analysis. He seems to have been the first to have made the face the mirror of the soul. His most famous pupil, Sandro Botticelli (1444–1510), carried the method of psychological treatment even farther. In spite of his sensitive feeling for nature which led him to paint with such delicate skill the subtle loveliness of youth, the summer sky, and the tender bloom of spring, Botticelli was really more deeply interested in the spiritual beauty of the soul. Like others of his time, he was strongly influenced by Neo-Platonism and dreamed of the reconciliation of pagan and Christian thought. As a consequence many of the countenances he painted reveal a pensive sadness, a mystic yearning for the divine. But by no means all of his work had a religious import. His *Allegory of Spring* and *Birth of Venus* are based entirely upon classical mythology and suggest little more than an absorbing pleasure in the unfolding of life and a romantic longing for the glories of ancient Greece and Rome.

Fra Lippo Lippi and Botticelli

See color plates at pages 380, 381

Perhaps the greatest of the Florentine painters was Leonardo da Vinci (1452–1519), one of the most talented and versatile geniuses who ever lived. Not only was he a gifted painter but a sculptor, musician, and architect of outstanding ability and a brilliant mathematician, scientist, and philosopher. The son of an illicit union of a prominent lawyer and a woman of humble station, he was placed by his father at an early age under the instruction of Verrocchio, a sculptor and painter of some renown and the most celebrated teacher of art in Florence. By the time he was twenty-five Leonardo was already sufficiently distinguished as a painter to win the favor of Lorenzo the Magnificent. But after five or six years he appears to have become dissatisfied with the intellectual and artistic views of the Medici and gladly accepted an offer of regular employment at the court of the Sforza in Milan. It was under the patronage of the Sforza that he produced some of the finest achievements of his life. His work, which embraces the late years of the fifteenth century and the first two decades of the sixteenth, marks the beginning of the so-called High Renaissance in Italy.

Leonardo da Vinci

As a painter Leonardo da Vinci was impatient with the established tradition of striving to imitate classical models. He believed that all art should have as its basis a scientific study of nature. But he had no intention of confining his interests to the mere surface appearances of things. He was convinced that the secrets of nature are deeply hidden, and that the artist must examine the structure of a plant or probe into the emotions of a human soul as painstakingly as the anatomist would dissect a body. He appears especially to have

Leonardo's artistic approach

397

been fascinated by the grotesque and unusual in nature. Yawning fissures in the earth, jagged pinnacles of rocks, rare plants and animals, embryos, and fossils—these were the phenomena he loved to ponder, evidently in the belief that this mysterious universe yields more of its secrets in the fantastic and unaccustomed than in the things that are commonplace and obvious. For the same reason he devoted much time to the study of exceptional human types, often wandering the streets for hours in quest of some face which would reveal the beauty and terror, the sincerity and hypocrisy, of the personality behind it. As a result of this deliberate selection of subjects, the paintings of Leonardo have a quality of realism decidedly at variance with the ordinary type. He did not generally portray the aspects of nature as they appear to the casual observer but strove to present them as symbols of his own philosophic reflections. He was one of the most profoundly intellectual of painters.

Leonardo's famous paintings

It is generally agreed that Leonardo da Vinci's masterpieces are his *Virgin of the Rocks*, his *Last Supper*, and his *Mona Lisa*. The first represents not only his marvelous technical skill but also his passion for science and his belief in the universe as a well-ordered place. The figures are arranged in geometric composition with every rock and plant depicted in accurate detail. The *Last Supper*, painted on the walls of the rectory of Santa Maria delle Grazie in Milan, is a study of psychological reactions. A serene Christ, resigned to his terrible fate, has just announced to his disciples that one of them will betray him. The purpose of the artist is to portray the mingled emotions of surprise, horror, and guilt revealed in the faces of the disciples as they gradually perceive the meaning of their master's statement. The third of Leonardo's major triumphs, the *Mona Lisa*, reflects a similar interest in the varied moods of the human soul. Although it is true that the *Mona Lisa* (or *Monna Lisa*, i.e., "my Lady Lisa") is a portrait of an actual woman, the wife of Francesco del Giocondo, a Neapolitan, it is more than a mere photographic likeness. The distinguished art critic and historian Bernard Berenson has said of it, "Who like Leonardo has depicted . . . the inexhaustible fascination of the woman in her years of mastery? . . . Leonardo is the one artist of whom it may be said with perfect literalness: 'Nothing that he touched but turned into a thing of eternal beauty.' " [5] Also distinguishing the *Mona Lisa* are its "stimulating" and "convincing" tactile values and the fact that it is the supreme embodiment of the artist's skill in depicting the play of light and shade. In place of the old technique of showing a gradual transition from light to dark, Leonardo introduced a new method of punctuating darker areas with little spots of light, and *vice versa*. The effect was to surround the faces in many of his paintings with a gentle haze, accentuating their tender and pensive look. For him the interplay of light and shadow was an even more significant manifestation

See color plates at pages 380, 381

[5] *Italian Painters of the Renaissance* (Meridian Books), p. 107.

of nature than color and outline. His emphasis upon this phenomenon had the result of illuminating some of the figures in the background of his paintings and of giving a suggestion of dark mystery to other figures.

The late Quattrocento, or the beginning of the High Renaissance, was marked by the rise of another celebrated school of Italian painting, the so-called Venetian school. Its chief representatives included Titian (1477–1576), Giorgione (1478–1510), and Tintoretto (1518–1594). Of the three, Titian was perhaps the greatest. The work of all these men reflected the luxurious life and the pleasure-loving interests of the thriving commercial city of Venice. The Venetian painters had none of the preoccupation with philosophical and psychological themes which had characterized the Florentine school. Their aim was to appeal to the senses rather than to the mind. They delighted in painting idyllic landscapes and gorgeous symphonies of color. For their subject matter they chose not merely the opulent beauty of Venetian sunsets and the shimmering silver of lagoons in the moonlight but also the man-made splendor of sparkling jewels, richly colored satins and velvets, and gorgeous palaces. In this subordination of form and meaning to color and elegance there were mirrored not only the sumptuous tastes of a wealthy bourgeoisie but also definite traces of Oriental influence which had filtered through from Byzantium during the late Middle Ages.

The Venetian painters

See color plates at pages 412, 413

The remaining great painters of the High Renaissance all lived their active careers in the Cinquecento. It was in this period that the evolution of art reached its peak, and the first signs of decay began to appear. Rome was now almost the only artistic center of importance on the mainland of the Italian peninsula, although the traditions of the Florentine school still exerted a potent influence. Among the eminent painters of this period at least two must be given more than passing attention. One of the most noted of them was Raphael (1483–1520), a native of Urbino, and perhaps the most popular artist of the entire Renaissance. The lasting appeal of his style is due primarily to its charm, its simple humanism, rather than to any power of thought or emotional fervor behind it. Although Raphael was an ardent admirer of Leonardo da Vinci and copied many technical features of his work, for the most part he remained loyal to the ideals of sweetness and piety inherited from his earlier teachers. He was inclined to glorify form and color for their own sake and to despise intellectual meaning. Never disturbed by the mental perplexities of Leonardo da Vinci or the emotional torments of Michelangelo, he devoted himself to the cultivation of an ideal type of beauty as an end in itself and to the expression of religious sentiments. Among his greatest works are the *School of Athens* and the *Sistine Madonna*.

The painters of the late Renaissance: Raphael

The towering giant of the Cinquecento in painting was Michel-

Michelangelo, *The Creation of Adam*. One of a series of fresco paintings on the ceiling of the Sistine Chapel in Rome. Suggesting philosophical inquiries into the meaning of life and the universe, it represents Renaissance realism at its height.

Michelangelo

See color plates at page 413

angelo (1475–1564). Beset by the hardships of poverty, harassed by grasping relatives, and torn by the emotional conflicts of his own tempestuous nature, Michelangelo appears as one of the most tragic figures in the history of art. His dark presentiments were often reflected in his work, with the result that some of his paintings are overwrought and almost morbidly pessimistic. Nevertheless, the sense of tragedy he implanted in the scenes he portrayed was not really personal but universal. After the manner of the Greek dramatists he conceived of the tragic fate of mortals as something external to man himself, a product of the cosmic order of things. If there was any one theme which dominated all of his work, it was humanism in its most intense and eloquent form. He considered the pathos and nobility of man as the only legitimate subjects of art. Rocks and trees and flowers meant nothing to him, not even as background. Michelangelo's grandest achievement as a painter was the series of frescoes he produced on the ceiling of the Sistine Chapel and on the wall above the altar. The sheer physical labor required to complete the task was prodigious. For four and a half years he toiled on a lofty scaffold, most of the time face upward, covering the six thousand square feet of ceiling with nearly

400

four hundred figures, many of them as much as ten feet in stature. The series embraces a number of scenes in the mighty epic of the human race according to Christian legend. Among them are *God Dividing the Light from the Darkness, God Creating the Earth, The Creation of Adam, The Fall of Man, The Deluge,* and so on. The culminating scene is *The Last Judgment,* which Michelangelo finished some thirty years later on the wall back of the altar. Sometimes referred to as the most famous painting in the world, this scene depicts a Herculean Christ damning the great mass of mankind to perdition. Although the subject matter is Christian, the spirit is thoroughly pagan, as indicated by the naked and muscular figures and the suggestion of a ruthless deity who punishes men beyond their deserts. Nowhere else is Michelangelo's conception of universal tragedy more strongly expressed than in this work of his lonely old age.

Medieval sculpture, as we have already seen, was not an inde-

Statue of John the Baptist by Donatello, at the Metropolitan Opera in Siena. A fine example of the realistic sculpture of the Italian Renaissance. The forerunner of the Christ is shown as a primitive holy man clad in goatskins and with warts and an impish smile on his face.

pendent art but a mere adjunct of architecture. During the Italian Renaissance a gradual evolution began which ultimately had the effect of freeing sculpture from its bondage to architecture and establishing its status as a separate art frequently devoted to secular purposes. Though the work of a number of earlier artists pointed the way to this evolution, the first great master of Renaissance sculpture was Donatello (1386?–1466). He emancipated his art from Gothic mannerisms and introduced a more vigorous note of individualism than did any of his predecessors. His statue of David standing triumphant over the body of the slain Goliath established a precedent of naturalism and of glorification of the nude which sculptors for many years afterward were destined to follow. Donatello also produced the first monumental equestrian statue in bronze since the time of the Romans, a commanding figure of the *condottiere*, Gattamelata.

One of the greatest sculptors of the Italian Renaissance, and probably of all time, was Michelangelo. Sculpture, in fact, was the artistic field of Michelangelo's personal preference. Despite his success as a painter he considered himself unfitted for that work. Whether he was ever particularly happy as a sculptor might be open to debate, for he smashed some of the works upon which he had spent months of labor and invested others with the same quality of hopeless pessimism that characterized much of his painting. The dominant purpose which motivated all of his sculpture was the expression of thought in stone. His art was above mere naturalism, for he subordinated nature to the force and sweep of his ideas. Other features of his work included the use of distortion for powerful effect, preoccupation with themes of disillusionment and tragedy, and a tendency to express his philosophical ideas in allegorical form. Most of his great masterpieces were done for the embellishment of tombs, a fact significantly in harmony with his absorbing interest in death, especially in his later career. On the tomb of Pope Julius II, which was never finished, he carved his famous figures of the *Bound Slave* and *Moses*. The first, which is probably in some degree autobiographical, represents tremendous power and talent restrained by the bonds of fate. The statue of Moses is perhaps the leading example of Michelangelo's sculpture showing his use of anatomical distortion to heighten the effect of emotional intensity. Its purpose was evidently to express the towering rage of the prophet on account of the disloyalty of the children of Israel to the faith of their fathers.

Some other examples of Michelangelo's work as a plastic artist create an even more striking impression. On the tombs of the Medici in Florence he produced a number of allegorical figures representing such abstractions as sorrow and despair. Two of them are known by the traditional titles of *Dawn* and *Sunset*. The first is that of a female figure, turning and raising her head like someone called from a dreamless sleep to awake and suffer. *Sunset* is the figure

Pietà, by Michelangelo. This portrayal of tragedy was made by the sculptor for his own tomb. Note the distortion for effect exemplified by the elongated body and left arm of the Christ. The figure in the rear is Nicodemus, but was probably intended to stand as a symbol of Michelangelo himself. Original in the Cathedral of Florence.

of a powerful man who appears to sink under the load of human misery around him. Whether these allegorical figures were intended to symbolize the disasters which had overtaken the republic of Florence or merely to express the artist's own sense of the repletion of disappointment and defeat in the world is unknown. As Michelangelo's life drew toward its close, he tended to introduce into his sculpture a more exaggerated and spectacular emotional quality. This was especially true of his *Pietà*, intended for his own tomb. The *Pietà* is a statue of the Virgin Mary grieving over the body of the dead Christ. The figure standing behind the Virgin is probably intended to represent Michelangelo himself contemplating the stark tragedy which seemed to epitomize the reality of life. It is perhaps fitting that this profound but overwrought interpretation of human existence should have brought the Renaissance epoch in sculpture to a close.

To a much greater extent than either sculpture or painting, Renaissance architecture had its roots in the past. The new building style was eclectic, a compound of elements derived from the Middle Ages and from pagan antiquity. It was not the Hellenic or the Gothic, however, but the Roman and the Romanesque which provided the inspiration for the architecture of the Italian Renaissance. Neither the Greek nor the Gothic had ever found a congenial soil in Italy. The Romanesque, by contrast, was able to flourish there, since it was more in keeping with Italian traditions, while the per-

Renaissance architecture

403

sistence of a strong admiration for Latin culture made possible
a revival of the Roman style. Accordingly, the great architects of
the Renaissance generally adopted their building plans from the
Romanesque churches and monasteries and copied their decorative
devices from the ruins of ancient Rome. The result was an architecture based upon the cruciform floor plan of transept and nave
and embodying the decorative features of the column and arch, or
the column and lintel, the colonnade, and frequently the dome.
Horizontal lines predominated; and, though many of the buildings
were churches, the ideals they expressed were the purely secular
ones of joy in this life and pride in human achievement. The finest
example of Renaissance architecture is St. Peter's church in Rome,
built under the patronage of Popes Julius II and Leo X and designed
by the most celebrated architects of the time—Bramante, Raphael,
and Michelangelo. Profusely decorated with costly paintings and
sculpture, it remains to this day the most magnificent church in the
world.

III. PHILOSOPHY AND SCIENCE The Common impression that the
Renaissance represented in every way a marked improvement over
the Middle Ages is not strictly true. Such was especially not the case
in the realm of philosophy. The early philosophers of the Italian
Renaissance rejected Scholasticism, which had given a very high
place to the exercise of human reason, and wallowed in a mass of
childish superstitions and mystical puerilities. Since the Scholastics
had made Aristotle their intellectual god, the majority of the early
humanists decided to go back to Plato. The leaders in this movement
were such men as Marsiglio Ficino (1433–1499), and Pico della
Mirandola (1463–1494), both of whom were members of the Pla-
tonic Academy founded by Cosimo de' Medici. Unfortunately the
Platonism of these men was far from being the pure variety. The
bulk of it was made up of the Neo-Platonist teachings of Plotinus
together with various mythological accretions which had been
accumulated throughout the Middle Ages. The exponents of this
philosophy were as blindly uncritical in following what they believed to be the teachings of Plato as any medievalist in his devotion to Aristotle. Indeed, one of the great aims of the Academy was
to reconcile Platonism and Christianity and thereby to build a new
faith in which worship of the pagan past would hold equal sway
with the promise of a life to come. Pico della Mirandola went one
step farther and urged a universal religion composed of a mixture
of Platonism, Christianity, and the Jewish Kabbala, that fantastic
compound of magic, numerology, and mysticism which had been
elaborated mainly by followers of Philo and the Neo-Pythagoreans
from the pre-Christian era to the end of the Middle Ages.

*Italian Renais-
sance philoso-
phy: the Neo-
Platonists*

But not all the Italian humanists were ecstatic worshipers of Plato.
Some in their zeal for a revival of pagan culture sought to reawaken
an interest in Aristotle for his own sake and not as a bulwark of

THE ITALIAN RENAISSANCE IN ARCHITECTURE

The Villa Rotonda of Palladio near Vicenza. A Renaissance building combining the Roman features of a square floor plan and a central dome with the Greek features of Ionic columns and colonnades.

Church of San Spirito in Florence. Michelangelo is buried here. Noteworthy are the classical features of the interior of this church.

The Cathedral of Florence. Completed by Filippo Brunelleschi in the Fifteenth Century, the Cathedral of Florence is a prime example of Renaissance architecture. With its majestic dome, massive construction, and horizontal lines, it harks back to the Romans. The bell tower, or campanile, however, begun by Giotto, reflects medieval influence.

*Lorenzo Valla
and Leonardo
da Vinci*

*Machiavelli's
political phi-
losophy*

Christianity. Others became Stoics, Epicureans, or Skeptics. The most original philosophers of the Italian Renaissance were Lorenzo Valla, Leonardo da Vinci, and Niccolo Machiavelli. The fearless and sensational ventures of Lorenzo Valla into the field of historical criticism have already been noted. He was equally unconventional as a philosopher. Declaring himself a follower of Epicurus, he avowed the highest good to be tranquil pleasure, condemned asceticism as utterly vain and worthless, and insisted that it is irrational to die for one's country. Although Leonardo da Vinci wrote nothing that could be called a philosophical treatise, he may yet be considered a philosopher in the true sense of the word; for he was one of the first to condemn unequivocally the reliance upon authority as a source of truth, and he urged the use of the inductive method. It may be worth while also in these troublous times to take note of his strictures on war, which he called "that most bestial madness." He wrote that "It is an infinitely atrocious thing to take away the life of a man," and he even refused to divulge the secret of one of his inventions for fear it might be used by unscrupulous rulers to increase the barbarity of war.[6]

Niccolo Machiavelli is by far the most famous—and also the most infamous—political philosopher of the Italian Renaissance. No man did more than he to overturn the basic political doctrines of the Middle Ages, especially the ideas of limited government and the ethical basis of politics. He frankly avowed his preference for absolutism as necessary to solidify and strengthen the state, and he expressed his profoundest contempt for the medieval idea of a moral law limiting the authority of the ruler. For him, the state was an end in itself. The supreme obligation of the ruler was to maintain the power and safety of the country over which he ruled. Whatever the means necessary to enable him to fulfill that obligation, the prince should not shrink from adopting them. No considerations of justice or mercy or the sanctity of treaties should be allowed to stand in the way. Cynical in his views of human nature, Machiavelli maintained that all men are prompted exclusively by motives of self-interest, particularly by desires for personal power and material prosperity. The head of the state should therefore take nothing for granted as to the loyalty or affection of his subjects. He should assume that all men are his potential rivals and should endeavor to play them off one against another for his own advantage. Machiavelli also rejected the medieval notion that a static society is desirable. He affirmed, on the contrary, that a state must either expand and develop or undergo the certainty of decay.[7] Notwithstanding the reproaches that have been heaped upon Machiavelli for his unmoral

---

[6] Edward MacCurdy, ed., *The Notebooks of Leonardo da Vinci*, Vol. I, p. 24.
[7] Machiavelli's political ideas are found mainly in *The Prince* and in his *Discourses on Livy*. In the latter work he condemned feudalism and defended the republican form of government as preferable to monarchy for most states.

teachings, he remains a significant figure in the history of political theory. Not only his divorce of politics from ethics, but also his suggestion of a positive law created by the state and maintained by physical force, in place of the law of nature, serves to make him the real progenitor of modern conceptions of government. He is significant also as the first important realist in political theory since the time of Polybius. He described the state not in accordance with some lofty ideal but as it actually was in his own day. And it is a deplorable fact that the essential parts of his description would fit the official practices of most rulers ever since.

Not only did the narrow attitude of the early humanists in Italy retard the progress of philosophy; it also hindered for some time the advancement of science. The early humanists, as we have seen, were not critical minded. They accepted the authority of the Neo-Platonists with a gullibility worthy of the Dark Ages. Moreover, their interests were in art and literature, not in science. Part of this emphasis may undoubtedly be attributed to the fact that the leaders of the Renaissance for some time had only a limited knowledge of Greek achievements. The early pagan revival was predominantly a revival of Latin antiquity. And it will be recalled that the contributions of the Romans to science were exceedingly few and mediocre. But in spite of the unfavorable influence of early humanism, Italy became by the fifteenth century the most important center of scientific discovery in Renaissance Europe. Men from all over the continent came to study in her universities and to profit from the researches of her eminent scholars. The foundations for nearly every major discovery of the fifteenth and sixteenth centuries were laid in Italy. Such was notably the case in the fields of astronomy, mathematics, physics, and medicine.

Science in the Italian Renaissance

The achievement *par excellence* in astronomy was the revival and demonstration of the heliocentric theory. Contrary to popular opinion, this was the work not of any one man but of several. It will be remembered that the idea of the sun as the center of our universe had originally been set forth by the Hellenistic astronomer Aristarchus in the third century B.C. But then, some four hundred years later, the theory of Aristarchus had been superseded by the geocentric explanation of Ptolemy. For more than twelve centuries thereafter the Ptolemaic theory was the universally accepted conclusion as to the nature of the physical universe. The Romans seem never to have questioned it, and it was adopted as a cardinal dogma by the Saracenic and Scholastic philosophers. It was first openly challenged about the middle of the fifteenth century by Nicholas of Cusa, who argued that the earth is not the center of the universe. Soon afterward Leonardo da Vinci taught that the earth rotates on its axis and denied that the apparent revolutions of the sun actually occur. In 1496 the now famous Pole, Nicholas Copernicus, came down into Italy to complete his education in civil and canon

The revival of the heliocentric theory

law. For ten years he studied in the universities of Bologna, Padua, and Ferrara, adding to his course in the law such subjects as mathematics and medicine. He also acquired an interest in astronomy and studied and worked for some years with the leading professors of that science. Upon returning to Poland he established his own observatory and devoted many weary nights to a study of the heavens. Lacking a telescope, he was able to make only a few observations with crude instruments he had devised for measuring the height and position of the sun and various stars. His conclusion that the planets revolve around the sun was based primarily upon mathematical calculations and upon hints received from Italian scientists and from the works of ancient astronomers. Fearing the hostility of the church, he refrained from publishing the results of his work until 1543. The proof sheets of his book, *On the Revolutions of the Heavenly Spheres,* were brought to him on his deathbed.

Galileo's achievements in astronomy

The most important astronomical evidence for the heliocentric theory was furnished by the greatest of Italian scientists, Galileo Galilei (1564–1642). With a telescope which he had perfected to a magnifying power of thirty times, he discovered the satellites of Jupiter, the rings of Saturn, and spots on the sun.[8] He was able also to determine that the Milky Way is a collection of celestial bodies independent of our solar system and to form some idea of the enormous distances of the fixed stars. Though there were many who held out against them, these discoveries of Galileo gradually convinced the majority of scientists that the main conclusion of Copernicus was true. The final triumph of this idea is commonly called the Copernican Revolution. Few more significant events have occurred in the intellectual history of the world; for it overturned the medieval world-view and paved the way for modern conceptions of mechanism, skepticism, and the infinity of time and space. Unfortunately it contributed also to the decline of humanism and the degradation of man, since it swept man out of his majestic position at the center of the universe and reduced him to a mere particle of dust in an endless cosmic machine.

The Copernican Revolution

Leonardo da Vinci and Galileo, greatest of Renaissance physicists

In the front rank among the physicists of the Renaissance were Leonardo da Vinci and Galileo. If Leonardo da Vinci had failed completely as a painter, his contributions to science would entitle him to everlasting fame. Not the least of these were his achievements in physics. His researches in the fields of hydraulics and hydrostatics went far beyond anything previously attempted. His conclusion that "every weight tends to fall toward the center by the shortest way" contained the kernel of the law of gravitation.[9] In addition to his accomplishments in pure science he worked out

[8] Galileo was not the original inventor of the telescope. That honor is usually accorded to Johannes Lippershey, an obscure optician who lived in the Low Countries about the beginning of the seventeenth century. Galileo learned of Lippershey's invention and improved upon it in a single night.
[9] Edward MacCurdy. ed., *The Notebooks of Leonardo da Vinci,* Vol. I, p. 18.

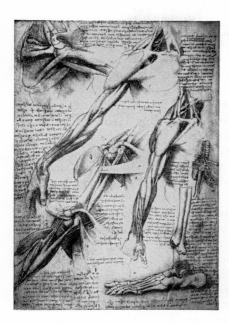

Studies of the Shoulder.

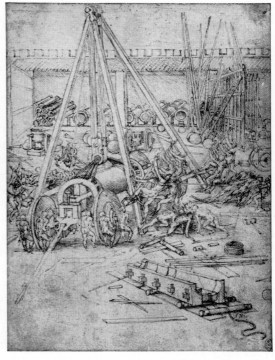

Cannon Foundry.

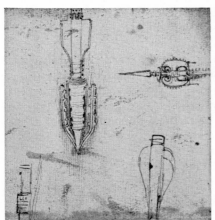

Designs for Weapons.

War Machines.

SKETCHES FROM THE NOTEBOOKS OF LEONARDO DA VINCI

the principles of an astonishing variety of inventions, including a diving boat, a steam engine, an armored fighting car, and a marble saw. Galileo is especially noted as a physicist for his law of falling bodies. Skeptical of the traditional theory that bodies fall with a speed directly proportional to their weight, he demonstrated by dropping weights from various heights that the distance covered in the fall increases as the square of the time involved. Rejecting the Scholastic notions of absolute gravity and absolute levity, he taught that these are purely relative terms, that all bodies have weight, even those which like the air are invisible, and that in a vacuum all objects would fall with equal velocity. Galileo seems to have had a broader conception of a universal force of gravitation than Leonardo da Vinci, for he perceived that the power which holds the moon in the vicinity of the earth and causes the satellites of Jupiter to circulate around that planet is essentially the same as the force which enables the earth to draw bodies to its surface. He never formulated this principle as a law, however, nor did he realize all of its implications as did Newton some fifty years later.

*Progress
in anatomy and
medicine*

The record of Italian achievements in the various sciences related to medicine is also an impressive one. As early as the fourteenth century a physician by the name of Mundinus introduced the practice of dissection at the University of Bologna as the only proper source of anatomical knowledge. Somewhat later Fallopio discovered the human oviducts, or Fallopian tubes, and Eustachio described the anatomy of the teeth and rediscovered the tube which bears his name, leading from the middle ear to the throat. A number of Italian physicians contributed valuable information pertaining to

*The circulation
of the blood*

the circulation of the blood. One of them described the valves of the heart, the pulmonary artery, and the aorta, while another located the valves in the veins. Even more significant was the work of certain foreigners who lived and taught in Italy. Andreas Vesalius, a native of Brussels, issued the first careful description of the human body based upon actual investigation. As a result of his extensive dissections he was able to correct many ancient superstitions, including the one about a single incorruptible bone supposed to be the necessary nucleus of the resurrection of the body. He is commonly considered the father of the modern science of anatomy. Two other physicians of foreign nationality who were heavily indebted to Italian progress in medicine were the Spaniard, Michael Servetus (1511–1553), and the Englishman, William Harvey (1578–1657). Servetus discovered the lesser or pulmonary circulation of the blood. In his work entitled *Errors concerning the Trinity* (his major interest was theology, but he practiced medicine for a living), he described how the blood leaves the left ventricle of the heart, is carried to the lungs to be purified, then returns to the heart and is conveyed from that organ to all parts of the body. But he had no idea of the return of the blood to the heart through the veins. It was left for William Harvey, who had studied under Italian physicians at Padua, to complete the discovery. This he did after his return to England about 1610. In his *Dissertation upon the Movement of the Heart* he described how an artery bound by a ligature would fill with blood in the section nearer the heart, while the portion away from the heart would empty, and how exactly the opposite results would occur when a ligature was placed on a vein. By such experiments he reached the conclusion that the blood is in constant process of circulation from the heart to all parts of the body and back again.

Palace of the Doge, Venice. Since Venice was the richest city in the world during the Renaissance, it was fitting that her public buildings should be noted for their opulence. The palace of the Doge, or Duke, was built of creamy white Istrian stone and red Verona marble. The style combined Moslem, Byzantine, and Gothic elements.

The Palazzo Vecchio, Florence. The residence of the Medici, the Palazzo Vecchio was built in the Fourteenth and Fifteenth Centuries. The design shows the inspiration of the medieval fortress. Savonarola was burned to death in front of this palace in 1498.

3. The Waning of the Italian Renaissance

Soon after 1550 the Renaissance in Italy came to an end after two and a half centuries of glorious history. The causes of its sudden demise are far from being perfectly clear. Possibly at the head of the list should be placed the loss of economic supremacy. It seems beyond question that the brilliant culture of the Italian cities had rested very largely on a foundation of commercial prosperity resulting from their monopoly of trade with the Near East after the downfall of the Moslem and Byzantine empires. But the discovery of the New World at the end of the fifteenth century led to a

Reasons for the decline of the Renaissance in Italy

411

rapid shift of the centers of trade from the Mediterranean area to the Atlantic coast. As a result, the life-blood of Italian culture was drained away. Among the other causes of decline may be mentioned the Catholic Reformation and political instability. The effects of the first of these in promoting dogmatism and clerical authority will be discussed in the chapter on The Age of the Reformation. The instability of Italian political life grew out of the unbridled individualism of the time and the jealousy among petty states. Most of the city-republics were governed by despots, who sometimes maintained themselves in power by methods worthy of a modern gangster. Although several of these rulers possessed remarkable ability, they all too frequently bequeathed their authority to weak and incompetent heirs. By way of illustration, the death of Lorenzo the Magnificent in 1492 was followed by the accession of his charming but incredibly stupid son Piero as dictator of Florence.

The Savonarola affair

Perhaps still another cause of the decay of Renaissance culture in Italy may be found in the persistence of ignorance and superstition among the masses. Despite the fact that it was possible for men of humble status to push their way upward into the charmed circle of intellectual and artistic genius, few, of course, ever did so. And those who managed to scale the heights were generally inclined to scorn the multitude left behind. With no system of universal education, it was inevitable that the great mass of the common people should have remained benighted. Underneath the proud structure of Italian art and learning were smoldering embers of superstition ready to be kindled into flame by the first fanatic who happened along. This fact probably contains the real explanation of the Savonarola affair. Girolamo Savonarola was born in Ferrara in 1452, the son of a shiftless and spendthrift father. Though he lived in a gay and worldly city, his early education, directed by his mother and grandfather, seems to have been chiefly religious. At the age of nineteen he fell passionately in love with the daughter of an aristocratic neighbor. The young lady spurned him contemptuously, and soon afterward he decided to renounce the world and fled to a Dominican monastery at Bologna. In 1482 he was transferred to Florence, where Lorenzo the Magnificent was then at the height of his power. The longer Savonarola remained in Florence, the more he was dismayed by the frivolity and paganism he saw all around him. Within two or three years he began preaching in the cloister garden and in the churches of the city, burning into the hearts of his hearers the terrible wrath that would overtake them if they did not flee from their sins. His fiery eloquence and gaunt and unearthly appearance attracted great hordes of frightened people. By 1494 his power over the mob had reached such proportions that he became virtual dictator of Florence. And then for four long years the gay Tuscan metropolis was subjected to a puritanical rule surpassing in austerity anything that Italy had witnessed since the

Madonna and Child, Luca della Robbia (1400–1482). This enameled terra cotta plaque is typical of the work of the della Robbia family. (MMA)

Pope Paul III and His Nephews, Titian (1477–1576). This painting, with its rich harmony of color, is unusual in being both a group portrait and a study of action. (National Museum, Naples)

Portrait of a Young Man, Giovanni Bellini (1430–1516). Though noted for opulence and color, artists of the Venetian school also excelled in portrait painting. (MMA)

The Madonna of the Chair, Raphael (1483–1520). Raphael's art was distinguished by warmth and serenity, and by an uncritical acceptance of the traditions and conventions of his time. (Pitti Palace, Florence)

Portrait of a Girl, Domenico Veneziano (1400–1461). Though born and probably trained in Venice, Domenico was strongly influenced by the technical achievements of the Florentines. (MMA)

Young Man, Bronzino (1502-1572).
The portrait displays the typical Re-
aissance spirit of the proud young m-
who glories in his achievemen-
(MMA)

"Christ and Madonna." From *The Last Judgment*, Michelangelo
(1475-1564). This painting above the altar in the Sistine Chapel,
Rome, shows Christ as judge condemning sinners to perdition.
Even the Madonna at His side seems to shrink from His wrath.

Rospigliosi Cup. Attributed to Benvenuto Cellini (1500-1571). Cellini
was not only an adventurer and writer, but also a talented goldsmith.
The cup shown was intended to hold salt. (MMA)

Boy with a Greyhound,
Veronese (1528-1588).
Veronese personifies con-
summate artistic skill with
little attention to meaning.
(MMA)-

The Doge Presented to the Redeemer, Tintoretto (1518-1594). This dramatic painting
commemorates a pledge by the Doge in 1576
to build a temple to the Redeemer if Venice
were saved from the plague. (MMA)

Four Saints, Corregg-
(1494-1534). Correggio w-
noted for his skill in con-
position and technical deta-
He painted the *Four Sain-*
while still in his teen-
(MMA)

A View of Florence Showing the
Burning of Savonarola. The Vecchio Palace is in the right center
and a portion of the Cathedral at
the extreme left. From a painting
by an artist of the Sixteenth (?)
Century.

days of Gregory the Great. Half the year was devoted to Lenten
abstinence, and even marriage was discouraged. Citizens were commanded to surrender their articles of luxury and their books and
paintings alleged to be immoral; all of these works of the devil
were cast into the flames in the public square in the celebrated "burning of the vanities." But in time the people wearied of the rule of
the haggard monk; his enemies plotted against him, and he was
finally condemned to death in 1498 at the instance of the Pope on
trumped-up charges of heresy. While the Savonarola affair was not
in itself a primary cause of the decline of Renaissance civilization,
it is important as an evidence of the uneven diffusion of learning, and therefore of the shaky foundations upon which the civilization was built.

Selected Readings—GENERAL

· Items so designated are available in paperbound editions.

· Allen, J. W., Political Thought in the Sixteenth Century, London, 1951.
(Barnes & Noble) The standard work on the subject.
· Berenson, Bernard, The Italian Painters of the Renaissance, New York, 1957.
(Meridian) Accurate and interesting.

413

· Burckhardt, Jacob, *The Civilization of the Renaissance in Italy*, new edn., New York, 1929. (Mentor; Torchbooks, 2 vols.) One of the great classics of Renaissance history.
· Butterfield, Herbert, *The Origins of Modern Science*, New York, 1951. (Collier)
Chubb, T. C., *The Life of Giovanni Boccaccio*, New York, 1930.
Ferguson, W. K., *The Renaissance*, New York, 1940. A splendid introduction.
· Gilmore, M., *The World of Humanism*, New York, 1952. (Torchbooks) An excellent general account.
· Huizinga, J., *The Waning of the Middle Ages*, London, 1924. (Anchor) A good analysis of the decline of feudalism.
Lang, Paul, *Music in Western Civilization*, New York, 1941. The best survey yet published.
Lucas, Henry S., *The Renaissance and the Reformation*, New York, 1934.
Owen, John, *The Skeptics of the Italian Renaissance*, London, 1893.
· Pater, Walter, *The Renaissance*, New York. (Mentor) Excellent for interpretation.
Randall, J. H., Jr., *The Making of the Modern Mind*, Boston, 1926, Chs. VI and IX.
Roeder, R., *The Man of the Renaissance*, New York, 1933.
Schevill, Ferdinand, *The First Century of Italian Humanism*, New York, 1928. Scholarly and stimulating.
· Sellery, George Clarke, *The Renaissance: Its Nature and Origins*, Madison, Wis., 1950. (Wisconsin) A good interpretation.
Shipp, Horace, *The Italian Masters*, New York, 1930.
Sichel, Edith, *The Renaissance*, New York, 1914.
Smith, Preserved, *A History of Modern Culture*, New York, 1930, Vol. I. Thorough and scholarly.
Symonds, J. A., *A Short History of the Renaissance in Italy*, New York, 1893. Provocative but contains some doubtful interpretations.
Taylor, H. O., *Thought and Expression in the Sixteenth Century*, London, 1920. Reliable and suggestive.
Thorndike, Lynn, *A History of Magic and Experimental Science in the Fourteenth and Fifteenth Centuries*, New York, 1934, 2 vols. Detailed but authoritative.
———, *Science and Thought in the Fifteenth Century*, New York, 1929.
· Vallentin, Antonina, *Leonardo da Vinci*, New York, 1938. (Grosset and Dunlap)
Van Dyke, Paul, *The Age of the Renascence*, New York, 1912.
· Wolf, A., *A History of Science, Technology and Philosophy in the XVIth and XVIIth Centuries*, New York, 1935. (Torchbooks, 2 vols.)
Wilkins, Ernest H., *A History of Italian Literature*, Cambridge, Mass., 1954. One of the best accounts of Italian writing since Dante.
Young, G. F., *The Medici*, New York, 1933. Readable but not entirely dependable.

Source Materials

Baumer, F. L. V., *Main Currents of Western Thought*, New York, 1952.
Galileo Galilei, *The Sidereal Messenger*.
MacCurdy, Edward, ed., *The Notebooks of Leonardo da Vinci*, 2 vols.
Machiavelli, Niccolo, *The Prince*, especially Chs. 15–21, 26.
———, *Discourses on Livy*, especially Book I, Chs. 3, 4, 6, 9, 11, 12, 25, 32, 33, 34, 47, 53, 55, 58, 59; Book II, Chs. 2, 5, 13, 19, 22.
Robinson, J. H., and Rolfe, H. W., *Petrarch, the First Modern Scholar and Man of Letters*.
Willis, Robert, tr., *The Works of William Harvey, M. D.*

The Expansion of the Renaissance

Art and sciences are not cast in a mould, but are formed and perfected by degrees, by often handling and polishing, as bears leisurely lick their cubs into form.

—Michel de Montaigne, *Works* II.xii

If a rock falls on your head, that is clearly painful; but shame, disgrace, and curses hurt only so far as they are felt. What isn't noticed isn't troublesome. So long as you applaud yourself what harm are the hisses of the world? And folly is the only key to this happiness.

—Erasmus, *The Praise of Folly*, II, The Powers and Pleasures of Folly

That a movement as vigorous as the Italian Renaissance should have spread into other countries was a result no less than inevitable. For years there had been a continuous procession of northern European students coming down into Italy to bask in the genial intellectual climate of Florence, Milan, and Rome. Moreover, the economic and social changes in northern and western Europe had roughly paralleled those of Italy for some time. Everywhere feudalism was being supplanted by a capitalist economy, and a new individualism was superseding the corporate structure of society sanctified by the church in the Middle Ages. Common economic and social interests fostered the growth of a similar culture. But it must not be supposed that the Renaissance in northern and western Europe was exactly the same as that in the south. The Italian and the Teuton differed markedly in temperament and in historical background. Joyous, carefree, and lacking in moral earnestness, the Italian was disposed to find in art and literature the most suitable media of self-expression. Besides, he was the heir of classical traditions, which also enhanced his aesthetic interests. The northern European, on the other hand, by reason of his harder struggle for existence, was inclined toward more serious and more practical pursuits. He tended to view the problems of life from a moral or religious angle. Everything mattered for good or evil; nothing could be esteemed as worthy merely because it was beautiful. As a result of these differences the northern European Renaissance was much less distinctly an artistic movement than the Renaissance in the south. Though painting flourished in the Low Countries, elsewhere it had no more than a limited scope, while sculpture was largely neglected. The

The spread of the Renaissance

415

main efforts of the northern peoples were concentrated in literature and philosophy, often with some religious or practical purpose. Furthermore, the northern humanist did not follow his Italian predecessor down the primrose path of paganism but generally remained loyal to the Christian faith, however sharply he might criticize the organized church.

The political history of the countries of northern and western Europe during the age of the Renaissance was characterized by developments somewhat similar to those which had occurred in Italy. There was the same transition from the weak and decentralized feudal regime to the concentrated rule of despotic princes. There was also the destruction of the political power of the guilds and the absorption of their prerogatives of sovereignty by the state. The chief difference was to be found in the fact that many of the states outside of Italy were beginning to take on the character of national units. Each of them occupied a territory of considerable size and embraced a population knit together by bonds of language and a vague consciousness of unity as a people. But for the most part these great political organisms were the creations of ambitious monarchs, who broke the power of local nobles and welded their petty principalities into huge dynastic empires. In England this process was abetted by the so-called Wars of the Roses, a series of bloody struggles beginning about 1455 between rival factions of barons. So many were the nobles killed in these wars, and so profound was the disgust with the long period of disorder, that the Tudor dynasty, founded by Henry VII in 1485, was soon able to crush completely the remnants of feudal power. The most noted members of this dynasty, Henry VIII and Queen Elizabeth, were the real founders of despotic government in England—with the support of the middle classes, who desired more protection for their commercial interests than the feudal regime could give.

The political background of the Renaissance outside of Italy

The growth of strong government in England

Conditions in France, Spain, and Germany

In the case of France it was also a war which led to the establishment of a consolidated state—but an international war rather than an internal squabble. The struggle which enabled the French kings to stamp out feudal sovereignty was the Hundred Years' War (1337–1453), fought primarily to expel the English from France and to break their commercial alliance with the Flemish cities. As a result of this conflict a national consciousness was aroused in the French people, the nobles who had followed their own selfish ambitions were discredited, and the monarchy was extolled for having saved the country from ruin. Within thirty years the shrewd but unscrupulous Louis XI (1461–1483) extended the royal domain over all of France with the exception of Flanders and Brittany. His policies paved the way for the absolute rule of the Bourbons. Still another important country of western Europe began its emergence as a nation-state toward the end of the fifteenth century. This country was Spain, united partly as a result of the marriage of Ferdinand of Aragon

See color plates at page 285

and Isabella of Castile in 1469 and partly through the exigencies of the long war against the Moors. Under Philip II (1556–1598) Spain rose to a place in the very front rank of European powers. Aside from Italy, the only major country of western Europe which was not united into a consolidated state during the age of the Renaissance was Germany. Though it is true that political authority in some of the individual German kingdoms was solidified, the country as a whole remained merely a part of the Holy Roman Empire, now headed by the Hapsburg monarchs of Austria. The sovereignty of the Holy Roman Emperors was a mere fiction, mainly because during the Middle Ages they had wasted their energies in a vain attempt to extend their control over Italy, thereby enabling the German dukes to entrench themselves in power.

1. The Intellectual and Artistic Renaissance in Germany

One of the first countries to receive the full impact of the Italian humanist movement was Germany. This was a natural development not only because of the proximity of the two countries, but also because of the large-scale migration of German students to the Italian universities. But the influence of this humanism was short-lived and its fruits rather scanty and mediocre. What the results might have been if Germany had not been hurled so soon into the maelstrom of religious contention cannot be determined. The fact remains, however, that the Protestant Revolution stirred up passions of hate and intolerance which could not be other than inimical to the humanist ideal. A premium was now set upon bigotry and faith, while anything resembling the worship of man or reverence for pagan antiquity was almost certain to be regarded as a work of the devil.

The limited scope of the German Renaissance

To fix a date for the beginning of the German Renaissance is practically impossible. In such prosperous cities of the south as Augsburg, Nuremberg, Munich, and Vienna there was a lively humanist movement, imported from Italy, as early as 1450. By the beginning of the sixteenth century it had taken firm root in university circles, particularly in the cities of Heidelberg, Erfurt, and Cologne. Its most notable representatives were Ulrich von Hutten (1488–1523) and Crotus Rubianus (1480–1539). Both were less interested in the literary aspects of humanism than in its possibilities as an expression of religious and political protest. Von Hutten, especially, made use of his gifts as a writer to satirize the worldliness and greed of the clergy and to indite fiery defenses of the German people against their enemies. He was himself an embittered rebel against almost every institution of the established order. The chief title of von Hutten and Rubianus to fame is their authorship of the *Letters of Obscure Men*, one of the wittiest satires in the history

German humanism: the Letters of Obscure Men

of literature. The circumstances under which it was written are so strikingly like those which frequently occur in the evolution of nations that they deserve to be recounted here. A learned humanist at the University of Heidelberg by the name of Johann Reuchlin had developed a passionate enthusiasm for the study of Hebrew writings. Because he criticized some of the theologians' interpretations of the Old Testament, he was savagely attacked by Christian fanatics and was finally haled before the Inquisitor-General for the Catholic church in Germany. Numerous pamphlets were published on both sides of the controversy, and the issue was soon sharply drawn between freedom and tolerance, on the one hand, and authoritarianism and bigotry on the other. When it became apparent that rational argument was accomplishing nothing, the friends of Reuchlin decided to make use of ridicule. Rubianus and von Hutten published a series of letters purporting to have been written by some of Reuchlin's opponents, with such ridiculous signatures as Ziegenmelker (Goat-milker), Honiglecker (Honey-licker), and Mistlader (Dung-loader). Heinrich Shafmaul (Sheep's mouth), the supposed writer of one of the letters, professed to be worried lest he had sinned grievously by eating an egg which contained a chick on Friday. The author of another of the letters boasted of his brilliant "discovery" that Julius Caesar could not have written the *Commentaries on the Gallic Wars* because he was too busy with his military exploits ever to have learned the Latin language. How much effect these letters had in undermining the influence of the Catholic hierarchy in Germany is impossible to say, but it must have been considerable, for they enjoyed a wide circulation.

German painting: Dürer and Holbein

The German Renaissance in art was limited entirely to painting and engraving, represented chiefly by the work of Albrecht Dürer (1471–1528) and Hans Holbein (1497–1543). Both of these artists were profoundly influenced by Italian traditions, though much of the Germanic spirit of somber realism is also expressed in their work. Dürer's best-known paintings are his *Adoration of the Magi*, the *Four Apostles*, and *The Crucified Christ*. The last is a study in tragic gloom. It shows the body of the pale Galilean stretched on the cross against a bleak and sinister sky. The glimmer of light on the horizon merely adds to the somber effect of the scene. Some of Dürer's best-known engravings exhibit similar qualities. His *Melancholy* represents a female figure, with wings too small to lift her body, meditating hopelessly on the problems of life, which appear to defy all solution. A compass is in her hand, and various other implements upon which man has relied for the control of his environment lie strewn about the floor. Hans Holbein, the other great artist of the German Renaissance, derives his renown primarily from his portraits and drawings. His portraits of Erasmus, of Henry VIII, of Jane Seymour, and of Anne of Cleves are among the most famous in the world. An impressive example of his drawings is the

See color
plates at
page 476

Portrait of Henry VIII by Hans Holbein the Younger. In the Palazzo Corsini, Rome.

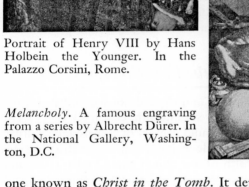

Melancholy. A famous engraving from a series by Albrecht Dürer. In the National Gallery, Washington, D.C.

one known as *Christ in the Tomb*. It depicts the body of the Son of God, with staring eyes and mouth half open, as neglected in death as the corpse of an ordinary criminal. The artist's purpose was probably to express the utter degradation which the Savior had suffered for the redemption of man. In his later career Holbein also drew many religious pictures satirizing the abuses in the Catholic church which were believed to be the chief justification for the Protestant Revolution. He was one of the few prominent artists to devote his talents to the Protestant cause.

The only German during the age of the Renaissance to make any significant contribution to science was Johann Kepler (1571–1630). An ardent adherent of the teachings of Copernicus, he improved the theory of the distinguished Pole by proving that the planets move in elliptical, rather than circular, orbits around the sun. Thus he may be said to have destroyed the last important vestige of the Ptolemaic astronomy, which had assumed the planets to be imbedded in perfect crystalline spheres. In addition, the laws of planetary motion which Kepler formulated were of tremendous value in suggesting to Newton his principle of universal gravitation. There was another scientist of German nationality whose work can be appropriately discussed in this connection, though he was actually born in the vicinity of Zürich, about the end of the fifteenth century. The name of this man was Theophrastus von Hohenheim, but

German science: Kepler and Paracelsus

419

he chose to call himself Paracelsus to indicate his own belief in his superiority to Celsus, the great Roman physician. Although Paracelsus is often referred to as a quack and an impostor, there is really comparatively little evidence that this was the case. He was at least sufficiently skillful as a practitioner of healing to be appointed professor of medicine at the University of Basel and town physician in 1527. Moreover, it is his special merit that he went straight to the book of experience for his knowledge of diseases and their cures. Instead of following the teachings of ancient authorities, he traveled widely, studying cases of illness in different environments and experimenting with innumerable drugs. He denied that the quest for the philosopher's stone should be the function of the chemist and insisted upon the close interrelation of chemistry and medicine. Perhaps his most important specific contribution was his discovery of the relation between cretinism in children and the presence of goiter in their parents.

2. Renaissance Culture in the Low Countries

The derivation and character of Renaissance culture in the Low Countries

Despite the fact that the Low Countries did not win independence of foreign domination until the seventeenth century,[1] they were nevertheless one of the most splendid centers of Renaissance culture on the Continent of Europe outside of Italy. The explanation is to be found primarily in the wealth of the Dutch and Flemish cities and in the important trade connections with southern Europe. As early as 1450 there were significant attainments in art in the Low Countries, including the development of painting in oil. Here also some of the first books were printed. While it is true that the Renaissance in the Low Countries was no broader in scope than in several other areas of northern Europe, its achievements were generally of surpassing brilliance.

Erasmus, the most civilized man of his age

The history of Renaissance literature and philosophy in the Low Countries begins and ends with Desiderius Erasmus, universally acclaimed as the Prince of the Humanists. The son of a priest and a servant girl, Erasmus was born near Rotterdam probably in the year 1466. For his early education he had the benefit of the excellent training given in the school of the Brethren of the Common Life at Deventer.[2] Later, after his father and mother were both dead, his guardians placed him in an Augustinian monastery. Here the young Erasmus found little religion or formal instruction of any kind but plenty of freedom to read what he liked. He devoured all the classics he could get his hands on and the writings of many of the Church Fathers. When he was about thirty years of age, he

---

[1] They were ruled by the Duchy of Burgundy until 1506 when they were inherited by Charles, the young king of Spain, whose grandfather had married the sole heiress of the Burgundian duke.

[2] See The Renaissance in Religion, §7 in this chapter.

obtained permission to leave the monastery and enroll in the University of Paris, where he completed the requirements for the degree of bachelor of divinity. But Erasmus never entered upon the active duties of a priest, choosing rather to make his living by teaching and writing. By extensive reading of the classics he achieved a style of Latin expression so remarkable for its wit and urbanity that everything he wrote was widely read. But Erasmus' love of the classics was not born of pedantic interest. He admired the ancient authors because they gave voice to the very ideals of naturalism, tolerance, and humanitarianism which held so exalted a place in his own mind. He was wont to believe that such pagans as Cicero and Socrates were far more deserving of the title of Saint than many a Christian canonized by the Pope. In 1536 Erasmus died in Basel at the end of a long and unfaltering career in defense of scholarship, high standards of literary taste, and the life of reason. He has rightfully been called the most civilized man of his age.

As a philosopher of humanism Erasmus was the incarnation of the finest ideals of the northern Renaissance. Convinced of the inherent goodness of man, he believed that all misery and injustice would eventually disappear if only the pure sunlight of reason could be allowed to penetrate the noisome caverns of ignorance, superstition, and hate. With nothing of the fanatic about him, he stood for liberality of mind, for reasonableness and conciliation, rather than for fierce intolerance of evil. He shrank from the violence and passion of war, whether between systems, classes, or nations. Much of his teaching and writing was dedicated to the cause of religious reform. The ceremonial, dogmatic, and superstitious extravagances in sixteenth-century Catholic life repelled him. But it was alien to his temper to lead any crusade against them. He sought rather by gentle irony, and occasionally by stinging satire, to expose irrationalism in all of its forms and to propagate a humanist religion of simple piety and noble conduct based upon what he called the "philosophy of Christ." Although his criticism of the Catholic faith had considerable effect in hastening the Protestant Revolution, he recoiled in disgust from the bigotry of the Lutherans. Neither did he have much sympathy for the scientific revival of his time. Like most of the humanists he believed that an emphasis upon science would serve to promote a crude materialism and to detract men's interests from the ennobling influence of literature and philosophy. The chief writings of Erasmus were his *Praise of Folly*, in which he satirized pedantry, the dogmatism of theologians, and the ignorance and credulity of the masses; and his *Familiar Colloquies* and *The Handbook of the Christian Knight*, in which he condemned ecclesiastical Christianity and argued for a return to the simple teachings of Jesus, "who commanded us nothing save love for one another." In a less noted work entitled *The Complaint of Peace*, he expressed his abhorrence of war and his contempt for despotic princes.

The liberal phi losophy of Erasmus

The writings of Erasmus

421

See color
plates at
page 476

The artistic Renaissance in the Low Countries was confined almost entirely to painting; and in this field the outstanding achievements were those of the Flemish school. Flemish painting derived no small measure of its excellence from the fact that it was an indigenous art. Here there were no classical influences, no ancient statues to imitate, and no living traditions from the Byzantine or Saracenic cultures. Until comparatively late, even the Italian influence was of little consequence. The painting of Flanders was rather the spontaneous product of a virile and prosperous urban society dominated by aspiring merchants interested in art as a symbol of luxurious tastes. The work of nearly all the leading painters—the van Eycks, Hans Memling, and Roger van der Weyden—betrayed this flair for depicting the solid and respectable virtues of their patrons. It was distinguished also by powerful realism, by a relentless attention to the details of ordinary life, by brilliant coloring, and by a deep and uncritical piety. Hubert and Jan van Eyck are noted for their *Adoration of the Lamb,* an altarpiece produced for a church in Ghent soon after the beginning of the fifteenth century. Described by some critics as the noblest achievement of the Flemish school, it portrays a depth of religious feeling and a background of ordinary experience unmatched in Italian art. It was the first great work of the Renaissance to be done by the new method of painting in oil, a process believed to have been invented by the van Eycks. The other two Flemish painters of the fifteenth century, Hans Memling and Roger van der Weyden, are noted, respectively, for naturalism and for the expression of emotional intensity. About a hundred years later came the work of Peter Breughel, the most independent and the most socially conscious of the northern artists. Spurning the religious and bourgeois traditions of his predecessors, Breughel chose to depict the life of the common man. He loved to portray the boisterous pleasures of peasant folk at their wedding feasts and village fairs or to illustrate proverbs with scenes from the lives of humble people close to the earth. While he was enough of a realist never to idealize the characters in his paintings, his attitude toward them was definitely sympathetic. He employed his talents for the purpose also of condemning the tyranny of the Spanish regime in the Low Countries. One of his paintings, *The Massacre of the Innocents,* pictures the slaughter of women and children by Spanish soldiers. Seldom has great art been used more effectively as a weapon of political protest.

3. The French Renaissance

Despite the strong aesthetic interests of the French people, as evidenced by their perfection of Gothic architecture during the Middle Ages, the achievements of their artists in the age of the Renaissance were of comparatively little importance. There was some minor progress in sculpture and a modest advancement in architecture. It was during this time that the Louvre was built, on the site of an earlier structure bearing the same name, while numerous châteaux erected throughout the country represented a more or less successful attempt to combine the grace and elegance of the Italian style with the solidity of the medieval castle. Nor was science entirely neglected, although the major accomplishments were few. They included the contributions of François Viète (1540–1603) to mathematics and of Ambroise Paré (1517?–1590) to surgery. The former invented modern algebraic symbols and elaborated the theory of equations, for which the ground had been prepared by the work of the Italians, Niccolò Tartaglia (1500–1557) and Girolamo Cardan (1501–1576). Paré improved upon the method of treating gunshot wounds by substituting bandages and unguents for applications of boiling oil. He was also responsible for introducing the ligature of arteries as a means of controlling the flow of blood in major amputations.

But the outstanding achievements of the French Renaissance were in literature and philosophy, illustrated especially by the writings of François Rabelais (1490?–1553) and Michel de Montaigne (1533–1592). Like Erasmus, Rabelais was educated as a monk, but soon after taking holy orders he left the monastery to study medicine at the University of Montpellier. He finished the course for the bachelor's degree in the short space of six weeks and obtained his doctorate about five years later, in the meantime having served for a period as public physician in Lyon in addition to lecturing and editing medical writings. He seems from the start to have interspersed his professional activities with literary endeavors of one sort and another. He wrote almanacs for the common people, satires against quacks and astrologers, and burlesques of popular superstitions. In 1532 Rabelais published his first edition of *Gargantua*, which he later revised and combined with another book bearing the title of *Pantagruel*. Gargantua and Pantagruel were originally the names of legendary medieval giants noted for their prodigious strength and their gross appetites. Rabelais' account of their adventures served as a vehicle for his robust, sprawling wit and for the expression of his philosophy of exuberant humanism. In language far from delicate he satirized the practices of the church, ridiculed Scholasticism, scoffed at superstitions, and pilloried every form of bigotry and repression. No man of the Renaissance was a more uncompromising individualist or exhibited more zeal in glorifying the human and the natural. For him every instinct of man was healthy, provided it was not directed toward tyranny over others. In common with Erasmus he believed in the inherent goodness of man, but unlike the great Prince of the Humanists he was a thoroughgoing pagan, rejecting not only Christian dogma but Christian morality as well. Any degree of restraint, intellectual or moral, was repugnant to Rabelais. His celebrated description of the abbey of Theleme, built by Gargantua, was intended to show the contrast between his conception of freedom and the Christian ascetic ideal. At Theleme there were no clocks summoning to duties and no vows of celibacy or perpetual membership. The inmates could leave when they liked; but while they remained they dwelt together "according to their own free will and pleasure. They rose out of their beds when they thought good; they did eat, drink, labour, sleep, when they had a mind to it, and were disposed for it. None did awake them, none did offer to constrain them . . . for so Gargantua had established it. In all their Rule and strictest tie of their order there was but this one clause to be observed, *Do what thou wilt*." [3]

Montaigne

A man of far different temperament and background was Michel de Montaigne (1533–1592). His father was a Catholic, his mother a Jewess who had become a Protestant. Almost from the day of his birth their son was subjected to an elaborate system of training. Every morning he was awakened by soft music, and he was attended throughout the day by servants who were forbidden to speak any language but Latin. When he was six years old he was ready for the College of Guienne at Bordeaux and at the age of thirteen began the study of law. After practicing law for a time and serving in various public offices, he retired at thirty-seven to his ancestral estate to devote the remainder of his life to study, contemplation, and writing. Always in delicate health, he found it necessary now more than ever to conserve his strength. Besides, he was repelled by the bitterness and strife he saw all around him and for that reason all the more anxious to find a refuge in a world of intellectual seclusion.

Montaigne's philosophy of skepticism and disenchantment

Montaigne's ideas are contained in his famous *Essays*, written during his years of retirement. The essence of his philosophy is skepticism in regard to all dogma and final truth. He knew too much about the diversity of beliefs among men, the welter of strange customs revealed by geographic discoveries, and the disturbing conclusions of the new science ever to accept the idea that any one sect had exclusive possession of "the Truth delivered once for all to the saints." It seemed to him that religion and morality were as much the product of custom as styles of dress or habits of eating. He taught that God is unknowable, and that it is as foolish to "weep that we shall not exist a hundred years hence as it would be to weep that we had not lived a hundred years ago." Man should be encouraged to despise death and to live nobly and delicately in this life rather than to yearn piously for an after-existence that is doubtful at best. Montaigne was just as skeptical in regard to any assumption of final truth in philosophy or science. The conclusions of reason, he taught, are sometimes fallacious, and the senses often deceive us. The sooner men come to realize that there is no certainty anywhere the better chance they will have to escape the tyranny which flows from

[3] *Works of Rabelais* (Urquhart and Motteux, trans.), First Book, p. 165.

superstition and bigotry. The road to salvation lies in doubt, not in faith. A second element in Montaigne's philosophy was cynicism. He could see no real difference between the morals of Christians and those of infidels. All sects, he pointed out, fight each other with equal ferocity, except that "there is no hatred so absolute as that which is Christian." Neither could he see any value in crusades or revolutions for the purpose of overthrowing one system and establishing another. All human institutions in his judgment were about equally futile, and he therefore considered it fatuous that man should take them so seriously as to wade through slaughter in order to substitute one for its opposite. No ideal, he maintained, is worth burning your neighbor for. In his attitude toward questions of ethics Montaigne was not such a ribald champion of carnality as Rabelais; yet he had no sympathy for asceticism. He believed it ridiculous that men should attempt to deny their physical natures and pretend that everything connected with sense is unworthy. "Sit we upon the highest throne in the world," he declared, "yet we do but sit upon our own behind." The philosophy of Montaigne, tinctured as it was with escapism and disenchantment, marked a fitting close of the Renaissance in France. But in spite of his negative attitude he did more good in the world than most of his contemporaries who founded new faiths or invented new excuses for absolute monarchs to enslave their subjects. Not only did his ridicule help to quench the flames of the cruel hysteria against witches, but the influence of his skeptical teachings had no small effect in combating fanaticism generally and in paving the way for a more generous tolerance in the future.

Montaigne's tolerance

4. The Spanish Renaissance

During the sixteenth and early seventeenth centuries Spain was at the height of her glory. Her conquests in the Western Hemisphere brought wealth to her nobles and merchants and gave her a proud position in the front rank of European states. Notwithstanding these facts the Spanish nation was not one of the leaders in Renaissance culture. Apparently her citizens were too deeply absorbed in plundering the conquered territories to devote much attention to intellectual or artistic pursuits. Moreover, the long war with the Moors had engendered a spirit of bigotry, the position of the church was too strong, while the expulsion of the Jews at the end of the fifteenth century had deprived the country of talent it could ill afford to lose. For these reasons the Spanish Renaissance was limited to a very few achievements in painting and literature, albeit some of these rank in brilliance with the best that other countries produced.

Reasons for the backwardness of Spain in the Renaissance

Spanish painting bore the deep impression of the bitter struggle between Christian and Moor. As a result it expressed an intense preoccupation with religion and with themes of anguish and tragedy. **425**

*The character
of Spanish
painting*

El Greco

*See color
plates at
page 476*

*Spanish litera-
ture: the drama*

*The satirical
novel of Cer-
vantes*

426

Its background was medieval, upon which were engrafted certain influences from Flanders and later from Italy. The first of the eminent Spanish painters was Luis de Morales (1517–1586), frequently called "The Divine." His Madonnas, Crucifixions, and Mater Dolorosas typified that earnest devotion to Catholic orthodoxy regarded by many Spaniards of this time as a duty both religious and patriotic. But the most talented artist of the Spanish Renaissance was not a native of Spain at all, but an immigrant from the island of Crete. His real name was Domenico Theotocopuli, but he is commonly called El Greco. After studying for some time under Titian in Venice, El Greco settled in Toledo about 1575, to live there until his death in 1614. A stern individualist in temperament, he seems to have imbibed but little of the warmth of color and serene joy in satin splendor of the Venetian school. Instead, nearly all of his art is characterized by fevered emotionalism, stark tragedy, or enraptured flights into the supernatural and mystical. His figures are often those of gaunt, half-crazed fanatics; his colors are cold and ashen; while his scenes of suffering and death seem deliberately contrived to produce an impression of horror. Among his famous works are *The Burial of the Count of Orgaz, Pentecost,* and *The Apocalyptic Vision.* Better than any other artist, El Greco expresses the fiery religious zeal of the Spanish people during the heyday of the Jesuits and the Inquisition.

Literature in the Spanish Renaissance displayed tendencies not dissimilar to those in painting. This was notably true of drama, which frequently took the form of allegorical plays depicting the mystery of transubstantiation or appealing to some passion of religious fervor. Others of the dramatic productions dwelt upon themes of political pride or sang the praises of the bourgeoisie and expressed contempt for the dying world of feudalism. The colossus among the Spanish dramatists was Lope de Vega (1562–1635), the most prolific author of plays the literary world has seen. He is supposed to have written no fewer than 1500 comedies and more than 400 religious allegories. Of the total about 500 survive to this day. His secular dramas fall mainly into two classes: (1) the "cloak and sword plays," which depict the violent intrigues and exaggerated ideals of honor among the upper classes; and (2) the plays of national greatness, which celebrate the glories of Spain in her prime and represent the king as the protector of the people against a vicious and degenerate nobility.

Few would deny that the most gifted writer of the Spanish Renaissance was Miguel de Cervantes (1547–1616). His great masterpiece, *Don Quixote,* has even been described as "incomparably the best novel ever written." Composed in the best tradition of Spanish satirical prose, it recounts the adventures of a Spanish gentleman (Don Quixote) who has been slightly unbalanced by constant reading of chivalric romances. His mind filled with all kinds of fantastic adventures, he finally sets out at the age of fifty upon the slippery road of knight-errantry. He imagines windmills to be glowering giants and flocks of sheep to be armies of infidels, whom it is his duty to rout with his spear. In his disordered fancy he mistakes inns for castles and the serving-wenches within them for courtly ladies on fire with love of him. The advances they have no intention of making he must graciously repel in order to prove his devotion to his own Dulcinea. Set off in bold contrast to the ridiculous knight-errant is the figure of his faithful squire, Sancho Panza. The latter represents the ideal of the practical man, with his feet on the ground and content with the substantial pleasures of eating, drinking, and sleeping. The book as a whole is a pungent satire on feudalism, especially on the pretensions of the nobles as the champions of honor and right. Its enormous popularity was convincing proof that medieval civilization was largely extinct even in Spain.

5. The Renaissance in England

In common with Spain, England also enjoyed a golden age in the sixteenth and early seventeenth centuries. Though her vast colonial empire had not yet been established, she was nevertheless reaping big profits from the production of wool and from her trade with the Continent. Her government, recently consolidated under the rule of the Tudors, was making the prosperity of the middle class the object of its special solicitude. Through the elimination of foreign traders, the granting of favors to English shipping, and the negotiation of reciprocal commercial treaties, the English merchant classes were given exceptional advantages over their rivals in other countries. The growth of a national consciousness, the awakening of pride in the power of the state, and the spread of humanism from Italy, France, and the Low Countries also contributed toward the flowering of a brilliant culture in England. Nevertheless, the English Renaissance was confined primarily to philosophy and literature. The arts did not flourish; perhaps because of the Calvinist influence, which began to make itself felt in Britain by the middle of the sixteenth century.

The economic and political foundations of the Renaissance in England

The earliest philosophers of the English Renaissance may best be described simply as humanists. But while they were not unmindful of the value of classical studies, they were interested chiefly in the more practical aspects of humanism. Most of them desired a simpler and more rational Christianity and looked forward to an educational system freed from the dominance of medieval logic. Others were concerned primarily with individual freedom and the correction of social abuses. The greatest of these early thinkers was Sir Thomas More, esteemed by contemporary humanists as "excellent above all his nation." Following a successful career as a lawyer and as Speaker of the House of Commons, More was appointed in 1529

The early English humanists

*The philosophy
of Sir Thomas
More*

Lord Chancellor of England. He was not long in this position, however, until he incurred the enmity of his royal master, Henry VIII. More was loyal to Catholic universalism and did not sympathize with the king's design of establishing a national church under subjection to the state. When in 1534 he refused to take the Oath of Supremacy acknowledging the king as the head of the Church of England, he was thrown into the Tower. A year later he was tried before a packed jury, convicted, and beheaded. More's philosophy is contained in his *Utopia*, which he published in 1516. Purporting to describe an ideal society on an imaginary island, the book is really an indictment of the glaring abuses of the time—of poverty undeserved and wealth unearned, of drastic punishments, religious persecution, and the senseless slaughter of war. The inhabitants of Utopia hold all their goods in common, work only six hours a day so that all may have leisure for intellectual pursuits, and practice the natural virtues of wisdom, moderation, fortitude, and justice. Iron is the precious metal "because it is useful," war and monasticism are abolished, and tolerance is granted to all creeds that recognize the existence of God and the immortality of the soul. Despite criticism of the *Utopia* as deficient in wit and originality, the conclusion seems justified that the author's ideals of humanity and tolerance were considerably in advance of those of most other men of his time.

Sir Francis Bacon

The thinker who has gone down in history as the greatest of all English Renaissance philosophers is Sir Francis Bacon. Born in 1561, the son of a high government official, Bacon was nurtured in the lap of luxury until the age of seventeen when the death of his father compelled him to work for a living. Thereafter the dominating ambition of his life was to obtain some profitable position with the government which would enable him to pursue his intellectual interests. Probably it was this mania for security which accounts for the shady morality of his public career. When occasion arose, he did not shrink from concealing his true beliefs, from disloyalty to his friends, or from sharing in graft. In 1618 he was appointed Lord Chancellor, but after a scant three years in this office he was impeached for accepting bribes. Despite his protestations that the taking of money from litigants had never influenced his decisions, he was convicted and sentenced to pay a fine of $200,000 and to undergo imprisonment in the Tower "at the king's pleasure." King James I remitted the fine and limited the term of imprisonment to four days. Bacon devoted the remaining five years of his life to writing, especially to the completion of the third and enlarged edition of his essays. Among his most valuable works are the *Novum Organum* and *The Advancement of Learning*.

Bacon's inductive philosophy

Bacon's monumental contribution to philosophy was the glorification of the inductive method. He was by no means the discoverer of that method, but he trumpeted it forth as the indispensable ground of accurate knowledge. He believed that all seekers of truth in the past had stumbled in darkness because they were slaves of precon-

428

ceived ideas or prisoners in the dungeons of Scholastic logic. He
argued that in order to overcome these obstacles the philosopher
should turn to the direct observation of nature, to the accumulation
of facts about things and the discovery of the laws that govern
them. Induction alone, he believed, was the magic key which would
unlock the secrets of truth. Authority, tradition, and syllogistic logic
should be as sedulously avoided as the plague. But admirable as these
teachings are, they were honored by Bacon himself almost as much
in the breach as in the observance. He believed in astrology, divination, and witchcraft. However successful he may have been in
clearing his mind of ancient dogma, he was not a good enough
scientist to perceive the validity of the Copernican theory. Moreover, the distinction he drew between ordinary knowledge and
the truths of religion was hardly in keeping with his stanch defense
of induction. "The senses," he wrote, "are like the sun, which displays the face of the earth, but shuts up that of the heavens." For
our voyage to the realm of celestial truth, we must "quit the small
vessel of human reason and put ourselves on board the ship of the
Church, which alone possesses the divine needle for justly shaping
the course. The stars of philosophy will be of no further service to
us. As we are obliged to obey the divine law, though our will mur-
mur against it, so we are obliged to believe in the word of God,
though our reason is shocked at it. The more absurd and incredible
any divine mystery is, the greater honor we do God in believing
it." It was not such a far cry after all from Roger Bacon in the thirteenth century to Francis Bacon in the seventeenth.

In literature, also, the English followed much more closely in the
footsteps of their medieval forerunners than did the Renaissance
writers in any other country with the exception of Italy. Indeed, it
is difficult to say just when the English Renaissance in literature
began. Chaucer's great work, the *Canterbury Tales*, written toward
the end of the fourteenth century, is commonly considered medieval; yet it breathed a spirit of earthiness and of lusty contempt for
the mystical quite as pronounced as anything to be found in the
writings of Shakespeare. If there were any essential differences between the English literature of the Renaissance and that produced
during the late Middle Ages, they would consist in a bolder individualism, a stronger sense of national pride, and a deeper interest
in themes of philosophic import. The first great poet in England
after the time of Chaucer was Edmund Spenser (1552?–1599). His
immortal creation, *The Faërie Queene*, is a colorful epic of England's greatness in the days of Queen Elizabeth. Though written as
a moral allegory to express the author's desire for a return to the
virtues of chivalry, it celebrates also the joy in conquest and much
of the gorgeous sensuousness typical of Renaissance humanism. The
rich music of its style and its wealth of picturesque incident have
endowed the poem with lasting popularity.

*English Renais-
sance literature*

But the most splendid achievements of the English in the Eliza-   **429** bethan Age were in the realm of drama. Not since the days of the Greeks had the writing of tragedies and comedies attained such heights as were reached in England during the sixteenth and early seventeenth centuries. Especially after 1580 a galaxy of playwrights appeared whose work outshone that of all their predecessors in nearly two thousand years. Included in this galaxy were such luminaries as Christopher Marlowe, Beaumont and Fletcher, Ben Jonson, and Shakespeare, of whom the first and the last are chiefly significant to the historian. Better than anyone else in his time, Christopher Marlowe embodies the insatiable egoism of the Renaissance—the everlasting craving for the fullness of life, for unlimited knowledge and experience. His brief but stormy career was a succession of scandalous escapades and fiery revolts against the restraints of convention until it was terminated by his death in a tavern brawl before he was thirty years old. The best known of his plays, entitled *Doctor Faustus*, is based upon the legend of Faust, in which the hero sells his soul to the devil in return for the power to feel every possible sensation, experience every possible triumph, and know all the mysteries of the universe.

The life and
writings of
William
Shakespeare

William Shakespeare, the most talented genius in the history of drama since Euripides, was born in 1564 into the family of a petty tradesman in the provincial market town of Stratford-on-Avon. His life is enshrouded in more mists of obscurity than the careers of most other great men. It is known that he left his native village when he was about twenty years old, and that ultimately he drifted to London to find employment in the theater. Tradition relates that for a time he earned his living by holding the horses of the more prosperous patrons of the drama. How he eventually became an actor and still later a writer of plays is unknown, but there is evidence that by the time he was twenty-eight he had already acquired a reputation as an author sufficient to excite the jealousy of his rivals. Before he retired to his native Stratford about 1610 to spend the rest of his days in ease, he had written or collaborated in writing nearly forty plays, to say nothing of 150 sonnets and two narrative poems.

The character
of Shakespeare's
work

In paying homage to the universality of Shakespeare's genius, we must not lose sight of the fact that he was also a child of the Renaissance. His work bore the deep impression of most of the virtues and defects of Renaissance humanism. Almost as much as Boccaccio or Rabelais, he personified that intense love of things human and earthly which had characterized most of the great writers since the close of the Middle Ages. Moreover, like the majority of the humanists, he showed a limited concern with the problems of politics and the values of science. Virtually the only political theory that interested him greatly was whether a nation had a better chance of prospering under a good king who was weak or under a bad king who was
strong. Though his knowledge of the sciences of his time was ex-

William Shakespeare. Portrait
made for the First Folio edition of
his works, 1623.

tensive, he regarded them as consisting primarily of alchemy, astrology, and medicine.[4] But the force and range of Shakespeare's intellect were far from being bounded by the narrow horizons of the age when he lived. While few of the works of his contemporaries are now widely read, the plays of Shakespeare still hold their rank as a kind of secular Bible wherever the English language is spoken. The reason lies not only in the author's unrivaled gift of expression, but especially in his scintillating wit and his profound analysis of human character assailed by the storms of passion and tried by the whims of fate.

Shakespeare's dramas fall rather naturally into three main groups. Those written during his earlier years conformed to the traditions of existing plays and generally reflected his own confidence in personal success. They include such comedies as *A Midsummer Night's Dream* and *The Merchant of Venice*, a number of historical plays, and the lyrical tragedy, *Romeo and Juliet*. Shortly before 1600 Shakespeare seems to have experienced a change of mood. The restrained optimism of his earlier plays was supplanted by some deep disillusion which led him to distrust human nature and to indict the whole scheme of the universe. The result was a group of dramas characterized by bitterness, overwhelming pathos, and a troubled searching into the mysteries of things. The series begins with the tragedy of intellectual idealism represented by *Hamlet*, goes on to the cynicism of *Measure for Measure* and *All's Well That Ends Well*, and culminates in the cosmic tragedies of *Macbeth* and *King Lear*. Perhaps the famous speech of Gloucester in the last of these plays may be taken to illustrate the depths of the author's pessimism at this time:

Types of Shakespeare's plays

[4] In psychology, however, he gives evidence of being ahead of his time, especially in his treatment of insanity. Perhaps this was natural in view of his profound interest in human emotions, in man's conflict with himself and with the universe of which he is a part.

431

As flies to wanton boys are we to the gods;
They kill us for their sport.[5]

The final group of dramas includes those written during the closing years of Shakespeare's life, probably after his retirement. Among them are *The Winter's Tale* and *The Tempest*. All of them may be described as idyllic romances. Trouble and grief are now assumed to be only the shadows in a beautiful picture. Despite individual tragedy, the divine plan of the universe is somehow benevolent and just.

6. Renaissance Developments in Music

Renaissance music compared with its medieval antecedents

Music in western Europe in the fifteenth and sixteenth centuries reached such a high point of development that it constitutes, together with painting and sculpture, one of the most brilliant aspects of Renaissance activity. While the visual arts were stimulated by the study of ancient models, music flowered naturally from an independent evolution which had long been in progress in medieval Christendom. As earlier, leadership was supplied by men trained in the service of the church, but the value of folk music was now appreciated, and its principles were combined with those of sacred music to bring a decided gain in color and emotional appeal. The distinction between sacred and profane became less sharp; most composers did not restrict their activities to either field. While the contrapuntal treatment of voices held the center of interest, some writing for instruments was attempted, and the use of instruments for accompaniment steadily increased. Music was no longer regarded merely as a diversion or an adjunct to worship but as an independent art.

The leading schools of composition

Different sections of Europe vied with one another for musical leadership. As with the other arts, advance was related to the increasingly generous patronage made possible by the expansion of commerce, and was centered in the prosperous towns. During the fifteenth century first rank was held by the cities of the Netherlands and Burgundy. The Netherlands school carried vocal counterpoint to a technical perfection. While its members inclined toward a display of excessive ingenuity, they nevertheless rendered a real service by providing models of excellent workmanship. In the sixteenth century the Italians were able to duplicate the skill of their northern masters and far surpassed them in the subordination of technique to artistic effect. In Italy for the first time warmth, color, and sheer beauty became conspicuous features in choral art. In the splendidly Byzantine St. Mark's cathedral of Venice the tendency toward sensuous and brilliant effects was most pronounced, and was emphasized by the use of double choirs singing antiphonally. Thus

[5] *King Lear*, Act IV, scene 1.

a similarity is apparent between the Venetian schools of music and
painting. At Rome, on the other hand, especially as reflected in the
papal choir, there was a stricter adherence to tradition and an emphasis upon the element of worship. The greatest exponent of the Roman school and the composer whose work marks the culmination
of the music of the age in its religious aspect was Palestrina (1526–
1594). In his masses and motets technical skill and intensity of purpose are so perfectly blended that the results meet the most exacting
artistic standards. Palestrina's music, though employing rich har-
monies and sometimes intricate in structure, constantly avoids ex-

Palestrina

Musical Instruments in the Sixteenth Century. In the lower left
is shown a small pipe organ, with a
bellows operated by the man seated
opposite the player. The boxlike
instrument on the table is a clavi-
chord. The triangular shaped tube
in the lower right corner is a
trumsheit, or German "drum log."

travagance and possesses a clarity and tonal purity which appeal
immediately to the listener. In its restraint, dignity, and moods of
devout meditation or elation, it exemplifies not the secular ideals
of Renaissance humanism but a profound religious dedication. Comparable developments to those in Italy were taking place in Austria
and in southern Germany. Orlandus Lassus, court choirmaster at
Munich from 1560 to 1590, was the equal of Palestrina in his handling of the contrapuntal style and exhibited a greater breadth of
interests and variety of styles. Progress in England was facilitated
by the patronage of the music-loving Tudor monarchs. The commercial ties between England and the Flemish cities may have provided an initial stimulus, but the English composers had enough
fertility and originality to keep from being mere imitators of Continental models. The English school takes pre-eminence for the

Orlandus Lassus

433

development of the *madrigal,* in which the subtlety and sustained interest of the perfected contrapuntal technique were applied to secular themes. Because of their vitality and freshness, these madrigals have never ceased to charm. The general level of musical proficiency seems to have been higher in Queen Elizabeth's day than in ours: the singing of part-songs was a popular pastime in homes and at informal social gatherings, and the ability to read a part at sight was expected of a well-bred person.

Renaissance music a magnificent achievement

In conclusion, it may be observed that while counterpoint had matured, our modern harmonic system had been born, and thus a way was opened for fresh experimentation. At the same time one should realize that the music of the Renaissance constitutes not merely a stage in evolution but a magnificent achievement in itself, with masters who rank among the great of all time. The composers Palestrina and Lassus are as truly representative of the artistic triumph of the Renaissance as are the painters Raphael and Michelangelo. The fifteenth and sixteenth centuries, fittingly called the "golden age of song," have never been surpassed in the realization of the possibilities for beauty inherent in the human voice. Their heritage, long neglected except at a few ecclesiastical centers, has within recent years begun to be appreciated, and is now gaining in popularity as interested groups of musicians devote themselves to its revival.

7. *The Renaissance in Religion*

The Christian Renaissance

No account of the age of the Renaissance would be complete without some attention to the Renaissance in religion, or the Christian Renaissance as it is commonly called. This was a movement almost entirely independent of the Protestant Revolution, which will be discussed in the next chapter. The leaders of the Christian Renaissance were generally humanists, not Protestants. Few of them ever deserted the Catholic faith; their aim was to purify that faith from within, not to overthrow it. Most of them found the bigotry of early Protestantism as repugnant to their religious ideals as any of the abuses in the Catholic church. The original impetus for the Christian Renaissance appears to have come from the Brethren of the Common Life, a group of pious laymen who maintained schools in the Low Countries and in western Germany. Their aim was to propagate a simple religion of practical piety, as free as possible from dogmatism and ritual. The most noted of their early followers was Thomas à Kempis, who wrote or edited about 1425 a book entitled *The Imitation of Christ.* Though profoundly mystical in tone, the book nevertheless repudiated the extreme otherworldliness of medieval mystics and urged a life of simple devotion to the teachings of Jesus. For over a century the *Imitation* was more widely read in Europe than any other book with the exception of the Bible.

By 1500 the Christian Renaissance had become definitely associated with northern humanism. Writers and philosophers in every country lent their support to the movement. Prominent among them were Sebastian Brant in Germany, Sir Thomas More in England, Erasmus in the Low Countries, and figures of lesser renown in France and Spain. The religious teachings of these men were thoroughly in keeping with the humanist ideal as it was understood in northern Europe. Believing that religion should function for the good of man and not for the benefit of an organized church or even for the glory of an ineffable God, they interpreted Christianity primarily in ethical terms. Many of the theological and supernatural elements in it they regarded as superfluous, if not positively harmful. They likewise had little use for ceremonies of any kind, and they ridiculed the superstitions connected with the veneration of relics and the sale of indulgences. While they recognized the necessity of a limited amount of ecclesiastical organization, they denied the absolute authority of the Pope and refused to admit that priests were really essential as intermediaries between man and God. In fine, what most of these Christian humanists really desired was the superiority of reason over faith, the primacy of conduct over dogma, and the supremacy of the individual over the organized system. They believed that this simple and rational religion could best be achieved, not through violent revolt against the Catholic church, but through the gradual conquest of ignorance and the elimination of abuses.

Stultifera Nauis,

qua omnium mortalium narratur ſtultitia, admodum vtilis & neceſſaria ab omnibus ad ſuam ſalutem perlegenda, è Latino ſermone in noſtrum vulgarem verſa, & iam diligenter impreſſa. An. Do. 1 5 7 0.

The Ship of Fooles, wherin is ſhewed the folly of all Eſtates, with diuers other workes adioyned vnto the ſame, very profitable and fruitfull for all men. Tranſlated out of Latin into Engliſhe by Alexander Barclay Prieſt.

Title Page of an English Translation of Sebastian Brant's Allegorical Satire *Das Narrenschiff* (*Ship of Fools*), 1494.

THE EXPANSION
OF THE
RENAISSANCE

*The decline
of the Renais-
sance outside
of Italy*

The decline of Renaissance culture in the countries of northern and western Europe came much less abruptly than in Italy. Indeed, the change in some respects was so gradual that there was simply a fusion of the old with the new. The achievements in science, for example, were merely extended, although with a definite shift of emphasis as time went on from the mathematical and physical branches to the biological. The Renaissance art of northern Europe, moreover, gradually evolved into the baroque, which dominated the seventeenth and early eighteenth centuries. On the other hand, humanism, in its Renaissance meaning of the worship of man and indifference to everything else, practically died out after the sixteenth century. In philosophy there has since been a tendency to exalt the universe and to relegate man to a place of insignificance as the helpless victim of an all-powerful destiny. When the end of the northern Renaissance did finally come, it probably resulted chiefly from the heritage of bitterness and unreason left by the Protestant Revolt. But that is a subject which can be discussed more appropriately in the chapter that follows.

Selected Readings

· *Items so designated are available in paperbound editions.*

Allen, P. S., *The Age of Erasmus*, New York, 1914.
· Beard, M. R., *A History of the Business Man*, New York, 1938. (Ann Arbor) Interesting sketches of Renaissance capitalists.
Bush, D., *The Renaissance and English Humanism*, Toronto, 1939. A brief but excellent introduction.
Elton, G. R., *England Under the Tudors*, London, 1955.
· Gilmore, M., *The World of Humanism*, New York, 1952. (Torchbooks) An excellent general account.
Gray, Cecil, *The History of Music*, 2nd edn., New York, 1931.
· Huizinga, Johan, *The Waning of the Middle Ages*, London, 1924. (Anchor)
Hyma, Albert, *The Christian Renaissance*, New York, 1924. The most authoritative work on this subject.
———, *Erasmus and the Humanists*, New York, 1930.
Lang, Paul, *Music in Western Civilization*, New York, 1941. The best survey yet published.
Lucas, Henry S., *The Renaissance and the Reformation*, New York, 1934.
McGinn, D. F., *Shakespeare and the Drama of His Age*, New Brunswick, N.J., 1938.
Oxford History of Music, Vols. I–II.
Panofsky, *Early Netherlandish Painting; Its Origins and Character*, Cambridge, Mass., 1954. Valuable for an understanding of Flemish painters.
· Pater, Walter, *The Renaissance*, New York. (Mentor, Meridian) A thoughtful interpretation.
Randall, J. H., Jr., *The Making of the Modern Mind*, Boston, 1926, Chs. VI and IX.
Reese, Gustave, *Music in the Renaissance*, New York, 1954.
Sichel, Edith, *The Renaissance*, New York, 1914.
Smith, Preserved, *A History of Modern Culture*, New York, 1930, Vol. I. Thorough and scholarly.
———, *Erasmus, A Study of His Life, Ideals and Place in History*, New York, 1923.

Taylor, H. O., *Thought and Expression in the Sixteenth Century*, London, 1920. Reliable and suggestive.

Thorndike, Lynn, *A History of Magic and Experimental Science in the Fourteenth and Fifteenth Centuries*, New York, 1934, 2 vols. Detailed and authoritative.

——, *Science and Thought in the Fifteenth Century*, New York, 1929.

Tilley, A. A., *Studies in the French Renaissance*, New York, 1923.

Van Dyke, Paul, *The Age of the Renascence*, New York, 1912.

· Wolf, A., *A History of Science, Technology and Philosophy in the XVIth and XVIIth Centuries*, New York, 1935. (Torchbooks, 2 vols.)

Source Materials

Bacon, Sir Francis, *The Great Instauration*, Preface.

Erasmus, Desiderius, *The Complaint of Peace.*

——, *The Handbook of a Christian Knight.*

——, *The Praise of Folly.*

Montaigne, Michel de, *Essays.*

More, Sir Thomas, *Utopia*, especially Book II.

Rabelais, François, *Gargantua and Pantagruel*, especially Book I.

CHAPTER 17

The Age of the Reformation
(1517-ca.1600)

> For the word of God cannot be received and honored by any
> works, but by faith alone.
> —Martin Luther, *On Christian Liberty*

> In conformity to the clear doctrine of the Scripture, we assert
> that by an eternal and immutable counsel, God has once for all
> determined both whom he would admit to salvation and whom
> he would condemn to destruction. . . . In the elect, we consider
> calling as an evidence of election, and justification as another
> token of its manifestation, till they arrive in glory, which consti-
> tutes its completion.
> —John Calvin, *Institutes* III.xxi

*The later
stages of the
Renaissance
accompanied by
a religious revo-
lution*

Preceding chapters have described the unfolding of a marvelous
culture which marked the transition from the Middle Ages to the
modern world. It became apparent that this culture, known as the
Renaissance, was almost as peculiarly an echo of the past as a herald
of the future. Much of its literature, art, and philosophy, and all of
its superstitions, had roots which were deeply buried in classical
antiquity or in the fabulous centuries of the Middle Ages. Even its
humanism breathed veneration for the past. Only in science and
politics and in the vigorous assertion of the right of the individual
to live as unconventionally and as dangerously as he liked was there
much that was really new. But the Renaissance in its later stages
was accompanied by the growth of another movement, the Reformation, which somewhat more accurately foreshadowed the
modern age. This movement included two principal phases: the
Protestant Revolution, which broke out in 1517 and resulted in the
secession of most of northern Europe from the Roman faith; and
the Catholic Reformation, which reached its height about 1560. Although the latter is not called a revolution, it really was such in
nearly every sense of the term; for it effected a profound alteration
of some of the notable features of late medieval Catholicism.

*The relation
between the
Renaissance and
the Reforma-
tion*

In a number of ways the Renaissance and the Reformation were
closely related. Both were products of that powerful current of individualism which wrought such havoc to the established order in
the fourteenth and fifteenth centuries. Each had a similar background of economic causes in the growth of capitalism and in the
rise of a bourgeois society. Both partook of the character of a
return to original sources: in the one case, to the literary and artistic
achievements of the Greeks and Romans; in the other, to the

Scriptures and the doctrines of the Church Fathers. But in spite of these important resemblances, it is misleading to think of the Reformation as merely the religious aspect of the Renaissance. The guiding principles of the two movements really had little in common. The essence of the Renaissance was enjoyment of this life and indifference to the supernatural. The spirit of the Reformation was otherworldliness and contempt for the things of the flesh as vastly inferior to the spiritual. In the judgment of the humanist, man's nature was inherently good; in the view of the Reformer, it was unspeakably corrupt and depraved. The leaders of the Renaissance believed in reason and tolerance; the followers of Luther and Calvin emphasized faith and conformity. While both the Renaissance and the Reformation aimed at a recovery of the past, each was really oriented in an altogether different direction. The past which the humanists strove to revive was Greek and Roman antiquity, though they actually continued a much larger number of late medieval traditions, especially in literature, than they were willing to admit. The Reformers, by contrast, were interested chiefly in a return to the teachings of St. Paul and St. Augustine; not only did they reject the humanist idea of a revival of pagan achievements, but the Protestants among them, at least, proposed to throw overboard practically the whole body of late medieval institutions and doctrines.

For reasons such as these it seems justifiable to conclude that the Reformation was not really a part of the Renaissance movement. In actual fact, it represented a much sharper break with the civilization of the Feudal Age than ever did the movement led by the humanists. The radical Reformers would have nothing to do with the basic theories and practices of thirteenth-century Christianity. Even the simple religion of love and selflessness for the betterment of man, as taught by St. Francis of Assisi, appeared to repel them almost as much as the mysteries of the sacramental theory or the bombastic claims of Innocent III to spiritual and temporal power. In the main, the religious results of this clash with medieval Christianity have endured to this day. Moreover, the Reformation was intimately bound up with certain political trends which have persisted throughout the modern era. Nationalism, as we shall see, was one of the principal causes of the Protestant Revolution. While it is true that several of the humanists wrote under the influence of national pride, perhaps the majority were swayed by altogether different considerations. Many were scornful of politics, being interested solely in man as an individual; others, the great Erasmus among them, were thoroughly international in their outlook. But the Protestant Reformers could scarcely have gained much of a hearing if they had not associated their cause with the powerful groundswell of national resentment in northern Europe against an ecclesiastical system which had come to be recognized as largely Italian in character. For this

The Reformation not really a part of the Renaissance

439

THE AGE
OF THE
REFORMATION
1517–ca. 1600

*The Christian
Renaissance*

as well as for the reasons mentioned previously, it would seem not unwarranted to regard the Reformation as a gateway to the modern world. And when we speak of the Renaissance in religion, we should think, not of the Reformation, but of the so-called Christian Renaissance, initiated by the Brethren of the Common Life and carried to its highest fulfillment in the teachings of Sir Thomas More and Erasmus. The common assumption that Luther hatched the egg which Erasmus had laid is true only in a very limited sense. The bird which Luther hatched belonged to a much tougher and wilder breed than any that could have descended from the Prince of the Humanists.

1. *The Protestant Revolution*

The Protestant Revolution sprang from a multiplicity of causes, most of them closely related to the political and economic conditions of the age. Nothing could be more grossly inaccurate than to think of the revolt against Rome as exclusively a religious movement. Had it not been for the basic political changes in northern Europe and the growth of new economic interests, Roman Catholicism would probably have undergone no more than a gradual evolution, perhaps in line with the teachings of the Christian Renaissance. Nevertheless, since the religious causes were the most obvious ones, it will be well to consider them first.

To the majority of Luther's early followers the movement he launched was chiefly a rebellion against abuses in the Catholic church. That such abuses existed no careful historian would deny, regardless of his religious affiliations. For example, many of the Roman clergy were incredibly ignorant. Some, having obtained their positions through irregular means, were unable to understand the Latin of the mass they were required to celebrate. There were even alleged to be cases of priests who could not repeat the Lord's Prayer or the creed in *any* language. Further, a considerable number of the clergy led scandalous lives. While some of the Popes and bishops were living in princely magnificence, the lowly priests occasionally sought to eke out the incomes from their parishes by keeping taverns, gaming houses, or other establishments for profit. Not only did some monks habitually ignore their vows of chastity, but a few indifferent members of the secular clergy surmounted the hardships of the rule of celibacy by keeping mistresses. Alexander VI, one of the most famous Popes on the eve of the Protestant Revolution, was known to have had eight illegitimate children, seven of them born before his election to the papacy. There were numerous evils also in connection with the sale of religious offices and dispensations. As in the case of most civil positions, offices in the church during the Renaissance period were commonly sold to the highest bidder. It

is estimated that Pope Leo X enjoyed an income of more than a million dollars a year from the sale of more than two thousand ecclesiastical offices. This abuse was rendered more serious by the fact that the men who bought these positions were under a strong temptation to make up for their investment by levying high fees for their services. The sale of dispensations was a second malodorous form of ecclesiastical graft. A dispensation may be defined as an exemption from a law of the church or from some vow previously taken. On the eve of the Reformation the dispensations most commonly sold were exemptions from fasting and from the marriage laws of the church. By way of illustration, first cousins would be permitted to marry for the payment of a fee of one ducat; while for closer degrees of relationship—for example, uncle and niece—the fee might be as much as thirty times that amount, depending upon ability to pay.

But the abuses which seemed to arouse the most ardent pressure for reform were the sale of indulgences and the superstitious veneration of relics. An indulgence is a remission of all or of part of the temporal punishment due to sin—that is, of the punishment in this life and in purgatory; it is not supposed to have anything to do with the punishment in hell. The theory upon which the indulgence rests is the famous doctrine of the Treasure of Merit developed by Scholastic theologians in the thirteenth century. According to this doctrine, Jesus and the saints, by reason of their "superfluous" virtues on earth, accumulated an excess of merit in heaven. This excess constitutes a treasure of grace upon which the Pope can draw for the benefit of ordinary mortals. Originally indulgences were not issued for payments of money, but only for works of charity, fasting, going on crusades, and the like. It was the Renaissance Popes, with their insatiable greed for revenue, who first embarked upon the sale of indulgences as a profitable business. And the methods they employed were far from scrupulous. The traffic in "pardons" was often turned over to bankers on a commission basis. As an example, the Fuggers in Augsburg had charge of the sale of indulgences for Leo X, with permission to pocket one-third of the proceeds. Naturally, but one motive dominated the business—to raise as much money as possible. As a consequence, the agents of the bankers deluded ignorant people into believing that the indulgences were passports to heaven. By the sixteenth century the nefarious traffic had assumed the proportions of a gigantic scandal.

For centuries before the Reformation the veneration of sacred relics had been an important element in Catholic worship. It was believed that objects used by the Christ, the Virgin, or the saints possessed a miraculous healing and protective virtue for anyone who touched them or came into their presence. But it was inevitable that this belief should have opened the way for innumerable frauds. Superstitious peasants could be easily convinced that almost any ancient splinter of wood was a fragment of the true cross. And

The sale of church offices and dispensations

The sale of indulgences

Abuses connected with the veneration of sacred relics

441

there was evidently no dearth of relic-mongers quick to take advantage of such credulity. The results were fantastic beyond belief. According to Erasmus, the churches of Europe contained enough wood of the true cross to build a ship. No fewer than five shinbones of the ass on which Jesus rode to Jerusalem were on exhibition in different places, to say nothing of twelve heads of John the Baptist. Martin Luther declared in a pamphlet lampooning his enemy, the Archbishop of Mainz, that the latter claimed to possess "a whole pound of the wind that blew for Elijah in the cave on Mount Horeb and two feathers and an egg of the Holy Ghost." [1]

Abuses not the primary causes of the Protestant Revolution

Modern historians agree, however, that abuses in the Catholic church were not the primary religious cause of the Protestant Revolution. It was medieval Catholicism itself, not the abuses therein, to which the Reformers objected. Moreover, just before the revolt broke out, conditions had begun to improve. Many pious Catholics themselves had started an agitation for reform, which in time would probably have eliminated most of the glaring evils in the system. But as so often happens in the case of revolutions, the improvement had come too late. Other forces more irresistible in character had been gradually gathering momentum. Chief among these forces of a religious nature was the growing reaction against late medieval theology, with its elaborate sacramental theory, its belief in the necessity of good works to supplement faith, and its doctrine of divine authority in the hands of the priests.

The clash between two different systems of theology: the Augustinian system

From preceding chapters the reader will recall that two different systems of theology had developed within the medieval church.[2] The first was formulated mainly by followers of St. Augustine in the early Middle Ages, on the basis of teachings in the Pauline Epistles. It was predicated on the assumption of an omnipotent God, who sees the whole drama of the universe in the twinkling of an eye. Not even a sparrow falls to the ground except in accordance with the divine decree. Human nature is hopelessly depraved, and it is therefore as impossible for man to perform good works as for thistles to bring forth figs. Man is absolutely dependent upon God not only for grace to keep him from sin but also for his fate after death. Only those mortals can be saved whom God for reasons of His own has predestined to inherit eternal life. Such in its barest outlines was the system of doctrine commonly known as Augustinianism. It was a theology well suited to the age of chaos which followed the breakup of the classical world. Men in this time were prone to fatalism and otherworldliness, for they seemed to be at the mercy of forces beyond their control. But the system never wholly died out. It was preserved intact for centuries in certain areas, especially of Germany, where the progress of late medieval civilization was

---

[1] Preserved Smith, *The Age of the Reformation*, pp. 495–96.
[2] See the chapters on The Civilization of Early Medieval Europe and The Civilization of the Feudal Age: Religious and Intellectual Developments.

comparatively slow. To Luther and many of his followers it seemed the most logical interpretation of Christian belief.

With the growth of a more abundant life in the cities of southern and western Europe, it was natural that the pessimistic philosophy of Augustinianism should have been replaced by a system which would restore to man some measure of pride in his own estate. The change was accelerated also by the growth of a dominant church organization. The theology of Augustinianism, by placing man's fate entirely in the hands of God, had seemed to imply that the functions of an organized church were practically unnecessary. Certainly no sinner could rely upon the ministrations of priests to improve his chances of salvation, since those who were to be saved had already been "elected" by God from all eternity. The new system of belief was finally crystallized in the writings of Peter Lombard and St. Thomas Aquinas in the twelfth and thirteenth centuries. Its cardinal premise was the idea that man had been endowed by God with freedom of will, with power to choose the good and avoid the evil. Man could not make this choice, however, entirely unaided, for without the support of heavenly grace he would be likely to fall into sin. It was therefore necessary for him to receive the sacraments, the indispensable means for communicating the grace of God to man. Of the seven sacraments of the church, the three most important for the layman were baptism, penance, and the Eucharist. The first wiped out the stain of previous sin; the second absolved the contrite sinner from guilt; while the third was especially significant for its effect in renewing the saving grace of Christ's sacrifice on the cross. Aside from baptism, none of the sacraments could ever be administered by anyone outside the ranks of the priesthood. The members of the clergy, having inherited the power of the keys from the Apostle Peter, alone had the authority to co-operate with God in forgiving sins and in performing the miracle of the Eucharist, whereby the bread and wine were transubstantiated into the body and blood of the Savior.

The late medieval theology of Peter Lombard and St. Thomas Aquinas

The Protestant Revolution was in very large measure a rebellion against the second of these systems of theology. Although the doctrines of Peter Lombard and St. Thomas Aquinas had really become part of the official theology of the church, they had never been universally accepted. To Christians who had been brought up under Augustinian influence, they seemed to detract from the sovereignty of God and to contradict the plain teachings of Paul that man's will is in bondage and his nature unspeakably vile. Worse still, in the opinion of these critics, was the fact that the new theology greatly strengthened the authority of the priesthood. In sum, what the Reformers wanted was a return to a more primitive Christianity than that which had prevailed since the thirteenth century. Any doctrine or practice not expressly sanctioned in the Scriptures, especially in the Pauline Epistles, or not recognized by

The Protestant Revolution a rebellion against the late medieval system of theology

443

the Fathers of the Church, they were strongly inclined to reject. It was for this reason that they condemned not only the theory of the priesthood and the sacramental system of the church, but also such medieval additions to the faith as the worship of the Virgin, the belief in purgatory, the invocation of saints, the veneration of relics, and the rule of celibacy for the clergy. Motives of rationalism or skepticism had comparatively little to do with it. While it is true that Luther ridiculed the worship of relics as a form of superstition, in the main the early Protestants were even more suspicious of reason than the Catholics. Their religious ideal rested upon the Augustinian dogmas of original sin, the total depravity of man, predestination, and the bondage of the will—which were certainly more difficult to justify on a rational basis than the liberalized teachings of St. Thomas.

Influence of the "Babylonian Captivity" of the papacy and the Great Schism

A few remaining religious causes deserve at least passing mention. One was the decline of respect for the papacy in consequence of the so-called "Babylonian Captivity" and the Great Schism. The "Babylonian Captivity" grew out of a quarrel between King Philip IV of France and Pope Boniface VIII at the beginning of the fourteenth century. The soldiers of the king arrested the Pope, and soon afterward Boniface died from the effects of the humiliation. A short

St. John Lateran, the Pope's Cathedral in Rome. The "Mother Church" of Catholic Christendom, it derives its name from Plautius Lateranus, a rich nobleman whose property in this area was confiscated by Nero.

time later King Philip's own candidate was elected to St. Peter's throne, and the papal capital was transferred to Avignon in the Rhone valley, where it remained for nearly seventy years. Surrounded by French influences, the Popes who reigned at Avignon were unable to escape the charge of subservience to French interests. In the minds of many Christians the papacy had ceased to be an international institution and had been degraded into the mere plaything of a secular power. In 1378 the head of the church suffered an even greater loss of prestige. An effort to restore the papacy to its original capital led to the election of two Popes, one at Avignon and one at Rome, each loudly proclaiming himself the rightful successor of the Apostle Peter. The resulting division of the church into two factions, supporting respectively the claims of the French and Italian Popes, is known as the Great Schism. Though finally healed by the Council of Constance in 1417, its effect in weakening the position of the papacy could hardly be overestimated.

Still another factor of some importance in hastening the Protestant Revolution was the influence of the mystics and early reformers. For more than two centuries before the time of Luther, mysticism had become one of the most popular forms of religious expression in northern Europe. And it is not without significance that the vast majority of the mystics were Germans or natives of the Low Countries. Pre-eminent among them was Meister Eckhart, who lived in the fourteenth century. Though none of the mystics preached open rebellion against the Catholic system, they were vehemently opposed to the ritualistic route to salvation sponsored by the medieval church. Their version of religion was one in which the individual would attain the highest heaven through extinction of selfish desires and absolute surrender of the soul to God. No sacraments or priestly miracles would be necessary. Faith and a deep emotional piety would accomplish more wonders in reconciling sinful man to God than all the masses in the calendar of the church. Along with the mystics a number of pre-Reformation reformers exerted considerable influence in preparing the ground for the Protestant Revolt. At the end of the fourteenth century an Oxford professor by the name of John Wyclif launched an attack upon the Catholic system which anticipated much of the thunder of Luther and Calvin. He denounced the immorality of the clergy, condemned indulgences and the temporal power of the church, recommended marriage of the clergy, insisted upon the supreme authority of the Scriptures as the source of belief, and denied transubstantiation, though admitting as Luther did later that Christ is actually present in the bread and wine. Most of Wyclif's teachings were ultimately carried to central Europe by Czech students from Oxford. They were actively propagated in Bohemia by John Huss, who was burned at the stake in 1415. Luther acknowledged his deep indebtedness to the Bohemian martyr.

Influence of the mystics and early reformers

Wyclif and Huss

As a political movement the Protestant Revolt was mainly the result of two causes: first, the growth of a national consciousness in northern Europe; and second, the rise of despotic governments. Ever since the late Middle Ages there had been a growing spirit of independence among many of the peoples outside of Italy. They had come to regard their own national life as unique and to resent interference from any external source. The Pope in particular they were inclined to view as a foreigner, who had no right to meddle with local affairs in England, France, or Germany. This feeling was manifested in England as early as the middle of the fourteenth century, when the famous Statutes of Provisors and Praemunire were passed. The first prohibited appointments by the Pope to church offices in England, while the second forbade the appeal of cases from the English courts to Rome. A law more extreme than either of these was issued by the king of France in 1438. The French law, known

The political causes of the Protestant Revolution: the growth of nationalism

as the Pragmatic Sanction of Bourges, practically abolished all papal authority in the country, including the appointive authority and the right to raise revenue. To the civil magistrates was given the power to regulate religious affairs within their own districts. A subsequent decree provided the death penalty for any agent of the Pope who should bring a bull into the country contradicting the Pragmatic Sanction. In Germany, despite the fact that there was no solid political unity, national feeling was by no means absent. It expressed itself in violent attacks upon the clergy by the Imperial Diet and in numerous decrees by the rulers of separate states prohibiting ecclesiastical appointments and the sale of indulgences without their consent.

The rise of despotic governments

The growth of a consciousness of national independence in all of these countries went hand in hand with the rise of despotic governments. Indeed, it would be difficult to say how much of the sense of nationality was spontaneous and how much of it was stimulated by ambitious princes intent upon increasing their power. At any rate it is certain that the claims of rulers to absolute authority were bound to result in defiance of Rome. No despot could long be expected to tolerate the exclusion of religion from his sphere of control. He could not be a despot so long as there was a double jurisdiction within his realm. The appetite of princes for control over the church was whetted originally by the revival of the Roman law, with its doctrine that the people had delegated *all* of their power to the secular ruler. To this must be added the effect of the teaching of Wyclif in England and Pierre Dubois (1250–1312) in France that the temporal power of the Pope should be transferred to the king. From this doctrine it was a comparatively easy step to the idea that all of the Pope's authority could be properly assumed by the head of the state. But whatever the reasons for its growth, there can be no doubt that the ambition of secular princes to establish churches under their own control was a primary cause of the mounting antagonism against Rome.

Economic causes: the desire to confiscate the wealth of the Catholic church

Finally, there were the economic causes of the Protestant Revolution. Foremost among these were the desire to get possession of the wealth of the church and resentment against papal taxation. In the course of its history from the beginning of the Middle Ages, the church had grown into a vast economic empire. It was by far the largest landowner in western Europe, to say nothing of its enormous movable wealth in the form of rich furnishings, jewels, precious metals, and the like. Estimates of the amount of land held by bishoprics and monasteries in the sixteenth century range as high as one-third of the total in Germany and one-fifth in France. Some of these possessions had been acquired by the church through grants by kings and nobles, but most of them came from the gifts and bequests of pious citizens. Legacy-hunting was a favorite occupation of the clergy as early as the twelfth century, as evidenced by a decree of Pope Alexander III declaring that no will could be valid unless made in the presence of a priest.[3] The existence of so much wealth in the hands of the church was a galling grievance not only to the ascetic reformers of the sixteenth century, but to thousands of laymen as well. Kings, panting for big armies and navies, had an urgent need for more revenue. But Catholic law prohibited the taxing of church property. The exemption of episcopal and monastic property from taxation meant a heavier burden on the possessions of individual owners, especially on the property of merchants and bankers. Moreover, the lesser nobles in Germany were being threatened with extinction on account of the collapse of the manorial economy. Many of them looked with covetous eyes upon the lands of the church. If only some excuse could be found for expropriating these, their difficult situation might be relieved.

Papal taxation, by the eve of the Protestant Revolution, had assumed a baffling variety of irritating forms. The most nearly universal, if not the most burdensome, was the so-called *Peter's pence*, an annual levy on every household in Christendom.[4] It must be understood that this tax was in addition to the *tithe*, which was supposed to be one-tenth of every Christian's income paid for the support of the parish church. Then there were the innumerable fees paid into the papal treasury for indulgences, dispensations, appeals of judicial decisions, and so on. In a very real sense the moneys collected for the sale of church offices and the *annates*, or commissions levied on the first year's income of every bishop and priest, were also forms of papal taxation, since the officials who paid them eventually reimbursed themselves through increased collections from the people. But the main objection to these taxes was not that they were so numerous and burdensome. The famous accusation of some modern Catholic writers that the Protestants simply wanted a cheaper religion has no good foundation in fact. The real basis of grievance against the papal levies was their effect in draining the northern countries of so much of their wealth for the enrichment of Italy. Economically the situation was almost exactly the same as if the nations of northern Europe had been conquered by a foreign prince and tribute imposed upon them. Some Germans and Englishmen were scandalized also by the fact that most of the money collected was not being spent for religious purposes, but was being squandered by worldly Popes to maintain a luxurious court. The reason for the resentment, however, was probably as much financial as moral.

Resentment against papal taxation

A third important economic cause of the Protestant Revolt was

[3] J. W. Thompson, *An Economic and Social History of the Middle Ages*, p. 688.

[4] Peter's pence derived its name from the fact that it was a tax of one penny. But the English penny at the end of the Middle Ages was the equivalent in purchasing power of slightly more than one dollar of our money. H. E. Barnes, *An Economic History of the Western World*, p. 121.

Conflicts be-
tween middle-
class ambitions
and the ascetic
ideals of the
church

the conflict between the ambitions of the new middle class and the ascetic ideals of medieval Christianity. It was shown in a preceding chapter that the Catholic philosophers of the late Middle Ages had developed an elaborate theory designed for the guidance of the Christian in matters of production and trade.[5] This theory was founded upon the assumption that business for the sake of profit is essentially immoral. No one has a right to any more than a reasonable wage for the service he renders to society. All wealth acquired in excess of this amount should be given to the church to be distributed for the benefit of the needy. The merchant or craftsman who strives to get rich at the expense of the people is really no better than a common thief. To gain an advantage over a rival in business by cornering the market or beating down wages is contrary to all law and morality. Equally sinful is the damnable practice of usury —the charging of interest on loans where no actual risk is involved. This is sheer robbery, for it deprives the person who uses the money of earnings that are justly his; it is contrary to nature, for it enables the man who lends the money to live without labor.

Effects of the
rise of competi-
tive capitalism

While it is far from true that these doctrines were universally honored even by the church itself, they nevertheless remained an integral part of the Catholic ideal down to the end of the Renaissance period. Even to this day they have not been entirely abandoned, as our study of liberal Catholicism in the nineteenth and twentieth centuries will show.[6] However, the age of the Renaissance was accompanied by the growth of an economic pattern distinctly incompatible with most of these doctrines. A ruthless, dynamic capitalism, based upon the principle of "dog eat dog," was beginning to supplant the old static economy of the medieval guilds. No longer were merchants and manufacturers content with a mere "wage" for the services they rendered to society. They demanded profits, and they could not see that it was any business of the church to decide what a man's earnings should be. Wages were fit only for hirelings, who had neither the wit nor the industry to go after the big rewards. In addition to all this, the growth of banking meant an even more violent conflict with the ascetic ideal of the church. As long as the business of moneylending was in the hands of Jews and Moslems, it mattered little that usury should be branded as a sin. But now that Christians were piling up riches by financing the exploits of kings and merchants, the shoe was on another foot. The new crop of bankers resented being told that their lucrative trade in cash was contrary to the laws of God. This seemed to them like an attempt of spokesmen for an outmoded past to dictate the standards for a new age of progress. But how was it that Italy did not break with

---

[5] See the chapter on The Civilization of the Feudal Age: Political and Economic Institutions.

[6] See the paragraphs on Christian Socialism at the end of the chapter on the Industrial Revolution of the Nineteenth and Twentieth Centuries.

the Catholic church in view of the extensive development of banking and commerce in such cities as Florence, Genoa, and Milan as early as the fourteenth century? The explanation is probably to be found in the stronger influence of paganism in Renaissance Italy than in any other country of Europe. Great bankers like the Medici of Florence were Christians in nothing but name. Even the Italians who remained something more than nominal Christians did not generally take their beliefs very seriously. Their view of religion was like that of the ancient Romans—external and mechanical, not ethical or spiritual. To the northern European, by contrast, religion had a much deeper significance. He conceived of it very largely as a system of morality ordained by a wrathful God. He was therefore profoundly disturbed by any inconsistency between his worldly life and the doctrines of the faith. When such a conflict arose, he could do only one of two things: either modify his personal conduct to conform to the faith or get a new religion. When the choice was one between ascetic denial and destruction of the system that frowned upon riches, it is not difficult to see which road he would take.

Before leaving this subject of causes, it is important to consider briefly the reasons why the Protestant Revolution began in Germany. First, there was the fact that Germany was somewhat more *Why the Protestant Revolution began in Germany* backward than most other areas of western Europe. The Renaissance had touched her but lightly, and the legacy of the Dark Ages was still very strong. As a consequence, religious-mindedness was more deeply rooted than in Italy, France, or England. Second, Germany was the victim of Catholic abuses to a greater extent than most other countries. The kings of France and England had successfully defied the Pope on appointments to religious offices and on appeals of cases to the Roman *curia*. But Germany had no powerful ruler to defend her interests. It was mainly for this reason that Leo X selected Germany as the most likely field for the sale of indulgences. The evils connected with this traffic would probably have been a stench in the nostrils of any nation. Finally, economic factors were very important. The church in Germany held an enormous proportion of the best agricultural lands, and the country was seething with discontent on account of a too rapid transition from a feudal society to an economy of profits and wages. The grievances of knights and peasants alike made an explosion of some sort inevitable. The petty nobility were threatened with ruin by the concentration of land in large estates, while the peasants were ground between the upper and nether millstones of rising prices and the loss of manorial privileges. Faced with such hardships, both classes turned against the church as their richest and most grievous oppressor. The merchants and bankers, for reasons quite different but just as compelling, were not slow in lending support.

I. THE LUTHERAN REVOLT IN GERMANY By the dawn of the sixteenth century Germany was ripe for religious revolution. All

*The early ca-
reer of Martin
Luther*

*Justification by
faith alone*

*Luther's revolt
against the sale
of indulgences*

that was necessary was to find a leader who could unite the dissatisfied elements and give a suitable theological gloss to their
grievances. Such a leader was not long in appearing. His name was
Martin Luther, and he was born in Thuringia in 1483. His parents
were originally peasants, but his father had left the soil soon after
his marriage to work in the mines of Mansfeld. Here he managed
to become moderately prosperous and served in the village council.
Nevertheless, young Martin's early environment was far from ideal.
He was whipped at home for trivial offenses until the blood came,
and his mind was filled with hideous terrors of demons and witches.
Some of these superstitions clung to him until the end of his life.
His parents intended that he should become a lawyer, and with this
end in view they placed him at the age of eighteen in the University
of Erfurt. During his first four years at the university, Luther
worked hard, gaining more than an ordinary reputation as a scholar.
But in 1505, while returning from a visit to his home, he was overtaken by a violent storm and felled to the ground by a bolt of
lightning. In terror lest an angry God strike him dead, he vowed
to St. Anne to become a monk. Soon afterward he entered the
Augustinian monastery at Erfurt. Here he gave himself up to earnest
reflection on the state of his soul. Obsessed with the idea that his
sins were innumerable, he strove desperately to attain a goal of
spiritual peace. He engaged in long vigils and went for days on end
without a morsel of food. But the more he fasted and tortured
himself, the more his anguish and depression increased. Told that
the way of salvation lies in love of God, he was ready to give up in
despair. How could he love a Being who is not even just, who saves
only those whom it pleases Him to save? "Love Him?" he said to
himself, "I do not love Him. I hate Him." But in time, as he pon-
dered the Scriptures, especially the story of the crucifixion, he
gained a new insight into the mysteries of the Christian theology. He
was profoundly impressed by the humiliation of the Savior's death
upon the cross. For the benefit of sinful humanity, the Christ, the
God-man, had shared the fate of common criminals. Why had He
done so except out of love for His creatures? The God of the storm
whose chief attribute appeared to be anger had revealed Himself
as a Father who pities His children. Here was a miracle which no
human reason could understand. It must be taken on faith; and by
faith alone, Luther concluded, can man be justified in the sight of
God. This doctrine of justification by faith alone, as opposed to
salvation by "good works," quickly became the central doctrine
of the Lutheran theology.

But long before Luther had completed his theological system, he
was called to lecture on Aristotle and the Bible at the University of
Wittenberg, which had recently been founded by Frederick the
Wise of Saxony. While serving in this capacity, he was confronted
by an event which furnished the spark for the Protestant Revolution.

450

Portrait of Martin Luther, by Melchior Lorch, 1548.

In 1517 an unprincipled Dominican friar by the name of Tetzel appeared in Germany as a hawker of indulgences. Determined to raise as much money as possible for Pope Leo X and the Archbishop of Mainz who had employed him, Tetzel deliberately represented the indulgences as tickets of admission to heaven. Though forbidden to enter Saxony, he came to the borders of that state, and many natives of Wittenberg rushed out to buy salvation at so attractive a price. Luther was appalled by such brazen deception of ignorant people. Accordingly, he drew up a set of ninety-five theses or statements attacking the sale of indulgences, and posted them, after the manner of the time, on the door of the castle church on October 31, 1517. Later he had them printed and sent to his friends in a number of cities. Soon it became evident that the Ninety-five Theses had voiced the sentiments of a nation. All over Germany, Luther was hailed as a leader whom God had raised to break the power of an arrogant and hypocritical clergy. A violent reaction against the sale of indulgences was soon in full swing. Tetzel was mobbed and driven from the country. The revolt against Rome had begun.

With the revenue from indulgences cut off, it was inevitable that the Pope should take action. Early in 1518 he commanded the general of the Augustinian order to make the rebellious friar recant. Luther not only refused but published a sermon stating his views more strongly than ever. That no more stringent measures were taken against him at this time was a result of the fact that Leo X was absorbed in the coming imperial election. For more than two years the impetuous friar enjoyed an immunity from persecution, protected by his friend, the Elector Frederick of Saxony. He made use of this time in writing pamphlets to expand his doctrines and to

The condemnation and excommunication of Luther

451

keep the enthusiasm of his supporters from flagging. Forced by his critics to answer questions on many points other than indulgences, he gradually came to realize that his own religion was utterly irreconcilable with that of the Roman church. There was no alternative except to break with the Catholic faith entirely. In 1520 his teachings were formally condemned in a bull promulgated by Leo X, and he was ordered to recant within sixty days or be dealt with as a heretic. Luther replied by publicly burning the Pope's proclamation. For this he was excommunicated and ordered to be turned over to the secular arm for punishment. Germany at this time was still under the technical rule of the Holy Roman Empire. Charles V, who had recently been elevated to the throne of this ramshackle state, was anxious to be rid of the insolent rebel at once, but he dared not act without the approval of the Imperial Diet. Accordingly, in 1521, Luther was summoned to appear before a meeting of this body at Worms. Since many of the princes and electors who composed the Diet were themselves hostile toward the church, nothing in particular was done, despite Luther's stubborn refusal to retract any of the things he had said. Finally, after a number of the members had gone home, the Emperor forced through an edict branding the obstreperous friar as an outlaw. But Luther had already been hidden away in the castle of his friend, the Elector of Saxony. Here he remained until all danger of arrest by the Emperor's soldiers had passed. Charles soon afterward withdrew to conduct his war with France, and the Edict of Worms was never enforced.

Founding the Lutheran church; Luther's doctrines

Thenceforth until his death in 1546 Luther was occupied with his work of building an independent German church. Despite the fundamental conflict between his own beliefs and Catholic theology, he nevertheless retained a good many of the elements of the Roman system. With the passing of the years he became more conservative than many of his own followers and compared some of them to Judas betraying his Master. Though he had originally denounced transubstantiation, he eventually came around to adopting a doctrine which bore at least a superficial resemblance to the Catholic theory. Theologians call this doctrine "consubstantiation," meaning that the body and blood of Christ are really present *along with* the bread and wine. He maintained that the words imputed to the Christ in the New Testament, "This is my body," were literally true, even if contrary to reason. He denied, however, that any change in the substance of the bread and wine occurred as the result of a priestly miracle. The function of the clergyman is simply to *reveal* the presence of God in the bread and wine. In like manner, Luther retained the Catholic practice of elevating the "host," or consecrated wafer of the Eucharist, for the adoration of the faithful. Still, the changes he made were drastic enough to preserve the revolutionary character of the new religion. He substituted German for Latin in the services of the church. He rejected the entire ecclesiastical system of Pope, archbishops, bishops, and priests as custodians of the keys to the kingdom of heaven. By abolishing monasticism and insisting upon the right of priests to marry, he went far toward destroying the barrier which had separated clergy from laity and given the former their special status as representatives of God on earth. He eliminated all of the sacraments with the exception of baptism and the Eucharist, and he denied that even these had any supernatural effect in bringing down grace from heaven. Since he

Luther Preaching. With one hand he points to popes, monks, and cardinals going down hell's mouth. Hell is a beast with snout, tusk, and eye. With the other hand Luther points to the crucifix. The Lord's Supper is being administered, both the bread and the wine to the laity. The chalice on the table emphasizes the evangelical practice of giving the cup to the laity. The people are not taking the elements into their own hands.

continued to emphasize faith rather than good works as the road to salvation, he naturally discarded such formalized practices as fasts, pilgrimages, the veneration of relics, and the invocation of saints. On the other hand, the doctrines of predestination and the supreme authority of the Scriptures were given in the new religion a higher place than they had ever enjoyed in the old. Last of all, Luther abandoned the Catholic idea that the church should be supreme over the state. Instead of having bishops subject to the Pope as the Vicar of Christ, he organized his church under superintendents who were essentially agents of the government.

Of course, Luther was not alone responsible for the success of the Protestant Revolution. In molding the tenets of the new faith he was ably assisted by Philip Melanchthon, a teacher of Greek and originally a humanist at the University of Wittenberg. It was Melanchthon who drafted the Augsburg Confession (1530), which is still accepted as the creed of the Lutheran church. The overthrow of Catholicism in Germany was also abetted by the outbreak of social revolt. In 1522–1523 there occurred a ferocious rebellion of

The outbreak of social revolution; the revolt of the knights

453

the knights. These petty nobles, as we have seen, were being impoverished by competition from the great estates and by the change to a capitalist economy. They saw as the chief cause of their misery the concentration of landed wealth in the hands of the great princes of the church. Intensely nationalistic, they dreamed of a united Germany free from the domination of powerful landlords and grasping priests. The leaders of the movement were Ulrich von Hutten, who had turned from a humanist into a fierce partisan of Luther, and Franz von Sickingen, a notorious robber baron and soldier of fortune. To these men the gospel of Luther seemed to provide an excellent program for a war on behalf of German liberty. Although their rebellion was speedily crushed by the armies of the archbishops and richer nobles, it apparently had considerable effect in persuading the pillars of the old regime that too much resistance to the Lutheran movement would scarcely be wise.

The uprising of the lower classes

The revolt of the knights was followed by a much more violent uprising of the lower classes in 1524–1525. Though most who took part were peasants, a great many poor workmen from the cities were attracted to the movement also. The causes of this second rebellion were somewhat similar to those of the first: the rising cost of living, the concentration of holdings of land, and the religious radicalism inspired by Luther's teachings. But the peasants and urban workers were stirred to action by many other factors as well. The decay of the feudal regime had eliminated the paternal relationship between noble and serf. In its place had grown up a mere cash nexus between employer and worker. The sole obligation now of the upper classes was to pay a wage. When sickness or unemployment struck, the laborer had to make shift with his slender resources as best he could. Furthermore, most of the old privileges which the serf had enjoyed on the manorial estate, of pasturing his flocks on the common lands and gathering wood in the forest, were being rapidly abolished. To make matters worse, landlords were attempting to meet advancing prices by exacting higher rents from the peasants. Finally, the lower classes were angered by the fact that the revival of the Roman law had the effect of bolstering property rights and of strengthening the power of the state to protect the interests of the rich.

The Anabaptists

Many of the downtrodden folk who participated in the so-called Peasants' Revolt belonged to a religious sect known as the Anabaptists. The name means re-baptizers, and was derived from the fact that the members of the sect held infant baptism to be ineffectual and insisted that the rite should be administered only when the individual had reached the age of reason. But a belief in adult baptism was not really their principal doctrine. The Anabaptists were extreme individualists in religion. Luther's teaching that every man has a right to follow the dictates of his own conscience they took exactly as it stood. Not only did they reject the Catholic theory of the priesthood, but they denied the necessity of any clergy at all, maintaining that every individual should follow the guidance of the "inner light." They refused to admit that God's revelation to man had ceased with the writing of the last book of the New Testament, but they insisted that He continues to speak directly to certain of His chosen followers. They attached much importance to literal interpretation of the Bible, even of its most occult portions. They believed that the church should be a community of saints and required of their followers abstention from lying, profanity, gluttony, lewdness, and drinking intoxicating liquors. Many of the members looked forward to the early destruction of this world and the establishment of Christ's kingdom of justice and peace, in which they would have a prominent place. But the Anabaptists were not merely a group of religious extremists; they represented as well the most radical social tendencies of their time. Though it is certainly an exaggeration to call them communists, they did denounce the accumulation of wealth and taught that it was the duty of Christians to share their goods with one another. In addition, they declined to recognize any distinctions of rank or class, declaring all men equal in the sight of God. Many of them also abominated the taking of oaths, condemned military service, and refused to pay taxes to governments that engaged in war. They abstained in general from political life and demanded the complete separation of church and state. Their doctrines represented the extreme manifestation of the revolutionary fervor generated by the Protestant movement.

The Peasants' Revolt of 1524–1525 began in southern Germany and spread rapidly to the north and west until most of the country was involved. At first it had more of the character of a strike than *The Peasants' Revolt of 1524-1525* a revolution. The rebels contented themselves with drafting petitions and attempting peaceably to persuade their masters to grant them relief from oppression. But before many months had passed, the movement came under the control of such fanatics as Thomas Münzer, who urged the use of fire and sword against the wicked nobles and clergy. In the spring of 1525 the misguided rustics began plundering and burning cloisters and castles and even murdering some of their more hated opponents. The nobles now turned against them with fiendish fury, slaughtering indiscriminately both those who resisted and those who were helpless. Strange as it may seem, the lords were encouraged in this savagery by several of the Reformers, including the great Luther himself. In a pamphlet *Against the Thievish, Murderous Hordes of Peasants* he urged everyone who could to hunt the rebels down like mad dogs, to "strike, strangle, stab secretly or in public, and let him remember that nothing can be more poisonous, harmful, or devilish than a man in rebellion." [7] To Luther's credit, it should perhaps be added that he

[7] Quoted by H. S. Lucas, *The Renaissance and the Reformation*, p. 457.

feared anarchy more than he did the particular doctrines of the Anabaptists. He believed that the use of force by anyone except the lawful authorities would result in the destruction of the social order.

Suppression of the Peasants' Revolt

But the brutal suppression of the Peasants' Revolt did not mark the end of revolutionary activities on the part of the submerged classes. In 1534 a group of Anabaptists gained control of the episcopal city of Münster in Westphalia. Thousands of their fellow believers from the surrounding country came pouring in, and Münster became a New Jerusalem where all of the accumulated vagaries of the lunatic fringe of the movement were put into practice. The property of unbelievers was confiscated, and polygamy was introduced. A certain John of Leyden assumed the title of king, proclaiming himself the successor of David with a mission to conquer the world and destroy the heathen. But after a little more than a year of this, Münster was recaptured by its bishop, and the leaders of Zion were put to death by horrible tortures. This second disaster proved to be the turning point in the revolt of the have-nots of the

A Page from the Bible Translated by Luther into German. The engraving shows several episodes of the story of Jonah in a single composite picture.

sixteenth century. Convinced of the futility of violence, they now abandoned the fanatical dogmas of their fallen leaders and returned to the religious quietism of earlier years. Most of the radical economic teachings were also dropped. Some of the survivors of the persecutions now joined the sect of Mennonites, so called from Menno Simons (1492–1559), whose teachings were partly derived from those of the original Anabaptists. Others fled to England to become the spiritual ancestors of the Quakers.

II. THE ZWINGLIAN AND CALVINIST REVOLTS IN SWITZERLAND

The special form of Protestantism developed by Luther did not prove to be particularly popular beyond its native environment. Outside of Germany, Lutheranism became the official religion only in Denmark, Norway, and Sweden. But the force of the Lutheran revolt made itself felt in a number of other lands. Such was especially the case in Switzerland, where nationalism had been gathering strength for centuries. At the close of the Middle Ages the gallant herdsmen and peasants of the Swiss cantons had challenged the right of the Austrians to rule over them, and finally in 1499 had compelled the Emperor Maximilian to recognize their independence, not only of the house of Hapsburg but of the Holy Roman Empire as well. Having thrown off the yoke of a foreign Emperor, the Swiss were not likely to submit indefinitely to an alien Pope. Moreover, the cities of Zürich, Basel, Berne, and Geneva had grown into flourishing centers of trade. Their populations were dominated by solid burghers who were becoming increasingly contemptuous of the Catholic ideal of glorified poverty. Here also northern humanism had found welcome lodgment in cultivated minds, with the effect of creating a healthy distrust of priestly superstitions. Erasmus had lived for a number of years in Basel. Lastly, Switzerland had been plucked by the indulgence peddlers to an extent only less grievous than Germany, while the city of Berne had been the scene of some particularly flagrant monkish frauds.

Causes of the Protestant Revolution in Switzerland

The father of the Protestant Revolution in Switzerland was Ulrich Zwingli. Only a few weeks younger than Luther, he was the son of a well-to-do magistrate, who was able to provide him with an excellent education. He attended the Universities of Vienna and Basel, completing the course for the master's degree at the latter. As a student he devoted nearly all of his time to philosophy and literature, with no interest in religion save in the practical reforms of the Christian humanists. Although he took holy orders at the age of twenty-two, his purpose in entering the priesthood was mainly the opportunity it would give him to cultivate his literary tastes. For some eight years thereafter he continued to accept the patronage of the Pope and to take his vows of celibacy exceedingly lightly. In 1519, however, he experienced one of those sudden conversions so typical of the careers of religious reformers. For this change of heart there seem to have been two main causes: a serious attack of the

Ulrich Zwingli

Portrait of Ulrich Zwingli (1484–1531). Sixteenth Century wood-cut by an unknown master.

plague and the influence of Luther. Which of these causes came first is unknown, but both had a powerful effect. From this time on Zwingli became a fervid crusader, not merely for a purer religion but for a break with the Catholic church. He accepted nearly all of the teachings of Luther with the exception of consubstantiation. Zwingli maintained that the bread and wine are mere symbols of the body and blood, and he reduced the sacrament of Holy Communion to a simple memorial service. So ably did he marshal the anti-Catholic forces that by 1528 nearly all of northern Switzerland had deserted the ancient faith. But when he attempted to extend his crusade into the conservative forest cantons, he encountered stiff opposition. In 1529 civil war broke out, resulting after two years in the defeat of the Zwinglian forces and in the death of their leader. By the Peace of Kappel (1531) the Protestants agreed that the choice of a religion for the several areas of Switzerland should be made by the cantonal governments.

The spread of the Protestant Revolt to Geneva

From the northern cantons the Protestant Revolt in Switzerland spread to Geneva. This beautiful city, located on a lake of the same name near the French border, had the doubtful advantage of a double government. The people owed allegiance to two feudal suzerains, the local bishop and the Count of Savoy. When these high-born chieftains conspired to make their power more absolute, the citizens rebelled against them. The result was their expulsion from the town about 1530 and the establishment of a free republic. But the movement could hardly have been successful without some aid from the northern cantons. Thus it was not long until Protestant preachers from Zürich and Berne began arriving in Geneva. Furthermore, since the leaders of the political revolution were excommunicated for defying their bishop, it was natural that they should be favorably disposed toward a new religion for their city.

It was under this constellation of events that John Calvin arrived **458** in Geneva. Although destined to play so prominent a role in the history of Switzerland, he was not a native of that country but of France. He was born at Noyon in Picardy in 1509. His mother died when he was very young, and his father, who did not like children, turned him over to the care of an aristocratic friend. For his higher education he was sent to the University of Paris, where, because of his bilious disposition and fault-finding manner, he was dubbed "the accusative case." Later he shifted at his father's wish to the study of law at Orléans. Here he came under the influence of disciples of Luther, evidently to a sufficient extent to cause him to be suspected of heresy. Consequently, in 1534, when the government began an attack on the wavering ones, Calvin fled to Switzerland. He settled for a time in Basel and then moved on to Geneva, which was still in the throes of political revolution. He began preaching and organizing at once, and by 1541 both government and religion had fallen completely under his sway. Until his death from asthma and dyspepsia in 1564 he ruled the city with a rod of iron. History contains few examples of men more dour in temperament and more stubbornly convinced of the rightness of their own ideas.

Under Calvin's rule Geneva was transformed into a religious oligarchy. The supreme authority was vested in the Congregation of the clergy, who prepared all legislation and submitted it to the Consistory to be ratified. The latter body, composed, in addition to the clergy, of twelve elders representing the people, had as its principal function the supervision of public and private morals. This function was carried out, not merely by the punishment of antisocial conduct but by a persistent snooping into the private life of every individual. The city was divided into districts, and a committee of the Consistory visited each household without warning to conduct an inquisition into the habits of its members. Even the

Portrait of John Calvin (1509–1564) after Susterman. Original in Boyman's Museum, Rotterdam.

459

mildest forms of human folly were strictly prohibited. Dancing, card-playing, attending the theater, working or playing on the Sabbath—all were outlawed as major crimes. Innkeepers were forbidden to allow anyone to consume food or drink without first saying grace, or to permit any patron to sit up after nine o'clock unless he was spying on the conduct of others. Needless to say, penalties were severe. Not only murder and treason were classified as capital crimes, but also adultery, witchcraft, blasphemy, and heresy; and the last of these especially was susceptible to a broad interpretation.

The Fury of the Reformation Brandishing Its Three Main Villains, Calvin, Luther, and Beza. Contemporary anti-reform woodcut.

During the first four years after Calvin became ruler of Geneva, there were no fewer than fifty-eight executions out of a total population of only 16,000.[8] But the good accomplished by all of this harshness seems to have been small indeed. According to Preserved Smith, there were more cases of vice in Geneva after the Reformation than before.[9]

The essentials of Calvin's theology are contained in his *Institutes of the Christian Religion,* which was published originally in 1536 and revised and enlarged several times thereafter. His ideas resemble those of St. Augustine more than any other theologian. He conceived of the universe as utterly dependent upon the will of an Almighty God, who created all things for His greater glory. Because of Adam's transgression all men are sinners by nature, bound hand and foot to an evil inheritance they cannot escape. Nevertheless, God for reasons of His own has predestined some for eternal salvation and damned all the rest to the torments of hell. Nothing that human beings may do can alter their fate; their souls are stamped with God's blessing or curse before they are born. But this did not

Calvin's theology

---

[8] Preserved Smith, *The Age of the Reformation,* p. 171.
[9] *Ibid.,* p. 174.

mean, in Calvin's opinion, that the Christian could be indifferent to his conduct on earth. If he were among the elect, God would have implanted in him the desire to live right. Abstemious conduct is a sign, though not an infallible one, that he who practices it has been chosen to sit at the throne of glory. Public profession of faith and participation in the sacraments are also presumptive evidences of election to be saved. But most of all, the Calvinists required an active life of piety and good morality as a solemn obligation resting upon members of the Christian Commonwealth. Like the ancient Hebrews, they conceived of themselves as chosen instruments of God with a mission to help in the fulfillment of His purposes on earth. Their duty was not to strive for their souls' salvation but for the glory of God. Thus it will be seen that the Calvinist system did not encourage its followers to sit with folded hands serene in the knowledge that their fate was sealed. No religion has fostered a more abundant zeal in the conquest of nature, in missionary activity, or in the struggle against political tyranny. Doubtless the reason lies in the Calvinist's belief that as the chosen instrument of God he must play a part in the drama of the universe worthy of his exalted status. And with the Lord on his side he was not easily frightened by whatever lions lurked in his path.

The religion of Calvin differed from that of Luther in a number of ways. First, it was more legalistic. Whereas the Wittenberg Reformer had emphasized the guidance of individual conscience, the dictator of Geneva stressed the sovereignty of law. He thought of God as a mighty legislator who had handed down a body of rules in the Scriptures which must be followed to the letter. Secondly, the religion of Calvin was more nearly an Old Testament faith than that of Luther. This can be illustrated in the attitude of the two men toward Sabbath observance. Luther's conception of Sunday was similar to that which prevails in modern Continental Europe. He insisted, of course, that his followers should attend church, but he did not demand that during the remainder of the day they should refrain from all pleasure or work. Calvin, on the other hand, revived the old Jewish Sabbath with its strict taboos against anything faintly resembling worldliness. In the third place, the religion of Geneva was more closely associated with the ideals of the new capitalism. Luther's sympathies lay with the nobles, and on at least one occasion he sharply censured the tycoons of finance for their greed. Calvin sanctified the ventures of the trader and the moneylender and gave an exalted place in his ethical system to the business virtues of thrift and diligence. Finally, Calvinism as compared to Lutheranism represented a more radical phase of the Protestant Revolution. As we have seen, the Wittenberg friar retained a good many features of Roman worship and even some Catholic dogmas. Calvin rejected everything he could think of that smacked of "popery." The organization of his church was con-

The religion of Calvin compared with that of Luther

461

structed in such a way as to exclude all traces of the episcopal system. Congregations were to choose their own elders and preachers, while an association of ministers at the top would govern the entire church. Ritual, instrumental music, stained glass windows, pictures, and images were ruthlessly eliminated, with the consequence that the religion was reduced to "four bare walls and a sermon." Even the observance of Christmas and Easter was sternly prohibited.

The spread of Calvinism

The popularity of Calvinism was not limited to Switzerland. It spread into most countries of western Europe where trade and finance had become leading pursuits. The Huguenots of France, the Puritans of England, the Presbyterians of Scotland, and the members of the Reformed church in Holland were all Calvinists. It was pre-eminently the religion of the bourgeoisie; though, of course, it drew converts from other strata as well. Its influence in molding the ethics of modern times and in bolstering the revolutionary courage of the middle class was enormous. Members of this faith had much to do with the initial revolts against despotism in England and France, to say nothing of their part in overthrowing Spanish tyranny in the Netherlands.

III. THE PROTESTANT REVOLUTION IN ENGLAND The original blow against the Roman church in England was not struck by a religious enthusiast like Luther or Calvin but by the head of the government. This does not mean, however, that the English Reformation was exclusively a political movement. Henry VIII could not have succeeded in establishing an independent English church if such action had not had the endorsement of large numbers of his subjects. And there were plenty of reasons why this endorsement was readily given. Though the English had freed themselves in some measure from papal domination, national pride had reached such a point that any degree of subordination to Rome was resented. Besides, England had been the scene for some time of lively agitation for religious reform. The memory of Wyclif's scathing attacks upon the avarice of the priests, the temporal power of Popes and bishops, and the sacramental system of the church had lingered since the fourteenth century. The influence of the Christian humanists, notably Sir Thomas More, in condemning the superstitions in Catholic worship, had also been a factor of considerable importance. Finally, soon after the outbreak of the Protestant Revolt in Germany, Lutheran ideas were brought into England by wandering preachers and through the circulation of printed tracts. As a result, the English monarch, in severing the ties with Rome, had no lack of sympathy from some of the most influential of his subjects.

Underlying causes of the Protestant Revolution in England

Henry VIII's domestic difficulties

The clash with the Pope was precipitated by Henry VIII's domestic difficulties. For eighteen years he had been married to Catherine of Aragon and had only a sickly daughter to succeed him. The death of all the sons of this marriage in infancy was a grievous disappointment to the king, who desired a male heir to perpetuate the Tudor dynasty. But this was not all, for Henry later became deeply infatuated with the dark-eyed lady-in-waiting, Anne Boleyn, and determined to make her his queen. He therefore appealed in 1527 to Pope Clement VII for an annulment of the marriage to Catherine. The law of the church did not sanction divorce, but it did provide that a marriage could be annulled if proof could be presented that conditions existing at the time of the marriage made it unlawful. Queen Catherine had previously been married to Henry's older brother, Arthur, who had died a few months after the ceremony was performed. Recalling this fact, Henry's lawyers found a passage in the Book of Leviticus which pronounced a curse of childlessness upon the man who should marry his deceased brother's wife. The Pope was now in a difficult position. If he rejected the king's appeal, England would probably be lost to the Catholic faith, for Henry was apparently firmly convinced that the Scriptural curse had blighted his chances of perpetuating his dynasty. On the other hand, if the Pope granted the annulment he would provoke the wrath of the Emperor Charles V, who was a nephew of Catherine. Charles had already invaded Italy and was threatening the Pope with a loss of his temporal power. There seemed nothing for Clement to do but to procrastinate. At first he made a pretense of having the question settled in England, and empowered his own legate and Cardinal Wolsey to hold a court of inquiry to determine whether the marriage to Catherine had been legal. Then after long delay the case was suddenly transferred to Rome. Henry lost patience and resolved to take matters into his own hands. In 1531 he convoked an assembly of the clergy and, by threatening to punish them for violating the Statute of Praemunire in submitting to the papal legate, he induced them to recognize himself as the head of the English church, "as far as the law of Christ allows." Next he persuaded Parliament to enact a series of laws abolishing all payments of revenue to the Pope and proclaiming the Anglican church an independent, national unit, subject to the exclusive authority of the king. By 1534 the last of the bonds uniting the English church to Rome had been cut.

The Anglican church

But the enactments put through by Henry VIII did not really make England a Protestant country. Though the abolition of papal authority was followed by the gradual dissolution of the monasteries and confiscation of their wealth, the church remained Catholic in doctrine. The Six Articles, adopted by Parliament at the king's behest in 1539, left no room for doubt as to official orthodoxy. Auricular confession, masses for the dead, and clerical celibacy were all confirmed, while death by burning was made the penalty for denying the Catholic dogma of the Eucharist. Yet the influence of a minority of Protestants at this time cannot be ignored. Their numbers were steadily increasing, and during the reign of Henry's successor, Edward VI, they actually gained the ascendancy. Since the

Activities of the radical Protestants

new king was only nine years old when he inherited the crown, it was inevitable that the policies of the government should be dictated by powers behind the throne. The men most active in this work were Thomas Cranmer, Archbishop of Canterbury, and the Dukes of Somerset and Northumberland, who successively dominated the council of regency. All three of these officials had strong Protestant leanings. As a result, the creeds and ceremonies of the Church of England were given some drastic revision. Priests were permitted to marry; English was substituted for Latin in the services; the use of images was abolished; and new articles of belief were drawn up repudiating all sacraments except baptism and the Lord's Supper and affirming the Lutheran dogma of justification by faith. When the youthful Edward died in 1553, it looked as if England had definitely entered the Protestant camp.

The Catholic reaction under Mary

Surface appearances, however, are frequently deceiving. They were never more so than in England at the end of Edward's reign. The majority of the people had refused to be weaned away from the usages of their ancient faith, and a reaction had set in against the high-handed methods of the radical Protestants. Moreover, the English during the time of the Tudors had grown accustomed to obeying the will of their sovereign. It was an attitude fostered by nationalism and the desire for order and prosperity. The successor of Edward VI was Queen Mary, the forlorn and graceless daughter of Henry VIII and Catherine. It was inevitable that Mary should have been a Catholic, and that she should have abhorred the revolt against Rome, for the origin of the movement was painfully associated with her mother's sufferings. Consequently, it is not strange that upon coming to the throne she should have attempted to turn the clock back. Not only did she restore the celebration of the mass and the rule of clerical celibacy, but she prevailed upon Parliament to vote the unconditional return of England to papal allegiance. But her policies ended in lamentable failure for several reasons. First of all, she fell into the same error as her predecessors in forcing through changes that were too radical for the temper of the times. The people of England were not ready for a Lutheran or Calvinist revolution, but neither were they in a mood to accept immediate subjection to Rome. Probably a more serious cause of her failure was her marriage to Philip, the ambitious heir to the Spanish throne. Her subjects feared that this union might lead to foreign complications, if not actual domination by Spain. When the queen allowed herself to be drawn into a war with France, in which England was compelled to surrender Calais, her last foothold on the Continent of Europe, the nation was almost ready for rebellion. Death ended Mary's inglorious reign in 1558.

The question whether England was to be Catholic or Protestant

was left to be settled by Mary's successor, her half-sister Elizabeth, daughter of the vivacious Anne Boleyn. Though reared as a Protestant, Elizabeth had no deep religious convictions. Her primary interest was statecraft, and she did not intend that her kingdom should be rent in twain by sectarian strife. Therefore she decided upon a policy of moderation, refusing to ally herself with either the extreme Catholics or the fanatical Protestants. So carefully did she hew to this line that for some years she deceived the Pope into thinking that she might turn Catholic. Nevertheless, she was enough of a nationalist to refuse even to consider a revival of allegiance to Rome. One of the first things she did after becoming queen was to order the passage of a new Act of Supremacy declaring the English sovereign to be the "supreme governor" of the independent Anglican church. The final settlement, completed about 1570, was a typical English compromise. The church was made Protestant, but certain articles of the creed were left vague enough so that a moderate Catholic might accept them without too great a shock to his conscience. Moreover, the episcopal form of organization was retained and much of the Catholic ritual. Long after Elizabeth's death in 1603 this settlement remained in effect. Indeed, most elements in it have survived to this day. And it is a significant fact that the modern Church of England is broad enough to include within its ranks such diverse factions as the Anglo-Catholics, who differ from their Roman brethren only in rejecting papal supremacy, and the "low-church" Anglicans, who are as radical in their Protestantism as the Lutherans.

While England was engaged in the process of mediating between the extremes of Catholicism and Protestantism, her northern neighbor Scotland was embroiled in a more violent break with the past. The Scottish branch of the Catholic church at the turn of the sixteenth century was one of the most corrupt in Europe. Enjoying the fruits of their vast possessions, the clergy divided their time between luxurious idleness and political intrigue. But this state of affairs could not long continue. Scotland had a greedy and untamed nobility eager to pounce upon the lands of the church at the first convenient opportunity. Besides, the political situation was far from satisfactory to the patriotic elements of the nation. The queen, Mary Stuart, was a mere child when she succeeded to the throne in 1542, and a regency had been assumed by her mother, who belonged to the French family of Guise. Since the Guises were determined Catholics, Catholicism came to be associated in the minds of many people with the Guises and thus with French domination. In 1557 a revolt broke out, and two years later the whole kingdom was ablaze. Leadership of the movement soon fell to a vigorous and stiff-necked preacher by the name of John Knox, who had sat at the feet of Calvin in Geneva. Knox uprooted every vestige of Catholicism in Scotland and established a Presbyterian church on a

The Elizabethan compromise

The establishment of Presbyterianism in Scotland

radical Calvinist basis.[10] So ripe was the country for a change that upon the death of the regent in 1560 Presbyterianism was proclaimed the official religion of the Scottish nation.

2. The Catholic Reformation

*The begin-
nings of Cath-
olic reform*

As noted at the beginning of this chapter, the Protestant Revolution was only one of the phases of the great movement known as the Reformation. The other was the Catholic Reformation, or the Counter Reformation as it used to be called, on the assumption that the primary purpose of its leaders was to cleanse the Catholic church in order to check the growth of Protestantism. Modern historians have shown, however, that the beginnings of the movement for Catholic reform were entirely independent of the Protestant Revolt. In Spain, during the closing years of the fifteenth century, a religious revival inaugurated by Cardinal Ximenes, with the approval of the monarchy, stirred that country to the depths. Schools were established, abuses were eliminated from the monasteries, and priests were goaded into accepting their responsibilities as shepherds of their flocks. Though the movement was launched primarily for the purpose of strengthening the church in the war against heretics and infidels, it nevertheless had considerable effect in regenerating the spiritual life of the nation. In Italy also, since the beginning of the sixteenth century, a number of earnest clerics had been laboring to make the priests of their church more worthy of their Christian calling. The task was a difficult one on account of the paganism of the Renaissance and the example of profligacy set by the papal court. In spite of these obstacles the movement did lead to the founding of several religious orders dedicated to high ideals of piety and social service. Outstanding among them were the Theatine Order and the Capuchin Order. The first was an organization of priests who took monastic vows of poverty, chastity, and obedience, while the second was an order of friars pledged to follow in the footsteps of St. Francis.

*The climax
of the Catholic
Reformation;
the reform
Popes*

But the fires of Catholic reform burned rather low until after the Protestant Revolution began to make serious inroads upon the ancient faith. Not until it appeared that the whole German nation was likely to be swept into the Lutheran orbit did any of the Popes become seriously concerned about the need for reform. The first of the Holy Fathers to attempt a purification of the church was Adrian VI of Utrecht, the only non-Italian to be elected to the papal throne in nearly a century and a half, and the last in history. But his reign of only twenty months was too short to enable him to accomplish much, and in 1523 he was succeeded by a Medici

[10] The name Presbyterian comes from "presbytery," the assembly of ministers and lay elders which Knox set up to govern the churches of a particular area in place of a bishop.

(Clement VII), who ruled for eleven years. The campaign against abuses in the church was not renewed until the reign of Paul III (1534–1549). He and three of his successors, Paul IV (1555–1559), Pius V (1566–1572), and Sixtus V (1585–1590), were the most zealous crusaders for reform who had presided over the See of Peter since the days of Gregory VII. They reorganized the papal finances, filled the church offices with priests renowned for austerity, and dealt drastically with those clerics who persisted in idleness and vice. It was under these Popes that the Catholic Reformation reached its height. Unfortunately they were also responsible for reviving the Inquisition, which had fallen into disuse during the Italian Renaissance.

These direct activities of the Popes were supplemented by the decrees of a great church council convoked in 1545 by Paul III, which met in the city of Trent (modern Trento), at intervals be- *The Council of* tween 1545 and 1563. This council was one of the most important *Trent* in the history of the church. The main purpose for which it had been summoned was to re-define the doctrines of the Catholic faith, and several of the steps in this direction were highly significant. Without exception the dogmas challenged by the Protestant Reformers were reaffirmed. Good works were held to be as necessary for salvation as faith. The theory of the sacraments as indispensable means of grace was upheld. Likewise, transubstantiation, the apostolic succession of the priesthood, the belief in purgatory, the invocation of saints, and the rule of celibacy for the clergy were all confirmed as essential elements in the Catholic system. On the much-debated question as to the proper source of Christian belief, the Bible and the traditions of apostolic teaching were held to be of equal authority. Not only was papal supremacy over every bishop and priest expressly maintained, but there was more than a faint suggestion that the authority of the Pope transcended that of the church council itself. By this admission the government of the church was reconstituted as monarchical in form. The great movement of the fourteenth and fifteenth centuries which had attempted to establish the superior authority of the general council was ignored entirely.

The Council of Trent did not confine its attention to matters of dogma. It passed important legislation also for the elimination of abuses and for reinforcing the discipline of the church over its *Reforms of* members. The sale of indulgences was flatly prohibited, and even *the Council of* their issuance for considerations other than money was restricted *Trent* temporarily. Bishops and priests were forbidden to hold more than one benefice, so that none could grow rich from a plurality of incomes. To eliminate the evil of an ignorant priesthood it was provided that a theological seminary must be established in every diocese. Toward the end of its deliberations the Council decided upon a censorship of books to prevent heretical ideas from corrupting the minds of those who still remained in the faith. A commission was appointed to draw up an index or list of writings which ought not to be read. The publication of this list by the Pope in 1564 resulted in the formal establishment of the Index of Prohibited Books as a part of the machinery of the church. Later a permanent agency known as the Congregation of the Index was set up to revise the list from time to time. Altogether more than forty such revisions have been made. The majority of the books condemned have been theological treatises, and probably the effect in retarding the progress of learning has been slight. Nonetheless, the establishment of the Index must be taken as a symptom of the malignant cancer of intolerance which had come to infect both Catholics and Protestants.

Ignatius of Loyola founds the Society of Jesus

The Catholic Reformation would never have been as thorough or as successful as it was if it had not been for the activities of the Jesuits, or members of the Society of Jesus. They did most of the rough political work in the Council of Trent which enabled the Popes to dominate that body in its later and more important sessions. The Jesuits also were largely responsible for winning Poland and southern Germany back into the Catholic fold. The founder of the Society of Jesus was Ignatius of Loyola, a Spanish nobleman from the Basque country. His early career seems not to have been particularly different from that of other Spaniards of his class—a life of philandering and marauding as a soldier of the king. But about the time the Protestant Revolution was getting well under way in Germany, he was painfully wounded in a battle with the French. While waiting for his injuries to heal, he read a pious biography of Jesus and some legends of the saints which profoundly changed his emotional nature. Overwhelmed by a consciousness of his wasted life, he determined to become a soldier of Christ. After a period of morbid self-tortures, in which he saw visions of Satan, Jesus, and the Trinity, he went to the University of Paris to learn more about

Portrait of Ignatius Loyola, Founder of the Society of Jesus. Engraving by Lucas Vorsterman, 1621.

the faith he intended to serve. Here he gathered around him a small group of devoted disciples, with whose aid in 1534 he founded the Society of Jesus. The members took monastic vows and pledged themselves to go on a pilgrimage to Jerusalem. With this aim in view they set out for Italy, intending to embark from Venice. Finding their pilgrimage blocked by a war with the Turks, they enlisted in the crusade for Catholic reform which was just then beginning in Italy. In 1540 their organization was approved by Pope Paul III. From then on it grew rapidly. When Loyola died in 1556, it could boast of no fewer than 1500 members.

The Society of Jesus was by far the most militant of the religious orders fostered by the spiritual zeal of the sixteenth century. It was not merely a monastic society but a company of soldiers sworn to defend the faith. Their weapons were not to be bullets and spears but eloquence, persuasion, instruction in the right doctrines, and if necessary more worldly methods of exerting influence. The organization was patterned after that of a military company, with a general as commander-in-chief and an iron discipline enforced on the members. All individuality was suppressed, and a soldierlike obedience to the general was exacted of the rank and file. Only the highest of the four classes of members had any share in the government of the order. This little group, known as the Professed of the Four Vows, elected the general for life and consulted with him on important matters. They were also bound to implicit obedience.

Organization of the Society of Jesus

As suggested already, the activities of the Jesuits were numerous and varied. First and foremost, they conceived of themselves as the defenders of true religion. For this object they obtained authority from the Pope to hear confessions and grant absolution. Many of them became priests in order to gain access to the pulpit and expound the truth as the oracles of God. Still others served as agents of the Inquisition in the relentless war against heresy. In all of this work they followed the leadership of Mother Church as their infallible guide. They raised no questions and attempted to solve no mysteries. Loyola taught that if the church ruled that white was black, it would be the duty of her sons to believe it. But the Jesuits were not satisfied merely to hold the field against the attacks of Protestants and heretics; they were anxious to propagate the faith in the farthest corners of the earth—to make Catholics out of Buddhists, Moslems, the Parsees of India, and even the untutored savages of the newly discovered continents. Long before the Reformation had ended, there were Jesuit missionaries in Africa, in Japan and China, and in North and South America. Yet another important activity of Loyola's soldiers of Christ was education. They founded colleges and seminaries by the hundreds in Europe and America and obtained positions in older institutions as well. Until the Society ran into conflict with several monarchs and was finally suppressed by the Pope in 1773, it had a monopoly of education in Spain and

Activities of the Jesuits

a near-monopoly in France. That the Catholic church recovered so much of its strength in spite of the Protestant secession was due in large measure to the manifold and aggressive activities of the Jesuits.

3. The Reformation Heritage

The most obvious result of the Reformation was the division of western Christendom into a multitude of hostile sects. No longer was there one fold and one shepherd for the whole of Latin and Teutonic Europe as had been true in the Middle Ages. Instead, northern Germany and the Scandinavian countries had become Lutheran; England had adopted a compromise Protestantism of her own; while Calvinism had triumphed in Scotland, Holland, and French Switzerland. In the vast domain once owing allegiance to the Vicar of Christ only Italy, Austria, France, Spain and Portugal, southern Germany, Poland, and Ireland were left; and even in several of these countries aggressive Protestant minorities were a thorn in the side of the Catholic majority. Strange as it may seem, this splintering of Christianity into rival factions was ultimately a source of some good to man. It worked in the long run to curb ecclesiastical tyranny and thereby to promote religious freedom. As the sects multiplied in various countries, it gradually became evident that no one of them could ever become strong enough to enforce its will upon the rest. Mutual toleration was made necessary in order for any of them to survive. To be sure, this was an incidental and long-delayed result, but its importance cannot be denied. If we follow the reasoning of James Madison, the mutiplication of sects was almost the only source of religious toleration in the United States.

If there were any other beneficial results of the Reformation, they would probably consist in an added momentum to individualism and in the expansion of popular education. By asserting the right of private judgment and by simplifying ritual and organization, the leaders of the Protestant Revolution liberated man from some of the constraints of medieval ecclesiasticism. It would be a mistake, however, to assume that Lutherans, Calvinists, and Anglicans really believed at this time in genuine religious freedom. They had no interest whatever in tolerating anyone who disagreed with their own respective orthodoxies. About all they did was to set a new and stronger precedent for challenging the authority and beliefs of a universal church. By so doing they promoted self-assertion in the religious sphere in somewhat the same degree as it already existed in the political and economic spheres. A third beneficial consequence of the Reformation was its effect in promoting the education of the masses. The Renaissance, with its absorbing interest in the classics, had had the unfortunate effect of distorting the curricula of the schools into an exaggerated emphasis upon Greek and Latin and of restricting education to the aristocracy. The Lutherans, Cal-

Results of the Reformation: the effect in promoting religious toleration

Other beneficial results

470

vinists, and Jesuits changed all of this. Ambitious to propagate their respective doctrines, they established schools for the masses, where even the son of the cobbler or peasant might learn to read the Bible and theological tracts. Practical subjects were often introduced in place of Greek and Latin, and it is a significant fact that some of these schools eventually opened their doors to the new science.

A good case can be made for the theory that the Reformation furthered democracy, in the form, at least, of limited government. Every one of the sects, whether Protestant or Catholic, raised arguments against the absolute state. Even the Lutherans, despite their adoption of St. Paul's doctrine that "the powers that be are ordained of God," nevertheless recognized the right of the German princes to rebel against the Holy Roman Empire. Luther wrote that disobedience was a greater sin than murder, unchastity, dishonesty, or theft; but what he meant was the disobedience of ordinary men. He never denied the right of princes and kings to protect their subjects, by armed rebellion if necessary, against a tyrant. A similar attitude, that rebellion can be lawfully waged only by lower magistrates, was the position originally taken by the Calvinists. From such a position, however, it was a comparatively easy step to the doctrine that the people themselves have the right to rebel against intolerable oppression. Calvinists in France, England, and the Low Countries not only asserted the right of revolution but actively practiced it. Jesuit philosophers taught that the authority of the secular ruler is derived from the people, and some even affirmed the right of the ordinary citizen to kill a tyrant. Among the leaders of almost every sect, efforts were made to revive the medieval idea of a higher law of nature, embodying principles of right and justice, which should be recognized as an automatic limitation upon the power of rulers. To this day religious bodies have played an important role in movements to restrict the authority of the omnipotent state.

Limitation upon the power of rulers

But we cannot look upon all the results of the Reformation and pronounce them good. One of the evil fruits was a series of religious wars which kept Europe in turmoil for two score years. The first to break out was the Schmalkaldic War (1546–1547), waged by Charles V in an effort to restore the unity of the Holy Roman Empire under the Catholic faith. In a few months he succeeded in cowing the Protestant princes of Germany into submission, but he was unable to force their subjects back into the Roman religion. The strife was ultimately settled by a compromise treaty, the Religious Peace of Augsburg (1555), under which each German prince was to be free to choose either Lutheranism or Catholicism as the faith of his people. The religion of each state was thus made to depend upon the religion of its ruler—a settlement typically in harmony with the despotic traditions of the time. A much more sanguinary struggle took place in France between 1562 and 1593. Here the

Evil fruits of the Reformation: religious wars

The Cities of the Schmalkaldic League Surrendering to Charles V. Engraving by Hieronymus Cock, 1560.

Protestants, or Huguenots as they were called, were decidedly in the minority, but they included some of the ablest and most influential members of the commercial and financial classes. Besides, they composed a political party involved in machinations against the Catholics for control of the government. In 1562 a faction of ultra-Catholics under the leadership of the Duke of Guise forced their way into power and, by their threats of persecution of the Huguenots, plunged the country into civil war. The struggle culminated ten years later in the frightful massacre of St. Bartholomew's Day. The regent, Catherine de' Medici, in a desperate effort to put an end to the strife, plotted with the Guises to murder the Protestant chiefs. The conspiracy unloosed the ugly passions of the Paris mob, with the result that in a single night two thousand Huguenots were slain. The war dragged on until 1593 when Henry IV became a Catholic in order to please the majority of his subjects, but the religious issue did not approach a settlement until 1598 when Henry issued the Edict of Nantes guaranteeing freedom of conscience to Protestants.

The Revolt of the Nether-lands

To a large extent the Revolt of the Netherlands was also an episode in the religious strife stirred up by the Reformation. Long after the Protestant Revolution began in Germany, the countries now known as Belgium and Holland were still being governed as dominions of the Spanish crown. Though Lutheranism and Calvinism had gained a foothold in the cities, the Protestants of the Netherlands were yet but a fraction of the total population. With the passage of time, however, the numbers of Calvinists increased until they included a majority of the townsmen, at least, in the Dutch provinces of the north. Interference by the Spanish government with their freedom of religion led to a desperate revolt in 1565. Religious causes were of course not the only ones. Nationalist feeling was a leading factor also, particularly since the Spanish king, Philip II, persisted in treating the Netherlands as mere subject provinces. In addition, there were serious economic grievances—high taxation and the restriction of commerce for the benefit of Spanish merchants. On the other hand, it was religious hatred that was largely responsible for the bitterness of the struggle. Philip II regarded all Protestants as traitors, and he was determined to root them out of every territory over which he ruled. In 1567 he sent the bigoted Duke of Alva with ten thousand soldiers to quell the revolt in the Netherlands. For six years Alva terrorized the land, putting hundreds of the rebels to death and torturing or imprisoning thousands of others. The Protestants retaliated with almost equal savagery, and the war continued its barbarous course until 1609. It ended in victory for the Protestants, largely through the bravery and self-sacrifice of their original leader, William the Silent. The chief result of the war was the establishment of an independent Dutch Republic comprising the territories now included in Holland. The southern or Belgian provinces, where the majority of the people were Catholics, returned to Spanish rule.

Actual warfare between nations and sects was not the only type of barbarity which the Reformation directly encouraged. For other examples we need only recall the atrocities perpetrated by the Catholic Inquisition, the savage persecution of Anabaptists in Germany, and the fierce intolerance of Calvinists against Catholics. The horrible witchcraft persecution, which will be discussed in the next chapter, was also in large measure the product of the seeds of fanaticism sown by the Reformation. On the whole, the amount of intolerance was now much greater than at any other time in the history of Christianity, not excepting the age of the Crusades. In more than one instance the victims of persecution were distinguished philosophers or scientists, whose talents the world of that day could ill afford to lose. The most eminent of the martyrs to the new learning put to death by the Catholics was Giordano Bruno. Despite his philosophy of mystical pantheism, Bruno set forth in startling fashion a number of the cardinal axioms of modern science. He taught the eternity of the universe, revived the atomic theory of matter, and denied that the heavenly bodies contain any superior element not found in the earth. Partly for these teachings and partly also for his pantheism and for his rejection of miracles, he was haled before the Inquisition and burned at the stake in 1600. One of the victims of Calvinist persecution at Geneva was Michael Servetus, the discoverer of the lesser circulation of the blood. Servetus was convicted of rejecting the doctrines of the Trinity and predestina-

Bigotry, witchcraft, and persecution

tion and of teaching that Palestine is a barren country in defiance of the Old Testament description as a land flowing with milk and honey. In 1553 he was condemned to be burned at the stake by slow fire. Some admirers of Calvin have argued that the Genevan Reformer opposed the burning of Servetus: he wanted him beheaded! But even the evidence for this rather doubtful display of mercy is not conclusive.

Aside from the persecution of men of learning, the Reformation was a blow to the progress of enlightenment in still other ways. The aim of the Protestant Reformers was to encourage an absolute reliance upon faith and a belief in the Bible as the final source of religion and truth. This led them to despise intellectual activity as a brazen attempt to assert man's independence of God. Luther blasted against reason as "the devil's harlot" and adjured his followers to "keep to revelation and don't try to understand." [11] Both Luther and Melanchthon condemned the Copernican astronomy on the ground that it was contrary to the Scriptures. The attitude of the leaders of the Catholic Reformation was no better. The Council of Trent included the following in its official decrees: "When God commands us to believe, he does not propose to have us search into his divine judgments, nor to inquire their reasons and causes, but demands an immutable faith. . . . Faith, therefore, excludes not only all doubt, but even the desire of subjecting its truth to demonstration." [12] This seemed to shift the emphasis from one of the cardinal principles of the Catholic philosophy of the late Middle Ages. "Subjecting its truth to demonstration" was the very thing which the great masters of thirteenth-century Scholasticism had considered most essential.

The attacks upon reason and science

Finally, the Reformation had a baneful effect upon art. Although Luther had some gifts of aesthetic appreciation, his followers were too deeply absorbed in theological controversy to care whether art survived or perished. Calvin took a more positive stand. Everything that appealed to the senses he utterly deplored as godless and immoral. He believed that the use of any pictures or images in his churches would profane the worship of God. Even the Catholic reformers were only slightly less hostile, despite the splendid traditions of their church as a patron of Renaissance art. The Council of Trent adopted severe restrictions against representation of the human form, and a second-rate artist was employed to paint breeches and skirts on the naked figures in Michelangelo's *Last Judgment*. In view of such attitudes as these, reflecting the bigotry and intolerance of the Reformers, it is rather difficult to believe that the movement they led was a milestone of human progress. If the reforms in the Catholic church could have been accomplished through

The effects upon art

[11] Preserved Smith, *The Age of the Reformation*, pp. 625–626.
[12] Catechism of the Council of Trent.

the enlightened philosophy of the Christian humanists instead of by religious revolution, the tragic aftermath of violence and unreason might well have been avoided. But the logic of political and economic events in the fifteenth and sixteenth centuries perhaps made revolution inevitable.

Selected Readings

· *Items so designated are available in paperbound editions.*

· Bainton, R. H., *The Age of the Reformation*, New York, 1957. (Anvil) The best short treatise. Half of it consists of documents.
· ———, *Here I Stand: A Life of Martin Luther*, Nashville, 1950. (Apex, New American Library)
Bax, E. B., *The Peasants' War in Germany*, New York, 1899. The best account in English but not especially scholarly.
· Beard, C., *The Reformation of the Sixteenth Century in Its Relation to Modern Thought and Knowledge*, New York, 1927. (Ann Arbor)
Bury, J. B., *History of the Freedom of Thought*, New York, 1913.
· Harkness, G. E., *John Calvin: the Man and His Ethics*, New York, 1931. (Apex)
· Huizinga, Johan, *Erasmus and the Age of Reformation*, New York, 1957. (Torchbooks)
Hulme, E. M., *The Renaissance, the Protestant Revolution and the Catholic Reformation in Continental Europe*, New York, 1914.
Jenkins, B. A., *The World's Debt to Protestantism*, Boston, 1930.
· Jones, R. M., *The Spiritual Reformers of the Sixteenth and Seventeenth Centuries*, New York, 1914. (Beacon)
Kidd, B. J., *The Counter-Reformation, 1550–1600*, New York, 1933. A complete account of the Jesuits, the Inquisition, and the Council of Trent.
Latourette, K. S., *A History of Christianity*, New York, 1953.
Lindsay, T. M., *History of the Reformation*, New York, 1928, 2 vols. Complete and scholarly.
Lucas, H. S., *The Renaissance and the Reformation*, New York, 1934.
· McGiffert, A. C., *Protestant Thought before Kant*, New York, 1911. (Torchbooks)
McNeill, J. T., *The History and Character of Calvinism*, New York, 1954. A general interpretation.
Marti, O. A., *The Economic Causes of the Reformation in England*, New York, 1930.
Nelson, E. N., *The Idea of Usury*, Princeton, 1949.
Randall, J. H., Jr., *The Making of the Modern Mind*, New York, 1926, Ch. VII.
Schwiebert, E. G., *Luther and His Times*, St. Louis, 1952. Valuable for background material.
Smith, Preserved, *The Age of the Reformation*, New York, 1920. The best general survey.
———, *The Life and Letters of Martin Luther*, New York, 1914.
Smithson, Robert, *The Anabaptists*, London, 1935.
· Tawney, R. H., *Religion and the Rise of Capitalism*, New York, 1926. (Mentor) Thoughtful and provocative.
Van Dyke, P., *Ignatius Loyola, The Founder of the Jesuits*, New York, 1926.
· Weber, Max, *The Protestant Ethic and the Spirit of Capitalism*, New York, 1948. (Scribner's) A stimulating sociological and psychological interpretation.

Source Materials

Baumer, F. L. V., *Main Currents of Western Thought*, New York, 1952.

Calvin, John, *Institutes of the Christian Religion*, especially Book II, Chs. 1–3; Book III, Chs. 19, 21–25; Book IV, Chs. 3, 14, 17, 20.

Catechism of the Council of Trent.

Luther, Martin, *Works* (Jacobs, tr.), "On Trade and Usury," Vol. IV.

———, *On Christian Liberty.*

———, *Address to the Christian Nobility of the German Nation.*

The Harvesters, Pieter Breughel the Elder (1520–1569). Spurning the religious and bourgeois traditions of most of the other Flemish painters, Breughel chose to depict the life of humble people close to the earth. (MMA)

The Virgin and Chancellor Rolin, Jan van Eyck (1390–1444). The early Flemish painters loved to present scenes of piety in the sumptuous surroundings of wealthy burghers. (Louvre)

The Betrothal of St. Catherine, Hans Memling (1430–1494). The infant Jesus in the lap of the Virgin is shown placing on the finger of St. Catherine the ring of betrothal to Christ and His Church. (MMA)

Erasmus, Hans Holbein the Younger (1497–1543). This portrait by the German Holbein is generally regarded as the best representation of the character and personality of the Prince of the Humanists. (Louvre)

Burial of the Count of Orgaz, El Greco (1541–1614). El Greco's masterpiece immortalizes the character of the people among whom he dwelt. The elongated figures, gaunt faces, and bold and dramatic colors are typical of his work. (Iglesia S. Tomé, Toledo, Spain)

The Marchessa Durazzo, Anthony Van Dyck (1599-1641). This portrait of a Genoese noblewoman suggests the Italian Renaissance sophistication admired by the Flemish burghers. (MMA)

Queen Mariana of Austria, Diego Velásquez (1599-1660). Velasquez's portraits celebrate the pomp and power of the Spanish court, but also emit the breath and life of real people. (Prado)

England and Scotland Crowning Charles I, Peter Paul Rubens (1577-1640). This voluptuous scene with classical setting was part of a series painted by Rubens in Whitehall Palace, London, to glorify the Stuart family. (Minneapolis Inst. of Art)

Index

Guide to Pronunciation

The sounds represented by the diacritical marks used in this Index are illustrated by the following common words:

āle	ēve	īce	ōld	ūse	bo͞ot
ăt	ĕnd	ĭll	ŏf	ŭs	fo͝ot
fâtality	êvent		ôbey	ûnite	
câre			fôrm	ûrn	
ärm					
ȧsk					

Vowels that have no diacritical marks are to be pronounced "neutral," for example: Aegean = ê-jē'an, Basel = bäz'el, Basil = bȧ'zil, common = kŏm'on, Alcaeus = ăl-sē'us. The combinations ou and oi are pronounced as in "out" and "oil."

477

Subjects indexed for pages 1–476 will be found in Volume 1; subjects indexed for pages 477–1042 will be found in Volume 2.

Subjects indexed for pages 1–476 will be found in Volume 1; subjects indexed for pages 477–1042 will be found in Volume 2.

Subjects indexed for pages 1–476 will be found in Volume 1; subjects indexed for pages 477–1042 will be found in Volume 2.

Subjects indexed for pages 1–476 will be found in Volume 1; subjects indexed for pages 477–1042 will be found in Volume 2.

Subjects indexed for pages 1–476 will be found in Volume 1; subjects indexed for pages 477–1042 will be found in Volume 2.

Subjects indexed for pages 1-476 will be found in Volume 1; subjects indexed for pages 477-1042 will be found in Volume 2.

*Subjects indexed for pages 1–476 will be found in Volume 1; subjects indexed for pages 477–1042 will
be found in Volume 2.*

Subjects indexed for pages 1–476 will be found in Volume 1; subjects indexed for pages 477–1042 will be found in Volume 2.

Subjects indexed for pages 1–476 will be found in Volume 1; subjects indexed for pages 477–1042 will be found in Volume 2.

Subjects indexed for pages 1–476 will be found in Volume 1; subjects indexed for pages 477–1042 will be found in Volume 2.

Subjects indexed for pages 1–476 will be found in Volume 1; subjects indexed for pages 477–1042 will be found in Volume 2.

Subjects indexed for pages 1-476 will be found in Volume 1; subjects indexed for pages 477-1042 will be found in Volume 2.

*Subjects indexed for pages 1–476 will be found in Volume 1; subjects indexed for pages 477–1042 will
be found in Volume 2.*

Subjects indexed for pages 1–476 will be found in Volume 1; subjects indexed for pages 477–1042 will be found in Volume 2.

Subjects indexed for pages 1–476 will be found in Volume 1; subjects indexed for pages 477–1042 will be found in Volume 2.

Subjects indexed for pages 1–476 will be found in Volume 1; subjects indexed for pages 477–1042 will
be found in Volume 2.

Subjects indexed for pages 1–476 will be found in Volume 1; subjects indexed for pages 477–1042 will be found in Volume 2.